Deviant Behavior

READINGS IN
THE SOCIOLOGY OF DEVIANCE

Deviant Behavior

READINGS IN
THE SOCIOLOGY OF DEVIANCE

Delos H. Kelly
CALIFORNIA STATE UNIVERSITY, LOS ANGELES

ST. MARTIN'S PRESS
NEW YORK

Library of Congress Catalog Card Number: 78-65242

Manufactured in the United States of America.

32109
fedcba

For information, write St. Martin's Press, Inc.,
175 Fifth Avenue, New York, N.Y. 10010

cover design: Tom McKeveny
typography: Judith Woracek

cloth ISBN: 0–312–19757–8
paper ISBN: 0–312–19758–6

Acknowledgments

Acknowledgments and copyrights continue at the back of the book on pages 767–769, which constitute an extension of the copyright page.

Selections from *Outsiders* by Howard S. Becker reprinted with permission of Macmillan Publishing Co. Inc. Copyright © 1963 by The Free Press of Glencoe, a Division of The Macmillan Company.

"Reactions to Deviance in a Junior High School: Student Views of the Labeling Process" by Robert W. Balch and Delos H. Kelly is reprinted with permission of V-U Publishing Company from the *Journal of Instructional Psychology,* Vol. 1, No. 1, Copyright, 1974.

Selection from *The Rules of Sociological Method* by Emile Durkheim translated by Sarah A. Solovay and John H. Mueller and edited by George E. C. Catlin reprinted with permission of Macmillan Publishing Co., Inc. Copyright © 1938 by George E. C. Catlin, renewed 1966 by Sarah A. Solovay, John H. Mueller and George E. C. Catlin.

"The Functions of Deviance in Groups" by Robert A. Dentler and Kai T. Erikson is reprinted with the permission of the authors and The Society for the Study of Social Problems from *Social Problems,* 7:2 (Fall, 1959).

"The Conflict of Conduct Norms" from *Culture, Conflict and Crime,* a report of the Subcommittee on Delinquency of the Committee on Personality and Culture, Social Science Research Council Bulletin 41 (New York, 1938) by Thorsten Sellin is reprinted courtesy of the Social Science Research Council.

"Lower Class Culture as a Generating Milieu of Gang Delinquency" by Walter B. Miller is reprinted with the permission of the author and The Society for the Psychological Study of Social Issues from *The Journal of Social Issues,* Vol. 14, No. 3 (1958).

Selection from *Criminology* by Edwin H. Sutherland and Donald R. Cressey reprinted by permission of the publisher, J. B. Lippincott Company. Copyright © 1970.

"Techniques of Neutralization: A Theory of Delinquency" by Gresham M. Sykes and David Matza is reprinted with the permission of the authors and The American Sociological Association from *American Sociological Review,* Vol. 22, 1957.

"Social Structure and Anomie" by Robert K. Merton is reprinted with the permission of The American Sociological Association from *American Sociological Review,* Vol. 3, 1938.

To Brett and Jane

Preface

Some anthologies dealing with the subject of deviance emphasize the ways in which society responds to deviant behavior. Others, by examining why certain individuals violate the social norm, focus on the motivational element. And a few trace the evolution of deviant categories. *Deviant Behavior: Readings in the Sociology of Deviance* has been designed to integrate and balance these concerns in a single volume—to explore, through carefully selected readings, the ramifications of deviance for both the individual (the *actor*) and for society.

Part One considers the ways society defines deviance and the deviant. Of particular interest is the role that specific individuals—especially those who hold political power or who serve as enforcers of the law—play in the labeling of actors and acts as deviant. It will become clear to the reader that no individual and no behavior is inherently deviant: it is society's perception of an actor or an act as deviant that affixes the label. Deviance, in other words, is in the eye of the beholder.

Why does socially prohibited behavior occur—and persist, despite society's efforts to eliminate or discourage it? How can we make sense of deviance? Sociologists approach these questions from a number of different theoretical perspectives. Part Two presents readings by major theorists representing the most important of these perspectives. The introduction to the section furnishes students with the theoretical framework upon which to build an understanding and an appreciation of these key thinkers.

Part Three follows the evolving *career* of the social deviant: it traces the steps by which he or she becomes identified by society as a deviant. It depicts, for example, the efforts of relatives to cope with the increasingly bizarre behavior of a family member. Frequently, of course, attempts to manage the deviant at home fail, and the family turns to institutions and agencies of social control for help. The couple in the article by Marian Radke Yarrow and others, "The Psychological Meaning of Mental Illness in the Family," exemplifies such an eventuality, as a woman responds to the growing awareness that her husband can no longer be counted upon to act rationally.

Once deviants have been institutionalized, their career is determined, to a great extent, by their experiences within the institution. Part Four explores the workings of several people-processing and people-changing facilities—ranging from juvenile court to mental hospital—to examine how such structures deal with clients and how clients, in turn, adapt their behavior and their self-concept to their surroundings. Students may find the article by Donald P. Jewell, "A Case of a 'Psychotic' Navaho Indian Male," particularly revealing: because the staff mistook the Navaho's culturally learned stoicism for schizophrenia, and because he could speak little English, the young man was assumed to by psychotic.

For certain types of deviance, institutional controls are far less significant than the traditions and norms of deviant subcultures. Part Five examines the ways in which such norms shape the career of the skid row alcoholic, the prostitute, the gang member, and others.

Finally, Part Six analyzes the processes by which deviant behavior and deviant careers may be redirected. The first three articles describe personal and institutional barriers that confront those who desire to move from a deviant to a nondeviant status—in particular, society's reluctance to accept as "normal' anyone who has borne the stigma of deviance. The remaining articles present examples of strategies that the deviant may use in an attempt to overcome prejudice against violators of society's conventions.

Overall, then, this book explores the establishment and maintenance of deviant categories; the motivations behind deviant behavior; the identification as deviant of individuals and of particular segments of society, by formal and informal means; the effects of institutionalization upon the deviant; and the efforts of deviants to eradicate the label society has placed upon them.

I would like to thank several people for their help in preparing this volume, particularly my editor, Bert Lummus. I am grateful as well for the contributions of Peter Iadicola and Ted Cote.

Delos H. Kelly

Contents

Part 5 / Noninstitutional Deviance   441

/ **General Introduction**

We all carry in our minds images of deviance and the deviant. To some, deviants are murderers and rapists. Others would include in the list prostitutes, child molesters, wife beaters, and homosexuals. As far as the motivations behind deviant behavior, some of us would place the blame on the family, while others would emphasize genetic factors or social factors, especially poverty.

CREATING DEVIANCE

Regardless of what kind of behavior we consider deviant or what factors we believe cause deviance, we must recognize that deviance *and* the deviant emerge out of a continuous process of interaction among people. For deviance to become a public fact, however, several conditions need to be satisfied: (1) some deviant category (e.g., mores and laws) must exist; (2) a person must be viewed as violating the category; and (3) someone must attempt to enforce the violation of the category. If the individual demanding enforcement is successful in his or her efforts to label the violator, the social deviant has been created.

The Creation of Deviant Categories

As far as deviant categories are concerned, relatively little attention has been focused upon their evolution. The formal and informal codes of conduct are generally accepted as "givens," and investigators concentrate on the examination of *why* the categories are violated and *how* they are enforced. An approach of this kind is inadequate, however, particularly in view of the fact that new categories are continually evolving and old ones are being modified. Obviously, as the definitions or categories of deviance change, the picture of deviance must also be altered. The rapidly changing content of the laws governing marijuana provides an example. If there are no penalties for possessing and smoking marijuana, one cannot be formally charged and processed for doing so.

1

In studying deviance, then, a central question needs to be raised: How (and why) do *acts* become defined as deviant?[1] Providing answers to this question requires an examination of how deviance is defined, how the definitions are maintained, and how violators of the definitions are processed and treated. What is entailed is both a historical and an ongoing analysis of those legislative and political processes that affect the evolution, modification, and enforcement of deviant categories. Central focus must be placed on those who possess the power and resources not only to define deviance and the deviant but to apply a label of deviance to a violator and to make the label stick. These processes are highlighted in part one and will be evident in the discussion of the "conflict model" in part two, as well as in several selections—for instance, the one on white-collar crime in part five.

Reactions to Violators of Deviant Categories

In terms of the *actor*, an equally important question can be asked: How (and why) do violators of various types of deviant categories (mores, laws, and regulations) become labeled as deviant? Answering this question requires an examination of the interaction occurring between an actor and an audience. A simple paradigm (Figure 1) can illustrate how the deviant is reacted to and thus socially created. This paradigm, it should be noted, can be applied to each of the selections in this volume.

The Interactional Paradigm A young man (the social *actor*) is seen smoking marijuana (the *act*, a violation of a deviant category) by a police officer (a social *audience*, an enforcer of the deviant category) and is arrested. The youth's deviation thus becomes a matter of public record, and a deviant career is initiated—a career which may be solidified and perpetuated by legal and institutional processing. Another officer, however, ignores the offense. In the first case, then, the violator is initially labeled as a "deviant," while in the second he is not. Figure 1 indicates that not only is audience response critical, but it depends upon several factors. The example also helps to underscore the fact that there is nothing inherently deviant about any act or actor—their meanings are derived from the interpretations *others* place upon them. Hence the notion that "deviance lies in the eyes of the beholder." This example can be extended by incorporating a concern for the fourth element of the paradigm: *third parties* or witnesses.

Specifically, the young man may be observed smoking grass by a peer, and the peer may choose to ignore the offense. Another peer, however, may not only consider the act illegal or deviant but may

Figure 1 / Interactional Paradigm

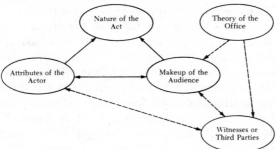

decide to do something about it. The peer lacks the power to arrest; he can, however, bring in third parties in an effort to create a shared attitude toward the smoker—namely, that he is a "criminal" or "deviant." The peer may turn to other peers, and they may decide to call the police and have the smoker arrested. If this happens, the male's "deviance" becomes a public fact.

Thus, the label "deviant" is a status conferred upon a person by an observer or observers. Although an understanding of this process requires an examination of the way the four basic elements of the paradigm interact with one another, such an examination is not sufficient. An awareness of the *theory of the office* that a particular agent or audience operates out of is also necessary, especially if the occupant of the office is an agent of social control. The preceding example, as well as the "organizational paradigm" highlighted in Figure 2, can be used to illustrate this requirement. (This paradigm represents a refinement of the "interactional paradigm" described in Figure 1. Here I am focusing upon the audience, particularly in terms of how the institution expects certain outcomes on the part of its agents. The paradigm can and will be generally applied throughout this volume.)

Figure 2 / Organizational Paradigm

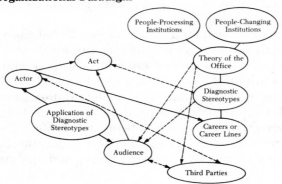

The Organizational Paradigm   Although it might be assumed that
the police officer in our examples operates on the basis of his or her
own initiative, this is frequently far from the truth. The officer, like
any institutional agent concerned with the processing (through the
courts) or rehabilitating (in correctional facilities) of clients, is guided
and generally constrained by a theory of the office, or "working ideology." The officer, through informal (contacts with other officers) and
formal (police academies) socialization experiences, learns how to
identify and classify deviants or suspected deviants. These institutional, or "diagnostic," stereotypes (Scheff, 1966) comprise a basic
ingredient of a department's official perspective. The officer, for
example, learns how to recognize the "typical" case of child molesta-
tion, runaway, or rape. These "normal crimes" (Sudnow, 1965) or
"social type designations" not only help the officer make sense out of
events; they also provide criteria upon which a suspect can be initially
identified, classified, and then selected out to play the role of the
deviant.

An institution's stereotypes are basic to the *rate production
process*—the creation of a body of institutional statistics. If, for example, a chief feels that homosexual behavior is morally wrong or criminal, not only will this one individual's conception become embedded
within the theory of the office, but the officers will be required to
zero in on such activity. This will produce a set of crime statistics
exhibiting an unusually high arrest rate for homosexual exchanges.
Similarly, if a chief formally or informally communicates to his departmental personnel that blacks, Mexicans, Indians, and other
minorities constitute the "real" deviants, delinquents, and criminals,
such people will be disproportionately selected out to play the role of
the deviant—that is, they will become more vulnerable to institutional processing. This, too, will produce a set of statistics reflecting a
heavy concentration of these individuals. The statistics can, in turn,
serve as justification for heavy and continued surveillance in areas
containing such groups. Examples like these could be multiplied
dramatically.

If we are to approach an understanding of what causes deviance,
and particularly of the ways in which institutional careers arise and
are perpetuated, then we need initially to analyze and dissect the
existing structure of the institutions of social control. To obtain an
understanding of how institutions operate requires, as suggested by
Paradigm 2, sensitization to several basic organizational elements
and processes: (1) the institution's theory of the office, (2) the content
of the institutional stereotypes embedded within the theory of the
office and used to identify clients for typing and processing, (3) the

existing careers or career lines (and associated role expectations) into which the identified clients are placed, (4) the socialization of institutional agents and their application of diagnostic stereotypes to clients, and (5) the effects of institutional typing and processing, both from the perspective of the client and the institution.

UNDERSTANDING DEVIANCE

In the discussion of the creation of deviance it was argued that some deviant category must exist, a person must be viewed as violating the category, and someone must make a demand for enforcement. Thus far, too, the focus has been upon the evolution and change of deviant categories, as well as on the interactional aspects—how and why violators of categories may be reacted to. Missing from this analysis, however, is a concern for the motivational aspects—the reasons why people may violate deviant categories. This concern, it may be noted, has been generally ignored by the labeling or interactionist proponents. Their main interest revolves around examining audience reactions and their impact upon people. Implicit in such a stand is the unwarranted suggestion that behavior is relatively unimportant. If, however, we are to approach a more complete understanding of deviance from a dynamic perspective, a major focus must also be given to motivation. Such a view provides us with an opportunity continually to analyze how behavior and labels interact with each other.

Violations of Deviant Categories

Traditionally, writers have placed a heavy emphasis on trying to explain why people may violate various types of deviant categories. Some have spent their time trying to explain group or structural rates of deviance, while others have concentrated on those processes by which individuals learn culture and traditions. These efforts have produced many schools of thought, each with its own set of assumptions. The "anomie" theorists, for example, argue that blocked opportunity can produce a strain toward deviation. The "conflict" theorists, by contrast, contend that the powerless may consciously violate the laws formulated by the powerful. Understanding deviance, then, requires that we investigate those reasons why people may violate deviant categories and by their violations bring upon themselves the labeling or "status degradation ceremony." The selections in part two offer some representative attempts to explore this question.

BECOMING DEVIANT

As far as becoming deviant, an initial distinction can be made between private and public settings. A husband may violate a particular set of expectations by acting strangely. The wife may try to make sense out of such behavior by rationalizing or neutralizing it away. She may argue to herself and others that he has experienced some personal setbacks and that the peculiar behavior will pass. At this stage the wife is trying to develop a counterdefinition of the situation, and she is also refusing to impute a deviant label to her spouse. The husband's behavior may grow increasingly violent, though, to the point where the wife finds it necessary to bring in agents of social control. She may call the police (third parties) or ultimately have her husband committed to a mental institution. If this should happen, not only have the wife's tolerance limits been exceeded but her attempts at various strategies of *accommodation* (such as neutralization or rationalization) have failed. The husband may then be typed, for example, as a schizophrenic and processed in accordance with the establishment's expectations of what the schizophrenic career should entail. The patient is expected, thereafter, to live up to his institutional role—to accept the label and act accordingly. The case of McMurphy in *One Flew Over the Cuckoo's Nest* (Kesey, 1962) describes what may happen when a patient protests against his assigned label. Because McMurphy rejects the "sick role," he becomes embroiled in a running battle with Big Nurse, the institution's agent. In our example, a similar situation may evolve with respect to the husband's response: he may repudiate the institutional tag, he may try to ignore it, or he may accept it. His response, like the response of observers, is frequently difficult to predict.

In terms of the preceding, it should be noted that attempts may be made to regulate and control behavior in private settings, and the efforts may be successful. However, once third parties or social control agents (such as the police or psychiatrists) are called in, the individual is frequently on his or her way to becoming an institutional deviant—that is, the organizational paradigm becomes operative, not only from the institution's viewpoint but from the actor's perspective. In particular, if a mental institution is involved, the client becomes viewed as a "mental patient"; this label becomes the patient's *master status* (Becker, 1963), and people will then react to the person on the basis of the label and not as a sane or "normal" person. The changing of one's status, or the *status degradation ceremony* (Garfinkel, 1956), also affects the views others have of the "deviant" (one's public identity), as well as how the actor views him- or herself (one's personal identity). It frequently affects one's self-esteem (how one views self, positively or negatively, relative to others on selected criteria).

INSTITUTIONAL AND NONINSTITUTIONAL CAREERS

An important distinction should be made between *institutional* and *noninstitutional* careers. A noninstitutional career is one which a person pursues primarily as a matter of choice. The individual takes an active role in structuring and presenting a specific image of self to others. The bookie, gambler, con artist, nudist, skid row alcoholic, and homosexual provide examples. Such individuals generally progress through some semblance of a career: once they gain entry or exposure, they begin to learn the existing culture and traditions. The bookie, for instance, may start out as a runner, "learn the ropes," and then move into other phases of the bookmaking operation. Similarly, if the skid row alcoholic wants to become an accepted member of the "bottle gang culture," he will become familiar with the norms prevalent among the skid rowers, particularly those that relate to the procurement and consumption of alcohol. Violations of the normative code are frequently responded to by exclusion from the group (Rubington, 1973). As with the sanctioning of "deviants" by "nondeviants," the "labeled deviants" have ways of punishing their "deviants."

Institutional careers, by contrast, involve those in which the individual plays a relatively passive role. Here, the career is initiated and perpetuated by some socializing or social control institution; this process was briefly noted in the discussion of how one becomes deviant. The careers of the "school misfit," mental patient, delinquent, and criminal are of this type. The major difference between institutional careers and noninstitutional careers concerns the role of the actor, particularly in the matter of choice and in the means of gaining entry. Once the institutional career begins, though, the mental patient, like the skid row alcoholic, is expected to learn and act in accordance with any existing culture and traditions.

It should be noted that institutional and noninstitutional careers are not always mutually exclusive. Frequently, a degree of overlap exists between the two. The skid row alcoholic, for example, may be arrested and sent to an alcoholic ward, where his or her behavior becomes subject to institutional control. Similarly, the prostitute may be arrested and taken to jail. In both instances the activities become a matter of institutional knowledge and record. A secret homosexual, by contrast, may never directly experience the effects of institutional processing.

The Effects of Institutional and Noninstitutional Careers

The distinction between institutional and noninstitutional careers provides a backdrop against which a person's reactions can be assessed. How, for example, is a person likely to respond to institutional typing and processing as a deviant? Will he or she reject or accept the institutional label? Answering these questions requires a consideration of how the "status degradation ceremony" affects an actor's personal and public identity. If the deviant rejects the label, a discrepancy (or *identity crisis*) occurs between one's personal and public identities—that is, between one's view of oneself as normal and the institution's view of one as a deviant. Obviously, unless some personal gain can be realized, such as the enhancement of one's prestige or status in the eyes of others, most persons will reject a deviant label imputed to them. Maintaining an image of self that is at odds with the institution's is not without its costs, though, and eventually the individual may come to accept the label and bring his or her behavior into line with institutional expectations. Lemert (1951) argues that *acceptance of the label* is a critical step on the way to secondary or *career* deviance. Not only do some individuals change their view of self—for instance, from that of "normal" to that of "schizophrenic"—but they often change their mode of dress, mannerisms, and circle of acquaintances. Acceptance of the label, it should be noted, is an important precondition to being certified as being "sane" or "rehabilitated" by institutions.

Involvement is noninstitutional careers or activities also affects the participants and other members of society as well. The covert lesbian teacher, for example, engages in sexual activity that some would consider deviant, and a discrepancy may evolve between her personal and public identities. Privately she may view herself as a lesbian and normal female but publicly she is viewed and responded to as a teacher. As with the institutional deviant, however, an identity crisis may arise. She may decide to "come out" and admit her sexual preference to others. Such a strategy is not without its costs. She may be ostracized by her family, friends, and acquaintances; and, more than likely, she will either be discriminated against on her job or fired. In view of these possibilities, the lesbian may decide to keep her sexual preference hidden and perhaps become involved in a gay culture. Such involvement can provide her with a degree of social support, as well as appropriate rationalizations to legitimize her way of life. Still, she (and other noninstitutional deviants) is aware that not only is she engaging in potentially discrediting behavior but must operate in a society in which there are many hostile elements.

CHANGING DEVIANCE

Identity problems do not cease when one leaves the institution or decides to go straight. Public or known ex-deviants, whether of the institutional or noninstitutional variety, continue to be viewed as "deviants." What Simmons (1969) calls a "lingering of traces" quite frequently occurs, especially among those who carry an institutionally bestowed label. Institutions, it has been pointed out, are most efficient in assigning deviant labels; they are notoriously inefficient when it comes to removing labels and their associated "stigma" (Goffman, 1963). Former deviants must continue to bear the brunt of the label—with the result that their behavioral patterns are much less likely to change.

The probability of rehabilitating someone who does not view his or her activity or career as deviant is poor. Many noninstitutional deviants—such as prostitutes, gamblers, and homosexuals—feel little need to "repent"; they believe that personal pressures and difficulties result from the intolerance of society. In fact, many of these individuals feel strongly that it is society that should be rehabilitated. On the other hand, some noninstitutional deviants, as well as some institutional deviants, such as mental patients, criminals, and delinquents, may try to transform their "deviant" identity. If they do, they can expect to encounter certain barriers. Job applications, for example, frequently require prospective employees to list any arrests, convictions, or periods of institutionalization—circumstances that bar entry into many occupations. Such roadblocks can produce feelings of frustration and inferiority. What many ex-deviants soon realize is that even if they change, they will still be effectively discriminated against because of past activities or involvement with stigmatizing institutions; they also learn very quickly that the social and political establishment is virtually unchanging—that the burden of change falls upon *them*.

SUMMARY AND ORGANIZATION OF THIS VOLUME

This book explores the subject of deviance in a number of ways—by focusing in turn on society, on the individual, and on institutions of control and rehabilitation. Part one describes how deviant categories evolve and how people who violate deviant categories become defined as social deviants. Part two analyzes why people may elect to violate deviant categories—violations that initiate the defining or labeling process. Part three deals with the deviant career, particularly as it arises in private, noninstitutional settings. Part four describes how careers may become initiated and perpetuated by institutions, while part five examines the rise and furtherance of noninstitutional careers. Finally, part six discusses how careers and activities may be terminated. Throughout, a major focus is given to the impact that involvement in institutional as well as noninstitutional activities and careers has upon actors, audiences, and third parties.

Note

1. For an excellent discussion of questions such as these, see particularly Ronald L. Akers, "Problems in the Sociology of Deviance: Social Definitions and Behavior," *Social Forces*, 46 (June 1968), 455–465.

References

Becker, Howard S. *Outsiders: Studies in the Sociology of Deviance.* New York: Free Press, 1963.

Garfinkel, Harold. "Conditions of Successful Degradation Ceremonies." *American Journal of Sociology*, 61 (March 1956), 420–424.

Goffman, Erving. *Stigma: Notes on the Management of Spoiled Identity.* Englewood Cliffs, N.J.: Prentice-Hall, 1963.

_____. "The Moral Career of the Mental Patient," *Psychiatry*, 22 (1959), 123–142.

Kesey, Ken. *One Flew Over the Cuckoo's Nest.* New York: Viking, 1962.

Lemert, Edwin. *Social Pathology.* New York: McGraw-Hill, 1951.

Rubington, Earl. "Variations in Bottle-Gang Controls." In Earl Rubington and Martin S. Weinberg, eds., *Deviance: The Interactionist Perspective.* New York: Macmillan, 1973.

Scheff, Thomas J. "Typification in the Diagnostic Practices of Rehabilitation Agencies." In Marvin B. Sussman, ed., *Sociology and Rehabilitation.* Washington, D.C.: American Sociological Association, 1966.

Simmons, J. L. *Deviants.* Berkeley: Glendessary, 1969.

Sudnow, David. "Normal Crimes: Sociological Features of the Penal Code," *Social Problems*, 12 (Winter 1965), 255–270.

Part 1 / Creating Deviance

As was briefly suggested in the general introduction, the process of creating deviance requires the satisfaction of several conditions. This may have been most apparent in my discussions of the evolution of deviant categories and the ways in which violators of the categories may be perceived and responded to. For deviance to become a social fact, however, a person must be viewed as violating some deviant category and thereafter labeled as deviant by a social observer. The selections in this section introduce a more systematic concern for the two basic processes involved: (1) the creation of deviant categories and (2) the reactions to violators of deviant categories.

The excerpt by Howard S. Becker, "Moral Entrepreneurs: The Creation and Enforcement of Deviant Categories," provides an excellent general overview of how deviant categories, particularly rules, evolve. Central to his analysis is the role of *moral entrepreneurs*, whom he categorizes into *rule creators* and *rule enforcers*. Rule creators are individuals who see some "evil" in society and feel that the evil can be corrected only by legislating against it. Frequently their efforts may result in the passage of a new law—that is, the creation of a new deviant category. Becker offers several interesting examples that describe this legislative-political phenomenon. He argues that a successful crusade will not only result in "the creation of a new set of rules" but will often give rise to "a new set of enforcement agencies and officials." It becomes the function of these officials to enforce the new rules. Becker concludes his analysis by offering several comments relating to rule enforcers. He contends, for example, that enforcers are concerned primarily with enforcing the law and not its contents; they are also interested in justifying their own position in the organization, as well as in gaining respect from their clients. Many of these same notions, it should be stated, can be applied to several of the selections that follow, especially those that deal with the topic of institutional incarceration and deviance.

The study by Robert W. Balch and Delos H. Kelly, "Reactions to

Deviance in a Junior High School: Student Views of the Labeling Process," unlike Becker's general discussion of the role of rule enforcers, provides a more concrete and graphic illustration of how audiences may *actually* respond to those individuals who violate certain rules and regulations. The research is focused upon a specific institution: a junior high school. The results offer a rather clear pattern: Students feel that teachers do, in fact, respond differently to actual or perceived deviants. Responses seem to be a function not only of the infraction involved, but of the particular label the actor is thought to possess. Several pieces of data are offered in support of this observation. Overall, the investigation provides both an account of the way institutional personnel react to deviants, and an introduction to many of the concepts underlying the "societal reactions," "labeling," or "interactionist" perspective. There is, for example, a discussion of the important contributions of Erikson, Lemert, Tannenbaum, Becker, and others. Several of these contributions and notions are more systematically dealt with in part two.

1 / Moral Entrepreneurs: The Creation and Enforcement of Deviant Categories

HOWARD S. BECKER

RULE CREATORS

The prototype of the rule creator, but not the only variety as we shall see, is the crusading reformer. He is interested in the content of rules. The existing rules do not satisfy him because there is some evil which profoundly disturbs him. He feels that nothing can be right in the world until rules are made to correct it. He operates with an absolute ethic; what he sees is truly and totally evil with no qualification. Any means is justified to do away with it. The crusader is fervent and righteous, often self-righteous.

It is appropriate to think of reformers as crusaders because they typically believe that their mission is a holy one. The prohibitionist serves as an excellent example, as does the person who wants to suppress vice and sexual delinquency or the person who wants to do away with gambling.

These examples suggest that the moral crusader is a meddling busybody, interested in forcing his own morals on others. But this is a one-sided view. Many moral crusades have strong humanitarian over-tones. The crusader is not only interested in seeing to it that other people do what he thinks right. He believes that if they do what is right it will be good for them. Or he may feel that his reform will prevent certain kinds of exploitation of one person by another. Pro-hibitionists felt that they were not simply forcing their morals on others, but attempting to provide the conditions for a better way of life for people prevented by drink from realizing a truly good life. Abolitionists were not simply trying to prevent slave owners from doing the wrong thing; they were trying to help slaves to achieve a better life. Because of the importance of the humanitarian motive, moral crusaders (despite their relatively single-minded devotion to their particular cause) often lend their support to other humanitarian crusades. Joseph Gusfield has pointed out that:

13

The American temperance movement during the 19th century was a part of a general effort toward the improvement of the worth of the human being through improved morality as well as economic conditions. The mixture of the religious, the equalitarian, and the humanitarian was an outstanding facet of the moral reformism of many movements. Temperance supporters formed a large segment of movements such as sabbatarianism, abolition, woman's rights, agrarianism, and humanitarian attempts to improve the lot of the poor. . . .

In its auxiliary interests the WCTU revealed a great concern for the improvement of the welfare of the lower classes. It was active in campaigns to secure penal reform, to shorten working hours and raise wages for workers, and to abolish child labor and in a number of other humanitarian and equalitarian activities. In the 1880's the WCTU worked to bring about legislation for the protection of working girls against the exploitation by men.[1]

As Gusfield says,[2] "Moral reformism of this type suggests the approach of a dominant class toward those less favorably situated in the economic and social structure." Moral crusaders typically want to help those beneath them to achieve a better status. That those beneath them do not always like the means proposed for their salvation is another matter. But this fact—that moral crusades are typically dominated by those in the upper levels of the social structure—means that they add to the power they derive from the legitimacy of their moral position, the power they derive from their superior position in society.

Naturally, many moral crusades draw support from people whose motives are less pure than those of the crusader. Thus, some industrialists supported Prohibition because they felt it would provide them with a more manageable labor force.[3] Similarly, it is sometimes rumored that Nevada gambling interests support the opposition to attempts to legalize gambling in California because it would cut so heavily into their business, which depends in substantial measure on the population of Southern California.[4]

The moral crusader, however, is more concerned with ends than with means. When it comes to drawing up specific rules (typically in the form of legislation to be proposed to a state legislature or the Federal Congress), he frequently relies on the advice of experts. Lawyers, expert in the drawing of acceptable legislation, often play this role. Government bureaus in whose jurisdiction the problem falls may also have the necessary expertise, as did the Federal Bureau of Narcotics in the case of the marihuana problem.

As psychiatric ideology, however, becomes increasingly acceptable, a new expert has appeared—the psychiatrist. Sutherland, in his discussion of the natural history of sexual psychopath laws, pointed to the psychiatrist's influence.[5] He suggests the following as the conditions under which the sexual psychopath law, which provides that a person "who is diagnosed as a sexual psychopath may be confined for an indefinite period in a state hospital for the insane,"[6] will be passed.

First, these laws are customarily enacted after a state of fear has been aroused in a community by a few serious sex crimes committed in quick succession. This is illustrated in Indiana, where a law was passed following three or four sexual attacks in Indianapolis, with murder in two. Heads of families bought guns and watch dogs, and the supply of locks and chains in the hardware stores of the city was completely exhausted. . . .

A second element in the process of developing sexual psychopath laws is the agitated activity of the community in connection with the fear. The attention of the community is focused on sex crimes, and people in the most varied situations envisage dangers and see the need of and possibility for their control. . . .

The third phase in the development of those sexual psychopath laws has been the appointment of a committee. The committee gathers the many conflicting recommendations of persons and groups of persons, attempts to determine "facts," studies procedures in other states, and makes recom-mendations, which generally include bills for the legislature. Although the general fear usually subsides within a few days, a committee has the formal duty of following through until positive action is taken. Terror which does not result in a committee is much less likely to result in a law.[7]

In the case of sexual psychopath laws, there usually is no govern-ment agency charged with dealing in a specialized way with sexual deviations. Therefore, when the need for expert advice in drawing up legislation arises, people frequently turn to the professional group most closely associated with such problems:

In some states, at the committee stage of the development of a sexual psychopath law, psychiatrists have played an important part. The psychia-trists, more than any others, have been the interest group back of the laws. A committee of psychiatrists and neurologists in Chicago wrote the bill which became the sexual psychopath law of Illinois; the bill was sponsored by the Chicago Bar Association and by the state's attorney of Cook County and was enacted with little opposition in the next session of the State Legislature. In Minnesota all the members of the governor's committee except one were psychiatrists. In Wisconsin the Milwaukee Neuropsychiat-ric Society shared in pressing the Milwaukee Crime Commission for the enactment of a law. In Indiana the attorney-general's committee received from the American Psychiatric Association copies of all the sexual psychopath laws which had been enacted in other states.[8]

The influence of psychiatrists in other realms of the criminal law has increased in recent years.

In any case, what is important about this example is not that psychia-trists are becoming increasingly influential, but that the moral crusader, at some point in the development of his crusade, often requires the services of a professional who can draw up the appropriate rules in an appropriate form. The crusader himself is often not concerned with such details. Enough for him that the main point has been won; he leaves its implementation to others.

By leaving the drafting of the specific rule in the hands of others, the crusader opens the door for many unforeseen influences. For those who draft legislation for crusaders have their own interests, which may affect the legislation they prepare. It is likely that the sexual psychopath laws drawn by psychiatrists contain many features never intended by the citizens who spearheaded the drives to "do something about sex crimes," features which do however reflect the professional interests of organized psychiatry.

THE FATE OF MORAL CRUSADES

A crusade may achieve striking success, as did the Prohibition movement with the passage of the Eighteenth Amendment. It may fail completely, as has the drive to do away with the use of tobacco or the anti-vivisection movement. It may achieve great success, only to find its gains whittled away by shifts in public morality and increasing restrictions imposed on it by judicial interpretations; such has been the case with the crusade against obscene literature.

One major consequence of a successful crusade, of course, is the establishment of a new rule or set of rules, usually with the appropriate enforcement machinery being provided at the same time. I want to consider this consequence at some length later. There is another consequence, however, of the success of a crusade which deserves mention.

When a man has been successful in the enterprise of getting a new rule established—when he has found, so to speak, the Grail—he is out of a job. The crusade which has occupied so much of his time, energy, and passion is over. Such a man is likely, when he first began his crusade, to have been an amateur, a man who engaged in a crusade because of his interest in the issue, in the content of the rule he wanted established. Kenneth Burke once noted that a man's occupation may become his preoccupation. The equation is also good the other way around. A man's preoccupation may become his occupation. What started as an amateur interest in a moral issue may become an almost full-time job; indeed, for many reformers it becomes just this. The success of the crusade, therefore, leaves the crusader without a vocation. Such a man, at loose ends, may generalize his interest and discover something new to view with alarm, a new evil about which something ought to be done. He becomes a professional discoverer of wrongs to be righted, of situations requiring new rules.

When the crusade has produced a large organization devoted to its cause, officials of the organization are even more likely than the individual crusader to look for new causes to espouse. This process occurred dramatically in the field of health problems when the National Foundation for Infantile Paralysis put itself out of business by discovering a vaccine that eliminated epidemic poliomyelitis. Taking the less constraining name of The National Foundation, officials quickly discovered other health problems to which the organization could devote its energies and resources.

The unsuccessful crusade, either the one that finds its mission no longer attracts adherents or the one that achieves its goal only to lose it again, may follow one of two courses. On the one hand, it may simply give up its original mission and concentrate on preserving what remains of the organization that has been built up. Such, according to one study, was the fate of the Townsend Movement.[9] Or the failing movement may adhere rigidly to an increasingly less popular mission, as did the Prohibition Movement. Gusfield has described present-day members of the WCTU as "moralizers-in-retreat."[10] As prevailing opinion in the United States becomes increasingly anti-temperance, these women have not softened their attitude toward drinking. On the contrary, they have become bitter at the formerly "respectable" people who no longer will support a temperance movement. The social class level from which WCTU members are drawn has moved down from the upper-middle class to the lower-middle class. The WCTU now turns to attack the middle class it once drew its support from, seeing this group as the locus of acceptance of moderate drinking. The following quotations from Gusfield's interviews with WCTU leaders give some of the flavor of the "moralizer-in-retreat":

> When this union was first organized, we had many of the most influential ladies of the city. But now they have got the idea that we ladies who are against taking a cocktail are a little queer. We have an undertaker's wife and a minister's wife, but the lawyer's and the doctor's wives shun us. They don't want to be thought queer.
> We fear moderation more than anything. Drinking has become so much a part of everything—even in our church life and our colleges.
> It creeps into the official church boards. They keep it in their iceboxes. . . . The minister here thinks that the church has gone far, that they are doing too much to help the temperance cause. He's afraid that he'll stub some influential toes.[11]

Only some crusaders, then, are successful in their mission and create, by creating a new rule, a new group of outsiders. Of the successful, some find they have a taste for crusades and seek new problems to attack. Other crusaders fail in their attempt and either support the organization they have created by dropping their distinc-

tive mission and focusing on the problem of organizational maintenance itself or become outsiders themselves, continuing to espouse
and preach a doctrine which sounds increasingly queer as time goes
on.

RULE ENFORCERS

The most obvious consequence of a successful crusade is the creation
of a new set of rules. With the creation of a new set of rules we often
find that a new set of enforcement agencies and officials is established. Sometimes, of course, existing agencies take over the administration of the new rule, but more frequently a new set of rule
enforcers is created. The passage of the Harrison Act presaged the
creation of the Federal Narcotics Bureau, just as the passage of the
Eighteenth Amendment led to the creation of police agencies charged
with enforcing the Prohibition Laws.

With the establishment of organizations of rule enforcers, the
crusade becomes institutionalized. What started out as a drive to
convince the world of the moral necessity of a new rule finally becomes an organization devoted to the enforcement of the rule. Just as
radical political movements turn into organized political parties and
lusty evangelical sects become staid religious denominations, the
final outcome of the moral crusade is a police force. To understand,
therefore, how the rules creating a new class of outsiders are applied
to particular people we must understand the motives and interests of
police, the rule enforcers.

Although some policemen undoubtedly have a kind of crusading
interest in stamping out evil, it is probably much more typical for the
policeman to have a certain detached and objective view of his job. He
is not so much concerned with the content of any particular rule as he
is with the fact that it is his job to enforce the rule. When the rules are
changed, he punishes what was once acceptable behavior just as he
ceases to punish behavior that has been made legitimate by a change
in the rules. The enforcer, then, may not be interested in the content of
the rule as such, but only in the fact that the existence of the rule
provides him with a job, a profession, and a *raison d'être*.

Since the enforcement of certain rules provides justification for his
way of life, the enforcer has two interests which condition his
enforcement activity: first, he must justify the existence of his position
and, second, he must win the respect of those he deals with.

These interests are not peculiar to rule enforcers. Members of all
occupations feel the need to justify their work and win the respect of
others. Musicians, as we have seen, would like to do this but have

difficulty finding ways of successfully impressing their worth on customers. Janitors fail to win their tenants' respect, but develop an
ideology which stresses the quasi-professional responsibility they
have to keep confidential the intimate knowledge of tenants they
acquire in the course of their work.[12] Physicians, lawyers, and other
professionals, more successful in winning the respect of clients, develop elaborate mechanisms for maintaining a properly respectful
relationship.

In justifying the existence of his position, the rule enforcer faces a
double problem. On the one hand, he must demonstrate to others that
the problem still exists: the rules he is supposed to enforce have some
point, because infractions occur. On the other hand, he must show that
his attempts at enforcement are effective and worthwhile, that the evil
he is supposed to deal with is in fact being dealt with adequately.
Therefore, enforcement organizations, particularly when they are
seeking funds, typically oscillate between two kinds of claims. First,
they say that by reason of their efforts the problem they deal with is
approaching solution. But, in the same breath, they say the problem is
perhaps worse than ever (though through no fault of their own) and
requires renewed and increased effort to keep it under control.
Enforcement officials can be more vehement than anyone else in their
insistence that the problem they are supposed to deal with is still with
us, in fact is more with us than ever before. In making these claims,
enforcement officials provide good reason for continuing the existence of the position they occupy.

We may also note that enforcement officials and agencies are inclined to take a pessimistic view of human nature. If they do not
actually believe in original sin, they at least like to dwell on the
difficulties in getting people to abide by rules, on the characteristics of
human nature that lead people toward evil. They are skeptical of
attempts to reform rule-breakers.

The skeptical and pessimistic outlook of the rule enforcer, of course,
is reinforced by his daily experience. He sees, as he goes about his
work, the evidence that the problem is still with us. He sees the
people who continually repeat offenses, thus definitely branding
themselves in his eyes as outsiders. Yet it is not too great a stretch of
the imagination to suppose that one of the underlying reasons for the
enforcer's pessimism about human nature and the possibilities of
reform is that fact that if human nature were perfectible and people
could be permanently reformed, his job would come to an end.

In the same way, a rule enforcer is likely to believe that it is
necessary for the people he deals with to respect him. If they do not, it
will be very difficult to do his job; his feeling of security in his work
will be lost. Therefore, a good deal of enforcement activity is devoted

not to the actual enforcement of rules, but to coercing respect from the people the enforcer deals with. This means that one may be labeled as deviant not because he has actually broken a rule, but because he has shown disrespect to the enforcer of the rule.

Westley's study of policemen in a small industrial city furnishes a good example of this phenomenon. In his interview, he asked policemen, "When do you think a policeman is justified in roughing a man up?" He found that "at least 37% of the men believed that it was legitimate to use violence to coerce respect."[13] He gives some illuminating quotations from his interviews:

> Well, there are cases. For example, when you stop a fellow for a routine questioning, say a wise guy, and he starts talking back to you and telling you you are no good and that sort of thing. You know you can take a man in on a disorderly conduct charge, but you can practically never make it stick. So what you do in a case like that is to egg the guy on until he makes a remark where you can justifiably slap him and, then, if he fights back, you can call it resisting arrest.

> Well, a prisoner deserves to be hit when he goes to the point where he tries to put you below him.

> You've gotta get rough when a man's language becomes very bad, when he is trying to make a fool of you in front of everybody else. I think most policemen try to treat people in a nice way, but usually you have to talk pretty rough. That's the only way to set a man down, to make him show a little respect.[14]

What Westley describes is the use of an illegal means of coercing respect from others. Clearly, when a rule enforcer has the option of enforcing a rule or not, the difference in what he does may be caused by the attitude of the offender toward him. If the offender is properly respectful, the enforcer may smooth the situation over. If the offender is disrespectful, then sanctions may be visited on him. Westley has shown that this differential tends to operate in the case of traffic offenses, where the policeman's discretion is perhaps at a maximum.[15] But it probably operates in other areas as well.

Ordinarily, the rule enforcer has a great deal of discretion in many areas, if only because his resources are not sufficient to cope with the volume of rule-breaking he is supposed to deal with. This means that he cannot tackle everything at once and to this extent must temporize with evil. He cannot do the whole job and knows it. He takes his time, on the assumption that the problems he deals with will be around for a long while. He establishes priorities, dealing with things in their turn, handling the most pressing problems immediately and leaving others for later. His attitude toward his work, in short, is professional. He lacks the naive moral fervor characteristic of the rule creator.

If the enforcer is not going to tackle every case he knows of at once, he must have a basis for deciding when to enforce the rule, which persons committing which acts to label as deviant. One criterion for selecting people is the "fix." Some people have sufficient political influence or know-how to be able to ward off attempts at enforcement, if not at the time of apprehension then at a later stage in the process. Very often, this function is professionalized; someone performs the job on a full-time basis, available to anyone who wants to hire him. A professional thief described fixers this way:

> There is in every large city a regular fixer for professional thieves. He has no agents and does not solicit and seldom takes any case except that of a professional thief, just as they seldom go to anyone except him. This centralized and monopolistic system of fixing for professional thieves is found in practically all of the large cities and many of the small ones.[16]

Since it is mainly professional thieves who know about the fixer and his operations, the consequence of this criterion for selecting people to apply the rules to is that amateurs tend to be caught, convicted, and labeled deviant much more frequently than professionals. As the professional thief notes:

> You can tell by the way the case is handled in court when the fix is in. When the copper is not very certain he has the right man, or the testimony of the copper and the complainant does not agree, or the prosecutor goes easy on the defendant, or the judge is arrogant in his decisions, you can always be sure that someone has got the work in. This does not happen in many cases of theft, for there is one case of a professional to twenty-five or thirty amateurs who know nothing about the fix. These amateurs get the hard end of the deal every time. The coppers bawl out about the thieves, no one holds up his testimony, the judge delivers an oration, and all of them get credit for stopping a crime wave. When the professional hears the case immediately preceding his own, he will think, "He should have got ninety years. It's the damn amateurs who cause all the heat in the stores." Or else he thinks, "Isn't it a damn shame for that copper to send that kid away for a pair of hose, and in a few minutes he will agree to a small fine for me for stealing a fur coat?" But if the coppers did not send the amateurs away to strengthen their records of convictions, they could not sandwich in the professionals whom they turn loose.[17]

Enforcers of rules, since they have no stake in the content of particular rules themselves, often develop their own private evaluation of the importance of various kinds of rules and infractions of them. This set of priorities may differ considerably from those held by the general public. For instance, drug users typically believe (and a few policemen have personally confirmed it to me) that police do not consider the use of marihuana to be as important a problem or as dangerous a practice as the use of opiate drugs. Police base this conclusion on the fact that, in their experience, opiate users commit other crimes (such as theft or prostitution) in order to get drugs, while marihuana users do not.

Enforcers, then, responding to the pressures of their own work situation, enforce rules and create outsiders in a selective way. Whether a person who commits a deviant act is in fact labeled a deviant depends on many things extraneous to his actual behavior: whether the enforcement official feels that at this time he must make some show of doing his job in order to justify his position, whether the misbehaver shows proper deference to the enforcer, whether the "fix" has been put in, and where the kind of act he has committed stands on the enforcer's list of priorities.

The professional enforcer's lack of fervor and routine approach to dealing with evil may get him into trouble with the rule creator. The rule creator, as we have said, is concerned with the content of the rules that interest him. He sees them as the means by which evil can be stamped out. He does not understand the enforcer's long-range approach to the same problems and cannot see why all the evil that is apparent cannot be stamped out at once.

When the person interested in the content of a rule realizes or has called to his attention the fact that enforcers are dealing selectively with the evil that concerns him, his righteous wrath may be aroused. The professional is denounced for viewing the evil too lightly, for failing to do his duty. The moral entrepreneur, at whose instance the rule was made, arises again to say that the outcome of the last crusade has not been satisfactory or that the gains once made have been whittled away and lost.

Notes

1. Joseph R. Gusfield, "Social Structure and Moral Reform: A Study of the Woman's Christian Temperance Union," *American Journal of Sociology*, LXI (November, 1955), 223.

2. *Ibid.*

3. See Raymond G. McCarthy, editor, *Drinking and Intoxication* (New Haven and New York: Yale Center of Alcohol Studies and The Free Press of Glencoe, 1959), pp. 395–396.

4. This is suggested in Oscar Lewis, *Sagebrush Casinos: The Story of Legal Gambling in Nevada* (New York: Doubleday and Co., 1953), pp. 233–234.

5. Edwin H. Sutherland, "The Diffusion of Sexual Psychopath Laws," *American Journal of Sociology*, LVI (September, 1950), 142–148.

6. *Ibid.*, p. 142.

7. *Ibid.*, pp. 143–145.

8. *Ibid.*, pp. 145–146.

9. Sheldon Messinger, "Organizational Transformation: A Case Study of a Declining Social Movement," *American Sociological Review*, XX (February, 1955), 3–10.

10. Gusfield, *op. cit.*, pp. 227–228.

11. *Ibid.*, pp. 227, 229–230.

12. See Ray Gold, "Janitors Versus Tenants: A Status-Income Dilemma," *American Journal of Sociology*, LVII (March, 1952), 486–493.

13. William A. Westley, "Violence and the Police," *American Journal of Sociology*, LIX (July, 1953), 39.

14. *Ibid.*

15. See William A. Westley, "The Police: A Sociological Study of Law, Custom, and Morality" (unpublished Ph.D. dissertation, University of Chicago, Department of Sociology, 1951).

16. Edwin H. Sutherland (editor), *The Professional Thief* (Chicago: University of Chicago Press, 1937), pp. 87–88.

17. *Ibid.*, pp. 91–92.

2 / Reactions to Deviance in a Junior High School: Student Views of the Labeling Process

ROBERT W. BALCH
DELOS H. KELLY

The study of deviant behavior has traditionally focused on deviant individuals as if they existed in a world apart from the agencies which define them as deviant. Delinquents, for example, are viewed as the unfortunate products of their families, friends, and communities. Not until recently have social scientists begun to realize that delinquency is created by a continuous process of interaction between children and the agents of social control, be they parents, teachers, or policemen. We need to be aware of the complex process by which children are progressively defined as troublemakers, as well as the kinds of reactions they elicit from others once so defined. As Erikson (1964) points out:

> "Deviance is not a property *inherent* in certain forms of behavior; it is a property *conferred upon* these forms by the audiences which directly or indirectly witness them. The critical variable in the study of deviance, then, is the social audience rather than the individual actor, since it is the audience which eventually determines whether or not any episode or behavior or any class of episodes is labeled deviant." [p. 11]

Lemert (1967) had a similar perspective in mind when he proposed a risk-taking model of deviant behavior. People, he said, are always engaging in behavior that runs the risk of being labeled criminal or delinquent. Why they deviate in the first place is less important than what happens to them after their aberrant behavior is discovered. The point is that most people at one time or another run this risk, but only a few of them are ever labeled deviant.

In the pages that follow we will discuss a new perspective on deviant behavior and then demonstrate its relevance to educational problems with data drawn from a large junior high school. We call this perspective an *interactional* approach to deviance because it deals directly with the interaction between deviants and the agents of social control (Rubington & Weinberg, 1968; Schafer, 1972).

24

AN INTERACTIONAL APPROACH
TO THE STUDY OF DEVIANCE

As long ago as 1938 Frank Tannenbaum suggested that deviant labels play a major role in the genesis of criminal behavior.

> There is a persistent demand for consistency in character. The community cannot deal with people it cannot define. Reputation is this sort of public definition. Once it is established, then unconsciously all agencies combine to maintain this definition even when they apparently and consciously attempt to deny their own implicit judgment.

> The process of making the criminal, therefore, is a process of tagging, defining, identifying, segregating, describing, emphasizing, making conscious and self-conscious; it becomes a way of stimulating, suggesting, emphasizing, and evoking the very traits that are complained of. [Tannenbaum, 1938, pp. 18-20.]

Advocates of Tannenbaum's version of the labeling process want to know how deviants react to their designations as criminal or delinquent. How do they come to adopt deviant roles? What changes in their group affiliations take place? And to what extent do they change their self conceptions to accord with their new social identity?

Central to the labeling perspective is the process of social typing. Assignment to a deviant category constitutes a collective attempt to come to terms with a pattern of apparently deviant acts. It is puzzling when a "good" boy breaks the rules, but when a "bad" boy does, no one is surprised. Everyone expects it *because he is a bad boy.* Thus labels help us make sense of the behavior of others. They explain the "real reasons" for a person's conduct.

The labeling perspective, as an etiological theory of deviance, depends heavily on the concept of the self-fulfilling prophecy. Processes set in motion by the act of labeling presumably confirm and strengthen one's deviant identity. According to Becker (1963) and Tannenbaum (1938), once an individual has been cast as a deviant, his other identities fade into the background. As Becker put it, deviance is a "master status" which overrides all others. Once a person has been labeled deviant, he is differentiated from others, segregated, and may eventually be excluded from conventional society. Just as the deviant is defined as an outsider by others, he learns to define others as outsiders, and eventually he may even accept his deviant role as a normal way of acting.

The process of exclusion often begins with selective perception, misperception, and the reintrepretation of deviant acts. Once a person has been labeled "homosexual," for example, it is hard to see him any other way.

> . . . when an individual's sexual "normality" is called into question, by whatever evidence, the imputation of homosexuality is documented by *retrospective interpretations* of the deviant's behavior, a process by which the subject re-interprets the individual's past behavior in the light of the new information concerning his sexual deviance. [Kitsuse, 1962, p. 253]

Mechanic (1962) and Scheff (1964) have concluded that psychiatrists who screen incoming mental patients often operate with a presumption of mental illness which determines how they see their patients. According to Mechanic, bias against prospective mental patients is built into the screening process. The psychiatrist has neither the time nor the criteria to make a definitive diagnosis, and frequently his theories are such that he presumes mental illness from the outset. No matter how "healthy" one appears on the surface, there may always be some pathology lurking somewhere in the background. Thus when someone is referred to the hospital by his family, the courts, or whatever, the psychiatrist finds it hard *not* to assume he is mentally disturbed. As one psychiatrist interviewed by Scheff (1964) put it: "The petition cases are pretty *automatic*. If the patient's own family wants to get rid of him you know there is something wrong [p. 410]." Once the assumption of mental illness is made, it is easy to "discover" pathological symptoms that confirm what everyone already suspects. Mechanic studied two mental hospitals over a three-month period, and not once did he find a case where the attending psychiatrist told a patient that he did not need help.

Scheff noticed that during their examinations many psychiatrists would search until they found "bad" answers which became conclusive proof of pathology, no matter how many good answers had gone before. The examining psychiatrists seemed to place an inordinate amount of weight on responses that confirmed their expectations. Some of them even seemed to be grasping at straws. One psychiatrist, after recommending that a girl be committed, explained she had said that bananas, apples, and oranges were all "something to eat" rather than fruit. The presumption of illness generates its own circular logic which virtually assures hospitalization. If patients admit they are mentally ill, they confirm what the psychiatrist already knew. If they deny their illness or demand legal counsel, they are said to lack "insight" into their condition or reveal signs of paranoia (Scheff, 1964; Szasz, 1970).

Deviant labels not only influence the way we "see" those who have been labeled, but how we react to them as well. Schwartz and Skolnick (1962) found that employers were reluctant to hire qualified applicants with a court record even when they had been acquitted and possessed a letter from the judge reaffirming their innocence. A study of Phillips (1963) reveals how association with another kind of labeling institution—the mental hospital—also leads to rejection. He found that a person described as psychologically normal but who had been in a mental hospital was rejected more severely on a social distance scale than a schizophrenic who sought no psychiatric help. Ray (1961) found that ex-heroin addicts frequently have difficulty returning to "straight" society because people still treat them as if they were addicts—"once a junkie, always a junkie."

Edwin Schur (1965) has demonstrated how the application of deviant labels leads to the segregation of drug users and homosexuals. Drug use and homosexuality are "crimes without victims" because they involve a willing exchange of goods and services. This is a critical point because the prohibition of such exchanges leads to the "secondary elaboration" of deviance. Although Schur never defines the term, it is very similar to Lemert's (1951) concept of "secondary deviance." Secondary deviance refers to deviant behavior which is a response to societal reactions to one's initial or "primary" deviant acts. For example, drug addiction is primary deviance. Society disapproves and makes drug use illegal. It becomes more difficult to obtain drugs, prices rise, and the addict must steal to support his habit. This is secondary deviation. Another form of secondary deviation is the prosperous illicit drug trade. Schur, however, prefers the more general term, "secondary elaboration" of deviance. The homosexual and drug subcultures are examples of such elaboration. They arise because deviants need continuous contact with each other to carry out their deviant acts. Gay bars offer homosexuals the mutual acceptance and moral support they are denied elsewhere. Eventually occasional homosexuals become regular participants. The homosexual community provides justifications for their behavior and denies the legitimacy of conventional definitions of homosexuality.

The concept of secondary deviation is worth pursuing. According to Lemert (1951, 1967), primary deviation is polygenetic. People violate social norms for all sorts of reasons, be they social, cultural, mental, or physiological. However, the initial cause of deviant behavior is less important than the reactions deviance evokes from other people. Secondary deviance springs from "a continuing sense of injustice, which is reinforced by job rejections, police cognizance, and strained interaction with normals [Lemert, 1967, p. 46]." It is the societal reaction to deviant behavior that is primarily responsible for the development of deviant careers. Consider the highly publicized case of Mary Ann Vecchio:

> The dark-haired girl first dropped into the news in an anonymous photograph, kneeling in horror over the body of Jeffrey Miller after National Guard bullets had cut him down at Kent State last May. She was soon identified as *Mary Ann Vecchio,* a runaway from Florida, only 14 but mature-looking and 6 feet tall. Back she went to a tearful reunion with her family in Opa-Locka, north of Miami, but Mary has had problems ever since. She was swamped with abusive letters, one calling her a "hippie Communist bitch" and another saying: "You dirty tramp. It's too bad it wasn't you that was shot." Parents warned their children to stay away from her. "No matter where Mary went, in a restaurant or anywhere, she was harassed," says her father. "She was told she was not welcome." Finally, after running away again and being picked up in a girl friend's apartment, she has been committed to a juvenile home for six months [*Newsweek,* April 5, 1971, p. 49]

Mary Ann's behavior obviously cannot be understood apart from the reactions of others all across the United States and especially in her hometown of Opa-Locka. Her case is a classic example of secondary deviation.

According to Rubington and Weinberg (1968), the final state in the ideal deviant career is the transformation of identity whereby the deviant finally admits that he "really is" a drug addict, a delinquent, or whatever. Like his conventional persecutors, he may even reinterpret his past to prove to himself that he has always been deviant— deep down inside if not overtly (Garfinkle, 1967). In the homosexual argot this is known as "coming out." The transformation of identity is not easy, however. Most deviants are marginal men, only secretly violating conventional norms. They move back and forth between deviant and conventional worlds, participating in both but belonging to neither. In a world of conformers it is not easy to be a deviant. In his study of systematic check forgers, Lemert (1967) found that being a "phony" day after day imposes serious identity problems that become unbearable after a while. For some, imprisonment is almost a welcome relief from the constant strain of pretending to be someone else. Here, of course, is where the deviant subculture plays an invaluable role, at least from the deviant's point of view. It provides him with an audience that will certify and support his deviant identity, that helps him "reject his rejectors" (McCorkle & Korn, 1954) and convinces him that he truly belongs in the deviant world.

The labeling process can be formal or informal. There is no law against being black, but Negroes are effectively excluded from many aspects of American society simply because of their color. Even color is often not as important as the ethnic label itself since Negroes who pass for white are quickly redefined and excluded when their racial background is discovered. Although there are laws prohibiting homosexuality, suspected sexual inverts need not have a long list of convictions to be rejected by straight society. Feminine demeanor or a vicious rumor may be just as effective as being arrested for propositioning a plain-clothes policeman. Thus deviants can be identified and singled out for special treatment by anyone. On the whole, however, officially sanctioned formal procedures for processing deviants are far more effective than informal measures (Rubington & Weinberg, 1968). The police, the courts, prisons, mental hospitals, and other agencies of social control have tremendous power to regulate the lives of citizens. A homosexual can always leave his home town for a fresh start, but he may never escape the police record he acquired there. For many people, contact with stigmatizing institutions is proof of a deviant character. The studies by Phillips (1963) and Schwartz and Skolnick (1962) are good illustrations. The critical role of formal labeling institutions has been summarized nicely by Szasz (1970).

> . . . just as the ordinary man in the Middle Ages had no way of knowing who was a witch, and recognized her only from her identification by inquisitors—so, in our day, the ordinary man has no way of knowing who is a madman, and recognizes him only from his identification by mental health workers. [pp. 235, 236]

LABELING IN SCHOOL

The school is an excellent place to observe the labeling process. Cicourel and Kitsuse (1963) have proposed a labeling explanation for much of the "deviant" behavior that counselors deal with in high schools. They point out that high school counselors occupy a marginal status somewhere between clinical psychologists and social workers. In order to justify their position, they must carve out a new area of concern not fully dealt with by either of the more established disciplines. Consequently they have begun to identify emotional and behavioral "problems" among the students that previously went unnoticed. These problems are duly noted in the students' records and follow them around for years, often determining whether they are placed in college-bound or remedial tracks.

Placement in a high or low track can have serious consequences for a student's career. In one intriguing study. Rosenthal and Jacobson (1968) showed how teachers' expectations can influence their students' academic performance. They randomly assigned elementary students to experimental and control conditions. Teachers in the experimental group were told to expect "unusual intellectual gains" from their students since they were all supposed to be academic "spurters." Teachers in the control group were told nothing. After eight months the students in the experimental condition showed significantly greater intellectual improvement than the control students. Not only that, but the experimental students were described as more interesting, curious, and happy. Their teachers also believed they had a significantly better chance of becoming successful in the future. This study reveals how ability grouping can become a self-fulfilling prophecy. Teachers expect, and therefore get, more from students in the college-bound track. Conversely they expect poorer performance from students in the lower tracks, and they are rarely disappointed.

Elder (1965) has reviewed some early studies of "streaming" (tracking) in England which show that placement in a lower stream can have serious detrimental effects, including damaged self-esteem and poor academic performance. Perhaps the best study of streaming in England was conducted by David Hargreaves (1967) at Lumley Secondary School. The top stream was the *raison d' etre* for Lumley. Boys in this stream were groomed for the rigorous grammar school qualifying exam, and Lumley's prestige as an educational institution depended largely on the number of students who passed. Top stream boys were neat, intelligent, and polite. They received constant recognition and approval from their teachers. On the other hand, the faculty took a dim view of boys in the lower streams. These boys cheated on exams and "messed around" in class just to spite their teachers. In turn, their teachers rated them low in appearance and behavior, and regarded their jobs as more custodial than anything else. Each stream's orientation was continually reinforced by the actions of the faculty. Low-stream boys were treated as if they were incapable of assuming responsibility, while the top-stream boys were carefully prepared for their exams. Streams were constantly compared with each other, and for the upper-stream boys, these comparisons were used as a means of social control. For example, a sign in one classroom read: "We must always remember to behave as an A class [Hargreaves, 1967, p. 94]." Interaction was also stream-bound, since each stream had its own teachers, met in its own classes, and participated in its own activities.

Given the pattern of social segregation and the invidious distinctions made by the teachers, it is not surprising that Hargreaves found that academic achievement, educational aspirations, and delinquent involvement varied by stream. Because of their troublemaking character, Hargreaves labeled the culture of the lower streams "delinquescent."

Hargreaves believed the differences between the streams were caused by the streaming process itself, and his argument is similar to that used by writers in the labeling tradition. Consistent with his hypothesis, he found that the second-year streams displayed practically none of the differences he found in the fourth year. Thus it appears that these differences were more likely to appear the longer the boys had been in the system.

Unfortunately Hargreaves' study is subject to alternative explanations. Briefly, stream assignment was positively (although not strongly) related to social class. More importantly, the parents of the high-stream boys tended to have a middle-class outlook—for example, greater concern for their sons' school achievement and eventual job success. Another alternative explanation is suggested in passing by Hargreaves. The streams could have become more homogeneous over time as "good" boys were promoted and "bad" ones dropped.

Fortunately a study by Schafer and Olexa (1971) has eliminated some of these problems. Their data show that when social class, I.Q., and past performance were held constant, there were still significant differences between the high and low tracks of two midwestern high schools. Students in the lower track were more likely to receive low grades, drop out of school, and become delinquent.

Even without a formal tracking system, the labeling process can have unfortunate consequences (Schafer, 1972; Schafer & Polk, 1967).

> . . . many schools unknowingly support formal and informal "mechanisms" whereby negative reputations of students are diffused among other staff. All too often the teachers' lounge or coffee room is the burying ground for students' success chances, as teachers openly inform each other about students "to watch out for," or confirm each other's negative assessments of so and so's attitude or conduct. [Schafer & Polk, 1967, p. 252]

Some schools even circulate lists of troublemakers among their teachers, and most keep formal records that help determine school careers. Unfortunately, at least as far as official records are concerned, it is much easier to acquire a bad reputation than a good one (Vinter & Sarri, 1965). Once defined as a troublemaker, the gradual process of exclusion is set in motion. Deviant students may be assigned to special classrooms, given low grades, or excluded from extracurricular activities (Schafer & Polk, 1967). Rather than reinvolving deviant students, schools may unwittingly force them out of the system.

HOW STUDENTS SEE THE LABELING PROCESS: AN EMPIRICAL STUDY

The data reported in the following pages are drawn from a broader study of the labeling process in a junior high school (Balch, 1972). In order to find out how students perceive the process of defining and punishing "troublemakers," we administered a brief questionnaire to 105 ninth-grade students attending a large junior high school on the Pacific Coast.[1] Our questionnaire contained seven vignettes, each describing a junior high school boy. Subjects were told to imagine that each boy had been caught in the hall during class time without a pass. After reading each vignette, the students were asked how "most teachers" would punish the boy. One boy had a reputation as a troublemaker around school, but he had not been in trouble with the police. The second boy was every teacher's ideal—a clean-cut reliable student council member. The third boy was simply a good quiet student, at least in the eyes of his teachers. The fourth was also a good student, but he became defiant when he was caught without his pass. The fifth boy was described as a a hippie. The sixth was a work-experience student,[2] a hard worker but not too interested in school. The last boy had repeatedly been in trouble with the police but had managed to stay "clean" at school. The same students were also asked to explain their answers. Although this question was optional, over half of them made comments, some quite extensive.

The results are presented in Table 1. The students clearly believed that teachers punish differently depending on the character of the offending student. Eighty-one percent of the students said that most teachers would be harder on the boy known as a troublemaker around school than they would be on other students caught without a pass. Although this boy had never been in trouble with the police, his teachers knew he was "a guy to watch out for." He enjoyed aggravating his teachers in class and he had been caught smoking in the restroom several times during the year. One student wrote that the teachers "would probably try to nail some rap on him for all the trouble he's caused." Several others said that teachers would probably be harder on him because they would question his motives. If a troublemaker is in the hall without a pass, he is up to no good, but a "good" student probably has a legitimate reason.

Not surprisingly 82 percent said that the student council member would be treated more easily than other students. As one put it, "They would probably joke with him a minute and let him go." Some reasons:

Because he's a good guy and doesn't tell his teachers what he thinks, so they like him.

Teachers like to be popular. They won't be if they give popular kids a rough time.

Because no one would believe he doesn't have a good reason for being there.

Table 1 / How Students Think Teachers Would React If They Caught a Student in the Hall Without a Pass

Perceived Response by Teachers	Kind of Student						
	TROUBLE IN SCHOOL	ALL-AROUND GUY	GOOD QUIET STUDENT	GOOD STUDENT BUT DEFIANT	HIPPIE	WORK-STUDY STUDENT	TROUBLE WITH POLICE
Most teachers would be easier on him than other guys	2	82	64	6	4	23	4
Most teachers would be harder on him than other guys	81	1	2	81	75	2	49
Most teachers would punish him about the same as they would anyone else	17	17	34	13	21	75	48
Total	100	100	100	100	100	100	101

Note: Figures rounded to nearest whole percent. N = 105.

Although the percentage is not as high, most students (64 percent) thought their teachers would also be more lenient with the quiet, withdrawn student who never caused any trouble. Of course a good reputation is no guarantee that teachers will be lenient. The boy described in the fourth vignette was a good student, an athlete, and all his teachers liked him. But he became defiant and shouted at the teacher when he was caught without a pass. Eighty-one percent of the students said that most teachers would punish him more severely than other students. Thus the nature of the offense clearly plays a big role in the treatment of the offender.

Seventy-five percent said that teachers would be more punitive with the boy who had been labeled a hippie. This boy had long hair and occasionally wore a headband to keep it out of his eyes. Although he could afford better, he wore an old army jacket and a pair of worn-out jeans. He also was reputed to be a drug user. According to one student, the nonconformist cannot win no matter what he does:

A lot of teachers purposely pick out kids with long hair and continuously pick on them and embarrass them in front of everybody. Pretty soon that person will lose interest or just give up because everyone already thinks he's a failure. Then the teachers start in again saying, "I knew he would flunk out. If the dirty hippie would get his hair cut maybe he could see some of the things going on in the classroom." Lots of times the kids get their hair cut out of desperation that maybe the teachers will bug off. That's a big laugh. The teachers will only bug him more and say things like, "Hey lookie!!! The fairy got his hair cut." I know, I've seen it happen before.

Most students (75 percent) thought that the work-experience student would be treated about the same as anyone else, but a sizeable minority (23 percent) believed that teachers would be more lenient with him. Nevertheless a few students made revealing comments about the work-study program. According to one girl:

I was going to be in work-experience but I didn't because I knew what the teacher would think. I get the impression from the teachers that if you're in work-experience you're poor (financially), you're a poor student, you get lousy grades, you're dirty, and you take it just to get out of school.

Another girl shared this opinion:

I think work-experience leaves a huge influence on teachers about the kid. They will act differently towards them . . . They actually single a person out if he has work-experience. They think that the kid is probably in trouble all the time and doesn't even care about going to college and is lazy and just wants to get out of class.

The greatest amount of disagreement was expressed over the boy with the police record. He had been caught breaking windows, stealing a case of beer, and even selling marijuana. He had not been in trouble at school, however. Forty-nine percent of the students said most teachers would be harder on him than other students while 48 percent said they would treat him about the same as anyone else. One student described how several boys had been treated after they were "busted" for using mescaline.

[The teachers] kept an eye on them. They didn't trust them any more. The counselors would ask their teachers how they were doing in their classes. If the kid was goofing off or acting strange they would call them in. The teachers, I could tell, didn't like them very well either. One of the guys was a cadet teacher and the teacher he worked for made him write a 500 [word] essay on what a cadet teacher should be.

It may be significant that the differences in punitiveness are clear-cut for every boy described in the questionnaire except the boy who had a police record. He was the only student whose deviant behavior did not take place in the school. Almost 50 percent of the students said he would be treated about the same as any other student, and many remarked that teachers would not bother him as long as he stayed out of trouble in his classes. As one student put it, "If he was clean at school and not like he was in town, they think of [his police record] as a minor detail." The students' replies suggest that teachers seem to be most sensitive to deviance when it is school-related, that is, when it threatens to disrupt the day-to-day routine of the school system.

We also asked the students what specific actions teachers would take against a boy with a reputation for "hassling" his teachers (Table 2). Eight alternatives (plus an open-ended response) were provided and the students were told to check as many items as they wished. Three responses were checked most frequently: "They would send him to the office more often" (71 percent); "They would lower his grade because of his bad attitude" (67 percent); and "They would

Table 2 / How Students Think Teachers Would Treat a Boy With a Reputation as a Troublemaker

Item	Percent Agreeing
They would treat him like any other student	18
They would be more lenient with him	14
They would make cutting remarks to him	59
They would try to keep him out of clubs and activities	36
They would try to have him transferred out of their classes	35
They would send him to the office more often	71
They would lower his grade because of his bad attitude	67
They would give him special help	21

Note: Figures rounded to nearest whole percent. Multiple responses were permitted. N = 105.

make cutting remarks to him" (59 percent). One of the students in a remedial English class wanted to know what "cutting remarks" were. Another student replied, "That's the way Mr. _____ talks to us." According to the teacher who administered the questionnaire, the student understood immediately. While 36 percent said that teachers would try to keep troublemakers out of clubs and activities, the exclusion of deviant students may happen more often than the students realize. For example, once a girl was not allowed to become a cheerleader because the faculty sponsors believed she would cause trouble. After the tryouts, the students voted for the girls they thought would make the best cheerleaders. The girl in question was elected, but the sponsors awarded the position to another girl. The students, of course, never knew because they did not count the votes. An example from another school in the same state illustrates how programs can be structured in such a way that undesirable students will be excluded. An English teacher working in a suburb of a large city was in charge of a field trip to a Shakespearean festival. Too many students had signed up for the trip, including many "dummies" and "dingalings" who would probably get in trouble and who "wouldn't benefit from the trip anyhow." In order to eliminate the undesirables, the teacher established stiff prerequisites for the trip. She made several heavy reading and writing assignments about the English theater with little time to complete them. Her stated purpose (at least in her conversations with other teachers) was to weed out the troublemakers and to limit the program to only the best students. (At the time, however, she was quite discouraged because all the students, including the "dingalings," were completing her assignments).[3]

The students also mentioned a wide variety of other ways that trouble-makers are treated. One of the most frequent responses was *close surveillance.* Many students said that teachers watch a known troublemaker more closely than other students so they are more likely to notice if he steps out of line again. Others said he would always be the prime suspect whenever there is trouble.

Every time there was trouble and he was around he would get questioned about it.

They would watch him more closely to get him in more trouble.

They would probably talk about him and accuse him of things that weren't really his fault.

Blame everything that happens in class on him.

He would be the first suspect if anything happened.

They would actually hope he would do something so they could get him for it.

A smattering of other students gave responses like the following:

Not pay attention when he asks questions.

They wouldn't be friendly with him.

They wouldn't call on them as much in class.

They would use him as an example in class.

Of course many students also said it was difficult to judge teachers generally because their styles of teaching or dealing with students are so varied. Many students mentioned the names of teachers they thought were especially unfair, and the same names kept recurring throughout their responses. Perhaps the trouble is not with "most teachers" as the questionnaire suggested, but with a few notorious individuals.

Interestingly enough, a few students said that most teachers would be more *lenient* with serious troublemakers than with other students.

Most teachers treat kids like they are a lost cause if they know they have been in trouble. Sometimes they will even refrain from getting them into trouble, because they have been before. These kids can get away with anything.

Rather than being more severe, some teachers may ignore trou-blemakers unless they are seriously disruptive. In effect they say, "What's the point of punishing him? It won't do any good." Punish-ment is viewed as therapeutic. Sending a student to the office may "put a good scare into him" unless the student has been there so many times that the prospect no longer frightens him. At that point some teachers may choose to ignore him if at all possible. Only a minority of students said that teachers would treat the troublemaker "like any other student" (18 percent) or give him special help (21 percent).

Earlier we indicated that people may be labeled deviant simply because they have been to see a psychiatrist or have been in a mental hospital. Several students described an interesting parallel. Students who come to the main office for whatever reason must sit and wait outside the counselor's offices. However, teachers who see a student waiting in the office during class time assume he is in trouble. The assumption is understandable since troublemakers are constantly being sent to the office for disciplinary action, yet the consequences can be unfortunate. One student described what can happen.

I was in front of [a counselor's] office to get my eighth period Journalism class changed to cadet teaching. Then along came Mr. _____. He saw me sitting there in front of the closed door of [the counselor's] office and said, "Well, Bill, what kind of trouble did you get in this time." I was so mad that I took my green transfer slip out of my pocket and held it in front of his face. He walked away and as he was going he turned and said, "Maybe not this time, but you'll get the shaft one of these days." This whole time I hadn't said one single word to him.

While our data strongly suggest that troublemakers are treated more harshly than "good" students, they also reveal that differential treatment is an extremely complex process. A delinquent does not have to be punished more severely than other students for the same offenses to feel the weight of discriminatory treatment. He knows he has been singled out whenever a teacher refuses to call on him in class, or whenever a teacher makes a cutting remark about the length of his hair—the same kind of "smart" remark he might get in trouble for if he had said it himself.

Of course, a certain amount of caution is in order. Our questionnaire only dealt with *students' perceptions* of the teachers' behavior, and there was no attempt to disguise the purpose of the study. As one girl pointed out, many students use discrimination as an excuse whenever they get into trouble.

Everyone is different and naturally you're going to be treated different. I think kids may be going against the teachers just because they didn't get the grade they wanted, and are blaming it on discrimination.

Nevertheless, even if many students are exaggerating, there still is strong evidence that troublemakers are treated much differently than other students. Furthermore, as students interact with their teachers, their behavior will be determined by their perceptions of the student-teacher relationship. As W. I. Thomas (1923) pointed out long ago, if people define a situation as real, it will be real in its consequences.

CONCLUSION

The implications of these data are very important. As students pass through the school system, they acquire reputations—good or bad—which precede them wherever they go. When a student's reputation precedes him, teachers may be predisposed to see only the bad side of the student—or the good side as the case may be. Although their unfavorable impressions may not initially lead to discriminatory behavior, their limited perception of the labeled student could lead to an accumulation of undesirable information about that student which may eventually be used to justify discriminatory treatment. If they already know that so-and-so is a "bad kid," they may try to keep him out of their classes, or they could make it difficult for him to join the clubs they sponsor. By avoiding contact with him, they begin or reinforce a gradual process of exclusion whereby the boy is quietly eased out of the mainstream of school society. They also reduce their chances of correcting their first impressions. Of course in real life teachers have many more cues available to them on which to base their impressions —e.g., the length of a student's hair, his demeanor, and his style of dress. All of these cues influence a teacher's decision about a student: Is he basically a good kid who has a few problems? or is he genuinely bad?

When teachers are unable to avoid contact with the student, they may unwittingly evoke the very responses they expected to see in the first place. For example, one boy described an experience he had after a teacher had seen him sitting in the office. The boy was there to have his schedule changed, but the teacher assumed he was in trouble.

. . . the next day that same teacher walked by in the hall and when I was about to pass him he grabbed me and said he would like to have a talk with me and he went through a lot of stuff saying like whatever you tell me it won't get out . . . He humiliated me in front of all my friends.

The boy went on to explain how he "got smart" with the teacher because what he had been doing in the office was none of the teacher's business. Perhaps the boy had every right to be upset, but his response probably only confirmed the teacher's suspicions.

Once a student has been typed, it is difficult for him to change his image because other people perceive him selectively. As many students indicated, known troublemakers are always the first suspects whenever anything bad happens. Teachers watch them more closely than other students because they expect them to get in trouble, and therefore they are more apt to notice if the students step out of line again. Of course deviant behavior occurs all the time. Good students as well as bad ones break the rules. But, as many of the students pointed out, some teachers respond very differently depending on what they "know" about the offender. If a "good" student is caught in the hall without a pass during class time, the teachers might "joke with him a minute and let him go." They would assume he had a good reason for being there. But if a "troublemaker" were caught in the same situation, they would probably assume he was cutting class. When good students deviate, we assume their behavior is either accidental or justified by the circumstances. It is hard to impute malicious intent to a basically good person.

We suggest, in conclusion, that one cannot understand deviance in the school system unless he first understands the process by which students are labeled as troublemakers. Deviance is, after all, not just something someone does. It is a status conferred on him by the agents of social control, and the reactions the deviant elicits from others may have a profound impact on his outlook and subsequent school career. As Schafer (1972) points out, highly coercive or degrading sanctions may have the immediate outcome of curbing deviant behavior, but

> in the long run it is likely that their result will be further deterioration of the student's educational commitment—further alienation from school personnel, ideals, and norms. Such unintended by-products of sanctioning practices may in fact contribute to the very problems which the sanctions are designed to alleviate. Thus the school itself may, through its own activities, sustain or even generate the deviance it seeks so hard to reduce. [p. 158]

References

Balch, R. W. Negative reactions to delinquent labels in a junior high school. Unpublished doctoral dissertation, University of Oregon, 1972.

Becker, H. S. *Outsiders: Studies in the sociology of deviance.* New York: Free Press, 1963.

Cicourel, A. V., and Kitsuse, J. I. *The educational decision-makers.* Indianapolis: Bobbs-Merrill, 1963.

Elder, G. H., Jr. Life opportunity and personality: Some consequences of stratified secondary education in Great Britain. *Sociology of Education,* 1965, *38,* 173–202.

Erikson, K. T. Notes on the sociology of deviance. In H. S. Becker (Ed.). *The other side: Perspectives on deviance.* New York: Free Press, 1964.

Garfinkle, H. *Studies in ethnomethodology.* Englewood Cliffs, N.J.: Prentice-Hall, 1967.

Hargreaves, D. *Social relations in a secondary school.* New York: Humanities Press, 1967.

Kitsuse, J. I. Societal reaction to deviant behavior. *Social Problems,* 1962, *9,* 247–256.

Lemert, E. M. *Social pathology.* New York: McGraw-Hill, 1951.

————. *Human deviance, social problems and social control.* Englewood Cliffs, N.J.: Prentice Hall, 1967.

McCorkle, L. W., and Korn, R. Resocialization within walls. *Annals of the American Academy of Political and Social Science,* 1954, *293,* 88–98.

Mechanic, D. Some factors in identifying and defining mental illness. *Mental Hygiene*, 1962, *46*, 66–74.

Newsweek, April 5, 1971, p. 49 (untitled).

Phillips, D. L. Rejection: A possible consequence of seeking help for mental disorders. *American Sociological Review*, 1963, *28*, 963–972.

Ray, M. The cycle of abstinence and relapse among heroin addicts. *Social Problems*, 1961, *9*, 132–140.

Rosenthal, R., and Jacobson, J. Self-fulfilling prophecies in the classroom: Teachers' expectations as unintended determinants for pupils' intellectual competence. In M. Deutsch, I. Katz, and A. R. Jensen (Eds.), *Social class, race, and psychological development.* New York: Holt, Rinehart & Winston, 1968.

Rubington, E., and Weinberg, M. S. *Deviance: The interactionist perspective.* New York: Macmillan, 1968.

Schafer, W. E. Deviance in the public school: An interactional view. In K. Polk and W. E. Schafer (Eds.), *Schools and delinquency.* Englewood Cliffs, N.J.: Prentice-Hall, 1972.

Schafer, W. E., and Olexa, C. *Tracking and opportunity: The locking-out process and beyond.* Scranton, Pa.: Chandler, 1971.

Schafer, W. E., and Polk, K. Delinquency and the schools. In President's Commission on Law Enforcement and Administration of Justice, *Task force report: Juvenile delinquency and youth crime.* Washington, D.C.: U.S. Government Printing Office, 1967.

Scheff, T. J. The societal reaction to deviance: Ascriptive elements in the psychiatric screening of mental patients in a midwestern state. *Social Problems*, 1964, *11*, 401–413.

Schur, E. M. *Crimes without victims.* Englewood Cliffs, N.J.: Prentice-Hall, 1965.

Schwartz, R. D., and Skolnick, J. H. Two studies of legal stigma. *Social Problems*, 1962, *10*, 133–138.

Szasz, T. S. *The manufacture of madness.* New York: Harper & Row, 1970.

Tannenbaum, F. *Crime and the community.* New York: Columbia University, 1938.

Thomas, W. I. *The unadjusted girl.* Boston: Little, Brown, 1923.

Vinter, R. D., and Sarri, R. S. Malperformance in the public school: A group work approach. *Social Work*, 1965, *10*, 3–13.

Notes

1. The school is located in a town of approximately 6,000 people, but it also serves several nearby rural communities. The population is primarily blue-collar, a fact reflected by the socio-economic status of our student sample. Seventy-two percent of the students had fathers employed as unskilled, semi-skilled, or skilled workers. Only 20 percent came from white-collar families, and the remainder either had unemployed fathers or did not respond to the question. The sample consisted of four ninth-grade English classes and one ninth-grade Spanish class. The questionnaire took about 15 to 20 minutes to complete.

2. Work-experience students attended classes in the morning but have a part-time job at a local business during the afternoon.

3. These examples were provided by a teacher employed at the junior high school.

Part 2 / Understanding Deviance: Theories and Perspectives

In the preceding section I introduced a specific concern for the ways in which deviant categories arise, as well as the ways in which violators of existing categories may be reacted to. Missing from this introduction was a concern for *why* actors may exhibit behavior in violation of established norms, rules, regulations, and laws — violations which may ultimately result in their being initially labeled as deviants. I have argued previously that if we are to approach a more complete understanding of deviance in terms of social processes, we must not only analyze the creation of deviant categories and the reactions to violators of categories; we must also examine the motivations for deviance. The selections in this part represent some of the major attempts to do so.

Explanations of the motivations for deviance have taken various forms. Some observers would place the blame on defective family structure or arrested personality adjustment; others would emphasize such conditions as poverty or racism; and there are proponents of the thesis that individuals are born deviant. It should be recognized, however, that no single factor can adequately explain why actors commit deviant acts. For example, what we generally find in the area of delinquency research is that a combination of family, school, and peer variables seems to make the most sense in providing motivations for youth crime and deviance.

The actual attempts at understanding or explaining can, for our purposes, be roughly grouped into six categories: (1) functionalist, (2) culture conflict, (3) cultural transmission, (4) anomie, (5) conflict theory, and (6) interactionist. Of these particular approaches, it should be noted that functionalism, culture conflict, and anomie are basically structural. Some who pursue this model seek to explain why crime and deviance exist in the social system, while others analyze societal-structural conditions that seem to produce pressures toward deviation. The cultural transmission view is concerned primarily with how, through social-psychological-symbolic processes, actors learn existing cultures and traditions. The conflict theorists, by contrast, investigate how the powerful influence the creation of deviant categories, and point out, as well, their frequent application to the less powerful. Finally, the interactionists analyze the labeling ceremony and its impact upon individuals. It should be noted, too, that while each of these approaches explicitly emphasizes certain underlying themes, concepts, or processes, there is frequently an implied or direct degree of overlap between or among the various models. Such linkages are evident in the representative statements of each model that follow.

The Functionalist Perspective

Social scientists who pursue a functionalist model contend that deviance is an integral part of any social system and that such behavior satisfies some societal need. In terms of sociological analysis, they maintain, deviance serves the important function of demarcating and maintaining current boundaries of acceptable behavior. These particular conceptions are embedded in Emile Durkheim's work.

In his statement "The Normal and the Pathological," Durkheim argues that not only is crime present in all societies, but serves a useful function for the collective conscience, particularly in maintaining the social system. And while forms and definitions of criminal and deviant behavior (i.e., the *collective types* or deviant categories) may vary from society to society, they do provide members with a basis upon which to punish violators of the prevailing normative codes. Punishment serves as an important reminder to others that certain behaviors are acceptable while others are not. Thus, to achieve an understanding of deviance and its categories requires an examination of the prevailing definitions of conformity.

A somewhat similar position has been advanced by Robert A. Dentler and Kai T. Erikson. In "The Functions of Deviance in Groups," they focus on social groups, especially with regard to the way in which deviance affects groupings or collectivities. They postulate that (1) groups tend to induce, sustain, and permit deviant behavior; (2) deviant behavior functions in enduring groups to help maintain group equilibrium; and (3) groups will resist any trend toward alienation of a member whose behavior is deviant. They attempt to substantiate their propositions by analyzing Quaker work projects and Army basic training units. One gains an understanding, from their study, of the ways in which various types of deviant activity actually affect group stability and maintenance.

It should be noted that Durkheim, and Dentler and Erikson, make no real attempt to explain why actors engage in activities that may result in their being labeled as deviants. The next perspective, however, considers the question of motivation more directly; in so doing, it enters the realm of social-psychological, or interactional, processes, particularly those aspects concerned with the inculcation of values and traditions within members of a society.

The Culture Conflict Perspective

A basic premise underlying this perspective is the notion that, because socializing influences and experiences vary a great deal, people are frequently confronted with conflicting definitions of a situation. Furthermore, if they act in accordance with their own values, they may be defined as deviants by those who are operating from a different set of values.

These ideas are elaborated upon by Thorsten Sellin. In "Culture Conflict and Crime," he argues that actors are members of numerous groups and are, therefore, exposed to many different sets of conduct norms and values. Among those who migrate from one society to another, the sense of cultural conflict may be particularly severe. Migrants frequently find themselves constrained and regulated by a new, and unfamiliar, set of values. Sellin cites, as an example, the case in which a father kills the seducer of his daughter. In Sicily, killing a seducer is acceptable; in the United States it is considered murder. A lack of consensus with respect to existing norms, then, may not only give rise to cultural conflict of various types but may result in the application of deviant labels to those who violate deviant categories.

The next selection, "Lower Class Culture as a Generating Milieu of Gang Delinquency," provides a more graphic illustration of how cultural conflict may lead to behavior that can be termed criminal, delinquent, or deviant by representatives of the larger, dominant culture—a culture that possesses the power and resources to define people as deviants. In this study Walter B. Miller, in examining the reasons why actors engage in delinquent or deviant acts, focuses upon the structure of the family. Central to his argument is the belief that growing up in a female-based household can create an identity problem in adolescent males. Miller contends that teenage youths may deal with actual or potential identity crises by becoming involved with spontaneous, single-sex peer groups. By aligning themselves with what Miller terms "focal concerns"—that is, by participating in activities which provide a certain degree of tension and excitement—the youths automatically violate the rules, regulations, and laws of the dominant, middle-class culture.

Cultural Transmission Theory

A central tenet underlying the cultural transmission model is the idea that one learns cultural traditions and values through symbolic communication with others. Probably the most famous representatives of this position are Edwin H. Sutherland and Donald R. Cressey.

In "Differential Association Theory," they seek to explain the ways in which deviant, and particularly criminal, behavior arises. Central to their analysis is the notion that as we learn to become conformists, we must also learn to become criminals. Basic to this learning process is the concept of social interaction, whereby actors, relating to one another in small, intimate groups, become socialized into the ways of the existing cultures and traditions. As part of socialization, one may learn that violation of the law is unacceptable, or one may be taught that it is acceptable, even desirable. It is argued, thereafter, that it is those individuals who have learned that violation is acceptable who will engage in criminal activities. Another important point concerns the *content* of learning. Individuals learn not only the appropriate "motives, drives, rationalizations, and attitudes" for committing crimes but the specific techniques for doing so.

The next statement, by Gresham M. Sykes and David Matza, also relates directly to cultural transmission theory, especially to those aspects dealing with the content of learning—that is, definitions of the legal codes and rationalizations. In "Techniques of Neutralization: A Theory of Delinquency," Sykes and Matza argue that contrary to the theory of Cohen especially, juveniles do not really reject middle-class values. Rather, because the existing normative structure has a certain flexibility, actors can "bend" the laws to fit their needs. Also basic to this thesis is the idea that when actors contemplate the commission of a delinquent or criminal act, they must come to grips with any immediate or potential threats to their identity. Developing an effective system of "neutralization" or rationalization is one way of accomplishing this. Sykes and Matza assert, moreover, that an attitude of self-justification is necessary not only before the commission of the offense; rationalization is operative during and after the act as well. The writers make the additional point that we all use rationalizations, whether we are involved in deviant activities or not.

Several of the articles discussed thus far (e.g., Sutherland and Cressey) have been concerned rather directly with the way in which socialization processes may bring about behavior that can be labeled as deviant. However, with one notable exception (Miller's theory), none of these writers has systematically examined the conditions that may lead to an exploration of nonconformist adaptations. The next perspective offers a more specific attempt to do so.

Anomie or Opportunity Theory

Those who subscribe to anomie theory are concerned primarily with the social conditions that may produce a strain toward deviation. Of particular focus is the way actors posture themselves relative to the existing social structure. Robert K. Merton's article "Social Structure and Anomie" represents what many consider the classic study, within anomie theory, of the emergence of deviant behavior.

Basic to Merton's explanation is the contention that any society can be characterized in terms of its structure, particularly its goals and its means. A well-integrated society, he reasons, displays a balance between these elements. Thus, when people want to obtain societal goals, they will use the appropriate institutionalized means for doing so. American society, according to Merton, does not maintain this sort of balance. It is a society in which there is an almost exclusive emphasis placed upon the achievement of goals—regardless of the methods used to attain them. Those affected the most by the imbalance are the *lower classes*. Most members of the lower classes accept the American dream of attaining success; when they attempt to realize their goals through legitimate means, however, they find themselves blocked, mainly because they do not possess the necessary resources. They may substitute other means—for instance, stealing or robbing. Merton refers to these individuals as "innovators." He argues, further, that when there is a disjunction between goals and means, the result may be cultural chaos, or *anomie*. In this situation predictability and regulation of behavior become tenuous.

Richard A. Cloward and Lloyd E. Ohlin, in "Differential Opportunity and Delinquent Subcultures," extend Merton's theory by incorporating a direct concern for the notion of *illegitimate opportunity structures*; they also make a significant contribution to the literature on the formation of deviant subcultures. The authors argue specifically that, just as there are differentials in access to legitimate means (Merton), so there are differentials in access to illegitimate means (Sutherland and Cressey). What this means is that illegitimate avenues are not necessarily open or freely available to those unable to obtain goals through legitimate channels. Not everyone, for instance, can become a successful con artist or embezzler. Cloward and Ohlin substantiate their thesis by showing how status-deprived, lower-class males learn the necessary skills associated with a particular type of criminal activity. Whether a specific activity or subculture evolves, however, is a function of the existing structure of the neighborhood, especially the relative availability of legitimate and illegitimate opportunity structures. For example, in a setting which exhibits a high degree of integration, or interplay, between legitimate and illegitimate structures, a criminal subculture is likely to evolve. Such a subculture furnishes the deprived with a source of material gain and provides them with a setting in which they can become socialized into the ways of an existing culture and traditions.

Although several of the statements thus far have offered hypotheses as to why deviance exists in a social system—and why actors commit deviant acts—none has provided an overall framework that can be used to understand how deviant categories arise, why they are violated, and how they are enforced. (The major exception is Becker's general statement in part one.) The next perspective, however, addresses these concerns in a more systematic, integrated manner.

Conflict Theory

Conflict theorists study groups, particularly the ways in which their interests and needs influence the definitions and policies that evolve. The statement by George B. Vold, "Group Conflict Theory as an Explanation of Crime," is representative of this position. Vold argues that group conflict can be used to explain the incidence of certain types of crime. Society, he believes, exhibits an uneasy equilibrium "of balanced forces in opposition." These groups, he contends, frequently come into conflict with each other when their purposes clash; this often occurs in competitive situations. Furthermore, as they line up against each other, groups invariably seek the assistance of the state "to help them defend their 'rights' and protect their interests." In essence, Vold argues that the political process of law making, law breaking, and law enforcement is "a direct reflection of deep-seated and fundamental conflicts between interest groups and their more general struggles for control of the police power of the state." Vold provides content to his thesis by analyzing why those who do not possess the power and influence to make the laws, but who frequently feel the brunt of the laws, may elect to violate the laws. Understanding this model thus requires an examination of the *total* political process and its outcomes.

A similar but somewhat more explicit statement of the conflict perspective is provided by Richard Quinney in his selection, "The Social Reality of Crime." In developing his explanation of crime, Quinney offers several assumptions about man and society, particularly in the areas of (1) process, (2) conflict, (3) power, and (4) social action. Of major concern is the role that interest groups play in the shaping of public policy. As Vold does, Quinney argues that public policy actually represents the interests and values of the powerful. He contends further that the interests of the powerful determine both how society defines criminal activity (the establishment of criminal or deviant categories) and how it treats those labeled as criminals (the enforcement of deviant categories). He also suggests some reasons why actors may violate deviant or criminal categories (why those defined as criminals may accept the label and then play the role of the criminal).

The last perspective to be considered in this section—the interactionist—is not specifically concerned with the evolution of deviant categories or their violation. Rather, this model explores the ways in which people who violate deviant categories (for whatever reasons) are responded to by formal and informal agents of social control. In this respect, definitional and interactional processes are given central focus. As explicated and refined by the interactional and organizational paradigms in the general introduction, this perspective is applied systematically throughout the remainder of this volume.

The Interactionist, Societal Reactions, or Labeling Perspective

Individuals who subscribe to the interactionist, or labeling, school examine those social and psychological, or interactional, processes that take place among actors, audiences, and third parties, particularly in terms of their impact upon the personal and social-public identity of the actor. Their main concern, then, is with definitional processes and products, and their effects.

The statement by Frank Tannenbaum, "Definition and the Dramatization of Evil," represents one of the earliest attempts at describing how individuals may be singled out for special treatment by the community. His basic thesis is that two opposing definitions of the situation may arise. For example, what may be viewed as play or fun by the young actor may be seen as a form of evil or delinquency by community members. Gradually there may occur a shift "from definition of the specific acts as evil to a definition of the individual as evil." This defining process is not without its effects. To the community, the individual has become a bad or evil person. To the individual, a sense of injustice emerges; this forces him to realize that he is different from other boys in the neighborhood, school, street, and community. Tannenbaum suggests further that such a person may not only change his personal identity—that is, come to view himself as a young criminal or delinquent—but may become part of a group or subculture that shares his activities. Primarily as a result of the self-fulfilling prophecy discussed by Balch and Kelly (part one), then, he may begin to act in accordance with the expectations associated with his label. He may, moreover, move into a pattern of career deviance or crime.

These processes and contingencies have been explored more systematically by Edwin M. Lemert, whose major focus in "Primary and Secondary Deviation" is the "sequence of interaction" that takes place between actors and audiences—especially those aspects that ultimately give rise to secondary or career deviance. Central to this process are the actor's perceptions and reactions to the negative social reactions he or she encounters. Quite often the actor's response to negative sanctions (or punishments) leads to the application of additional penalties. This type of reciprocal relationship, and its gradual deterioration, can reach the point at which the deviant actually accepts the imputed status or label. The acceptance of this particular status and associated label frequently results in other significant changes. The deviant may, for example, buy new clothes and change his or her speech, posture, and mannerisms to fit the new role.

Howard S. Becker has explored the concept of career, the major orienting focus of this volume, in some depth. He also introduces some important analytical distinctions. In "Career Deviance," he argues that public labeling is generally the most crucial step in building a long-term deviant career. Not only does being branded a deviant affect one's continued social participation, but it frequently produces notable changes in the actor's self-image. The most drastic change, however, seems to occur with respect to the actor's public identity— that is, how others view him or her. All of a sudden, in the eyes of others he or she has become a *different* person; this new status can be effectively referred to as a *master status*. In offering an important distinction between master and subordinate statuses, Becker argues that master statuses assume a certain priority and appear to override most other status considerations.

The status of deviant is one such status. In relating to a deviant, people will frequently respond to the label and not to the individual. Treatment of an actor in this fashion—as if he or she is generally deviant and not specifically deviant—can serve as a self-fulfilling prophecy whereby attempts are made to mold the actor into the image others have of him or her. Deliberate attempts may be made, for example, to exclude the deviant from any meaningful social intercourse. The actor may respond negatively to such treatment, and, over time, exclusion and its associated reactions can actually give rise to more deviance. The treatment situation, Becker claims, is especially likely to produce such a result. Many of these processes, as well as those described by Tannenbaum and Lemert, will become even more evident in my discussion of the initiation and perpetuation of deviant careers, particularly those careers that are subject to institutional processing (part four).

3 / The Normal and the Pathological

EMILE DURKHEIM

Crime is present not only in the majority of societies of one particular species but in all societies of all types. There is no society that is not confronted with the problem of criminality. Its form changes; the acts thus characterized are not the same everywhere; but, everywhere and always, there have been men who have behaved in such a way as to draw upon themselves penal repression. If, in proportion as societies pass from the lower to the higher types, the rate of criminality, i.e., the relation between the yearly number of crimes and the population, tended to decline, it might be believed that crime, while still normal, is tending to lose this character of normality. But we have no reason to believe that such a regression is substantiated. Many facts would seem rather to indicate a movement in the opposite direction. From the beginning of the [nineteenth] century, statistics enable us to follow the course of criminality. It has everywhere increased. In France the increase is nearly 300 per cent. There is, then, no phenomenon that presents more indisputably all the symptoms of normality, since it appears closely connected with the conditions of all collective life. To make of crime a form of social morbidity would be to admit that morbidity is not something accidental, but, on the contrary, that in certain cases it grows out of the fundamental constitution of the living organism; it would result in wiping out all distinction between the physiological and the pathological. No doubt it is possible that crime itself will have abnormal forms, as, for example, when its rate is unusually high. This excess is, indeed, undoubtedly morbid in nature. What is normal, simply, is the existence of criminality, provided that it attains and does not exceed, for each social type, a certain level, which it is perhaps not impossible to fix in conformity with the preceding rules.[1]

Here we are, then, in the presence of a conclusion in appearance quite paradoxical. Let us make no mistake. To classify crime among the phenomena of normal sociology is not to say merely that it is an inevitable, although regrettable phenomenon, due to the incorrigible wickedness of men; it is to affirm that it is a factor in public health, an integral part of all healthy societies. This result is, at first glance, surprising enough to have puzzled even ourselves for a long time. Once this first surprise has been overcome, however, it is not difficult to find reasons explaining this normality and at the same time confirming it.

In the first place crime is normal because a society exempt from it is utterly impossible. Crime, we have shown elsewhere, consists of an act that offends certain very strong collective sentiments. In a society in which criminal acts are no longer committed, the sentiments they offend would have to be found without exception in all individual consciousnesses, and they must be found to exist with the same degree as sentiments contrary to them. Assuming that this condition could actually be realized, crime would not thereby disappear; it would only change its form, for the very cause which would thus dry up the sources of criminality would immediately open up new ones.

Indeed, for the collective sentiments which are protected by the penal law of a people at a specified moment of its history to take possession of the public conscience or for them to acquire a stronger hold where they have an insufficient grip, they must acquire an intensity greater than that which they had hitherto had. The community as a whole must experience them more vividly, for it can acquire from no other source the greater force necessary to control these individuals who formerly were the most refractory. For murderers to disappear, the horror of bloodshed must become greater in those social strata from which murderers are recruited; but, first it must become greater throughout the entire society. Moreover, the very absence of crime would directly contribute to produce this horror; because any sentiment seems much more respectable when it is always and uniformly respected.

One easily overlooks the consideration that these strong states of the common consciousness cannot be thus reinforced without reinforcing at the same time the more feeble states, whose violation previously gave birth to mere infraction of convention—since the weaker ones are only the prolongation, the attenuated form, of the stronger. Thus robbery and simple bad taste injure the same single altruistic sentiment, the respect for that which is another's. However, this same sentiment is less grievously offended by bad taste than by robbery; and since, in addition, the average consciousness has not sufficient intensity to react keenly to the bad taste, it is treated with greater tolerance. That is why the person guilty of bad taste is merely blamed, whereas the thief is punished. But, if this sentiment grows stronger, to the point of silencing in all consciousnesses the inclination which disposes man to steal, he will become more sensitive to the offenses which, until then, touched him but lightly. He will react against them, then, with more energy; they will be the object of greater opprobrium, which will transform certain of them from the simple moral faults that they were and give them the quality of crimes. For example, improper contracts, or contracts improperly executed, which only incur public blame or civil damages, will become offenses in law.

Imagine a society of saints, a perfect cloister of exemplary individuals. Crimes, properly so called, will there be unknown; but faults which appear venial to the layman will create there the same scandal that the ordinary offense does in ordinary consciousnesses. If, then, this society has the power to judge and punish, it will define these acts as criminal and will treat them as such. For the same reason, the perfect and upright man judges his smallest failings with a severity that the majority reserve for acts more truly in the nature of an offense. Formerly, acts of violence against persons were more frequent than they are today, because respect for individual dignity was less strong. As this has increased, these crimes have become more rare; and also, many acts violating this sentiment have been introduced into the penal law which were not included there in primitive times.[2]

In order to exhaust all the hypotheses logically possible, it will perhaps be asked why this unanimity does not extend to all collective sentiments without exception. Why should not even the most feeble sentiment gather enough energy to prevent all dissent? The moral consciousness of the society would be present in its entirety in all the individuals, with a vitality sufficient to prevent all acts offending it—the purely conventional faults as well as the crimes. But a uniformity so universal and absolute is utterly impossible; for the immediate physical milieu in which each one of us is placed, the hereditary antecedents, and the social influences vary from one individual to the next, and consequently diversify consciousnesses. It is impossible for all to be alike, if only because each one has his own organism and that these organisms occupy different areas in space. That is why, even among the lower peoples, where individual originality is very little developed, it nevertheless does exist.

Thus, since there cannot be a society in which the individuals do not differ more or less from the collective type, it is also inevitable that, among these divergences, there are some with a criminal character. What confers this character upon them is not the intrinsic quality of a given act but that definition which the collective conscience lends them. If the collective conscience is stronger, if it has enough authority practically to suppress these divergences, it will also be more sensitive, more exacting; and, reacting against the slightest deviations with the energy it otherwise displays only against more considerable infractions, it will attribute to them the same gravity as formerly to crimes. In other words, it will designate them as criminal.

Crime is, then, necessary; it is bound up with fundamental conditions of all social life, and by that very fact it is useful, because these conditions of which it is a part are themselves indispensable to the normal evolution of morality and law.

Indeed, it is no longer possible today to dispute the fact that law and morality vary from one social type to the next, nor that they change within the same type if the conditions of life are modified. But, in order that these transformations may be possible, the collective sentiments at the basis of morality must not be hostile to change, and consequently must have but moderate energy. If they were too strong, they would no longer be plastic. Every pattern is an obstacle to new patterns, to the extent that the first pattern is inflexible. The better a structure is articulated, the more it offers a healthy resistance to all modification; and this is equally true of functional, as of anatomical, organization. If there were no crimes, this condition could not have been fulfilled; for such a hypothesis presupposes that collective sentiments have arrived at a degree of intensity unexampled in history. Nothing is good indefinitely and to an unlimited extent. The authority which the moral conscience enjoys must not be excessive; otherwise no one would dare criticize it, and it would too easily congeal into an immutable form. To make progress, individual originality must be able to express itself. In order that the originality of the idealist whose dreams transcend his century may find expression, it is necessary that the originality of the criminal, who is below the level of his time, shall also be possible. One does not occur without the other.

Nor is this all. Aside from this indirect utility, it happens that crime itself plays a useful role in this evolution. Crime implies not only that the way remains open to necessary changes but that in certain cases it directly prepares these changes. Where crime exists, collective sentiments are sufficiently flexible to take on a new form, and crime sometimes helps to determine the form they will take. How many times, indeed, it is only an anticipation of future morality—a step toward what will be! According to Athenian law, Socrates was a criminal, and his condemnation was no more than just. However, his crime, namely, the independence of his thought, rendered a service not only to humanity but to his country. It served to prepare a new morality and faith which the Athenians needed, since the traditions by which they had lived until then were no longer in harmony with the current conditions of life. Nor is the case of Socrates unique; it is reproduced periodically in history. It would never have been possible to establish the freedom of thought we now enjoy if the regulations prohibiting it had not been violated before being solemnly abrogated. At that time, however, the violation was a crime, since it was an offense against sentiments still very keen in the average conscience.

And yet this crime was useful as a prelude to reforms which daily became more necessary. Liberal philosophy had as its precursors the heretics of all kinds who were justly punished by secular authorities during the entire course of the Middle Ages and until the eve of modern times.

From this point of view the fundamental facts of criminality present themselves to us in an entirely new light. Contrary to current ideas, the criminal no longer seems a totally unsociable being, a sort of parasitic element, a strange and unassimilable body, introduced into the midst of society.[3] On the contrary, he plays a definite role in social life. Crime, for its part, must no longer be conceived as an evil that cannot be too much suppressed. There is no occasion for self-congratulation when the crime rate drops noticeably below the average level, for we may be certain that this apparent progress is associated with some social disorder. Thus, the number of assault cases never falls so low as in times of want.[4] With the drop in the crime rate, and as a reaction to it, comes a revision, or the need of a revision in the theory of punishment. If, indeed, crime is a disease, its punishment is its remedy and cannot be otherwise conceived; thus, all the discussions it arouses bear on the point of determining what the punishment must be in order to fulfil this role of remedy. If crime is not pathological at all, the object of punishment cannot be to cure it, and its true function must be sought elsewhere.

Notes

1. From the fact that crime is a phenomenon of normal sociology, it does not follow that the criminal is an individual normally constituted from the biological and psychological points of view. The two questions are independent of each other. This independence will be better understood when we have shown, later on, the difference between psychological and sociological facts.

2. Calumny, insults, slander, fraud, etc.

3. We have ourselves committed the error of speaking thus of the criminal, because of a failure to apply our rule (*Division du travail social*, pp. 395–96).

4. Although crime is a fact of normal sociology, it does not follow that we must not abhor it. Pain itself has nothing desirable about it; the individual dislikes it as society does crime, and yet it is a function of normal physiology. Not only is it necessarily derived from the very constitution of every living organism, but it plays a useful role in life, for which reason it cannot be replaced. It would, then, be a singular distortion of our thought to present it as an apology for crime. We would not even think of protesting against such an interpretation, did we not know to what strange accusations and misunderstandings one exposes oneself when one undertakes to study moral facts objectively and to speak of them in a different language from that of the layman.

4 / The Functions of Deviance in Groups

ROBERT A. DENTLER
KAI T. ERIKSON

Although sociologists have repeatedly noted that close similarities exist between various forms of social marginality, research directed at these forms has only begun to mark the path toward a social theory of deviance. This slow pace may in part result from the fact that deviant behavior is too frequently visualized as a product of organizational failure rather than as a facet of organization itself.

Albert Cohen has recently attempted to specify some of the assumptions and definitions necessary for a sociology of deviant behavior (3). He has urged the importance of erecting clearly defined concepts, devising a homogeneous class of phenomena explainable by a unified system of theory, and developing a sociological rather than a psychological framework—as would be the case, for example, in a central problem which was stated: "What is it about the structure of social systems that determines the kinds of criminal acts that occur in these systems and the way in which such acts are distributed within the systems?" (3, p. 462). Cohen has also suggested that a theory of deviant behavior should account simultaneously for deviance and conformity; that is, the explanation of one should serve as the explanation of the other.

In this paper we hope to contribute to these objectives by presenting some propositions about the sources and functions of deviant behavior in small groups. Although we suspect that the same general processes may well characterize larger social systems,[1] this paper will be limited to small groups, and more particularly to enduring task and primary groups. Any set of propositions about the functions of deviance would have to be shaped to fit the scope of the social unit chosen for analysis, and we have elected to use the small group unit in this exploratory paper primarily because a large body of empirical material dealing with deviance in groups has accumulated which offers important leads into the study of deviance in general.

With Cohen, we define deviance as "behavior which violates institutionalized expectations, that is, expectations which are shared and recognized as legitimate within a social system" (3, p. 462). Our guiding assumption is that deviant behavior is a reflection not only of the personality of the actor, but the structure of the group in which the behavior was enacted. The violations of expectation which the group experiences, as well as the norms which it observes, express both cultural and structural aspects of the group. While we shall attend to cultural elements in later illustrations, our propositions are addressed primarily to the structure of groups and the functions that deviant behavior serves in maintaining this structure.

PROPOSITION ONE

Our first proposition is that *groups tend to induce, sustain, and permit deviant behavior.* To say that a group *induces* deviant behavior, here, is to say that as it goes through the early stages of development and structures the range of behavior among its members, a group will tend to define the behavior of certain members as deviant. A group *sustains* or *permits* this newly defined deviance in the sense that it tends to institutionalize and absorb this behavior into its structure rather than eliminating it. As group structure emerges and role specialization takes place, one or more role categories will be differentiated to accommodate individuals whose behavior is occasionally or regularly expected to be deviant. It is essential to the argument that this process be viewed not only as a simple group adjustment to individual differences, but also as a requirement of group formation, analogous to the requirement of leadership.

The process of role differentiation and specialization which takes place in groups has been illuminated by studies which use concepts of sociometric rank. Riecken and Homans conclude from this evidence: "The higher the rank of a member the closer his activities come to realizing the norms of the group . . . and there is a tendency toward 'equilibration of rank' " (11, p. 794). Thus the rankings that take place on a scale of social preference serve to identify the activities that members are expected to carry out: each general rank represents or contains an equivalent role which defines that member's special relationship to the group and its norms. To the extent that a group ranks its members preferentially, it distributes functions differentially. The proposition, then, simply notes that group members who violate norms will be given low sociometric rank; that this designation carries with it an appropriate differentiation of the functions that such members are expected to perform in respect to the group; and that the roles contained in these low-rank positions become institutionalized and are retained in the structure of the group.

The most difficult aspect of this proposition is the concept of *induc-*

tion of deviance. We do not mean to suggest that the group creates the motives for an individual's deviant behavior or compels it from persons not otherwise disposed toward this form of expression. When a person encounters a new group, two different historical continuities meet. The individual brings to the group a background of private experience which disposes him to certain patterns of conduct; the group, on the other hand, is organized around a network of role priorities to which each member is required to conform. While the individual brings new resources into the group and alters its potential for change and innovation, the group certainly operates to rephrase each member's private experience into a new self-formula, a new sense of his own needs.

Thus any encounter between a group and a new member is an event which is novel to the experience of both. In the trial-and-error behavior which issues, both the functional requirements of the group and the individual needs of the person will undergo certain revisions, and in the process the group plays an important part in determining whether those already disposed toward deviant behavior will actually express it overtly, or whether those who are lightly disposed toward deviating styles will be encouraged to develop that potential. *Inducing* deviance, then, is meant to be a process by which the group channels and organizes the deviant possibilities contained in its membership.

The proposition argues that groups induce deviant behavior in the same sense that they induce other group qualities like leadership, fellowship, and so on. These qualities emerge early and clearly in the formation of new groups, even in traditionless laboratory groups, and while they may be diffusely distributed among the membership initially they tend toward specificity and equilibrium over time. In giving definition to the end points in the range of behavior which is brought to a group by its membership, the group establishes its boundaries and gives dimension to its structure. In this process, the designation of low-ranking deviants emerges as surely as the designation of high-ranking task leaders.

PROPOSITION TWO

Bales has written:

> The displacement of hostilities on a scapegoat at the bottom of the status structure is one mechanism, apparently, by which the ambivalent attitudes toward the ... "top man" ... can be diverted and drained off. These patterns, culturally elaborated and various in form, can be viewed as particular cases of mechanisms relevant to the much more general problem of equilibrium (2, p. 454).

This comment provides a bridge between our first and second propositions by suggesting that deviant behavior may serve important functions for groups — thereby contributing to, rather than disrupting, equilibrium in the group. Our second proposition, accordingly, is that *deviant behavior functions in enduring groups to help maintain group equilibrium.* In the following discussion we would like to consider some of the ways this function operates.

Group Performance. The proposition implies that deviant behavior contributes to the maintenance of optimum levels of performance, and we add at this point that this will particularly obtain where a group's achievement depends upon the contributions of all its members.

McCurdy and Lambert devised a laboratory task which required full group participation in finding a solution to a given problem (7). They found that the performance of their groups compared unfavorably with that of individual problem-solvers, and explained this by noting the high likelihood that a group would contain at least one member who failed to attend to instructions. The group, they observed, may prove no stronger than its weakest member. The implication here, as in the old adage, seems to be that the group would have become correspondingly stronger if its weakest link were removed. Yet this implication requires some consideration: to what extent can we say that the inattentive member was acting in the name of the group, performing a function which is valuable to the group over time? To what extent can we call this behavior a product of group structure rather than a product of individual eccentricity?

As roles and their equivalent ranks become differentiated in a group, some members will be expected to perform more capably than others; and in turn the structure of the group will certainly be organized to take advantage of the relative capabilities of its members — as it demonstrably does in leadership choice. These differentials require testing and experimentation: the norms about performance in a group cannot emerge until clues appear as to how much the present membership can accomplish, how wide the range of variation in performance is likely to be, and so on. To the extent that group structure becomes an elaboration and organization of these differentials, certainly the "weak link" becomes as essential to this process as the high-producer. Both are outside links in the communication system which feeds back information about the range of group performance and the limits of the differentiated structure.

As this basis for differentiation becomes established, then, the group moves from a state in which pressure is exerted equally on all members to conform to performance norms, and moves toward a state in which these norms become a kind of anchor which locates the center of wide variations in behavior. The performance "mean" of a group is of course expected to be set at a level dictated by "norms"; and this mean is not only achieved by the most conforming members but by a balance of high and low producers as well. It is a simple calculation that the loss of a weak link, the low producer, would raise the mean output of the group to a point where it no longer corresponded to original norms unless the entire structure of the group shifted as compensation. In this sense we can argue that neither role differentiation nor norm formation could occur and be maintained without the "aid" of regular deviations.

Rewards. Stated briefly, we would argue that the process of distributing incentives to members of the group is similarly dependent upon the recurrence of deviant behavior. This is an instance where, as Cohen has urged, an explanation of conformity may lead to an explanation of deviance. Customarily, conformance is rewarded while deviance is either unrewarded or actively punished. The rewards of conformity, however, are seen as "rewarding" in comparison to other possible outcomes, and obviously the presence of a deviant in the group would provide the continual contrast without which the reward structure would have little meaning. The problem, then, becomes complex: the reward structure is set up as an incentive for conformity, but depends upon the outcome that differentials in conformity will occur. As shall be pointed out later, the deviant is rewarded in another sense for his role in the group, which makes it "profitable" for him to serve as a contrast in the conventional reward structure. Generally speaking, comparison is as essential in the maintenance of norms as is conformity: a norm becomes most evident in its occasional violation, and in this sense a group maintains "equilibrium" by a controlled balance of the relations which provide comparison and those which assure conformity.

Boundaries. Implicit in the foregoing is the argument that the presence of deviance in a group is a boundary-maintaining function. The comparisons which deviance makes possible help establish the range in which the group operates, the extent of its jurisdiction over behavior, the variety of styles it contains, and these are among the essential dimensions which give a group identity and distinctiveness. In Quaker work camps, Riecken found that members prided themselves on their acceptance of deviations, and rejected such controls as ridicule and rejection (10, pp. 57–67). Homans has noted that men in the Bank Wiring Group employed certain sanctions against deviant behavior which were felt to be peculiar to the structure of the group (5). A group is distinguished in part by the norms it creates for handling deviance and by the forms of deviance it is able to absorb and contain. In helping, then, to give members a sense of their group's distinctiveness, deviant behavior on the group's margins provides an important boundary-maintaining function.

PROPOSITION THREE

Kelley and Thibault have asserted:

> It is common knowledge that when a member deviates markedly from a group standard, the remaining members of the group bring pressures to bear on the deviate to return to conformity. If pressure is of no avail, the deviate is rejected and cast out of the group. The research on this point is consistent with common sense (6, p. 768).

Apparently a deviating member who was *not* rejected after repeated violations would be defined as one who did not deviate markedly enough. While there is considerable justification to support this common-sense notion, we suggest that it overattends to rejection and neglects the range of alternatives short of rejection. The same focus is evident in the following statement by Rossi and Merton:

> What the individual experiences as estrangement from a group tends to be experienced by his associates as repudiation of the group, and this ordinarily evokes a hostile response. As social relations between the individual and the rest of the group deteriorate, the norms of the group become less binding for him. For since he is progressively seceding from the group and being penalized by it, he is the less likely to experience rewards for adherence to . . . norms. Once initiated, this process seems to move toward a cumulative detachment from the group (2, p. 270).

While both of the above quotations reflect current research concerns in their attention to the group's rejection of the individual and his alienation from the group, our third proposition focuses on the common situation in which the group works to prevent elimination of a deviant member. *Groups will resist any trend toward alienation of a member whose behavior is deviant.* From the point of view of the group majority, deviants will be retained in the group up to a point where the deviant expression becomes critically dangerous to group solidarity. This accords with Kelley and Thibault's general statement, if not with its implication; but we would add that the point at which deviation becomes "markedly" extreme—and dangerous to the group—cannot be well defined in advance. This point is located by the group as a result of recurrent interaction between conforming members who respect the central norms of the group and deviating members who test its boundaries. This is the context from which the group derives a conception of what constitutes "danger," or what variations from the norm shall be viewed as "marked."

From the point of view of the deviant, then, the testing of limits is an exercise of his role in the group; from the point of view of the group, pressures are set into motion which secure the deviant in his "testing" role, yet try to assure that his deviation will not become pronounced enough to make rejection necessary. Obviously this is a delicate balance to maintain, and failures are continually visible. Yet there are a great many conditions under which it is worth while for the group to retain its deviant members and resist any trend which might lead the majority membership and other deviant members to progressive estrangement.

ILLUSTRATIONS OF PROPOSITIONS

Each of the authors of this paper has recently completed field research which illuminates the propositions set forth here. Dentler studied the relative effectiveness of ten Quaker work projects in influencing conformity with norms of tolerance, pacifism, democratic group relations, and related social attitudes (4). One interesting sidelight in this study was the finding that while all ten groups were highly solidary, those with relatively higher numbers of sociometric isolates exhibited higher degrees of favorable increased conformity.

Case study of five of the ten groups, using interviews and participant observation, revealed that the two groups achieving the greatest favorable changes in tolerance, democratism, pacifism, and associated attitudes not only had the highest proportions of social isolates, but some of the isolates were low-ranking deviants. Of course none of the groups was without at least one isolate and one deviant, and these roles were not always occupied by the same member. But in the two high-change groups low-rank deviants were present.

In one group, one of these members came from a background that differed radically from those of other members. Although these were cooperative living and work projects, this member insisted upon separately prepared special food and complained loudly about its quality. Where three-fourths of the group members came from professional and managerial families, and dressed and acted in conformity with upper-middle-class standards, this deviant refused to wear a shirt to Sunday dinner and often came to meals without his shoes. He could not hold a job and lost two provided by the group leader during the first two weeks of the program.

His social and political attitudes also differed radically from group norms, and he was often belligerently assertive of his minority perspectives. He had no allies for his views. In an interview one of the group's leaders described the group's response to this deviant:

At first we didn't know how to cope with him though we were determined to do just that. After he came to Sunday dinner in his undershirt, and after he smashed a bowl of food that had been fixed specially for him—as usual— we figured out a way to set down certain firm manners for him. There were some rules, we decided, that no one was going to violate. We knew he was very new to this kind of life and so we sought to understand him. We never rejected him. Finally, he began to come to terms; he adapted, at least enough so that we can live with him. He has begun to conform on the surface to some of our ways. It's been very hard to take that he is really proud of having lost his first two jobs and is not quiet about it. Things have gone better since we made a birthday cake for him, and I feel proud of the way our group has managed to handle this internal problem.

The same group sustained another deviant and even worked hard to retain him when he decided to leave the group. Here a group leader discusses group relations with this member:

X left our group after the first four weeks of the eight-week program. He had never been away from home before although he was about 21 years old. He couldn't seem to adjust to his job at the day camp, and he just couldn't stand doing his share of the housework and cooking. This lack of doing his share was especially hard on us, and we often discussed privately whether it would be good for him to relieve him of any household chores. We decided that wouldn't be right, but we still couldn't get him to work. Funny, but this sort of made housework the center of our group life. We are proud that no one else has shirked his chores; there is no quibbling now. . . . Anyway, X kept being pressured by his mother and brother to come home, but we gave him tremendous support. We talked it all out with him. We let him know we really wanted him to stay. This seemed to unify our group. It was working out the problem of X that seemed to unify our group. It was working out the problem of X that seemed to help us build some group standards. He began to follow some of our standards but he also stayed free to dissent. His mother finally forced him to come home.

In the second high-change group, there were also two extreme deviants. Here a group leader comments on one of them:

I've never got over feeling strongly antagonistic toward K. K has been a real troublemaker and we never really came to terms with him or controlled him significantly. He is simply a highly neurotic, conflicted person as far as life in our group goes. Personally, I've resented the fact that he has mo- nopolized Z, who without him would have been a real contributor but who has become nothing more than a sort of poor imitation of K. After we had been here about half the summer, incidentally, a professional came out from staff headquarters and after observing our meetings he asked why K hadn't been dismissed or asked to leave the group early in the summer. But K didn't leave, of course, and most of us wouldn't want him to leave.

Finally a group leader described the reaction to the departure of its second deviant, who was repeatedly described in interviews as "kind of obnoxious":

On the night N was upstairs talking with your interviewer, the group got together downstairs suddenly to talk about getting up a quick party, a farewell party for him. In 15 minutes, like a whirlwind, we decorated the house and some of the fellows wrote a special song of farewell for N. We also wrote a last-minute appeal asking him to stay with the group and people ran about asking, "What are you doing for N?" There seemed to be a lot of guilt among us about his leaving. We felt that maybe we hadn't done enough to get him more involved in the life of our group. I think there was some hidden envy too. After he had left, a joke began to spread around that went like this: If you leave now maybe we'll have a party for you.

The group with the lowest amount of change during the summer contained two low-ranking members, one of whom deviated from the group's norms, occasionally, but no evidence came to light to indicate that this group achieved the same intensity in social relationships or the same degree of role differentiation as did groups with more extremely deviant members. Members of this low-change group reflected almost without exception the views expressed in this typical quotation:

Objectively, this is a good, congenial group of individuals. Personally they leave me a little cold. I've been in other project groups, and this is the most congenial one I've been in; yet, I don't think there will be any lasting friendships.

All these quotations reflect strong impressions embodied in our observational reports. Taken as a whole they illustrate aspects of our three postulates. While this material does not reveal the sense in which a group may induce deviance—and this is perhaps the most critical proposition of all—it does show how groups will make great efforts to keep deviant members attached to the group, to prevent full alienation. By referring to our findings about attitude change we have hoped to suggest the relevance of deviance to increasing conformity, a functional relationship of action and reaction.

In 1955–6, Erikson participated in a study of schizophrenia among basic trainees in the U. S. Army, portions of which have been published elsewhere (1). Through various interview and questionnaire techniques, a large body of data was collected which enabled the investigators to reconstruct short histories of the group life shared by the future schizophrenic and his squad prior to the former's hospitalization. There were eleven subjects in the data under consideration. The bulk of the evidence used for this short report comes from loosely structured interviews which were conducted with the entire squad in attendance, shortly after it had lost one of its members to the psychiatric hospital.

The eleven young men whose breakdown was the subject of the

interviews all came from the north-eastern corner of the United States, most of them from rural or small-town communities. Typically, these men had accumulated long records of deviation in civilian life: while few of them had attracted psychiatric attention, they had left behind them fairly consistent records of job failure, school truancy, and other minor difficulties in the community. Persons in the community took notice of this behavior, of course, but they tended to be gently puzzled by it rather than attributing distinct deviant motives to it.

When such a person enters the service, vaguely aware that his past performance did not entirely live up to expectations current in his community, he is likely to start negotiating with his squad mates about the conditions of his membership in the group. He sees himself as warranting special group consideration, as a consequence of a deviant style which he himself is unable to define; yet the group has clear-cut obligations which require a high degree of responsibility and coordination from everyone. The negotiation seems to go through several successive stages, during which a reversal of original positions takes place and the individual is fitted for a role which is clearly deviant.

The first stage is characteristic of the recruit's first days in camp. His initial reaction is likely to be an abrupt attempt to discard his entire "civilian" repertoire to free himself for adoption of new styles and new ways. His new uniform for daily wear seems to become for him a symbolic uniform for his sense of identity: he is, in short, overconforming. He is likely to interpret any gesture of command as a literal moral mandate, sometimes suffering injury when told to scrub the floor until his fingers bleed, or trying to consciously repress thoughts of home when told to get everything out of his head but the military exercise of the moment.

The second stage begins shortly thereafter as he fails to recognize that "regulation" reality is different from the reality of group life, and that the circuits which carry useful information are contained within the more informal source. The pre-psychotic is, to begin with, a person for whom contacts with peers are not easy to establish, and as he tries to find his way into these circuits, looking for cues to the rhythm of group life, he sees that a fairly standard set of interaction techniques is in use. There are ways to initiate conversation, ways to impose demands, and so on. Out of this cultural lore, then, he chooses different gambits to test. He may learn to ask for matches to start discussion, be ready with a supply of cigarettes for others to "bum," or he may pick up a local joke or expression and repeat it continually. Too often, however, he misses the context in which these interaction cues are appropriate, so that his behavior, in its over-literal simplicity, becomes almost a caricature of the sociability rule he is trying to follow. We may cite the "specialist" in giving away cigarettes:

I was out of cigarettes and he had a whole pack. I said, "Joe, you got a smoke?" He says "yes," and Jesus, he gave me about twelve of them. At other times he used to offer me two or three packs of cigarettes at a time when I was out.

Or the "specialist" in greetings:

He'd go by you in the barracks and say, "What do you say, Jake?" I'd say, "Hi, George, how are you?" and he'd walk into the latrine. And he'd come by not a minute later, and it's the same thing all over again, "What do you say, Jake?" It seemed to me he was always saying "hi" to someone. You could be sitting right beside him for ten minutes and he would keep on saying it.

These clumsy overtures lead the individual and the group into the third stage. Here the recruit, almost hidden from group view in his earlier overconformity, has become a highly visible group object: his behavior is clearly "off beat," anomalous; he has made a presentation of himself to the squad, and the squad has had either to make provisions for him in the group structure or begin the process of eliminating him. The pre-psychotic is clearly a low producer, and in this sense he is potentially a handicap. Yet the group neither exerts strong pressures on him to conform nor attempts to expel him from the squad. Instead, he is typically given a wide license to deviate from both the performance and behavior norms of the group, and the group in turn forms a hard protective shell around him which hides him from exposure to outside authorities.

His duties are performed by others, and in response the squad only seems to ask of him that he be at least consistent in his deviation—that he be consistently helpless and consistently anomalous. In a sense, he becomes the ward of the group, hidden from outside view but the object of friendly ridicule within. He is referred to as "our teddy bear," "our pet," "mascot," "little brother," "toy," and so on. In a setting where having buddies is highly valued, he is unlikely to receive any sociometric choices at all. But it would be quite unfortunate to assume that he is therefore isolated from the group or repudiated by it: an accurate sociogram would have the deviant individual encircled by the interlocking sociometric preferences, sheltered by the group structure, and an important point of reference for it.

The examples just presented are weak in that they include only failures of the process described. The shell which protected the deviant from visibility leaked, outside medical authorities were notified, and he was eventually hospitalized. But as a final note it is interesting to observe that the shell remained even after the person for whom it was erected had withdrawn. Large portions of every squad interview were devoted to arguments, directed at a psychiatrist, that the departed member was not ill and should never have been hospitalized.

DISCUSSION

The most widely cited social theories of deviant behavior which have appeared in recent years—notably those of Merton and Parsons (8; 9)—have helped turn sociologists' attention from earlier models of social pathology in which deviance was seen as direct evidence of disorganization. These newer models have attended to the problem of how social structures exert pressure on certain individuals rather than others toward the expression of deviance. Yet the break with the older social disorganization tradition is only partial, since these theories still regard deviance from the point of view of its value as a "symptom" of dysfunctional structures. One aim of this paper is to encourage a functional approach to deviance, to consider the contributions deviant behavior may make toward the development of organizational structures, rather than focusing on the implicit assumption that structures must be somehow in a state of disrepair if they produce deviant behavior.

Any group attempts to locate its position in social space by defining its symbolic boundaries, and this process of self-location takes place not only in reference to the central norms which the group develops but in reference to the *range* of possibilities which the culture makes available. Specialized statuses which are located on the margins of the group, chiefly high-rank leaders and low-rank deviants, become critical referents for establishing the end points of this range, the group boundaries.

As both the Quaker and Army illustrations suggest, deviant members are important targets toward which group concerns become focused. Not only do they symbolize the group's activities, but they help give other members a sense of group size, its range and extent, by marking where the group begins and ends in space. In general, the deviant seems to help give the group structure a visible "shape." The deviant is someone about whom something should be done, and the group, in expressing this concern, is able to reaffirm its essential cohesion and indicate what the group is and what it can do. Of course the character of the deviant behavior in each group would vary with the group's general objectives, its relationship to the larger culture, and so on. In both the Quaker groups and Army squads, nurturance was a strong element of the other members' reaction to their deviant fellow. More specifically in the Army material it is fairly sure that the degree of helplessness and softness supplied by the pre-psychotic introduced emotional qualities which the population—lacking women and younger persons—could not otherwise afford.

These have been short and necessarily limited illustrations of the propositions advanced. In a brief final note we would like to point out how this crude theory could articulate with the small group research tradition by suggesting one relatively ideal laboratory procedure that might be used. Groups composed of extremely homogeneous members should be assigned tasks which require group solution but which impose a high similarity of activity upon all members. If role differentiation occurs, then, it would be less a product of individual differences or the specific requirements of the task than a product of group formation. We would hypothesize that such differentiation would take place, and that one or more roles thus differentiated would be reserved for deviants. The occupants of these deviant roles should be removed from the group. If the propositions have substance, the group—and this is the critical hypothesis—would realign its members so that these roles would become occupied by other members. While no single experiment could address all the implications of our paradigm, this one would confront its main point.

This paper, of course, has deliberately neglected those group conditions in which deviant behavior becomes dysfunctional: it is a frequent group experience that deviant behavior fails to provide a valued function for the structure and helps reduce performance standards or lower levels of interaction. We have attempted here to present a side of the coin which we felt was often neglected, and in our turn we are equally—if intentionally—guilty of neglect.

Summary

This paper has proposed the following interpretations of deviant behavior in enduring primary and task groups:

1. Deviant behavior tends to be induced, permitted, and sustained by a given group.

2. Deviant behavior functions to help maintain group equilibrium.

3. Groups will resist any trend toward alienation of a member whose behavior is deviant.

The substance of each proposition was discussed heuristically and illustrated by reference to field studies of deviant behavior in Quaker work projects and Army basic training squads. A laboratory test was suggested as one kind of critical test of the paradigm. The aim of the presentation was to direct attention to the functional interdependence of deviance and organization.

References

1. Artiss, Kenneth L., ed., *The Symptom as Communication in Schizophrenia* (New York: Grune and Stratton, 1959).

2. Bales, Robert F., "The Equilibrium Problem in Small Groups," in *Small Groups*, A. Paul Hare, et al., eds. (New York: Knopf, 1955), 424–456.
3. Cohen, Albert K., "The Study of Social Disorganization and Deviant Behavior," in *Sociology Today*, Robert K. Merton, et al., eds. (New York: Basic Books, 1959), 461–484.
4. Dentler, Robert, *The Young Volunteers* (Chicago: National Opinion Research Center Report, 1959).
5. Homans, George W., *The Human Group* (New York: Harcourt, Brace, 1950).
6. Kelley, Harold H., and John W. Thibault, "Experimental Studies of Group Problem Solving and Process," in *Handbook of Social Psychology*, Vol. II, Gardner Lindzey, ed. (Cambridge: Addison-Wesley, 1954), 759–768.
7. McCurdy, Harold G., and Wallace E. Lambert, "The Efficiency of Small Human Groups in the Solution of Problems Requiring Genuine Cooperation," *Journal of Personality*, 20 (June, 1952), 478–494.
8. Merton, Robert K., *Social Theory and Social Structure*, rev. ed. (Glencoe: Free Press, 1957).
9. Parsons, Talcott, *The Social System* (Glencoe: Free Press, 1951), 256–267, 321–325; and Talcott Parsons, Robert F. Bales and Edward A. Shils, *Working Papers in the Theory of Action* (Glencoe: Free Press, 1953), 67–78.
10. Riecken, Henry, *Volunteer Work Camp* (Cambridge: Addison-Wesley, 1952), 57–67.
11. Riecken, Henry, and George W. Homans, "Psychological Aspects of Social Structure," in *Handbook of Social Psychology*, Vol. II. Gardner Lindzey, ed. (Cambridge: Addison-Wesley, 1954), 786–832.

Note

1. One of the authors (Erikson) is currently preparing a paper which deals with the broader implications of the problems discussed here.

5 / The Conflict of Conduct Norms

THORSTEN SELLIN

CULTURE CONFLICTS AS CONFLICTS OF CULTURAL CODES

. . . There are social groups on the surface of the earth which possess complexes of conduct norms which, due to differences in the mode of life and the social values evolved by these groups, appear to set them apart from other groups in many or most respects. We may expect conflicts of norms when the rural dweller moves to the city, but we assume that he has absorbed the basic norms of the culture which comprises both town and country. How much greater is not the conflict likely to be when Orient and Occident meet, or when the Corsican mountaineer is transplanted to the lower East Side of New York. Conflicts of cultures are inevitable when the norms of one cultural or subcultural area migrate to or come in contact with those of another.

Conflicts between the norms of divergent cultural codes may arise

1. when these codes clash on the border of contiguous culture areas;
2. when, as may be the case with legal norms, the law of one cultural group is extended to cover the territory of another; or
3. when members of one cultural group migrate to another.[1]

Speck, for instance, notes that "where the bands popularly known as Montagnais have come more and more into contact with Whites, their reputation has fallen lower among the traders who have known them through commercial relationships within that period. The accusation is made that they have become less honest in connection with their debts, less trustworthy with property, less truthful, and more inclined to alcoholism and sexual freedom as contacts with the frontier towns have become easier for them. Richard White reports in 1933 unusual instances of Naskapi breaking into traders' store houses."[2]

Similar illustrations abound in the works of the cultural anthropologists. We need only to recall the effect on the American

70

Indian of the culture conflicts induced by our policy of acculturation by guile and force. In this instance, it was not merely contact with the white man's culture, his religion, his business methods, and his liquor, which weakened the tribal mores. In addition, the Indian became subject to the white man's law and this brought conflicts as well, as has always been the case when legal norms have been imposed upon a group previously ignorant of them. Maunier[3] in discussing the diffusion of French law in Algeria, recently stated: "In introducing the *Code Penal* in our colonies, as we do, we transform into offenses the ancient usages of the inhabitants which their customs permitted or imposed. Thus, among the Khabyles of Algeria, the killing of adulterous wives is ritual murder committed by the father or brother of the wife and not by her husband, as elsewhere. The woman having been sold by her family to her husband's family, the honor of her relatives is soiled by her infidelity. Her father or brother has the right and the duty to kill her in order to cleanse by her blood the honor of her relatives. Murder in revenge is also a duty, from family to family, in case of murder of or even in case of insults to a relative: the vendetta, called the *rekba* in Khabylian, is imposed by the law of honor. But these are crimes in French law! Murder for revenge, being premeditated and planned, is assassination, punishable by death! . . . What happens, then, often when our authorities pursue the criminal, guilty of an offense against public safety as well as against morality: public enemy of the French order, but who has acted in accord with a respected custom? The witnesses of the assassination, who are his relatives, or neighbors, fail to lay charges against the assassin; when they are questioned, they pretend to know nothing; and the pursuit is therefore useless. A French magistrate has been able to speak of the conspiracy of silence among the Algerians; a conspiracy aiming to preserve traditions, always followed and obeyed, against their violation by our power. This is the tragic aspect of the conflict of laws. A recent decree forbids the husband among the Khabyles to profit arbitrarily by the power given him according to this law to repudiate his wife, demanding that her new husband pay an exorbitant price for her—this is the custom of the *lefdi*. Earlier, one who married a repudiated wife paid nothing to the former husband. It appears that the first who tried to avail himself of the new law was killed for violating the old custom. The abolition of the ancient law does not always occur without protest or opposition. That which is a crime was a duty; and the order which we cause to reign is sometimes established to the detriment of 'superstition'; it is the gods and the spirits, it is believed, that would punish any one who fails to revenge his honor."

When Soviet law was extended to Siberia, similar effects were observed. Anossow[4] and Wirschubski[5] both relate that women among the Siberian tribes, who in obedience to the law, laid aside their veils were killed by their relatives for violating one of the most sacred norms of their tribes.

We have noted that culture conflicts are the natural outgrowth of processes of social differentiation, which produce an infinity of social groupings, each with its own definitions of life situations, its own interpretations of social relationships, its own ignorance or misunderstanding of the social values of other groups. The transformation of a culture from a homogeneous and well-integrated type to a heterogeneous and disintegrated type is therefore accompanied by an increase of conflict situations. Conversely, the operation of integrating processes will reduce the number of conflict situations. Such conflicts within a changing culture may be distinguished from those created when different cultural systems come in contact with one another, regardless of the character or stage of development of these systems. In either case, the conduct of members of a group involved in the conflict of codes will in some respects be judged abnormal by the other group.

THE STUDY OF CULTURE CONFLICTS

In the study of culture conflicts, some scholars have been concerned with the effect of such conflicts on the conduct of specific persons, an approach which is naturally preferred by psychologists and psychiatrists and by sociologists who have used the life history technique. These scholars view the conflict as internal. Wirth[6] states categorically that a culture "conflict can be said to be a factor in delinquency only if the individual feels it or acts as if it were present." Culture conflict is mental conflict, but the character of this conflict is viewed differently by the various disciplines which use this term. Freudian psychiatrists[7] regard it as a struggle between deeply rooted biological urges which demand expression and the culturally created rules which give rise to inhibitive mechanisms which thwart this expression and drive them below the conscious level of the mind, whence they rise either by ruse in some socially acceptable disguise, as abnormal conduct when the inhibiting mechanism breaks down, or as neuroses when it works too well. The sociologist, on the other hand, thinks of mental conflict as being primarily the clash between antagonistic conduct norms incorporated in personality. "Mental conflict in the person," says Burgess in discussing the case presented by Shaw in *The Jack-Roller*, "may always be explained in terms of the conflict of divergent cultures."[8]

If this view is accepted, sociological research on culture conflict and its relationships to abnormal conduct would have to be strictly limited to a study of the personality of cultural hybrids. Significant studies could be conducted only by the life-history case technique applied to persons in whom the conflict is internalized, appropriate control groups being utilized, of course. . . .

The absence of mental conflict, in the sociological sense, may, however, be well studied in terms of culture conflict. An example may make this clear. A few years ago a Sicilian father in New Jersey killed the sixteen-year-old seducer of his daughter, expressing surprise at his arrest since he had merely defended his family honor in a traditional way. In this case a mental conflict in the sociological sense did not exist. The conflict was external and occurred between cultural codes or norms. We may assume that where such conflicts occur violations of norms will arise merely because persons who have absorbed the norms of one cultural group or area migrate to another and that such conflict will continue so long as the acculturation process has not been completed. . . . Only then may the violations be regarded in terms of mental conflict.

If culture conflict may be regarded as sometimes personalized, or mental, and sometimes as occurring entirely in an impersonal way solely as a conflict of group codes, it is obvious that research should not be confined to the investigation of mental conflicts and that contrary to Wirth's categorical statement that it is impossible to demonstrate the existence of a culture conflict "objectively . . . by a comparison between two cultural codes"[9] this procedure has not only a definite function, but may be carried out by researches employing techniques which are familiar to the sociologist.

The emphasis on the life history technique has grown out of the assumption that "the experiences of one person at the same time reveals the life activities of his group" and that "habit in the individual is an expression of custom in society."[10] This is undoubtedly one valid approach. Through it we may hope to discover generalizations of a scientific nature by studying persons who (1) have drawn their norms of conduct from a variety of groups with conflicting norms, or (2) who possess norms drawn from a group whose code is in conflict with that of the group which judges the conduct. In the former case alone can we speak of mental or internal culture conflict; in the latter, the conflict is external.

If the conduct norms of a group are, with reference to a given life situation, inconsistent, or if two groups possess inconsistent norms, we may assume that the members of these various groups will individually reflect such group attitudes. Paraphrasing Burgess, the experiences of a group will reveal the life activities of its members. While these norms can, no doubt, be best established by a study of a sufficient number of representative group members, they may for some groups at least be fixed with sufficient certainty to serve research purposes by a study of the social institutions, the administration of justice, the novel, the drama, the press, and other expressions of group attitudes. The identification of the groups in question having been made, it might be possible to determine to what extent such conflicts are reflected in the conduct of their members. Comparative studies based on the violation rates of the members of such groups, the trends of such rates, etc., would dominate this approach to the problem.

In conclusion, then, culture conflict may be studied either as mental conflict or as a conflict of cultural codes. The criminologist will naturally tend to concentrate on such conflicts between legal and nonlegal conduct norms. The concept of conflict fails to give him more than a general framework of reference for research. In practice, it has, however, become nearly synonymous with conflicts between the norms of cultural systems or areas. Most researches which have employed it have been done on immigrant or race groups in the United States, perhaps due to the ease with which such groups may be identified, the existence of more statistical data recognizing such groupings, and the conspicuous differences between some immigrant norms and our norms.

Notes

1. This is unfortunately not the whole story, for with the rapid growth of impersonal communication, the written (press, literature) and the spoken word (radio, talkie), knowledge concerning divergent conduct norms no longer grows solely out of direct personal contact with their carriers. And out of such conflicts grow some violations of custom and of law which would not have occurred without them.

2. Speck, Frank G. "Ethical Attributes of the Labrador Indians." *American Anthropologist*. N. S. 35:559–94. October–December 1933. P. 559.

3. Maunier, René, "La diffusion du droit français en Algérie." Harvard Tercentenary Publications, *Independence, Convergence, and Borrowing in Institutions, Thought, and Art*. Cambridge: Harvard University Press. 1937. Pp. 84–85.

4. Anossow, J. J. "Die volkstümlichen Verbrechen im Strafkodex der USSR." *Monatsschrift für Kriminalpsychologie und Strafrechtsreform*. 24: 534–37. September 1933.

5. Wirschubski, Gregor. "Der Schutz der Sittlichkeit im Sowjetstrafrecht." *Zeitschrift für die gesamte Strafrechtswissenschaft*. 51: 317–28. 1931.

6. Wirth, Louis. "Culture Conflict and Misconduct." *Social Forces*. 9: 484–92. June 1931. P. 490. Cf. Allport, Floyd H. "Culture Conflict versus the Individual as Factors in Delinquency." *Ibid*. Pp. 493–97.

7. White, William A. *Crimes and Criminals*. New York: Farrar & Rinehart. 1933. Healy, William. *Mental Conflict and Misconduct*. Boston: Little, Brown & Co. 1917. Alexander, Franz and Healy, William. *Roots of Crime*. New York: Alfred A. Knopf. 1935.

8. Burgess, Ernest W. in Clifford R. Shaw's *The Jack-Roller*. Chicago: University of Chicago Press. 1930. Pp. 184–197, p. 186.

9. Wirth, Louis. *Op. cit*. P. 490. It should be noted that Wirth also states that culture should be studied "on the objective side" and that "the sociologist is not primarily interested in personality but in culture."

10. Burgess, Ernest W. *Op. cit*. P. 186.

6 / Lower Class Culture as a Generating Milieu of Gang Delinquency

WALTER B. MILLER

The etiology of delinquency has long been a controversial issue and is particularly so at present. As new frames of reference for explaining human behavior have been added to traditional theories, some authors have adopted the practice of citing the major postulates of each school of thought as they pertain to delinquency, and of going on to state that causality must be conceived in terms of the dynamic interaction of a complex combination of variables on many levels. The major sets of etiological factors currently adduced to explain delinquency are, in simplified terms, the physiological (delinquency results from organic pathology), the psycho-dynamic (delinquency is a "behavioral disorder" resulting primarily from emotional disturbance generated by a defective mother-child relationship), and the environmental (delinquency is the product of disruptive forces, "disorganization," in the actor's physical or social environment).

This paper selects one particular kind of "delinquency"[1]—law-violating acts committed by members of adolescent street corner groups in lower class communities—and attempts to show that the dominant component of motivation underlying these acts consists in a directed attempt by the actor to adhere to forms of behavior, and to achieve standards of value, as they are defined within that community. It takes as a premise that the motivation of behavior in this situation can be approached most productively by attempting to understand the nature of cultural forces impinging on the acting individual as they are perceived *by the actor himself*—although by no means only that segment of these forces of which the actor is consciously aware—rather than as they are perceived and evaluated from the reference position of another cultural system. In the case of "gang" delinquency, the cultural system which exerts the most direct influence on behavior is that of the lower class community itself—a long-established, distinctively patterned tradition with an integrity of its own—rather than a so-called "delinquent subculture" which has arisen through conflict with middle class culture and is oriented to the deliberate violation of middle class norms.

The bulk of the substantive data on which the following material is based was collected in connection with a service-research project in the control of gang delinquency. During the service aspect of the project, which lasted for three years, seven trained social workers maintained contact with twenty-one corner group units in a "slum" district of a large eastern city for periods of time ranging from ten to thirty months. Groups were Negro and white, male and female, and in early, middle, and late adolescence. Over eight thousand pages of direct observational data on behavior patterns of group members and other community residents were collected; almost daily contact was maintained for a total time period of about thirteen worker years. Data include workers' contact reports, participant observation reports by the writer—a cultural anthropologist—and direct tape recordings of group activities and discussions.[2]

FOCAL CONCERNS OF LOWER CLASS CULTURE

There is a substantial segment of present-day American society whose way of life, values, and characteristic patterns of behavior are the product of a distinctive cultural system which may be termed "lower class." Evidence indicates that this cultural system is becoming increasingly distinctive, and that the size of the group which shares this tradition is increasing.[3] The lower class way of life, in common with that of all distinctive cultural groups, is characterized by a set of focal concerns—areas or issues which command widespread and persistent attention and a high degree of emotional involvement. The specific concerns cited here, while by no means confined to the American lower classes, constitute a distinctive *patterning* of concerns which differs significantly, both in rank order and weighting, from that of American middle class culture. Chart 1 presents a highly schematic and simplified listing of six of the major concerns of lower class culture. Each is conceived as a "dimension" within which a fairly wide and varied range of alternative behavior patterns may be followed by different individuals under different situations. They are listed roughly in order of the degree of *explicit* attention accorded each and, in this sense, represent a weighted ranking of concerns. The "perceived alternatives" represent polar positions which define certain parameters within each dimension. As will be explained in more detail, it is necessary in relating the influence of these "concerns" to the motivation of delinquent behavior to specify *which* of its aspects is oriented to, whether orientation is *overt* or *covert, positive* (conforming to or seeking the aspect) or *negative* (rejecting or seeking to avoid the aspect).

Chart 1 / Focal Concerns of Lower Class Culture

Area	Perceived alternatives (state, quality, condition)	
1. Trouble:	law-abiding behavior	law-violating behavior
2. Toughness:	physical prowess, skill; "masculinity";	weakness, ineptitude; effeminacy;
	fearlessness, bravery, daring	timidity, cowardice, caution
3. Smartness:	ability to outsmart, dupe, "con";	gullibility, "con-ability";
	gaining money by "wits";	gaining money by hard work;
	shrewdness, adroitness in repartee	slowness, dull-wittedness, verbal maladroitness
4. Excitement:	thrill;	boredom;
	risk, danger;	"deadness," safeness;
	change, activity	sameness, passivity
5. Fate:	favored by fortune, being "lucky"	ill-omened, being "un-lucky"
6. Autonomy:	freedom from external constraint;	presence of external constraint;
	freedom from superordinate authority;	presence of strong authority;
	independence	dependency, being "cared for"

The concept "focal concern" is used here in preference to the concept "value" for several interrelated reasons: (1) It is more readily derivable from direct field observation. (2) It is descriptively neutral—permitting independent consideration of positive and negative valences as varying under different conditions, whereas "value" carries a built-in positive valence. (3) It makes possible more refined analysis of subcultural differences, since it reflects actual behavior, whereas "value" tends to wash out intracultural differences since it is colored by notions of the "official" ideal.

Trouble

Concern over "trouble" is a dominant feature of lower class culture. The concept has various shades of meaning; "trouble" in one of its aspects represents a situation or a kind of behavior which results in unwelcome or complicating involvement with official authorities or agencies of middle class society. "Getting into trouble" and "staying out of trouble" represent major issues for male and female, adults and children. For men, "trouble" frequently involves fighting or sexual adventures while drinking; for women, sexual involvement with disadvantageous consequences. Expressed desire to avoid behavior which violates moral or legal norms is often based less on an explicit commitment to "official" moral or legal standards than on a desire to avoid "getting into trouble," e.g., the complicating consequences of the action.

The dominant concern over "trouble" involves a distinction of critical importance for the lower class community—that between "law-abiding" and "non-law-abiding" behavior. There is a high degree of sensitivity as to where each person stands in relation to these two classes of activity. Whereas in the middle class community a major dimension for evaluating a person's status is "achievement" and its external symbols, in the lower class personal status is very frequently gauged along the law-abiding–non-law-abiding dimension. A mother will evaluate the suitability of her daughter's boyfriend less on the basis of his achievement potential than on the basis of his innate "trouble" potential. This sensitive awareness of the opposition of "trouble-producing" and "non-trouble-producing" behavior represents both a major basis for deriving status distinctions and an internalized conflict potential for the individual.

As in the case of other focal concerns, which of two perceived alternatives—"law-abiding" or "non-law-abiding"—is valued varies according to the individual and the circumstances; in many instances there is an overt commitment to the "law-abiding" alternative, but a covert commitment to the "non-law-abiding." In certain situations, "getting into trouble" is overtly recognized as prestige-conferring; for example, membership in certain adult and adolescent primary groupings ("gangs") is contingent on having demonstrated an explicit commitment to the law-violating alternative. It is most important to note that the choice between "law-abiding" and "non-law-abiding" behavior is still a choice *within* lower class culture; the distinction between the policeman and the criminal, the outlaw and the sheriff, involves primarily this one dimension; in other respects they have a high community of interests. Not infrequently brothers raised in an identical cultural milieu will become police and criminals respectively.

For a substantial segment of the lower class population "getting into trouble" is not in itself overtly defined as prestige-conferring, but is implicitly recognized as a means to other valued ends, e.g., the covertly valued desire to be "cared for" and subject to external constraint, or the overtly valued state of excitement or risk. Very frequently "getting into trouble" is multi-functional and achieves several sets of valued ends.

Toughness

The concept of "toughness" in lower class culture represents a compound combination of qualities or states. Among its most important components are physical prowess, evidenced both by demonstrated possession of strength and endurance and by athletic skill; "masculinity," symbolized by a distinctive complex of acts and avoidances (bodily tattooing, absence of sentimentality, non-concern with "art," "literature," conceptualization of women as conquest objects, etc.); and bravery in the face of physical threat. The model for the "tough guy"—hard, fearless, undemonstrative, skilled in physical combat—is represented by the movie gangster of the thirties, the "private eye," and the movie cowboy.

The genesis of the intense concern over "toughness" in lower class culture is probably related to the fact that a significant proportion of lower class males are reared in a predominantly female household and lack a consistently present male figure with whom to identify and from whom to learn essential components of a "male" role. Since women serve as a primary object of identification during pre-adolescent years, the almost obsessive lower class concern with "masculinity" probably resembles a type of compulsive reaction-formation. A concern over homosexuality runs like a persistent thread through lower class culture. This is manifested by the institutionalized practice of baiting "queers," often accompanied by violent physical attacks, an expressed contempt for "softness" or frills, and the use of the local term for "homosexual" as a generalized pejorative epithet (e.g., higher class individuals or upwardly mobile peers are frequently characterized as "fags" or "queers"). The distinction between "overt" and "covert" orientation to aspects of an area of concern is especially important in regard to "toughness." A positive overt evaluation of behavior defined as "effeminate" would be out of the question for a lower class male; however, built into lower class culture is a range of devices which permit men to adopt behaviors and concerns which in other cultural milieux fall within the province of women, and at the same time to be defined as "tough" and manly. For example, lower class men can be professional short-order cooks in a diner and still be regarded as "tough." The highly intimate circumstances of the street corner gang involve the recurrent expression of strongly affectionate feelings towards other men. Such expressions, however, are disguised as their opposite, taking the form of ostensibly aggressive verbal and physical interaction (kidding, "ranking," roughhousing, etc.).

Smartness

"Smartness," as conceptualized in lower class culture, involves the capacity to outsmart, outfox, outwit, dupe, "take," "con" another or others and the concomitant capacity to avoid being outwitted, "taken," or duped oneself. In its essence, smartness involves the capacity to achieve a valued entity—material goods, personal status—through a maximum use of mental agility and a minimum use of physical effort. This capacity has an extremely long tradition in lower class culture and is highly valued. Lower class culture can be characterized as "non-intellectual" only if intellectualism is defined specifically in terms of control over a particular body of formally learned knowledge involving "culture" (art, literature, "good" music, etc.), a generalized perspective on the past and present conditions of our own and other societies, and other areas of knowledge imparted by formal educational institutions. This particular type of mental attainment is, in general, overtly disvalued and frequently associated with effeminacy; "smartness" in the lower class sense, however, is highly valued.

The lower class child learns and practices the use of this skill in the street corner situation. Individuals continually practice duping and outwitting one another through recurrent card games and other forms of gambling, mutual exchanges of insults, and "testing" for mutual "con-ability." Those who demonstrate competence in this skill are accorded considerable prestige. Leadership roles in the corner group are frequently allocated according to demonstrated capacity in the two areas of "smartness" and "toughness"; the ideal leader combines both, but the "smart" leader is often accorded more prestige than the "tough" one—reflecting a general lower class respect for "brains" in the "smartness" sense.[4]

The model of the "smart" person is represented in popular media by the card shark, the professional gambler, the "con" artist, the promoter. A conceptual distinction is made between two kinds of people: "suckers," easy marks, "lushes," dupes, who work for their money and are legitimate targets of exploitation; and sharp operators, the "brainy" ones, who live by their wits and "getting" from the suckers by mental adroitness.

Involved in the syndrome of capacities related to "smartness" is a dominant emphasis in lower class culture on ingenious aggressive repartee. This skill, learned and practiced in the context of the corner group, ranges in form from the widely prevalent semi-ritualized teasing, kidding, razzing, "ranking," so characteristic of male peer group interaction, to the highly ritualized type of mutual insult interchange known as "the dirty dozens," "the dozens," "playing house," and other terms. This highly patterned cultural form is practiced on its most advanced level in adult male Negro society, but less polished variants are found throughout lower class culture—practiced, for example, by white children, male and female, as young as four or five. In essence, "doin' the dozens" involves two antagonists who vie with each other in the exchange of increasingly inflammatory insults, with incestuous and perverted sexual relations with the mother a dominant theme. In this form of insult interchange, as well as on other less ritualized occasions for joking, semi-serious, and serious mutual invective, a very high premium is placed on ingenuity, hair-trigger responsiveness, inventiveness, and the acute exercise of mental faculties.

Excitement

For many lower class individuals the rhythm of life fluctuates between periods of relatively routine or repetitive activity and sought situations of great emotional stimulation. Many of the most characteristic features of lower class life are related to the search for excitement or "thrill." Involved here are the highly prevalent use of alcohol by both sexes and the widespread use of gambling of all kinds—playing the numbers, betting on horse races, dice, cards. The quest for excitement finds what is perhaps its most vivid expression in the highly patterned practice of the recurrent "night on the town." This practice, designated by various terms in different areas ("honky-tonkin' "; "goin' out on the town"; "bar hoppin' "), involves a patterned set of activities in which alcohol, music, and sexual adventuring are major components. A group or individual sets out to "make the rounds" of various bars or night clubs. Drinking continues progressively throughout the evening. Men seek to "pick up" women, and women play the risky game of entertaining sexual advances. Fights between men involving women, gambling, and claims of physical prowess, in various combinations, are frequent consequences of a night of making the rounds. The explosive potential of this type of adventuring with sex and aggression, frequently leading to "trouble," is semi-explicitly sought by the individual. Since there is always a good likelihood that being out on the town will eventuate in fights, etc., the practice involves elements of sought risk and desired danger.

Counterbalancing the "flirting with danger" aspect of the "excitement" concern is the prevalence in lower class culture of other well-established patterns of activity which involve long periods of relative inaction or passivity. The term "hanging out" in lower class culture refers to extended periods of standing around, often with peer mates, doing what is defined as "nothing," "shooting the breeze," etc. A definite periodicity exists in the pattern of activity relating to the two aspects of the "excitement" dimension. For many lower class individuals the venture into the high risk world of alcohol, sex, and fighting occurs regularly once a week, with interim periods devoted to accommodating to possible consequences of these periods, along with recurrent resolves not to become so involved again.

Fate

Related to the quest for excitement is the concern with fate, fortune, or luck. Here also a distinction is made between two states—being "lucky" or "in luck" and being unlucky or jinxed. Many lower class individuals feel that their lives are subject to a set of forces over which they have relatively little control. These are not directly equated with the supernatural forces of formally organized religion, but relate more to a concept of "destiny," or man as a pawn of magical powers. Not infrequently this often implicit world view is associated with a conception of the ultimate futility of directed effort towards a goal: if the cards are right, or the dice good to you, or if your lucky number comes up, things will go your way; if luck is against you, it's not worth trying. The concept of performing semi-magical rituals so that one's "luck will change" is prevalent; one hopes as a result to move from the state of being "unlucky" to that of being "lucky." The element of fantasy plays an important part in this area. Related to and complementing the notion that "only suckers work" (Smartness) is the idea that once things start going your way, relatively independent of your own effort, all good things will come to you. Achieving great material rewards (big cars, big houses, a roll of cash to flash in a fancy night club), valued in lower class as well as in other parts of American culture, is a recurrent theme in lower class fantasy and folk lore; the cocaine dreams of Willie the Weeper or Minnie the Moocher present the components of this fantasy in vivid detail.

The prevalence in the lower class community of many forms of gambling, mentioned in connection with the "excitement" dimension, is also relevant here. Through cards and pool which involve skill, and thus both "toughness" and "smartness"; or through race horse betting, involving "smartness"; or through playing the numbers, involving predominantly "luck," one may make a big killing with a minimum of directed and persistent effort within conventional occupational channels. Gambling in its many forms illustrates the fact that many of the persistent features of lower class culture are multi-functional—serving a range of desired ends at the same time. Describing some of the incentives behind gambling has involved mention of all of the focal concerns cited so far—Toughness, Smartness, and Excitement, in addition to Fate.

Autonomy

The extent and nature of control over the behavior of the individual—an important concern in most cultures—has a special significance and is distinctively patterned in lower class culture. The discrepancy between what is overtly valued and what is covertly sought is particularly striking in this area. On the overt level there is a strong and frequently expressed resentment of the idea of external controls, restrictions on behavior, and unjust or coercive authority. "No, one's gonna push *me* around," or "I'm gonna tell him he can take the job and shove it. . . ." are commonly expressed sentiments. Similar explicit attitudes are maintained to systems of behavior-restricting rules, insofar as these are perceived as representing the injunctions and bearing the sanctions of superordinate authority. In addition, in lower class culture a close conceptual connection is made between "authority" and "nurturance." To be restrictively or firmly controlled is to be cared for. Thus the overtly negative evaluation of superordinate authority frequently extends as well to nurturance, care, or protection. The desire for personal independence is often expressed in such terms as "I don't need *nobody* to take care of me. I can take care of myself!" Actual patterns of behavior, however, reveal a marked discrepancy between expressed sentiment and what is covertly valued. Many lower class people appear to seek out highly restrictive social environments wherein stringent external controls are maintained over their behavior. Such institutions as the armed forces, the mental hospital, the disciplinary school, the prison or correctional institution, provide environments which incorporate a strict and detailed set of rules, defining and limiting behavior and enforced by an authority system which controls and applies coercive sanctions for deviance from these rules. While under the jurisdiction of such systems, the lower class person generally expresses to his peers continual resentment of the coercive, unjust, and arbitrary exercise of authority. Having been released, or having escaped from these milieux, however, he will often act in such a way as to insure recommitment, or choose recommitment voluntarily after a temporary period of "freedom."

Lower class patients in mental hospitals will exercise considerable ingenuity to insure continued commitment while voicing the desire to get out; delinquent boys will frequently "run" from a correctional institution to activate efforts to return them; to be caught and returned means that one is cared for. Since "being controlled" is equated with "being cared for," attempts are frequently made to "test" the severity or strictness of superordinate authority to see if it remains firm. If intended or executed rebellion produces swift and firm punitive sanctions, the individual is reassured, at the same time that he is complaining bitterly at the injustice of being caught and punished. Some environmental milieux, having been tested in this fashion for the "firmness" of their coercive sanctions, are rejected, ostensibly for being too strict, actually for not being strict enough. This is frequently so in the case of "problematic" behavior by lower class youngsters in the public schools, which generally cannot command the coercive controls implicitly sought by the individual.

A similar discrepancy between what is overtly and covertly desired is found in the area of dependence-independence. The pose of tough rebellious independence often assumed by the lower class person frequently conceals powerful dependency cravings. These are manifested primarily by obliquely expressed resentment when "care" is not forthcoming rather than by expressed satisfaction when it is. The concern over autonomy-dependency is related both to "trouble" and "fate." Insofar as the lower class individual feels that his behavior is controlled by forces which often propel him into "trouble" in the face of an explicit determination to avoid it, there is an implied appeal to "save me from myself." A solution appears to lie in arranging things so that his behavior will be coercively restricted by an externally imposed set of controls strong enough to forcibly restrain his inexplicable inclination to get into trouble. The periodicity observed in connection with the "excitement" dimension is also relevant here; after involvement in trouble-producing behavior (assault, sexual adventure, a "drunk"), the individual will actively seek a locus of imposed control (his wife, prison, a restrictive job); after a given period of subjection to this control, resentment against it mounts, leading to a "break away" and a search for involvement in further "trouble."

FOCAL CONCERNS OF THE LOWER CLASS ADOLESCENT STREET CORNER GROUP

The one-sex peer group is a highly prevalent and significant structural form in the lower class community. There is a strong probability that the prevalence and stability of this type of unit is directly related to the prevalence of a stabilized type of lower class child-rearing unit—the "female-based" household. This is a nuclear kin unit in which a male parent is either absent from the household, present only sporadically, or, when present, only minimally or inconsistently involved in the support and rearing of children. This unit usually consists of one or more females of childbearing age and their offspring. The females are frequently related to one another by blood or marriage ties, and the unit often includes two or more generations of women, e.g., the mother and/or aunt of the principal childbearing female.

The nature of social groupings in the lower class community may be clarified if we make the assumption that it is the *one-sex peer unit* rather than the two-parent family unit which represents the most significant relational unit for both sexes in lower class communities. Lower class society may be pictured as comprising a set of age-graded one-sex groups which constitute the major psychic focus and reference group for those over twelve or thirteen. Men and women of mating age leave these groups periodically to form temporary marital alliances, but these lack stability, and after varying periods of "trying out" the two-sex family arrangement, they gravitate back to the more "comfortable" one-sex grouping, whose members exert strong pressure on the individual *not* to disrupt the group by adopting a two-sex household pattern of life.[5] Membership in a stable and solidary peer unit is vital to the lower class individual precisely to the extent to which a range of essential functions—psychological, educational, and others—are not provided by the "family" unit.

The adolescent street corner group represents the adolescent variant of this lower class structural form. What has been called the "delinquent gang" is one subtype of this form, defined on the basis of frequency of participation in law-violating activity; this subtype should not be considered a legitimate unit of study per se, but rather as one particular variant of the adolescent street corner group. The "hanging" peer group is a unit of particular importance for the adolescent male. In many cases it is the most stable and solidary primary group he has ever belonged to; for boys reared in female-based households the corner group provides the first real opportunity to learn essential aspects of the male role in the context of peers facing similar problems of sex-role identification.

The form and functions of the adolescent corner group operate as a selective mechanism in recruiting members. The activity patterns of the group require a high level of intragroup solidarity; individual members must possess a good capacity for subordinating individual desires to general group interests as well as the capacity for intimate and persisting interaction. Thus highly "disturbed" individuals, or those who cannot tolerate consistently imposed sanctions on "deviant" behavior cannot remain accepted members; the group itself will extrude those whose behavior exceeds limits defined as "normal." This selective process produces a type of group whose members possess to an unusually high degree both the *capacity* and *motivation* to conform to perceived cultural norms, so that the nature of the system of norms and values oriented to is a particularly influential component of motivation.

Focal concerns of the male adolescent corner group are those of the general cultural milieu in which it functions. As would be expected, the relative weighting and importance of these concerns pattern somewhat differently for adolescents than for adults. The nature of this patterning centers around two additional "concerns" of particular importance to this group—concern with "belonging," and with "status." These may be conceptualized as being on a higher level of abstraction than concerns previously cited, since "status" and "belonging" are achieved *via* cited concern areas of Toughness, etc.

Belonging

Since the corner group fulfills essential functions for the individual, being a member in good standing of the group is of vital importance for its members. A continuing concern over who is "in" and who is not involves the citation and detailed discussion of highly refined criteria for "in-group" membership. The phrase "he hangs with us" means "he is accepted as a member in good standing by current consensus"; conversely, "he don't hang with us" means he is not so accepted. One achieves "belonging" primarily by demonstrating knowledge of and determination to adhere to the system of standards and valued qualities defined by the group. One maintains membership by acting in conformity with valued aspects of Toughness, Smartness, Autonomy, etc. In those instances where conforming to norms of this reference group at the same time violates norms of other reference groups (e.g., middle class adults, institutional "officials"), immediate reference group norms are much more compelling since violation risks invoking the group's most powerful sanction: exclusion.

Status

In common with most adolescents in American society, the lower class corner group manifests a dominant concern with "status." What differentiates this type of group from others, however, is the particular set of criteria and weighting thereof by which "status" is defined. In general, status is achieved and maintained by demonstrated possession of the valued qualities of lower class culture—Toughness, Smartness, expressed resistance to authority, daring, etc. It is important to stress once more that the individual orients to these concerns *as they are defined within lower class society;* e.g., the status-conferring potential of "smartness" in the sense of scholastic achievement generally ranges from negligible to negative.

The concern with "status" is manifested in a variety of ways. Intragroup status is a continued concern and is derived and tested constantly by means of a set of status-ranking activities; the intragroup "pecking order" is constantly at issue. One gains status within the group by demonstrated superiority in Toughness (physical prowess, bravery, skill in athletics and games such as pool and cards), Smartness (skill in repartee, capacity to "dupe" fellow group members), and the like. The term "ranking," used to refer to the pattern of intragroup aggressive repartee, indicates awareness of the fact that this is one device for establishing the intragroup status hierarchy.

The concern over status in the adolescent corner group involves in particular the component of "adultness," the intense desire to be seen as "grown up," and a corresponding aversion to "kid stuff." "Adult" status is defined less in terms of the assumption of "adult" responsibility than in terms of certain external symbols of adult status—a car, ready cash, and, in particular, a perceived "freedom" to drink, smoke, and gamble as one wishes and to come and go without external restrictions. The desire to be seen as "adult" is often a more significant component of much involvement in illegal drinking, gambling, and automobile driving than the explicit enjoyment of these acts as such.

The intensity of the corner group member's desire to be seen as "adult" is sufficiently great that he feels called upon to demonstrate qualities associated with adultness (Toughness, Smartness, Autonomy) to a much greater degree than a lower class adult. This means that he will seek out and utilize those avenues to these qualities which he perceives as available with greater intensity than an adult and less regard for their "legitimacy." In this sense the adolescent variant of lower class culture represents a maximization or an intensified manifestation of many of its most characteristic features.

Concern over status is also manifested in reference to other street corner groups. The term "rep" used in this regard is especially significant and has broad connotations. In its most frequent and explicit connotation, "rep" refers to the "toughness" of the corner group as a whole relative to that of other groups; a "pecking order" also exists among the several corner groups in a given interactional area, and there is a common perception that the safety or security of the group and all its members depends on maintaining a solid "rep" for toughness vis-a-vis other groups. This motive is most frequently advanced as a reason for involvement in gang fights: "We *can't* chicken out on this fight; our rep would be shot!"; this implies that the group would be relegated to the bottom of the status ladder and become a helpless and recurrent target of external attack.

On the other hand, there is implicit in the concept of "rep" the recognition that "rep" has or may have a dual basis—corresponding to the two aspects of the "trouble" dimension. It is recognized that group as well as individual status can be based on both "law-abiding" and "law-violating" behavior. The situational resolution of the persisting conflict between the "law-abiding" and "law-violating" bases of status comprises a vital set of dynamics in determining whether a "delinquent" mode of behavior will be adopted by a group, under what circumstances, and how persistently. The determinants of this choice are evidently highly complex and fluid, and rest on a range of factors including the presence and perceptual immediacy of different community reference-group loci (e.g., professional criminals, police, clergy, teachers, settlement house workers), the personality structures and "needs" of group members, the presence in the community of social work, recreation, or educational programs which can facilitate utilization of the "law-abiding" basis of status, and so on.

What remains constant is the critical importance of "status" both for the members of the group as individuals and for the group as a whole insofar as members perceive their individual destinies as linked to the destiny of the group, and the fact that action geared to attain status is much more acutely oriented to the fact of status itself than to the legality or illegality, morality or immorality of the means used to achieve it.

LOWER CLASS CULTURE AND THE MOTIVATION OF DELINQUENT BEHAVIOR

The customary set of activities of the adolescent street corner group includes activities which are in violation of laws and ordinances of the legal code. Most of these center around assault and theft of various types (the gang fight; auto theft; assault on an individual; petty pilfering and shoplifting; "mugging"; pocketbook theft). Members of street corner gangs are well aware of the law-violating nature of these acts; they are not psychopaths, or physically or mentally "defective"; in fact, since the corner group supports and enforces a rigorous set of standards which demand a high degree of fitness and personal competence, it tends to recruit from the most "able" members of the community.

Why, then, is the commission of crimes a customary feature of gang activity? The most general answer is that the commission of crimes by members of adolescent street corner groups is motivated primarily by the attempt to achieve ends, states, or conditions which are valued and to avoid those that are disvalued within their most meaningful cultural milieu, through those culturally available avenues which appear as the most feasible means of attaining those ends.

The operation of these influences is well illustrated by the gang fight—a prevalent and characteristic type of corner group delinquency. This type of activity comprises a highly stylized and culturally patterned set of sequences. Although details vary under different circumstances, the following events are generally included. A member or several members of group A "trespass" on the claimed territory of group B. While there they commit an act or acts which group B defines as a violation of their rightful privileges, an affront to their honor, or a challenge to their "rep." Frequently this act involves advances to a girl associated with group B; it may occur at a dance or party; sometimes the mere act of "trespass" is seen as deliberate provocation. Members of group B then assault members of group A, if they are caught while still in B's territory. Assaulted members of group A return to their "home" territory and recount to members of their group details of the incident, stressing the insufficient nature of the provocation ("I just *looked* at her! Hardly even said anything!"), and the unfair circumstances of the assault ("About *twenty* guys jumped just the *two* of us!"). The highly colored account is acutely inflammatory; group A, perceiving its honor violated and its "rep" threatened, feels obligated to retaliate in force. Sessions of detailed planning now occur; allies are recruited if the size of group A and its potential allies appears to necessitate larger numbers; strategy is plotted, and messengers dispatched. Since the prospect of a gang fight is frightening to even the "toughest" group members, a constant rehearsal of the provocative incident or incidents and declamations of the essentially evil nature of the opponents accompany the planning process to bolster possibly weakening motivation to fight. The excursion into "enemy" territory sometimes results in a full scale fight; more often group B cannot be found, or the police appear and stop the fight, "tipped off" by an anonymous informant. When this occurs, group members express disgust and disappointment; secretly there is much relief; their honor has been avenged without incurring injury; often the anonymous tipster is a member of one of the involved groups.

The basic elements of this type of delinquency are sufficiently stabilized and recurrent as to constitute an essentially ritualized pattern, resembling both in structure and expressed motives for action classic forms such as the European "duel," the American Indian tribal war, and the Celtic clan feud. Although the arousing and "acting out" of individual aggressive emotions are inevitably involved in the gang fight, neither its form nor motivational dynamics can be adequately handled within a predominantly personality-focused frame of reference.

It would be possible to develop in considerable detail the processes by which the commission of a range of illegal acts is either explicitly supported by, implicitly demanded by, or not materially inhibited by factors relating to the focal concerns of lower class culture. In place of such a development, the following three statements condense in general terms the operation of these processes:

1. Following cultural practices which comprise essential elements of the total life pattern of lower class culture automatically violates certain legal norms.

2. In instances where alternate avenues to similar objectives are available, the non-law-abiding avenue frequently provides a relatively greater and more immediate return for a relatively smaller investment of energy.

3. The "demanded" response to certain situations recurrently engendered within lower class culture involves the commission of illegal acts.

The primary thesis of this paper is that the dominant component of the motivation of "delinquent" behavior engaged in by members of lower class corner groups involves a positive effort to achieve states, conditions, or qualities valued within the actor's most significant cultural milieu. If "conformity to immediate reference group values" is the major component of motivation of "delinquent" behavior by gang members, why is such behavior frequently referred to as negativistic, malicious, or rebellious? Albert Cohen, for example, in *Delinquent Boys* (Glencoe, Ill.: Free Press, 1955) describes behavior which violates school rules as comprising elements of "active spite and malice, contempt and ridicule, challenge and defiance." He ascribes to the gang "keen delight in terrorizing 'good' children, and in general making themselves obnoxious to the virtuous." A recent national conference on social work with "hard-to-reach" groups characterized lower class corner groups as "youth groups in conflict with the culture of their (*sic*) communities." Such characterizations are obviously the result of taking the middle class community and its institutions as an implicit point of reference.

A large body of systematically interrelated attitudes, practices, behaviors, and values characteristic of lower class culture are designed to support and maintain the basic features of the lower class way of life. In areas where these differ from features of middle class culture, action oriented to the achievement and maintenance of the lower class system may violate norms of middle class culture and be perceived as deliberately non-conforming or malicious by an observer strongly cathected to middle class norms. This does not mean, however, that violation of the middle class norm is the dominant component of motivation; it is a by-product of action primarily oriented to the lower class system. The standards of lower class culture cannot be seen merely as a reverse function of middle class culture — as middle class standards "turned upside down"; lower class culture is a distinctive tradition many centuries old with an integrity of its own.

From the viewpoint of the acting individual, functioning within a field of well-structured cultural forces, the relative impact of "conforming" and "rejective" elements in the motivation of gang delinquency is weighted preponderantly on the conforming side. Rejective or rebellious elements are inevitably involved, but their influence during the actual commission of delinquent acts is relatively small compared to the influence of pressures to achieve what is valued by the actor's most immediate reference groups. Expressed awareness by the actor of the element of rebellion often represents only that aspect of motivation of which he is explicitly conscious; the deepest and most compelling components of motivation — adherence to highly meaningful group standards of Toughness, Smartness, Excitement, etc. — are often unconsciously patterned. No cultural pattern as well established as the practice of illegal acts by members of lower class corner groups could persist if buttressed primarily by negative, hostile, or rejective motives; its principal motivational support, as in the case of any persisting cultural tradition, derives from a positive effort to achieve what is valued within that tradition, and to conform to its explicit and implicit norms.

Notes

1. The complex issues involved in deriving a definition of "delinquency" cannot be discussed here. The term "delinquent" is used in this paper to characterize behavior or acts committed by individuals within specified age limits which if known to official authorities could result in legal action. The concept of a "delinquent" individual has little or no utility in the approach used here; rather, specified types of *acts* which may be committed rarely or frequently by few or many individuals are characterized as "delinquent."

2. A three-year research project is being financed under National Institutes of Health Grant M-1414 and administered through the Boston University School of Social Work. The primary research effort has subjected all collected material to a uniform data-coding process. All information bearing on some seventy areas of behavior (behavior in reference to school, police, theft, assault, sex, collective athletics, etc.) is extracted from the records, recorded on coded data cards, and filed under relevant categories. Analysis of these data aims to ascertain the actual nature of customary behavior in these areas and the extent to which the social work effort was able to effect behavioral changes.

3. Between 40 and 60 per cent of all Americans are directly influenced by lower class culture, with about 15 per cent, or twenty-five million, comprising the "hard core"

lower class group—defined primarily by its use of the "female-based" household as the basic form of child-rearing unit and of the "serial monogamy" mating pattern as the primary form of marriage. The term "lower class culture" as used here refers most specifically to the way of life of the "hard core" group; systematic research in this area would probably reveal at least four to six major subtypes of lower class culture, for some of which the "concerns" presented here would be differently weighted, especially for those subtypes in which "law-abiding" behavior has a high overt valuation. It is impossible within the compass of this short paper to make the finer intracultural distinctions which a more accurate presentation would require.

4. The "brains-brawn" set of capacities are often paired in lower class folk lore or accounts of lower class life, e.g., "Brer Fox" and "Brer Bear" in the Uncle Remus stories, or George and Lennie in "Of Mice and Men."

5. Further data on the female-based household unit (estimated as comprising about 15 per cent of all American "families") and the role of one-sex groupings in lower class culture are contained in Walter B. Miller, Implications of Urban Lower Class Culture for Social Work. *Social Service Review*, 1959, 33, No. 3.

7 / Differential Association Theory

EDWIN H. SUTHERLAND
DONALD R. CRESSEY

THE PROBLEM FOR CRIMINOLOGICAL THEORY

If criminology is to be scientific, the heterogeneous collection of "multiple factors" known to be associated with crime and criminality should be organized and integrated by means of explanatory theory which has the same characteristics as the scientific theory in other fields of study. That is, the conditions which are said to cause crime should always be present when crime is present, and they should always be absent when crime is absent. Such a theory or body of theory would stimulate, simplify, and give direction to criminological research, and it would provide a framework for understanding the significance of much of the knowledge acquired about crime and criminality in the past. Furthermore, it would be useful in control of crime, provided it could be "applied" in much the same way that the engineer "applies" the scientific theories of the physicist.

There are two complementary procedures which may be used to put order into criminological knowledge, to develop a causal theory of criminal behavior. The first is logical abstraction. Negroes, urban-dwellers, and young adults all have comparatively high crime rates. What do they have in common that results in these high crime rates? Research studies have shown that criminal behavior is associated, in greater or lesser degree, with the social and personal pathologies, such as poverty, bad housing, slum-residence, lack of recreational facilities, inadequate and demoralized families, mental retardation, emotional instability, and other traits and conditions. What do these conditions have in common which apparently produces excessive criminality? Research studies have also demonstrated that many persons with those pathological traits and conditions do not commit crimes and that persons in the upper socioeconomic class frequently violate the law, although they are not in poverty, do not lack recreational facilities, and are not mentally retarded or emotionally unstable. Obviously, it is not the conditions or traits themselves which cause crime, for the conditions are sometimes present when criminality does not occur, and they also are sometimes absent when criminality does occur. A causal explanation of criminal behavior can be reached by abstracting, logically, the mechanisms and processes which are common to the rich and the poor, the Negroes and the whites, the urban- and the rural-dwellers, the young adults and the old adults, and the emotionally stable and the emotionally unstable who commit crimes.

In arriving at these abstract mechanisms and processes, criminal behavior must be precisely defined and carefully distinguished from noncriminal behavior. The problem in criminology is to explain the criminality of behavior, not behavior, as such. The abstract mechanisms and processes common to the classes of criminals indicated above should not also be common to noncriminals. Criminal behavior is human behavior, has much in common with noncriminal behavior, and must be explained within the same general framework used to explain other human behavior. However, an explanation of criminal behavior should be a specific part of a general theory of behavior. Its specific task should be to differentiate criminal from noncriminal behavior. Many things which are necessary for behavior are not for that reason important to the criminality of behavior. Respiration, for instance, is necessary for any behavior, but the respiratory process cannot be used in an explanation of criminal behavior, for it does not differentiate criminal behavior from noncriminal behavior.

The second procedure for putting order into criminological knowledge is differentiation of levels of analysis. This means that the problem is limited to a particular part of the whole situation, largely in terms of chronology. The causal analysis must be held at a particular level. For example, when physicists stated the law of falling bodies, they were not concerned with the reasons why a body began to fall except as this might affect the initial momentum. It made no difference to the physicist whether a body began to fall because it was dropped from the hand of an experimental physicist or rolled off the edge of a bridge because of vibration caused by a passing vehicle. Also, a round object would have rolled off the bridge more readily than a square object, but this fact was not significant for the law of falling bodies. Such facts were considered as exsisting on a different level of explanation and were irrelevant to the problem with which the physicists were concerned.

Much of the confusion regarding criminal behavior is due to a failure to define and hold constant the level of explanation. By analogy, many criminologists would attribute some degree of causal power to the "roundness" of the object in the above illustration. However, consideration of time sequences among the conditions associated with crime and criminality may lead to simplicity of statement. In the heterogeneous collection of factors associated with criminal behavior, one factor often occurs prior to another factor (in much the way that "roundness" occurs prior to "vibration," and "vibration" occurs prior to "rolling off a bridge"), but a theoretical statement about criminal behavior can be made without referring to those early factors. By holding the analysis at one level, the early factors are combined with or differentiated from later factors or conditions, thus reducing the number of variables which must be considered in a theory.

A motion picture several years ago showed two boys engaged in a minor theft; they ran when they were discovered; one boy had longer legs, escaped, and became a priest; the other had shorter legs, was caught, committed to a reformatory, and became a gangster. In this comparison, the boy who became a criminal was differentiated from the one who did not become a criminal by the length of his legs. But "length of legs" need not be considered in a criminological theory, for there is no significant relationship between criminality and length of legs; certainly many persons with short legs are law-abiding, and some persons with long legs are criminals. The length of the legs does not determine criminality and has no necessary relation to criminality. In the illustration, the differential in the length of the boys' legs may be observed to be significant to subsequent criminality or noncriminality only to the degree that it determined the subsequent experiences and associations of the two boys. It is in these experiences and associations, then, that the mechanisms and processes which are important to criminality or noncriminality are to be found. A "one-level" theoretical explanation of crime would be concerned solely with these mechanisms and processes, not with the earlier factor, "length of legs."

TWO TYPES OF EXPLANATIONS OF CRIMINAL BEHAVIOR

Scientific explanations of criminal behavior may be stated either in terms of the processes which are operating at the moment of the occurrence of crime or in terms of the processes operating in the earlier history of the criminal. In the first case, the explanation may be called "mechanistic," "situational," or "dynamic"; in the second, "historical" or "genetic." Both types of explanation are desirable. The mechanistic type of explanation has been favored by physical and biological scientists, and it probably could be the more efficient type of explanation of criminal behavior. However, criminological explanations of the mechanistic type have thus far been notably unsuccessful, perhaps largely because they have been formulated in connection with the attempt to isolate personal and social pathologies among criminals. Work from this point of view has, at least, resulted in the conclusion that the immediate determinants of criminal behavior lie in the person-situation complex.

The objective situation is important to criminality largely to the extent that it provides an opportunity for a criminal act. A thief may steal from a fruit stand when the owner is not in sight but refrain when the ower is in sight; a bank burglar may attack a bank which is poorly protected but refrain from attacking a bank protected by watchmen and burglar alarms. A corporation which manufactures automobiles seldom violates the pure food and drug laws, but a meat-packing corporation might violate these laws with great frequency. But in another sense, a psychological or sociological sense, the situation is not exclusive of the person, for the situation which is important is the situation as defined by the person who is involved. That is, some persons define a situation in which a fruit-stand owner is out of sight as a "crime-committing" situation, while others do not so define it. Furthermore, the events in the person-situation complex at the time a crime occurs cannot be separated from the prior life experiences of the criminal. This means that the situation is defined by the person in terms of the inclinations and abilities which he has acquired. For example, while a person could define a situation in such a manner that criminal behavior would be the inevitable result, his past experiences would, for the most part, determine the way in which he defined the situation. An explanation of criminal behavior made in terms of these past experiences is an historical or genetic explanation.

The following paragraphs state such a genetic theory of criminal behavior on the assumption that a criminal act occurs when a situation appropriate for it, as defined by the person, is present. The theory should be regarded as tentative, and it should be tested by the factual information presented in the later chapters and by all other factual information and theories which are applicable.

GENETIC EXPLANATION OF CRIMINAL BEHAVIOR

The following statements refer to the process by which a particular person comes to engage in criminal behavior.

1. *Criminal behavior is learned.* Negatively, this means that criminal behavior is not inherited, as such; also, the person who is not already trained in crime does not invent criminal behavior, just as a person does not make mechanical inventions unless he has had training in mechanics.

2. *Criminal behavior is learned in interaction with other persons in a process of communication.* This communication is verbal in many respects but includes also "the communication of gestures."

3. *The principal part of the learning of criminal behavior occurs within intimate personal groups.* Negatively, this means that the impersonal agencies of communication, such as movies and newspapers, play a relatively unimportant part in the genesis of criminal behavior.

4. *When criminal behavior is learned, the learning includes (a) techniques of committing the crime, which are sometimes very complicated, sometimes very simple; (b) the specific direction of motives, drives, rationalizations, and attitudes.*

5. *The specific direction of motives and drives is learned from definitions of the legal codes as favorable or unfavorable.* In some societies an individual is surrounded by persons who invariably define the legal codes as rules to be observed, while in others he is surrounded by persons whose definitions are favorable to the violation of the legal codes. In our American society these definitions are almost always mixed, with the consequence that we have culture conflict in relation to the legal codes.

6. *A person becomes delinquent because of an excess of definitions favorable to violation of law over definitions unfavorable to violation of law.* This is the principle of differential association. It refers to both criminal and anticriminal associations and has to do with counteracting forces. When persons become criminal, they do so because of contacts with criminal patterns and also because of isolation from anticriminal patterns. Any person inevitably assimilates the surrounding culture unless other patterns are in conflict; a southerner does not pronounce *r* because other southerners do not pronounce *r*. Negatively, this proposition of differential association means that associations which are neutral so far as crime is concerned have little or no effect on the genesis of criminal behavior. Much of the experience of a person is neutral in this sense, e.g., learning to brush one's teeth. This behavior has no negative or positive effect on criminal behavior except as it may be related to associations which are concerned with the legal codes. This neutral behavior is important especially as an occupier of the time of a child so that he is not in contact with criminal behavior during the time he is so engaged in the neutral behavior.

7. *Differential associations may vary in frequency, duration, priority, and intensity.* This means that associations with criminal behavior and also associations with anticriminal behavior vary in those respects. "Frequency" and "duration" as modalities of associations are obvious and need no explanation. "Priority" is assumed to be important in the sense that lawful behavior developed in early childhood may persist throughout life, and also that delinquent be-

havior developed in early childhood may persist throughout life. This tendency, however, has not been adequately demonstrated, and priority seems to be important principally through its selective influence. "Intensity" is not precisely defined, but it has to do with such things as the prestige of the source of a criminal or anticriminal pattern and with emotional reactions related to the associations. In a precise description of the criminal behavior of a person, these modalities would be rated in quantitative form and a mathematical ratio [would] be reached. A formula in this sense has not been developed, and the development of such a formula would be extremely difficult.

8. *The process of learning criminal behavior by association with criminal and anticriminal patterns involves all of the mechanisms that are involved in any other learning.* Negatively, this means that the learning of criminal behavior is not restricted to the process of imitation. A person who is seduced, for instance, learns criminal behavior by association, but this process would not ordinarily be described as imitation.

9. *While criminal behavior is an expression of general needs and values, it is not explained by those general needs and values, since noncriminal behavior is an expression of the same needs and values.* Thieves generally steal in order to secure money, but likewise honest laborers work in order to secure money. The attempts by many scholars to explain criminal behavior by general drives and values, such as the happiness principle, striving for social status, the money motive, or frustration, have been, and must continue to be, futile, since they explain lawful behavior as completely as they explain criminal behavior. They are similar to respiration, which is necessary for any behavior, but which does not differentiate criminal from noncriminal behavior.

It is not necessary, at this level of explanation, to explain why a person has the associations he has; this certainly involves a complex of many things. In an area where the delinquency rate is high, a boy who is sociable, gregarious, active, and athletic is very likely to come in contact with the other boys in the neighborhood, learn delinquent behavior patterns from them, and become a criminal; in the same neighborhood the psychopathic boy who is isolated, introverted, and inert may remain at home, not become acquainted with the other boys in the neighborhood and not become delinquent. In another situation, the sociable, athletic, aggressive boy may become a member of a scout troop and not become involved in delinquent behavior. The person's associations are determined in general context of social organization. A child is ordinarily reared in a family; the place of residence of the family is determined largely by family income; and the delinquency rate is in many respects related to the rental value of the houses. Many other aspects of social organization affect the kinds of associations a person has.

The preceding explanation of criminal behavior purports to explain the criminal and noncriminal behavior of individual persons. As indicated earlier, it is possible to state sociological theories of criminal behavior which explain the criminality of a community, nation, or other group. The problem, when thus stated, is to account for variations in crime rates and involves a comparison of the crime rates of various groups or the crime rates of a particular group at different times. The explanation of a crime rate must be consistent with the explanation of the criminal behavior of the person, since the crime rate is a summary statement of the number of persons in the group who commit crimes and the frequency with which they commit crimes. One of the best explanations of crime rates from this point of view is that a high crime rate is due to social disorganization. The term *social disorganization* is not entirely satisfactory, and it seems preferable to substitute for it the term *differential social organization*. The postulate on which this theory is based, regardless of the name, is that crime is rooted in the social organization and is an expression of that social organization. A group may be organized for criminal behavior or organized against criminal behavior. Most communities are organized for both criminal and anticriminal behavior, and, in that sense the crime rate is an expression of the differential group organization. Differential group organization as an explanation of variations in crime rates is consistent with the differential association theory of the processes by which persons become criminals.

8 / Techniques of Neutralization: A Theory of Delinquency

GRESHAM M. SYKES
DAVID MATZA

In attempting to uncover the roots of juvenile delinquency, the social scientist has long since ceased to search for devils in the mind or stigma of the body. It is now largely agreed that delinquent behavior, like most social behavior, is learned and that it is learned in the process of social interaction.

The classic statement of this position is found in Sutherland's theory of differential association, which asserts that criminal or delinquent behavior involves the learning of (a) techniques of committing crimes and (b) motives, drives, rationalizations, and attitudes favorable to the violation of law.[1] Unfortunately, the specific content of what is learned—as opposed to the process by which it is learned—has received relatively little attention in either theory or research. Perhaps the single strongest school of thought on the nature of this content has centered on the idea of a delinquent sub-culture. The basic characteristic of the delinquent sub-culture, it is argued, is a system of values that represents an inversion of the values held by respectable, law-abiding society. The world of the delinquent is the world of the law-abiding turned upside down, and its norms constitute a countervailing force directed against the conforming social order. Cohen[2] sees the process of developing a delinquent sub-culture as a matter of building, maintaining, and reinforcing a code for behavior which exists by opposition, which stands in point by point contradiction to dominant values, particularly those of the middle class. Cohen's portrayal of delinquency is executed with a good deal of sophistication, and he carefully avoids overly simple explanations such as those based on the principle of "follow the leader" or easy generalizations about "emotional disturbances." Furthermore, he does not accept the delinquent sub-culture as something given, but instead systematically examines the function of delinquent values as a viable solution to the lower-class, male child's problems in the area of social status. Yet in spite of its virtues, this image of juvenile delinquency as a form of behavior based on competing or countervailing values and norms appears to suffer from a number of serious defects. It is the nature of these defects and a possible alternative or modified explanation for a large portion of juvenile delinquency with which this paper is concerned.

The difficulties in viewing delinquent behavior as springing from a set of deviant values and norms—as arising, that is to say, from a situation in which the delinquent defines his delinquency as "right"—are both empirical and theoretical. In the first place, if there existed in fact a delinquent sub-culture such that the delinquent viewed his illegal behavior as morally correct, we could reasonably suppose that he would exhibit no feelings of guilt or shame at detection or confinement. Instead, the major reaction would tend in the direction of indignation or a sense of martyrdom.[3] It is true that some delinquents do react in the latter fashion, although the sense of martyrdom often seems to be based on the fact that others "get away with it," and indignation appears to be directed against the chance events or lack of skill that led to apprehension. More important, however, is the fact that there is a good deal of evidence suggesting that many delinquents *do* experience a sense of guilt or shame, and its outward expression is not to be dismissed as a purely manipulative gesture to appease those in authority. Much of this evidence is, to be sure, of a clinical nature or in the form of impressionistic judgments of those who must deal first hand with the youthful offender. Assigning a weight to such evidence calls for caution, but it cannot be ignored if we are to avoid the gross stereotype of the juvenile delinquent as a hardened gangster in miniature.

In the second place, observers have noted that the juvenile delinquent frequently accords admiration and respect to law-abiding persons. The "really honest" person is often revered, and if the delinquent is sometimes overly keen to detect hypocrisy in those who conform, unquestioned probity is likely to win his approval. A fierce attachment to a humble, pious mother or a forgiving upright priest (the former, according to many observers, is often encountered in both juvenile delinquents and adult criminals) might be dismissed as rank sentimentality, but at least it is clear that the delinquent does not necessarily regard those who abide by the legal rules as immoral. In a similar vein, it can be noted that the juvenile delinquent may exhibit great resentment if illegal behavior is imputed to "significant others" in his immediate social environment or to heroes in the world of sport and entertainment. In other words, if the delinquent does hold to a set of values and norms that stand in complete opposition to those of respectable society, his norm-holding is of a peculiar sort. While supposedly thoroughly committed to the deviant system of the delinquent subculture, he would appear to recognize the moral validity of the dominant normative system in many instances.[4]

In the third place, there is much evidence that juvenile delinquents often draw a sharp line between those who can be victimized and those who cannot. Certain social groups are not to be viewed as "fair game" in the performance of supposedly approved delinquent acts while others warrant a variety of attacks. In general, the potentiality for victimization would seem to be a function of the social distance between the juvenile delinquent and others, and thus we find implicit maxims in the world of the delinquent such as "don't steal from friends" or "don't commit vandalism against a church of your own faith."[5] This is all rather obvious, but the implications have not received sufficient attention. The fact that supposedly valued behavior tends to be directed against disvalued social groups hints that the "wrongfulness" of such delinquent behavior is more widely recognized by delinquents than the literature has indicated. When the pool of victims is limited by considerations of kinship, friendship, ethnic group, social class, age, sex, etc., we have reason to suspect that the virtue of delinquency is far from unquestioned.

In the fourth place, it is doubtful if many juvenile delinquents are totally immune from the demands for conformity made by the dominant social order. There is a strong likelihood that the family of the delinquent will agree with respectable society that delinquency is wrong, even though the family may be engaged in a variety of illegal activities. That is, the parental posture conductive to delinquency is not apt to be a positive prodding. Whatever may be the influence of parental example, what might be called the "Fagin" pattern of socialization into delinquency is probably rare. Furthermore, as Redl has indicated, the idea that certain neighborhoods are completely delinquent, offering the child a model for delinquent behavior without reservations, is simply not supported by the data.[6]

The fact that a child is punished by parents, school officials, and agencies of the legal system for his delinquency may, as a number of observers have cynically noted, suggest to the child that he should be more careful not to get caught. There is an equal or greater probability, however, that the child will internalize the demands for conformity. This is not to say that demands for conformity cannot be counteracted. In fact, as we shall see shortly, an understanding of how internal and external demands for conformity are neutralized may be crucial for understanding delinquent behavior. But it is to say that a complete denial of the validity of demands for conformity and the substitution of a new normative system is improbable, in light of the child's or adolescent's dependency on adults and encirclement by adults inherent in his status in the social structure. No matter how deeply enmeshed in patterns of delinquency he may be and no matter how much this involvement may outweigh his associations with the law-abiding, he cannot escape the condemnation of his deviance. Somehow the demands for conformity must be met and answered; they cannot be ignored as part of an alien system of values and norms.

In short, the theoretical viewpoint that sees juvenile delinquency as a form of behavior based on the values and norms of a deviant subculture in precisely the same way as law-abiding behavior is based on the values and norms of the larger society is open to serious doubt. The fact that the world of the delinquent is embedded in the larger world of those who conform cannot be overlooked, nor can the delinquent be equated with an adult thoroughly socialized into an alternative way of life. Instead, the juvenile delinquent would appear to be at least partially committed to the dominant social order in that he frequently exhibits guilt or shame when he violates its proscriptions, accords approval to certain conforming figures, and distinguishes between appropriate and inappropriate targets for his deviance. It is to an explanation for the apparently paradoxical fact of his delinquency that we now turn.

As Morris Cohen once said, one of the most fascinating problems about human behavior is why men violate the laws in which they believe. This is the problem that confronts us when we attempt to explain why delinquency occurs despite a greater or lesser commitment to the usages of conformity. A basic clue is offered by the fact that social rules or norms calling for valued behavior seldom if ever take the form of categorical imperatives. Rather, values or norms appear as *qualified* guides for action, limited in their applicability in terms of time, place, persons, and social circumstances. The moral injunction against killing, for example, does not apply to the enemy during combat in time of war, although a captured enemy comes once again under the prohibition. Similarly, the taking and distributing of scarce goods in a time of acute social need is felt by many to be right, although under other circumstances private property is held inviolable. The normative system of a society, then, is marked by what Williams has termed *flexibility*, it does not consist of a body of rules held to be binding under all conditions.[7]

This flexibility is, in fact, an integral part of the criminal law in that measures for "defenses to crimes" are provided in pleas such as nonage, necessity, insanity, drunkenness, compulsion, self-defense, and so on. The individual can avoid moral culpability for his criminal action—and thus avoid the negative sanctions of society—if he can prove that criminal intent was lacking. *It is our argument that much delinquency is based on what is essentially an unrecognized extension of defenses to crimes, in the form of justifications for deviance that are seen as valid by the delinquent but not by the legal system or society at large.*

These justifications are commonly described as rationalizations. They are viewed as following deviant behavior and as protecting the individual from self-blame and the blame of others after the act. But there is also reason to believe that they precede deviant behavior and make deviant behavior possible. It is this possibility that Sutherland mentioned only in passing and that other writers have failed to exploit from the viewpoint of sociological theory. Disapproval flowing from internalized norms and conforming others in the social environment is neutralized, turned back, or deflected in advance. Social controls that serve to check or inhibit deviant motivational patterns are rendered inoperative, and the individual is freed to engage in delinquency without serious damage to his self-image. In this sense, the delinquent both has his cake and eats it too, for he remains committed to the dominant normative system and yet so qualifies its imperatives that violations are "acceptable" if not "right." Thus the delinquent represents not a radical opposition to law-abiding society but something more like an apologetic failure, often more sinned against than sinning in his own eyes. We call these justifications of deviant behavior techniques of neutralization; and we believe these techniques make up a crucial component of Sutherland's "definitions favorable to the violation of law." It is by learning these techniques that the juvenile becomes delinquent, rather than by learning moral imperatives, values, or attitudes standing in direct contradiction to those of the dominant society. In analyzing these techniques, we have found it convenient to divide them into five major types.

The Denial of Responsibility

Insofar as the delinquent can define himself as lacking responsibility for his deviant actions, the disapproval of self or others is sharply reduced in effectiveness as a restraining influence. As Justice Holmes has said, even a dog distinguishes between being stumbled over and being kicked, and modern society is no less careful to draw a line between injuries that are unintentional, i.e., where responsibility is lacking, and those that are intentional. As a technique of neutralization, however, the denial of responsibility extends much further than the claim that deviant acts are an "accident" or some similar negation of personal accountability. It may also be asserted that delinquent acts are due to forces outside of the individual and beyond his control such as unloving parents, bad companions, or a slum neighborhood. In effect, the delinquent approaches a "billiard ball" conception of himself in which he sees himself as helplessly propelled into new situations. From a psychodynamic viewpoint, this orientation toward one's own actions may represent a profound alienation from self, but it is important to stress the fact that interpretations of responsibility are cultural constructs and not merely idiosyncratic beliefs. The similarity between this mode of justifying illegal behavior assumed by the delinquent and the implications of a "sociological" frame of reference or a "humane" jurisprudence is readily apparent.[8] It is not the validity of this orientation that concerns us here, but its function of deflecting blame attached to violations of social norms and its relative independence of a particular personality structure.[9] By learning to view himself as more acted upon than acting, the delinquent prepares the way for deviance from the dominant normative system without the necessity of a frontal assault on the norms themselves.

The Denial of Injury

A second major technique of neutralization centers on the injury or harm involved in the delinquent act. The criminal law has long made a distinction between crimes which are *mala in se* and *mala prohibita* —that is between acts that are wrong in themselves and acts that are illegal but not immoral—and the delinquent can make the same kind of distinction in evaluating the wrongfulness of his behavior. For the delinquent, however, wrongfulness may turn on the question of whether or not anyone has clearly been hurt by his deviance, and this matter is open to a variety of interpretations. Vandalism, for example, may be defined by the delinquent simply as "mischief"—after all, it may be claimed, the persons whose property has been destroyed can well afford it. Similarly, auto theft may be viewed as "borrowing," and gang fighting may be seen as a private quarrel, an agreed upon duel between two willing parties, and thus of no concern to the community at large. We are not suggesting that this technique of neutralization, labeled the denial of injury, involves an explicit dialectic. Rather, we are arguing that the delinquent frequently, and in a hazy fashion, feels that his behavior does not really cause any great harm despite the fact that it runs counter to law. Just as the link between the individual and his acts may be broken by the denial of responsibility, so may the link between acts and their consequences be broken by the denial of injury. Since society sometimes agrees with the delinquent, e.g., in matters such as truancy, "pranks," and so on, it merely reaffirms the idea that the delinquent's neutralization of social controls by means of qualifying the norms is an extension of common practice rather than a gesture of complete opposition.

The Denial of the Victim

Even if the delinquent accepts the responsibility for his deviant actions and is willing to admit that his deviant actions involve an injury or hurt, the moral indignation of self and others may be neutralized by an insistence that the injury is not wrong in light of the circumstances. The injury, it may be claimed, is not really an injury; rather, it is a form of rightful retaliation or punishment. By a subtle alchemy the delinquent moves himself into the position of an avenger and the victim is transformed into a wrong-doer. Assaults on homosexuals or suspected homosexuals, attacks on members of minority groups who are said to have gotten "out of place," vandalism as revenge on an unfair teacher or school official, thefts from a "crooked" store owner—all may be hurts inflicted on a transgressor, in the eyes of the delinquent. As Orwell has pointed out, the type of criminal admired by the general public has probably changed over the course of years and Raffles no longer serves as a hero;[10] but Robin Hood, and his latter day derivatives such as the tough detective seeking justice outside the law, still capture the popular imagination, and the delinquent may view his acts as part of a similar role.

To deny the existence of the victim, then, by transforming him into a person deserving injury is an extreme form of a phenomenon we have mentioned before, namely, the delinquent's recognition of appropriate and inappropriate targets for his delinquent acts. In addition, however, the existence of the victim may be denied for the delinquent, in a somewhat different sense, by the circumstances of the delinquent act itself. Insofar as the victim is physically absent, unknown, or a vague abstraction (as is often the case in delinquent acts committed against property), the awareness of the victim's existence is weakened. Internalized norms and anticipations of the reactions of others must somehow be activated if they are to serve as guides for behavior; and it is possible that a diminished awareness of the victim plays an important part in determining whether or not this process is set in motion.

The Condemnation of the Condemners

A fourth technique of neutralization would appear to involve a condemnation of the condemners or, as McCorkle and Korn have phrased it, a rejection of the rejectors.[11] The delinquent shifts the focus of attention from his own deviant acts to the motives and behavior of those who disapprove of his violations. His condemners, he may claim, are hypocrites, deviants in disguise, or impelled by personal spite. This orientation toward the conforming world may be of particular importance when it hardens into a bitter cynicism directed against those assigned the task of enforcing or expressing the norms of the dominant society. Police, it may be said, are corrupt, stupid, and brutal. Teachers always show favoritism and parents always "take it out" on their children. By a slight extension, the rewards of conformity—such as material success—become a matter of pull or luck, thus decreasing still further the stature of those who stand on the side of the law-abiding. The validity of this jaundiced viewpoint is not so important as its function in turning back or deflecting the negative sanctions attached to violations of the norms. The delinquent, in effect, has changed the subject of the conversation in the dialogue between his own deviant impulses and the reactions of others; and by attacking others, the wrongfulness of his own behavior is more easily repressed or lost to view.

The Appeal to Higher Loyalties

Fifth, and last, internal and external social controls may be neutralized by sacrificing the demands of the larger society for the demands of the smaller social groups to which the delinquent belongs, such as the sibling pair, the gang, or the friendship clique. It is important to note that the delinquent does not necessarily repudiate the imperatives of the dominant normative system, despite his failure to follow them. Rather, the delinquent may see himself as caught up in a dilemma that must be resolved, unfortunately, at the cost of violating the law. One aspect of this situation has been studied by Stouffer and Toby in their research on the conflict between particularistic and universalistic demands, between the claims of friendship and general social obligations, and their results suggest that "it is possible to classify people according to a predisposition to select one or the other horn of a dilemma in role conflict."[12] For our purposes, however, the most important point is that deviation from certain norms may occur not because the norms are rejected but because other norms, held to be more pressing or involving a higher loyalty, are accorded precedence. Indeed, it is the fact that both sets of norms are believed in that gives meaning to our concepts of dilemma and role conflict.

The conflict between the claims of friendship and the claims of law, or a similar dilemma, has of course long been recognized by the social scientist (and the novelist) as a common human problem. If the juvenile delinquent frequently resolves his dilemma by insisting that he must "always help a buddy" or "never squeal on a friend," even when it throws him into serious difficulties with the dominant social order, his choice remains familiar to the supposedly law-abiding. The delinquent is unusual, perhaps, in the extent to which he is able to see the fact that he acts in behalf of the smaller social groups to which he belongs as a justification for violations of society's norms, but it is a matter of degree rather than of kind.

"I didn't mean it." "I didn't really hurt anybody." "They had it coming to them." "Everybody's picking on me." "I didn't do it for myself." These slogans or their variants, we hypothesize, prepare the juvenile for delinquent acts. These "definitions of the situation" represent tangential or glancing blows at the dominant normative system rather than the creation of an opposing ideology; and they are extensions of patterns of thought prevalent in society rather than something created *de novo*.

Techniques of neutralization may not be powerful enough to fully shield the individual from the force of his own internalized values and the reactions of conforming others, for as we have pointed out, juvenile delinquents often appear to suffer from feelings of guilt and shame when called into account for their deviant behavior. And some delinquents may be so isolated from the world of conformity that techniques of neutralization need not be called into play. Nonetheless, we would argue that techniques of neutralization are critical in lessening the effectiveness of social controls and that they lie behind a large share of delinquent behavior. Empirical research in this area is scattered and fragmentary at the present time, but the work of Redl,[13] Cressey,[14] and others has supplied a body of significant data that has done much to clarify the theoretical issues and enlarge the fund of supporting evidence. Two lines of investigation seem to be critical at this stage. First, there is need for more knowledge concerning the differential distribution of techniques of neutralization, as operative patterns of thought, by age, sex, social class, ethnic group, etc. On a priori grounds it might be assumed that these justifications for deviance will be more readily seized by segments of society for whom a discrepancy between common social ideals and social practice is most apparent. It is also possible, however, that the habit of "bending" the dominant normative system—if not "breaking" it—cuts across our cruder social categories and is to be traced primarily to patterns of social interaction within the familial circle. Second, there is need for a greater understanding of the internal structure of techniques of neutralization, as a system of beliefs and attitudes, and its relationship to various types of delinquent behavior. Certain techniques of neutralization would appear to be better adapted to particular deviant acts than to others, as we have suggested, for example, in the case of offenses against property and the denial of the victim. But the issue remains far from clear and stands in need of more information.

In any case, techniques of neutralization appear to offer a promising line of research in enlarging and systematizing the theoretical grasp of juvenile delinquency. As more information is uncovered concerning techniques of neutralization, their origins, and their consequences, both juvenile delinquency in particular and deviation from normative systems in general may be illuminated.

Notes

1. E. H. Sutherland, *Principles of Criminology*, revised by D. R. Cressey, Philadelphia: Lippincott, 1955, pp. 77–80.

2. Albert K. Cohen, *Delinquent Boys*, Glencoe, Ill.: The Free Press, 1955.

3. This form of reaction among the adherents of a deviant sub-culture who fully believe in the "rightfulness" of their behavior and who are captured and punished by the agencies of the dominant social order can be illustrated, perhaps, by groups such as Jehovah's Witnesses, early Christian sects, nationalist movements in colonial areas, and conscientious objectors during World Wars I and II.

4. As Weber has pointed out, a thief may recognize the legitimacy of legal rules without accepting their moral validity. Cf. Max Weber, *The Theory of Social and Economic Organization* (translated by A. M. Henderson and Talcott Parsons), New York: Oxford University Press, 1947, p. 125. We are arguing here, however, that the juvenile delinquent frequently recognizes *both* the legitimacy of the dominant social order and its moral "rightness."

5. Thrasher's account of the "Itschkies"—a juvenile gang composed of Jewish boys—and the immunity from "rolling" enjoyed by Jewish drunkards is a good illustration. Cf. F. Thrasher, *The Gang*, Chicago: The University of Chicago Press, 1947, p. 315.

6. Cf. Solomon Kobrin, "The Conflict of Values in Delinquency Areas," *American Sociological Review*, 16 (October, 1951), pp. 653–661.

7. Cf. Robin Williams, Jr., *American Society*, New York: Knopf, 1951, p. 28.

8. A number of observers have wryly noted that many delinquents seem to show a surprising awareness of sociological and psychological explanations for their behavior and are quick to point out the causal role of their poor environment.

9. It is possible, of course, that certain personality structures can accept some techniques of neutralization more readily than others, but this question remains largely unexplored.

10. George Orwell, *Dickens, Dali, and Others*, New York: Reynal, 1946.

11. Lloyd W. McCorkle and Richard Korn, "Resocialization Within Walls," *The Annals of the American Academy of Political and Social Science*, 293 (May, 1954), pp. 88–98.

12. See Samuel A. Stouffer and Jackson Toby, "Role Conflict and Personality," in *Toward a General Theory of Action*, edited by Talcott Parsons and Edward A. Shils, Cambridge, Mass.: Harvard University Press, 1951, p. 494.

13. See Fritz Redl and David Wineman, *Children Who Hate*, Glencoe, Ill.: The Free Press, 1956.

14. See D. R. Cressey, *Other People's Money*, Glencoe, Ill.: The Free Press, 1953.

9 / Social Structure and Anomie

ROBERT K. MERTON

There persists a notable tendency in sociological theory to attribute the malfunctioning of social structure primarily to those of man's imperious biological drives which are not adequately restrained by social control. In this view, the social order is solely a device for "impulse management" and the "social processing" of tensions. These impulses which break through social control, be it noted, are held to be biologically derived. Nonconformity is assumed to be rooted in original nature.[1] Conformity is by implication the result of a utilitarian calculus or unreasoned conditioning. This point of view, whatever its other deficiencies, clearly begs one question. It provides no basis for determining the nonbiological conditions which induce deviations from prescribed patterns of conduct. In this paper, it will be suggested that certain phases of social structure generate the circumstances in which infringement of social codes constitutes a "normal" response.[2]

The conceptual scheme to be outlined is designed to provide a coherent, systematic approach to the study of socio-cultural sources of deviate behavior. Our primary aim lies in discovering how some social structures *exert a definite pressure* upon certain persons in the society to engage in noncomformist rather than conformist conduct. The many ramifications of the scheme cannot all be discussed; the problems mentioned outnumber those explicitly treated.

Among the elements of social and cultural structure, two are important for our purposes. These are analytically separable although they merge imperceptibly in concrete situations. The first consists of culturally defined goals, purposes, and interests. It comprises a frame of aspirational reference. These goals are more or less integrated and involve varying degrees of prestige and sentiment. They constitute a basic, but not the exclusive, component of what Linton aptly has called "designs for group living." Some of these cultural aspirations are related to the original drives of man, but they are not determined by them. The second phase of the social structure defines, regulates, and controls the acceptable modes of achieving these goals. Every social group invariably couples its scale of desired ends with moral or institutional regulation of permissible and required procedures for attaining these ends. These regulatory norms and moral imperatives do not necessarily coincide with technical or efficiency norms. Many procedures which form the standpoint of *particular individuals* would be most efficient in securing desired values, e.g., illicit oil-stock schemes, theft, fraud, are ruled out of the institutional area of permitted conduct. The choice of expedients is limited by the institutional norms.

To say that these two elements, culture goals and institutional norms, operate jointly is not to say that the ranges of alternative behaviors and aims bear some constant relation to one another. The emphasis upon certain goals may vary independently of the degree of emphasis upon institutional means. There may develop a disproportionate, at times, a virtually exclusive, stress upon the value of specific goals, involving relatively slight concern with the institutionally appropriate modes of attaining these goals. The limiting case in this direction is reached when the range of alternative procedures is limited only by technical rather than institutional considerations. Any and all devices which promise attainment of the all important goal would be permitted in this hypothetical polar case.[3] This constitutes one type of cultural malintegration. A second polar type is found in groups where activities originally conceived as instrumental are transmuted into ends in themselves. The original purposes are forgotten, and ritualistic adherence to institutionally prescribed conduct becomes virtually obsessive.[4] Stability is largely ensured while change is flouted. The range of alternative behaviors is severely limited. There develops a tradition-bound, sacred society characterized by neophobia. The occupational psychosis of the bureaucrat may be cited as a case in point. Finally, there are the intermediate types of groups where a balance between culture goals and institutional means is maintained. These are the significantly integrated and relatively stable, though changing, groups.

An effective equilibrium between the two phases of the social structure is maintained as long as satisfactions accrue to individuals who conform to both constraints, viz., satisfactions from the achievement of the goals and satisfactions emerging directly from the institutionally canalized modes of striving to attain these ends. Success, in such equilibrated cases, is twofold. Success is reckoned in terms of the product and in terms of the process, in terms of the outcome and in terms of activities. Continuing satisfactions must derive from sheer *participation* in a competitive order as well as from eclipsing one's competitors if the order itself is to be sustained. The occasional sacrifices involved in institutionalized conduct must be compensated by socialized rewards. The distribution of statuses and roles through

competition must be so organized that positive incentives for conformity to roles and adherence to status obligations are provided *for
every position* within the distributive order. Aberrant conduct, therefore, may be viewed as a symptom of dissociation between culturally
defined aspirations and socially structured means.

Of the types of groups which result from the independent variation
of the two phases of the social structure, we shall be primarily concerned with the first, namely, that involving a disproportionate accent
on goals. This statement must be recast in a proper perspective. In no
group is there an absence of regulatory codes governing conduct, yet
groups do vary in the degree to which these folkways, mores, and
institutional controls are effectively integrated with the more diffuse
goals which are part of the culture matrix. Emotional convictions may
cluster about the complex of socially acclaimed ends, meanwhile
shifting their support from the culturally defined implementation of
these ends. As we shall see, certain aspects of the social structure may
generate countermores and antisocial behavior precisely because of
differential emphases on goals and regulations. In the extreme case,
the latter may be so vitiated by the goal-emphasis that the range of
behavior is limited only by considerations of technical expediency.
The sole significant question then becomes, which available means is
most efficient in netting the socially approved value?[5] The technically
most feasible procedure, whether legitimate or not, is preferred to the
institutionally prescribed conduct. As this process continues, the integration of the society becomes tenuous and anomie ensues.

Thus, in competitive athletics, when the aim of victory is shorn of its
institutional trappings and success in contests becomes construed as
"winning the game" rather than "winning through circumscribed
modes of activity," a premium is implicitly set upon the use of illegitimate but technically efficient means. The star of the opposing
football team is surreptitiously slugged; the wrestler furtively inca-
pacitates his opponent through ingenious but illicit techniques; university alumni covertly subsidize "students" whose talents are largely
confined to the athletic field. The emphasis on the goal has so attenuated the satisfactions deriving from sheer participation in the
competitive activity that these satisfactions are virtually confined to a
successful outcome. Through the same process, tension generated by
the desire to win in a poker game is relieved by successfully dealing
oneself four aces, or, when the cult of success has become completely
dominant, by sagaciously shuffling the cards in a game of solitaire.
The faint twinge of uneasiness in the last instance and the surrepti-
tious nature of public delicts indicate clearly that the institutional
rules of the game are *known* to those who evade them, but that the
emotional supports of these rules are largely vitiated by cultural

exaggeration of the success-goal.[6] They are microcosmic images of the social macrocosm.

Of course, this process is not restricted to the realm of sport. The process whereby exaltation of the end generates a *literal demoralization*, i.e., a deinstitutionalization, of the means is one which characterizes many[7] groups in which the two phases of the social structure are not highly integrated. The extreme emphasis upon the accumulation of wealth as a symbol of success[8] in our own society militates against the completely effective control of institutionally regulated modes of acquiring a fortune.[9] Fraud, corruption, vice, crime, in short, the entire catalogue of proscribed behavior, becomes increasingly common when the emphasis on the *culturally induced* success-goal becomes divorced from a coordinated institutional emphasis. This observation is of crucial theoretical importance in examining the doctrine that antisocial behavior most frequently derives from biological drives breaking through the restraints imposed by society. The difference is one between a strictly utilitarian interpretation which conceives man's ends as random and an analysis which finds these ends deriving from the basic values of the culture.[10]

Our analysis can scarcely stop at this juncture. We must turn to other aspects of the social structure if we are to deal with the social genesis of the varying rates and types of deviate behavior characteristic of different societies. Thus far, we have sketched three ideal types of social orders constituted by distinctive patterns of relations between culture ends and means. Turning from these types of *culture patterning*, we find five logically possible, alternative modes of adjustment or adaptation *by individuals* within the culture-bearing society or group.[11] These are schematically presented in the following table, where (+) signifies "acceptance," (−) signifies "elimination," and (±) signifies "rejection and substitution of new goals and standards."

		Culture goals	Institutionalized means
I.	Conformity	+	+
II.	Innovation	+	−
III.	Ritualism	−	+
IV.	Retreatism	−	−
V.	Rebellion[12]	±	±

Our discussion of the relation between these alternative responses and other phases of the social structure must be prefaced by the observation that persons may shift from one alternative to another as they engage in different social activities. These categories refer to role adjustments in specific situations, not to personality *in toto*. To treat the development of this process in various spheres of conduct would introduce a complexity unmanageable within the confines of this paper. For this reason, we shall be concerned primarily with economic activity in the broad sense, "the production, exchange, distribution, and consumption of goods and services" in our competitive society, wherein wealth has taken on a highly symbolic cast. Our task is to search out some of the factors which exert presure upon individuals to engage in certain of these logically possible alternative responses. This choice, as we shall see, is far from random.

In every society, Adaptation I (conformity to both culture goals and means) is the most common and widely diffused. Were this not so, the stability and continuity of the society could not be maintained. The mesh of expectancies which constitutes every social order is sustained by the modal behavior of its members falling within the first category. Conventional role behavior oriented toward the basic values of the group is the rule rather than the exception. It is this fact alone which permits us to speak of a human aggregate as comprising a group or society.

Conversely, Adaptation IV (rejection of goals and means) is the least common. Persons who "adjust" (or maladjust) in this fashion are, strictly speaking, *in* the society but not *of* it. Sociologically, these constitute the true "aliens." Not sharing the common frame of orientation, they can be included within the societal population merely in a fictional sense. In this category are *some* of the activities of psychotics, psychoneurotics, chronic autists, pariahs, outcasts, vagrants, vagabonds, tramps, chronic drunkards, and drug addicts.[13] These have relinquished, in certain spheres of activity, the culturally defined goals, involving complete aim-inhibition in the polar case, and their adjustments are not in accord with institutional norms. This is not to say that in some cases the source of their behavioral adjustments is not in part the very social structure which they have in effect repudiated nor that their very existence within a social area does not constitute a problem for the socialized population.

This mode of "adjustment" occurs, as far as structural sources are concerned, when both the culture goals and institutionalized procedures have been assimilated thoroughly by the individual and imbued with affect and high positive value, but where those institutionalized procedures which promise a measure of successful attainment of the goals are not available to the individual. In such instances, there results a two-fold mental conflict insofar as the moral obligation for adopting institutional means conflicts with the pressure to resort to illegitimate means (which may attain the goal) and inasmuch as the individual is shut off from means which are both legitimate *and* effective. The competitive order is maintained, but the frustrated and handicapped individual who cannot cope with this order drops out. Defeatism, quietism, and resignation are manifested in escape mechanisms which ultimately lead the individual to "escape" from the requirements of the society. It is an expedient which arises from continued failure to attain the goal by legitimate measures and from an inability to adopt the illegitimate route because of internalized prohibitions and institutionalized compulsives, *during which process the supreme value of the success-goal has as yet not been renounced.* The conflict is resolved by eliminating *both* precipitating elements, the goals and means. The escape is complete, the conflict is eliminated, and the individual is associated.

Be it noted that where frustration derives from the inaccessibility of effective institutional means for attaining economic or any other type of highly valued "success," that Adaptations II, II, and V (innovation, ritualism, and rebellion) are also possible. The result will be determined by the particular personality, and thus, the *particular* cultural background, involved. Inadequate socialization will result in the innovation response whereby the conflict and frustration are eliminated by relinquishing the institutional means and retaining the success-aspiration; an extreme assimilation of institutional demands will lead to ritualism wherein the goal is dropped as beyond one's reach but conformity to the mores persists; and rebellion occurs when emancipation from the reigning standards, due to frustration or to marginalist perspectives, leads to the attempt to introduce a "new social order."

Our major concern is with the illegitimacy adjustment. This involves the use of conventionally proscribed but frequently effective means of attaining at least the simulacrum of culturally defined success,—wealth, power, and the like. As we have seen, this adjustment occurs when the individual has assimilated the cultural emphasis on success without equally internalizing the morally prescribed norms governing means for its attainment. The question arises, Which phases of our social structure predispose toward this mode of adjustment? We may examine a concrete instance, effectively analyzed by Lohman,[14] which provides a clue to the answer. Lohman has shown that specialized areas of vice in the near north side of Chicago constitute a "normal" response to a situation where the cultural emphasis upon pecuniary success has been absorbed, but where there is little access to conventional and legitimate means for attaining such success. The conventional occupational opportunities of persons in this area are almost completely limited to manual labor. Given our cultural stigmatization of manual labor, and its correlate, the prestige of white collar work, it is clear that the result is a strain toward innovational practices. The limitation of opportunity to unskilled labor and the resultant low income cannot compete *in terms of conventional stan-*

dards of achievement with the high income from organized vice.

For our purposes, this situation involves two important features. First, such antisocial behavior is in a sense "called forth" by certain conventional values of the culture *and* by the class structure involving differential access to the approved opportunities for legitimate, prestige-bearing pursuit of the culture goals. The lack of high integration between the means-and-end elements of the cultural pattern and the particular class structure combine to favor a heightened frequency of antisocial conduct in such groups. The second consideration is of equal significance. Recourse to the first of the alternative responses, legitimate effort, is limited by the fact that actual advance toward desired success-symbols through conventional channels is, despite our persisting open-class ideology,[15] relatively rare and difficult for those handicapped by little formal education and few economic resources. The dominant pressure of group standards of success is, therefore, on the gradual attenuation of legitimate, but by and large ineffective, strivings and the increasing use of illegitimate, but more or less effective, expedients of vice and crime. The cultural demands made on persons in this situation are incompatible. On the one hand, they are asked to orient their conduct toward the prospect of accumulating wealth and on the other, they are largely denied effective opportunities to do so institutionally. The consequences of such structural inconsistency are psychopathological personality, and/or antisocial conduct, and/or revolutionary activities. The equilibrium between culturally designated means and ends becomes highly unstable with the progressive emphasis on attaining the prestige-laden ends by any means whatsoever. Within this context, Capone represents the triumph of amoral intelligence over morally prescribed "failure," when the channels of vertical mobility are closed or narrowed[16] *in a society which places a high premium on economic affluence and social ascent for* all *its members.*[17]

This last qualification is of primary importance. It suggests that other phases of the social structure besides the extreme emphasis on pecuniary success must be considered if we are to understand the social sources of antisocial behavior. A high frequency of deviate behavior is not generated simply by "lack of opportunity" or by this exaggerated pecuniary emphasis. A comparatively rigidified class structure, a feudalistic or caste order, may limit such opportunities far beyond the point which obtains in our society today. It is only when a system of cultural values extols, virtually above all else, certain *common* symbols of success *for the population at large* while its social structure rigorously restricts or completely eliminates access to approved modes of acquiring these symbols *for a considerable part of the same population* that antisocial behavior ensues on a considerable scale. In other words, our egalitarian ideology denies by implication the existence of noncompeting groups and individuals in the pursuit of pecuniary success. The same body of success-symbols is held to be desirable for all. These goals are held to *transcend class lines*, not to be bounded by them, yet the actual social organization is such that there exist class differentials in the accessibility of these *common* success-symbols. Frustration and thwarted aspiration lead to the search for avenues of escape from a culturally induced intolerable situation; or unrelieved ambition may eventuate in illicit attempts to acquire the dominant values.[18] The American stress on pecuniary success and ambitiousness for all thus invites exaggerated anxieties, hostilities, neuroses, and antisocial behavior.

This theoretical analysis may go far toward explaining the varying correlations between crime and poverty.[19] Poverty is not an isolated variable. It is one in a complex of interdependent social and cultural variables. When viewed in such a context, it represents quite different states of affairs. Poverty as such, and consequent limitation of opportunity, are not sufficient to induce a conspicuously high rate of criminal behavior. Even the often mentioned "poverty in the midst of plenty" will not necessarily lead to this result. Only insofar as poverty and associated disadvantages in competition for the culture values approved for *all* members of the society are linked with the assimilation of a cultural emphasis on monetary accumulation as a symbol of success is antisocial conduct a "normal" outcome. Thus, poverty is less highly correlated with crime in southeastern Europe than in the United States. The possibilities of vertical mobility in these European areas would seem to be fewer than in this country, so that neither poverty *per se* nor its association with limited opportunity is sufficient to account for the varying correlations. It is only when the full configuration is considered, poverty, limited opportunity, and a commonly shared system of success symbols, that we can explain the higher association between poverty and crime in our society than in others where rigidified class structure is coupled with *differential class symbols of achievement*.

In societies such as our own, then, the pressure of prestige-bearing success tends to eliminate the effective social constraint over means employed to this end. "The-end-justifies-the-means" doctrine becomes a guiding tenet for action when the cultural structure unduly exalts the end and the social organization unduly limits possible recourse to approved means. Otherwise put, this notion and associated behavior reflect a lack of cultural coordination. In international relations, the effects of this lack of integration are notoriously apparent. An emphasis upon national power is not readily coordinated with an inept organization of legitimate, i.e., internationally defined and accepted, means for attaining this goal. The result is a tendency toward the abrogation of international law, treaties become scraps of paper, "undeclared warfare" serves as a technical evasion, the bombing of civilian populations is rationalized,[20] just as the same societal situation induces the same sway of illegitimacy among individuals.

The social order we have described necessarily produces this "strain toward dissolution." The pressure of such an order is upon outdoing one's competitors. The choice of means within the ambit of institutional control will persist as long as the sentiments supporting a competitive system, i.e., deriving from the possibility of outranking competitors and hence enjoying the favorable response of others, are distributed throughout the entire system of activities and are not confined merely to the final result. A stable social structure demands a balanced distribution of affect among its various segments. When there occurs a shift of emphasis from the satisfactions deriving from competition itself to almost exclusive concern with successful competition, the resultant stress leads to the breakdown of the regulatory structure.[21] With the resulting attenuation of the institutional imperatives, there occurs an approximation of the situation erroneously held by utilitarians to be typical of society generally wherein calculations of advantage and fear of punishment are the sole regulating agencies. In such situations, as Hobbes observed, force and fraud come to constitute the sole virtues in view of their relative efficiency in attaining goals—which were for him, of course, not culturally derived.

It should be apparent that the foregoing discussion is not pitched on a moralistic plane. Whatever the sentiments of the writer or reader concerning the ethical desirability of coordinating the means-and-goals phases of the social structure, one must agree that lack of such coordination leads to anomie. Insofar as one of the most general functions of social organization is to provide a basis for calculability and regularity of behavior, it is increasingly limited in effectiveness as these elements of the structure become dissociated. At the extreme, predictability virtually disappears and what may be properly termed cultural chaos or anomie intervenes.

This statement, being brief, is also incomplete. It has not included an exhaustive treatment of the various structural elements which predispose toward one rather than another of the alternative responses open to individuals; it has neglected, but not denied the relevance of, the factors determining the specific incidence of these responses; it has not enumerated the various concrete responses which are constituted by combinations of specific values of the analytical variables; it has omitted, or included only by implication, any consideration of the social functions performed by illicit responses; it has not tested the full explanatory power of the analytical scheme by examining a large number of group variations in the frequency of deviate and conformist behavior; it has not adequately dealt with rebellious conduct which seeks to refashion the social framework radically; it has not examined the relevance of cultural conflict for an analysis of culture-goal and institutional-means malintegration. It is suggested that these and related problems may be profitably analyzed by this scheme.

Notes

1. E.g., Ernest Jones, *Social Aspects of Psychoanalysis*, 28, London, 1924. If the Freudian notion is a variety of the "original sin" dogma, then the interpretation advanced in this paper may be called the doctrine of "socially derived sin."

2. "Normal" in the sense of a culturally oriented, if not approved, response. This statement does not deny the relevance of biological and personality differences which may be significantly involved in the *incidence* of deviate conduct. Our focus of interest is the social and cultural matrix; hence we abstract from other factors. It is in this sense, I take it, that James S. Plant speaks of the "normal reaction of normal people to abnormal conditions." See his *Personality and the Cultural Pattern*, 248, New York, 1937.

3. Contemporary American culture has been said to tend in this direction. See André Siegfried, *America Comes of Age*, 26–37, New York, 1927. The alleged extreme(?) emphasis on the goals of monetary success and material prosperity leads to dominant concern with technological and social instruments designed to produce the desired result, inasmuch as institutional controls become of secondary importance. In such a situation, innovation flourishes as the *range of means* employed is broadened. In a sense, then, there occurs the paradoxical emergence of "materialists" from an "idealistic" orientation. Cf. Durkheim's analysis of the cultural conditions which predispose toward crime and innovation, both of which are aimed toward efficiency, not moral norms. Durkheim was one of the first to see that "contrairement aux idées courantes le criminel n'apparait plus comme un être radicalement insociable, comme une sorte d'elément parasitaire, de corps étranger et inassimilable, introduit au sein de la société; c'est un agent régulier de la vie sociale." See *Les Règles de la Méthode Sociologique*, 86–89, Paris, 1927.

4. Such ritualism may be associated with a mythology which rationalizes these actions so that they appear to retain their status as means, but the dominant pressure is in the direction of strict ritualistic conformity, irrespective of such rationalizations. In this sense, ritual has proceeded farthest when such rationalizations are not even called forth.

5. In this connection, one may see the relevance of Elton Mayo's paraphrase of the title of Tawney's well-known book. "Actually the problem *is not that of the sickness of an acquisitive society; it is that of the acquisitiveness of a sick society.*" *Human Problems of an Industrial Civilization*, 153, New York, 1933. Mayo deals with the process through which wealth comes to be a symbol of social achievement. He sees this as arising from a state of anomie. We are considering the unintegrated monetary-success goal as an element in producing anomie. A complete analysis would involve both phases of this system of interdependent variables.

6. It is unlikely that interiorized norms are completely eliminated. Whatever residuum persists will induce personality tensions and conflict. The process involves a certain degree of ambivalence. A manifest rejection of the institutional norms is coupled with some latent retention of their emotional correlates. "Guilt feelings," "sense of sin," "pangs of conscience" are obvious manifestations of this unrelieved tension; symbolic adherence to the nominally repudiated values or rationalizations constitute a more subtle variety of tensional release.

7. "Many," and not all, unintegrated groups, for the reason already mentioned. In groups where the primary emphasis shifts to institutional means, i.e., when the range of

alternatives is very limited, the outcome is a type of ritualism rather than anomie.

8. Money has several peculiarities which render it particularly apt to become a symbol of prestige divorced from institutional controls. As Simmel emphasized, money is highly abstract and impersonal. However acquired, through fraud or institutionally, it can be used to purchase the same goods and services. The anonymity of metropolitan culture, in conjunction with this peculiarity of money, permits wealth, the sources of which may be unknown to the community in which the plutocraft lives, to serve as a symbol of status.

9. The emphasis upon wealth as a success-symbol is possibly reflected in the use of the term "fortune" to refer to a stock of accumulated wealth. This meaning becomes common in the late sixteenth century (Spenser and Shakespeare). A similar usage of the Latin *fortuna* comes into prominence during the first century B.C. Both these periods were marked by the rise to prestige and power of the "bourgeoisie."

10. See Kingsley Davis, "Mental Hygiene and the Class Structure," *Psychiatry*, 1928, 1: esp. 62–63; Talcott Parsons, *The Structure of Social Action*, 59–60, New York, 1937.

11. This is a level intermediate between the two planes distinguished by Edward Sapir; namely, culture patterns and personal habit systems. See his "Contribution of Psychiatry to an Understanding of Behavior in Society," *Amer. J. Sociol.*, 1937, 42:862–870.

12. This fifth alternative is on a plane clearly different from that of the others. It represents a *transitional* response which seeks to *institutionalize* new procedures oriented toward revamped cultural goals shared by the members of the society. It thus involves efforts to *change* the existing structure rather than to perform accommodative actions *within* this structure, and introduces additional problems with which we are not at the moment concerned.

13. Obviously, this is an elliptical statement. These individuals may maintain some orientation to the values of their particular differentiated groupings within the larger society or, in part, of the conventional society itself. Insofar as they do so, their conduct cannot be classified in the "passive rejection" category (IV). Nels Anderson's description of the behavior and attitudes of the bum, for example, can readily be recast in terms of our analytical scheme. See *The Hobo*, 93–98, *et passim*, Chicago, 1923.

14. Joseph D. Lohman, "The Participant Observer in Community Studies," *Amer. Sociol. Rev.*, 1937, 2:890–898.

15. The shifting historical role of this ideology is a profitable subject for exploration. The "office-boy-to-president" stereotype was once in approximate accord with the facts. Such vertical mobility was probably more common then than now, when the class structure is more rigid. (See the following note.) The ideology largely persists, however, possibly because it still performs a useful function for maintaining the *status quo*. For insofar as it is accepted by the "masses," it constitutes a useful sop for those who might rebel against the entire structure, were this consoling hope removed. This ideology now serves to lessen the probability of Adaptation V. In short, the role of this notion has changed from that of an approximately valid empirical theorem to that of an ideology, in Mannheim's sense.

16. There is a growing body of evidence, though none of it is clearly conclusive, to the effect that our class structure is becoming rigidified and that vertical mobility is declining. Taussig and Joslyn found that American business leaders are being *increasingly* recruited from the upper ranks of our society. The Lynds have also found a "diminished chance to get ahead" for the working classes in Middletown. Manifestly, these objective changes are not alone significant; the individual's subjective evaluation of the situation is a major determinant of the response. The extent to which this change in opportunity for social mobility has been recognized by the least advantaged classes is still conjectural, although the Lynds present some suggestive materials. The writer suggests that a case in point is the increasing frequency of cartoons which observe in a tragi-comic vein that "my old man says everybody can't be President. He says if ya can get three days a week steady on W.P.A. work ya ain't doin' so bad either." See F. W. Taussig and C. S. Joslyn, *American Business Leaders*, New York, 1932; R. S. and H. M. Lynd, *Middletown in Transition*, 67 ff., chap. 12, New York, 1937.

17. The role of the Negro in this respect is of considerable theoretical interest. Certain elements of the Negro population have assimilated the dominant caste's values of pecuniary success and social advancement, but they also recognize that social ascent is at present restricted to their own caste almost exclusively. The pressures upon the Negro which would otherwise derive from the structural inconsistencies we have noticed are hence not identical with those upon lower class whites. See Kingsley Davis, *op. cit.*, 63; John Dollard, *Caste and Class in a Southern Town*, 66 ff., New Haven, 1936; Donald Young, *American Minority Peoples*, 581, New York, 1932.

18. The psychical coordinates of these processes have been partly established by the experimental evidence concerning *Anspruchsniveaus* and levels of performance. See Kurt Lewin, *Vorsatz, Willie und Bedurfnis*, Berlin, 1926; N. F. Hoppe, "Erfolg und Misserfolg," *Psychol. Forschung*, 1930, 14:1–63; Jerome D. Frank, "Individual Differences in Certain Aspects of the Level of Aspiration," *Amer. J. Psychol.*, 1935, 47:119–128.

19. Standard criminology texts summarize the data in this field. Our scheme of analysis may serve to resolve some of the theoretical contradictions which P. A. Sorokin indicates. For example, "not everywhere nor always do the poor show a greater proportion of crime . . . many poorer countries have had less crime than the richer countries . . . . The [economic] improvement in the second half of the nineteenth century, and the beginning of the twentieth, has not been followed by a decrease of crime." See his *Contemporary Sociological Theories*, 560–561, New York, 1928. The crucial point is, however, that poverty has varying social significance in different social structures, as we shall see. Hence, one would not expect a linear correlation between crime and poverty.

20. See M. W. Royse, *Aerial Bombardment and the International Regulation of War*, New York, 1928.

21. Since our primary concern is with the socio-cultural aspects of this problem, the psychological correlates have been only implicitly considered. See Karen Horney, *The Neurotic Personality of Our Time*, New York, 1937, for a psychological discussion of this process.

10 / Differential Opportunity and Delinquent Subcultures

RICHARD A. CLOWARD
LLOYD E. OHLIN

THE AVAILABILITY OF ILLEGITIMATE MEANS

Social norms are two-sided. A prescription implies the existence of a prohibition, and *vice versa*. To advocate honesty is to demarcate and condemn a set of actions which are dishonest. In other words, norms that define legitimate practices also implicitly define illegitimate practices. One purpose of norms, in fact, is to delineate the boundary between legitimate and illegitimate practices. In setting this boundary, in segregating and classifying various types of behavior, they make us aware not only of behavior that is regarded as right and proper but also of behavior that is said to be wrong and improper. Thus the criminal who engages in theft or fraud does not invent a new way of life; the possibility of employing alternative means is acknowledged, tacitly at least, by the norms of the culture.

This tendency for proscribed alternatives to be implicit in every prescription, and *vice versa*, although widely recognized, is nevertheless a reef upon which many a theory of delinquency has foundered. Much of the criminological literature assumes, for example, that one may explain a criminal act simply by accounting for the individual's readiness to employ illegal alternatives of which his culture, through its norms, has already made him generally aware. Such explanations are quite unsatisfactory, however, for they ignore a host of questions regarding the *relative availability* of illegal alternatives to various potential criminals. The aspiration to be a physician is hardly enough to explain the fact of becoming a physician; there is much that transpires between the aspiration and the achievement. This is no less true of the person who wants to be a successful criminal. Having decided that he "can't make it legitimately," he cannot simply choose among an array of illegitimate means, all equally available to him. As we have noted earlier, it is assumed in the theory of anomie that access to conventional means is differentially distributed, that some individuals, because of their social class, enjoy certain advantages that are denied to those elsewhere in the class structure. For example, there are variations in the degree to which members of various classes are fully exposed to and thus acquire the values, knowledge, and skills that facilitate upward mobility. It should not be startling, therefore, to suggest that there are socially structured variations in the availability of illegitimate means as well. In connection with delinquent subcultures, we shall be concerned principally with differentials in access to illegitimate means within the lower class.

Many sociologists have alluded to differentials in access to illegitimate means without explicitly incorporating this variable into a theory of deviant behavior. This is particularly true of scholars in the "Chicago tradition" of criminology. Two closely related theoretical perspectives emerged from this school. The theory of "cultural transmission," advanced by Clifford R. Shaw and Henry D. McKay, focuses on the development in some urban neighborhoods of a criminal tradition that persists from one generation to another despite constant changes in population.[1] In the theory of "differential association," Edwin H. Sutherland described the processes by which criminal values are taken over by the individual.[2] He asserted that criminal behavior is learned, and that it is learned in interaction with others who have already incorporated criminal values. Thus the first theory stresses the value systems of different areas; the second, the systems of social relationships that facilitate or impede the acquisition of these values.

Scholars in the Chicago tradition, who emphasized the processes involved in learning to be criminal, were actually pointing to differentials in the availability of illegal means—although they did not explicitly recognize this variable in their analysis. This can perhaps best by seen by examining Sutherland's classic work, *The Professional Thief*. "An inclination to steal," according to Sutherland, "is not a sufficient explanation of the genesis of the professional thief."[3] The "self-made" thief, lacking knowledge of the ways of securing immunity from prosecution and similar techniques of defense, "would quickly land in prison; . . . a person can be a professional thief only if he is recognized and received as such by other professional thieves." But recognition is not freely accorded: "Selection and tutelage are the two necessary elements in the process of acquiring recognition as a professional thief. . . . A person cannot acquire recognition as a professional thief until he has had tutelage in professional theft, *and tutelage is given only to a few persons selected from the total population*." For one thing, "the person must be appreciated by the professional thieves. He must be appraised as having an adequate equipment of wits, front, talking-ability, honesty, reliability, nerve and determination." Furthermore, the aspirant is judged by high standards of performance, for only "a very small percentage of those who start on this process ever reach the stage of professional thief. . . ." Thus motivation and pressures toward deviance do not fully account for deviant behavior any more than motivation and pressures toward conformity account for conforming behavior. The individual must have access to a learning environment and, once having been trained, must be allowed to perform his role. Roles, whether conforming or deviant in content, are not necessarily freely available; access to them depends upon a variety of factors, such as one's socioeconomic position, age, sex, ethnic affiliation, personality characteristics, and the like. The potential thief, like the potential physician, finds that access to his goal is governed by many criteria other than merit and motivation.

What we are asserting is that access to illegitimate roles is not freely available to all, as is commonly assumed. Only those neighborhoods in which crime flourishes as a stable, indigenous institution are fertile criminal learning environments for the young. Because these environments afford integration of different age-levels of offender, selected young people are exposed to "differential association" through which tutelage is provided and criminal values and skills are acquired. To be prepared for the role may not, however, ensure that the individual will ever discharge it. One important limitation is that more youngsters are recruited into these patterns of differential associations than the adult criminal structure can possibly absorb. Since there is a surplus of contenders for these elite positions, criteria and mechanisms of selection must be evolved. Hence a certain proportion of those who aspire may not be permitted to engage in the behavior for which they have prepared themselves.

Thus we conclude that access to illegitimate roles, no less than access to legitimate roles, is limited by both social and psychological factors. We shall here be concerned primarily with socially structured differentials in illegitimate opportunities. Such differentials, we contend, have much to do with the type of delinquent subculture that develops.

LEARNING AND PERFORMANCE STRUCTURES

Our use of the term "opportunities," legitimate or illegitimate, implies access to both learning and performance structures. That is, the individual must have access to appropriate environments for the acquisition of the values and skills associated with the performance of a particular role, and he must be supported in the performance of the role once he has learned it.

Tannenbaum, several decades ago, vividly expressed the point that criminal role performance, no less than conventional role performance, presupposes a patterned set of relationships through which the requisite values and skills are transmitted by established practitioners to aspiring youth:

> It takes a long time to make a good criminal, many years of specialized training and much preparation. But training is something that is given to people. People learn in a community where the materials and the knowledge are to be had. A craft needs an atmosphere saturated with purpose and promise. The community provides the attitudes, the point of view, the philosophy of life, the example, the motive, the contacts, the friendships, the incentives. No child brings those into the world. He finds them here and available for use and elaboration. The community gives the criminal his materials and habits, just as it gives the doctor, the lawyer, the teacher, and the candlestick-maker theirs.[4]

Sutherland systematized this general point of view, asserting that opportunity consists, at least in part, of learning structures. Thus "criminal behavior is learned" and, furthermore, it is learned "in interaction with other persons in a process of communication." However, he conceded that the differential-association theory does not constitute a full explanation of criminal behavior. In a paper circulated in 1944, he noted that "criminal behavior is partially a function of opportunities to commit [*i.e.*, to perform] specific classes of crime, such as embezzlement, bank burglary, or illicit heterosexual intercourse." Therefore, "while opportunity may be partially a function of association with criminal patterns and of the specialized techniques thus acquired, it is not determined entirely in that manner, and consequently differential association is not the sufficient cause of criminal behavior."[5]

To Sutherland, then, illegitimate opportunity included conditions favorable to the performance of a criminal role as well as conditions favorable to the learning of such a role (differential associations). These conditions, we suggest, depend upon certain features of the social structure of the community in which delinquency arises.

We believe that each individual occupies a position in both legitimate and illegitimate opportunity structures. This is a new way of defining the situation. The theory of anomie views the individual primarily in terms of the legitimate opportunity structure. It poses questions regarding differentials in access to legitimate routes to success-goals; at the same time it assumes either that illegitimate avenues to success-goals are freely available or that differentials in their availability are of little significance. This tendency may be seen in the following statement by Merton:

> Several researches have shown that specialized areas of vice and crime constitute a "normal" response to a situation where the cultural emphasis upon pecuniary success has been absorbed, but where there is little access to conventional and legitimate means for becoming successful. The occupational opportunities of people in these areas are largely confined to manual labor and the lesser white-collar jobs. Given the American stigmatization of manual labor *which has been found to hold rather uniformly for all social classes,* and the absence of realistic opportunities for advancement beyond this level, the result is a marked tendency toward deviant behavior. The status of unskilled labor and the consequent low income cannot readily compete *in terms of established standards of worth* with the promises of power and high income from organized vice, rackets and crime. . . . [Such a situation] leads toward the gradual attenuation of legitimate, but by and large ineffectual, strivings and the increasing use of illegitimate, but more or less effective, expedients.[6]

The cultural-transmission and differential-association tradition, on the other hand, assumes that access to illegitimate means is variable, but it does not recognize the significance of comparable differentials in access to legitimate means. Sutherland's "ninth proposition" in the theory of differential association states:

> *Though criminal behavior is an expression of general needs and values, it is not explained by those general needs and values since non-criminal behavior is an expression of the same needs and values.* Thieves generally steal in order to secure money, but likewise honest laborers work in order to secure money. The attempts by many scholars to explain criminal behavior by general drives and values, such as the happiness principle, striving for social status, the money motive, or frustration, have been and must continue to be futile since they explain lawful behavior as completely as they explain criminal behavior.[7]

In this statement, Sutherland appears to assume that people have equal and free access to legitimate means regardless of their social position. At the very least, he does not treat access to legitimate means as variable. It is, of course, perfectly true that "striving for social status," "the money motive," and other socially approved drives do not fully account for either deviant or conforming behavior. But if goal-oriented behavior occurs under conditions in which there are socially structured obstacles to the satisfaction of these drives by legitimate means, the resulting pressures, we contend, might lead to deviance.

The concept of differential opportunity structures permits us to unite the theory of anomie, which recognizes the concept of differentials in access to legitimate means, and the "Chicago tradition," in which the concept of differentials in access to illegitimate means is implicit. We can now look at the individual, not simply in relation to one or the other system of means, but in relation to both legitimate and illegitimate systems. This approach permits us to ask, for example, how the relative availability of illegitimate opportunities affects the resolution of adjustment problems leading to deviant behavior. We believe that the way in which these problems are resolved may depend upon the kind of support for one or another type of illegitimate activity that is given at different points in the social structure. If, in a given social location, illegal or criminal means are not readily available, then we should not expect a criminal subculture to develop among adolescents. By the same logic, we should expect the manipulation of violence to become a primary avenue to higher status only in areas where the means of violence are not denied to the young. To give a third example, drug addiction and participation in subcultures organized around the consumption of drugs presuppose that persons can secure access to drugs and knowledge about how to use them. In some parts of the social structure, this would be very difficult; in others, very easy. In short, there are marked differences from one part of the social structure to another in the types of illegitimate adaptation that are available to persons in search of solutions to problems of adjustment arising from the restricted availability of legitimate means.[8] In this sense, then, we can think of individuals as being located in two opportunity structures—one legitimate, the other illegitimate. Given limited access to success-goals by legitimate means, the nature of the delinquent response that may result will vary according to the availability of various illegitimate means.[9]

VARIETIES OF DELINQUENT SUBCULTURE

As we have noted, there appear to be three major types of delinquent subculture typically encountered among adolescent males in lower-class areas of large urban centers. One is based principally upon criminal values; its members are organized primarily for the pursuit of material gain by such illegal means as extortion, fraud, and theft. In the second, violence is the keynote; its members pursue status ("rep") through the manipulation of force or threat of force. These are the "warrior" groups that attract so much attention in the press. Finally, there are subcultures which emphasize the consumption of drugs. The participants in these drug subcultures have become alienated from conventional roles, such as those required in the family or the occupational world. They have withdrawn into a restricted world in which the ultimate value consists in the "kick." We call these three subcultural forms "criminal," "conflict," and "retreatist," respectively.[10]

These shorthand terms simply denote the *principal* orientation of each form of adaptation from the perspective of the dominant social order; although one can find many examples of subcultures that fit accurately into one of these three categories, subcultures frequently appear in somewhat mixed form. Thus members of a predominantly conflict subculture may also on occasion engage in systematic theft; members of a criminal subculture may sometimes do combat in the streets with rival gangs. But this should not obscure the fact that these subcultures tend to exhibit essentially different orientations.

The extent to which the delinquent subculture organizes and controls a participant's allegiance varies from one member to another. Some members of the gang are almost totally immersed in the perspectives of the subculture and bring them into play in all their contacts; others segregate this aspect of their lives and maintain other roles in the family, school, and church. The chances are relatively slight, however, that an adolescent can successfully segregate delinquent and conforming roles for a long period of time. Pressures emanate from the subculture leading its members to adopt unfavorable attitudes toward parents, school teachers, policemen, and other adults in the conventional world. When he is apprehended for delinquent acts, the possibility of the delinquent's maintaining distinctly separate role involvements breaks down, and he is confronted with the necessity of choosing between law-abiding and delinquent styles of life. Since family, welfare, religious, educational, law-enforcement, and correctional institutions are arrayed against the appeal of his delinquent associates, the decision is a difficult one, frequently requiring either complete acceptance or complete rejection of one or the other system of obligations.[11]

At any one point in time, however, the extent to which the norms of the delinquent subculture control behavior will vary from one member to another. Accordingly, descriptions of these subcultures must be stated in terms of the fully indoctrinated member rather than the average member. Only in this way can the distinctiveness of delinquent styles of life be made clear. It is with this understanding that we offer the following brief empirical characterizations of the three main types of delinquent subculture.

The Criminal Pattern

The most extensive documentation in the sociological literature of delinquent behavior patterns in lower-class culture describes a tradition which integrates youthful delinquency with adult criminality.[12]

In the central value orientation of youths participating in this tradition, delinquent and criminal behavior is accepted as a means of achieving success-goals. The dominant criteria of in-group evaluation stress achievement, the use of skill and knowledge to get results. In this culture, prestige is allocated to those who achieve material gain and power through avenues defined as illegitimate by the larger society. From the very young to the very old, the successful "haul"—which quickly transforms the penniless into a man of means—is an ever-present vision of the possible and desirable. Although one may also achieve material success through the routine practice of theft or fraud, the "big score" remains the symbolic image of quick success.

The means by which a member of a criminal subculture achieves success are clearly defined for the aspirant. At a young age, he learns to admire and respect older criminals and to adopt the "right guy" as his role-model. Delinquent episodes help him to acquire mastery of the techniques and orientation of the criminal world and to learn how to cooperate successfully with others in criminal enterprises. He exhibits hostility and distrust toward representatives of the larger society. He regards members of the conventional world as "suckers," his natural victims, to be exploited when possible. He sees successful people in the conventional world as having a "racket"—e.g., big businessmen have huge expense accounts, politicians get graft, etc. This attitude successfully neutralizes the controlling effect of conventional norms. Toward the in-group the "right guy" maintains relationships of loyalty, honesty, and trustworthiness. He must prove himself reliable and dependable in his contacts with his criminal associates although he has no such obligations toward the out-group of noncriminals.

One of the best ways of assuring success in the criminal world is to cultivate appropriate "connections." As a youngster, this means running with a clique composed of other "right guys" and promoting an apprenticeship or some other favored relationship with older and successful offenders. Close and dependable ties with income-producing outlets for stolen goods, such as the wagon peddler, the junkman, and the fence, are especially useful. Furthermore, these intermediaries encourage and protect the young delinquent in a criminal way of life by giving him a jaundiced perspective on the private morality of many functionaries in conventional society. As he matures, the young delinquent becomes acquainted with a new world made up of predatory bondsmen, shady lawyers, crooked policemen, grafting politicians, dishonest businessmen, and corrupt jailers. Through "connections" with occupants of these half-legitimate, half-illegitimate roles and with "big shots" in the underworld, the aspiring criminal validates and assures his freedom of movement in a world made safe for crime.

The Conflict Pattern[13]

The role-model in the conflict pattern of lower-class culture is the "bopper" who swaggers with his gang, fights with weapons to win a wary respect from other gangs, and compels a fearful deference from the conventional adult world by his unpredictable and destructive assaults on persons and property. To other gang members, however, the key qualities of the bopper are those of the successful warrior. His performance must reveal a willingness to defend his personal integrity and the honor of the gang. He must do this with great courage and displays of fearlessness in the face of personal danger.

The immediate aim in the world of fighting gangs is to acquire a reputation for toughness and destructive violence. A "rep" assures not only respectful behavior from peers and threatened adults but also admiration for the physical strength and masculinity which it symbolizes. It represents a way of securing access to the scarce resources for adolescent pleasure and opportunity in underprivileged areas.

Above all things, the bopper is valued for his "heart." He does not "chicken out," even when confronted by superior force. He never defaults in the face of a personal insult or a challenge to the integrity of his gang. The code of the bopper is that of the warrior who places great stress on courage, the defense of his group, and the maintenance of honor.

Relationships between bopping gang members and the adult world are severely attenuated. The term that the bopper uses most frequently to characterize his relationships with adults is "weak." He is unable to find appropriate role-models that can designate for him a structure of opportunities leading to adult success. He views himself as isolated and the adult world as indifferent. The commitments of adults are to their own interests and not to his. Their explanations of why he should behave differently are "weak," as are their efforts to help him.

Confronted by the apparent indifference and insincerity of the adult world, the ideal bopper seeks to win by coercion the attention and opportunities he lacks and cannot otherwise attract. In recent years the street-gang worker who deals with the fighting gang on its own "turf" has come to symbolize not only a recognition by conventional adult society of the gang's toughness but also a concession of opportunities formerly denied. Through the alchemy of competition between gangs, this gesture of attention by the adult world to the "worst" gangs is transformed into a mark of prestige. Thus does the manipulation of violence convert indifference into accommodation and attention into status.

The Retreatist Pattern

Retreatism may include a variety of expressive, sensual, or consummatory experiences, alone or in a group. In this analysis, we are interested only in those experiences that involve the use of drugs and that are supported by a subculture. We have adopted these limitations in order to maintain our focus on subcultural formations which are clearly recognized as delinquent, as drug use by adolescents is. The retreatist preoccupation with expressive experiences creates many varieties of "hipster" cult among lower-class adolescents which foster patterns of deviant but not necessarily delinquent conduct.

Subcultural drug-users in lower-class areas perceive themselves as culturally and socially detached from the life-style and everyday preoccupations of members of the conventional world. The following characterization of the "cat" culture, observed by Finestone in a lower-class Negro area in Chicago, describes drug use in the more general context of "hipsterism."[14] Thus it should not be assumed that this description in every respect fits drug cultures found elsewhere. We have drawn heavily on Finestone's observations, however, because they provide the best descriptions available of the social world in which lower-class adolescent drug cultures typically arise.

The dominant feature of the retreatist subculture of the "cat" lies in the continuous pursuit of the "kick." Every cat has a kick—alcohol, marijuana, addicting drugs, unusual sexual experiences, hot jazz, cool jazz, or any combination of these. Whatever its content, the kick is a search for ecstatic experiences. The retreatist strives for an intense awareness of living and a sense of pleasure that is "out of this world." In extreme form, he seeks an almost spiritual and mystical knowledge that is experienced when one comes to know "it" at the height of one's kick. The past and the future recede in the time perspective of the cat, since complete awareness in present experience is the essence of the kick.

The successful cat has a lucrative "hustle" which contrasts sharply with the routine and discipline required in the ordinary occupational tasks of conventional society. The many varieties of the hustle are characterized by a rejection of violence or force and a preference for manipulating, persuading, outwitting, or "conning" others to obtain resources for experiencing the kick. The cat begs, borrows, steals, or engages in some petty con-game. He caters to the illegitimate cravings of others by peddling drugs or working as a pimp. A highly exploitative attitude toward women permits the cat to view pimping as a prestigeful source of income. Through the labor of "chicks" engaged in prostitution or shoplifting, he can live in idleness and concentrate his entire attention on organizing, scheduling, and experiencing the esthetic pleasure of the kick. The hustle of the cat is secondary to his interest in the kick. In this respect the cat differs from his fellow delinquents in the criminal subculture, for whom income-producing activity is a primary concern.

The ideal cat's appearance, demeanor, and taste can best be characterized as "cool." The cat seeks to exhibit a highly developed and sophisticated taste for clothes. In his demeanor, he struggles to reveal a self-assured and unruffled manner, thereby emphasizing his aloofness and "superiority" to the "squares." He develops a colorful, discriminating vocabulary and ritualized gestures which express his sense of difference from the conventional world and his solidarity with the retreatist subculture.

The word "cool" also best describes the sense of apartness and detachment which the retreatist experiences in his relationships with the conventional world. His reference group is the "society of cats," and "elite" group in which he becomes isolated from conventional society. Within this group, a new order of goals and criteria of achievement are created. The cat does not seek to impose this system of values on the world of the squares. Instead, he strives for status and deference within the society of cats by cultivating the kick and the hustle. Thus the retreatist subculture provides avenues to success-goals, to the social admiration and the sense of well-being or oneness with the world which the members feel are otherwise beyond their reach.

Notes

1. See esp. C. R. Shaw, *The Jack-Roller* (Chicago: University of Chicago Press, 1930); Shaw, *The Natural History of a Delinquent Career* (Chicago: University of Chicago Press, 1931); Shaw *et al.*, *Delinquency Areas* (Chicago: University of Chicago Press, 1940); and Shaw and H. D. McKay, *Juvenile Delinquency and Urban Areas* (Chicago: University of Chicago Press, 1942).

2. E. H. Sutherland, ed., *The Professional Thief* (Chicago: University of Chicago Press, 1937); and Sutherland, *Principles of Criminology*, 4th Ed. (Philadelphia: Lippincott, 1947).

3. All quotations on this page are from *The Professional Thief*, pp. 211–13. Emphasis added.

4. Frank Tannenbaum, "The Professional Criminal," *The Century*, Vol. 110 (May-Oct. 1925), p. 577.

5. See A. K. Cohen, Alfred Lindesmith, and Karl Schuessler, eds., *The Sutherland Papers* (Bloomington, Ind.: Indiana University Press, 1956), pp. 31–35.

6. R. K. Merton, *Social Theory and Social Structure*, Rev. and Enl. Ed. (Glencoe, Ill.: Free Press, 1957), pp. 145–46.

7. *Principles of Criminology, op. cit.*, pp. 7–8.

8. For an example of restrictions on access to illegitimate roles, note the impact of racial definitions in the following case: "I was greeted by two prisoners who were to be

my cell buddies. Ernest was a first offender, charged with being a 'hold-up' man. Bill, the other buddy, was an older offender, going through the machinery of becoming a habitual criminal, in and out of jail. . . . The first thing they asked me was, 'What are you in for?' I said, 'Jack-rolling.' The hardened one (Bill) looked at me with a superior air and said, 'A hoodlum, eh? An ordinary sneak thief. Not willing to leave jack-rolling to the niggers, eh? That's all they're good for. Kid, jack-rolling's not a white man's job.' I could see that he was disgusted with me, and I was too scared to say anything." (Shaw, *The Jack-Roller, op. cit.,* p. 101).

9. For a discussion of the way in which the availability of illegitimate means influences the adaptations of inmates to prison life, see R. A. Cloward, "Social Control in the Prison," *Theoretical Studies of the Social Organization of the Prison,* Bulletin No. 15 (New York: Social Science Research Council, March 1960), pp. 20–48.

10. It should be understood that these terms characterize these delinquent modes of adaptation from the reference position of conventional society; they do not necessarily reflect the attitudes of members of the subcultures. Thus the term "retreatist" does not necessarily reflect the attitude of the "cat." Far from thinking of himself as being in retreat, he defines himself as among the elect.

11. Tannenbaum summarizes the community's role in this process of alienation by the phrase "dramatization of evil" (Frank Tannenbaum, *Crime and the Community* [New York: Columbia University Press, 1938], pp. 19–21). For a more detailed account of this process, see Chap. 5, *infra.*

12. See esp. C. R. Shaw, *The Jack Roller* (Chicago: University of Chiago Press, 1930); Shaw, *The Natural History of a Delinquent Career* (Chicago: University of Chicago Press, 1940); Shaw and H. D. McKay, *Juvenile Delinquency and Urban Areas* (Chicago: University of Chicago Press, 1942); E. H. Sutherland, ed., *The Professional Thief (Chicago: University of Chicago Press, 1937);* Sutherland, *Principles of Criminology,* 4th ed. (Philadelphia: J. P. Lippincott Co., 1947); and Sutherland, *White Collar Crime* (New York: Dryden Press, 1949).

13. For descriptions of conflict groups, see Harrison Salisbury, *The Shook-up Generation* (New York: Harper & Bros., 1958); *Reaching the Unreached,* a Publication of the New York City Youth Board, 1952; C. K. Myers, *Light the Dark Streets* (Greenwich, Conn.: Seabury Press, 1957); Walter Bernstein, "The Cherubs Are Rumbling," *The New Yorker,* Sept. 21, 1957; Sam Glane, "Juvenile Gangs in East Side Los Angeles," *Focus,* Vol. 29 (Sept. 1959), pp. 136–41; Dale Kramer and Madeline Karr, *Teen-Age Gangs* (New York: Henry Holt, 1953); S. V. Jones, "The Cougars—Life with a Brooklyn Gang," *Harper's,* Vol. 209 (Nov. 1954), pp. 35–43; P. C. Crawford, D. I. Malamud, and J. R. Dumpson, *Working with Teen-Age Gangs* (New York Welfare Council, 1950); Dan Wakefield, "The Gang That Went Good," *Harper's,* Vol. 216 (June 1958), pp. 36–43.

14. Harold Finestone, "Cats, Kicks and Color," *Social Problems,* Vol. 5 (July 1957), pp. 3–13.

11 / Group Conflict Theory as Explanation of Crime

GEORGE B. VOLD

1. BASIC CONSIDERATIONS IN CONFLICT THEORY

The social-psychological orientation for conflict theory rests on social interaction theories of personality formation and the 'social process' conception of collective behavior.[1] Implicit to this new view is the assumption that man always is a group-involved being whose life is both a part of, and a product of his group associations. Implicit also is the view of society as a congerie of groups held together in a shifting but dynamic equilibrium of opposing group interests and efforts.[2]

This continuity of group interaction, the endless series of moves and counter-moves, of checks and cross checks, is the essential element in the concept of social process. It is this continuous on-going of interchanging influence, in an immediate and dynamically maintained equilibrium, that gives special significance to the designation 'collective behavior,' as opposed to the idea of simultaneously behaving individuals.[3] It is this fluid flow of collective action that provides opportunity for a continuous possibility of shifting positions, of gaining or losing status, with the consequent need to maintain an alert defense of one's position, and also always with the ever-present and appealing chance of improving on one's status relationship. The end result is a more or less continuous struggle to maintain, or to defend, the place of one's own group in the interaction of groups, always with due attention to the possibility of improving its relative status position. Conflict is viewed, therefore, as one of the principal and essential social processes upon which the continuing on-going of society depends.[4]

As social interaction processes grind their way through varying kinds of uneasy adjustment to a more or less stable equilibrium of balanced forces in opposition, the resulting condition of relative stability is what is usually called social order or social organization. But it is the adjustment, one to another, of the many groups of varying strengths and of different interests that is the essence of society as a functioning reality.

The normal principle of social organization is that groups are formed out of situations in which members have common interests and common needs that can be best furthered through collective action.[5] In other words, groups arise out of important needs of group members, and groups must serve the needs of the members or they soon wither away and disappear. New groups are therefore continuously being formed as new interests arise, and existing groups weaken and disappear when they no longer have a purpose to serve.[6]

Groups come into conflict with one another as the interests and purposes they serve tend to overlap, encroach on one another, and become competitive. In other words, conflicts between groups occur principally when the groups become competitive by attempting to operate in the same general field of interaction. There is never any serious conflict between groups whose operations can be channeled so that they perform satisfactorily without moving in on one another's territory of common interests and common purposes.[7]

The danger that any existing group must protect itself against, when in contact with any other group in the same area of interests and needs, is the ever-present one of being taken over, of being replaced. A group must always be in a position to defend itself in order to maintain its place and position in the world of constantly changing adjustments. The principal goal, therefore, of one group in contact with another, is to keep from being replaced. Where there is no problem of competition and replacement, there is little likelihood of serious inter-group conflict, be it between nations, races, religions, economic systems, labor unions, or any other type of group organization.

Groups become effective action units through the direction and coordination of the activities of their members. For the members, the experience of participation in group activity and the sharing of troubles and satisfactions operate to make the individual a group-conscious person. It is out of this experience background that group identification and group loyalty become psychological realities. The loyalty of the group member to his group is one of the most profoundly significant facts of social psychology, though there is no assured explanation of *why* the loyalty and identification develop. Both loyalty and identification tend to be emotionally toned attachments not closely related to any rational understanding the individual may have of the place or significance of a particular group in the general scheme of things.[8]

It has long been realized that conflict between groups tends to develop and intensify the loyalty of the group members to their respective groups.[9] This is clearly one of the important elements in developing *esprit de corps* and 'group-mindedness' attitudes on the part of individual members. The individual is most loyal to the group for which he has had to fight the hardest, and to which he has had to give the greatest measure of self for the common end of group achievement.[10]

Nothing promotes harmony and self-sacrifice within the group quite as effectively as a serious struggle with another group for survival. Hence, patriotic feeling runs high in war time, and the more desperate the situation (short of collapse and the chaos of defeat and despair) in battle, the higher runs the feeling that nothing is too great a sacrifice for the national good. A group crisis, in which the member must stand up and be counted, is an age-old device for separating the men from the boys. It needs to be remembered that groups have always paid tribute to 'service beyond the call of duty.' Thus it is that some of our finest ideals of character and manhood are the off-shoots of group conflict where the individual has had opportunity to serve the common purpose and not merely to serve his own selfish ends.[11]

The logical outcome of group conflict should be either, on the one hand, conquest and victory for one side with the utter defeat and destruction or subjugation for the other side; or, on the other hand, something less conclusive and decisive, a stalemate of compromise and withdrawal to terminate the conflict with no final settlement of the issues involved. It should be noted that, generally speaking, there is never any compromise with a position of weakness—the weak, as a rule, are quickly overwhelmed, subjugated to and integrated with the victors in some subordinate and inferior capacity. The group that will survive and avoid having to go down in defeat is the one strong enough to force some compromise settlement of the issues in conflict. This general pattern has been a commonplace occurrence in the conflicts between national groups and also between political factions within the nation.[12]

2. CRIME AND THE CONFLICT PROCESS

The foregoing brief sketch of some of the elements involved in the conflicts of groups should be sufficient to alert the thoughtful reader to further applications of these general group relationships to more specific situations. For example, politics, as it flourishes in a democracy, is primarily a matter of finding practical compromises between antagonistic groups in the community at large.[13] The prohibitionist wishes to outlaw the manufacture and sale of alcoholic beverages; the distillers and brewers wish unrestricted opportunity to make and sell a product for which there is a genuine economic demand (i.e. 'demand' in the sense of not only having a desire for the product but also having the ability to pay for it). The complicated collection of regulations that American communities know so well, including special taxes, special licensing fees and regulations, special inspections, and special rules for closing hours etc., are all part of the compromise settlement in the clash of these incompatible interests in the political organization of society.

As political groups line up against one another, they seek the assistance of the organized state to help them defend their 'rights' and protect their interests. Thus the familiar cry, 'there ought to be a law' (to suppress the undesirable) is understandable as the natural recourse of one side or the other in a conflict situation. Yet for exactly the same reason such action has a necessary logical opposition which resists the proposed legislation. Whichever group interest can marshal the greatest number of votes will determine whether or not there is to be a new law to hamper and curb the interests of some opposition group.[14]

Suppose, for purposes of illustration, that a new law has been enacted by a normal, legal, legislative majority. Those who opposed it and fought it before adoption are understandably not in sympathy with its provisions, and do not take kindly to efforts at law enforcement. In other words, the whole political process of law making, law breaking, and law enforcement becomes a direct reflection of deep-seated and fundamental conflicts between interest groups and their more general struggles for the control of the police power of the state. Those who produce legislative majorities win control over the police power and dominate the policies that decide who is likely to be involved in violation of the law.[15]

The struggle between those who support the law and those who violate it existed in the community before there was legislative action; it was the basis for the battle in the legislature; it is then continued through the judicial proceedings of prosecution and trial; and it culminates eventually in the prison treatment of the violators by those who wish to have the law enforced. The principle of compromise from positions of strength operates at every stage of this conflict process. Hence, there is bargaining in the legislature to get the law passed; there is bargaining between prosecution and defense in connection with the trial; between prison officials and inmates; and between parole agent and parolee. This is the background for Sutherland's famous 'sociological definition' of crime as a social situation, as a set of relationships rather than as an act of behavior under specific legal definition.[16]

3. CRIME AS MINORITY GROUP BEHAVIOR

Crime and delinquency as group behavior is a familiar topic in criminology that has long been observed and discussed. Shaw and

McKay[17] reported that from 80 to 90 per cent (depending on the offense) of 5,480 juvenile offenders before the Cook County Juvenile Court in 1928 had committed their offenses with one or more associates. The Gluecks reported that about 70 per cent of their 100 juvenile offenders[18] had had companions in crime; for their reformatory group of 500 older offenders[19] the proportion was nearly 60 per cent. From their more recent and more carefully controlled study[20] the Gluecks reported that nearly all delinquents, in contrast to only a very few non-delinquents, preferred to chum with, or pal around with, other delinquents, while more than one-half of the delinquents, as compared with less than 1 per cent of the non-delinquents, were members of gangs.

Such statistics, however, report only the formal aspects of the extent to which prosecution has become aware of shared experience and group participation in situations that the criminal law ordinarily prefers to view as individual wrongdoing, and a matter for which the individual should be held responsible. From a more general point of view, however, this prevalence of collective action in crime may reasonably be interpreted as an indication of the banding together for protection and strength of those who in some way are at odds with organized society and with the police forces maintained by that society. The delinquent boys' gang is clearly a 'minority group' in the sense that it cannot achieve its objectives through regular channels, making use of, and relying for protection on, the police powers of the state.

The gang, therefore, resorts to direct action with the typical social-psychological reaction of a conflict group (e.g. loyalty to group and leaders, subordination of individual wishes to group ends, adherence to an 'approved code' of values and behavior etc.) which has purposes to achieve that are at variance with those set up for it by the elements in control of the official police powers of the state.[21] The juvenile gang, in this sense, is nearly always a 'minority group,' out of sympathy with and in more or less direct opposition to the rules and regulations of the dominant majority; that is, the established world of adult values and power. The police ordinarily represent the power and values of the adult world, while the gang seeks to operate to get benefits and advantages not permitted it under the adult code. When, in the course of time, members of a gang become adults, many of the gang activities are sometimes continued under the color of a political party name (e.g. as a 'Young Republican Club' or a 'Fourth Ward Democratic Club' etc.) with political influence now giving it police protection and support, since it now is part of the majority group in control of power.[22]

What happens to members of a minority group with a strong

ideological orientation out of sympathy with the established majority pattern is well illustrated by the experiences of 'conscientious objectors' in time of war.[23] While not a very large proportion of those in prison, the actual numbers nevertheless added up to a considerable total for the United States in World War II. In the war years, 1940–45, there were over 5000 persons who served prison sentences in federal institutions for the 'crime' of having convictions which led them to refuse to participate in any way in war activity. This was in addition to the much larger number (over 9000) who registered under the draft as 'conscientious objectors' but accepted assignment to non-military service of some kind.[24]

The full import of the social-psychological fact of minority group orientation, which remains utterly oblivious to and unmoved by continuous contact with an 'out-group' majority officially dedicated to changing it, is made abundantly clear in an interesting account of prison experiences by one of the conscientious objectors who served a sentence in the federal institution at Lewisburg, Pennsylvania. *The Diary of a Self-Made Convict* by Alfred Hassler[25] is the story of prison life by a skilled professional writer who, both before and after imprisonment, devoted himself to the task of writing and editorial work for the Fellowship of Reconciliation. His book is intended as an account of the realities of prison life, as lived in a 'good' modern prison that practices all the 'gimmicks' of contemporary penology. Its intention is not in any way to deal with the problem of the conscientious objector, or with his ideas. Yet the book is completely revealing in its portrayal of the psychological orientation of the author. It is obvious throughout his account of the day to day happenings of prison life that he never had any question in his mind but that his own particular role in becoming a convict was wholly and completely honorable. His title is equally revealing—a 'self-made' convict; that is, a convict by his own free choice, a choice of which he obviously was proud.

This is another demonstration of the simple, stubborn fact that minority group members, whose criminal behavior has been consistent with minority group views, are not changed easily by coercive measures applied by the majority group. Every prisoner-of-war stockade in the world testifies to this same general ineffectiveness of majority group pressure on the attitudes and loyalties of minority group members whose 'crimes' consist of the fact that they have been overwhelmed in the battle for power. The failure of court conviction, sentence, and prison experience to change Hassler's general self-satisfaction with the rightness of his own course of action is by no means unique with conscientious objectors. It is not only the convinced pacifist who rejects the moral justification for his conviction or who constructs a rationale of his own course of action such that he can remain loyal and faithful to his minority group ideology. Criminals of all kinds who have significant group identification to bolster their morale react in very much the same manner. Well-intentioned efforts at rehabilitation, in these cases, are usually no more effective.

This kind of reaction is one of the logical consequences of the formal organization of political society. This basic relationship between the individual and his group, however, is of genuine significance for criminological theory, and must be given due consideration. Those who reject the majority view and refuse to follow required behavior patterns are inevitably defined as, and treated as, criminals, be they conscientious religious persons, like Hassler, or be they only conscientious devotees of the economic principle of private profit who refuse to accept or follow required practices under a system of government control of consumer prices.[26] Members of such a minority group do not accept the definition of themselves, or of their behavior, as criminal. Looking at their own group of like-thinking associates, they readily persuade themselves that their course of action has been acceptable and, from their point of view, entirely honorable. The more basic problem, therefore, is the conflict of group interests and the struggle for the control of power that is always present in the political organization of any society.

4. THE POLITICAL NATURE OF MUCH CRIMINAL BEHAVIOR

Many kinds of criminal acts must be recognized as representing primarily behavior on the front-line fringes of direct contact between groups struggling for the control of power in the political and cultural organization of society. To surface appearance, the offenses may seem to be the ordinary common-law ones involving persons and property, but on closer examination they often are revealed as the acts of good soldiers fighting for a cause and against the threat of enemy encroachment. The age-old psychological principle of all group centered conflict activity comes to the fore, namely, the end justifies the means, and the end object is the maintenance of the group position.

The fact that the means used may be less than honorable, that they may involve outright criminal behavior is viewed as unfortunate but not therefore to be shirked, if necessary to the accomplishment of group ends. Hence, at the point of contact between groups in conflict all manner of blustering violence, deceit, treachery, and pious disingenuousness become a relatively commonplace part of the struggle. Closer examination of a few type-situations will help make clear some of the ramifications of this aspect of criminal behavior.

1. Numerous crimes result from the direct political reform type of protest movement. Such reform activity often has recourse to violence, the ultimate form of which is rebellion or revolution. A successful revolution makes criminals out of the government officials previously in power, and an unsuccessful revolution makes its leaders into traitors subject to immediate execution. Murder, sabotage, seizures of private property, and many other offenses against the ordinary criminal code are commonplace accompaniments of political rebellion.[27]

But revolutions are by no means the only occasions under which political activity sets the stage for or calls forth a certain amount of criminal activity. Many an election, in many a democratic country, has brought about the direct, physical collision of opposing groups with resulting personal violence and many kinds of personal dishonesty, bribery, perjury, and sometimes outright burglary and theft, all for the sake of winning the election and gaining (or keeping) control of political power.[28] Such conduct will always be deprecated publicly, but its persistence in one form or another in every country in the world where popular elections have significance in the contest for the control of power is further testimony to the important relation between some kinds of crime and the group struggle for the control of power.[29]

2. Many crimes result directly from the clash of interests of company management and labor unions in that form of industrial conflict that we call strikes or lockouts. If management tries to bring in non-striking employees (strike-breakers), these must cross picket lines and are often forcefully kept out of company property. Each side may use force, and in the resulting fights heads may be broken and property may be destroyed.[30] The company's legal ownership of property usually brings in the police to protect it and prevent its usurpation by non-owners. This has often in the past led to direct physical clashes between police and strikers. In such battles there often have been casualties on both sides, including the killing or maiming of individuals and the destruction of property, both private and public.[31]

Obviously such episodes involve long lists of actual crimes by any ordinary rule of law. Yet there are relatively few instances of successful prosecution of such lawlessness, presumably for the good and sufficient reason that the criminal acts are recognized to be incidental to what is more basically a battle between politically powerful groups whose full power is much more extensive than that exerted on any particular instance of clashing force. The public interest is often ignored, or even brazenly outraged, in these clashes. Public streets and highways, always of direct interest to government and to public convenience, may be closed, or their use made dependent upon an appropriate 'permit' from some 'strike committee.'[32] The general object of any strike or lockout is to bring enough pressure to bear on the other side, through the reaction of an outraged public, so that satisfactory settlement will be reached.

The point of these illustrations is simply that the participants on either side of a labor dispute condone whatever criminal behavior is deemed 'necessary' for the maintenance of their side of the struggle. The end justifies the means, and the individual in the struggle does his duty as a good soldier, even if what he has to do is contrary to law and something he would not otherwise do. Thus, as a picket, a labor union member may carry a piece of pipe as a club, swing it on a strikebreaker's head, and be guilty technically of murder or manslaughter, though in reality he has only carried out his duty assignment as a faithful member of his group.

3. Similar in nature but with a different focus for the conflict, numerous crimes result as incidental episodes in the jurisdictional disputes between different labor unions. Such disputes often involve intimidation and personal violence, and sometimes they become entangled with the 'rackets' and gang warfare of the criminal underworld. The point to be emphasized is that the violence and criminal behavior of some members of labor unions, in these instances, are part of the general conflict behavior of the group. Any particular individual involved has the psychological advantage of feeling assured of group support. He operates as a soldier in a war—sorry that he has to be nasty and unpleasant, always hoping for an early peace settlement that will be favorable to his union.

4. Numerous kinds of crimes result from the clashes incidental to attempts to change, or to upset the caste system of racial segregation in various parts of the world, notably in the United States and in the Union of South Africa. To the dominant white, the Negro is acceptable and desirable only 'in his place,' a place of obvious social inferiority. In the economic sphere, he is regarded as a source of cheap labor and not as a skilled professional or as a technician. Regardless of personal qualities or qualifications, to the white majority his place must be one recognizably subordinate to that of the white majority.[33] Again, no one subscribes publicly to violence or to open intimidation as the desirable method of maintaining the status quo, but in practice such lawless action is often supported as 'necessary.'

The type-situation illustrations above have been elaborated in order to emphasize an important kind of criminal behavior, one whereby, technically under the law, individuals are charged with ordinary common-law crimes, yet the specific criminal behavior involved represented for the individual loyal service to a social-political group struggling to maintain, or to improve its position in the struggle for the control of power. Criminological theories based on notions of individual choice and responsibility are not germane to the underlying problem of group conflict involved in this type of situation. Such an individualistic theory, applied to this kind of crime, is like holding the individual soldier in an army at war responsible for the violence he may have inflicted on an enemy in the course of battle. Victorious nations in war sometimes react in this manner in dealing with the top leaders of defeated enemy forces — witness the 'war crimes trials' that have dotted the pages of history — but usually the ordinary soldier is guilty primarily of doing his duty as ordered. In the conflict of groups within a society, the analogy with crime and the criminal has genuine psychological significance.

5. IMPLICATIONS AND LIMITATIONS

Criminal behavior that involves the kind of situations discussed in this chapter obviously has far-reaching implications for any kind of general criminological theory. It points to one of the fundamental conditions of life in organized political society. It suggests the probability that there are many situations in which criminality is the normal, natural response of normal, natural human beings struggling in understandably normal and natural situations for the maintenance of the way of life to which they stand committed.

Defectiveness and abnormality hypotheses are clearly inapplicable to the type of situation here discussed. Yet the criminal behavior involved is readily understood and easily explained as the kind of behavior necessary to protect and defend the interests of the individual's group in conflict with other groups. Criminological theory, in this type of situation, becomes a specialized application of the more general theory of a sociology of conflict. The behavior of the individual is viewed as incidental to the course of action required for the group to maintain its place in the struggle with other groups.

On the other hand, it is also clear that group conflict theory is strictly limited to those kinds of situations in which the individual criminal acts flow from the collision of groups whose members are loyally upholding the in-group position. Such theory does not serve to explain many kinds of impulsive, irrational acts of a criminal nature that are quite unrelated to any battle between different interest groups in organized society. Other theories, with different emphases on other factors, need to be considered for such situations.

Like the defectiveness hypothesis, or the hypothesis of individual differences, the group conflict hypothesis should not be stretched too far. Yet there seems to be little doubt but that a considerable amount of crime is intimately related to the course of group conflict situations, and that for these situations the principles of a sociology of conflict become also the solid bases for understanding and explaining this kind of criminal behavior.

Notes

1. Cf. Robert E. Park and Ernest W. Burgess, *Introduction to Science of Sociology*, University of Chicago Press, Chicago, 1924. 'Competition,' pp. 504–10; 'Conflict,' pp. 574–9; 'Collective Behavior,' pp. 865–74.
2. Cf. Arthur F. Bentley, *The Process of Government*, University of Chicago Press, Chicago, 1908, 'Social Pressures,' pp. 258–96.
3. R. E. Park and E. W. Burgess, op. cit. p. 865; also Muzafer Sherif, op. cit. ch. 5, 'Properties of Group Situations,' pp. 98–121.
4. For a discussion of the relation between the principal social processes and the resulting social order, see R. E. Park and E. W. Burgess, op. cit. pp. 506–10.
5. Cf. Albion W. Small, *General Sociology*, University of Chicago Press, Chicago, 1905, pp. 495–500.
6. Cf. Charles H. Cooley, *Social Organization*, Scribner, New York, 1924, 'Primary Aspects of Organization,' pp. 3–57.
7. Charles H. Cooley, op. cit. 'Hostile Feelings between Classes,' pp. 301–9.
8. Muzafer Sherif, *An Outline of Social Psychology*, Harper, New York, 1948, ch. 13, 'Adolescent Attitudes and Identification,' pp. 314–38.
9. Walter Bagehot, *Physics and Politics*, 1869, reprinted by Knopf, New York, 1948, 'The Use of Conflict,' pp. 44–84.
10. Muzafer Sherif, op. cit. ch. 7, 'The Formation of Group Standards or Norms,' pp. 156–82.
11. Ibid. ch. 12, 'Ego-Involvement in Personal and Group Relationships,' pp. 282–313; also ch. 16, 'Men in Critical Situations,' pp. 401–424.
12. Cf. Park and Burgess, op. cit., p. 575; also Hadley Cantril, *The Psychology of Social Movements*, Wiley, New York, 1941, chs. 8 and 9, 'The Nazi Party,' pp. 210–70.
13. Walter Bagehot, op. cit. chs. 3 and 4, 'Nation-Making,' pp. 85–160.
14. E. H. Sutherland and Donald R. Cressey, *Principles of Criminology*, 5th ed., Lippincott, New York, 1955, ch. 1, 'Criminology and the Criminal Law,' pp. 3–22.
15. E. H. Sutherland, 'Crime and the Conflict Process,' *Journal of Juvenile Research*, 13:38–48, 1929.
16. Sutherland and Cressey, op. cit. p. 15.
17. C. R. Shaw and H. D. McKay, 'Social Factors in Juvenile Delinquency,' *Report on the Causes of Crime*, vol. II, no. 13, of the Report of the National Commission on Law Observance and Law Enforcement, Washington, D.C., June 26, 1931, pp. 192–8.
18. Sheldon and Eleanor Glueck, *One Thousand Juvenile Delinquents*, Harvard University Press, Cambridge, 1934, pp. 100–101.
19. Sheldon and Eleanor Glueck, *Five Hundred Criminal Careers*, Knopf, New York, 1930, p. 152.
20. Sheldon and Eleanor Glueck, *Unraveling Juvenile Delinquency*, Commonwealth Fund, New York, 1950, p. 278.
21. Cf. William F. Whyte, *Street Corner Society*, University of Chicago Press, Chicago, 1943; also Solomon Kobrin, 'The Conflict of Values in Delinquency Areas,' *American Sociological Review*, 16:653–62, October 1951.
22. These are well-documented facts in the celebrated studies of big city gangs such as Frederick Thrasher, *The Gang*, 2nd ed. rev., University of Chicago Press, Chicago, 1936; Herbert Asbury, *The Gangs of New York*, Knopf, New York, 1928; and his more recent study of Chicago—*Gem of the Prairie*, Knopf, New York, 1940.
23. A well-documented and reasonably objective account of the prison aspects of this problem for the United States for World War II may be found in Mulford Q. Sibley and Ada Wardlaw, *Conscientious Objectors in Prison, 1940–1945*, The Pacifist Research Bureau, Ithaca, New York, 1945.
24. See Mabel Elliott, *Crime in Modern Society*, Harper, New York, 1952, pp.

179–97, for a good brief account of the main facts relating to the political criminal and the conscientious objector in the United States in and since World War II.

25. Alfred Hassler, *The Diary of a Self-Made Convict*, Foreword by Henry Elmer Barnes, Regnery, Chicago, 1954. The Fellowship of Reconciliation is a Christian pacifist group organized in 1914 in Cambridge, England, and reported to have about 15,000 members in the United States at the present time.

26. Cf. Marshall Clinard, *The Black Market*, Rinehart, New York, 1952. This is a study of and report on the attempt to control consumer prices during war rationing of food and other scarce commodities in the United States during World War II.

27. Hadley Cantril, *The Psychology of Social Movements*, Wiley, New York, 1941, chs. 8 and 9, 'The Nazi Party,' pp. 210–270.

28. Cf. Lincoln Steffens, *The Shame of the Cities*, McClure, Phillips, New York, 1904.

29. Cf. Jack Lait and Lee Mortimer, *New York Confidential*, 1949; *Chicago Confidential*, 1950; *Washington Confidential*, 1951. These three books were published by Crown Publishers, New York.

30. See, for example, Oscar Lewis, *The Big Four*, Knopf, New York, 1938, pp. 370–84, for the account of the John L. Davie *vs.* Southern Pacific Railroad battle over waterfront rights in the Oakland, California, area.

31. See Mary Heaton Vorse, *Labor's New Millions*, Modern Age Books, New York, 1938, pp. 118–27, for a short account of the 'Chicago Massacre,' i.e. the violent encounters between police and workers at the Republic Steel Plant, May 26–30, 1937, that resulted in an eventual death list of 17 killed, and many more seriously wounded.

32. Cf. Charles Rumford Walker, *American City: A Rank and File History*, New York, Farrar and Rinehart, 1937. Detailed account of the Minneapolis truck strike of 1934 in which a strike committee completely usurped the power of government over streets and highway, so that passage into the city was 'on permit' from the committee.

33. For illustrations of the more recent episodes in this continuing conflict in the United States, often beset with violence and crime, see the issues of *Life* for August and September 1956. Specifically, 'Segregation,' September 24, 1956, pp. 98–114, and 'School Battle Turns to Law,' October 1, 1956, pp. 51–2. Illustrated accounts of the violence in Little Rock, Arkansas may be found in *Life* for September 23, September 30, and October 7, 1957.

12 / The Social Reality of Crime

RICHARD QUINNEY

ASSUMPTIONS: MAN AND SOCIETY IN A THEORY OF CRIME

In studying any social phenomenon we must hold to some general perspective. Two of those used by sociologists, and by most social analysts for that matter, are the *static* and the *dynamic* interpretations of society. Either is equally plausible, though most sociologists take the static viewpoint.[1] This emphasis has relegated forces and events, such as deviance and crime, which do not appear to be conducive to stability and consensus, to the pathologies of society.

My theory of crime, however, is based on the dynamic perspective. The theory is based on these assumptions about man and society: (1) process, (2) conflict, (3) power, and (4) social action.

Process

The dynamic aspect of social relations may be referred to as "social process." Though in analyzing society we use static descriptions, that is, we define the structure and function of social relations, we must be aware that social phenomena fluctuate continually.[2]

We apply this assumption to all social phenomena that have duration and undergo change, that is, all those which interest the sociologist. A social process is a continuous series of actions, taking place in time, and leading to a special kind of result: "a system of social change taking place within a defined situation and exhibiting a particular order of change through the operation of forces present from the first within the situation."[3] Any particular phenomenon, in turn, is viewed as contributing to the dynamics of the total process. As in the "modern systems approach," social phenomena are seen as generating out of an interrelated whole.[4] The methodological implication of the process assumption is that any social phenomenon may be viewed as part of a complex network of events, structures, and underlying processes.

Conflict

In any society conflicts between persons, social units, or cultural elements are inevitable, the normal consequences of social life. Conflict is especially prevalent in societies with diverse value systems and normative groups. Experience teaches that we cannot expect to find consensus on all or most values and norms in such societies.

Two models of society contrast sharply: one is regarded as "conflict" and the other, "consensus." With the consensus model we describe social structure as a functionally integrated system held together in equilibrium. In the conflict model, on the other hand, we find that societies and social organizations are shaped by diversity, coercion, and change. The differences between these contending but complementary conceptions of society have been best characterized by Dahrendorf.[5] According to his study, we assume in postulating the consensus (or integrative) model of society that: (1) society is a relatively persistent, stable structure, (2) it is well integrated, (3) every element has a function — it helps maintain the system, and (4) a functioning social structure is based on a consensus on values. For the conflict (or coercion) model of society, on the other hand, we assume that: (1) at every point society is subject to change, (2) it displays at every point dissensus and conflict, (3) every element contributes to change, and (4) it is based on the coercion of some of its members by others. In other words, society is held together by force and constraint and is characterized by ubiquitous conflicts that result in continuous change: "values are ruling rather than common, enforced rather than accepted, at any given point of time."[6]

Although in society as a whole conflict may be general, according to the conflict model, it is still likely that we will find stability and consensus on values among subunits in the society. Groups with their own cultural elements are found in most societies, leading to social differentiation with conflict between the social units; nonetheless integration and stability may appear within specific social groups: "Although the total larger society may be diverse internally and may form only a loosely integrated system, within each subculture there may be high integration of institutions and close conformity of individuals to the patterns sanctioned by their own group."[7]

Conflict need not necessarily disrupt society. Some sociologists have been interested in the *functions* of social conflict, "that is to say, with those consequences of social conflict which make for an increase rather than a decrease in the adaptation or adjustment of particular social relationships or groups."[8] It seems that conflict can promote cooperation, establish group boundaries, and unite social factions. Furthermore, it may lead to new patterns that may in the long run be beneficial to the whole society or to parts of it.[9] Any doubts about its functional possibilities have been dispelled by Dahrendorf: "I would suggest . . . that all that is creativity, innovation, and development in the life of the individual, his group, and his society is due, to no small extent, to the operation of conflicts between group and group, individual and individual, emotion and emotion within one individual. This fundamental fact alone seems to me to justify the value judgment that conflict is essentially 'good' and 'desirable.' "[10] Conflict is not always the disruptive agent in a society; at certain times it may be meaningful to see it as a cohesive force.

Power

The conflict conception of society leads us to assume that coherence is assured in any social unit by coercion and constraint. In other words, *power* is the basic characteristic of social organization. "This means that in every social organization some positions are entrusted with a right to exercise control over other positions in order to ensure effective coercion; it means, in other words, that there is a differential distribution of power and authority."[11] Thus, conflict and power are inextricably linked in the conception of society presented here. The differential distribution of power produces conflict between competing groups, and conflict, in turn, is rooted in the competition for power. Wherever men live together conflict and a struggle for power will be found.

Power, then, is the ability of persons and groups to determine the conduct of other persons and groups.[12] It is utilized not for its own sake, but is the vehicle for the enforcement of scarce values in society, whether the values are material, moral, or otherwise. The use of power affects the distribution of values and values affect the distribution of power. The "authoritative allocation of values" is essential to any society.[13] In any society, institutional means are used to officially establish and enforce sets of values for the entire population.

Power and the allocation of values are basic in forming *public policy*. Groups with special *interests* become so well organized that they are able to influence the policies that are to affect all persons. These interest groups exert their influence at every level and branch of government in order to have their own values and interests represented in the policy decisions.[14] Any interest group's ability to influence public policy depends on the group's position in the political power structure. Furthermore, access to the formation of public policy is unequally distributed because of the structural arrangements of the political state. "Access is one of the advantages unequally distributed by such arrangements; that is, in consequence of the structural peculiarities of our government some groups have better and more varied opportunities to influence key points of decision than do others."[15] Groups that have the power to gain access to the decision-making process also inevitably control the lives of others.

A major assumption in my conception of society, therefore, is the importance of interest groups in shaping public policy. Public policy is formed so as to represent the interests and values of groups that are in positions of power. Rather than accept the pluralistic conception of the political process, which assumes that all groups make themselves heard in policy decision-making, I am relying upon a conception that assumes an unequal distribution of power in formulating and administering public policy.[16]

Social Action

An assumption of man that is consistent with the conflict-power conception of society asserts that man's actions are purposive and meaningful, that man engages in voluntary behavior. This *humanistic* conception of man contrasts with the oversocialized conception of man. Man is, after all, capable of considering alternative actions, of breaking from the established social order.[17] Once he gains an awareness of self, by being a member of society, he is able to choose his actions. The extent to which he does conform depends in large measure upon his own self-control.[18] Nonconformity may also be part of the process of finding self-identity. It is thus *against* something that the self can emerge.[19]

By conceiving of man as able to reason and choose courses of action, we may see him as changing and becoming, rather than merely being.[20] The kind of culture that man develops shapes his ability to be creative. Through his culture he may develop the capacity to have greater freedom of action.[21] Not only is he shaped by his physical, social, and cultural experiences, he is able to select what he is to experience and develop. The belief in realizing unutilized human potential is growing and should be incorporated in a contemporary conception of human behavior.[22]

The *social action* frame of reference that serves as the basis of the humanistic conception of man is drawn from the work of such writers as Weber, Znaniecki, MacIver, Nadel, Parsons, and Becker.[23] It was originally suggested by Max Weber: "Action is social in so far as, by virtue of the subjective meaning attached to it by the acting individual (or individuals), it takes account of the behavior of others and is thereby oriented in its own course."[24] Hence, human behavior is *intentional*, has *meaning* for the actors, is *goal-oriented*, and takes place with an *awareness* of the consequences of behavior.

Because man engages in social action, a *social reality* is created. That is, man in interaction with others constructs a meaningful world of everyday life.

> It is the world of cultural objects and social institutions into which we are all born, within which we have to find our bearings, and with which we have to come to terms. From the outset, we, the actors on the social scene, experience the world we live in as a world both of nature and of culture, not as a private but as an intersubjective one, that is, as a world common to all of us, either actually given or potentially accessible to everyone; and this involves intercommunication and language.[25]

Social reality consists of both the social meanings and the products of the subjective world of persons. Man, accordingly, constructs activities and patterns of actions as he attaches meaning to his everyday existence.[26] Social reality is thus both a *conceptual reality* and a *phenomenal reality*. Having constructed social reality, man finds a world of meanings and events that is real to him as a conscious social being.

THEORY: THE SOCIAL REALITY OF CRIME

The theory contains six propositions and a number of statements within the propositions. With the first proposition I define crime. The next four are the explanatory units. In the final proposition the other five are collected to form a composite describing the social reality of crime. The propositions and their integration into a theory of crime reflect the assumptions about explanation and about man and society outlined above.[27]

Proposition 1 (definition of crime) Crime is a definition of human conduct that is created by authorized agents in a politically organized society.

This is the essential starting point in the theory—a definition of crime—which itself is based on the concept of definition. Crime is a *definition* of behavior that is conferred on some persons by others. Agents of the law (legislators, police, prosecutors, and judges), representing segments of a politically organized society, are responsible for formulating and administering criminal law. Persons and behaviors, therefore, become criminal because of the *formulation* and *application* of criminal definitions. Thus, *crime is created.*

ST. MARTIN'S PRESS, INC.

175 FIFTH AVENUE — NEW YORK, N. Y. 10010

DESK OR EXAMINATION COPIES FOR

| PROFESSOR DAVID RADEN | 032955 1 287 |
| PURDUE UNIVERSITY CALUMET CAMPUS | 49240 101279 |

QTY.	NUMBER AND TITLE
01	197586 DEVIANT BEHAVIOR: RDGS SOC DEV PAPER

YOUR COMMENTS ON OUR BOOKS HELP US ESTIMATE PRINTING REQUIREMENTS, ASSIST US IN PREPARING REVISIONS, AND GUIDE US IN SHAPING FUTURE BOOKS TO YOUR NEEDS. WILL YOU PLEASE TAKE A MOMENT TO FILL OUT AND RETURN THIS POSTPAID CARD?

☐ I PLAN TO ADOPT THIS BOOK   ☐ I AM CONSIDERING ADOPTING THIS BOOK

COURSE TITLE _____ ENROLLMENT_____

COMMENTS

MAY WE QUOTE YOU? YES☐ NO☐   FOLD, TAPE, AND MAIL

FOLD, TAPE, AND MAIL

By viewing crime as a definition, we are able to avoid the commonly used "clinical perspective," which leads one to concentrate on the quality of the act and to assume that criminal behavior is an individual pathology.[28] Crime is not inherent in behavior, but is a judgment made by some about the actions and characteristics of others.[29] This proposition allows us to focus on the formulation and administration of the criminal law as it touches upon the behaviors that become defined as criminal. Crime is seen as a result of a process which culminates in the defining of persons and behaviors as criminal. It follows, then, that *the greater the number of criminal definitions formulated and applied, the greater the amount of crime.*

Proposition 2 (formulation of criminal definitions) Criminal definitions describe behaviors that conflict with the interests of the segments of society that have the power to shape public policy.

Criminal definitions are formulated according to the interests of those *segments* (types of social groupings) of society which have the *power* to translate their interests into *public policy*. The interests — based on desires, values, and norms — which are ultimately incorporated into the criminal law are those which are treasured by the dominant interest groups in the society.[30] In other words, those who have the ability to have their interests represented in public policy regulate the formulation of criminal definitions.

That criminal definitions are formulated is one of the most obvious manifestations of *conflict* in society. By formulating criminal law (including legislative statutes, administrative rulings, and judicial decisions), some segments of society protect and perpetuate their own interests. Criminal definitions exist, therefore, because some segments of society are in conflict with others.[31] By formulating criminal definitions these segments are able to control the behavior of persons in other segments. It follows that *the greater the conflict in interests between the segments of a society, the greater the probability that the power segments will formulate criminal definitions.*

The interests of the power segments of society are reflected not only in the content of criminal definitions and the kinds of penal sanctions attached to them, but also in the *legal policies* stipulating how those who come to be defined as "criminal" are to be handled. Hence, procedural rules are created for enforcing and administering the criminal law. Policies are also established on programs for treating and punishing the criminally defined and for controlling and preventing crime. In the initial criminal definitions or the subsequent procedures, and in correctional and penal programs or policies of crime control and prevention, the segments of society that have power and interests to protect are instrumental in regulating the behavior of those who have conflicting interests and less power.[32] Finally, law changes with modifications in the interest structure. When the interests that underlie a criminal law are no longer relevant to groups in power, the law will be reinterpreted or altered to incorporate the dominant interests. Hence, *the probability that criminal definitions will be formulated is increased by such factors as (1) changing social conditions, (2) emerging interests, (3) increasing demands that political, economic, and religious interests be protected, and (4) changing conceptions of the public interest.* The social history of law reflects changes in the interest structure of society.

Proposition 3 (application of criminal definitions) Criminal definitions are applied by the segments of society that have the power to shape the enforcement and administration of criminal law.

The powerful interests intervene in all stages in which criminal definitions are created. Since interests cannot be effectively protected by merely formulating criminal law, enforcement and administration of the law are required. The interests of the powerful, therefore, operate in *applying* criminal definitions. Consequently, crime is "political behavior and the criminal becomes in fact a member of a 'minority group' without sufficient public support to dominate the control of the police power of the state."[33] Those whose interests conflict with the interests represented in the law must either change their behavior or possibly find it defined as "criminal."

The probability that criminal definitions will be applied varies according to the extent to which the behaviors of the powerless conflict with the interests of the power segments. Law enforcement efforts and judicial activity are likely to be increased when the interests of the powerful are threatened by the opposition's behavior. Fluctuations and variations in the application of criminal definitions reflect shifts in the relations of the various segments in the power structure of society.

Obviously, the criminal law is not applied directly by the powerful segments. They delegate enforcement and administration of the law to authorized *legal agents*, who, nevertheless, represent their interests. In fact, the security in office of legal agents depends on their ability to represent the society's dominant interests.

Because the interest groups responsible for creating criminal definitions are physically separated from the groups to which the authority to enforce and administer law is delegated, local conditions affect the manner in which criminal definitions are applied.[34] In particular, communities vary in the law enforcement and administration of justice they expect. Application is also affected by the visibility of acts in a community and by its norms about reporting possible offenses. Especially important are the occupational organization and ideology of the legal agents.[35] Thus, *the probability that criminal definitions will be applied is influenced by such community and organizational factors as (1) community expectations of law enforcement and administration, (2) the visibility and public reporting of offenses, and (3) the occupational organization, ideology, and actions of the legal agents to whom the authority to enforce and administer criminal law is delegated.* Such factors determine how the dominant interests of society are implemented in the application of criminal definitions.

The probability that criminal definitions will be applied in *specific situations* depends on the actions of the legal agents. In the final analysis, a criminal definition is applied according to an *evaluation* by someone charged with the authority to enforce and administer the law. In the course of "criminalization," a criminal label may be affixed to a person because of real or fancied attributes: "Indeed, a person is evaluated, either favorably or unfavorably, not because he *does* something, or even because he *is* something, but because others react to their perceptions of him as offensive or inoffensive."[36] Evaluation by the definers is affected by the way in which the suspect handles the situation, but ultimately their evaluations and subsequent decisions determine the criminality of human acts. Hence, *the more legal agents evaluate behaviors and persons as worthy of criminal definition, the greater the probability that criminal definitions will be applied.*

Proposition 4 (development of behavior patterns in relation to criminal definitions) Behavior patterns are structured in segmentally organized society in relation to criminal definitions, and within this context persons engage in actions that have relative probabilities of being defined as criminal.

Although behavior varies, all behaviors are similar in that they represent the *behavior patterns* of segments of society. Therefore, all persons—whether they create criminal definitions or are the objects of criminal definitions—act according to *normative systems* learned in relative social and cultural settings.[37] Since it is not the quality of the behavior but the action taken against the behavior that makes it criminal, that which is defined as criminal in any society is relative to the behavior patterns of the segments of society that formulate and apply criminal definitions. Consequently, *persons in the segments of society whose behavior patterns are not represented in formulating and applying criminal definitions are more likely to act in ways that will be defined as criminal than those in the segments that formulate and apply criminal definitions.*

Once behavior patterns are established with some regularity within the respective segments of society, individuals are provided with a framework for developing *personal action patterns*. These patterns continually develop for each person as he moves from one experience to another. It is the development of these patterns that gives his behavior its own substance in relation to criminal definitions.

Man constructs his own patterns of action in participating with others. It follows, then, that *the probability that a person will develop action patterns that have a high potential of being defined as criminal depends on the relative substance of (1) structured opportunities, (2) learning experiences, (3) interpersonal associations and identifications, and (4) self-conceptions.* Throughout his experiences, each person creates a conception of himself as a social being. Thus prepared, he behaves according to the anticipated consequences of his actions.[38]

During experiences shared by the criminal definers and the criminally defined, personal action patterns develop among the criminally defined because they are so defined. After such persons have had continued experience in being criminally defined, they learn to manipulate the application of criminal definitions.[39]

Furthermore, those who have been defined as criminal begin to conceive of themselves as criminal; as they adjust to the definitions imposed upon them, they learn to play the role of the criminal.[40] Because of others' reactions, therefore, persons may develop personal action patterns that increase the likelihood of their being defined as criminal in the future. That is, *increased experience with criminal definitions increases the probability of developing actions that may be subsequently defined as criminal.*

Thus, both the criminal definers and the criminally defined are involved in reciprocal action patterns. The patterns of both the definers and the defined are shaped by their common, continued, and related experiences. The fate of each is bound to that of the other.

Proposition 5 (construction of criminal conceptions) Conceptions of crime are constructed and diffused in the segments of society by various means of communication.

The "real world" is a social construction: man with the help of others creates the world in which he lives. Social reality is thus the world a group of people create and believe in as their own. This reality is constructed according to the kind of "knowledge" they develop, the ideas they are exposed to, the manner in which they select information to fit the world they are shaping, and the manner in which they interpret these conceptions.[41] Man behaves in reference to the *social meanings* he attaches to his experiences.

Among the constructions that develop in a society are those which

Figure 1 / Model of the Social Reality of Crime

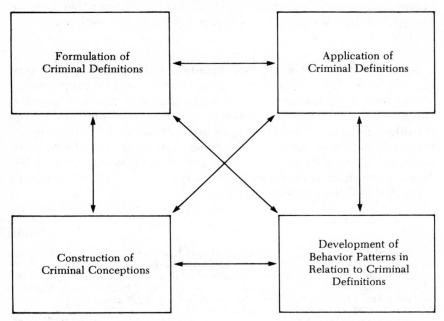

determine what man regards as crime. Wherever we find the concept of crime, there we will find conceptions about the relevance of crime, the offender's characteristics, and the relation of crime to the social order.[42] These conceptions are constructed by communication. In fact, *the construction of criminal conceptions depends on the portrayal of crime in all personal and mass communications.* By such means, criminal conceptions are constructed and diffused in the segments of a society. The most critical conceptions are those held by the power segments of society. These are the conceptions that are certain of becoming incorporated into the social reality of crime. In general, then, *the more the power segments are concerned about crime, the greater the probability that criminal definitions will be created and that behavior patterns will develop in opposition to criminal definitions.* The formulation and application of criminal definitions and the development of behavior patterns related to criminal definitions are thus joined in full circle by the construction of criminal conceptions.

Proposition 6 (the social reality of crime) The social reality of crime is constructed by the formulation and application of criminal definitions, the development of behavior patterns related to criminal definitions, and the construction of criminal conceptions.

These five propositions can be collected into a composite. The theory, accordingly, describes and explains phenomena that increase the probability of crime in society, resulting in the social reality of crime.

Since the first proposition is a definition and the sixth is a composite, the body of the theory consists of the four middle propositions. These form a model, as diagrammed in Figure 1, which relates the propositions into a theoretical system. Each proposition is related to the others forming a theoretical system of developmental propositions interacting with one another. The phenomena denoted in the propositions and their relationships culminate in what is regarded as the amount and character of crime in a society at any given time, that is, in the social reality of crime.

Notes

1. See Robert A. Nisbet, *The Sociological Tradition* (New York: Basic Books, 1966); Reinhard Bendix and Bennett Berger, "Images of Society and Problems of Concept Formation in Sociology," in Gross, *Symposium on Sociological Theory*, pp. 92–118.

2. Howard Becker, *Systematic Sociology on the Basis of the Beziehungslehre and Gebildelehre of Leopold von Wiess* (New York: John Wiley & Sons, 1932).

3. Robert MacIver, *Social Causation* (New York: Ginn, 1942), p. 130.

4. Walter Buckley, "A Methodological Note," in Thomas J. Scheff, *Being Mentally Ill* (Chicago: Aldine, 1966), pp. 201–205.

5. Ralf Dahrendorf, *Class and Class Conflict in Industrial Society* (Stanford: Stanford University Press, 1959), pp. 161–162.

6. Ralf Dahrendorf, "Out of Utopia: Toward a Reorientation in Sociological Analysis," *American Journal of Sociology*, 67 (September, 1958), p. 127.

7. Robin M. Williams, Jr., *American Society*, 2nd ed. (New York: Alfred A. Knopf, 1960), p. 375.

8. Lewis A. Coser, *The Functions of Social Conflict* (New York: The Free Press, 1956), p. 8.

9. Lewis A. Coser, "Social Conflict and the Theory of Social Change," *British Journal of Sociology*, 8 (September, 1957), pp. 197–207.

10. Dahrendorf, *Class and Class Conflict in Industrial Society*, p. 208. The importance of conflict in society is also discussed in, among other works, George Simmel, *Conflict*, trans. Kurt H. Wolff (New York: The Free Press, 1955); Irving Louis Horowitz, "Consensus, Conflict and Cooperation: A Sociological Inventory," *Social Forces*, 41 (December, 1962), pp. 177–188; Raymond W. Mack, "The Components of Social Conflict," *Social Problems*, 12 (Spring, 1965), pp. 388–397.

11. Dahrendorf, *Class and Class Conflict in Industrial Society*, p. 165.

12. Max Weber, *From Max Weber: Essays in Sociology*, trans. H. H. Gerth and C. Wright Mills (New York: Oxford University Press, 1946); Hans Gerth and C. Wright Mills, *Character and Social Structure* (New York: Harcourt, Brace, 1953), especially pp. 192–273; C. Wright Mills, *The Power Elite* (New York: Oxford University Press, 1956); George Simmel, *The Sociology of George Simmel*, trans. Kurt H. Wolff (New York: The Free Press, 1950), pp. 181–186; Robert Bierstedt, "An Analysis of Social Power," *American Sociological Review*, 15 (December, 1950), pp. 730–738.

13. David Easton, *The Political System* (New York: Alfred A. Knopf, 1953), p. 137. Similar ideas are found in Harold D. Lasswell, *Politics: Who Gets What, When, How* (New York: McGraw-Hill, 1936); Harold D. Lasswell and Abraham Kaplan, *Power and Society* (New Haven: Yale University Press, 1950).

14. Among the vast amount of literature on interest groups, see Donald C. Blaisdell, *American Democracy Under Pressure* (New York: Ronald Press, 1957); V. O. Key, Jr., *Politics, Parties, and Pressure Groups* (New York: Thomas Y. Crowell, 1959); Earl Latham, *Group Basis of Politics* (Ithaca, N.Y.: Cornell University Press, 1952); David Truman, *The Governmental Process* (New York: Alfred A. Knopf, 1951); Henry W. Ehrmann (ed.), *Interest Groups on Four Continents* (Pittsburgh: University of Pittsburgh Press, 1958); Henry A. Turner, "How Pressure Groups Operate," *Annals of the American Academy of Political and Social Science*, 319 (September, 1958), pp. 63–72; Richard W. Gable, "Interest Groups as Policy Shapers," *Annals of the American Academy of Political and Social Science*, 319 (September, 1958), pp. 84–93; Murray S. Stedman, "Pressure Group and the American Tradition," *Annals of the American Academy of Political and Social Science*, 319 (September, 1958), pp. 123–219. For documentation on the influence of specific interest groups, see Robert Engler, *The Politics of Oil* (New York: Macmillan, 1961); Oliver Garceau, *The Political Life of the American Medical Association* (Cambridge: Harvard University Press, 1941); Charles M. Hardin, *The Politics of Agriculture: Soil Conservation and the Struggle for Power in Rural America* (New York: The Free Press of Glencoe, 1962); Grant McConnell, *Private Power and American Democracy* (New York: Alfred A. Knopf, 1966); Harry A. Millis and Royal E. Montgomery, *Organized Labor* (New York: McGraw-Hill, 1945); Warner Schilling, Paul Y. Hammond, and Glenn H. Snyder, *Strategy, Politics and Defense* (New York: Columbia University Press, 1962); William R. Willoughby, *The St. Lawrence Waterway: A Study in Politics and Diplomacy* (Madison: University of Wisconsin Press, 1961).

15. Truman, *The Governmental Process*, p. 322.

16. Evaluations of the pluralistic and power approaches are found in Peter Bachrach and Morton S. Baratz, "Two Faces of Power," *American Political Science Review*, 61 (December, 1962), pp. 947–952; Thomas I. Cook, "The Political System: The Stubborn Search for a Science of Politics," *Journal of Philosophy*, 51 (February, 1954), pp. 128–137; Charles S. Hyneman, *The Study of Politics* (Urbana: University of Illinois Press, 1959); William C. Mitchell, "Politics as the Allocation of Values: A Critique," *Ethics*, 71 (January, 1961), pp. 79–89; Talcott Parsons, "The Distribution of Power in American Society," *World Politics*, 10 (October, 1957), pp. 123–143; Charles Perrow, "The Sociological Perspective and Political Pluralism," *Social Research*, 31 (Winter, 1964), pp. 411–422.

17. For essentially this aspect of man see Peter Berger, *Invitation to Sociology: A Humanistic Perspective* (New York: Doubleday, 1963), chap. 6; Max Mark, "What Image of Man for Political Science?" *Western Political Quarterly*, 15 (December, 1962), pp. 593–604; Dennis Wrong, "The Oversocialized Conception of Man in Modern Sociology," *American Sociological Review*, 26 (April, 1961), pp. 183–193.

18. Tamotsu Shibutani, *Society and Personality: An Interactionist Approach to Social Psychology* (Englewood Cliffs, N.J.: Prentice-Hall, 1961), especially pp. 60, 91–94, 276–278. Also see S. F. Nadel, "Social Control and Self-Regulation," *Social Forces*, 31 (March, 1953), pp. 265–273.

19. Erving Goffman, *Asylums* (New York: Doubleday, 1961), pp. 318–320.

20. Richard A. Schermerhorn, "Man the Unfinished," *Sociological Quarterly*, 4 (Winter, 1963), pp. 5–17; Gordon W. Allport, *Becoming: Basic Considerations for a Psychology of Personality* (New Haven: Yale University Press, 1955).

21. Herbert J. Muller, *The Uses of the Past* (New York: Oxford University Press, 1952), especially pp. 40–42.

22. Julian Huxley, *New Bottles for New Wines* (New York: Harper, 1957).

23. Florian Znaniecki, *Social Actions* (New York: Farrar and Rinehart, 1936); MacIver, *Social Causation*; S. F. Nadel, *Foundations of Social Anthropology* (New York: The Free Press, 1951); Talcott Parsons, *The Structure of Social Action* (New York: The Free Press, 1949); Howard Becker, *Through Values to Social Interpretation* (Durham: Duke University Press, 1950).

24. Max Weber, *The Theory of Social and Economic Organization*, trans. A. M. Henderson and Talcott Parsons (New York: The Free Press), p. 88.

25. Alfred Schutz, *The Problem of Social Reality: Collected Papers I* (The Hague: Martinus Nijhoff, 1962), p. 53.

26. See Peter L. Berger and Thomas Luckmann, *The Social Construction of Reality* (Garden City, N.Y.: Doubleday, 1966).

27. For earlier background material, see Richard Quinney, "A Conception of Man and Society for Criminology," *Sociological Quarterly*, 6 (Spring, 1965), pp. 119–127; Quinney, "Crime in Political Perspective," *American Behavioral Scientist*, 8 (December, 1964), pp. 19–22; Quinney, "Is Criminal Behavior Deviant Behavior?" *British Journal of Criminology*, 5 (April, 1965), pp. 132–142.

28. See Jane R. Mercer, "Social System Perspective and Clinical Perspective: Frames of Reference for Understanding Career Patterns of Persons Labelled as Mentally Retarded," *Social Problems*, 13 (Summer, 1966), pp. 18–34.

29. This perspective in the study of social deviance has been developed in Becker, *Outsiders*; Kai T. Erikson, "Notes on the Sociology of Deviance," *Social Problems*, 9 (Spring, 1962), pp. 307–314; John I. Kitsuse, "Societal Reactions to Deviant Behavior: Problems of Theory and Method," *Social Problems*, 9 (Winter, 1962), pp. 247–256. Also see Ronald L. Akers, "Problems in the Sociology of Deviance: Social Definitions and Behavior," *Social Forces*, 46 (June, 1968), pp. 455–465; David J. Bordua, "Recent Trends: Deviant Behavior and Social Control," *Annals of the American Academy of Political and Social Science*, 369 (January, 1967), pp. 149–163; Jack P. Gibbs, "Conceptions of Deviant Behavior: The Old and the New," *Pacific Sociological Review*, 9 (Spring, 1966), pp. 9–14; Clarence R. Jeffrey, "The Structure of American Criminological Thinking," *Journal of Criminal Law, Criminology and Police Science*, 46 (January–February, 1956), pp. 658–672; Austin T. Turk, "Prospects for Theories of Criminal Behavior," *Journal of Criminal Law, Criminology and Police Science*, 55 (December, 1964), pp. 454–461.

30. See Richard C. Fuller, "Morals and the Criminal Law," *Journal of Criminal Law, Criminology and Police Science*, 32 (March–April, 1942), pp. 624–630; Thorsten Sellin, *Culture Conflict and Crime* (New York: Social Science Research Council, 1938), pp. 21–25; Clarence R. Jeffery, "Crime, Law and Social Structure," *Journal of Criminal Law, Criminology and Police Science*, 47 (November–December, 1956), pp. 423–435; John J. Honigmann, "Value Conflict and Legislation," *Social Problems*, 7 (Summer, 1959), pp. 34–40; George Rusche and Otto Kirchheimer, *Punishment and Social Structure* (New York: Columbia University Press, 1939); Roscoe Pound, *An Introduction to the Philosophy of Law* (New Haven: Yale University Press, 1922).

31. I am obviously indebted to the conflict formulation of George B. Vold, *Theoretical Criminology* (New York: Oxford University Press, 1958), especially pp. 203–242. A recent conflict approach to crime is found in Austin T. Turk, "Conflict and Criminality," *American Sociological Review*, 31 (June, 1966), pp. 338–352.

32. Considerable support for this proposition is found in the following studies: William J. Chambliss, "A Sociological Analysis of the Law of Vagrancy," *Social Problems*, 12 (Summer, 1964), pp. 66–77; Kai T. Erikson, *Wayward Puritans* (New York: John Wiley, 1966); Jerome Hall, *Theft, Law and Society*, 2nd ed. (Indianapolis: Bobbs-Merrill, 1952); Clarence R. Jeffery, "The Development of Crime in Early England," *Journal of Criminal Law, Criminology and Police Science*, 47 (March–April, 1957), pp. 647–666; Alfred R. Lindesmith, *The Addict and the Law* (Bloomington: Indiana University Press, 1965); Rusche and Kirchheimer, *Punishment and Social Structure*; Andrew Sinclair, *Era of Excess: A Social History of the Prohibition Movement* (New York: Harper & Row, 1964); Edwin H. Sutherland, "The Sexual Psychopath Law," *Journal of Criminal Law, Criminology and Police Science*, 40 (January–February, 1950), pp. 543–554.

33. Vold, *Theoretical Criminology*, p. 202. Also see Irving Louis Horowitz and Martin Liebowitz, "Social Deviance and Political Marginality: Toward a Redefinition of the Relation Between Sociology and Politics," *Social Problems*, 15 (Winter, 1968), pp. 280–296.

34. See Michael Banton, *The Policeman and the Community* (London: Tavistock, 1964); Egon Bittner, "The Police on Skid-Row: A Study of Peace Keeping," *American Sociological Review*, 32 (October, 1967), pp. 699–715; John P. Clark, "Isolation of the Police: A Comparison of the British and American Situations," *Journal of Criminal Law, Criminology and Police Science*, 56 (September, 1965), pp. 307–319; Nathan Goldman, *The Differential Selection of Juvenile Offenders for Court Appearance*

(New York National Council on Crime and Delinquency, 1963); James Q. Wilson, *Varieties of Police Behavior* (Cambridge: Harvard University Press, 1968).

35. Abraham S. Blumberg, *Criminal Justice* (Chicago: Quadrangle Books, 1967); David J. Bordua and Albert J. Reiss, Jr., "Command, Control and Charisma: Reflections on Police Bureaucracy," *American Journal of Sociology*, 72 (July, 1966), pp. 68–76; Aaron V. Cicourel, *The Social Organization of Juvenile Justice* (New York: John Wiley, 1968); Arthur Niederhoffer, *Behind the Shield: The Police in Urban Society* (Garden City, N.Y.: Doubleday, 1967); Jerome H. Skolnick, *Justice Without Trial: Law Enforcement in Democratic Society* (New York: John Wiley, 1966); Arthur L. Stinchcombe, "Institutions of Privacy in the Determination of Police Administrative Practice," *American Journal of Sociology*, 69 (September, 1963), pp. 150–160; David Sudnow, "Normal Crimes: Sociological Features of the Penal Code in a Public Defender Office," *Social Problems*, 12 (Winter, 1965), pp. 255–276; William A. Westley, "Violence and the Police," *American Journal of Sociology*, 59 (July, 1953), pp. 34–41; Arthur Lewis Wood, *Criminal Lawyer* (New Haven: College & University Press, 1967).

36. Turk, "Conflict and Criminality," p. 340. For research on the evaluation of suspects by policemen, see Irving Piliavin and Scott Briar, "Police Encounters with Juveniles," *American Journal of Sociology*, 70 (September, 1964), pp. 206–214.

37. Assumed within the theory of the social reality of crime is Sutherland's theory of differential association. See Edwin H. Sutherland, *Principles of Criminology*, 4th ed. (Philadelphia: J. B. Lippincott, 1947). An analysis of the differential association theory is found in Melvin L. De Fleur and Richard Quinney, "A Reformulation of Sutherland's Differential Association Theory and a Strategy for Empirical Verification," *Journal of Research in Crime and Delinquency*, 3 (January, 1966), pp. 1–22.

38. On the operant nature of criminally defined behavior, see Robert L. Burgess and Ronald L. Akers, "A Differential Association-Reinforcement Theory of Criminal Behavior," *Social Problems*, 14 (Fall, 1966), pp. 128–147; C. R. Jeffery, "Criminal Behavior and Learning Theory," *Journal of Criminal Law, Criminology and Police Science*, 56 (September, 1965), pp. 294–300.

39. A discussion of the part the person plays in manipulating the deviant defining situation is found in Judith Lorber, "Deviance as Performance: The Case of Illness," *Social Problems*, 14 (Winter, 1967), pp. 302–310.

40. Edwin M. Lemert, *Human Deviance, Social Problems, and Social Control* (Englewood Cliffs, N.J.: Prentice-Hall, 1964), pp. 40–64; Edwin M. Lemert, *Social Pathology* (New York: McGraw-Hill, 1951), pp. 3–98. A related and earlier discussion is in Frank Tannenbaum, *Crime and the Community* (New York: Columbia University Press, 1938), pp. 3–81.

41. See Berger and Luckmann, *The Social Construction of Reality*. Relevant research on the diffusion of information is discussed in Everett M. Rogers, *Diffusion of Innovations* (New York: The Free Press of Glencoe, 1962).

42. Research on public conceptions of crime is only beginning. See Alexander L. Clark and Jack P. Gibbs, "Social Control: A Reformulation," *Social Problems*, 12 (Spring, 1965), pp. 398–415; Thomas E. Dow, Jr., "The Role of Identification in Conditioning Public Attitude Toward the Offender," *Journal of Criminal Law, Criminology and Police Science*, 58 (March, 1967), pp. 75–79; William P. Lentz, "Social Status and Attitudes Toward Delinquency Control," *Journal of Research in Crime and Delinquency*, 3 (July, 1966), pp. 147–154; Jennie McIntyre, "Public Attitudes Toward Crime and Law Enforcement," *Annals of the American Academy of Political and Social Science*, 374 (November, 1967), pp. 34–46; Anastassios D. Mylonas and Walter C. Reckless, "Prisoners' Attitudes Toward Law and Legal Institutions," *Journal of Criminal Law, Criminology and Police Science*, 54 (December, 1963), pp. 479–484; Elizabeth A. Rooney and Don C. Gibbons, "Social Reactions to 'Crimes Without Victims,' " *Social Problems*, 13 (Spring, 1966), pp. 400–410.

13 / Definition and the Dramatization of Evil

FRANK TANNENBAUM

In the conflict between the young delinquent and the community there develop two opposing definitions of the situation. In the beginning the definition of the situation by the young delinquent may be in the form of play, adventure, excitement, interest, mischief, fun. Breaking windows, annoying people, running around porches, climbing over roofs, stealing from pushcarts, playing truant—all are items of play, adventure, excitement. To the community, however, these activities may and often do take on the form of a nuisance, evil, delinquency, with the demand for control, admonition, chastisement, punishment, police court, truant school. This conflict over the situation is one that arises out of a divergence of values. As the problem develops, the situation gradually becomes redefined. The attitude of the community hardens definitely into a demand for suppression. There is a gradual shift from the definition of the specific acts as evil to a definition of the individual as evil, so that all his acts come to be looked upon with suspicion. In the process of identification his companions, hang-outs, play, speech, income, all his conduct, the personality itself, become subject to scrutiny and question. From the community's point of view, the individual who used to do bad and mischievous things has now become a bad and unredeemable human being. From the individual's point of view there has taken place a similar change. He has gone slowly from a sense of grievance and injustice, of being unduly mistreated and punished, to a recognition that the definition of him as a human being is different from that of other boys in his neighborhood, his school, street, community. This recognition on his part becomes a process of self-identification and integration with the group which shares his activities. It becomes, in part, a process of rationalization; in part, a simple response to a specialized type of stimulus. The young delinquent becomes bad because he is defined as bad and because he is not believed if he is good. There is a persistent demand for consistency in character. The community cannot deal with people whom it cannot define. Reputation is this sort of public definition. Once it is established, then unconsciously all agencies combine to maintain this definition even when they apparently and consciously attempt to deny their own implicit judgment.

Early in his career, then, the incipient professional criminal develops an attitude of antagonism to the regulated orderly life that he is required to lead. This attitude is hardened and crystallized by opposition. The conflict becomes a clash of wills. And experience too often has proved that threats, punishments, beatings, commitments to institutions, abuse and defamation of one sort or another, are of no avail. Punishment breaks down against the child's stubbornness. What has happened is that the child has been defined as an "incorrigible" both by his contacts and by himself, and an attempt at a direct breaking down of will generally fails.

The child meets the situation in the only way he can, by defiance and escape—physical escape if possible, or emotional escape by derision, anger, contempt, hatred, disgust, tantrums, destructiveness, and physical violence. The response of the child is just as intelligent and intelligible as that of the schools, of the authorities. They have taken a simple problem, the lack of fitness of an institution to a particular child's needs, and have made a moral issue out of it with values outside the child's ken. It takes on the form of war between two wills, and the longer the war lasts, the more certainly does the child become incorrigible. The child will not yield because he cannot yield—his nature requires other channels for pleasant growth; the school system or society will not yield because it does not see the issues involved as between the incompatibility of an institution and a child's needs, sometimes physical needs, and will instead attempt to twist the child's nature to the institution with that consequent distortion of the child which makes an unsocial career inevitable. The verbalization of the conflict in terms of evil, delinquency, incorrigibility, badness, arrest, force, punishment, stupidity, lack of intelligence, truancy, criminality, gives the innocent divergence of the child from the straight road a meaning that it did not have in the beginning and makes its continuance in these same terms by so much the more inevitable.

The only important fact, when the issue arises of the boy's inability to acquire the specific habits which organized institutions attempt to impose upon him, is that this conflict becomes the occasion for him to acquire another series of habits, interests, and attitudes as a substitute. These habits become as effective in motivating and guiding conduct as would have been those which the orderly routine social institutions attempted to impose had they been acquired.

This conflict gives the gang its hold, because the gang provides escape, security, pleasure, and peace. The gang also gives room for the motor activity which plays a large role in a child's life. The attempt to break up the gang by force merely strengthens it. The arrest of the children has consequences undreamed-of, for several reasons.

First, only some of the children are caught though all may be equally guilty. There is a great deal more delinquency practiced and committed by the young groups than comes to the attention of the police. The boy arrested, therefore, is singled out in specialized treatment. This boy, no more guilty than the other members of his group, discovers a world of which he knew little. His arrest suddenly precipitates a series of institutions, attitudes, and experiences which the other children do not share. For this boy there suddenly appear the police, the patrol wagon, the police station, the other delinquents and criminals found in the police lock-ups, the court with all its agencies such as bailiffs, clerks, bondsmen, lawyers, probation officers. There are bars, cells, handcuffs, criminals. He is questioned, examined, tested, investigated. His history is gone into, his family is brought into court. Witnesses make their appearance. The boy, no different from the rest of his gang, suddenly becomes the center of a major drama in which all sorts of unexpected characters play important roles. And what is it all about? about the accustomed things his gang has done and has been doing for a long time. In this entirely new world he is made conscious of himself as a different human being than he was before his arrest. He becomes classified as a thief, perhaps, and the entire world about him has suddenly become a different place for him and will remain different for the rest of his life. . . .

The first dramatization of the "evil" which separates the child out of his group for specialized treatment plays a greater role in making the criminal than perhaps any other experience. It cannot be too often emphasized that for the child the whole situation has become different. He now lives in a different world. He has been tagged. A new and hitherto non-existent environment has been precipitated out for him.

The process of making the criminal, therefore, is a process of tagging, defining, identifying, segregating, describing, emphasizing, making conscious and self-conscious; it becomes a way of stimulating, suggesting, emphasizing, and evoking the very traits that are complained of. If the theory of relation of response to stimulus has any meaning, the entire process of dealing with the young delinquent is mischievous in so far as it identifies him to himself or to the environment as a delinquent person.

The person becomes the thing he is described as being. Nor does it seem to matter whether the valuation is made by those who would punish or by those who would reform. In either case the emphasis is upon the conduct that is disapproved of. The parents or the policeman, the older brother or the court, the probation officer or the juvenile institution, in so far as they rest upon the thing complained of, rest upon a false ground. Their very enthusiasm defeats their aim. The harder they work to reform the evil, the greater the evil grows under their hands. The persistent suggestion, with whatever good intentions, works mischief, because it leads to bringing out the bad behavior that it would suppress. The way out is through a refusal to dramatize the evil. The less said about it the better. The more said about something else, still better.

> The hard-drinker who keeps thinking of not drinking is doing what he can to initiate the acts which lead to drinking. He is starting with the stimulus to his habit. To succeed he must find some positive interest or line of action which will inhibit the drinking series and which by instituting another course of action will bring him to his desired end.[1]

The dramatization of the evil therefore tends to precipitate the conflict situation which was first created through some innocent maladjustment. The child's isolation forces him into companionship with other children similarly defined, and the gang becomes his means of escape, his security. The life of the gang gives it special mores, and the attack by the community upon these mores merely overemphasizes the conflict already in existence, and makes it the source of a new series of experiences that lead directly to a criminal career.

In dealing with the delinquent, the criminal, therefore, the important thing to remember is that we are dealing with a human being who is responding normally to the demands, stimuli, approval, expectancy, of the group with whom he is associated. We are dealing not with an individual but with a group.

> In a study of 6,000 instances of stealing, with reference to the number of boys involved, it was found that in 90.4 per cent of the cases two or more boys were known to have been involved in the act and were consequently brought to court. Only 9.6 per cent of all the cases were acts of single individuals. Since this study was based upon the number of boys brought to court, and since in many cases not all of the boys involved were caught and brought to court, it is certain that the percentage of group stealing is therefore even greater than 90.4 per cent. It cannot be doubted that delinquency, particularly stealing, almost invariably involves two or more persons.[2]

That group may be a small gang, a gang of children just growing up, a gang of young "toughs" of nineteen or twenty, or a gang of older criminals of thirty. If we are not dealing with a gang we may be dealing with a family. And if we are not dealing with either of these especially we may be dealing with a community. In practice all these factors — the family, the gang, and the community — may be important in the development and the maintenance of that attitude towards the world which makes a criminal career a normal, an accepted and approved way of life.

Direct attack upon the individual in these circumstances is a dubious undertaking. By the time the individual has become a criminal his habits have been so shaped that we have a fairly integrated character whose whole career is in tune with the peculiar bit of the environment for which he has developed the behavior and habits that cause him to be apprehended. In theory isolation from that group ought to provide occasion for change in the individual's habit structure. It might, if the individual were transplanted to a group whose values and activities had the approval of the wider community, and in which the newcomer might hope to gain full acceptance eventually. But until now isolation has meant the grouping in close confinement of persons whose strongest common bond has been their socially disapproved delinquent conduct. Thus the attack cannot be made without reference to group life.

The attack must be on the whole group; for only by changing its attitudes and ideals, interests and habits, can the stimuli which it exerts upon the individual be changed. Punishment as retribution has failed to reform, that is, to change character. If the individual can be made aware of a different set of values for which he may receive approval, then we may be on the road to a change in his character. But such a change of values involves a change in stimuli, which means that the criminal's social world must be changed before he can be changed.

The point of view here developed rejects all assumptions that would impute crime to the individual in the sense that a personal shortcoming of the offender is the cause of the unsocial behavior. The assumption that crime is caused by any sort of inferiority, physiological or psychological, is here completely and unequivocally repudiated.

This of course does not mean that morphological or psychological techniques do not have value in dealing with the individual. It merely means that they have no greater value in the study of criminology than they would have in the study of any profession. If a poor IQ is a bad beginning for a career in medicine, it is also a poor beginning for a career in crime. If the psychiatrist can testify that a psychopath will make an irritable doctor he can prove the same for the criminal. But he can prove no more. The criminal differs from the rest of his fellows only in the sense that he has learned to respond to the stimuli of a very small and specialized group; but that group must exist or the criminal could not exist. In that he is like the mass of men, living a certain kind of life with the kind of companions that make that life possible.

This explanation of criminal behavior is meant to apply to those who more or less consistently pursue the criminal career. It does not necessarily presume to describe the accidental criminal or the man who commits a crime of passion. Here perhaps the theories that would seek the cause of crime in the individual may have greater application than in attempting to deal with those who follow a life of crime. But even in the accidental criminal there is a strong presumption that the accident is the outcome of a habit situation. Any habit tends to have a background of social conditioning.

A man with the habit of giving way to anger may show his habit by a murderous attack upon some one who has offended. His act is nonetheless due to habit because it occurs only once in his life. The essence of habit is an acquired predisposition to *ways* or modes of response, not to particular acts except as, under special conditions, these express a way of behaving. Habit means special sensitiveness or accessibility to certain classes of stimuli, standing predilections and aversions, rather than bare recurrence of specific acts. It means will.[3]

In other words, perhaps the accidental criminal also is to be explained in terms such as we use in discussing the professional criminal.

Notes

1. John Dewey, *Human Nature and Conduct*, p. 35. New York, 1922.
2. Clifford R. Shaw and Earl D. Myers, "The Juvenile Delinquent," *The Illinois Crime Survey*, pp. 662–663. Chicago, 1929.
3. Dewey, op. cit., p. 42.

14 / Primary and Secondary Deviation

EDWIN M. LEMERT

SOCIOPATHIC INDIVIDUATION

The deviant person is a product of differentiating and isolating processes. Some persons are individually differentiated from others from
the time of birth onward, as in the case of a child born with a congeni-
tal physical defect or repulsive appearance, and as in the case of a
child born into a minority racial or cultural group. Other persons grow
to maturity in a family or in a social class where pauperism, begging, or
crime are more or less institutionalized ways of life for the entire
group. In these latter instances the person's sociopsychological
growth may be normal in every way, his status as a deviant being
entirely caused by his maturation within the framework of social
organization and culture designated as "pathological" by the larger
society. This is true of many delinquent children in our society.[1]

> It is a matter of great significance that the delinquent child, growing up in
> the delinquency areas of the city, has very little access to the cultural
> heritages of the larger conventional society. His infrequent contacts with
> this larger society are for the most part formal and external. Quite naturally
> his conception of moral values is shaped and molded by the moral code
> prevailing in his play groups and the local community in which he lives . . .
> the young delinquent has very little appreciation of the meaning of the
> traditions and formal laws of society. . . . Hence the conflict between the
> delinquent and the agencies of society is, in its broader aspects, a conflict of
> divergent cultures.

The same sort of gradual, unconscious process which operates in
the socialization of the deviant child may also be recognized in the
acquisition of socially unacceptable behavior by persons after having
reached adulthood. However, with more verbal and sophisticated
adults, step-by-step violations of societal norms tend to be progressively rationalized in the light of what is socially acceptable.
Changes of this nature can take place at the level of either overt or
covert behavior, but with a greater likelihood that adults will preface
overt behavior changes with projective symbolic departures from

society's norms. When the latter occur, the subsequent overt changes may appear to be "sudden" personality modifications. However, whether these changes are completely radical ones is to some extent a moot point. One writer holds strongly to the opinion that sudden and dramatic shifts in behavior from normal to abnormal are seldom the case, that a sequence of small preparatory transformations must be the prelude to such apparently sudden behavior changes. This writer is impressed by the day-by-day growth of "reserve potentialities" within personalities of all individuals, and he contends that many normal persons carry potentialities for abnormal behavior, which, given proper conditions, can easily be called into play.[2]

Personality Changes Not Always Gradual

This argument is admittedly sound for most cases, but it must be taken into consideration that traumatic experiences often speed up changes in personality.[3] Nor can the "trauma" in these experiences universally be attributed to the unique way in which the person conceives of the experience subjectively. Cases exist to show that personality modifications can be telescoped or that there can be an acceleration of such changes caused largely by the intensity and variety of the social stimulation. Most soldiers undoubtedly have entirely different conceptions of their roles after intensive combat experience. Many admit to having "lived a lifetime" in a relatively short period of time after they have been under heavy fire in battle for the first time. Many generals have remarked that their men have to be a little "shooted" or "blooded" in order to become good soldiers. In the process of group formation, crises and interactional amplification are vital requisites to forging true, role-oriented group behavior out of individuated behavior.[4]

The importance of the person's conscious symbolic reactions to his or her own behavior cannot be overstressed in explaining the shift from normal to abnormal behavior or from one type of pathological behavior to another, particularly where behavior variations become systematized or structured into pathological roles. This is not to say that conscious choice is a determining factor in the differentiating process. Nor does it mean that the awareness of the self is a purely conscious perception. Much of the process of self-perception is doubtless marginal from the point of view of consciousness.[5] But however it may be perceived, the individual's self-definition is closely connected with such things as self-acceptance, the subordination of minor to major roles, and with the motivation involved in learning the skills, techniques, and values of a new role. *Self-definitions or self-realizations are likely to be the result of sudden perceptions and they are especially significant when they are followed immediately by overt demonstrations of the new role they symbolize.* The self-defining junctures are critical points of personality genesis and in the special case of the atypical person they mark a division between two different types of deviation.

Primary and Secondary Deviation

There has been an embarrassingly large number of theories, often without any relationship to a general theory, advanced to account for various specific pathologies in human behavior. For certain types of pathology, such as alcoholism, crime, or stuttering, there are almost as many theories as there are writers on these subjects. This has been occasioned in no small way by the preoccupation with the origins of pathological behavior and by the fallacy of confusing *original* causes with *effective* causes. All such theories have elements of truth, and the divergent viewpoints they contain can be reconciled with the general theory here if it is granted that original causes or antecedents of deviant behaviors are many and diversified. This holds especially for the psychological processes leading to similar pathological behavior, but it also holds for the situational concomitants of the initial aberrant conduct. A person may come to use excessive alcohol not only for a wide variety of subjective reasons but also because of diversified situational influences, such as the death of a loved one, business failure, or participating in some sort of organized group activity calling for heavy drinking of liquor. Whatever the original reasons for violating the norms of the community, they are important only for certain research purposes, such as assessing the extent of the "social problem" at a given time or determining the requirements for a rational program of social control. From a narrower sociological viewpoint the deviations are not significant until they are organized subjectively and transformed into active roles and become the social criteria for assigning status. The deviant individuals must react symbolically to their own behavior aberrations and fix them in their sociopsychological patterns. The deviations remain primary deviations or symptomatic and situational as long as they are rationalized or otherwise dealt with as functions of a socially acceptable role. Under such conditions normal and pathological behaviors remain strange and somewhat tensional bedfellows in the same person. Undeniably a vast amount of such segmental and partially integrated pathological behavior exists in our society and has impressed many writers in the field of social pathology.

Just how far and for how long a person may go in dissociating his sociopathic tendencies so that they are merely troublesome adjuncts of normally conceived roles is not known. Perhaps it depends upon the number of alternative definitions of the same overt behavior that he can develop; perhaps certain physiological factors (limits) are also involved. However, if the deviant acts are repetitive and have a high visibility, and if there is a severe societal reaction, which, through a process of identification is incorporated as part of the "me" of the individual, the probability is greatly increased that the integration of existing roles will be disrupted and that reorganization based upon a new role or roles will occur. (The "me" in this context is simply the subjective aspect of the societal reaction.) Reorganization may be the adoption of another normal role in which the tendencies previously defined as "pathological" are given a more acceptable social expression. The other general possibility is the assumption of a deviant role, if such exists; or, more rarely, the person may organize an aberrant sect or group in which he creates a special role of his own. *When a person begins to employ his deviant behavior or a role based upon it as a means of defense, attack, or adjustment to the overt and covert problems created by the consequent societal reaction to him, his deviation is secondary.* Objective evidences of this change will be found in the symbolic appurtenances of the new role, in clothes, speech, posture, and mannerisms, which in some cases heighten social visibility, and which in some cases serve as symbolic cues to professionalization.

Role Conceptions of the Individual Must Be Reinforced by Reactions of Others

It is seldom that one deviant act will provoke a sufficiently strong societal reaction to bring about secondary deviation, unless in the process of introjection the individual imputes or projects meanings into the social situation which are not present. In this case anticipatory fears are involved. For example, in a culture where a child is taught sharp distinctions between "good" women and "bad" women, a single act of questionable morality might conceivably have a profound meaning for the girl so indulging. However, in the absence of reactions by the person's family, neighbors, or the larger community, reinforcing the tentative "bad-girl" self-definition, it is questionable whether a transition to secondary deviation would take place. It is also doubtful whether a temporary exposure to a severe punitive reaction by the community will lead a person to identify himself with a pathological role, unless, as we have said, the experience is highly traumatic. Most frequently there is a progressive reciprocal relationship between the deviation of the individual and the societal reaction, with a compounding of the societal reaction out of the minute accretions in the deviant behavior, until a point is reached where ingrouping and outgrouping between society and the deviant is manifest.[6] At this point a stigmatizing of the deviant occurs in the form of name calling, labeling, or stereotyping.

The sequence of interaction leading to secondary deviation is roughly as follows: (1) primary deviation; (2) social penalties; (3) further primary deviation; (4) stronger penalties and rejections; (5) further deviation, perhaps with hostilities and resentment beginning to focus upon those doing the penalizing; (6) crisis reached in the tolerance quotient, expressed in formal action by the community stigmatizing of the deviant; (7) strengthening of the deviant conduct as a reaction to the stigmatizing and penalties; (8) ultimate acceptance of deviant social status and efforts at adjustment on the basis of the associated role.

As an illustration of this sequence the behavior of an errant schoolboy can be cited. For one reason or another, let us say excessive energy, the schoolboy enagages in a classroom prank. He is penalized for it by the teacher. Later, due to clumsiness, he creates another disturbance and again he is reprimanded. Then, as sometimes happens, the boy is blamed for something he did not do. When the teacher uses the tag "bad boy" or "mischief maker" or other invidious terms, hostility and resentment are excited in the boy, and he may feel that he is blocked in playing the role expected of him. Thereafter, there may be a strong temptation to assume his role in the class as defined by the teacher, particularly when he discovers that there are rewards as well as penalties deriving from such a role. There is, of course, no implication here that such boys go on to become delinquents or criminals, for the mischief-maker role may later become integrated with or retrospectively rationalized as part of a role more acceptable to school authorities.[7] If such a boy continues this unacceptable role and becomes delinquent, the process must be accounted for in the light of the general theory of this volume. There must be a spreading corroboration of a sociopathic self-conception and societal reinforcement at each step in the process.

The most significant personality changes are manifest when societal definitions and their subjective counterpart become generalized. When this happens, the range of major role choices becomes narrowed to one general class.[8] This was very obvious in the case of a young girl who was the daughter of a paroled convict and who was attending a small Middle Western college. She continually argued with herself and with the author, in whom she had confided, that in reality she belonged on the "other side of the railroad tracks" and that her life could be enormously simplified by acquiescing in this verdict and living accordingly. While in her case there was a tendency to dramatize her conflicts, nevertheless there was enough societal rein-forcement of her self-conception by the treatment she received in her relationship with her father and on dates with college boys to lend it a painful reality. Once these boys took her home to the shoddy dwelling in a slum area where she lived with her father, who was often in a drunken condition, they abruptly stopped seeing her again or else became sexually presumptive.

Notes

1. Shaw, C., *The Natural History of a Delinquent Career*, Chicago, 1941, pp. 75–76. Quoted by permission of the University of Chicago Press, Chicago.
2. Brown, L. Guy, *Social Pathology*, 1942, pp. 44–45.
3. Allport, G., *Personality, A Psychological Interpretation*, 1947, p. 57.
4. Slavson, S. R., *An Introduction to Group Psychotherapy*, 1943, pp. 10, 229*ff*.
5. Murphy, G., *Personality*, 1947, p. 482.
6. Mead, G., "The Psychology of Punitive Justice," *American Journal of Sociology*, 23 March, 1918, pp. 577–602.
7. Evidence for fixed or inevitable sequences from predelinquency to crime is absent. Sutherland, E. H., *Principles of Criminology*, 1939, 4th ed., p. 202.
8. Sutherland seems to say something of this sort in connection with the develop-ment of criminal behavior. *Ibid.*, p. 86.

15 / Career Deviance

HOWARD S. BECKER

One of the most crucial steps in the process of building a stable pattern of deviant behavior is likely to be the experience of being caught and publicly labeled as a deviant. Whether a person takes this step or not depends not so much on what he does as on what other people do, on whether or not they enforce the rule he has violated. . . . First of all, even though no one else discovers the nonconformity or enforces the rules against it, the individual who has committed the impropriety may himself act as an enforcer. He may brand himself as deviant because of what he has done and punish himself in one way or another for his behavior. This is not always or necessarily the case, but may occur. Second, there may be cases like those described by psychoanalysts in which the individual really wants to get caught and perpetrates his deviant act in such a way that it is almost sure he will be.

In any case, being caught and branded as deviant has important consequences for one's further social participation and self-image. The most important consequence is a drastic change in the individual's public identity. Committing the improper act and being publicly caught at it place him in a new status. He has been revealed as a different kind of person from the kind he was supposed to be. He is labeled a "fairy," "dope fiend," "nut" or "lunatic," and treated accordingly.

In analyzing the consequences of assuming a deviant identity let us make use of Hughes' distinction between master and auxiliary status traits.[1] Hughes notes that most statuses have one key trait which serves to distinguish those who belong from those who do not. Thus the doctor, whatever else he may be, is a person who has a certificate stating that he has fulfilled certain requirements and is licensed to practice medicine; this is the master trait. As Hughes points out, in our society a doctor is also informally expected to have a number of auxiliary traits: most people expect him to be upper middle class, white, male, and Protestant. When he is not there is a sense that he has in some way failed to fill the bill. Similarly, though skin color is the master status trait determining who is Negro and who is white, Negroes are informally expected to have certain status traits and not to have others; people are surprised and find it anomalous if a Negro turns out to be a doctor or a college professor. People often have the master status trait but lack some of the auxiliary, informally expected characteristics; for example, one may be a doctor but be female or Negro.

Hughes deals with this phenomenon in regard to statuses that are well thought of, desired and desirable (noting that one may have the formal qualifications for entry into a status but be denied full entry because of lack of the proper auxiliary traits), but the same process occurs in the case of deviant statuses. Possession of one deviant trait may have a generalized symbolic value, so that people automatically assume that its bearer possesses other undesirable traits allegedly associated with it.

To be labeled a criminal one need only commit a single criminal offense, and this is all the term formally refers to. Yet the word carries a number of connotations specifying auxiliary traits characteristic of anyone bearing the label. A man who has been convicted of house-breaking and thereby labeled criminal is presumed to be a person likely to break into other houses; the police, in rouding up known offenders for investigation after a crime has been committed, operate on this premise. Further, he is considered likely to commit other kinds of crimes as well, because he has shown himself to be a person without "respect for the law." Thus, apprehension for one deviant act exposes a person to the likelihood that he will be regarded as deviant or undesirable in other respects.

There is one other element in Hughes' analysis we can borrow with profit: the distinction between master and subordinate statuses.[2] Some statuses, in our society as in others, override all other statuses and have a certain priority. Race is one of these. Membership in the Negro race, as socially defined, will override most other status considerations in most other situations; the fact that one is a physician or middle-class or female will not protect one from being treated as a Negro first and any of these other things second. The status of deviant (depending on the kind of deviance) is this kind of master status. One receives the status as a result of breaking a rule, and the identification proves to be more important than most others. One will be identified as a deviant first, before other identifications are made. The question is raised: "What kind of person would break such an important rule?" And the answer is given: "One who is different from the rest of us, who cannot or will not act as a moral human being and therefore might break other important rules." The deviant identification becomes the controlling one.

Treating a person as though he were generally rather than specifically deviant produces a self-fulfilling prophecy. It sets in motion several mechanisms which conspire to shape the person in the image people have of him.[3] In the first place, one tends to be cut off, after being identified as deviant, from participation in more conventional groups, even though the specific consequences of the particular deviant activity might never of themselves have caused the isolation had there not also been the public knowledge and reaction to it. For example, being a homosexual may not affect one's ability to do office work, but to be known as a homosexual in an office may make it impossible to continue working there. Similarly, though the effects of opiate drugs may not impair one's working ability, to be known as an addict will probably lead to losing one's job. In such cases, the individual finds it difficult to conform to other rules which he had no intention or desire to break, and perforce finds himself deviant in these areas as well. The homosexual who is deprived of a "respectable" job by the discovery of his deviance may drift into unconventional, marginal occupations where it does not make so much difference. The drug addict finds himself forced into other illegitimate kinds of activity, such as robbery and theft, by the refusal of respectable employers to have him around.

When the deviant is caught, he is treated in accordance with the popular diagnosis of why he is that way, and the treatment itself may likewise produce increasing deviance. The drug addict, popularly considered to be a weak-willed individual who cannot forego the indecent pleasures afforded him by opiates, is treated repressively. He is forbidden to use drugs. Since he cannot get drugs legally, he must get them illegally. This forces the market underground and pushes the price of drugs up far beyond the current legitimate market price into a bracket that few can afford on an ordinary salary. Hence the treatment of the addict's deviance places him in a position where it will probably be necessary to resort to deceit and crime in order to support his habit.[4] The behavior is a consequence of the public reaction to the deviance rather than a consequence of the inherent qualities of the deviant act.

Notes

1. Everett C. Hughes, "Dilemmas and Contradictions of Status," *American Journal of Sociology*, L (March, 1945), 353–359.

2. *Ibid.*

3. See Marsh Ray, "The Cycle of Abstinence and Relapse Among Heroin Addicts," *Social Problems*, 9 (Fall, 1961), 132–140.

4. See *Drug Addiction: Crime or Disease?* Interim and Final Reports of the Joint Committee of the American Bar Association and the American Medical Association on Narcotic Drugs (Bloomington, Indiana: Indiana University Press, 1961).

Part 3 / Becoming Deviant

In part one I introduced a general concern for the way deviant categories arise and the way violators of categories may be reacted to. In part two I explored some of the major theories and perspectives that serve to explain why actors may commit deviant acts. In this section I will deal more systematically with reactions that may bring about early stages of deviant careers—careers which may ultimately become subject to institutional control and regulation (part four).

In the general introduction, I made a distinction between the initiation of the labeling ceremony in a private domain and in the public domain. A wife, for example, may try to accommodate herself to her husband's increasingly violent behavior. If she is successful, the deviance will remain primarily a matter of private knowledge, regulation, and management—although the wife herself may consider her husband to be deviant. If, on the other hand, the wife's accommodative strategies fail, she may find it necessary to bring in third parties (e.g., social control agents like the police) to regulate her husband's behavior. Not only have the wife's "tolerance limits" been exceeded, in this case, but behavior which had been managed in the private setting now becomes subject to institutional control. And the husband may be typed and processed as a mental patient.

The selections which follow explore the ways in which accommodative strategies operate, particularly those involved in the initial stages of deviance. Arnold Birenbaum, in "On Managing a Courtesy Stigma," describes the situation of possessing a "courtesy stigma," defined as being "regarded by others as having a spoiled identity because [they] share a web of affiliation with the stigmatized." Birenbaum focuses on mothers of the mentally retarded, especially in terms of the adjustments that have to be made in relation to the family, friends, and the community. For example, once family members become aware of the retardation, they usually visit their friends less frequently. Of particular interest, too, is the observation of what may happen to the retardate as he or she moves into adolescence and adulthood. Up to this time, the community has appeared to support the family's attempt to achieve normal parenthood; however, in later years, because the retardate lacks clear-cut social and occupational roles, community members "no longer confirm the normal-appearing character of the family." The problems of adjustment confronting the family may become so severe that members may be forced to institutionalize the retardate. If this happens, not only have the family's accommodative strategies failed, but the retardate becomes subject to institutional processing as a mental patient—and may well be on the road to becoming a career deviant, at least in the institutional sense. Birenbaum's research thus offers a rather clear pattern: Accommodative strategies may be successful only at certain stages in the life of the mental retardate. The success of specific attempts at accommodation depends, moreover, on the community's perception of the appropriate role for the retardate at particular periods in his or her life. As Birenbaum states succinctly, "In the case of all socially assigned identities, they may be regarded as having both a constructed and a precarious nature."

"The Adjustment of the Family to the Crisis of Alcoholism" by Joan K. Jackson provides an excellent account of how family members, particularly wives, try to adjust to the husband's alcoholism. Jackson's article provides a fruitful examination of how the accommodative process actually works. A wife may at first deny that a drinking problem exists by rationalizing it away, and she may be successful in her attempts. However, it may happen that not only does the drinking become progressively worse, but a family crisis develops. The wife may then decide that there is no real hope for the marriage and leave. Jackson maintains that even though many wives do leave their husbands, they frequently return; their return is often prompted by an increased understanding of alcoholism and by the need to lessen their feelings of guilt at leaving a sick man. When a wife returns, she will attempt to reorganize the family, while still relying upon accommodative strategies as necessary.

"The Psychological Meaning of Mental Illness in the Family" by Marion Radke Yarrow, Charlotte Green Schwartz, Harriet S. Murphy, and Leila Calhoun Deasy, offers a vivid description of how behavior that is managed initially in a private setting ultimately becomes the object of institutional control. The case of the thirty-five-year-old cabdriver serves as an excellent illustration of the process. The husband began to act bizarrely, and the wife tried, in various ways, to adjust to his behavior. She sought, in addition, to explain to herself—and to others—what might have motivated or produced the changes (job difficulties, for instance). As his behavior became more violent, however, the wife found it necessary to bring in agents of social control.

The moment the husband became the object of institutional process-ing marked the beginning of an involuntary, or institutional, career.

It should be noted that as family members seek to adjust to the increasingly maladaptive behavior of a relative, they frequently dis-play a reluctance to impute pathology to him or her. The wife's initial refusal to characterize her husband as mentally ill illustrates this point. A similar response was evident in the studies by Birenbaum and Jackson. Most of us would find it difficult to admit to ourselves and others that we are living with "weirdos" or "deviants," or that we, in some way, may have contributed to the deviance.

Edwin M. Lemert's work, "Paranoia and the Dynamics of Exclu-sion," also provides some insight into the way in which behavior that occurs in a private domain is reacted to by others. The focus is on an institutional setting and not the family. The research not only pro-vides a concrete illustration of how people may respond to perceived deviants; it illustrates how a sequence of negative interaction (part two) may actually instill feelings of paranoia. The humming of the tune "Dragnet" when the "institutional deviant" approached offers an excellent example of this. Lemert argues that interactional pro-cesses like this only served to produce a gradual estrangement be-tween the involved parties. He does not imply that the initial "para-noid" behavior may have been produced by the negative reactions— it is clear that it may have developed out of some psychopathology— but he suggests that the reactions of others played a major role in exacer-bating the subject's feelings of paranoia. In this regard, Lemert con-tends that the notion of a "paranoid pseudocommunity" does not seem to apply. This is apparent from the subject's observations and feelings that certain members were actually conspiring against him—feelings that were supported in terms of the data. The subject thus appeared to have a keen grasp of social reality. The article, it should be noted, also provides a useful alternative to explaining how *selected* cases of paranoia may arise. In this situation it appears that a personal crisis, when compounded by a sequence of negative interac-tion, can produce paranoia.

The research by Darrell J. Steffensmeier and Robert M. Terry in "Deviance and Respectability: An Observational Study of Reactions to Shoplifting" offers an interesting perspective on the selections discussed thus far. Their investigation specifically examines the ex-tent to which selected variables affect the probability that one cus-tomer will report another for shoplifting. The major finding concerns the type of interaction that takes place between the audience and the actor. The researchers maintain that reactions are not based solely upon the violation of a deviant category (e.g., laws against shoplifting). Rather, the demand for enforcement is frequently a function of who the actor is. Hippie shoplifters, in particular, were more likely than others to be reported to authorities for the *same* offense. This special vulnerability of selected actors to institutional processing has been commented upon previously (e.g., in my discussion in part two of conflict theory), and it will be given major focus in the next section.

16 / On Managing a Courtesy Stigma

ARNOLD BIRENBAUM

People who bear a courtesy stigma—those regarded by others as having a spoiled identity because they share a web of affiliation with the stigmatized (Goffman, 1963:30)—are in an ambiguous situation in society. They are "normal" yet "different." Their normality is obvious in their performance of conventional social roles; their differentness is occasionally manifested by their association with the stigmatized during encounters with normals, from conversations that barely skirt certain topics or clumsily touch upon these sensitive subjects. Since their stigma is affiliational and not physical, it is relatively easy for them to manage information about themselves. Despite the occasional revelation of differentness, many people who bear a courtesy stigma usually proffer an image of normality without any apparent effort to dissemble, and this image is ordinarily confirmed by others in interaction.

Courtesy stigmas abound in American society: There are friends or relatives of those publicly identified as radicals, homosexuals, criminals, or mental patients; parents of handicapped children or children of divorced or handicapped parents; and, finally, friends or lovers of members of pariah groups in society, as "nigger lovers," who become branded as not fully competent. These three kinds of courtesy stigma result from affiliations with those regarded as having biographical, physical, or tribal identities that are discrepant between the way they appear and the way they are expected to be (Goffman, 1963:4). For the actor with a courtesy stigma, his spoiled identity is *always* biographical in nature, being based on his affiliations with the fully stigmatized.

Some who bear a courtesy stigma do not attempt to convey a normal-appearing image, but seek to demonstrate through their actions and attitudes the extent to which they can accept those with spoiled identities and consequently lose their capacity to be regarded as "normal" by members of the conventional social order (Goffman, 1963:30). In contrast, others seek to erase all information about their affiliation with the stigmatized from the knowledge others acquire about them, thereby seeking to convey the impression of being unsoiled (Goffman, 1963:31).

Thus, there appear to be at least three types of adaptation possible for those with courtesy stigmas. Actors may move from one to another of these adaptations at different points in their careers, depending on the kinds of resources they have available to convey different impressions. It is not my purpose here, however, to examine the conditions under which one or another stance is chosen, but to show, on the level of interaction, how some actors with courtesy stigmas manage to achieve a "normal-appearing round of life."

The person successful in this adaptation, it will be demonstrated, seeks a careful balance between the world of the stigmatized and the world of the normal. To some extent this balance is predicated on the person's participation in the social organizations and culture of the world surrounding a particular stigma (Birenbaum, 1969). The orderliness found in this culture creates a useful parallel of conventionality from which one can convey impressions of managing an intolerable situation, thereby helping to reduce the now unpredictable nature of the conventional social order. Moreover, when accepting the primacy of conventional social roles, those with courtesy stigmas assiduously avoid overinvolvement in the world of the stigmatized, thereby minimizing the extent to which normals will regard them as deviant, even in the presence of stigmatized individuals.

The courtesy stigma is conceived here as a situationally induced social construct rather than a constant attribute of the person. It results from a failure of two or more actors, both the discreditable ones and the conventional, to establish shared definitions of the situation which would avoid the discrediting of the person with an immediate affiliation with a stigmatized person. Therefore, each encounter can result either in the renewed construction of the courtesy stigma or an avoidance of it. Moreover, the adaptation designed as "a normal-appearing round of life" may quite plausibly be the modal type for persons who bear a courtesy stigma, for it allows actors to take into account and use the most salient characteristic of the courtesy stigma—its situational variability.

Yet even when actors are aware of this property, the shared definitions created that do *not* generate stigma often include a mutual recognition of the differentness of the discreditable actor's obligations to the fully stigmatized. At the same time, these obligations are never regarded overtly by either party as a basis for the relationship between the person with the courtesy stigma and the conventional actor. Such relationships thrive on tactful inattention, strictly contrived to appear as if the objective fact of the courtesy stigma is of no major subjective importance. Alternatively, whether this claim is successfully upheld depends on the capacity of the discreditable actor to avoid situations in which his obligations to the fully stigmatized will become obtrusive. When their differentness becomes activated in everyday life, validation by others of the normal-appearing round of life will be markedly less. Under these conditions it is likely that a person with a courtesy stigma will either have to embrace the stigmatized or seek to dissociate himself from this affiliation.

Mothers of mentally retarded children provide an outstanding example of persons with courtesy stigmas who seek to maintain a normal-appearing round of life. Their actions and attitudes bring others in their communities to recognize and regard them and other members of the retardate's family as conventional members of that community. The family with a retarded child in addition proffers an image of conventionality so great that the family members are able to regard the family's continuity as a greater priority than the welfare of the retarded child. Thus, the concept "a normal-appearing round of life" denotes both the life style to which mothers aspire and the means by which members of the conventional social order are able to validate the conventional character of the family.

I studied the adaptations of mothers of mentally retarded children through interviews with 103 women, the majority of whose children were moderately retarded, and almost all of whom lived at home. The schedule was concerned with (1) how mothers learned their children were retarded; (2) their perspective on the child; (3) the extent of interaction with similarly situated others; (4) the condition of the child; and (5) background characteristics of the mother and the family. Respondents were drawn randomly from the membership lists of an agency, located in a large city, that was devoted to providing services for mentally retarded children, adolescents, and adults. The socioeconomic status of the majority of the women interviewed could be considered either lower middle class or working class. All interviews were conducted at the offices of the agency, and only one interview was terminated before completion, with much of the needed information in that case collected at a later time. About 10 per cent of the women approached for an interview refused to take part in the study (Birenbaum, 1968).

RELATIONS WITH FRIENDS AND RELATIVES

The effects of the presence of a mentally retarded child on the family's relations with others in the community are well documented in the literature. In their survey of 50 families of retarded children, Schonell and Watts report that "in fifty per cent of the cases, visits by the family to the houses of other people were curtailed." "Twenty-one per cent of the sample reported curtailment of the range of people invited to their homes. Twenty-six per cent reported self-imposed limits to vacation plans." Finally, "twenty-eight per cent moved to different residential areas because of the child . . ." (Schonell and Watts, 1956:217). The movement was to urban areas where facilities could be found to care for the child.

In a study of fifty families of mongoloid children, Elizabeth Kramm (1963:39) reports that only "twenty-two families said that their social activities had not been affected by having the child in the home; twelve said that theirs had been severely restricted; and sixteen that theirs had been restricted to some extent. Fourteen families felt that some old friends were less cordial than formerly."

Kramm (1963:16) also demonstrates the extent to which the parents are under stress in anticipation of, and during, community contacts: "The crisis-meeting resources of the parents were put to their hardest test when they had to explain for the first time to their families, neighbors, and friends that the child was mongoloid or was retarded. Many couples found it hard to tell members of their own family; many more found it even harder to tell neighbors and friends."

The stress of interaction with others in the community continues after the period in which the parents are first informed about the child's condition (Kramm, 1963:17): "Twenty-seven still found it hard to talk to any but very close neighbors and sixteen others still avoided neighborhood contacts. Several remarked that when they took their child on walks, the neighbors seemed so obviously uncomfortable in the child's presence that they felt undertain whether or not to explain."

Similarly, almost half the sample saw their friends less frequently after they found out the child was mentally retarded (Birenbaum, 1968:102). Furthermore, over one-third of the respondents considered relations with friends to have changed since learning that their children were mentally retarded, and most of them felt farther apart from their friends.

Despite these alterations in contact with others in the community, over three-fourths of the respondents considered their family life to be as good as that of parents of normal children. Mothers were asked to compare their family life—the amount of satisfaction they received from their husbands and children—with that of families with normal children whom they knew, and to state whether they thought they were better off, worse off, or about the same. Fifty-six per cent said their family life was the same as that of families with normal children. The remainder were equally divided between those who felt they were better off and those who felt they were worse off; 22 per cent were in each category.

Similarly, mothers were asked how their particular situation compared with that of other families with retarded children. Interestingly, over 55 per cent said they were better off than the comparison group. Only 25 per cent thought they were on the same level, and about 6 per cent said they were less well off. About 11 per cent did not know how they stood compared with other families with retarded children.

It is clear from this brief discussion that many more questions are raised by these findings than are answered. It seems important to examine not self-regard or the statistical distribution of altered relationships with others in the community, but their new and ongoing meanings to the actors, that is, the process of interaction by which some mothers of retarded children are able to regard themselves as more or less conventional members of the community.

To the extent that mothers of retardates are able to perform roles similar to those performed by mothers of normal children, the consequences of the courtesy stigma they bear are manageable. That is, what is regarded by community members as conventional activity is typically an extension of the generic role of mothering. Alternatively, the respondents eschewed activities that went beyond these boundaries. Yet when others in the community no longer produced validation for this strategy, it was not abandoned but continuously practiced. For it can be argued that the more mothers of retarded children conform to this model of conventional motherhood, the more difficult it becomes, especially in the child's later years, to maintain him in the community. More generally, all persons with courtesy stigmas who seek to convey and maintain an image of conventionality face the possibility, at one time or another, that their acceptance is something they and conventional actors construct for the moment. Most significantly for the study of courtesy stigmas, such failures to maintain conventional appearances, despite or as a result of conformity, are also strategic ways of locating and confirming the social components of successful management of this particular adaptation.

VALIDATION OF THE NORMAL-APPEARING ROUND OF LIFE

Mothers felt that relationships with friends had not changed, or they felt closer to friends, on receiving what they described as "consideration." Considerate individuals did not indicate by their actions that the family was being re-evaluated as a result of having a retarded child. Yet to the extent that such a situation was reached, mothers were unable or unwilling to verbalize about something that was, in their evaluation, continuing as in the past. The mother's recognition of the sources of stability in the relationship would be an obvious admission of change, an introduction of special concern from their friends focusing on the nonreciprocal nature of their continuing friendship.

"Consideration," then, is inferred as a polite recognition and acceptance of the plight of the family with the disabled child. It means that the situation will never be spoken about unless brought up in conversation by the parents of the retarded child. Furthermore, comparisons between normal and retarded children will be carefully avoided. On a behavioral level it means that all children will be treated equally, even if this means regarding a retarded child as a normal one. Finally and most importantly, it means that friends will anticipate, and thereby avoid, any situations that might result in awkwardness and embarrassment for both the family with the retarded child and the friends of the family.

The most revealing cases of "consideration" appear in its absence. Examining the tales told about the gaffes committed by ex-friends of the family reveals the unstated meaning of the mother's operational code of everyday interaction with community members. These stories are also a means for the mother to caution against, and remove herself from, situations that are stigma-producing. In this way situational failures protect the mother against similar encounters, thereby increasing the validity of this adaptation for her.

Mothers often found that their old friends and neighbors responded to the retarded child in ways they considered inappropriate. A frequent complaint was that friends and neighbors were condescending. Respondents terminated relationships with friends who acted in this manner. The relationships were characterized by a "drifting apart."

> Respondent: . . . we're different types. You know we think differently—the friends that I had before. We think differently, and don't like anybody telling me what to do with my child.
>
> Interviewer: Did they tell you what to do?
>
> Respondent: Well, I know one friend called up. I hadn't spoken to her in a long time. And I told her T. [the retardate] was going to school. And she said, "Oh, he goes all day?" And then she asked how my other (normal) son was—how's R. Like you know, she expected me to say, oh—you know, he's the same as T. So I just point out to her how T. has progressed and everything, you know. And she just tells me how her children are. That's it. Because I know with R.—how is R.? And my son R. was a late talker. And why don't you take him here? And he's not walking right. And he's not doing this. So I just tell them [laughter] to leave me alone.

Another mother considered relations to be strained when her friend did not reprimand both her own child and the retardate for misbehavior, but singled out the retardate:

> Interviewer: Do you see your friends who have retarded children more, less, or about the same as you do your other friends?
> Respondent: Oh, much less. Because I just want to tell you that the reason is because you're not making friends with somebody because of your son. You're making it because you get along with them. Ah, and you just—and usually you get along. I find if two—if any of my friends and I are very close, we sort of think along the same lines. And when our children are in contact with one—they play, you know, there's some sort of democratic way of playing. You know, it's not like, F. [the retardate], you did that. You know, I have a few—one girlfriend that I have (I like her very much), she's apt to do that . . . and there's a strained relationship just in there. Because she feels her children are above everyone else. I don't mean academically, even behavior-wise. Where my other friends will say, look, both of you stop it. You know, instead of singling one out. Now stop it, we don't want to hear any more. You know.

The presence of a retarded child also affected reciprocal visiting. Friends continued to visit the family, but visits to friends' houses were less frequent than in the past. Less awkwardness and embarrassment ensued when mothers could control the environment provided by their own homes. Some respondents said they found it more comfortable to receive guests in their home than to visit other people's houses, because they were afraid that the retarded child might cause damage to a friend's home.

The retarded child had a lesser impact on relations with relatives than on relations with friends. Friendship ties are likely to be based on residential propinquity and similarities in social identity. Consequently they are more easily disrupted by changes in social identity than are relations with relatives. Particularistic ties to relatives do not have to be reaffirmed or earned through the maintenance of similar styles of life. Age-graded expectations for members of the same family make similarities of life style an inappropriate means of affirming kinship ties.

While approximately 50 per cent of the respondents said they saw their friends less frequently than before they learned that their children were retarded, only 24 per cent said they saw their relatives less than before. Respondents felt that relationships with relatives had not changed, or they felt closer to them when they received "consideration" from their families. Those who felt farther apart from relatives since finding out about the child's condition attributed this state to the awkwardness and embarrassment demonstrated by relatives in the presence of family members. In general, however, mothers found relatives to be supportive, especially when the rules of "consideration" were observed.

> . . . there's never been any open discussion, let's put it that way. Everything is accepted as is, and everything—all conversation—proceeds normally. There is never any. . . . Naturally, he—when he does visit, he runs to the television set or whatever; and he has to be told what he should and shouldn't do. But other than that, there's no problem.

The presence of the retarded child always necessitates a differential response to the family. Therefore, relations with friends and relatives are always somewhat altered, even when they are continued. Mothers discontinued relationships with others who did not show "consideration." Still, those relationships that were maintained were a major source of conventional identity, while those that were avoided and/or terminated were stigma-producing. Thus, through a selection process, those relationships that can be "normalized" (Davis, 1964:132) validate the mother's conception of her own normality.

In this process, some bases for interaction are eliminated because they could convey stigma. For example, common features of motherhood that were previously shared, such as discussions of their children's successes in school, were avoided to prevent the mother of a retarded child from feeling she was being placed at a disadvantage. Condescension, described earlier, was regarded as producing stigma. Friends were also less likely to ask mothers of retarded children to do favors for them, while most respondents regarded friends and relatives as helpful. Despite, or perhaps because of, these nonreciprocal patterns of interaction, mothers regarded their friendships with others as more or less the same as before finding out about their child's condition.

RELATIONS WITH OTHER PARENTS OF RETARDED CHILDREN

Mothers of retarded children are often dependent on specialized facilities for school, diagnostic, recreational, and other services. Within the confines of these agencies, and at voluntary associations of those similarly situated, they come into contact with many other parents. One would expect such establishments to be natural breeding grounds for friendships, given parents' common interests and frequent disruption of prior friendship patterns.

While relationships with friends and relatives altered, in most instances, they continued. Few respondents established close ties with other mothers of retarded children. Friendships with others who are stigmatized do not support a normal-appearing round of life, since they can be misinterpreted by others as an identification with one's fate. In general, mothers regarded their participation in the organized world of mental retardation to be specifically for the child.

Most members of the sample said they made friends with other mothers of retarded children, but few found such relationships as intimate or rewarding as relationships with other friends. Sociability was focused around the retarded children through various organizations at which mothers came into contact. Mothers sought knowledge, advice, and occasionally sympathy from each other in generally collegial friendships. (Collegial relations may be a feature of all roles that are expressively rather than instrumentally oriented. Hence collegial relations will be characteristic of interactions between mothers of children the same age who frequent the same establishments such as parks, supermarkets, and pediatrician waiting rooms. Where such relationships exist, role performance is evaluated by a consensus among the similarly situated, rather than by rationalized criteria (McHugh, 1966).)

Few of the respondents said they met with other mothers of retardates on occasions when their retarded children were not present:

Interviewer: Since you found out your son is retarded, have you made any friends with other mothers of retarded children?
Respondent: Not social friends. Not to go out socially. No. But on the telephone. To keep in tab with what's going on. I'd say four, four girls.
Interviewer: You don't see them socially at all?
Respondent: No.
Interviewer: You never get together with your kid and their children?
Respondent: No, no.
Interviewer: Do you feel as close to these women as you do to your other friends?
Respondent: No.

Interaction among mothers of retarded children was often limited to discussions of their children's progress, or to their efforts to gain access to programs:

Interviewer: Since you found your child is retarded, have you made any friends with other parents of retarded children?

Respondent: Well, not to any great extent. Just that this one party who lives in the house approached me, and mentioned how well she thought my son was doing. And we've never gone out of our way to meet each other. If I would see her in the elevator or the laundry room, we'd talk about each other's children and that's about it. I know her daughter is on the waiting list at the Shield [of David] and I asked her if she heard anything. And that's about as far as it goes.

Respondents occasionally arranged to meet in order to provide their children with entertainment and opportunities to play together:

Interviewer: Since you found out your son is retarded, have you made any friends with other parents of retarded children?

Respondent: Are you talking about personal friends now?

Interviewer: Then what do you classify as other parents of retarded children?

Respondent: Oh, well, friends of E.'s that we have gotten together [with].

Interviewer: Do you feel as close to these friends of E.'s as you do to your other friends?

Respondent: No, no. Just one thing in common: when—when we do get together, that the children should have a good time, or what they're going to do, or—basically, it's all for the young adults.

Interviewer: Do you ever see these other parents when you don't have E. with you?

Respondent: It depends upon the occasion, which is also connected with the children.

Interviewer: I mean, aside from formal occasions like dinners and things like that.

Respondent: Not really, no. No.

Interviewer: You don't go to the movies, let's say?

Respondent: No, not really.

By becoming active in the organized field of mental retardation, mothers were able to lead a normal-appearing round of life. Yet, too strong an involvement in this world would threaten such a life style by accentuating the mother's identity as mother of a retarded child at the expense of her identity in the conventional social order. The mother must balance these two identities in relationships within the immediate family as well as with others in the community. Indeed, it is the maintenance of routine family life, despite the presence of a retarded child, that provides a claim to conventionality for the mother.

One way this claim is affirmed is through an ordering of priorities in the family so that the integrity of this group as a member of the community is never called into question.

FAMILY DECISIONS AND THE RETARDED CHILD

Conventional families in contemporary American society generally have available a wide range of community-sponsored facilities such as schools, which perform much of the task of socializing children. Parents of "normal" children channel their familial resources to provide for the scarce facilities important for status placement, such as college, that are not made available to all members of the community. Community-sponsored facilities for socialization cannot be taken for granted in the case of a retarded child, however. For example, there is no uniformity from one locale to another as to the extent, quality, or cost of special educational programs for retardates. When financial resources are limited, the capacity of a retardate's family to meet all the needs of its members is called into question. Respondents spoke of the need of their normal children to be "self-made men."

In an everyday way, the presence of a retarded child also raises problems for the family in its relations to the conventional families in the community. Moments of strain are created by the retardate's presence at encounters with normals, or when he is at play with other children. Appropriate parental behavior in situations where normal children are concerned is not always applicable where a retarded child is involved. Active intervention by a parent to protect his child in a squabble among youngsters is usually inappropriate, for example, yet the retardate may be incapable of asserting his claims in a group of children. Furthermore, it is impossible for parents to segregate their activities on behalf of the retardate from their other activities within the confines of the nuclear family. Mothers are frequently confronted with the need to make decisions for the family where the well-being or future situation of the retarded child is a major consideration.

As a means of locating the respondents' commitment to their retarded children as opposed to other family commitments, the women were presented with six plausible dilemmas facing the parents of a retarded child and asked to choose between two outcomes, one of which favors the mentally retarded child. Becker (1960) has introduced the concept of "commitment" in a discussion of how careers differ for different actors. A person who has made a commitment is said to have taken an action, which may or may not be directly related to the decision in question, that affects his actions in other spheres of life. The concept of commitment may be useful in linking personal decision-making and socially structured determinants. Two of the questions were related to decisions that might alter the mothers' relations with others in the community, such as neighbors, friends, and fellow church members. The other four questions concerned the extent to which the mother would forsake the economic interests of the family and her normal children for the retarded child. These questions touched on two traditional areas of interest for students of the family: (1) upward mobility and (2) status placement of the children. In order to make the situations appear hypothetical, questions were phrased so that respondents were supposedly giving advice to another set of parents. However, respondents considered the dilemmas as relevant to themselves and often claimed that they had faced a similar decision, or that they expected such a problem to arise in the future. A majority of respondents selected answers to each of the questions that supported a normal-appearing round of life for the family.

Mothers were asked what they would do if a playmate made fun of the retarded child. Fifty-six per cent of the sample said they would intervene in behalf of the retardate by talking to the child doing the teasing or to his parents. Thirty per cent said they would do nothing in such a situation, and over 15 per cent said they would comfort the retarded child or tell him to stop playing with the one who made fun of him.

Respondents were asked whether they thought the child should be sent to a program recommended by a professional in the field of retardation but run by a religious organization not of the family's faith, knowing that some compulsory religious instruction would be included. About 85 per cent of the sample said they would send the retarded child to such a program; the most common explanation offered was that any good program is worth the possible confusion that another religion would cause for the child or family. Furthermore, respondents often claimed that religious training would have little impact on a retarded child. In contrast, when respondents were asked occasionally during an interview if they would send a normal child to a college run by a religious organization not of their faith, not one mother considered this course of action appropriate (Birenbaum, 1968:119).

Members of the sample were asked whether they felt that their husbands should hire mentally retarded persons to fill menial jobs such as sweeper and dishwasher. They were informed that retardates could not perform these tasks as efficiently and quickly as normal persons. Thus they were warned that the retarded person might be a minor economic liability to the husband's business. Yet over 85 per cent of the women believed that retardates should be hired for these jobs. About half of those who advocated this solution said it should be done in order to give the mentally retarded adult a chance to work. Over one-third of those who would hire retarded employees said that the mentally retarded person would be trained for the job. (It is interesting to note that mothers employed the ideology of professionals to support their decisions in favor of hiring the mentally retarded. Over one-third claimed that vocational training is effective with the mentally retarded.) About 15 per cent suggested that the mentally retarded person would be more reliable than the normal one for this kind of job, since the retardate would appreciate the opportunity to work and would not be easily distracted.

Another situation had the parents invited to dinner by a business client of the husband. When they were about to leave, the retarded child became ill with an upset stomach. Respondents were asked whether they should go to the engagement or remain at home caring for the child. Over 60 per cent of the sample said they would keep the engagement, but most of these women qualified their answers by suggesting they would go only if a capable babysitter were caring for the child, or if the upset stomach were not severe. They then said they would follow these procedures with any child. Seven women said they would send their husbands and stay home with the child.

The availability of full-time day programs for retarded children was an important consideration if respondents had to decide whether to relocate the family. In a few cases cited by professionals in the field of mental retardation, families were known to have moved to neighboring counties in order to gain access to day programs. Therefore, the problem of maintaining or improving the economic position of the family at the expense of the retarded child was difficult for mothers to solve.

Mothers were presented with a dilemma in which the retarded child was in a special program where he was doing very well when the husband received a good job offer for which he had been hoping in another part of the country without such a program. When asked whether the offer should be accepted, over half the sample said the family should stay where the program was or go only if *some kind* of program existed for the retarded child. An additional 15 per cent of the sample suggested that the family should go, since a program could always be started by mothers of the retarded. Almost 30 per cent said flatly that the family should make the move, with the most common reasons offered relating to the priority of the family's livelihood over the needs of individual members.

Finally, mothers were asked to choose between sending the retardate to an excellent program recommended by professionals or sending a normal child to college, given that funds were available for only one of these projects. Mothers of retarded children were concerned that their normal children have every opportunity other normal children have. Respondents wanted their normal children to have a good education: Over 60 per cent of those with normal children hoped to support them in college. Many women felt they had not given enough attention to their normal child because the retarded child occupied a great deal of their time and was often a great expense to them. Over 55 per cent of the respondents said they would send the normal child to college rather than send the retarded child to a recommended special program. Most respondents who favored sending the normal child to college reasoned that an education was very important to the future of the normal child, while there was no guarantee that the retarded child would derive benefits from the special program. This can be shown in the following dialogue:

> Interviewer: What if nothing could be done? If you had to choose between sending G. to a special program or sending your oldest daughter to college?
> Respondent: Then I would send my older daughter to college, if I had to choose.
> Interviewer: Why would you do that?
> Respondent: I feel, let her get the most. Because I don't know what G. is going to gain.
> Interviewer: It's kind of risky with G.?
> Respondent: That's right.

Respondents' choices in these hypothetical dilemmas illustrate the limits of the mother's commitment to her retarded child. Mothers are faced with the problem of providing activities for the retardate without disrupting the conventional domestic life of the family. When this is not possible, respondents favored solutions that would maintain the normal-appearing round of life. Thus, mothers decided in favor of the retarded child only when the costs to the family were minor. For example, they believed the retarded child should be defended if a neighbor's child made fun of him. They strongly favored sending the retarded child to a program operated by a religious organization of a different faith if this were the only available program. They considered the benefits to the child to outweigh any possible disadvantages. Furthermore, the child's participation in full-time day programs was a major component in the maintenance of a normal-appearing round of life. To this end, the majority of respondents believed the family should live in an area where programs for the retarded could be found. Similarly, they regarded the employment of adult retardates as an important part of their care.

Respondents chose against the retarded child where the capacity of the family to maintain a normal-appearing life would be threatened by a decision in the child's favor. They would not cancel a dinner engagement with the father's business client if the child was not feeling well. Finally, the education of the normal child took precedence over the education or training of the retarded child, if there was no way to provide both.

DECREASING VALIDATION OF THE NORMAL-APPEARING ROUND OF LIFE

In summary, the acquisition of a courtesy stigma, that is, becoming a mother of a mentally retarded child, is accompanied by an alteration of the mother's relation to the community. The conventional social order, which encourages the mother to use the segregated facilities that are available for permanently disabled children, does not allow her to fully retain her former social identity.

Paradoxically, while participation in the organized world of mental retardation produces a sense of stigma for the mother, it also allows her to reaffirm her membership in the conventional part of the social order. A normal-appearing round of life can be created in the community to the extent that (1) others respond to the family with "consideration," a polite fiction in which others carefully ignore the child's disability; and (2) encounters that are stigma-producing can be avoided.

Most importantly, respondents showed that they recognized the primacy of conventional family norms despite the presence of a disabled member. In this regard, they minimized the differences between their family life and that of families without retarded children, while not closely identifying themselves with other families with retarded children. In so doing, they proffered a viable adaptation to this courtesy stigma.

Alternatively, this complex of behaviors and attitudes is validated as expected performance, for it is accepted and enforced by conventional community members. Community membership is maintained when conventional families and families with a retarded child are able to overlook their specific differences in everyday life. In other words, the formal similarities of family living override the substantive differences in the attributes of the particular members.

However, the cyclical character of conventional family living is arrested in the family with a mentally retarded child. When the retardate becomes an adult, or even when he becomes an adolescent, the

194 / ARNOLD BIRENBAUM

normal-appearing definition of the family is withdrawn by conventional community members as the parents lose their capacity to emulate conventional parenthood. The unavailability of socially valid adult roles for both persons so disabled (e.g., job or marriage) and, concomitantly, for his parents (e.g., mother-in-law or grandmother) makes it difficult to maintain him in the household and community. Conventional community members are uncertain about such atypical nonperformers of full-time social roles and so no longer confirm the normal-appearing character of the family. As a result of the eventual failure of this strategy, mothers come to regard the future of the family and the child as an uncertainty. In other words, the objective certainty of the retarded child's continued dependence and very likely removal from the community to a custodial residence is in stark contrast to the normal child's increasing independence. Thus, the assumed character of the life style is called into question during the child's later years.

The career of the bearer of a courtesy stigma, then, may involve adopting different strategies at different critical points. Thus, the three strategies specified at the beginning of this article should not be considered mutually exclusive adaptations. In this way the bearer of the courtesy stigma emulates the fully stigmatized person, who also experiences cycles of affiliation and dissociation from the community and those who are similarly situated. Most important, except for total withdrawal from the community and the establishment of a new community among those similarly situated, the style of life employed depends on its being both offered for acceptance and enforced by the conventional community. As in the case of all socially assigned identities, they may be regarded as having both a constructed and a precarious nature. Paradoxically, even continued emulation of conventional life styles can be regarded by conventional actors as calling attention to the discrepancy between the conventional and those who bear a courtesy stigma, thereby endangering the very adaptation they wish to conserve.

References

Becker, H.
    1960   "Notes on the concept of commitment." American Journal of Sociology 66 (July):35–36.
Birenbaum, Arnold.
    1968   Non-Institutionalized Roles and Role Formation: A Study of Mothers of Mentally Retarded Children. Unpublished Ph.D. dissertation, Columbia University.
    1969   "Helping mothers of mentally retarded children use specialized facilities." The Family Coordinator 18 (October):379–384.

Davis, F.
   1964   "Deviance disavowal: the management of strained interaction by
          the visibly handicapped." Pp. 119–137, in Howard S. Becker (ed.),
          The Other Side. New York: Free Press.
Goffman, Erving.
   1963   Stigma: Notes on the Management of Spoiled Identity. Englewood
          Cliffs: Prentice-Hall.
Kramm, Elizabeth.
   1963   Families of Mongoloid Children. Washington: The Children's
          Bureau (No. 401).
McHugh, P.
   1966   Structured Uncertainty: The Professional Actor. Paper delivered at
          the American Sociological Society Meetings, Miami. Mimeo.
Schonell, F. J., and B. H. Watts.
   1956   "A first survey of the effects of a subnormal child on the family unit."
          American Journal of Mental Deficiency 61 (July):210–219.

17 / The Adjustment of the Family to the Crisis of Alcoholism

JOAN K. JACKSON

... Over a 3-year period, the present investigator has been an active participant in the Alcoholics Anonymous Auxiliary in Seattle. This group is composed partly of women whose husbands are or were members of Alcoholics Anonymous, and partly of women whose husbands are excessive drinkers but have never contacted Alcoholics Anonymous. At a typical meeting one-fifth would be the wives of Alcoholics Anonymous members who have been sober for some time; the husband of another fifth would have recently joined the fellowship; the remainder would be equally divided between those whose husbands were "on and off" the Alcoholics Anonymous program and those whose husbands had as yet not had any contact with Alcoholics Anonymous.

At least an hour and a half of each formal meeting of this group is taken up with a frank discussion of the current family problems of the members. As in other meetings of Alcoholics Anonymous the questions are posed by describing the situation which gives rise to the problem and the answers are a narration of the personal experiences of other wives who have had a similar problem, rather than direct advice. Verbatim shorthand notes have been taken of all discussions, at the request of the group, who also make use of the notes for the group's purposes. Informal contact has been maintained with past and present members. In the past 3 years 50 women have been members of this group.

The families represented by these women are at present in many different stages of adjustment and have passed through several stages during the past few years. The continuous contact over a prolonged period permits generalizations about processes and changes in family adjustments.

In addition, in connection with research on hospitalized alcoholics, many of their wives have been interviewed. The interviews with the hospitalized alcoholics, as well as with male members of Alcoholics Anonymous, have also provided information on family interactions.

Further information has been derived from another group of wives, not connected with Alcoholics Anonymous, and from probation officers, social workers and court officials.

The following presentation is limited insofar as it deals only with families seeking help for the alcoholism of the husband. Other families are known to have solved the problem through divorce, often without having attempted to help the alcoholic member first. Others never seek help and never separate. There were no marked differences between the two groups seeking help, one through the hospital and one through the A.A. Auxiliary. The wives of hospitalized alcoholics gave a history of the family crisis similar to that given by women in the Auxiliary.

A second limitation is that only the families of male alcoholics are dealt with. It is recognized that the findings cannot be generalized to the families of alcoholic women without further research. Due to differences between men and women in their roles in the family as well as in the pattern of drinking, it would be expected that male and female alcoholics would in some ways have a different effect on family structure and function.

A third limitation is imposed for the sake of clarity and brevity: only the accounts of the wives of their attempts to stabilize their family adjustments will be dealt with. For any complete picture, the view of the alcoholic husband would also have to be included.

It must be emphasized that this paper deals with the definitions of the family situations by the wives, rather than with the actual situation. It has been noted that frequently wife and husband do not agree on what has occurred. The degree to which the definition of the situation by the wife or husband correlates with actual behavior is a question which must be left for further research.

The families represented in this study are from the middle and lower classes. The occupations of the husbands prior to excessive drinking include small business owners, salesmen, business executives, skilled and semiskilled workers. Prior to marriage the wives have been nurses, secretaries, teachers, saleswomen, cooks, or waitresses. The economic status of the childhood families of these husbands and wives ranged from very wealthy to very poor.

Method

From the records of discussions of the Alcoholics Anonymous Auxiliary, the statements of each wife were extracted and arranged in a time sequence. Notes on informal contacts were added at the point in the sequence where they occurred. The interviews with the wives of hospitalized alcoholics were similarly treated. These working records on individual families were then examined for uniformities of behavior and for regularities in changes over time.

The similarities in the process of adjustment to an alcoholic family member are presented here as stages of variable duration. It should be stressed that only the similarities are dealt with. Although the wives have shared the patterns dealt with here, there have been marked differences in the length of time between stages, in the number of stages passed through up to the present time, and in the relative importance to the family constellation of any one type of behavior. For example, all admitted nagging, but the amount of nagging was variable.

When the report of this analysis was completed it was read before a meeting of the Auxiliary with a request for correction of any errors in fact or interpretation. Corrections could be presented either anonymously or publicly from the floor. Only one correction was suggested and has been incorporated. The investigator is convinced that her relationship with the group is such that there would be no reticence about offering corrections. Throughout her contact with this group her role has been that of one who is being taught, very similar to the role of the new member. The overall response of the group to the presentation indicated that the members individually felt that they had been portrayed accurately.

The sense of having similar problems and similar experiences is indicated also in the reactions of new members to the Auxiliary's summarization of the notes of their discussions. Copies of these summaries are given to new members, who commonly state that they find it a relief to see that their problems are far from unique and that there are methods which successfully overcome them.

Statement of the Problem

For purposes of this presentation, the family is seen as involved in a cumulative crisis. All family members behave in a manner which they hope will resolve the crisis and permit a return to stability. Each member's action is influenced by his previous personality structure, by his previous role and status in the family group, and by the history of the crisis and its effects on his personality, roles and status up to that point. Action is also influenced by the past effectiveness of that particular action as a means of social control before and during the crisis. The behavior of family members in each phase of the crisis contributes to the form which the crisis takes in the following stages and sets limits on possible behavior in subsequent stages.

Family members are influenced, in addition, by the cultural definitions of alcoholism as evidence of weakness, inadequacy, or sinfulness; by the cultural prescriptions for the roles of family members; and by the cultural values of family solidarity, sanctity, and self-sufficiency. Alcoholism in the family poses a situation defined by the culture as shameful but for the handling of which there are no pre-scriptions which are effective or which permit direct action not in conflict with other cultural prescriptions. While in crises such as illness or death the family members can draw on cultural definitions of appropriate behavior for procedures which will terminate the crisis, this is not the case with alcoholism in the family. The cultural view has been that alcoholism is shameful and should not occur. Only recently has any information been offered to guide families in their behavior toward their alcoholic member and, as yet, this information resides more in technical journals than in the media of mass communication. Thus, in facing alcoholism, the family is in an unstructured situation and must find the techniques for handling it through trial and error.

STAGES IN FAMILY ADJUSTMENT TO AN ALCOHOLIC MEMBER

The Beginning of the Marriage

At the time marriage was considered, the drinking of most of the men was within socially acceptable limits. In a few cases the men were already alcoholics but managed to hide this from their fiancées. They drank only moderately or not at all when on dates and often avoided friends and relatives who might expose their excessive drinking. The relatives and friends who were introduced to the fiancée were those who had hopes that "marriage would straighten him out" and thus said nothing about the drinking. In a small number of cases the men spoke with their fiancées of their alcoholism. The women had no conception of what alcoholism meant, other than that it involved more than the usual frequency of drinking, and they entered the marriage with little more preparation than if they had known nothing about it.

Stage 1. Incidents of excessive drinking begin and, although they are sporadic, place strains on the husband-wife interaction. In at-tempts to minimize drinking, problems in marital adjustment not related to the drinking are avoided.

Stage 2. Social isolation of the family begins as incidents of exces-sive drinking multiply. The increasing isolation magnifies the im-portance of family interactions and events. Behavior and thought become drinking-centered. Husband-wife adjustment deteriorates and tension rises. The wife begins to feel self-pity and to lose her self-confidence as her behavior fails to stabilize her husband's drinking. There is an attempt still to maintain the original family structure, which is disrupted anew with each episode of drinking, and as a result the children begin to show emotional disturbance.

Stage 3. The family gives up attempts to control the drinking and begins to behave in a manner geared to relieve tension rather than achieve long-term ends. The disturbance of the children becomes more marked. There is no longer an attempt to support the alcoholic in his roles as husband and father. The wife begins to worry about her own sanity and about her inability to make decisions or act to change the situation.

Stage 4. The wife takes over control of the family and the husband is seen as a recalcitrant child. Pity and strong protective feelings largely replace the earlier resentment and hostility. The family becomes more stable and organized in a manner to minimize the disruptive behavior of the husband. The self-confidence of the wife begins to be rebuilt.

Stage 5: The wife separates from her husband if she can resolve the problems and conflicts surrounding this action.

Stage 6: The wife and children reorganize as a family without the husband.

Stage 7: The husband achieves sobriety and the family, which had become organized around an alcoholic husband, reorganizes to include a sober father and experiences problems in reinstating him in his former roles.

Stage 1. Attempts to Deny the Problem

Usually the first experience with drinking as a problem arises in a social situation. The husband drinks in a manner which is inappropriate to the social setting and the expectations of others present. The wife feels embarrassed on the first occasion and humiliated as it occurs more frequently. After several such incidents she and her husband talk over his behavior. The husband either formulates an explanation for the episode and assures her that such behavior will not occur again, or he refuses to discuss it at all. For a time afterward he drinks appropriately and drinking seems to be a problem no longer. The wife looks back on the incidents and feels that she has exaggerated them, feels ashamed of herself for her disloyalty and for her behavior. The husband, in evaluating the incident, feels shame also and vows such episodes will not recur. As a result, both husband and wife attempt to make it up to the other and, for a time, try to play their conceptions of the ideal husband and wife roles, minimizing or avoiding other difficulties which arise in the marriage. They thus create the illusion of a "perfect" marriage.

Eventually another inappropriate drinking episode occurs and the pattern is repeated. The wife worries but takes action only in the situations in which inappropriate drinking occurs, as each long intervening period of acceptable drinking behavior convinces her that a recurrence is unlikely. As time goes on, in attempting to cope with individual episodes, she runs the gamut of possible trial and error behaviors, learning that none is permanently effective.

If she speaks to other people about her husband's drinking, she is usually assured that there is no need for concern, that her husband can control his drinking and that her fears are exaggerated. Some friends possibly admit that his drinking is too heavy and give advice on how they handled similar situations with their husbands. These friends convince her that her problem will be solved as soon as she hits upon the right formula for dealing with her husband's drinking.

During this stage the husband-wife interaction is in no way "abnormal." In a society in which a large proportion of the men drink, most wives have at some time had occasion to be concerned, even though only briefly, with an episode of drinking which they considered inappropriate (7). In a society in which the status of the family depends on that of the husband, the wife feels threatened by any behavior on his part which might lower it. Inappropriate drinking is regarded by her as a threat to the family's reputation and standing in the community. The wife attempts to exert control and often finds herself blocked by the sacredness of drinking behavior to men in America. Drinking is a private matter and not any business of the wife's. On the whole, a man reacts to his wife's suggestion that he has not adequately controlled his drinking with resentment, rebelliousness, and a display of emotion which makes rational discussion difficult. The type of husband-wife interaction outlined in this stage has occurred in many American families in which the husband never became an excessive drinker.

Stage 2. Attempts to Eliminate the Problems

Stage 2 begins when the family experiences social isolation because of the husband's drinking. Invitations to the homes of friends become less frequent. When the couple does visit friends, drinks are not served or are limited, thus emphasizing the reason for exclusion from other social activities of the friendship group. Discussions of drinking begin to be sidestepped awkwardly by friends, the wife, and the husband.

By this time the periods of socially acceptable drinking are becoming shorter. The wife, fearing that the full extent of her husband's drinking will become known, begins to withdraw from social participation, hoping to reduce the visibility of his behavior, and thus the threat to family status.

Isolation is further intensified because the family usually acts in accordance with the cultural dictate that it should be self-sufficient and manage to resolve its own problems without recourse to outside aid. Any experiences which they have had with well-meaning outsiders, usually relatives, have tended to strengthen this conviction. The husband has defined such relatives as interfering and the situation has deteriorated rather than improved.

With increasing isolation, the family members begin to lose perspective on their interaction and on their problems. Thrown into closer contact with one another as outside contacts diminish, the behavior of each member assumes exaggerated importance. The drinking behavior becomes the focus of anxiety. Gradually all family difficulties become attributed to it. (For example, the mother who is cross with her children will feel that, if her husband had not been drinking, she would not have been so tense and would not have been angry.) The fear that the full extent of drinking may be discovered mounts steadily; the conceptualization of the consequences of such a discovery becomes increasingly vague and, as a result, more anxiety-provoking. The family feels different from others and alone with its shameful secret.

Attempts to cover up increase. The employer who calls to inquire about the husband's absence from work is given excuses. The wife is afraid to face the consequences of loss of the husband's pay check in addition to her other concerns. Questions from the children are evaded or they are told that their father is ill. The wife lives in terror of the day when the children will be told by others of the nature of the "illness." She is also afraid that the children may describe their father's symptoms to teachers or neighbors. Still feeling that the family must solve its own problems, she keeps her troubles to herself and hesitates to seek outside help. If her husband beats her, she will bear it rather than call in the police. (Indeed, often she has no idea that this is even a possibility.) Her increased isolation has left her without the advice of others as to sources of help in the community. If she knows of them, an agency contact means to her an admission of the complete failure of her family as an independent unit. For the middle-class woman particularly, recourse to social agencies and law enforcement agencies means a terrifying admission of loss of status.

During this stage, husband and wife are drawing further apart. Each feels resentful of the behavior of the other. When this resentment is expressed, further drinking occurs. When it is not, tension mounts and the next drinking episode is that much more destructive of family relationships. The reasons for drinking are explored frantically. Both husband and wife feel that if only they could discover the reason, all members of the family could gear their behavior to making drinking unnecessary. The discussions become increasingly unproductive, as it is the husband's growing conviction that his wife does not and cannot understand him.

On her part, the wife begins to feel that she is a failure, that she has been unable to fulfill the major cultural obligations of a wife to meet her husband's needs. With her increasing isolation, her sense of worth derives almost entirely from her roles as wife and mother. Each failure to help her husband gnaws away at her sense of adequacy as a person.

Periods of sobriety or socially acceptable drinking still occur. These periods keep the wife from making a permanent or stable adjustment. During them her husband, in his guilt, treats her like a queen. His behavior renews her hope and rekindles positive feelings toward him. Her sense of worth is bolstered temporarily and she grasps desperately at her husband's reassurance that she is really a fine person and not a failure and an unlovable shrew. The periods of sobriety also keep her family from facing the inability of the husband to control his drinking. The inaccuracies of the cultural stereotype of the alcoholic—particularly that he is in a constant state of inebriation— also contribute to the family's rejection of the idea of alcoholism, as the husband seems to demonstrate from time to time that he can control his drinking.

Family efforts to control the husband become desperate. There are no culturally prescribed behavior patterns for handling such a situation and the family is forced to evolve its own techniques. Many different types of behavior are tried but none brings consistent results; there seems to be no way of predicting the consequences of any action that may be taken. All attempts to stabilize or structure the situation to permit consistent behavior fail. Threats of leaving, hiding his liquor away, emptying the bottles down the drain, curtailing his money, are tried in rapid succession, but none is effective. Less punitive methods, as discussing the situation when he is sober, babying him during hangovers, and trying to drink with him to keep him in the home, are attempted and fail. All behavior becomes oriented around the drinking, and the thought of family members becomes obsessive on this subject. As no action seems to be successful in achieving its goal, the wife persists in trial-and-error behavior with mounting frustration. Long-term goals recede into the background and become secondary to just keeping the husband from drinking today.

There is still an attempt to maintain the illusion of husband-wife-children roles. When father is sober, the children are expected to give him respect and obedience. The wife also defers to him in his role as head of the household. Each drinking event thus disrupts family functioning anew. The children begin to show emotional disturbances as a result of the inconsistencies of parental behavior. During periods when the husband is drinking the wife tries to shield them from the knowledge and effects of his behavior, at the same time drawing them closer to herself and deriving emotional support from them. In sober periods, the father tries to regain their favor. Due to experiencing directly only pleasant interactions with their father, considerable affection is often felt for him by the children. This affection becomes increasingly difficult for the isolated wife to tolerate, and an additional source of conflict. She feels that she needs and deserves the love and support of her children and, at the same time, she feels it important to maintain the children's picture of their father. She counts on the husband's affection for the children to motivate a cessation of drinking as he comes to realize the effects of his behavior on them.

In this stage, self-pity begins to be felt by the wife, if it has not entered previously. It continues in various degrees throughout the succeeding stages. In an attempt to handle her deepening sense of inadequacy, the wife often tries to convince herself that she is right and her husband wrong, and this also continues through the following stages. At this point the wife often resembles what Whalen (5) describes as "The Sufferer."

Stage 3. Disorganization

The wife begins to adopt a "What's the use?" attitude and to accept her husband's drinking as a problem likely to be permanent. Attempts to understand one another become less frequent. Sober periods still engender hope, but hope qualified by skepticism; they bring about a lessening of anxiety and this is defined as happiness.

By this time some customary patterns of husband-wife-children interaction have evolved. Techniques which have had some effectiveness in controlling the husband in the past or in relieving pent-up frustration are used by the wife. She nags, berates or retreats into silence. Husband and wife are both on the alert, the wife watching for increasing irritability and restlessness which mean a recurrence of drinking, and the husband for veiled aspersions on his behavior or character.

The children are increasingly torn in their loyalties as they become tools in the struggle between mother and father. If the children are at an age of comprehension, they have usually learned the true nature of their family situation, either from outsiders or from their mother, who has given up attempts to bolster her husband's position as father. The children are often bewildered but questioning their parents brings no satisfactory answers as the parents themselves do not understand what is happening. Some children become terrified; some have increasing behavior problems within and outside the home; others seem on the surface to accept the situation calmly.[1]

During periods of the husband's drinking, the hostility, resentment and frustrations felt by the couple is allowed expression. Both may resort to violence — the wife in self-defense or because she can find no other outlet for her feelings. In those cases in which the wife retaliates to violence in kind, she feels a mixture of relief and intense shame at having deviated so far from what she conceives to be "the behavior of a normal woman."

When the wife looks at her present behavior, she worries about her "normality." In comparing the person she was in the early years of her marriage with the person she has become, she is frightened. She finds herself nagging and unable to control herself. She resolves to stand up to her husband when he is belligerent but instead finds herself cringing in terror and then despises herself for her lack of courage. If she retaliates with violence, she is filled with self-loathing at behaving in an "unwomanly" manner. She finds herself compulsively searching for bottles, knowing full well that finding them will change nothing, and is worried because she engages in such senseless behavior. She worries about her inability to take constructive action of any kind. She is confused about where her loyalty lies, whether with her husband or her children. She feels she is a failure as a wife, mother and person. She believes she should be strong in the face of adversity and instead feels herself weak.

The wife begins to find herself avoiding sexual contact with her husband when he has been drinking. Sex under these circumstances, she feels, is sex for its own sake rather than an indication of affection for her. Her husband's lack of consideration of her needs to be satisfied leaves her feeling frustrated. The lack of sexual responsiveness reflects her emotional withdrawal from him in other areas of family life. Her husband, on his part, feels frustrated and rejected; he accuses her of frigidity and this adds to her concern about her adequacy as a woman.[2]

By this time the opening wedge has been inserted into the self-sufficiency of the family. The husband has often been in difficulty with the police and the wife has learned that police protection is available. An emergency has occurred in which the seeking of outside help was the only possible action to take; subsequent calls for aid from outsiders do not require the same degree of urgency before they can be undertaken. However, guilt and a lessening of self-respect and self-confidence accompany this method of resolving emergencies.

The husband intensifies these feelings by speaking of the interference of outsiders, or of his night in jail.

In Stage 3 all is chaos. Few problems are met constructively. The husband and wife both feel trapped in an intolerable, unstructured situation which offers no way out. The wife's self-assurance is almost completely gone. She is afraid to take action and afraid to let things remain as they are. Fear is one of the major characteristics of this stage: fear of violence, fear of personality damage to the children, fear for her own sanity, fear that relatives will interfere, and fear that they will not help in an emergency. Added to this, the family feels alone in the world and helpless. The problems, and the behavior of family members in attempting to cope with them, seem so shameful that help from others is unthinkable. They feel that attempts to get help would meet only with rebuff, and that communication of the situation will engender disgust.

At this point the clinical picture which the wife presents is very similar to what Whalen (5) has described as "The Waverer."

Stage 4. Attempts to Reorganize in Spite of the Problems

Stage 4 begins when a crisis occurs which necessitates that action be taken. There may be no money or food in the house; the husband may have been violent to the children; or life on the level of Stage 3 may have become intolerable. At this point some wives leave, thus entering directly into Stage 5.

The wife who passes through Stage 4 usually begins to ease her husband out of his family roles. She assumes husband and father roles. This involves strengthening her role as mother and putting aside her role as wife. She becomes the manager of the home, the discipliner of the children, the decision-maker; she becomes somewhat like Whalen's (5) "Controller." She either ignores her husband as much as possible or treats him as her most recalcitrant child. Techniques are worked out for getting control of his pay check, if there still is one, and money is doled out to her husband on the condition of his good behavior. When he drinks, she threatens to leave him, locks him out of the house, refuses to pay his taxi bills, leaves him in jail overnight rather than pay his bail. Where her obligations to her husband conflict with those to her children, she decides in favor of the latter. As she views her husband increasingly as a child, pity and a sense of being desperately needed by him enter. Her inconsistent behavior toward him, deriving from the lack of predictability inherent in the situation up to now, becomes reinforced by her mixed feelings toward him.

In this stage the husband often tries to set his will against hers in decisions about the children. If the children have been permitted to stay with a friend overnight, he may threaten to create a scene unless they return immediately. He may make almost desperate efforts to gain their affection and respect, his behavior ranging from getting them up in the middle of the night to fondle them to giving them stiff lectures on children's obligations to fathers. Sometimes he will attempt to align the males of the family with him against the females. He may openly express resentment of the children and become belligerent toward them physically or verbally.

Much of the husband's behavior can be conceptualized as resulting from an increasing awareness of his isolation from the other members of the family and their steady withdrawal of respect and affection. It seems to be a desperate effort to regain what he has lost, but without any clear idea of how this can be accomplished—an effort to change a situation in which everyone is seen as against him; and, in reality, this is becoming more and more true. As the wife has taken over control of the family with some degree of success, he feels, and becomes, less and less necessary to the ongoing activity of the family. There are fewer and fewer roles left for him to play. He becomes aware that members of the family enjoy each other's company without him. When he is home he tries to enter this circle of warmth or to smash it. Either way he isolates himself further. He finds that the children discuss with the mother how to manage him and he sees the children acting on the basis of their mother's idea of him. The children refuse to pay attention to his demands: they talk back to him in the same way that they talk back to one another, adding pressure on him to assume the role of just another child. All this leaves him frustrated and, as a result, often aggressive or increasingly absent from home.

The children, on the whole, become more settled in their behavior as the wife takes over the family responsibilities. Decisions are made by her and upheld in the face of their father's attempts to interfere. Participation in activities outside the home is encouraged. Their patterns of interaction with their father are supported by the mother. Whereas in earlier stages the children often felt that there were causal connections between their actions and their father's drinking, they now accept his unpredictability. "Well," says a 6-year old, "I'll just have to get used to it. I have a drunken father."

The family is more stabilized in one way but in other ways insecurities are multiplied. Pay checks are received less and less regularly. The violence or withdrawal of the father increases. When he is away the wife worries about automobile accidents or injury in fights, which become more and more probable as time passes. The husband may begin to be seriously ill from time to time; his behavior may become quite bizarre. Both of these signs of increasing illness arouse anxiety in the family.

During this stage hopes may rise high for father's "reform" when he begins to verbalize wishes to stop drinking, admits off and on his inability to stop, and sounds desperate for doing something about his drinking. Now may begin the trek to sanitariums for the middle-class alcoholic, to doctors, or to Alcoholics Anonymous. Where just the promise to stop drinking has failed to revive hope, sobriety through outside agencies has the ability to rekindle it brightly. There is the feeling that at last he is "taking really constructive action." In failure the discouragement is deeper. Here another wedge has been inserted into the self-sufficiency of the family.

By this time the wedges are many. The wife, finding she has managed to bring some semblance or order and stability to her family, while not exactly becoming a self-assured person, has regained some sense of worth which grows a little with each crisis she meets successfully. In addition, the very fact of taking action to stabilize the situation brings relief. On some occasion she may be able to approach social agencies for financial help, often during a period when the husband has temporarily deserted or is incarcerated. She may have gone to the family court; she may have consulted a lawyer about getting a restraining order when the husband was in a particularly belligerent state. She has begun to learn her way around among the many agencies which offer help.

Often she has had a talk with an Alcoholics Anonymous member and has begun to look into what is known about alcoholism. If she has attended a few Alcoholics Anonymous meetings, her sense of shame has been greatly alleviated as she finds so many others in the same boat. Her hopes rise as she meets alcoholics who have stopped drinking, and she feels relieved at being able to discuss her problems openly for the first time with an audience which understands fully. She begins to gain perspective on her problem and learns that she herself is involved in what happens to her husband, and that she must change. She exchanges techniques of management with other wives and receives their support in her decisions.

She learns that her husband is ill rather than merely "ornery," and this often serves to quell for the time being thoughts about leaving him which have begun to germinate as she has gained more self-confidence. She learns that help is available but also that her efforts to push him into help are unavailing. She is not only supported in her recently evolved behavior of thinking first of her family, but now this course also emerges from the realm of the unconceptualized and is set in an accepted rationale. She feels more secure in having a reason and a certainty that the group accepts her as "doing the right thing." When she reports deviations from what the group thinks is the "right way," her reasons are understood; she receives solid support but there is also pressure on her to alter her behavior again toward the acceptable.

Blaming and self-pity are actively discouraged. In group discussions she still admits to such feelings but learns to recognize them as they arise and to go beyond them to more productive thinking.

How much her altered behavior changes the family situation is uncertain, but it helps her and gives her security from which to venture forth to further actions of a consistent and constructive type, constructive at least from the point of view of keeping her family on as even a keel as possible in the face of the disruptive influence of the husband. With new friends whom she can use as a sounding board for plans, and with her growing acquaintance with the alternatives and possible patterns of behavior, her thinking ceases to be circular and unproductive. Her anxiety about her own sanity is alleviated as she is reassured by others that they have experienced the same concern and that the remedy is to get her own life and her family under better control. As she accomplishes this, the difference in her feelings about herself convinces her that this is so.

Whether or not she has had a contact with wives of Alcoholics Anonymous members or other wives who have been through a similar experience and have emerged successfully, the very fact of taking hold of her situation and gradually making it more manageable adds to her self-confidence. As her husband is less and less able to care for himself or his family, she begins to feel that he needs her and that without her he would be destroyed. Such a feeling makes it difficult for her to think of leaving him. His almost complete social isolation at this point and his cries for help reinforce this conviction of being needed.

The drinking behavior is no longer hidden. Others obviously know about it, and this becomes accepted by the wife and children. Already isolated and insulated against possible rejection, the wife is often surprised to find that she has exaggerated her fears of what would happen were the situation known. However, the unpredictability of her husband's behavior makes her reluctant to form social relationships which could be violently disrupted or to involve others in the possible consequences of his behavior.

Stage 5. Efforts to Escape the Problems

Stage 5 may be the terminal one for the marriage. In this stage the wife separates from her husband. Sometimes the marriage is re-established after a period of sobriety, when it appears certain that the husband will not drink again. If he does revert to drinking, the marriage is sometimes finally terminated but with less emotional stress than the first time. If the husband deserts, being no longer able to tolerate his lack of status in his family, Stage 6 may be entered abruptly.

The events precipitating the decision to terminate the marriage may be near-catastrophic, as when there is an attempt by the husband to kill the wife or children, or they may appear trivial to outsiders, being only the last straw to an accumulation of years.

The problems in coming to the decision to terminate the marriage cannot be underestimated. Some of these problems derive from emotional conflicts; some are related to very practical circumstances in the situation; some are precipitated by the conflicting advice of outsiders. With several children dependent on her, the wife must decide whether the present situation is more detrimental to them than future situations she can see arising if she should leave her husband. The question of where the money to live on will come from must be thought out. If she can get a job, will there be enough to provide for child care also while she is away from home? Should the children, who have already experienced such an unsettled life, be separated from her to be cared for by others? If the family still owns its own home, how can she retain control of it? If she leaves, where can she go? What can be done to tide the family over until her first earnings come in? How can she ensure her husband's continued absence from the home and thus be certain of the safety of individuals and property in her absence? These are only a small sample of the practical issues that must be dealt with in trying to think her way through to a decision to terminate the marriage.

Other pressures act on her to impede the decision-making process. "If he would only stay drunk till I carry out what I intend to do," is a frequent statement. When the husband realizes that his wife really means to leave, he frequently sobers up, watches his behavior in the home, plays on her latent and sometimes conscious feelings of her responsibility for the situation, stresses his need for her and that without her he is lost, tears away at any confidence she has that she will be able to manage by herself, and threatens her and the children with injury or with his own suicide if she carries out her intention.

The children, in the meantime, are pulling and pushing on her emotions. They think she is "spineless" to stay but unfair to father's chances for ultimate recovery if she leaves. Relatives, who were earlier alienated in her attempts to shield her family but now know of the situation, do not believe in its full ramifications. They often feel she is exaggerating and persuade her to stay with him. Especially is this true in the case of the "solitary drinker." His drinking has been so well concealed that the relatives have no way of knowing the true nature of the situation. Other relatives, afraid that they will be called on for support, exert pressure to keep the marriage intact and the husband thereby responsible for debts. Relatives who feel she should leave him overplay their hands by berating the husband in such a manner as to evoke her defense of him. This makes conscious the positive aspects of her relationship with him, causing her to waver in her decision. If she consults organized agencies, she often gets conflicting advice. The agencies concerned with the well-being of the family may counsel leaving; those concerned with rehabilitating the husband may press her to stay. In addition, help from public organizations almost always involves delay and is frequently not forthcoming at the point where she needs it most.

The wife must come to terms with her own mixed feelings about her husband, her marriage and herself before she can decide on such a step as breaking up the marriage. She must give up hope that she can be of any help to her husband. She must command enough self-confidence, after years of having it eroded, to be able to face an unknown future and leave the security of an unpalatable but familiar past and present. She must accept that she has failed in her marriage, not an easy thing to do after having devoted years to stopping up the cracks in the family structure as they appeared. Breaking up the marriage involves a complete alteration in the life goals toward which all her behavior has been oriented. It is hard for her to rid herself of the feeling that she married him and he is her responsibility. Having thought and planned for so long on a day-to-day basis, it is difficult to plan for a long-term future.

Her taking over the family raises her self-confidence but failure to carry through on decisions undermines the new gains that she has made. Vacillation in her decisions tends to exasperate the agencies trying to help her, and she begins to feel that help from them may not be forthcoming if she finally decides to leave.

Some events, however, help her to arrive at a decision. During the absences of her husband she has seen how manageable life can be and how smoothly her family can run. She finds that life goes on without him. The wife who is working comes to feel that "my husband is a luxury I can no longer afford." After a few short-term separations in which she tries out her wings successfully, leaving comes to look more possible. Another step on the path to leaving is the acceptance of the idea that, although she cannot help her husband, she can help her family. She often reaches a state of such emotional isolation from her husband that his behavior no longer disturbs her emotionally but is only something annoying which upsets daily routines and plans.

Stage 6. Reorganization of Part of the Family

The wife is without her husband and must reorganize her family on this basis. Substantially the process is similar to that in other divorced families, but with some additions. The divorce rarely cuts her relationships to her husband. Unless she and her family disappear, her husband may make attempts to come back. When drunk, he may endanger her job by calls at her place of work. He may attempt violence against members of the family, or he may contact the children and work to gain their loyalty so that pressure is put on the mother to accept him again. Looking back on her marriage, she forgets the full impact of the problem situation on her and on the children and feels more warmly toward her husband, and these feelings can still be manipulated by him. The wide circulation of information on alcoholism as an illness engenders guilt about having deserted a sick man. Gradually, however, the family becomes reorganized.

Stage 7. Recovery and Reorganization of the Whole Family

Stage 7 is entered if the husband achieves sobriety, whether or not separation has preceded. It was pointed out that in earlier stages most of the problems in the marriage were attributed to the alcoholism of the husband, and thus problems in adjustment not related directly to the drinking were unrecognized and unmet. Also, the "sober personality" of the husband was thought of as the "real" personality, with a resulting lack of recognition of other factors involved in his sober behavior, such as remorse and guilt over his actions, leading him to act to the best of his ability like "the ideal husband" when sober. Irritation or other signs of growing tension were viewed as indicators of further drinking, and hence the problems giving rise to them were walked around gingerly rather than faced and resolved. Lack of conflict and lack of drinking were defined as indicating a perfect adjustment. For the wife and husband facing a sober marriage after many years of an alcoholic marriage, the expectations of what marriage without alcoholism will be are unrealistically idealistic, and the reality of marriage almost inevitably brings disillusionments. The expectation that all would go well and that all problems be resolved with the cessation of the husband's drinking cannot be met and this threatens the marriage from time to time.

The beginning of sobriety for the husband does not bring too great hope to the family at first. They have been through this before but are willing to help him along and stand by him in the new attempt. As the length of sobriety increases, so do the hopes for its permanence and efforts to be of help. The wife at first finds it difficult to think more than in terms of today, waking each morning with fear of what the day will bring and sighing with relief at the end of each sober day.

With the continuation of sobriety, many problems begin to crop up. Mother has for years managed the family, and now father again wishes to be reinstated in his former roles. Usually the first role re-established is that of breadwinner, and the economic problems of the family begin to be alleviated as debts are gradually paid and there is enough left over for current needs. With the resumption of this role, the husband feels that the family should also accept him at least as a partner in the management of the family. Even if the wife is willing to hand over some of the control of the children, for example, the children often are not able to accept this change easily. Their mother has been both parents for so long that it takes time to get used to the idea of consulting their father on problems and asking for his decisions. Often the father tries too hard to manage this change overnight, and the very pressure put on the children toward this end defeats him. In addition, he is unable to meet many of the demands the children make on him because he has never really become acquainted with them or learned to understand them and is lacking in much necessary background knowledge of their lives.

The wife, who finds it difficult to conceive of her husband as permanently sober, feels an unwillingness to let control slip from her hands. At the same time she realizes that reinstatement of her husband in his family roles is necessary to his sobriety. She also realizes that the closer his involvement in the family the greater the probability of his remaining sober. Yet she remembers events in the past in which his failure to handle his responsibilities was catastrophic to the family. Used to avoiding anything which might upset him, the wife often hesitates to discuss problems openly. At times, if she is suc-cessful in helping him to regain his roles as father, she feels resentful of his intrusion into territory she has come to regard as hers. If he makes errors in judgment which affect the family adversely, her former feelings of being his superior may come to the fore and affect her interaction with him. If the children begin to turn to him, she may feel a resurgence of self-pity at being left out and find herself attempt-ing to swing the children back toward herself. Above all, however, she finds herself feeling resentful that some other agency achieved what she and the children could not.

Often the husband makes demands for obedience, for consideration and for pampering which members of the family feel unable to meet. He may become rather euphoric as his sobriety continues and feel superior for a time.

Gradually, however, the drinking problem sinks into the past and marital adjustment at some level is achieved. Even when this has occurred, the drinking problem crops up occasionally, as when the time comes for a decision about whether the children should be permitted to drink. The mother at such times becomes anxious, sees in the child traits which remind her of her husband, worries whether these are the traits which mean future alcoholism. At parties, at first, she is watchful and concerned about whether her husband will take a drink or not. Relatives and friends may, in a party mood, make the husband the center of attention by emphasizing his nondrinking. They may unwittingly cast aspersions on his character by trying to convince him that he can now "drink like a man." Some relatives and friends have gone so far as secretly to "spike" a nonalcoholic drink and then cry "bottoms up!" without realizing the risk of reactivating patterns from the past.

If sobriety has come through Alcoholics Anonymous, the husband frequently throws himself so wholeheartedly into A.A. activities that his wife sees little of him and feels neglected. As she worries less about his drinking, she may press him to cut down on these activities. That this is dangerous, since A.A. activity is correlated with success in Alcoholics Anonymous, has been shown by Lahey (9). Also, the wife discovers that, though she has a sober husband, she is by no means free of alcoholics. In his Twelfth Step work, he may keep the house filled with men he is helping. In the past her husband has avoided self-searching; and now he may become excessively introspective, and it may be difficult for her to deal with this.

If the husband becomes sober through Alcoholics Anonymous and the wife participates actively in groups open to her, the thoughts of what is happening to her, to her husband and to her family will be verbalized and interpreted within the framework of the Alcoholics Anonymous philosophy and the situation will probably be more tolerable and more easily worked out.

SUGGESTIONS FOR FURTHER RESEARCH

The above presentation has roughly delineated sequences and characteristics of family adjustment to an alcoholic husband. A more detailed delineation of the stages is required. The extent to which these findings, based on families seeking help, can be generalized to other families of alcoholics needs to be determined, and differences between these families and others specified. Consideration should be given to the question of correspondence between the wife's definition of the situation and that which actually occurs.

Further research is needed on the factors which determine the rate of transition through the stages, and on the factors which retard such a transition, sometimes to the extent that the family seems to remain in the same stage almost permanently. In the group studied, the majority passed from one stage to the next but took different lengths of time to make the transition. Those wives whose husbands have been sober a long time had all passed through all the stages. None of the long-term members remained in the same stage throughout the time that the group was under study.

Other problems which require clarification are: (a) What are the factors within families which facilitate a return to sobriety or hamper it? (b) What variations in family behavior are determined by social class? (c) What problems are specific to the different types of drinking patterns of the husband—for example, the periodic drinker, the steady drinker, the solitary drinker, the sociable drinker, the drinker who becomes belligerent, and the drinker who remains calm? There are indications in the data gathered in the present study that such specific problems arise.

SUMMARY

The onset of alcoholism in a family member has been viewed as precipitating a cumulative crisis for the family. Seven critical stages have been delineated. Each stage affects the form which the following one will take. The family finds itself in an unstructured situation which is undefined by the culture. Thus it is forced to evolve techniques of adjustment by trial and error. The unpredictability of the situation, added to its lack of structure, engenders anxiety in family members which gives rise to personality difficulties. Factors in the culture, in the environment, and within the family situation prolong the crisis and deter the working out of permanent adjustment patterns. With the arrest of the alcoholism, the crisis enters its final stage. The family attempts to reorganize to include the ex-alcoholic and makes adjustments to the changes which have occurred in him.

It has been suggested that the clinical picture presented by the wife to helping agencies is not only indicative of a type of basic personality structure but also of the stage in family adjustment to an alcoholic. That the wives of alcoholics represent a rather limited number of personality types can be interpreted in two ways, which are not mutually exclusive.

(a) That women with certain personality attributes tend to select alcoholics or potential alcoholics as husbands in order to satisfy unconscious personality needs;

(b) That women undergoing similar experiences of stress, within similarly unstructured situations, defined by the culture and reacted to by members of the society in such a manner as to place limits on the range of possible behavior, will emerge from this experience showing many similar neurotic personality traits. As the situation evolves some of these personality traits will also change. Changes have been observed in the women studied which correlate with altered family interaction patterns. This hypothesis is supported also by observations on the behavior of individuals in other unstructured situations, in situations involving conflicting goals and loyalties, and in situations in which they were isolated from supporting group interaction. It is congruent also with the theory of reactions to increased and decreased stress.

Notes

1. Some effects of alcoholism of the father on children have been discussed by Newell (8).

2. It is of interest here that marriage counselors and students of marital adjustment are of the opinion that unhappy marriage results in poor sexual adjustment more often than poor sexual adjustment leads to unhappy marriage. If this proves to be true, it would be expected that most wives of alcoholics would find sex distasteful while their husbands are drinking. The wives of the inactive alcoholics report that their sexual adjustments with their husbands are currently satisfactory; many of those whose husbands are still drinking state that they enjoyed sexual relationships before the alcoholism was established.

References

1. Mowrer, H. R. A psychocultural analysis of the alcoholic. Amer. Sociol. Rev. 5:546–557, 1940.
2. Bacon, S. D. Excessive drinking and the institution of the family. In: Alcohol, Science and Society; Lecture 16. New Haven; Quarterly Journal of Studies on Alcohol; 1945.
3. Baker, S. M. Social case work with inebriates. In: Alcohol, Science and Society; Lecture 27. New Haven; Quarterly Journal of Studies on Alcohol; 1945.
4. Futterman, S. Personality trends in wives of alcoholics. J. Psychiat. Soc. Work 23:37–41, 1953.
5. Whalen, T. Wives of alcoholics: four types observed in a family service agency. Quart. J. Stud. Alc. 14:632–641, 1953.
6. Price, G. M. A study of the wives of 20 alcoholics. Quart. J. Stud. Alc. 5:620–627, 1945.
7. Club and Educational Bureaus of Newsweek. Is alcoholism everyone's problem? Platform, N.Y., p. 3, Jan. 1950.
8. Newell, N. Alcoholism and the father-image. Quart. J. Stud. Alc. 11: 92–96, 1950.
9. Lahey, W. W. A Comparison of Social and Personal Factors Identified with Selected Members of Alcoholics Anonymous. Master's Thesis; University of Southern California; 1950.

18 / The Psychological Meaning of Mental Illness in the Family

MARIAN RADKE YARROW
CHARLOTTE GREEN SCHWARTZ
HARRIET S. MURPHY
LEILA CALHOUN DEASY

The manifestations of mental illness are almost as varied as the spectrum of human behavior. Moreover, they are expressed not only in disturbance and functional impairment for the sick person but also in disruptive interactions with others. The mentally ill person is often, in his illness, a markedly deviant person, though certainly less so than the popular stereotype of the "insane." One wonders what were the initial phases of the impact of mental illness upon those within the ill person's social environment. How were the disorders of illness interpreted and tolerated? What did the patients, prior to hospitalization, communicate of their needs, and how did others— those closest to the ill persons—attempt, psychologically and behaviorally, to cope with the behavior? How did these persons come to be recognized by other family members as needing psychiatric help?

This paper presents an analysis of cognitive and emotional problems encountered by the wife in coping with the mental illness of the husband. It is concerned with the factors which lead to the reorganization of the wife's perceptions of her husband from a *well* man to a man who is mentally sick or in need of hospitalization in a mental hospital. The process whereby the wife attempts to understand and interpret her husband's manifestations of mental illness is best communicated by considering first the concrete details of a single wife's experiences. The findings and interpretations based on the total sample are presented following the case analysis.

ILLUSTRATIVE CASE

Robert F., a 35-year-old cab driver, was admitted to Saint Elizabeth's Hospital with a diagnosis of schizophrenia. How did Mr. F. get to the mental hospital? Here is a very condensed version of what his wife told an interviewer a few weeks later.

Mrs. F. related certain events, swift and dramatic, which led directly to the hospitalization. The day before admission, Mr. F. went shopping with his wife, which he never had done before, and expressed worry lest he lose her. This was in her words, "rather strange." (*His behavior is not in keeping with her expectations for him.*) Later that day, Mr. F. thought a TV program was about him and that the set was "after him." "Then I was getting worried." (*She recognizes the bizarre nature of his reactions. She becomes concerned.*)

That night, Mr. F. kept talking. He reproached himself for not working enough to give his wife surprises. Suddenly, he exclaimed he did have a surprise for her—he was going to kill her. "I was petrified and said to him, 'What do you mean?' Then, he began to cry and told me not to let him hurt me and to do for him what I would want him to do for me. I asked him what was wrong. He said he had cancer. . . . He began talking about his grandfather's mustache and said there was a worm growing out of it." She remembered his watching little worms in the fish bowl and thought his idea came from that. Mr. F. said he had killed his grandfather. He asked Mrs. F. to forgive him and wondered if she were his mother or God. She denied this. He vowed he was being punished for killing people during the war. "I thought maybe . . . worrying about the war so much . . . had gotten the best of him. (*She tries to understand his behavior. She stretches the range of normality to include it.*) I thought he should see a psychiatrist . . . I don't know how to explain it. He was shaking. I knew it was beyond what I could do . . . I was afraid of him . . . I thought he was losing his normal mental attitude and mentality, but I wouldn't say that he was insane or crazy, because he had always bossed me around before . . ." (*She shifts back and forth in thinking his problem is psychiatric and in feeling it is normal behavior that could he accounted for in terms of their own experience.*) Mr. F. talked on through the night. Sometime in the morning, he "seemed to straighten out" and drove his wife to work. (*This behavior tends to balance out the preceding disturbed activities. She quickly returns to a normal referent.*)

At noon, Mr. F. walked into the store where his wife worked as a clerk. "I couldn't make any sense of what he was saying. He kept getting angry because I wouldn't talk to him. . . . Finally, the boss' wife told me to go home." En route, Mr. F. said his male organs were blown up and little seeds covered him. Mrs. F. denied seeing them and announced she planned to call his mother. "He began crying and I had to promise not to. I said, . . . 'Don't you think you should go to a psychiatrist?' and he said, 'No, there is nothing wrong with me.' . . .

Then we came home, and I went to pay a bill . . ." (*Again she considers, but is not fully committed to, the idea that psychiatric help is needed.*)

Back at their apartment, Mr. F. talked of repairing his cab while Mrs. F. thought of returning to work and getting someone to call a doctor. Suddenly, he started chasing her around the apartment and growling like a lion. Mrs. F. screamed, Mr. F. ran out of the apartment, and Mrs. F. slammed and locked the door. "When he started roaring and growling, then I thought he was crazy. That wasn't a human sound. You couldn't say a thing to him . . ." Later, Mrs. F. learned that her husband went to a nearby church, created a scene, and was taken to the hospital by the police. (*Thoroughly threatened, she defines problem as psychiatric.*)

What occurred before these events which precipitated the hospitalization? Going back to their early married life, approximately three years before hospitalization, Mrs. F. told of her husband's irregular work habits and long-standing complaints of severe headaches. "When we were first married, he didn't work much and I didn't worry as long as we could pay the bills." Mrs. F. figured they were just married and wanted to be together a lot. (*Personal norms and expectations are built up.*)

At Thanksgiving, six months after marriage, Mr. F. "got sick and stopped working." During the war he contracted malaria, he explained, which always recurred at that time of year. "He wouldn't get out of bed or eat. . . . He thought he was constipated and he had nightmares. . . . What I noticed most was his perspiring so much. He was crabby. You couldn't get him to go to a doctor. . . . I noticed he was nervous. He's always been a nervous person. . . . Any little thing that would go wrong would upset him—if I didn't get a drawer closed right. . . . His friends are nervous, too. . . . I came to the conclusion that maybe I was happy-go-lucky and everyone else was a bundle of nerves. . . . For a cab driver, he worked hard—most cab drivers loaf. When he felt good, he worked hard. He didn't work so hard when he didn't." (*She adapts to his behavior. The atypical is normalized as his type of personality and appropriate to his subculture.*)

As the months and years went by, Mrs. F. changed jobs frequently, but she worked more regularly than did her husband. He continued to work sporadically, get sick intermittently, appear "nervous and tense" and refrain from seeking medical care. Mrs. F. "couldn't say what was wrong." She had first one idea, then another, about his behavior. "I knew it wasn't right for him to be acting sick like he did." Then, "I was beginning to think he was getting lazy because there wasn't anything I could see." During one period, Mrs. F. surmised he was carrying on with another woman. "I was right on the verge of going, until he explained it wasn't anyone else." (*There is a building up of deviant behavior to a point near her tolerance limits. Her interpretations shift repeatedly.*)

About two and a half years before admission, Mrs. F. began talking to friends about her husband's actions and her lack of success in getting him to a doctor. "I got disgusted and said if he didn't go to a doctor, I would leave him. I got Bill (the owner of Mr. F.'s cab) to talk to him. . . . I begged, threatened, fussed . . ." After that, Mr. F. went to a VA doctor for one visit, overslept for his second appointment and never returned. He said the doctor told him nothing was wrong.

When Mr. F. was well and working, Mrs. F. "never stopped to think about it." "You live from day to day. . . When something isn't nice, I don't think about it. If you stop to think about things, you can worry yourself sick. . . He said he wished he could live in my world. He'd never seem to be able to put his thinking off the way I do . . ." (*Her mode of operating permits her to tolerate his behavior.*)

Concurrently, other situations confronted Mrs. F. Off and on, Mr. F. talked of a coming revolution as a result of which Negroes and Jews would take over the world. If Mrs. F. argued that she didn't believe it, Mr. F. called her "dumb" and "stupid." "The best thing to do was to change the subject." Eighteen months before admission, Mr. F. began awakening his wife to tell of nightmares about wartime experiences, but she "didn't think about it." Three months later, he decided he wanted to do something besides drive a cab. He worked on an invention but discovered it was patented. Then, he began to write a book about his wartime experiences and science. "If you saw what he wrote, you couldn't see anything wrong with it. . . . He just wasn't making any money." Mrs. F. did think it was "silly" when Mr. F. went to talk to Einstein about his ideas and couldn't understand why he didn't talk to someone in town. Nevertheless, she accompanied him on the trip. (*With the further accumulation of deviant behavior, she becomes less and less able to tolerate it. The perceived seriousness of his condition is attenuated so long as she is able to find something acceptable or understandable in his behavior.*)

Three days before admission, Mr. F. stopped taking baths and changing clothes. Two nights before admission, he awakened his wife to tell her he had just figured out that the book he was writing had nothing to do with science or the world, only with himself. "He said he had been worrying about things for ten years and that writing a book solved what had been worrying him for ten years." Mrs. F. told him to burn his writings if they had nothing to do with science. It was the following morning that Mrs. F. first noticed her husband's behavior as "rather strange."

In the long prelude to Mr. F.'s hospitalization, one can see many of the difficulties which arise for the wife as the husband's behavior no longer conforms and as it strains the limits of the wife's expectations for him. At some stage the wife defines the situation as one requiring help, eventually psychiatric help. Our analysis is concerned primarily with the process of the wife's getting to this stage in interpreting and responding to the husband's behavior. In the preceding case are many reactions which appear as general trends in the data group. These trends can be systematized in terms of the following focal aspects of the process:

1. The wife's threshold for initially discerning a problem depends on the accumulation of various kinds of behavior which are not readily understandable or acceptable to her.
2. This accumulation forces upon the wife the necessity for examining and adjusting expectations for herself and her husband which permit her to account for his behavior.
3. The wife is in an "overlapping" situation, of problem—not problem or of normal—not normal. Her interpretations shift back and forth.
4. Adaptations to the atypical behavior of the husband occur. There is testing and waiting for additional cues in coming to any given interpretation, as in most problem solving. The wife mobilizes strong defenses against the husband's deviant behavior. These defenses take form in such reactions as denying, attenuating, balancing and normalizing the husband's problems.
5. Eventually there is a threshold point at which the perception breaks, when the wife comes to the relatively stable conclusion that the problem is a psychiatric one and/or that she cannot alone cope with the husband's behavior.

These processes are elaborated in the following analysis of the wives' responses.

METHOD OF DATA COLLECTION

Ideally, to study this problem one might like to interview the wives as they struggled with the developing illness. This is precluded, however, by the fact that the problem is not "visible" until psychiatric help is sought. The data, therefore, are the wives' reconstructions of their earlier experiences and accounts of their current reactions during the husband's hospitalization.

It is recognized that recollections of the prehospital period may well include systematic biases, such as distortions, omissions and increased organization and clarity. As a reliability check, a number of wives, just before the husband's discharge from the hospital, were asked again to describe the events and feelings of the prehospital period. In general, the two reports are markedly similar; often details are added and others are elaborated, but events tend to be substantially the same. While this check attests to the consistency of the wives' reporting, it has, of course, the contamination of overlearning which comes from many retellings of these events.

THE BEGINNINGS OF THE WIFE'S CONCERN

In the early interviews, the wife was asked to describe the beginnings of the problem which led to her husband's hospitalization. ("Could you tell me when you first noticed that your husband was different?") This question was intended to provide an orientation for the wife to reconstruct the sequence and details of events and feelings which characterized the period preceding hospitalization. The interviewer provided a minimum of structuring in order that the wife's emphases and organization could be obtained.

In retrospect, the wives usually cannot pinpoint the time the husband's problem emerged. Neither can they clearly carve it out from the contexts of the husband's personality and family expectations. The subjective beginnings are seldom localized in a single strange or disturbing reaction on the husband's part but rather in the piling up of behavior and feelings. We have seen this process for Mrs. F. There is a similar accumulation for the majority of wives, although the time periods and kinds of reported behavior vary. Thus, Mrs. Q. verbalizes the impact of a concentration of changes which occur within a period of a few weeks. Her explicit recognition of a problem comes when she adds up this array: her husband stays out late, doesn't eat or sleep, has obscene thoughts, argues with her, hits her, talks continuously, "cannot appreciate the beautiful scene," and "cannot appreciate me or the baby."

The problem behaviors reported by the wives are given in Table 1. They are ordered roughly; the behaviors listed first occurred primarily, but not exclusively, within the family; those later occurred in the more public domain. Whether the behavior is public or private does not seem to be a very significant factor in determining the wife's threshold for perceiving a problem.

There are many indications that these behaviors, now organized as a problem, have occurred many times before. This is especially true where alcoholism, physical complaints or personality "weaknesses" enter the picture. The wives indicate how, earlier, they had assimi-

Table 1 / Reported Problem Behavior at Time of the Wife's Initial Concern and at Time of the Husband's Admission to Hospital

Problem Behavior	INITIALLY		AT HOSPITAL ADMISSION	
	PSYCHOTICS N	PSYCHO-NEUROTICS N	PSYCHOTICS N	PSYCHO-NEUROTICS N
Physical problems, complaints, worries	12	5	7	5
Deviations from routines of behavior	17	9	13	9
Expressions of inadequacy or hopelessness	4	1	5	2
Nervous, irritable, worried	19	10	18	9
Withdrawal (verbal, physical)	5	1	6	1
Changes or accentuations in personality "traits" (slovenly, deceptive, forgetful)	5	6	7	6
Aggressive or assaultive and suicidal behavior	6	3	10	6
Strange or bizarre thoughts, delusions, hallucinations and strange behavior	11	1	15	2
Excessive drinking	4	7	3	4
Violation of codes of "decency"	3	1	3	2
Number of Respondents	23	10	23	10

lated these characteristics into their own expectations in a variety of ways: the characteristics were congruent with their image of their husbands, they fitted their differential standards for men and women (men being less able to stand up to troubles), they had social or environmental justifications, etc.

When and how behavior becomes defined as problematic appears to be a highly individual matter. In some instances, it is when the wife can no longer manage her husband (he will no longer respond to her usual prods); in others, when his behavior destroys the status quo (when her goals and living routines are disorganized); and, in still others, when she cannot explain his behavior. One can speculate that her level of tolerance for his behavior is a function of her specific personality needs and vulnerabilities, her personal and family value systems and the social supports and prohibitions regarding the husband's symptomatic behavior.

INITIAL INTERPRETATIONS OF HUSBAND'S PROBLEM

Once the behavior is organized as a problem, it tends also to be interpreted as some particular kind of problem. More often than not, however, the husband's difficulties are not seen initially as manifestations of mental illness or even as emotional problems (Table 2).

Table 2 / Initial Interpretations of the Husband's Behavior

Interpretation	PSYCHOTICS N	PSYCHONEUROTICS N
Nothing really wrong	3	0
"Character" weakness and "controllable" behavior (lazy, mean, etc.)	6	3
Physical problem	6	0
Normal response to crisis	3	1
Mildly emotionally disturbed	1	2
"Something" seriously wrong	2	2
Serious emotional or mental problem	2	2
Number of Respondents	23	10

Early interpretations often tend to be organized around physical difficulties (18% of cases) or "character" problems (27%). To a very marked degree, these orientations grow out of the wives' long-standing appraisals of their husbands as weak and ineffective or physically sick men. These wives describe their husbands as spoiled, lacking will-power, exaggerating little complaints and acting like babies. This is especially marked where alcoholism complicates the husband's symptomatology. For example, Mrs. Y., whose husband was chronically alcoholic, aggressive and threatening to her, "raving," and who "chewed his nails until they almost bled," interprets his difficulty thus: "He was just spoiled rotten. He never outgrew it. He told me when he was a child he could get his own way if he insisted, and he is still that way." This quotation is the prototype of many of its kind.

Some wives, on the other hand, locate the problem in the environment. They expect the husband to change as the environmental crisis subsides. Several wives, while enumerating difficulties and concluding that there is a problem, in the same breath say it is really nothing to be concerned about.

Where the wives interpret the husband's difficulty as emotional in nature, they tend to be inconsistently "judgmental" and "understanding." The psychoneurotics are more often perceived initially by their wives as having emotional problems or as being mentally ill than are the psychotics. This is true even though many more clinical signs (bizarre, confused, delusional, aggressive and disoriented behavior) are reported by the wives of the psychotics than of the psychoneurotics.

Initial interpretations, whatever their content, are seldom held with great confidence by the wives. Many recall their early reactions to their husbands' behaviors as full of puzzling confusion and uncertainty. Something is wrong, they know, but, in general, they stop short of a firm explanation. Thus, Mrs. M. reports, "He was kind of worried. He was kind of worried before, not exactly worried. . . ." She thought of his many physical complaints; she "racked" her "brain" and told her husband, "Of course, he didn't feel good." Finally, he stayed home from work with "no special complaints, just blah," and she "began to realize it was more deeply seated."

CHANGING PERCEPTIONS OF THE HUSBAND'S PROBLEM

The fog and uneasiness in the wife's early attempts to understand and cope with the husband's difficulties are followed, typically, by painful psychological struggles to resolve the uncertainties and to change the current situation. Usually, the wife's perceptions of the husband's problems undergo a series of changes before hospitalization is sought or effected, irrespective of the length of time elapsing between the beginnings of concern and hospitalization.

Viewing these changes macroscopically, three relatively distinct patterns of successive redefinitions of the husband's problems are apparent. One sequence (slightly less than half the cases) is characterized by a progressive intensification; interpretations are altered in a definite direction—toward seeing the problem as mental illness. Mrs. O. illustrates this progression. Initially, she thought her husband was "unsure of himself." "He was worried, too, about getting old."

These ideas moved to: "He'd drink to forget. . . . He just didn't have the confidence. . . . He'd forget little things. . . . He'd wear a suit weeks on end if I didn't take it away from him. . . . He'd say nasty things." Then, when Mr. O. seemed "so confused," "to forget all kinds of things . . . where he'd come from . . . to go to work," and made "nasty, cutting remarks all the time," she began to think in terms of a serious personality disturbance. "I did think he knew that something was wrong . . . that he was sick. He was never any different this last while and I couldn't stand it any more. . . . You don't know what a relief it was. . . ." (when he was hospitalized). The husband's drinking, his failure to be tidy, his nastiness, etc., lose significance in their own right. They move from emphasis to relief and are recast as signs of "something deeper," something that brought "it" on.

Some wives whose interpretations move in the direction of seeing their husbands as mentally ill hold conceptions of mental illness and of personality that do not permit assigning the husband all aspects of the sick role. Frequently, they use the interpretation of mental illness as an angry epithet or as a threatening prediction for the husband. This is exemplified in such references as: "I told him he should have his head examined," "I called him a half-wit," "I told him if he's not careful, he'll be a mental case." To many of these wives, the hospital is regarded as the "end of the road."

Other wives showing this pattern of change hold conceptions of emotional disturbance which more easily permit them to assign to their husbands the role of patient as the signs of illness become more apparent. They do not as often regard hospitalization in a mental hospital as the "last step." Nevertheless, their feelings toward their husbands may contain components equally as angry and rejecting as those of the wives with the less sophisticated ideas regarding mental illness.

A somewhat different pattern of sequential changes in interpreting the husband's difficulties (about one-fifth of the cases) is to be found among wives who appear to cast around for situationally and momentarily adequate explanations. As the situation changes or as the husband's behavior changes, these wives find reasons and excuses but lack an underlying or synthesizing theory. Successive interpretations tend to bear little relation to one another. Situational factors tend to lead them to seeing their husbands as mentally ill. Immediate, serious and direct physical threats or the influence of others may be the deciding factor. For example, a friend or employer may insist that the husband see a psychiatrist, and the wife goes along with the decision.

A third pattern of successive redefinitions (slightly less than one-third of the cases) revolves around an orientation outside the framework of emotional problems or mental illness. In these cases, the wife's specific explanations change but pivot around a denial that the husband is mentally ill.

A few wives seem not to change their interpretations about their husband's difficulties. They maintain the same explanation throughout the development of his illness, some within the psychiatric framework, others rigidly outside that framework.

Despite the characteristic shiftings in interpretations, in the group as a whole, there tend to be persisting underlying themes in the individual wife's perceptions that remain essentially unaltered. These themes are a function of her systems of thinking about normality and abnormality and about valued and devalued behavior.

THE PROCESS OF RECOGNIZING THE HUSBAND'S PROBLEM AS MENTAL ILLNESS

In the total situation confronting the wife, there are a number of factors, apparent in our data, which make it difficult for the wife to recognize and accept the husband's behavior in a mental-emotional-psychiatric framework. Many cross-currents seem to influence the process.

The husband's behavior itself is a fluctuating stimulus. He is not worried and complaining all of the time. His delusions and hallucinations may not persist. His hostility toward the wife may be followed by warm attentiveness. She has, then, the problem of deciding whether his "strange" behavior is significant. The greater saliency of one or the other of his responses at any moment of time depends in some degree upon the behavior sequence which has occurred most recently.

The relationship between husband and wife also supplies a variety of images and contexts which can justify varied conclusions about the husband's current behavior. The wife is likely to adapt to behavior which occurs in their day to day relationships. Therefore, symptomatic reactions which are intensifications of long-standing response patterns become part of the fabric of life and are not easily disentangled as "symptomatic."

Communications between husband and wife regarding the husband's difficulties act sometimes to impede and sometimes to further the process of seeing the difficulties within a psychiatric framework. We have seen both kinds of influences in our data. Mr. and Mrs. F. were quite unable to communicate effectively about Mr. F.'s problems. On the one hand, he counters his wife's urging that he see a doctor with denials that anything is wrong. On the other hand, in his own way through his symptoms, he tries to communicate his problems

. . . but she responds only to his verbalized statements, taking them at face value.

Mr. and Mrs. K. participate together quite differently, examining Mr. K.'s fears that he is being followed by the F.B.I., that their house has been wired and that he is going to be fired. His wife tentatively shares his suspicions. At the same time, they discuss the possibility of paranoid reactions.

The larger social context contributes, too, in the wife's perceptual tug of war. Others with whom she can compare her husband provide contrasts to his deviance, but others (Mr. F.'s nervous friends) also provide parallels to his problems. The "outsiders," seeing less of her husband, often discount the wife's alarm when she presses them for opinions. In other instances, the friend or employer, less adapted to or defended against the husband's symptoms, helps her to define his problem as psychiatric.

This task before the wife, of defining her husband's difficulties, can be conceptualized as an "overlapping" situation (in Lewin's terms), in which the relative potencies of the several effective influences fluctuate. The wife is responding to the various sets of forces simultaneously. Thus, several conclusions or interpretations of the problem are simultaneously "suspended in balance," and they shift back and forth in emphasis and relief. Seldom, however, does she seem to be balancing off clear-cut alternatives, such as physical versus mental. Her complex perceptions (even those of Mrs. F. who is extreme in misperceiving cues) are more "sophisticated" than the casual questioner might be led to conclude.

Thus far, we have ignored the personally threatening aspects of recognizing mental illness in one's spouse, and the defenses which are mobilized to meet this threat. It is assumed that it is threatening to the wife not only to realize that the husband is mentally ill but further to consider her own possible role in the development of the disorder, to give up modes of relating to her husband that may have had satisfactions for her and to see a future as the wife of a mental patient. Our data provide systematic information only on the first aspect of this problem, on the forms of defense against the recognition of the illness. One or more of the following defenses are manifested in three-fourths of our cases.

The most obvious form of defense in the wife's response is the tendency to *normalize* the husband's neurotic and psychotic symptoms. His behavior is explained, justified or made acceptable by seeing it also in herself or by assuring herself that the particular behavior occurs again and again among persons who are not ill. Illustrative of this reaction is the wife who reports her husband's hallucinations and assures herself that this is normal because she herself heard voices when she was in the menopause. Another wife responds to her husband's physical complaints, fears, worries, nightmares, and delusions with "A lot of normal people think there's something wrong when there isn't. I think men are that way; his father is that way."

When behavior cannot be normalized, it can be made to seem less severe or less important in a total picture than an outsider might see it. By finding some grounds for the behavior or someting explainable about it, the wife achieves at least momentary *attenuation* of the seriousness of it. Thus, Mrs. F. is able to discount partly the strangeness of her husband's descriptions of the worms growing out of his grandfather's mustache when she recalls his watching the worms in the fish bowl. There may be attenuation, too, by seeing the behavior as "momentary" ("You could talk him out of his ideas.") or by rethinking the problem and seeing it in a different light.

By *balancing* acceptable with unacceptable behavior or "strange" with "normal" behavior, some wives can conclude that the husband is not seriously disturbed. Thus, it is very important to Mrs. R. that her husband kissed her goodbye before he left for the hospital. This response cancels out his hostile feelings toward her and the possibility that he is mentally ill. Similarly, Mrs. V. reasons that her husband cannot be "out of his mind" for he had reminded her of things she must not forget to do when he went to the hospital.

Defense sometimes amounts to a thorough-going *denial*. This takes the form of denying that the behavior perceived can be interpreted in an emotional or psychiatric framework. In some instances, the wife reports vividly on such behavior as repeated thoughts of suicide, efforts to harm her and the like and sums it up with "I thought it was just a whim." Other wives bend their efforts toward proving the implausibility of mental illness.

After the husband is hospitalized, it might be expected that these denials would decrease to a negligible level. This is not wholly the case, however. A breakdown of the wives' interpretations just following the husband's admission to the hospital shows that roughly a fifth still interpret the husband's behavior in another framework than that of a serious emotional problem or mental illness. Another fifth ambivalently and sporadically interpret the behavior as an emotional or mental problem. The remainder hold relatively stable interpretations within this framework.

After the husband has been hospitalized for some time, many wives reflect on their earlier tendencies to avoid a definition of mental illness. Such reactions are almost identically described by these wives: "I put it out of my mind—I didn't want to face it—anything but a mental illness." "Maybe I was aware of it. But you know you push things away from you and keep hoping." "Now you think maybe you should have known about it. Maybe you should have done more than you did and that worries me."

DISCUSSION

The findings on the perceptions of mental illness by the wives of patients are in line with general findings in studies of perception. Behavior which is unfamiliar and incongruent and unlikely in terms of current expectations and needs will not be readily recognized, and stressful or threatening stimuli will tend to be misperceived or perceived with difficulty or delay.

We have attempted to describe the factors which help the wife maintain a picture of her husband as normal and those which push her in the direction of accepting a psychiatric definition of his problem. The kind and intensity of the symptomatic behavior, its persistence over time, the husband's interpretation of his problem, interpretations and defining actions of others, including professionals, all play a role. In addition, the wives come to this experience with different conceptions of psychological processes and of the nature of emotional illness, itself, as well as with different tolerances for emotional disturbance. As we have seen, there are also many supports in society for maintaining a picture of normality concerning the husband's behavior. Social pressures and expectations not only keep *behavior* in line but to a great extent *perceptions* of behavior as well.

There are implications of these findings both for those who are working in the field of prevention of mental illness and early detection of emotional disturbance as well as for the rehabilitation worker. They suggest that to acquaint the public with the nature of mental illness by describing psychotic behavior and emphasizing its non-threatening aspect is, after all, an intellectualization and not likely to be effective in dealing with the threatening aspects of recognizing mental illness which we have described. Further, it is not enough simply to recognize the fact that the rehabilitation of patients is affected by the attitudes and feelings of the family toward the patient and his illness. Perhaps a better acceptance of the patient can be developed if families who have been unable to deal with the problem of the illness are helped to work through this experience and to deal with their difficulties in accepting the illness and what remains of it after the patient leaves the hospital.

19 / Paranoia and the Dynamics of Exclusion[1]

EDWIN M. LEMERT

One of the few generalizations about psychotic behavior which sociologists have been able to make with a modicum of agreement and assurance is that such behavior is a result or manifestation of a disorder in communication between the individual and society. The generalization, of course, is a large one, and, while it can be illustrated easily with case history materials, the need for its conceptual refinement and detailing of the process by which disruption of communication occurs in the dynamics of mental disorder has for some time been apparent. Among the more carefully reasoned attacks upon this problem is Cameron's formulation of the paranoid pseudocommunity (1).

In essence, the conception of the paranoid pseudocommunity can be stated as follows:[2]

Paranoid persons are those whose inadequate social learning leads them in situations of unusual stress to incompetent social reactions. Out of the fragments of the social behavior of others the paranoid person symbolically organizes a pseudocommunity whose functions he perceives as focused on him. His reactions to this *supposed community* of response which he sees loaded with threat to himself bring him into open conflict with the actual community and lead to his temporary or permanent isolation from its affairs. The "real" community, which is unable to share in his attitudes and reactions, takes action through forcible restraint or retaliation *after* the paranoid person "bursts into defensive or vengeful activity" (1).

That the community to which the paranoid reacts is "pseudo" or without existential reality is made unequivocal by Cameron when he says:

"As he (the paranoid person) begins attributing to others the attitudes which he has towards himself, he unintentionally organizes these others into a functional community, a group unified in their supposed reactions, attitudes and plans with respect to him. He in this way organizes individuals, some of whom are actual persons and some only inferred or imagined, into a whole which satisfies for the time being his immediate need for explanation but which brings no assurance with it, and usually serves to increase his tensions. The community he forms not only fails to correspond to any organization shared by others but actually contradicts this consensus.

More than this, the actions ascribed by him to its personnel are not actually performed or maintained by them; *they are united in no common undertaking against him*" (1). (Italics ours.)

The general insightfulness of Cameron's analysis cannot be gainsaid and the usefulness of some of his concepts is easily granted. Yet a serious question must be raised, based upon empirical inquiry, as to whether in actuality the insidious qualities of the community to which the paranoid reacts are pseudo or a symbolic fabrication. There is an alternative point of view, which is the burden of this paper, namely that, while the paranoid person reacts differentially to his social environment, it is also true that "others" react differentially to him and this reaction commonly if not typically involves covertly organized action and conspiratorial behavior in a very real sense. A further extension of our thesis is that these differential reactions are reciprocals of one another, being interwoven and concatenated at each and all phases of a process of exclusion which arises in a special kind of relationship. Delusions and associated behavior must be understood in a context of exclusion which attenuates this relationship and disrupts communication.

By thus shifting the clinical spotlight away from the individual to a relationship and a process, we make an explicit break with the conception of paranoia as a disease, a state, a condition, or a syndrome of symptoms. Furthermore, we find it unnecessary to postulate trauma of early childhood or arrested psychosexual development to account for the main features of paranoia—although we grant that these and other factors may condition its expression.

This conception of paranoia is neither simple *a priori* theory nor is it a proprietary product of sociology. There is a substantial body of writings and empirical researches in psychiatry and psychology which question the sufficiency of the individual as primary datum for the study of paranoia. Tyhurst, for example, concludes from his survey of this literature that reliance upon intrapsychic mechanisms and the "isolated organism" have been among the chief obstacles to fruitful discoveries about this disorder (18). Significantly, as Milner points out, the more complete the investigation of the cases the more frequently do unendurable external circumstances make their appearance (13). More precisely, a number of studies have ended with the conclusions that external circumstances—changes in norms and values, displacement, strange environments, isolation, and linguistic separation—may create a paranoid disposition in the absence of any special character structure (15). The recognition of paranoid reactions in elderly persons, alcoholics, and the deaf adds to the data generally consistent with our thesis. The finding that displaced persons who withstood a high degree of stress during war and captivity subsequently developed paranoid reactions when they were isolated in a foreign environment commands special attention among data requiring explanation in other than organic or psychodynamic terms (7, 10).

From what has been said thus far, it should be clear that our formulation and analysis will deal primarily with what Tyhurst (18) calls paranoid patterns of behavior rather than with a clinical entity in the classical Kraepelinian sense. Paranoid reactions, paranoid states, paranoid personality disturbances, as well as the seldom-diagnosed "true paranoia," which are found superimposed or associated with a wide variety of individual behavior or "symptoms," all provide a body of data for study so long as they assume priority over other behavior in meaningful social interaction. The elements of behavior upon which paranoid diagnoses are based—delusions, hostility, aggressiveness, suspicion, envy, stubbornness, jealousy, and ideals of reference—are readily comprehended and to some extent empathized by others as social reactions, in contrast to the bizarre, manneristic behavior of schizophrenia or the tempo and affect changes stressed in manic-depressive diagnoses. It is for this reason that paranoia suggests, more than any other forms of mental disorder, the possibility of fruitful sociological analysis.

DATA AND PROCEDURE

The first tentative conclusions which are presented here were drawn from a study of factors influencing decisions to commit mentally disordered persons to hospitals, undertaken with the cooperation of the Los Angeles County Department of Health in 1952. This included interviews by means of schedules with members of 44 families in Los Angeles County who were active petitioners in commitment proceedings and the study of 35 case records of public health officer commitments. In 16 of the former cases and in seven of the latter, paranoid symptoms were conspicuously present. In these cases family members and others had plainly accepted or "normalized" paranoid behavior, in some instances longstanding, until other kinds of behavior or exigencies led to critical judgments that "there was something wrong" with the person in question, and, later, that hospitalization was necessary. Furthermore, these critical judgments seemed to signal changes in the family attitudes and behavior towards the affected persons which could be interpreted as contributing in different ways to the form and intensity of the paranoid symptoms.

In 1958 a more refined and hypothesis-directed study was made of eight cases of persons with prominent paranoid characteristics. Four of these had been admitted to the state hospital at Napa, California, where they were diagnosed as paranoid schizophrenic. Two other cases were located and investigated with the assistance of the district attorney in Martinez, California. One of the persons had previously been committed to a California state hospital, and the other had been held on an insanity petition but was freed after a jury trial. Added to these was one so-called "White House case," which had involved threats to a President of the United States, resulting in the person's commitment to St. Elizabeth's Hospital in Washington, D.C. A final case was that of a professional person with a history of chronic job difficulties, who was designated and regarded by his associates as "brash," "queer," "irritating," "hypercritical," and "thoroughly un-likeable."

In a very rough way the cases made up a continuum ranging from one with very elaborate delusions, through those in which fact and misinterpretation were difficult to separate, down to the last case, which comes closer to what some would call paranoid personality disturbance. A requirement for the selection of the cases was that there be no history or evidence of hallucinations and also that the persons be intellectually unimpaired. Seven of the cases were of males, five of whom were over 40 years of age. Three of the persons had been involved in repeated litigations. One man published a small, independent paper devoted to exposures of psychiatry and mental hospitals. Five of the men had been or were associated with organizations, as follows: a small-town high school, a government research bureau, an association of agricultural producers, a university, and a contracting business.

The investigations of the cases were as exhaustive as it was possible to make them, reaching relatives, work associates, employers, attorneys, police, physicians, public officials and any others who played significant roles in the lives of the persons involved. As many as 200 hours each were given to collecting data on some of the cases. Written materials, legal documents, publications and psychiatric histories were studied in addition to the interview data. Our procedure in the large was to adopt an interactional perspective which sensitized us to sociologically relevant behavior underlying or associated with the more apparent and formal contexts of mental disorder. In particular we were concerned to establish the order in which delusions and social exclusion occur and to determine whether exclusion takes conspiratorial form.

THE RELEVANT BEHAVIOR

In another paper (8) we have shown that psychotic symptoms as described in formal psychiatry are not relevant bases for predictions about changes in social status and social participation of persons in whom they appear. Apathy, hallucinations, hyperactivity, mood swings, tics, tremors, functional paralysis or tachychardias have no intrinsic social meanings. By the same token, neither do such imputed attributes as "lack of insight," "social incompetence" or "defective role-taking ability" favored by some sociologists as generic starting points for the analysis of mental disorders. Rather, it is behavior which puts strain on social relationships that leads to status changes: informal or formal exclusion from groups, definition as a "crank," or adjudication as insane and commitment to a mental hospital (8). This is true even where the grandiose and highly bizarre delusions of paranoia are present. Definition of the socially stressful aspects of this disorder is a minimum essential, if we are to account for its frequent occurrence in partially compensated or benign form in society, as well as account for its more familiar presence as an official psychiatric problem in a hospital setting.

It is necessary, however, to go beyond these elementary observations to make it pre-eminently clear that strain is an emergent product of a relationship in which the behaviors of two or more persons are relevant factors, and in which the strain is felt both by ego and *alter* or *alters*. The paranoid relationship includes reciprocating behaviors with attached emotions and meanings which, to be fully understood, must be described cubistically from at least two of its perspectives. On one hand the behavior of the individual must be seen from the perspective of others or that of a group, and conversely the behavior of others must be seen from the perspective of the involved individual.

From the vantage of others the individual in the paranoid relationship shows:

1. A disregard for the values and norms of the primary group, revealed by giving priority to verbally definable values over those which are implicit, a lack of loyalty in return for confidences, and victimizing and intimidating persons in positions of weakness.
2. A disregard for the implicit structure of groups, revealed by presuming to privileges not accorded him, and the threat or actual resort to formal means for achieving his goals.

The second items have a higher degree of relevancy than the first in an analysis of exclusion. Stated more simply, they mean that, to the group, the individual is an ambiguous figure whose behavior is uncertain, whose loyalty can't be counted on. In short, he is a person who can't be trusted because he threatens to expose informal power structures. This, we believe, is the essential reason for the frequently encountered idea that the paranoid person is "dangerous" (4).

If we adopt the perceptual set of ego and see others or groups through his eyes, the following aspects of their behavior become relevant:

1. the spurious quality of the interaction between others and himself or between others interacting in his presence;

2. the overt avoidance of himself by others;
3. the structured exclusion of himself from interaction.

The items we have described thus far—playing fast and loose with the primary group values by the individual, and his exclusion from interaction—do not alone generate and maintain paranoia. It is additionally necessary that they emerge in an interdependent relationship which requires trust for its fulfillment. The relationship is a type in which the goals of the individual can be reached only through cooperation from particular others, and in which the ends held by others are realizable if cooperation is forthcoming from ego. This is deduced from the general proposition that cooperation rests upon perceived trust, which in turn is a function of communication (11). When communication is disrupted by exclusion, there is a lack of mutually perceived trust and the relationship becomes dilapidated or paranoid. We will now consider the process of exclusion by which this kind of relationship develops.

THE GENERIC PROCESS OF EXCLUSION

The paranoid process begins with persistent interpersonal difficulties between the individual and his family, or his work associates and superiors, or neighbors, or other persons in the community. These frequently or even typically arise out of bona fide or recognizable issues centering upon some actual or threatened loss of status for the individual. This is related to such things as the death of relatives, loss of a position, loss of professional certification, failure to be promoted, age and physiological life cycle changes, mutilations, and changes in family and marital relationships. The status changes are distinguished by the fact that they leave no alternative acceptable to the individual, from whence comes their "intolerable" or "unendurable" quality. For example: the man trained to be a teacher who loses his certificate, which means he can never teach; or the man of 50 years of age who is faced with loss of a promotion which is a regular order of upward mobility in an organization, who knows that he can't "start over"; or the wife undergoing hysterectomy, which mutilates her image as a woman.

In cases where no dramatic status loss can be discovered, a series of failures often is present, failures which may have been accepted or adjusted to, but with progressive tension as each new status situation is entered. The unendurability of the current status loss, which may appear unimportant to others, is a function of an intensified commitment, in some cases born of an awareness that there is a quota placed on failures in our society. Under some such circumstances, failures have followed the person, and his reputation as a "difficult person" has preceded him. This means that he often has the status of a stranger on trial in each new group he enters, and that the groups or organizations willing to take a chance on him are marginal from the standpoint of their probable tolerance for his actions.

The behavior of the individual—arrogance, insults, presumption of privilege and exploitation of weaknesses in others—initially has a segmental or checkered pattern in that it is confined to status-committing interactions. Outside of these, the person's behavior may be quite acceptable—courteous, considerate, kind, even indulgent. Likewise, other persons and members of groups vary considerably in their tolerance for the relevant behavior, depending on the extent to which it threatens individual and organizational values, impedes functions, or sets in motion embarrassing sequences of social actions. In the early generic period, tolerance by others for the individual's aggressive behavior generally speaking is broad, and it is very likely to be interpreted as a variation of normal behavior, particularly in the absence of biographical knowledge of the person. At most, people observe that "there is something odd about him," or "he must be upset," or "he is just ornery," or "I don't quite understand him" (3).

At some point in the chain of interactions, a new configuration takes place in perceptions others have of the individual, with shifts in figure-ground relations. The individual, as we have already indicated, is an ambiguous figure, comparable to textbook figures of stairs or outlined cubes which reverse themselves when studied intently. From a normal variant the person becomes "unreliable," "untrustworthy," "dangerous," or some with whom others "do not wish to be involved." An illustration nicely apropos of this came out in the reaction of the head of a music department in a university when he granted an interview to a man who had worked for years on a theory to compose music mathematically:

> When he asked to be placed on the staff so that he could use the electronic computers of the University *I shifted my ground* ... when I offered an objection to his theory, he became disturbed, so I changed my reaction to "yes and no."

As is clear from this, once the perceptual reorientation takes place, either as the outcome of continuous interaction or through the receipt of biographical information, interaction changes qualitatively. In our words it becomes *spurious*, distinguished by patronizing, evasion, "humoring," guiding conversation onto selected topics, underreaction, and silence, all calculated either to prevent intense interaction or to protect individual and group values by restricting access to them. When the interaction is between two or more persons in the individual's presence it is cued by a whole repertoire of subtle expressive signs which are meaningful only to them.

The net effects of spurious interaction are to:

1. stop the flow of information to ego;
2. create a discrepancy between expressed ideas and affect among those with whom he interacts;
3. make the situation or the group image an ambiguous one for ego, much as he is for others.

Needless to say this kind of spurious interaction is one of the most difficult for an adult in our society to cope with, because it complicates or makes decisions impossible for him and also because it is morally invidious.[3]

The process from inclusion to exclusion is by no means an even one. Both individuals and members of groups change their perceptions and reactions, and vacillation is common, depending upon the interplay of values, anxieties and guilt on both sides. Members of an excluding group may decide they have been unfair and seek to bring the individual back into their confidence. This overture may be rejected or used by ego as a means of further attack. We have also found that ego may capitulate, sometimes abjectly, to others and seek group re-entry, only to be rejected. In some cases compromises are struck and a partial reintegration of ego into informal social relations is achieved. The direction which informal exclusion takes depends upon ego's reactions, the degree of communication between his interactors, the composition and structure of the informal groups, and the perceptions of "key others" at points of interaction which directly affect ego's status.

ORGANIZATIONAL CRISIS AND FORMAL EXCLUSION

Thus far we have discussed exclusion as an informal process. Informal exclusion may take place but leave ego's formal status in an organization intact. So long as this status is preserved and rewards are sufficient to validate it on his terms, an uneasy peace between him and others may prevail. Yet ego's social isolation and his strong commitments make him an unpredictable factor; furthermore the rate of change and internal power struggles, especially in large and complex organizations, means that preconditions of stability may be short lived.

Organizational crises involving a paranoid relationship arise in several ways. The individual may act in ways which arouse intolerable anxieties in others, who demand that "something be done." Again, by going to higher authority or making appeals outside the organization, he may set in motion procedures which leave those in power no other choice than to take action. In some situations ego remains relatively quiescent and does not openly attack the organization. Action against him is set off by growing anxieties or calculated motives of associates—in some cases his immediate superiors. Finally, regular organizational procedures incidental to promotion, retirement or reassignment may precipitate the crisis.

Assuming a critical situation in which the conflict between the individual and members of the organization leads to action to formally exclude him, several possibilities exist. One is the transfer of ego from one department, branch or division of the organization to another, a device frequently resorted to in the armed services or in large corporations. This requires that the individual be persuaded to make the change and that some department will accept him. While this may be accomplished in different ways, not infrequently artifice, withholding information, bribery, or thinly disguised threats figure conspicuously among the means by which the transfer is brought about. Needless to say, there is a limit to which transfers can be employed as a solution to the problem, contingent upon the size of the organization and the previous diffusion of knowledge about the transferee.

Solution number two we call encapsulation, which, in brief, is a reorganization and redefinition of ego's status. This has the effect of isolating him from the organization and making him directly responsible to one or two superiors who act as his intermediators. The change is often made palatable to ego by enhancing some of the material rewards of his status. He may be nominally promoted or "kicked upstairs," given a larger office, or a separate secretary, or relieved of onerous duties. Sometimes a special status is created for him.

This type of solution often works because it is a kind of formal recognition by the organization of ego's intense commitment to his status and in part a victory for him over his enemies. It bypasses them and puts him into direct communication with higher authority who may communicate with him in a more direct manner. It also relieves his associates of further need to connive against him. This solution is sometimes used to dispose of troublesome corporation executives, high-ranking military officers, and academic *personae non gratae* in universities.

A third variety of solutions to the problem of paranoia in an organization is outright discharge, forced resignation or non-renewal of appointment. Finally, there may be an organized move to have the individual in the paranoid relationship placed on sick leave, or to compel him to take psychiatric treatment. The extreme expression of this is pressure (as on the family) or direct action to have the person committed to a mental hospital.

The order of the enumerated solutions to the paranoid problem in a rough way reflects the amount of risk associated with the alternatives, both as to the probabilities of failure and of damaging repercussions to the organization. Generally, organizations seem to show a good deal of resistance to making or carrying out decisions which require expulsion of the individual or forcing hospitalization, regardless of his mental condition. One reason for this is that the person may have power within the organization, based upon his position, or monopolized skills and information,[4] and unless there is a strong coalition against him the general conservatism of administrative judgments will run in his favor. Herman Wouk's novel of *The Caine Mutiny* dramatizes some of the difficulties of cashiering a person from a position of power in an essentially conservative military organization. An extreme of this conservatism is illustrated by one case in which we found a department head retained in his position in an organization even though he was actively hallucinating as well as expressing paranoid delusions.[5] Another factor working on the individual's side is that discharge of a person in a position of power reflects unfavorably upon those who placed him there. Ingroup solidarity of administrators may be involved, and the methods of the opposition may create sympathy for ego at higher levels.

Even when the person is almost totally excluded and informally isolated within an organization, he may have power outside. This weighs heavily when the external power can be invoked in some way, or when it automatically leads to raising questions as to the internal workings of the organization. This touches upon the more salient reason for reluctance to eject an uncooperative and retaliatory person, even when he is relatively unimportant to the organization. We refer to a kind of negative power derived from the vulnerability of organizations to unfavorable publicity and exposure of their private lives that are likely if the crisis proceeds to formal hearings, case review or litigation. This is an imminent possibility where paranoia exists. If hospital commitment is attempted, there is a possibility that a jury trial will be demanded, which will force leaders of the organization to defend their actions. If the crisis turns into a legal contest of this sort, it is not easy to prove insanity, and there may be damage suits. Even if the facts heavily support the petitioners, such contests can only throw unfavorable light upon the organization.

THE CONSPIRATORIAL NATURE OF EXCLUSION

A conclusion from the foregoing is that organizational vulnerability as well as anticipations of retaliations from the paranoid person lay a functional basis for conspiracy among those seeking to contain or oust him. Probabilities are strong that a coalition will appear within the organization, integrated by a common commitment to oppose the paranoid person. This, the exclusionist group, demands loyalty, solidarity and secrecy from its members; it acts in accord with a common scheme and in varying degrees utilizes techniques of manipulation and misrepresentation.

Conspiracy in rudimentary form can be detected in informal exclusion apart from an organizational crisis. This was illustrated in an office research team in which staff members huddled around a water cooler to discuss the unwanted associate. They also used office telephones to arrange coffee breaks without him and employed symbolic cues in his presence, such as humming the Dragnet theme song when he approached the group. An office rule against extraneous conversation was introduced with the collusion of supervisors, ostensibly for everyone, actually to restrict the behavior of the isolated worker. In another case an interview schedule designed by a researcher was changed at a conference arranged without him. When he sought an explanation at a subsequent conference, his associates pretended to have no knowledge of the changes.

Conspiratorial behavior comes into sharpest focus during organizational crises in which the exclusionists who initiate action become an embattled group. There is a concerted effort to gain consensus for this view, to solidify the group and to halt close interaction with those unwilling to completely join the coalition. Efforts are also made to neutralize those who remain uncommitted but who can't be kept ignorant of the plans afoot. Thus an external appearance of unanimity is given even if it doesn't exist.

Much of the behavior of the group at this time is strategic in nature, with determined calculations as to "what we will do if he does this or that." In one of our cases, a member on a board of trustees spoke of the "game being played" with the person in controversy with them. Planned action may be carried to the length of agreeing upon the exact words to be used when confronted or challenged by the paranoid individual. Above all there is continuous, precise communication among exclusionists, exemplified in one case by mutual exchanging of copies of all letters sent and received from ego.

Concern about secrecy in such groups is revealed by such things as carefully closing doors and lowering of voices when ego is brought under discussion. Meeting places and times may be varied from normal procedures; documents may be filed in unusual places and certain telephones may not be used during a paranoid crisis.

The visibility of the individual's behavior is greatly magnified during this period; often he is the main topic of conversation among the exclusionists, while rumors of the difficulties spread to other groups, which in some cases may be drawn into the controversy. At a certain juncture steps are taken to keep the members of the ingroup continually informed of the individual's movements and, if possible, of his plans. In effect, if not in form, this amounts to spying. Members of one embattled group, for example, hired an outside person unknown to their accuser to take notes on a speech he delivered to enlist a community organization on his side. In another case, a person having an office opening onto that of a department head was persuaded to act as an informant for the nucleus of persons working to depose the head from his position of authority. This group also seriously debated placing an all-night watch in front of their perceived malefactor's house.

Concomitant with the magnified visibility of the paranoid individual, come distortions of his image, most pronounced in the inner coterie of exclusionists. His size, physical strength, cunning, and anecdotes of his outrages are exaggerated, with a central thematic emphasis on the fact that he is dangerous. Some individuals give cause for such beliefs in that previously they have engaged in violence or threats, others do not. One encounters characteristic contradictions in interviews on this point, such as: "No, he has never struck anyone around here—just fought with the policemen at the State Capitol," or "No, I am not afraid of him, but one of these days he will explode."

It can be said parenthetically that the alleged dangerousness of paranoid persons storied in fiction and drama has never been systematically demonstrated. As a matter of fact, the only substantial data on this, from a study of delayed admissions, largely paranoid, to a mental hospital in Norway, disclosed that "neither the paranoiacs nor paranoids have been dangerous, and most not particularly troublesome" (14). Our interpretation of this, as suggested earlier, is that the imputed dangerousness of the paranoid individual does not come from physical fear but from the organizational threat he presents and the need to justify collective action against him.[6]

However, this is not entirely tactical behavior—as is demonstrated by anxieties and tensions which mount among those in the coalition during the more critical phases of their interaction. Participants may develop fears quite analogous to those of classic conspirators. One leader in such a group spoke of the period of the paranoid crisis as a "week of terror," during which he was wracked with insomnia and "had to take his stomach pills." Projection was revealed by a trustee who, during a school crisis occasioned by discharge of an aggressive teacher, stated that he "watched his shadows," and "wondered if all would be well when he returned home at night." Such tensional states, working along with a kind of closure of communication within the group, are both a cause and an effect of amplified group interaction which distorts or symbolically rearranges the image of the person against whom they act.

Once the battle is won by the exclusionists, their version of the individual as dangerous becomes a crystallized rationale for official action. At this point misrepresentation becomes part of a more deliberate manipulation of ego. Gross misstatements, most frequently called "pretexts," become justifiable ways of getting his cooperation, for example, to get him to submit to psychiatric examination or detention preliminary to hospital commitment. This aspect of the process has been effectively detailed by Goffman, with his concept of a "betrayal funnel" through which a patient enters a hospital (5). We need not elaborate on this, other than to confirm its occurrence in the exclusion process, complicated in our cases by legal strictures and the ubiquitous risk of litigation.

THE GROWTH OF DELUSION

The general idea that the paranoid person symbolically fabricates the conspiracy against him is in our estimation incorrect or incomplete. Nor can we agree that he lacks insight, as is so frequently claimed. To the contrary, many paranoid persons properly realize that they are being isolated and excluded by concerted interaction, or that they are being manipulated. However, they are at a loss to estimate accurately or realistically the dimensions and form of the coalition arrayed against them.

As channels of communication are closed to the paranoid person, he has no means of getting feedback on consequences of his behavior, which is essential for correcting his interpretations of the social relationships and organization which he must rely on to define his status and give him identity. He can only read overt behavior without the informal context. Although he may properly infer that people are organized against him, he can only use confrontation or formal inquisitorial procedures to try to prove this. The paranoid person must provoke strong feelings in order to receive any kind of meaningful communication from others—hence his accusations, his bluntness, his insults. Ordinarily this is non-deliberate; nevertheless, in one complex case we found the person consciously provoking discussions to get readings from others on his behavior. This man said of himself: "Some people would describe me as very perceptive, others would describe me as very imperceptive."

The need for communication and the identity which goes with it does a good deal to explain the preference of paranoid persons for formal, legalistic, written communications, and the care with which many of them preserve records of their contacts with others. In some ways the resort to litigation is best interpreted as the effort of the individual to compel selected others to interact directly with him as equals, to engineer a situation in which evasion is impossible. The fact that the person is seldom satisfied with the outcome of his letters, his petitions, complaints and writs testifies to their function as devices for establishing contact and interaction with others, as well as "setting the record straight." The wide professional tolerance of lawyers for aggressive behavior in court and the nature of Anglo-Saxon legal institutions, which grew out of a revolt against conspiratorial or star-chamber justice, mean that the individual will be heard. Furthermore his charges must be answered; otherwise he wins by default. Sometimes he wins small victories, even if he loses the big ones. He may earn grudging respect as an adversary, and sometimes shares a kind of legal camaraderie with others in the courts. He gains an identity through notoriety.

REINFORCEMENT OF DELUSION

The accepted psychiatric view is that prognosis for paranoia is poor, that recoveries from "true" paranoia are rare, with the implication that the individual's delusions more or less express an unalterable pathological condition. Granting that the individual's needs and dispositions and his self-imposed isolation are significant factors in perpetuating his delusional reactions, nevertheless there is an important social context of delusions through which they are reinforced or strengthened. This context is readily identifiable in the fixed ideas and institutionalized procedures of protective, custodial, and treatment organizations in our society. They stand out in sharpest relief where paranoid persons have come into contact with law enforcement agencies or have been hospitalized. The cumulative and interlocking impacts of such agencies work strongly to nurture and sustain the massive sense of injustice and need for identity which underlie the delusions and aggressive behavior of the paranoid individual.

Police in most communities have a well-defined concept of cranks, as they call them, although the exact criteria by which persons are so judged are not clear. Their patience is short with such persons: in some cases they investigate their original complaints and if they conclude that the person in question is a crank they tend to ignore him thereafter. His letters may be thrown away unanswered, or phone calls answered with patronizing reassurance or vague promises to take steps which never materialize.

Like the police, offices of district attorneys are frequently forced to deal with persons they refer to as cranks or soreheads. Some offices delegate a special deputy to handle these cases, quaintly referred to in one office as the "insane deputy." Some deputies say they can spot letters of cranks immediately, which means that they are unanswered or discarded. However, family or neighborhood quarrels offer almost insoluble difficulties in this respect, because often it is impossible to determine which of two parties is delusional. In one office some complainants are called "fifty-fifty," which is jargon meaning that it is impossible to say whether they are mentally stable. If one person seems to be persistently causing trouble, deputies may threaten to have him investigated, which, however, is seldom if ever done.

Both police and district attorney staffs operate continuously in situations in which their actions can have damaging legal or political repercussions. They tend to be tightly ingrouped and their initial reaction to outsiders or strangers is one of suspicion or distrust until they are proved harmless or friendly. Many of their office procedures and general manner reflect this—such as carefully recording in a log book names, time, and reason for calling of those who seek official interviews. In some instances a complainant is actually investigated before any business will be transacted with him.

When the paranoid person goes beyond local police and courts to seek redress through appeals to state or national authorities, he may meet with polite evasion, perfunctory treatment of his case or formalized distrust. Letters to administrative people may beget replies up to a certain point, but therafter they are ignored. If letters to a highly placed authority carry threats, they may lead to an investigation by security agencies, motivated by the knowledge that assassinations are not unknown in American life. Sometimes redress is sought in legislatures, where private bills may be introduced, bills which by their nature can only be empty gestures.

In general, the contacts which the delusional person makes with formal organizations frequently disclose the same elements of shallow response, evasion or distrust which played a part in the generic process of exclusion. They become part of a selective or selected pattern of interaction which creates a social environment of uncertainty and ambiguity for the individual. They do little to correct and much to confirm his suspicion, distrust and delusional interpretations. Moreover, even the environment of treatment agencies may contribute to the furtherance of paranoid delusion, as Stanton and Schwartz have shown in their comments on communication within the mental hospital. They speak pointedly of the "pathology of communication" brought about by staff practices of ignoring explicit meanings in

246 / EDWIN M. LEMERT

statements or actions of patients and reacting to inferred or imputed meanings, thereby creating a type of environment in which "the paranoid feels quite at home" (17).

Some paranoid or paranoid-like persons become well known locally or even throughout larger areas to some organizations. Persons and groups in the community are found to assume a characteristic stance towards such people—a stance of expectancy and preparedness. In one such case, police continually checked the whereabouts of the man and, when the governor came to speak on the courthouse steps, two officers were assigned the special task of watching the man as he stood in the crowd. Later, whenever he went to the state capitol, a number of state police were delegated to accompany him when he attended committee hearings or sought interviews with state officials.[7] The notoriety this man acquired because of his reputed great strength in tossing officers around like tenpins was an obvious source of pleasure to him, despite the implications of distrust conveyed by their presence.

It is arguable that occupying the role of the mistrusted person becomes a way of life for these paranoids, providing them with an identity not otherwise possible. Their volatile contentions with public officials, their issuance of writings, publications, litigations in *persona propria*, their overriding tendency to contest issues which other people dismiss as unimportant or as "too much bother" become a central theme for their lives, without which they would probably deteriorate.

If paranoia becomes a way of life for some people, it is also true that the difficult person with grandiose and persecutory ideas may fulfill certain marginal functions in organizations and communities. One is his scapegoat function, being made the subject of humorous by-play or conjectural gossip as people "wonder what he will be up to next." In his scapegoat role, the person may help integrate primary groups within larger organizations by directing aggressions and blame towards him and thus strengthening feelings of homogeneity and consensus of group members.

There are also instances in which the broad, grapeshot charges and accusations of the paranoid person function to articulate dissatisfactions of those who fear openly to criticize the leadership of the community, organization, or state, or of the informal power structures within these. Sometimes the paranoid person is the only one who openly espouses values of inarticulate and politically unrepresented segments of the population (12). The "plots" which attract the paranoid person's attention—dope rings, international communism, monopolistic "interests," popery, Jewry, or "psychopoliticians"—

often reflect the vague and ill-formed fears and concerns of peripheral groups, which tend to validate his self-chosen role as a "protector." At times in organizational power plays and community conflicts his role may even be put to canny use by more representative groups as a means of embarrassing their opposition.

THE LARGER SOCIO-CULTURAL CONTEXT

Our comments draw to a close on the same polemic note with which they were begun, namely, that members of communities and organizations do unite in common effort against the paranoid person prior to or apart from any vindictive behavior on his part. The paranoid community is real rather than pseudo in that it is composed of reciprocal relationships and processes whose net results are informal and formal exclusion and attenuated communication.

The dynamics of exclusion of the paranoid person are made understandable in larger perspective by recognizing that decision making in America social organization is carried out in small, informal groups through casual and often subtle male interaction. Entree into such groups is ordinarily treated as a privilege rather than a right, and this privilege tends to be jealously guarded. Crucial decisions, including those to eject persons or to reorganize their status in larger formal organizations, are made secretly. The legal concept of "privileged communication" in part is a formal recognition of the necessity for making secret decisions within organizations.

Added to this is the emphasis placed upon conformity in our organization-oriented society and the growing tendency of organization elites to rely upon direct power for their purposes. This is commonly exercised to isolate and neutralize groups and individuals who oppose their policies both inside and outside of the organization. Formal structures may be manipulated or deliberately reorganized so that resistant groups and indivuduals are denied or removed from access to power or the available means to promote their deviant goals and values. One of the most readily effective ways of doing this is to interrupt, delay or stop the flow of information.

It is the necessity to rationalize and justify such procedures on a democratic basis which leads to concealment of certain actions, misrepresentation of their underlying meaning and even the resort to unethical or illegal means. The difficulty of securing sociological knowledge about these techniques, which we might call the "controls behind the controls," and the denials by those who use them that they exist are logical consequences of the perceived threat such knowledge and admissions become to informal power structures. The epiphenomena of power thus become a kind of shadowy world of our culture, inviting conjecture and condemnation.

CONCLUDING COMMENT

We have been concerned with a process of social exclusion and with the ways in which it contributes to the development of paranoid patterns of behavior. While the data emphasize the organizational forms of exclusion, we nevertheless believe that these are expressions of a generic process whose correlates will emerge from the study of paranoia in the family and other groups. The differential responses of the individual to the exigencies of organized exclusion are significant in the development of paranoid reactions only insofar as they partially determine the "intolerable" or "unendurable" quality of the status changes confronting him. Idiosyncratic life history factors of the sort stressed in more conventional psychiatric analyses may be involved, but equally important in our estimation are those which inhere in the status changes themselves, age being one of the more salient of these. In either case, once situational intolerability appears, the stage is set for the interactional process we have described.

Our cases, it will be noted, were all people who remained undeteriorated, in contact with others and carrying on militant activities oriented towards recognizable social values and institutions. Generalized suspiciousness in public places and unprovoked aggression against strangers were absent from their experiences. These facts, plus the relative absence of "true paranoia" among mental-hospital populations, leads us to conclude that the "pseudocommunity" associated with random aggression (in Cameron's sense) is a sequel rather than an integral part of paranoid patterns. They are likely products of deterioration and fragmentation of personality appearing, when and if they do, in the paranoid person after long or intense periods of stress and complete social isolation.

References

1. Cameron, N., "The Paranoid Pseudocommunity," *American Journal of Sociology*, 1943, 46, 33–38.
2. Cameron, N., "The Paranoid Pseudocommunity Revisited," *American Journal of Sociology*, 1959, 65, 52–58.
3. Cumming, E., and J. Cumming, *Closed Ranks*, Cambridge, Mass.: Harvard Press, 1957, Ch. VI.
4. Dentler, R. A., and K. T. Erikson, "The Functions of Deviance in Groups," *Social Problems*, 1959, 7, 102.

5. Goffman, E., "The Moral Career of the Mental Patient," *Psychiatry*, 1959, 22, 127 ff.
6. Jaco, E. G., "Attitudes Toward, and Incidence of Mental Disorder: A Research Note," *Southwestern Social Science Quarterly*, June, 1957, p. 34.
7. Kine, F. F., "Aliens' Paranoid Reaction," *Journal of Mental Science*, 1951, 98, 589–594.
8. Lemert, E., "Legal Commitment and Social Control," *Sociology and Social Research*, 1946, 30, 33–338.
9. Levenson, B., "Bureaucratic Succession," in *Complex Organizations*, A. Etzioni, (ed.), New York: Holt, Rinehart and Winston, 1961, 362–395.
10. Listivan, I., "Paranoid States: Social and Cultural Aspects," *Medical Journal of Australia*, 1956, 776–778.
11. Loomis, J. L., "Communications, The Development of Trust, and Cooperative Behavior," *Human Relations*, 1959, 12, 305–315.
12. Marmor, J., "Science, Health and Group Opposition" (mimeographed paper), 1958.
13. Milner, K. O., "The Environment as a Factor in the Etiology of Criminal Paranoia," *Journal of Mental Science*, 1949, 95, 124–132.
14. Ödegard, Ö., "A Clinical Study of Delayed Admissions to a Mental Hospital," *Mental Hygiene*, 1958, 42, 66–77.
15. Pederson, S., "Psychological Reactions to Extreme Social Displacement (Refugee Neuroses)," *Psychoanalytic Review*, 1946, 36, 344–354.
16. Sapir, E., "Abnormal Types of Speech in Nootka," *Canada Department of Mines, Memoir 62*, 1915, No. 5.
17. Stanton, A. H., and M. S. Schwartz, *The Mental Hospital*, New York: Basic Books, 1954, 200–210.
18. Tyhurst, J. S., "Paranoid Patterns," in A. H. Leighton, J. A. Clausen, and R. Wilson, (eds.), *Exploration in Social Psychiatry*, New York: Basic Books, 1957, Ch. II.

Notes

1. The research for this paper was in part supported by a grant from the California State Department of Mental Hygiene, arranged with the assistance of Dr. W. A. Oliver, Associate Superintendent of Napa State Hospital, who also helped as a critical consultant and made the facilities of the hospital available.
2. In a subsequent article Cameron (2) modified his original conception, but not of the social aspects of paranoia, which mainly concern us.
3. The interaction in some ways is similar to that used with children, particularly the *"enfant terrible."* The function of language in such interaction was studied by Sapir (16) years ago.
4. For a systematic analysis of the organizational difficulties in removing an "unpromotable" person from a position see (9).
5. One of the cases in the first study.
6. *Supra*, p. 3.
7. This technique in even more systematic form is sometimes used in protecting the President of the United States in "White House cases."

20 / Deviance and Respectability: An Observational Study of Reactions to Shoplifting

DARRELL J. STEFFENSMEIER
ROBERT M. TERRY

The interactionist-labeling perspective in deviance asserts that audience responses to deviant acts are crucial to the understanding of deviant behavior. Furthermore, to understand audience response — reactions toward various types of deviance — investigators need to discover the meaning these behaviors have for potential reactors. These meanings may vary with the deviant's other social identities, with situational factors such as social support and social setting, and the characteristics of potential reactors. Although some research relates these variables to audience reactions, few studies have manipulated such variables within a field setting.

A growing body of observational field studies treats the reactions of official control agents such as the police (e.g., Black, 1970; Piliavin and Briar, 1964) and courts to deviant actors (Emerson, 1969). But such research has generally lacked the kind of control that allows for experimental manipulation of variables and the systematic examination of posited relationships. In addition, studies examining the reactions of the general public have been largely ignored. With few exceptions (e.g., Darley and Latane, 1968; Denner, 1968; Freed et al., 1955; Lefkowitz et al., 1955), there is a dearth of experimental field research that systematically examines posited relationships between reactions of the general public and deviant behavior.

Current thinking in Sociology indicates that the study of deviant behavior must overcome problems in the validity of official statistics (see, especially, Douglas, 1971a; Kitsuse and Cicourel, 1963; Wheeler, 1967), must recognize that while official control agents are important it is the general public that usually initiates responses to deviant behavior (e.g., Black, 1970), and must study deviance in its natural setting rather than as mediated through the official reports and actions of formal control agents (e.g., Douglas, 1971b; Humphreys, 1970).

This research attempts to shed some light on the nature and basis of reactions to a particular kind of deviance and, in doing so, tries to overcome the aforementioned problems by (1) using field research methods, (2) ascertaining responses of the general public to instances of deviant behavior in real life situations, and (3) making direct observations of behavior of members of the social audience. Specifically, appearance and sex of the deviant are varied systematically in order to assess their effects upon the responses of the general public to observed instances of shoplifting.[1]

There is much theoretical support for the notion that the actor's social identity is a crucial determinant of reactions to deviant behavior (Douglas, 1970; Goffman, 1963; Lemert, 1951; Lofland, 1969). Two important aspects of social identity considered in this research are those of appearance and sex, both of which can be subsumed under the more abstract rubric of respectability.

Much of the literature in the interactionist-labeling perspective has argued that differential treatment is accorded persons with poor social backgrounds, less than perfect social identities, or "bad" reputations. Many analyses of deviant categories are founded on the assumption that particular classes of people are more likely to perform deviant acts and to be particular types of deviant persons (Hughes, 1945; Kitsuse, 1962; Lofland, 1969; Scheff, 1966; Simmons, 1965; Sudnow, 1965). Such studies are highly consistent in arguing that respectability decreases the likelihood of deviant imputations, whereas "unrespectability" has the opposite effect.

In this research, appearance and sex are used as indicators of respectability. Reports by Ball (1970) and Cameron (1964) have noted that a respectable appearance serves as a buffer against a deviant imputation. Lefkowitz *et al.* (1955) found that a respectable appearance was influential in inducing others to engage in deviant behavior (jaywalking). In a field experiment, Bickman (1971) found that persons who appeared to be of low status were treated more dishonestly by experimental subjects than were those of apparently higher status. It has been noted that one's appearance (kinds of clothing, hair style, and the like) is part and parcel of being a particular kind of person and also indicates, in a general sense, an individual's attitude toward community norms (Carey, 1968; Stone, 1962). In the current scene, commonsense distinctions between hippie and straight appearances are especially noteworthy.

Another of actor's social identities thought to affect reactions to deviance is one's sex. Consistent research findings show that females are less severely dealt with by formal control agents than are males and some evidence exists to support the notion that public attitudes and reactions toward the sexes tend to favor females (Pollak, 1961; Reckless, 1961; Ward and Kassebaum, 1965). Schur (1969) has argued that the greater attitude of protectiveness taken toward women in our society and more generally the nature of their social roles and situations permit women to exploit their sex for criminal purposes and to engage in various kinds of criminal behavior with relatively little fear of detection or prosecution.

The effect of sex status on deviant imputation can be fitted into Goffman's discussion of social identities and more specifically into the rubric of respectability. Goffman (1963) argues that an individual's biography is composed of both past and present events and characteristics which function so as to establish an individual's social identity. The latter refers to those attributes others can observe, providing thereby a basis for classifying an actor as a particular kind of person. Such attributes as age and sex are of primary importance in making such categorizations. Although none of these variables is inherently bound to the notion of respectability, the deviant behavior literature rather clearly indicates that being a male tends to be viewed as an unfavorable attribute by social control agents and increases a person's vulnerability to the imputation of deviance.

Our third independent variable, sex of subject, is ambiguously grounded in research that generally indicates that females are less tolerant of deviance than are males (Phillips, 1964; Westie and Martin, 1959; Williams, 1964); although there is conflicting evidence (Whatley, 1959). Traditional sex role differences, theoretically at least, have emphasized more support of stability and the ongoing system among females than among males. Thus, females should be less accepting of nonconforming behavior than males (Parsons and Bales, 1955) and therefore should be more likely to report deviant acts.

HYPOTHESES

On the basis of the foregoing, the following hypotheses are the targets of inquiry:

1. *Store customers will be more likely to report a shoplifting incident when the shoplifter has a hippie rather than a straight appearance.*
2. *Store customers will be more likely to report a shoplifting incident when the shoplifter is male rather than female.*

3. *Female store customers will be more likely to report a shoplifting incident than male store customers.*

METHODS

This research sought to discover factors related to reactions to shoplifting. "Reactions" was defined in terms of variations in the willingness of store customers to report behavior (shoplifting) which was blatantly illegal and deviant. In order to observe the reactions of a wide variety of subjects and simultaneously maintain some degree of control over the frequency of occurrence and consistency of the deviant behavior, a natural field experiment was designed. While this approach assured a rather high degree of external validity it presented some difficulties in settling on the variables determining societal reactions. For the experimental situation allowed us to investigate only those independent variables that were amenable to immediate observation in fleeting encounters: hence, sex and appearance.

The study was conducted in three preselected stores in a midwestern university city of 50,000. The experiment can best be described as a rigged shoplifting incident—i.e., its occurrence was prearranged. The store's manager and personnel had complete knowledge of the experiment and the researchers had their full cooperation in staging the shoplifting incidents.

A. Shoplifting Sequence

The main concern of this research was the extent to which customers were willing to report shoplifting to store personnel. In order to control the frequency and consistency of the shoplifting situation three accomplices were employed. One accomplice played the part of a shoplifter and two more accomplices played the parts of store employees. The experimental procedure is best understood through a discussion of the roles played by the accomplices.

The first accomplice played the part of a shoplifter. This accomplice was to place himself under the direct observation of a customer (the subject), and then steal some item of merchandise in an obvious and deliberate manner.[2] Having done his shoplifting, the first accomplice moved to another location where he remained out of hearing distance but within eyesight of the subject. This procedure avoided the possible intimidation of the subject and simultaneously eased identification of the shoplifter if the subject showed a willingness to report the incident. The appearance and sex of the shoplifter were varied systematically.

The second and third research accomplices played the parts of store employees.[3] The principal task of the second accomplice or first store employee was to make himself readily available should the subject wish to report the shoplifting incident. As soon as the shoplifter moved away to another location (after he had shoplifted) the first store employee had instructions to move into the immediate vicinity of the subject and act as though he were arranging merchandise on the shelves or counters. The accomplice remained in the area for a brief period of time in order to allow the subject ample opportunity to report. If the subject reported, then the store employee was instructed to "apprehend" the shoplifter and both of them moved backstage.[4] If the subject did not report the shoplifting, the accomplice left the area and signaled to a third accomplice to intervene.

The third accomplice played the part of a second store employee. He was instructed to act more directly and vigorously in order to increase the likelihood of reporting. He asked the subject for assistance in identifying a possible shoplifter by prompting the subject in two different ways. The first prompting was as follows: "Good afternoon (evening), sir (madam), we have been watching so-and-so (identifying description) for shoplifting. Did you happen to see anything?" If, in response to this first prompting the subject reported the shoplifter, then the employee "apprehended" him and they moved backstage. If the subject did not respond to the first prompting, the same store employee was instructed to intervene more forcefully to elicit reporting from the subject. The second prompting was as follows: "Gee, I was quite sure I saw him (her) take something (specify item) and put it down his coat. You didn't happen to see anything suspicious, did you?" If the subject still did not report, the accomplice left the vicinity and there was no further prompting of the subject.

After the experiment was completed each subject was immediately debriefed by another research assistant. Every conceivable effort was made to clarify to the subject the nature and the purpose of the deception. In addition, an attempt was made to interview the subject briefly as to his perception of and reaction to the experiment.[5]

B. Operationalization of the Dependent Variable

The dependent variable in this research is willingness to report a shoplifting incident. On a higher theoretical level we are getting at the willingness of potential reactors to impute a deviant label to presumably deviant actors. The use of prompting as a device to obtain variation in the dependent variable was suggested by the previous research of Latane and Darley (1969) and Denner (1968). As operationalized in this research, willingness to report could achieve four possible values:

1. If the subject reported the shoplifting incident to the first store employee this response was assigned a value of *high* willingness to report. As will be recalled, the first store employee took a passive stance toward the subject and made no direct attempt to encourage reporting. No prompting was used at this point.

2. If the subject reported the shoplifting incident to the second store employee in response to the first prompting, this behavior was held to indicate *medium high* willingness to report.

3. If the subject reported the shoplifting incident to the second store employee in response to the second prompting, this behavior was assigned a value of *medium low* willingness to report.

4. The category of *low* willingness to report consisted of all subjects who did not report the shoplifting incident.

Table 1 gives the distributions obtained for the sample on the dependent variable, willingness to report. As can be seen, we got good variance in type of response. A good deal of reporting took place even without prompting.

Table 1 / Frequency Distribution of Respondent Reporting Levels

Reporting	TOTAL SAMPLE (n = 212)	ADULTS (n = 191)	STUDENTS (n = 21)
High	62 (29.2)	61 (31.9)	1 (4.8)
Medium high	73 (34.4)	71 (37.2)	2 (9.5)
Medium low	28 (13.2)	25 (13.1)	3 (14.3)
Low	49 (23.1)	34 (17.8)	15 (71.4)

C. Research Sites

Stores were selected on the basis of several criteria. We thought it important to use stores of differing size and degree of bureaucratization.[6] Also, the stores had to retail merchandise that would be easy and obvious to steal. We also sought stores that had customers who represented the nonstudent population of a university-dominated city.

After considering these matters, we approached several store managers to determine their willingness to participate in the project. Some were encouraging and enthusiastic. Out of necessity, then, the stores finally selected as research sites were those at which most cooperation was offered. Fortunately, these stores varied along the relevant dimensions of size and bureaucratization. In addition, each store had certain unique features.

Store A was a small, older chain grocery store, located close to the downtown area. Patrons consisted largely of persons living in the immediate neiborhood, older people, and university students. Store B was a relatively new, large chain grocery store located in a fringe area shopping center. The patrons consisted chiefly of housewives. Store C was a very large discount department store located on the edge of the city. For a number of reasons (location, prices, variety of merchandise, store hours, etc.) this store was more likely to attract out-of-town customers than the other stores.[7]

We tried to get approximately equal numbers of subjects in each store. Except for persons later identified as college students, this aim was achieved, with 67 subjects exposed to shoplifting in Store A, 69 in Store B, and 55 in Store C. Since the stores differed in size and therefore in the number of customers during any given time period, trial runs were conducted on four separate occasions in Store A, on two separate occasions in Store B, and on one occasion in Store C. In addition, Store A was used to conduct all pretests for the experiment.

D. Experimental Design

A primary justification for the study of contrived rather than real shoplifting is the greater ability to manipulate the independent variables. Two identities of the shoplifters were systematically varied— appearance and sex. In addition, sex of the subject (shopper) was also varied across experimental events. Each variable is dichotomized,

Figure 1 / Representation of the Research Design

	Sex of Shoplifter			
	Male		Female	
	Appearance of Shoplifter		Appearance of Shoplifter	
Sex of Subject	Hippie	Straight	Hippie	Straight
Male				
Female				

resulting in an overall research design of the $2 \times 2 \times 2$ variety. Figure 1 illustrates the eight comparison groups produced by this design. Approximately 25 subjects are represented in each cell, with a total sample size of 212. Each subject was exposed to only one combination of the independent variables, sex of shoplifter and appearance of shoplifter. We tried to include proportionate numbers of male and female subjects from various age categories and backgrounds and to exclude persons who appeared to be college students. Of the total of 212 subjects, 191 were classifiable as nonstudent adults. All future tabulations of experimental data are based on these 191 subjects.[8]

E. Operationalizing the Independent Variables

The major independent variables in this research were appearance and sex. Appearance was varied: hippie vs. straight. Sex was varied by using male and female shoplifters. Attributes of the shoplifter presentation types are as follows:

(1) *Hippie shoplifter:*
    (a) *Male:* He wore soiled patched blue jeans, blue workman's shirt, and blue denim jacket; well-worn scuffed shoes with no socks. He had long and unruly hair with a ribbon tied around his forehead. He was unshaven and had a small beard.
    (b) *Female:* She wore soiled patched blue jeans, blue workman's shirt, and dirty blue denim jacket; well-worn ragged tennis shoes with no socks. She had long unruly and ratted hair. She wore no makeup.

(2) *Straight shoplifter:*
    (a) *Male:* He wore neatly pressed dress slacks, sport shirt and tie, sport jacket, shined shoes. He had short, trimly cut hair and was clean shaven.
    (b) *Female:* She wore a dress, shined shoes or boots, a fur coat. Her hair was well-styled. She wore makeup and was well groomed.

Other than the induced differences of grooming and dress, the shoplifters were about the same age, same height and build, and attractiveness.

RESULTS

Tables 2 and 3 analyze the effects on reporting levels of our three independent variables. Table 2 also shows the interaction effects

Table 2 / Three-way Analysis of Variance of Reporting Levels and Tests for Interaction Effects for Appearance of Shoplifter, Sex of Shoplifter, and Sex of Subject*

Source	SS	DF†	MS	F	Prob.
Total	235.1296	$(npqr - 1) = 190$			
Main effects					
Appearance of					
Shoplifter (A)	46.9782	$(q - 1) = 1$	46.9782	48.1186	<.001
Sex of shoplifter (B)	.0048	$(p - 1) = 1$	.0048	.0049	>.05 N.S.
Sex of subject (C)	2.7066	$(r - 1) = 1$	2.7066	2.7723	>.05 N.S.
Interactions					
AB interaction	.1688	$(q - 1)(p - 1) = 1$	.1688	.1728	>.05 N.S.
AC interaction	.5145	$(q - 1)(r - 1) = 1$	.5145	.5269	>.05 N.S.
BC interaction	4.6232	$(p - 1)(r - 1) = 1$	4.6232	4.7354	$.01 < p < .05$
ABC interaction	1.4594	$(q - 1)(p - 1)(r - 1) = 1$	1.4594	1.4948	>.05 N.S.
Error					
Error SS (W. cell)	178.6741	$pqr(\bar{n} - 1) = 183$	.9763		

* The analysis of variance procedures used in Table 2 was based on the "method of expected equal frequencies." According to this procedure, if cell Ns do not differ markedly, a fairly simple weighting procedure can be used to estimate what the cell sums and sums of squared scores would be if all Ns had been the same. (See Kohout, forthcoming; Schuessler, 1971, for cogent discussions of the procedure involved.)

† In computing the degrees of freedom, q = levels of A, p = levels of B, r = levels of C, and $\bar{n}$ = the average cell frequency.

Table 3 / Summary Correlation Table*

Zero-order	FIRST-ORDER	SECOND-ORDER
$r_{wy} = .465$	$r_{wy.x} = .465$	$r_{wy.xz} = .471$
(appearance of shoplifter)	$r_{wy.z} = .471$	
$r_{xy} = .012$	$r_{xy.w} = .016$	$r_{xy.wz} = .018$
(sex of shoplifter)	$r_{xy.z} = .014$	
$r_{zy} = .096$	$r_{zy.w} = .127$	$r_{zy.wx} = .127$
(sex of subject)	$r_{zy.x} = .096$	

* The measure of association reported is Pearson's coefficient of correlation.
 z = sex of subject
 x = sex of shoplifter
 w = appearance of shoplifter
 y = reporting level

among our three independent variables. The tests of hypotheses, which are treated separately below, are derived from the information presented in Tables 2 and 3.

Appearance and Reporting

Our hypothesis predicts that the level of reporting of a shoplifting incident will be higher for the hippie than for the straight shoplifter. The hypothesis is clearly supported in that the relationship $(r=.465)$ is large and in the expected direction and the F-test results are highly significant. In line with previous arguments, the shoplifter's appearance provides the potential reactor with information that enables him to locate the actor on a high-low evaluative continuum. Apparently a hippie appearance constitutes a negative identity that results in a greater willingness on the part of subjects to report the hippie over the straight shoplifter and, by extension, a greater willingness to impute a deviant label to a hippie rather than a straight actor. The effects of shoplifter's appearance on reporting levels is discussed in greater detail following presentation of other results.

Sex of Shoplifter and Reporting

Our hypothesis as to the effect of shoplifter's sex on reporting levels is not supported in the data. The relationship $(r=.012)$ is in the expected direction but is so small as to be non-existent. In addition, F-test results are not significant.

Explanations for this finding are easy to come by, although such explanations are speculative. First, the findings may be limited to shoplifting and may not be generalizable to other deviance. Also, the trend toward sexual equality may be narrowing sex differentials in attitudes and actions toward offenders and the protectiveness argument may be no longer feasible. Finally, findings of differential reactions to offenders on the basis of sex have focused upon the reactions of formal control agents rather than the general public. It may be that control agents discriminate whereas the public does not.

Sex of Subject and Reporting Levels

Our hypothesis asserts that females will be more likely to report than will males. The data offer little support for the hypothesis. As indicated in Tables 2 and 3, the relationship $(r=.096)$ is in the expected direction, but it is so small that we reject the hypothesis. In addition, F-test results are not significant. Again, it is possible that changing cultural definitions of female social roles and the increasing equalitarianism of women in general has had the effect of narrowing sexual differentials in reactions to deviance. Williams (1964) has argued that this is occurring with racial prejudice and discrimination, and a similar process might have produced these results with respect to deviance.

Interaction Effects

Table 2 shows the interaction effects on reporting levels of various combinations of our independent variables. Only the interaction effect between sex of shoplifter and sex of subject proved to be significant (*BC* Interaction: *.01< p< .05*). This interaction effect can be explained ex post facto by means of further analyses. The cell means for combinations of the independent variables were used to rank-order reporting levels for various categories of shoplifters and subjects. In addition, a new variable was derived by combining the sex of subject and sex of shoplifter. The derived variable yields a dichotomy—opposite sex vs. same sex reporting. The results are presented in Table 4, a table which neatly summarizes the results of this research.

First, the appearance of the shoplifter has the strongest and most clear-cut effect on reporting levels. Hippie shoplifters are always more likely to be reported than straight shoplifters. Second, for hippie shoplifters, female subjects report more than male subjects, irrespective of sex of shoplifter. For straight shoplifters, subject's willingness to report is greater when the shoplifter is of the opposite, rather than the same sex. According to these rank orders, straight shoplifters who are the same sex as the subject-witness are the least likely of all shoplifters to be reported.

Within categories of shoplifter's appearance we have a case of specification. For the hippie shoplifter, sex of subject has an indepen-

Table 4 / Mean Reporting Levels for Combinations of Independent Variables

Rank Order	SEX OF SUBJECT	SEX OF SHOPLIFTER	SEX OF SUBJECT AND SEX OF SHOPLIFTER	APPEARANCE OF SHOPLIFTER	MEAN REPORTING LEVEL
1	Female	Male	Opposite	Hippie	1.4347
2	Female	Female	Same	Hippie	1.5217
3	Male	Female	Opposite	Hippie	1.7173
4	Male	Male	Same	Hippie	1.9130
5	Female	Male	Opposite	Straight	2.2962
6	Male	Female	Opposite	Straight	2.5000
7	Female	Female	Same	Straight	2.8518
8	Male	Male	Same	Straight	2.9166

dent effect on reporting: females report more often than males. In the case of the straight shoplifter, the interaction of sex of subject and sex of shoplifter clearly affects the level of reporting. The simple finding of interaction between these two independent variables becomes more complicated than it at first appeared to be in Table 2.

This specification of different levels of reporting requires us to try to explain the results for each category, separately. For straight shoplifters, same sex reporting may be less than opposite sex reporting because subjects are more able to empathize with persons of the same sex. Another possibility is that subjects are more likely to report a member of the opposite sex because they feel less threatened. That is, subjects may feel that they are less likely to be attacked (physically or verbally) in a highly visible public situation by a member of the opposite sex than by a member of the same sex.

On the other hand, female subjects are more likely than male subjects to report the shoplifter who is a hippie because they are probably more offended by the overt violation of community norms and are more threatened by such attacks on the social order of the community. Females therefore are more likely than males to sanction persons with a nonrespectable appearance. The possibility that female subjects are more concerned with the appearance of respectability and with maintenance of social order explains the differential in reporting between male and female subjects when the shoplifter is a hippie.

DISCUSSION

The major results of this research are that sex of shoplifter and sex of subject had little effect on reporting levels, whereas appearance of shoplifter exerted a major independent effect on reporting levels. The importance of appearance merits further discussion: How to account for its significance?

The evidence presented clearly indicates that a hippie appearance constituted a highly salient basis for social differentiation. From the perspective of "middle class" America, hippies and other beatnik types are viewed as basically unstable, as lacking in ambition and ability, and as marginal contributors to the social system. By the mere fact of being a hippie the person has demonstrated his lack of moral worth, his unrespectability, from the dominant cultural perspective. As such, a hippie label represents a stigma, an extreme negative identity. Such an identity has been variously dealt with as a "master status" by Becker (1963), a "pivotal category" by Lofland (1969), or a "central trait" by Asch (1946). All of these concepts refer to a similar

phenomenon: an extreme negative identity can exercise a disproportionate influence in structuring perceptions and behaviors and, in
terms of this research, the reactions to shoplifting. A hippie identity or
label constitutes, for many subjects in this research, a master status, a
pivotal category, or a central trait, which greatly increases the individual's vulnerability to stigmatization as a deviant.[9]

Some anecdotal observations illustrate these notions. These observations also depict the less conscious, less deliberate reactions of the
subjects to the hippie identity than to the straight identity. In general,
most subjects appeared to be inclined *not* to report the shoplifting
incident and to avoid getting involved. When they witnessed the
incident and the shoplifter gave off no other negative cues or stimuli
they were apt to hesitate. Hesitation of this sort was likely to result in
disengagement and failure to report.

Subjects were more likely to hesitate when the shoplifter was
straight rather than hippie. A number of subjects, for instance, indicated that they considered reporting the straight shoplifter but thought
twice or hesitated before proceeding with a course of action. This
"thinking twice" or hesitating then often resulted in their deciding
simply to ignore the incident.

But in the case of hippie shoplifters, this hesitation was less likely to
occur. That is, when witnessing a hippie shoplifting the subject was
not only more likely to consider reporting but he was also less likely to
think twice about it and thus in reality he was more likely to proceed to
report. The hippie appearance seemed to tip the scales in the direction of increased reporting.

Further support for the importance of appearance comes from the
level of enthusiasm in reporting. In reporting the hippie shoplifter
some subjects were very excited—even enthusiastic. Although not
true of all subjects, reporting of hippie shoplifters (without prompting) frequently included such comments as "That hippie thing took a
package of lunchmeat," or "That son of a bitch hippie over there just
stuffed a banana down his coat." For these subjects, the high levels of
reporting of hippie shoplifters must be viewed within a particular
situational context wherein his undoing was not simply a result of his
being a shoplifter, but because he was both shoplifter *and* hippie.

CONCLUSIONS

Via the use of field research techniques combined with an experimental design we have provided clear support for the basic interactionist-
labeling contention that the imputation of deviance resides not only in

the *fact* of deviance per se; it also depends heavily on the meanings that the audience attach to the behavior and the actor. Willingness to report deviant acts can be assumed to depend on the "deviant's" other social identities, a significant clue to identity being provided by his appearance.

At the same time, however, some other identities that may seem to be important at first glance may actually prove to be unimportant aspects of the interpersonal relationships between offender and audience. This seemed to be the case with sex of shoplifter and sex of subject, although it is apparent that the complexity of the relationships involved necessitates additional research. Further research should also focus upon other aspects of the social identities of the offender, the situational contexts in which deviant acts occur, and the backgrounds and relevant identities of members of the social audience. At the very least we have demonstrated that in order to get at such problems it is possible and fruitful to utilize experimental field research techniques.

References

Alvarez, R. 1968. "Informal Reactions to Deviance in Simulated Work Organizations: A Laboratory Experiment." *American Sociological Review* 33 (December): 895–911.

Asch, S. E. 1946. "Forming Impressions of Personality." *Journal of Abnormal and Social Psychology* 41:258–90.

Ball, D. W. 1970. "The Problematics of Respectability." In Jack Douglas (ed.), *Respectability and Deviance*. New York: Basic Books.

Becker, Howard S. 1963. *Outsiders: Studies in the Sociology of Deviance*. New York: Free Press.

Bickman, L. 1971. "The Effect of Social Class on the Honesty of Others." *Journal of Social Psychology* 85:87–92.

Black, D. J. 1970. "Production of Crime Rates." *American Sociological Review* 35 (August): 733–48.

Black, D. J., and A. J. Reiss, Jr. 1970. "Police Control of Juveniles." *American Sociological Review* 35 (February): 63–77.

Cameron, Mary O. 1964. *The Booster and the Snitch*. Glencoe: Free Press.

Carey, James T. 1968. *The College Drug Scene*. Englewood Cliffs: Prentice-Hall.

Darley, J. M., and B. Latane. 1968. "Bystander Intervention in Emergencies: Diffusion of Responsibility." *Journal of Personality and Social Psychology* 8:377–83.

Denner, B. 1968. "Did a Crime Occur? Should I Inform Anyone? A Study of Deception." *Journal of Personality* 36:454–68.

Douglas, Jack (ed.). 1970. *Respectability and Deviance*. New York: Basic Books.

———. 1971a. *American Social Order*. New York: Free Press.

————. 1971b. (ed.). *Research on Deviance*. New York: Random House.

Emerson, Robert M. 1969. *Judging Delinquents*. Chicago: Aldine.

Freed, A., P. J. Chandler, R. R. Blake, and J. S. Mouton. 1955. "Stimulus and Background Factors in Sign Violation." *Journal of Personality* 23:499.

Goffman, Erving. 1963. *Stigma: Notes on the Management of Spoiled Identity*. Englewood Cliffs: Spectrum Books.

Hollander, E. P. 1958. "Conformity, Status, and Idiosyncrasy Credit." *Psychological Review* 65:117–27.

Homans, George C. 1961. *Social Behavior: Its Elementary Forms*. New York: Harcourt, Brace & World.

Hughes, E. C. 1945. "Dilemmas and Contradictions of Status." *American Journal of Sociology* 50 (March): 353–9.

Humphreys, Laud. 1970. *Tearoom Trade*. Chicago: Aldine.

Kitsuse, J. I. 1962. "Societal Reaction to Deviant Behavior: Problems of Theory and Method." *Social Problems* 9:247–56.

Kitsuse, J. I., and A. Cicourel. 1963. "A Note on the Uses of Official Statistics." *Social Problems* 11:131–9.

Kohout, Frank J. 1972. *Applied Statistics*. Forthcoming.

Latane, B., and J. Darley. 1969. "Bystander Apathy." *American Scientist* 57:244–68.

Lefkowitz, M., R. R. Blake, and J. S. Mouton. 1955. "Status Factors in Pedestrian Violation of Traffic Signals." *Journal of Abnormal and Social Psychology* 51:704–705.

Lemert, Edwin. 1951. *Social Pathology*. New York: McGraw-Hill.

Lofland, John. 1969. *Deviance and Identity*. Englewood Cliffs: Prentice-Hall.

Parsons, Talcott, and Robert F. Bales. 1955. *Family Socialization and Interaction Process*. Glencoe: Free Press.

Phillips, D. L. 1964. "Rejection of the Mentally Ill: The Influence of Behavior and Sex." *American Sociological Review* 29 (October): 679–87.

Piliavin, I., and S. Briar. 1964. "Police Encounters with Juveniles." *American Journal of Sociology* 70 (November): 206–14.

Pollak, Otto. 1961. *The Criminality of Women*. New York: Perpetua Books.

Reckless, Walter. 1961. *The Crime Problem*. New York: Appleton-Century-Crofts.

Scheff, Thomas J. 1966. *Being Mentally Ill: A Sociological Theory*. Chicago: Aldine.

Schuessler, Karl. 1971. *Analyzing Social Data*. Boston: Houghton Mifflin.

Schur, E. M. 1969. "Reactions to Deviance: A Critical Assessment." *American Sociological Review*.

Simmons, J. L. 1965. "Public Stereotypes of Deviants." *Social Problems* 13:223–32.

Stone, G. P. 1962. "Appearance and the Self." In Arnold Rose (ed.), *Human Behavior and Social Processes*. Boston: Houghton Mifflin.

Sudnow, D. 1965. "Normal Crimes: Sociological Features of the Penal Code in a Public Defender Office." *Social Problems* 12:255–76.

Ward, David A., and Gene Kassebaum. 1965. *Women's Prison: Sex and Social Structure*. Chicago: Aldine.

Westie, F. R., and J. C. Martin. 1959. "The Tolerant Personality." *American Sociological Review* 24 (August): 521–28.

Whatley, C. D. 1959. "Social Attitudes Toward Discharged Mental Patients." *Social Problems* 6:313–20.

Wheeler, S. 1967. "Criminal Statistics: A Reformulation of the Problem." *Journal of Criminal Law, Criminology, and Police Science* 58: 317–24.

Williams, Robin M., Jr. 1964. *Strangers Next Door*. Englewood Cliffs: Prentice-Hall.

Notes

1. Theoretically the choice of shoplifting is predicated on the assumption that it is a form of deviant behavior which elicits variable social reactions that are usually mild to moderate. Moreover, shoplifting is a sufficiently problematic form of deviance to allow for other deviant identities to influence reactions to it. Several practical considerations also determined the selection of shoplifting as the object of investigation. It was a behavior around which a field experiment could readily be constructed and that in turn allowed for the observation of a large number of subjects within a limited time period and simultaneously permitted the control and manipulation of the independent variables.

2. In the course of pretesting, we found that for subjects to be aware of the shoplifting as well as for them to be reasonably certain that it was shoplifting, our shoplifters had to be quite blatant and aggressive in their shoplifting. At least one member of the research team had to be reasonably certain that the subject saw the shoplifting.

3. The research accomplices who were assigned the roles of store employees were all males who appeared to be about 25–30 years old. To give as much credibility as possible to the experiment, these accomplices wore the same apparel as the regular store employees. In Stores A and B, long white aprons made the accomplices easily identifiable. However in Store C regular employees were less well differentiated and thus some minor modifications were introduced in our accomplices in order to ensure their proper identification by subjects. These modifications did not seem to create any noticeable differences in the experimental situation that would affect our interpretation of the data.

4. Backstage refers to an area of the store reserved for store personnel where the researcher and his associates were able to record each event as it happened and plan for the next event without being observed by subjects.

5. Studying behavior in the natural environment raises ethical questions about the deception of subjects and the invasion of their privacy. Should people be used in a social-psychological experiment without their permission or awareness? The question is difficult to answer. We feel that in the case of this study the permission of the subjects was not crucial. None of the subjects expressed hostility toward the experiment and most were highly cooperative. Note, for example, that 178 of the 191 adult subjects completed the postexperimental interview, and 171 of these 178 consented either to a mailed questionnaire or home interview. Careful and thorough pretesting enabled us to avoid numerous problems.

6. Subsequent reports will deal with the effects on reporting levels of size of store and degree of bureaucratization of the store. In general, these variables had little effect on reporting levels and did not affect the relationships between reporting levels and the three variables discussed in this article.

7. Since two of the stores studied were grocery stores, most things stolen were food items. The remainder consisted of articles of clothing, small appliances, cosmetics, etc. The items shoplifted were of relatively small value, most retailing for less than $3.00.

8. A subject was operationally defined as a student if he/she indicated that he/she attended the university full- or part-time and was less than 26 years old. Pretesting indicated that students were highly unlikely to report, irrespective of prompting.

9. Related notions have been dealt with in exchange theory wherein perceived statuses or identities are characterized in terms of positive and negative credits. In dealing with reactions to deviance the reasoning is as follows: the higher the perceived status of an individual the greater his "stock" of esteem, or accumulation of credits. Being involved in visibly deviant behaviors, such as shoplifting, reduces the absolute level of these accumulated credits. However, if a high- (straight-appearing actor) and low- (hippie-appearing actor) status individual commit the same deviant act the high-status person can retain some level of positive credits while the low-status person can go to zero or minus quantity of credits (Alvarez, 1968; Hollander, 1958; Homans, 1961). Thus having a high status or respectable identity served to "protect" the actor from being reported for shoplifting whereas having a low-status or less-than-respectable identity increases the likelihood of being reported. That is, a hippie appearance reduces actor's level of positive credits to a considerable degree, with the effect that when such an actor engages in deviant behavior, more positive credits are lost and his chances for being reported are greatly increased.

Part 4 / Institutional Deviance

In the preceding section I described how deviant behavior may initially be managed in a private setting. The material I presented demonstrated how such behavior may become subject to regulation by a social control agent or agency. (The case of the thirty-five-year-old cabdriver who threatened to kill his wife provided such an illustration). When this occurs, the actor's behavior is screened by the institution and its staff, and a label may be placed upon him or her. The individual then becomes an institutional deviant, expected, thereafter, to conform to the institution's definition of the label. Some will accept this labeling. In this event, not only does the person's public identity—how others view him or her—mesh with the personal identity—how the person views him- or herself—but we can speak of the secondary, or career, deviant (part two). Other deviants, however, will reject the label and attempt to structure and present to others a nondeviant image of self. The selections in this part explore such possibilities as these; they also illustrate clearly how institutional careers are initiated and perpetuated. Throughout the following discussion of the various articles, the "organizational paradigm" (general introduction) is applied.

Typing by Agents of Social Control

I have argued previously that it is difficult to understand deviance unless we first analyze the institution or organization out of which a specific social control agent operates; it is particularly important to know how the existing theory of the office (working ideology), existing deviant categories, and diagnostic stereotypes are applied to clients. The selection by James Q. Wilson, "The Police and the Delinquent in Two Cities," demonstrates how this thesis may operate in the field. Specifically, Wilson's research illustrates clearly how an institution's theory of the office affects the processing of deviants. For example, not only do the police officers in Western City, when compared with those in Eastern City, hold more complex attitudes about why juveniles violate deviant categories (part two), but they respond to juveniles differently. Youths in Eastern City are often reprimanded and taken home, whereas those in Western City are apt to be taken to the station. One reason for these differences can be found in the degree of professionalism within the two departments. Because of the more highly professional structure and specialization of their departments, Western City officers can arrest juveniles and then pass them on to juvenile officers. In Eastern City, which has a more fraternalistic department, the officers are involved in the cases to their disposition. An interesting finding also concerns the attitudes of Eastern City officers toward blacks. These officers appear to select blacks for special processing and treatment more readily. This does not seem to hold for Western City, where blacks and whites are treated much the same.

It should be noted, however, that once a person has been initially identified as a deviant or potential deviant, he or she frequently becomes subject to institutional control and scrutiny. Thomas J. Scheff's research, "The Societal Reaction to Deviance: Ascriptive Elements in the Psychiatric Screening of Patients in a Midwestern State," offers a vivid account of what may happen to those actors brought involuntarily before a psychiatric screening board.

Scheff notes that most patients are incarcerated. The fact that even though many "patients" did not meet the minimal criteria for admission, twenty-four out of the twenty-six cases examined were committed provides a strong measure of support for this observation. Scheff explains his finding by arguing that the theory of the office is predicated solidly upon the "presumption of mental illness," at least as far as it relates to the "involuntary patient." Thus, when such patients come before the board, they are invariably committed; this suggests that the commitment decision has already been made, with the psychiatrists seeming merely to go through the motions. This is apparent from the brief examinations given, the type of questions asked, and the comments offered by various psychiatric personnel. By committing, Scheff reasons, the psychiatrists are confirming the mental institution's expectations of how the involuntary actor should be typed; they are also able to deal with any uncertainty that may arise and thereby remove the threat of negative public reaction that may result if such patients are released.

"A Case of a 'Psychotic' Navaho Indian Male" by Donald P. Jewell, unlike Scheff's study, offers a more concrete example of how institutions frequently respond to people exhibiting certain attributes, especially those who lack power or occupy marginal positions in society. The institution's response made clear that the fact that the client was an Indian took priority over other status considerations. Not only did the institution hold certain stereotypes with respect to Indians, but it is obvious that the institutional personnel were not especially concerned with how Indians were typed, processed, and treated. Even when it was subsequently "discovered" that the subject was not psychotic, the treatment personnel displayed a reluctance to accept this judgment. It should be noted that the fact that the Indian was of a different cultural background only contributed further to his problems. In the Navaho culture, he was viewed as being conservative; however, in terms of psychiatric labels, his passivity and presumed inability to communicate were used to label the Indian psychotic. Many of these same notions were implicit in my discussion of several of the models in part two (e.g., the culture conflict model).

"The Role of Teachers' Nominations in the Perpetuation of Deviant Adolescent Careers," extends the theme being developed in this section, particularly in terms of how actors who occupy marginal positions, or who exhibit what institutions consider to be "stigma symbols," are selected out for placement in deviant career lines. My focus is upon the educational system. I initially describe the existing structure of the school, both in terms of deviant and nondeviant career lines, and then proceed to describe how students are actually selected and placed in deviant careers. A major observation concerns the role that "nonacademic" criteria play in the selection process. Specifically, instead of basing their selection on the basis of academic standards, many teachers used nonacademic measures—most notably, that of whether a student has experienced prior contact with some stigmatizing program.

Sanctioning and Treatment

Once individuals have been typed and screened, they frequently become subject to institutional sanctioning and treatment. Such processing increases the probability that a person will eventually become a career deviant, particularly in the manner described by Lemert (part two).

"Court Processing of Delinquents" by Robert M. Emerson provides an account of how the juvenile court is likely to react to those juveniles who violate deviant categories. An important finding concerns the role of the juveniles relative to court personnel. In particular, attempts are made, throughout the "denunciation" ceremony, to discredit the youths' "moral character" and to show that in spite of opportunities to reform, the juveniles still "messed up." This is the conception the probation officer frequently conveys to the judge—a conception that the judge will later use in rendering a decision. Emerson also notes that, given the marginal status of juveniles and their general lack of resources, it is virtually impossible to structure an effective "counter-denunciation."

Jacqueline P. Wiseman, in "Court Responses to Skid Row Alcoholics," describes the process of "platoon sentencing" whereby 50 to 250 men are sentenced within a very short period of time. Wiseman's classification of social types and probable sentences provides an excellent illustration of how institutional stereotypes relating to skid row alcoholics are actually applied. For example, the alcoholic who is gravely ill is frequently given a suspended sentence and taken to a hospital. Of interest, too, is the way court personnel, many of whom are ex-alcoholics, attempt to present a specific image of the alcoholic to the judge. It should be noted, however, that if the alcoholic is slated for institutional treatment, his behavior becomes regulated by some "people-changing institution" (e.g., an alcoholic ward or hospital). Furthermore, the alcoholic becomes subject to a different theory of the office (and associated institutional stereotypes) and set of institutional expectations. The alcoholic is also expected to act in accordance with his new status, and failure to do so may result in the application of various types of institutional sanctions.

"Characteristics of Total Institutions" by Erving Goffman provides a general overview of what, for example, the officially adjudicated alcoholic or deviant can expect to encounter in the treatment situation. Goffman presents a rough typology of five groups of "total institutions." The actual examples range from homes for the aged and blind to prisons and monasteries. A central feature of such institutions is the breakdown of barriers regulating the sleep, work, and play of inmates. This is accomplished most effectively by conducting all aspects of the clients' life "in the same place and under the same authority," as well as tightly regulating all aspects of the daily routine. Associated with such strategies is the "stripping process," in which all features of the inmates' personal identity and being are removed. Goffman terms this procedure the "mortification of the self." Inmates may react to the institutional experience by withdrawing, turning rebellious, becoming colonizers, or turning into converts of the system. Even though these variations in adjustments are made, Goffman contends that most inmates are probably concerned with "playing it cool"; this frequently means they will become involved in various aspects of the inmate culture.

The excerpt from Leo Carroll's research, "Blacks and Cons: The Working of the Prison Inmate Culture," provides an illustration of how inmates may generally respond to their incarceration. These observations are part of Carroll's fifteen-month study of 186 black and white prisoners in Eastern Correctional Institution (ECI), a facility located in an urban and highly industrialized eastern state. Of major focus is the web of relations surrounding the inmates' concern with drugs and sex. For example, not only does Carroll describe the transactions involved in obtaining drugs, but he also provides many useful insights into how the inmate culture operates. His analysis is also helpful in understanding the type of relationships that exist with respect to the culture, formal structure, and organization of the institution.

Effects of Institutional Processing

I have argued previously that the labeling ceremony or institutional processing can be viewed from two major perspectives: the institution's or the actor's. Thus far, not only have the selections dealt with processing from the institution's perspective, but very little direct focus has been given to the actor's perceptions and responses. If, however, we are to approach a more complete understanding of the effects of various types of processing, then we must try to assume the role of the affected. Erving Goffman's work, "The Moral Career of the Mental Patient," represents what many would consider to be a classic attempt to do so.

Goffman is concerned with analyzing the *moral career* of the mental patient, particularly in terms of how patients perceive and respond to their treatment. Of major concern, then, is the impact of the ward experience upon *self*. He points out initially, as indicated especially in the work by Yarrow et al. and Scheff (parts three and four), that very few patients come willingly to the hospital. Rather, many arrive as a result of family or police action. (In this sense, then, the article further substantiates the discussion of the way in which behavior in private domains may become regulated by some institution.) Goffman argues that the prepatient career can be analyzed in terms of an "extrusory model." What this means in essence is that the patient initially has certain relationships and rights; however, at admission, he or she ends up with very few. Throughout Goffman's insightful analysis one can obtain an excellent understanding of how the actor's public identity becomes transformed into a "deviant" identity — in this case, that of a mental patient. Important to this process are such phenomena as the "alienative coalition" and the "betrayal funnel." Goffman argues further that "the last step in the prepatient career can involve his realization—justified or not—that he has been deserted by society and turned out of relationships by those closest to him." At this stage the patient may begin to orient himself to the "ward system." Some may, for example, accept the "sick role" and develop a set of rationalizations to "explain" their hospitalization. Such strategies enable the patient to regain and sustain a certain semblance of self—a self that has been subjected to a frontal assault by the institution, its personnel, family members and relatives, and, frequently, other patients. With his or her acceptance of this label, the individual begins to take on the identity of the secondary or career deviant.

"Schizophrenic Patients in the Psychiatric Interview: An Experimental Study of Their Effectiveness at Manipulation" by Benjamin M. Braginsky and Dorothea D. Braginsky offers an interesting set of corollary findings to Goffman's observations. These researchers note, supporting Goffman's thesis, that how the patient responds to treatment is frequently a function of the interactional setting or context. If the setting is appropriate, the individual may play the "sick role." If not, he or she may attempt to play the "well role." Through the use of "impression management," patients can consciously construct and present a specific image of self to others. Such observations not only offer a challenge to some of the traditional assumptions concerning the role of the mental patient, but they also underscore the need to examine more carefully actors' perceptions and responses in various settings. The Braginskys' results demonstrate very clearly that some patients are critically aware of their plight. The evidence also indicates that many patients may not be as helpless as we would like to think they are.

"Two Studies of Legal Stigma" by Richard D. Schwartz and Jerome H. Skolnick, unlike Goffman's and the Braginskys' concern with the effects of processing upon the *actors* themselves, analyzes how *social observers*—that is, third parties and witnesses—may react to the *ex*-criminal or *ex*-deviant. Specifically, in the first study the researchers examine the effects that a criminal record may produce upon the probability of obtaining employment. Potential employers were asked if they would hire four categories of applicants, the only difference among them being whether or not they possessed a criminal label. The findings clearly indicate that contact with a stigmatizing institution or agency (i.e., the criminal justice system) reduces significantly the chances of being hired. This is apparent from the observation that only one subject with a record of conviction received a positive response, as compared with three positive responses for those without a letter, six responses for those acquitted with a letter, and nine for those with no record.

Significant, then, is the finding that even though subjects were acquitted, they still, as a group, would experience a reduction in their chances of obtaining jobs. The second study examined the effects that a malpractice suit produced upon the practices of doctors. Of the fifty-eight doctors interviewed, fifty-two reported no adverse effects upon their practice, and five of the remaining six said that their practices had actually improved as a result of the suit. The reactions in these two studies are not so much a function of the particular criminal or deviant category violated as of the status and attributes of the offenders. Obviously doctors, when compared with skilled workers, possess a higher degree of status and respect in our society; they also possess more power and resources. The research also underscores the irreversibility characteristic of a deviant label. Specifically, institutions are most efficient in stamping people with labels, while the reverse process of institutional delabeling, if it exists, is extremely inefficient. As a result, actors, audiences, and third parties continually impute a host of negative attributes to those who have experienced contact with "stigmatizing" programs and institutions.

Derek L. Phillips' research, "Rejection: A Possible Consequence of Seeking Help for Mental Disorders," parallels the efforts of Schwartz and Skolnick, especially in terms of how third parties are likely to respond to those who have experienced various types of contacts with institutions — in this case, people who have sought help for their mental illness. The results indicate that rejection is a function of the nature of the help obtained. Individuals who used a psychiatrist or had contact with a mental institution were most likely to be rejected. Those least likely to be rejected had either sought no help or had talked with a clergyman. Phillips also notes that his findings are a function of several factors, one of the most important of which seems to be whether or not knowledge of the illness is possessed by relatives.

21 / The Police and the Delinquent in Two Cities

JAMES Q. WILSON

. . . A juvenile is arrested and tried, not for committing a "crime" but for behavior that may eventuate in his being made a ward of the court. Although laws vary from state to state, the common practice (and the practice of the states in which are located the cities that we analyze here) is not to regard proceedings before a juvenile court as criminal but, in the language of one state statute, as intended to "secure for each minor under the jurisdiction of the juvenile court such care and guidance, preferably in his own home, as will serve the spiritual, emotional, mental, and physical welfare of the minor and the best interests of the State; to preserve and strengthen the minor's family ties whenever possible, removing him from the custody of his parents only when his welfare or safety and protection of the public cannot be adequately safeguarded without removal. . . ." In the words of another state statute, delinquent children "shall be treated, not as criminals, but as children in need of aid, encouragement and guidance."

These legal considerations and the customary practices that result from them confer on the authorities considerable discretion in the treatment of juveniles.[1] The police as well as the courts need not and, indeed, do not arrest and punish every child who has committed an act which, if he were an adult, would be a misdemeanor or a felony; the police are generally free to exercise their judgment as to which acts require arrest for the protection of society or the welfare of the child and which acts can be dealt with by other means, including police reprimands, unofficial warnings, or referral to parents or welfare agencies.

The two police departments compared here are those of what we shall call Eastern City and Western City. Both cities have substantially more than 300,000 inhabitants; they are heterogeneous in population and in economic base; both are free of domination by a political machine; and both have a substantial nonwhite population. Western City generally has a mild climate, which probably contributes to rates of crimes against property that are somewhat higher than the rates of

Eastern City, where severe winters assist the police in keeping thieves off the streets.

THE MEANING OF PROFESSIONALISM

The most important difference between the police of the two cities is that in Western City the police department is highly "professionalized." This does not mean that in Eastern City the police department is wholly corrupt and incompetent; far from it. But as any observer familiar with Eastern City will readily acknowledge, its police officers have been recruited, organized, and led in a way that falls considerably short of the standards set forth in the principal texts. Whether the standards of the texts are right is, of course, another matter. Since the meaning (to say nothing of the value) of professionalism is itself problematical, an effort will be made here to arrive at a general analytical definition and to specify the particular attributes of the police that professionalism implies and how the two police forces differ in these attributes.

A "professional" police department is one governed by values derived from general, impersonal rules which bind all members of the organization and whose relevance is independent of circumstances of time, place or personality.[2] A nonprofessional department (what will be called a "fraternal" department), on the other hand, relies to a greater extent on particularistic judgments—that is, judgments based on the significance to a particular person of his particular relations to particular others. The professional department looks outward to universal, externally valid, enduring standards; the nonprofessional department looks, so to speak, inward at the informal standards of a special group and distributes rewards and penalties according to how well a member conforms to them. The specific attributes that are consistent with these definitions include the following ones.

A professional, to a greater extent than a fraternal, department recruits members on the basis of achievement rather than ascriptive criteria. It relies more on standardized formal entrance examinations, open equally to all eligible persons. Thus the professional department recruits not only impartially as to political connections, race or religion; it recruits without regard to local residence. Nonprofessional departments often insist (or laws require them to insist) on recruitment only from among local citizens. Educational standards are typically higher for entrants to professional departments.

Professional departments treat equals equally; that is, laws are enforced without respect to person. In such departments "fixing" traffic tickets is difficult or impossible and the sons of the powerful cannot expect preferential treatment. Fraternal departments have a less formal sense of justice, either because the system of which they are a part encourages favoritism or because (and this is equally important) officers believe it is proper to take into account personal circumstances in dispensing justice. Concretely, we may expect to find less difference in the professional department between the proportion of white and nonwhite juvenile offenders who are arrested, as opposed to being let off with warnings or reprimands.

Professional departments are less open to graft and corruption and their cities will be more free of "tolerated" illegal enterprises (gambling, prostitution) than will cities with nonprofessional departments.

Professional departments seek, by formal training and indoctrination, to produce a force whose members are individually committed to generally applicable standards. Their traning will acquaint them with the writing and teaching of "experts" (that is, of carriers of generalized, professional norms). In fraternal departments, there is less formal training and what there is of it is undertaken by departmental officers who inculcate particularistic values and suggest "how to get along" on the force.

Within the professional department, authority attaches to the role and not to the incumbent to a greater extent than in nonprofessional departments. The essentially bureaucratic distribution of authority within the professional force is necessary because, due to the reliance on achievement, young officers are often promoted rapidly to positions of considerable authority (as sergeants and lieutenants in both line and staff bureaus).[3]

By these tests Western City has a highly professionalized force and Eastern City has not. An observer's first impressions of the two departments suggest the underlying differences: the Western City force has modern, immaculate, and expensive facilities, new buildings, and shiny cars; the officers are smartly dressed in clean, well-pressed uniforms; the routine business of the department is efficiently carried out. In Eastern City, the buildings are old and in poor repair; cars are fewer, many are old and worn; the officers are sometimes unkempt; routine affairs, particularly the keeping of records, are haphazardly conducted by harried or indifferent personnel.

In Western City, three-fourths of the officers were born outside the city and one-half outside the state (this is about the same as the proportion of all males in the city who were born outside the state). In Eastern City, the vast majority of officers were born and raised within the city they now serve, many in or near neighborhoods in which they now live. In Western City, over one-third of all officers had one year or more of college education; over one-fifth have two years or more; and one-tenth a college degree or better. In Eastern City, the proportion of officers educated beyond high school is far smaller.[4]

In Western City, there was little evidence of gambling or prostitution; Eastern City, while far from "wide open," has not made it difficult for a visitor to find a bookie or a girl. For several years at least, Western City has had a department free from the suspicion of political influence and a court system noted for its "no-fix" policy. In Eastern City, *reports* of influence and fixes are not infrequent (of course, a scholar without the power of subpoena cannot confirm such charges).

The chief of the Western City police department has been a high official of the International Association of Chiefs of Police (IACP); Eastern City's force, by contrast, has been the subject of a special comprehensive report by the IACP, contracted for by the local officials and containing recommendations for extensive reorganization and improvement. In sum, whether judged by subjective impression or objective measure, the police forces of the two cities are significantly different. The crucial question is the consequences of the differences upon the handling of juvenile offenders.

In Western City, justice, on the basis of fragmentary evidence, seems more likely to be blind than in Eastern City. Table 1 shows the

Table 1 / Proportion of Suspected Juvenile Offenders Arrested or Cited, by Race, for Selected Offenses in Western City (1962)

Offense	Total Offenses		Percent Arrested or Cited	
	WHITE	NEGRO	WHITE	NEGRO
Robbery	19	105	100.0	92.4
Aggravated assault	9	61	78.8	55.4
Burglary	199	331	87.9	92.8
Auto theft	124	142	93.6	86.6
Larceny	459	1119	56.2	56.6
Loitering	504	829	12.5	20.0
Drunk and disorderly	151	343	39.1	34.7
Malicious mischief	213	216	33.8	37.5
Assault and battery	93	306	58.1	65.3
Total	1771	3452	46.5	50.9

percentage of youths of each race arrested or cited in 1962 by Western City's police department for each of the most common offenses. Those not arrested or cited were disposed of, for the most part, by official reprimands. As the table indicates, Negro and white juveniles received remarkably similar treatment for all offenses but two; whites were more frequently arrested than Negroes for aggravated assault, and Negroes more frequently arrested than whites for loitering.

Table 2 gives similar though not precisely comparable information for Eastern City. This table is based on a random sample (1/25) of all

Table 2 / Proportion of Juveniles (in 1/25 Sample of All Those Processed) Taken to Court, by Race, for Selected Offenses in Eastern City (1959–1961)

	Total Offenses		Percent Taken to Court	
Offense	WHITE	NEGRO	WHITE	NEGRO
Assaults	26	12	11.5	25.0
Burglary	34	4	11.8	100.0
Auto theft	7	3	42.8	66.7
Larceny	98	27	24.5	52.0
Drunk and disorderly	33	4	0.0	0.0
Malicious mischief	69	9	4.4	0.0
Incorrigible	20	4	40.0	100.0
Total	287	63	15.7	42.9

juveniles processed by the Eastern City police over the four years since the juvenile bureau began keeping records. The data on offense and disposition were taken from cards for individual juveniles; thus, the figures in Table 2 show what proportion of *juveniles*, by race, were taken to court for various offenses, while the figures in Table 1 show what proportion of *juvenile offenses* (many juveniles being counted more than once), by race, resulted in a court disposition. Despite the lack of strict comparability, the differences are worth consideration. Although, in Western City, there was little difference in the probability of arrest for whites as compared to Negroes, in Eastern City the probability of court action (rather than warnings or reprimands) is almost three times higher for Negroes than for whites.

HANDLING THE DELINQUENT

The two police departments are systematically different both in their treatment of delinquents and in the way the members think and talk about delinquents; paradoxically, the differences in behavior do not correspond to the verbal differences. Interviews with approximately half the officers (selected at random) assigned to the juvenile bureaus of the police departments of Eastern and Western Cities reveal that Western City's officers have more complex attitudes toward delinquency and juveniles than their colleagues of Eastern City. The former's attitudes, at least superficially, tend to be less moralistic, less certain as to causal factors, more therapeutic, and more frequently couched in generalizations than in anecdotes. Eastern City's officers, by contrast, are more likely to interpret a problem as one of personal or familial morality rather than of social pathology, to urge restrictive and punitive rather than therapeutic measures, to rely on single explanations expressed with great conviction and certainty, and to confine discussions of juveniles almost exclusively to anecdotes and references to recent episodes than to generalizations, trends, or patterns.[5]

The behavior of the officers with respect to juveniles tends to be the opposite of what we might expect from their expressed sentiments. In Western City, the discretionary powers of the police are much more likely than in Eastern City to be used to restrict the freedom of the juvenile: Western City's officers process a larger proportion of the city's juvenile population as suspected offenders and, of those they process, arrest a larger proportion.

Table 3 shows the total number of juveniles processed in 1962 by the departments of Eastern and Western City, the rate per 100,000 juveniles in the populations of the two cities, and the percentage (and

Table 3 / Number and Rate of Juveniles Processed and Arrested in Western City and Eastern City, 1962

	Western City	Eastern City
Total juveniles processed (all offenses)	8,331	6,384
Rate per 100,000 children[a]	13,600	6,380
Number of juveniles arrested or cited (all offenses)	3,869	1,911
Percent arrested or cited	46.8	30.0
Rate per 100,000 children	6,365	1,910
Total juveniles processed, less those charged with loitering	6,685	6,384
Rate per 100,000 children	10,900	6,380
Number of juveniles arrested or cited, less loiterers	3,446	1,911
Percent arrested or cited	51.6	30.0
Rate per 100,000 children	5,623	1,910

[a] Rate is based on number of children, ages six through sixteen, in population of city according to the 1960 census of population.

rate) arrested or cited. By "processed" is meant that the youth came in contact with the police in a manner that required the latter to take official cognizance; a report was filed or a record entry made on the ground that the police had reasonable cause to believe that the youth had engaged in, or was a material witness to, acts which brought him under provisions of the state statutes. By "arrested or cited" is meant that the police brought formal action against the juvenile, either by taking him into custody and thence turning him over officially to the courts or to the probation officers or referees who can make a preliminary disposition, or by issuing an order or citation requiring him to appear before a court or official of the probation department. Such dispositions should be contrasted with all others in which the possibility of punitive action does not exist: officially reprimanding and releasing the child, referring him to another agency, returning him to his parents, and so forth. In short, the proportion arrested or cited is the proportion of all juveniles, suspected of having committed any offense, for whom the police make official punitive action a possibility—although not a certainty.

The rate of juveniles (Table 3) processed for *all* offenses by Western City's police was more than twice as great as the rate in Eastern City (13,600 per 100,000 as opposed to 6,380 per 100,000) and, of those processed, the proportion arrested or cited was more than 50 percent greater in Western than in Eastern City (46.8 percent as opposed to 30 percent). However, the laws of the two cities (and consequently the number of grounds on which juveniles can be processed by the police) differ, and therefore these raw figures must be modified by eliminating all juveniles processed for offenses unique to one place. The only type of offense that involved more than 1 percent of the juveniles was an antiloitering ordinance in effect in Western City but not in Eastern City. (The fact that Western City *has* such an ordinance—that forbids persons under the age of eighteen from loitering unaccompanied by a parent in public places between 10:00 p.m. and sunrise—is, it can be argued, in itself a manifestation of the difference in the conception of justice prevailing in each city. Not only does Eastern City not have such an ordinance but the head of the juvenile bureau at the time of this research was opposed to its adoption.) Table 3 gives the adjusted figures after deleting from Western City's totals all juveniles processed or arrested for violation of the antiloitering ordinance; yet both the processing rate and the arrest rate remain over 50 percent higher than in Eastern City.

In short, the young man or woman in Western City is one and one-half to two times as likely to come into contact with the police and, once in contact with the police, one and one-half times as likely to be arrested or cited rather than reprimanded or referred. One explanation of the contrast might be that, because of circumstances over which the police have no control, all the people there—the old as well as the young—are more likely to commit criminal acts. The more favorable climate, for example, might well explain why there were more crimes against property in Western City than in Eastern City. It can be argued that young people who are not professional thieves are even more likely than adults to be deterred by wind, snow, and freezing temperatures from stealing cars or breaking into hardware stores. Furthermore, Western City has a higher proportion of Negroes than Eastern City. If, in fact, Western City's youths are "more criminal" or have more opportunity for criminal acts, then differences in processing and arrest rates might reveal nothing about police attitudes or community norms.

In an effort to evaluate this objection, a more detailed comparison of crime and arrest rates for both juveniles and adults is given in Table 4. For each of the "Part I" offenses, the seven most serious offenses as

Table 4 / Crime Rates and Adult and Juvenile Arrest Rates per 100,000 Population for Western City (W) and Eastern City (E), 1962, by Major Offense

Offense	CRIME RATE		ADULT ARREST RATE		JUVENILE ARREST RATE		RATIO[a]	
	W	E	W	E	W	E	ADULT	JUV.
Homicide	8	7	10	11	3	0.2	0.9	17.0
Forcible rape	17	15	14	14	36	13	1.0	2.8
Robbery	167	104	115	71	197	63	1.6	3.1
Aggravated assault	105	117	85	107	69	73	0.8	0.9
Burglary	957	566	188	118	860	334	1.6	2.6
Larceny	458	420	576	240	1,580	664	2.4	2.4
Auto theft	357	855	71	127	450	316	0.6	1.4
Total	2,069	2,084	1,059	688	3,195	1,463	1.5	2.2

[a] These are the ratios of arrest rates in Western City to arrest rates in Eastern City for adults and juveniles. The ratio was calculated by dividing the Western City rate by the Eastern City rate. Values in excess of 1.0 are measured of the degree to which Western City rates exceed Eastern City rates.

defined by the FBI, overall crime rates (that is, offenses known to the police and arrest rates for both adults and juveniles) are given for both cities for 1962. In sum, the crime rates of the two cities are remarkably similar, although some considerable disparities are concealed in the totals. As one might predict, Western City has a substantially higher crime rate for robbery and burglary; unexpectedly, Eastern City has a substantially higher rate for auto theft. Crimes against the person—homicide, forcible rape, and aggravated assault—are quite similar in the two cities, crimes of passion being unfortunately less inhibited by adverse weather, probably because so many of them occur indoors. The arrest rates are a different story: the rates for both adults and juveniles are higher in Western City than in Eastern City, but the difference is greatest for the juveniles.

Western City's police arrest a greater proportion of the population than do Eastern City's but whereas the former's rate is 50 percent higher for adults, it is over 100 percent higher for juveniles. The last two columns in Table 4 summarize these differences by showing, for both adults and juveniles, the ratio between Western and Eastern City rates of arrest for each offense. Only for aggravated assault were the rates for juveniles of Eastern City higher than those of Western City; for all other offenses, Western City's rates were generally from 1.4 to 3.1 times greater. Particularly striking is the fact that, although the *auto theft rate* was over twice as high in Eastern City, the *juvenile arrest rate* for auto theft was 40 percent greater in Western City.

Thus, a juvenile in Western City is far less likely than one in Eastern City to be let off by the police with a reprimand. What the data indicate, interviews confirm. Police officers, social workers, and students of delinquency in Eastern City agree that the police there are well-known for what is called by many the "pass system." Unless the youth commits what the police consider a "vicious" crime—brutally assaulting an elderly person, for example, or engaging in wanton violence—he is almost certain to be released with a reprimand or warning on his first contact with the police and quite likely to be released on the second, third, and sometimes even on the fourth contact. It must be said that the juvenile officer who handles the case may consult a card file in his station showing previous police contacts for all juveniles in the precinct; a "pass" is not given out of ignorance.

The account of one Eastern City juvenile officer is typical of most accounts:

> Most of the kids around here get two or three chances. Let me give you an example. There was this fellow around here who is not vicious, not, I think, what you'd call bad; he's really sort of a good kid. He just can't move without getting into trouble. I don't know what there is about him . . . I'll read you his record. 1958—he's picked up for shop-lifting, given a warning. 1958—again a few months later was picked up for illegal possession [of dangerous weapons]. He had some dynamite caps and railroad flares. Gave him another warning. 1959—the next year he stole a bike. Got a warning. 1960—he broke into some freight cars. [Taken to court and] continued

without a finding [that is, no court action] on the understanding that he would pay restitution. Later the same year he was a runaway from home. No complaint was brought against him. Then in 1960 he started getting into some serious stuff. There was larceny and committing an unnatural act with a retarded boy. So, he went up on that one and was committed to [the reformatory] for nine months. Got out. In 1962 he was shot while attempting a larceny in a junk yard at night . . . Went to court, continued without a finding [that is, no punishment]. Now that's typical of a kid who just sort of can't stay out of trouble. He only went up once out of, let me see . . . eight offenses. . . . I wouldn't call him a bad kid despite the record . . . the bad kids: we don't have a lot of those.

In Eastern City, there are, of course, officers who have the reputation for being "tough." The "toughness" may be manifested, however, not so much in more frequent court appearances of youths, but in the greater ease of getting information. "Tough" and "soft" officers work as teams, the latter persuading juveniles to talk in order to save them from the former. In any case, the net effect of police discretion in Eastern City is unambiguous; only 17.5 percent of the first offenders included in a 1/25 random sample of all juveniles processed over a four-year period by the police department were referred to court. Indeed, Eastern City's officers occasionally mentioned that it was their understanding that officers "in the West" made arrests more frequently than they; Western City's officers sometimes observed that they had been told that officers "in the East" made arrests less frequently than they.

Observation of the operation of the two departments provided considerable evidence of the effect of the preceding on the day-to-day practice of police work. While cruising the city in patrol cars, Western City's officer would frequently stop to investigate youths "hanging" on street corners; the officers would check the youths' identification, question them closely, and often ask over the radio if they were persons for any reason wanted at headquarters. In Eastern City, officers would generally ignore young persons hanging around corners except to stop the car, lean out, and gruffly order them to "move along." "Sweeping" or "brooming" the corners was done with no real hope on the part of the police that it would accomplish much ("they'll just go around the block and come right back here in ten minutes") but they would ask, "what else can you do?"

Technically, of course, an officer in either city who takes a person into custody on the street is required by law to bring him to police headquarters or to a station house and to initiate a formal procedure whereby an arrest is effected, charges stated, certain rights guaranteed, and, if necessary, physical detention effected. In fact, and particularly with respect to juveniles, police officers sometimes take persons directly to their homes. In Eastern City this procedure is, in my judgment (naturally no conclusive evidence is available), much more common than in Western City.

THE CORRELATES OF DISCRETION

If, at least in this one case, a "professionalized" police department tends to expose a higher proportion of juveniles to the possibility of court action, despite the more "therapeutic" and sophisticated verbal formulas of its officers, it is important to ask why this occurs. Many reasons suggest themselves but, since this research is limited to an intensive examination of two departments, with a more cursory examination of two others, it is impossible to say how much of the variation in arrest rates can be accounted for by any single circumstance or by all circumstances together, or whether in other cities different relationships might be found. However, a rather strong argument can be made that, at the very least, the relationship is not accidental and, further, that professionalism itself in a variety of ways contributes to the result. Finally, what at first seems a paradox—the discrepancy between ideology and behavior—is not in fact a paradox at all, but simply the differing expression of a single state of affairs.

Certain structural and procedural dissimilarities undoubtedly account for some of the differences in arrests. In Eastern City the juvenile officer on the police force is also the prosecuting officer: he personally prepares and presents the case in court against the juvenile. In Western City, the juvenile officer (who, as in Eastern City, takes charge of the juvenile after a patrolman or detective has "brought him in") prepares an initial report but sends the report and, if detention seems warranted, the child himself, to an independent probation department which determines whether the suspect should be taken before the judge. In effect, Western City officers can "pass the buck," and even if the case goes to court, the officer himself only rarely is required to appear in court. In Eastern City, the police are involved right up to the moment when the judge actually makes a disposition, a police appearance being always required if there is to be a court hearing. Moreover, the probation department is not independent, but is an arm of the court which acts only *after* a court appearance. As a result of these arrangements, Eastern City's officers may have an incentive not to send the child to court because it requires more work; to Western City's officers, on the other hand, initiating a court appearance is relatively costless.

But such considerations do not explain why the *arresting* officer (who in most cases is *not* the juvenile officer who makes the ultimate disposition or the court appearance) should be less likely to make an arrest in one city than the other—unless, of course, there is some social pressure from juvenile officers in Eastern City to keep down the arrest rate. There is such pressure but, as will be shown, it does not come from juvenile officers but from the force as a whole.

It may be, of course, that the force as a whole is influenced by its perception of the probability that the court will actually punish the suspect, although it is by no means clear which way this influence might work. On the one hand, a lenient court might prove discouraging to the police, leading them to conclude that the "kid will get off anyway, so why should I go to the trouble of making an arrest?" On the other hand, a lenient court could as easily lead officers to argue that, since the kid will be "let off," there is no real danger to the suspect and, therefore, he may as well be arrested, whatever the merits of the case, as a way of throwing a harmless but perhaps useful "scare" into him.

This need not be solved, however, because the officers in both cities perceive the court, together with the probation authorities, as "excessively" lenient. And with good reason: in Eastern City, even though the police take only about 17.5 percent of all first offenders to court, only a third of these get any punishment at all and less than a tenth are sent to a reformatory. Those not committed to a reformatory are given suspended sentences or placed on probation. In sum, *only 1.6 percent* of first offenders see the inside of a correctional institution. In Western City, comparable figures are difficult to assemble. Generally speaking, however, the police are correct in their belief that only a small fraction of the youths they refer to the probation department will be sent on to court and that, of these, an even smaller fraction will be committed to a correctional institution. Of the more than eight thousand juveniles processed by the police in 1962, slightly less than half were referred, by arrest or citation, to the probation department. Of the juveniles referred, about one-third were ordered by the probation department to make a court appearance; of these, about one-sixth were sent to a public institution. In sum, *only about 2.8 percent* of the juveniles processed by the police were in some way confined. The differences in the probability of punishment in the two cities were so small as to make them a negligible influence on police behavior.

Far more important, it seems to me, than any mechanical differences between the two departments are the organizational arrangements, community attachments, and institutionalized norms which govern the daily life of the police officer himself, all of which might be referred to collectively as the "ethos" of the police force. It is this ethos which, in my judgment, decisively influences the police in the two places. In Western City, this is the ethos of a *professional* force; in Eastern City, the ethos of a *fraternal* force.

Western City's police officer works in an organizational setting which is highly centralized. Elaborate records are kept of all aspects of police work: each officer must, on a log, account for every minute of his time on duty; all contacts with citizens must be recorded in one form or another; and automatic data-processing equipment frequently issues detailed reports on police and criminal activity. The department operates out of a single headquarters; all juvenile offenders are processed in the office of the headquarters' juvenile bureau in the presence of a sergeant, a lieutenant, and, during the day shift, a captain. Dossiers on previously processed juveniles are kept and consulted at headquarters. Arresting officers bring all juveniles to headquarters for processing and their disposition is determined by officers of the juvenile bureau at that time.

In Eastern City, the force is highly decentralized. Officers are assigned to and, sometimes for their whole career, work in precinct station houses. Juvenile suspects are brought to the local station house and turned over to the officer of the juvenile bureau assigned there. These assignments are relatively constant: a patrolman who becomes a juvenile officer remains in the same station house. The juvenile officer is not supervised closely or, in many cases, not supervised at all; he works in his own office and makes his own dispositions. Whatever records the juvenile officer chooses to keep—and most keep some sort of record—is largely up to him. Once a week he is required to notify the headquarters of the juvenile bureau of his activities and to provide the bureau with the names and offenses of any juveniles he has processed. Otherwise, he is on his own.[6]

The centralized versus the decentralized mode of operations is in part dictated by differences in size of city—Eastern City has a larger population than Western City—but also in great part by a deliberate organizational strategy. Western City at one time had precincts, but they were abolished by a new, "reform" police chief as a way of centralizing control over the department in his hands. There had been some scandals before his appointment involving allegations of police brutality and corruption which he was determined would not occur again. Abolishing the precincts, centralizing the force, increasing the number and specificity of the rules and reporting procedures, and tightening supervision were all measures to achieve this objective. These actions all had consequences, many of them perhaps unintended, upon the behavior of the department. Officers felt the pressure: they were being watched, checked, supervised, and reported on. The force was becoming to a considerable extent "bureaucratized"—behavior more and more was to involve the nondiscretionary application of general rules to particular cases.[7] Some officers felt that their "productivity" was being measured—number of arrests made, citations written, field contact reports filed, and suspicious persons checked. Under these circumstances, it would be surprising if they did not feel they ought to act in such a way as to minimize any risk to themselves that might arise, not simply from being brutal or taking graft, but from failing to "make pinches" and "keep down the crime rate." In short, organizational measures intended to insure that police behave properly with respect to nondiscretionary matters (such as taking bribes) may also have the effect (perhaps unintended) of making them behave differently with respect to matters over which they *do* have discretion. More precisely, these measures tend to induce officers to convert discretionary to nondiscretionary matters—for example, to treat juveniles according to rule and without regard to person.

In Eastern City the nonprofessional, fraternal ethos of the force leads officers to treat juveniles primarily on the basis of personal judgment and only secondarily by applying formal rules. Although the department has had its full share of charges of corruption and brutality, at the time of this research there had been relatively few fundamental reforms. The local precinct captain is a man of great power; however, he rarely chooses to closely supervise the handling of juvenile offenders. His rules, though binding, are few in number and rarely systematic or extensive.

In Western City, the juvenile officers work as a unit; they meet together every morning for a line-up, briefing, and short training session; they work out of a common headquarters; they have their own patrol cars; and they work together in pairs. In Eastern City most, though not all, precincts have a single juvenile officer. He works in the station house in association with patrolmen and detectives; he has no car of his own, but must ride with other officers or borrow one of their cars; he rarely meets with other juvenile officers and there is practically no training for his job or systematic briefing while on it. In Western City, the juvenile officer's ties of association on and off the job are such that his fellow juvenile officers are his audience. He is judged by, and judges himself by, their standards and their opinions. In Eastern City, the relevant audience is much more likely to be patrolmen and detectives. In Western City, the primary relations of the juvenile officer are with "professional" colleagues; in Eastern City, the relations are with fraternal associates.

Eastern City's juvenile officer feels, and expresses to an interviewer, the conflicting and ambivalent standards arising out of his association with officers who do not handle juveniles. On the one hand, almost every juvenile officer in Eastern City complained that patrolmen and detectives did not "understand" his work, that they regarded him as a man who "chased kids," that they "kissed off" juvenile cases onto him and did not take them seriously, and that they did not think arresting a "kid" constituted a "good pinch." These attitudes might, in part, be explained by the patrolmen's reluctance to bring a juvenile into the station, even if they could then turn him over to the juvenile officer on duty; bringing the boy in meant bringing him in in front of their fellow patrolmen in the squad room of the station house. One patrolman's views on this were typical:

> A delinquent is not a good pinch—at least not for most officers. You get ribbed a lot and sort of ridiculed when you bring a kid in. Sort of grinds you down when you bring a kid in and the other officers start telling you, "Hey, look at the big man, look at the big guy with the little kid, hey, can you handle that kid all by yourself?" You get a little ribbing like that and finally you don't bring so many kids in for pinches.

Instead, the patrolmen or detectives often simply refer the juvenile's name to the juvenile officer and let the officer go out and handle the case from investigation to arrest. This not only places a larger work load on the juvenile officer; it places it on him under conditions that do not reward effective performance. He is given the "kid stuff" because patrolmen do not feel rewarded for handling it; at the same time, the patrolman lets it be known that he does not feel the juvenile officer ought to get much credit, either. At the same time, almost all patrolmen interviewed felt that the authorities, including in most cases the juvenile officer himself, were "too easy" on the kids. But this generalized commitment to greater punitiveness, although widely shared in Eastern City, rarely—for reasons to be discussed later— determines the fate of any particular juvenile. This being the case, the juvenile officer in Eastern City seems to allow his behavior to be influenced by associates, insofar as it is influenced by them at all, in the direction of permissive treatment.

Western City's juvenile officers, by contrast, are more insulated from or less dependent on the opinion of patrolmen and detectives. And the latter, when taking a juvenile into custody, can bring him to a central juvenile bureau staffed only by juvenile officers, rather than to a precinct station filled with fellow patrolmen and detectives. Neither juvenile officers nor arresting patrolmen are, in Western City, as directly exposed to or dependent upon the opinions of associates concerning whether a juvenile arrest is justified.

Even if Western City's officers should be so exposed, however, it is likely that they would still be more punitive than their counterparts in Eastern City. In Western City, the officer, both in and out of the juvenile bureau, is recruited and organized in a way that provides little possibility of developing a strong identification with either delinquents in general or with delinquents in some particular neighborhood. He is likely to have been raised outside the city and even outside the state; in many cases he was recruited by the representatives of the force who canvass the schools of police administration attached to western and midwestern universities. In only *one* case in Western City did I interview a juvenile officer who, when asked about his own youth, spoke of growing up in a "tough" neighborhood where juvenile gangs, juvenile misbehavior, and brushes with the police were common. There were, on the other hand, only one or two of Eastern City's officers who had *not* come from such backgrounds: they were almost all products not only of local neighborhoods but of neighborhoods where scrapes with the law were a common occurrence.

The *majority* of Eastern City's officers were not only "locals," but locals from lower or lower-middle-class backgrounds. Several times officers spoke of themselves and their friends in terms that suggested that the transition between being a street-corner rowdy and a police officer was not very abrupt. The old street-corner friends that they used to "hang" with followed different paths as adults but, to the officers, the paths were less a matter of choice than of accident, fates which were legally but not otherwise distinct. The officers spoke proudly of the fights they used to have, of youthful wars between the Irish and the Italians, and of the old gangs, half of whose alumni went to the state prison and the other half to the police and fire departments. Each section of the city has great meaning to these officers; they are nostalgic about some where the old life continues, bitter about others where new elements—particularly Negroes—have "taken over."

The *majority* of Western City's officers who were interviewed, almost without exception, described their own youth as free of violence, troubles with the police, broken homes, or gang behavior. The city in which they now serve has a particular meaning for only a very few. Many live outside it in the suburbs and know the city's neighborhoods almost solely from their police work. Since there are no precinct stations but only radio car routes, and since these are frequently changed, there is little opportunity to build up an intimate familiarity, much less an identificaton, with any neighborhood. The Western City police are, in a real sense, an army of occupation organized along paramilitary lines.

It would be a mistake to exaggerate these differences or to be carried away by neighborhood romanticism that attaches an undeservedly high significance to the folklore about the "neighborhood cop" walking his rounds—king of the beat, firm arbiter of petty grievances, and gruff but kind confidant of his subjects. The "oldtime beat cop," as almost all the Eastern City's officers are quick and sad to admit, is gone forever. But even short of romanticism, the differences remain and are important. Except for the downtown business district and the skid row area, there are no foot patrolmen in Western City; in Eastern City, in all the residential areas with high crime rates, officers walk their beats. Furthermore, the station houses in Eastern City receive a constant stream of local residents who bring their grievances and demands to the police; in Western City the imposing new police headquarters building is downtown and has no "front desk" where business obviously can be transacted. Although visitors are encouraged, upon entering the ground floor one is confronted by a bank of automatic elevators. Finally, officers on duty in Eastern City eat in diners and cafés in or close to their routes; in Western City officers often drive several miles to a restaurant noted for its reasonably-priced food rather than for its identification with the neighborhood.

These differences in style between the two police departments can perhaps be summarized by saying that in Western City the officer has a generalized knowledge of juveniles and of delinquency and that, although he, of course, becomes familiar with some children and areas, that generalized knowledge—whether learned in college, from departmental doctrine, from the statute books, or from the popular literature on juvenile behavior—provides the premises of his decisions. He begins with general knowledge and he is subjected to fewer particularizing influences than his counterpart in Eastern City. In Eastern City, the officer's knowledge or what he takes to be his knowledge about delinquency, crime, and neighborhood affairs is, from the first, specific, particular, indeed, *personal*, and the department is organized and run in a way that maintains a particularist orientation toward relations between officer and officer and between police and citizens.[8]

This Eastern City ethos exists side by side with the general moral absolutism of police attitudes toward delinquency *in general*. When asked about the cause, extent, or significance of delinquency *generally*, the officers usually respond, as has been indicated, with broad, flat, moral indictments of the modern American family, overly-indulged youth, weakened social bonds, corrupting mass media of communication, and pervasive irreligion and socialism. When the same officers are asked about delinquency in *their precinct*, they speak anecdotally of particular juveniles engaging in particular acts in particular circumstances, in dealing with whom they apply, not their expressed general moral absolutes, but their particular knowledge of the case in question and some rough standard of personal substantive justice.

The one striking exception arises when Negroes are involved. The white officer is not in any kind of systematic communication with Negroes; the Negro is the "invader," and—what may be statistically true—more likely to commit crimes. The officer sees the Negro as being often more vicious, certainly more secretive, and always alien. To the policemen of Eastern City, the Negro has no historical counterpart in his personal experience and, as a result, the Negro juvenile is more likely than the white to be treated, in accord not with particularist standards, but with the generalized and absolutist attitudes which express the officer's concern for the problem "as a whole."

One reason for the apparently higher proportion of arrests of Negro compared to white juveniles in Eastern City may have nothing to do with "prejudice." In addition to being perceived as an "alien," the Negro offender is also perceived as one who "has no home life." Eastern City officers frequently refer to (and deplore) the apparent weakness of the lower-class Negro family structure, the high proportion of female heads of households, and the alleged high incidence of welfare cases (notably Aid to Dependent Children). If a fraternal force is concerned as much with the maintenance of family authority as with breaking the law and if referring the child to the home is preferred to referring him to court, then the absence (or perceived absence) of family life among Negroes would lead to a greater resort to the courts.

Western City's officer, acting on essentially general principles, treats juveniles with more severity (concern with distinctions of person is less, though by no means entirely absent) but with less discrimination. Negroes and whites are generally treated alike and both are treated more severely. Because the officer in this city is more likely to be essentially of middle-class background and outlook and sometimes college educated as well, he is much more likely to be courteous, impersonal, and "correct" than the Eastern City officer.

These differences in organizational character are reinforced by the political and civic institutions of the cities. Eastern City has been governed for decades by "old-style" politics; personal loyalties, neighborhood interests, and party preferment are paramount. Western City is preeminently a "good government" community in all respects. The non-partisan city council and administration have, by and large, made every effort to make the management of the community honest and efficient. In this, they have been supported by the press and by business and civic groups. Western City's police chief enjoys strong support in his determined effort to maintain and extend professional standards in the force. Eastern City's chief is, of course, expected to perform creditably and avoid scandal but the whole tenor of the city's political life provides little evidence that anything more than routine competence is required or even wanted. . . .

Notes

1. On the general problems of police discretion, compare Joseph Goldstein, "Police Discretion Not to Invoke the Criminal Process: Low-Visibility Decisions," *Yale Law Journal*, 69, 534–594 (March 1960) and Herman Goldstein, "Police Discretion: The Ideal Versus the Real," *Public Administration Review*, 23, 140–148 (September 1963).

2. The following definitions are taken from, and treated in greater detail by James Q. Wilson, "The Police and Their Problems: A Theory," *Public Policy*, 12, 189–216 (1962).

3. There is a general tendency for authority to adhere more to the person than to the office in a police force as compared to other kinds of public agencies. See Robert L. Peabody, "Perceptions of Organizational Authority: A Comparative Analysis," *Administrative Science Quarterly*, 6, 477–480 (March 1962).

4. These differences are characteristic of entire regions and not simply of the two departments here studied. In one study it was found that almost 90 percent of the officers in police departments in the Pacific states, but only about two-thirds of those in New England and North Atlantic states, had a high school education. Similarly, 55 percent of those from the Pacific states, but only about 18 percent of those from New England and North Atlantic states, had attended college. See George W. O'Connor and Nelson A. Watson, *Juvenile Delinquency and Youth Crime: The Police Role* (Washington, D.C.: International Association of Chiefs of Police, 1964), pp. 78–79.

5. Compare these dichotomous attitudes with those classified in Walter B. Miller, "Inter-Institutional Conflict as a Major Impediment to Delinquency Prevention," *Human Organization*, 17 (3), 20–23 (Fall 1958); and Harold L. Wilensky and Charles N. Lebeaux, *Industrial Society and Social Welfare* (New York: Russell Sage Foundation, 1958), pp. 219–228.

6. The juvenile bureau of the Eastern City police department was only created after community concern over what appeared to be a serious incident involving a juvenile "gang" compelled it. The police commissioner at the time was reported to oppose the existence of such a bureau on the revealing grounds that "each beat officer should be his own juvenile officer." The fraternal force apparently resisted even the nominal degree of specialization and centralization represented by the creation of this bureau. This, again, is also a regional phenomenon. Over 80 percent of the police departments in Pacific states, but less than 58 percent of those in New England states, have specialized juvenile units. O'Connor and Watson, *op. cit.*, p. 84.

7. Compare the causes and consequences of bureaucratization in an industrial setting in Alvin W. Gouldner, *Patterns of Industrial Bureaucracy* (Glencoe, Ill.: Free Press, 1954).

8. The findings of O'Connor and Watson are consistent with this argument. They discovered that officers in Pacific police departments tended to have "tougher" attitudes toward the *means* to be employed in handling juvenile offenders than officers in New England or North Atlantic departments. The former were more likely to favor transporting juveniles in marked rather than unmarked police cars, to favor having a curfew, to oppose having the police get involved in community affairs concerning youth matters, to oppose destroying the police records of juveniles after they become adults, and to oppose having the police try to find jobs for juveniles who come to their attention. (*op. cit.*, pp. 91–97, 115–127.)

22 / The Societal Reaction to Deviance: Ascriptive Elements in the Psychiatric Screening of Mental Patients in a Midwestern State

THOMAS J. SCHEFF
DANIEL M. CULVER

The case for making the societal reaction to deviance a major independent variable in studies of deviant behavior has been succinctly stated by Kitsuse:

A sociological theory of deviance must focus specifically upon the interactions which not only define behaviors as deviant but also organize and activate the application of sanctions by individuals, groups, or agencies. For in modern society, the socially significant differentiation of deviants from the non-deviant population is increasingly contingent upon circumstances of situation, place, social and personal biography, and the bureaucratically organized activities of agencies of control.[1]

In the case of mental disorder, psychiatric diagnosis is one of the crucial steps which "organizes and activates" the societal reaction, since the state is legally empowered to segregate and isolate those persons whom psychiatrists find to be committable because of mental illness.

Recently, however, it has been argued that mental illness may be more usefully considered to be a social status than a disease, since the symptoms of mental illness are vaguely defined and widely distributed, and the definition of behavior as symptomatic of mental illness is usually dependent upon social rather than medical contingencies.[2] Furthermore, the argument continues, the status of the mental patient is more often an ascribed status, with conditions for status entry external to the patient, than an achieved status with conditions for status entry dependent upon the patient's own behavior. According to this argument, the societal reaction is a fundamentally important variable in all stages of a deviant career.

The actual usefulness of a theory of mental disorder based on the societal reaction is largely an empirical question: to what extent is entry to the status of mental patient independent of the behavior or "condition" of the patient? The present paper will explore this question for one phase of the societal reaction: the legal screening of persons alleged to be mentally ill. This screening represents the official phase of the societal reaction, which occurs after the alleged deviance has been called to the attention of the community by a complainant. This report will make no reference to the initial deviance or other situation which resulted in the complaint, but will deal entirely with procedures used by the courts after the complaint has occurred.

The purpose of the description that follows is to determine the extent of uncertainty that exists concerning new patients' qualifications for involuntary confinement in a mental hospital, and the reactions of the courts to this type of uncertainty. The data presented here indicate that, in the face of uncertainty, there is a strong presumption of illness by the court and the court psychiatrists.[3] In the discussion that follows the presentation of findings, some of the causes, consequences and implications of the presumption of illness are suggested.

The data upon which this report is based were drawn from psychiatrists' ratings of a sample of patients newly admitted to the public mental hospitals in a Midwestern state, official court records, interviews with court officials and psychiatrists, and our observations of psychiatric examinations in four courts. The psychiatrists' ratings of new patients will be considered first.

In order to obtain a rough measure of the incoming patient's qualifications for involuntary confinement, a survey of newly admitted patients was conducted with the cooperation of the hospital psychiatrists. All psychiatrists who made admission examinations in the three large mental hospitals in the state filled out a questionnaire for the first ten consecutive patients they examined in the month of June, 1962. A total of 223 questionnaires were returned by the 25 admission psychiatrists. Although these returns do not constitute a probability sample of all new patients admitted during the year, there were no obvious biases in the drawing of the sample. For this reason, this group of patients will be taken to be typical of the newly admitted patients in Midwestern State.

The two principal legal grounds for involuntary confinement in the United States are the police power of the state (the state's right to protect itself from dangerous persons) and *parens patriae* (the State's right to assist those persons who, because of their own incapacity, may not be able to assist themselves.)[4] As a measure of the first ground, the potential dangerousness of the patient, the questionnaire contained this item: "In your opinion, if this patient were released at the present time, is it likely he would harm himself or others?" The psychiatrists were given six options, ranging from Very Likely to Very Unlikely. Their responses were: Very Likely, 5%; Likely, 4%; Somewhat Likely, 14%; Somewhat Unlikely, 20%; Unlikely, 37%; Very Unlikely, 18%. (Three patients were not rated, 1%).

As a measure of the second ground, *parens patriae*, the questionnaire contained the item: "Based on your observations of the patient's behavior, his present degree of mental impairment is:

None_____   Minimal_____   Mild_____   Moderate_____
Severe_____" The psychiatrists' responses were: None, 2%; Minimal, 12%; Mild, 25%; Moderate, 42%; Severe, 17%. (Three patients were not rated, 1%).

To be clearly qualified for involuntary confinement, a patient should be rated as likely to harm self or others (Very Likely, Likely, or Somewhat Likely) and/or as Severely Mentally Impaired. However, voluntary patients should be excluded from this analysis, since the court is not required to assess their qualifications for confinement. Excluding the 59 voluntary admissions (26% of the sample), leaves a sample of 164 involuntary confined patients. Of these patients, 10 were rated as meeting both qualifications for involuntary confinement, 21 were rated as being severely mentally impaired, but not dangerous, 28 were rated as dangerous but not severely mentally impaired, and 102 were rated as not dangerous nor as severely mentally impaired. (Three patients were not rated.)

According to these ratings, there is considerable uncertainty connected with the screening of newly admitted involuntary patients in the state, since a substantial majority (63%) of the patients did not clearly meet the statutory requirements for involuntary confinement. How does the agency responsible for assessing the qualifications for confinement, the court, react in the large numbers of cases involving uncertainty?

On the one hand, the legal rulings on this point by higher courts are quite clear. They have repeatedly held that there should be a presumption of sanity. The burden of proof of insanity is to be on the petitioners, there must be a preponderance of evidence, and the evidence should be of a "clear and unexceptionable" nature.[5]

On the other hand, existing studies suggest that there is a presumption of illness by mental health officials. In a discussion of the "discrediting" of patients by the hospital staff, based on observations at St. Elizabeth's Hospital, Washington, D.C., Goffman states:

[The patient's case record] is apparently not regularly used to record occasions when the patient showed capacity to cope honorably and effectively with difficult life situations. Nor is the case record typically used to provide a rough average or sampling of his past conduct. [Rather, it extracts] from his whole life course a list of those incidents that have or might have had "symptomatic" significance. ... I think that most of the information gathered in case records is quite true, although it might seem also to be true that almost anyone's life course could yield up enough denigrating facts to provide grounds for the record's justification of commitment.[6]

Mechanic makes a similar statement in his discussion of two large mental hospitals located in an urban area in California:

In the crowded state or county hospitals, which is the most typical situation, the psychiatrist does not have sufficient time to make a very complete psychiatric diagnosis, nor do his psychiatric tools provide him with the equipment for an expeditious screening of the patient ...

In the two mental hospitals studied over a period of three months, the investigator never observed a case where the psychiatrist advised the patient that he did not need treatment. Rather, all persons who appeared at the hospital were absorbed into the patient population regardless of their ability to function adequately outside the hospital.[7]

A comment by Brown suggests that it is a fairly general understanding among mental health workers that state mental hospitals in the U.S. accept all comers.[8]

Kutner, describing commitment procedures in Chicago in 1962, also reports a strong presumption of illness by the staff of the Cook County Mental Health Clinic:

Certificates are signed as a matter of course by staff physicians after little or no examination ... The so-called examinations are made on an assembly-line basis, often being completed in two or three minutes, and never taking more than ten minutes. Although psychiatrists agree that it is practically impossible to determine a person's sanity on the basis of such a short and hurried interview, the doctors recommend confinement in 77% of the cases. It appears in practice that the alleged-mentally-ill is presumed to be insane and bears the burden of proving his sanity in the few minutes allotted to him ...[9]

These citations suggest that mental health officials handle uncertainty by presuming illness. To ascertain if the presumption of illness occurred in Midwestern State, intensive observations of screening procedures were conducted in the four courts with the largest volume of mental cases in the state. These courts were located in the two most populous cities in the state. Before giving the results of these observations, it is necessary to describe the steps in the legal procedures for hospitalization and commitment.

STEPS IN THE SCREENING OF PERSONS ALLEGED TO BE MENTALLY ILL

The process of screening can be visualized as containing five steps in Midwestern State:

1. The application for judicial inquiry, made by three citizens. This application is heard by deputy clerks in two of the courts (C and D), by a court reporter in the third court, and by a court commissioner in the fourth court.

2. The intake examination, conducted by a hospital psychiatrist.

3. The psychiatric examination, conducted by two psychiatrists appointed by the court.

4. The interview of the patient by the guardian *ad litem*, a lawyer appointed in three of the courts to represent the patient. (Court A did not use guardians *ad litem.*)

5. The judicial hearing, conducted by a judge.

These five steps take place roughly in the order listed, although in many cases (those cases designated as emergencies) step No. 2, the intake examination, may occur before step No. 1. Steps No. 1 and No. 2 usually take place on the same day or the day after hospitalization. Steps No. 3, No. 4, and No. 5 usually take place within a week of hospitalization. (In courts C and D, however, the judicial hearing is held only once a month.)

This series of steps would seem to provide ample opportunity for the presumption of health, and a thorough assessment, therefore, of the patient's qualifications for involuntary confinement, since there are five separate points at which discharge could occur. According to our findings, however, these procedures usually do not serve the function of screening out persons who do not meet statutory requirements. At most of these decision points, in most of the courts, retention of the patient in the hospital was virtually automatic. A notable exception to this pattern was found in one of the three state hospitals; this hospital attempted to use step No. 2, the intake examination, as a screening point to discharge patients that the superintendent described as "illegitimate," i.e., patients who do not qualify for involuntary confinement.[10] In the other two hospitals, however, this examination was perfunctory and virtually never resulted in a finding of health and a recommendation of discharge. In a similar manner, the other steps were largely ceremonial in character. For example, in court B, we observed twenty-two judicial hearings, all of which were conducted perfunctorily and with lightning rapidity. (The mean time of these hearings was 1.6 minutes.) The judge asked each patient two or three routine questions. Whatever the patient answered, however, the judge always ended the hearings and retained the patient in the hospital.

What appeared to be the key role in justifying these procedures was played by step No. 3, the examination by the court-appointed psychiatrists. In our informal discussions of screening with the judges and other court officials, these officials made it clear that although the statutes give the court the responsibility for the decision to confine or release persons alleged to be mentally ill, they would rarely if ever take the responsibility for releasing a mental patient without a medical recommendation to that effect. The question which is crucial, therefore, for the entire screening process is whether or not the court-appointed psychiatric examiners presume illness. The remainder of the paper will consider this question.

Our observations of 116 judicial hearings raised the question of the adequacy of the psychiatric examination. Eighty-six of the hearings failed to establish that the patients were "mentally ill" (according to the criteria stated by the judges in interviews).[11] Indeed, the behavior and responses of 48 of the patients at the hearings seemed completely unexceptionable. Yet the psychiatric examiners had not recommended the release of a single one of these patients. Examining the court records of 80 additional cases, there was still not a single recommendation for release.

Although the recommendation for treatment of 196 out of 196 consecutive cases strongly suggests that the psychiatric examiners were presuming illness, particularly when we observed 48 of these patients to be responding appropriately, it is conceivable that this is not the case. The observer for this study was not a psychiatrist (he was a first year graduate student in social work) and it is possible that he could have missed evidence of disorder which a psychiatrist might have seen. It was therefore arranged for the observer to be present at a series of psychiatric examinations, in order to determine whether the examinations appeared to be merely formalities or whether, on the other hand, through careful examination and interrogation, the psychiatrists were able to establish illness even in patients whose appearance and responses were not obviously disordered. The observer was instructed to note the examiners' procedures, the criteria they appeared to use in arriving at their decision, and their reaction to uncertainty.

Each of the courts discussed here employs the services of a panel of physicians as medical examiners. The physicians are paid a flat fee of ten dollars per examination, and are usually assigned from three to five patients for each trip to the hospital. In court A, most of the examinations are performed by two psychiatrists, who went to the hospital once a week, seeing from five to ten patients a trip. In court B,

C and D, a panel of local physicians was used. These courts seek to arrange the examinations so that one of the examiners is a psychiatrist, the other a general practitioner. Court B has a list of four such pairs, and appoints each pair for a month at a time. Courts C and D have a similar list, apparently with some of the same names as court B.

To obtain physicians who were representative of the panel used in these courts, we arranged to observe the examinations of the two psychiatrists employed by court A, and one of the four pairs of physicians used in court B, one a psychiatrist, the other a general practitioner. We observed 13 examinations in court A and 13 examinations in court B. The judges in courts C and D refused to give us the names of the physicians on their panels, and we were unable to observe examinations in these courts. (The judge in court D stated that he did not want these physicians harassed in their work, since it was difficult to obtain their services even under the best of circumstances.) In addition to observing the examinations by four psychiatrists, three other psychiatrists used by these courts were interviewed.

The medical examiners followed two lines of questioning. One line was to inquire about the circumstances which led to the patient's hospitalization, the other was to ask standard questions to test the patient's orientation and his capacity for abstract thinking by asking him the date, the President, Governor, proverbs, and problems requiring arithmetic calculation. These questions were often asked very rapidly, and the patient was usually allowed only a very brief time to answer.

It should be noted that the psychiatrists in these courts had access to the patient's record (which usually contained the Application for Judicial Inquiry and the hospital chart notes on the patient's behavior), and that several of the psychiatrists stated that they almost always familiarized themselves with this record before making the examination. To the extent that they were familiar with the patient's circumstances from such outside information, it is possible that the psychiatrists were basing their diagnoses of illness less on the rapid and peremptory examination than on this other information. Although this was true to some extent, the importance of the record can easily be exaggerated, both because of the deficiencies in the typical record, and because of the way it is usually utilized by the examiners.

The deficiencies of the typical record were easily discerned in the approximately one hundred applications and hospital charts which the author read. Both the applications and charts were extremely brief and sometimes garbled. Moreover, in some of the cases where the author and interviewer were familiar with the circumstances involved in the hospitalization, it was not clear that the complainant's testimony was any more accurate than the version presented by the patient. Often the original complaint was so paraphrased and condensed that the application seemed to have little meaning.

The attitude of the examiners toward the record was such that even in those cases where the record was ample, it often did not figure prominently in their decision. Disparaging remarks about the quality and usefulness of the record were made by several of the psychiatrists. One of the examiners was apologetic about his use of the record, giving us the impression that he thought that a good psychiatrist would not need to resort to any information outside his own personal examination of the patient. A casual attitude toward the record was openly displayed in 6 of the 26 examinations we observed. In these 6 examinations, the psychiatrist could not (or in 3 cases, did not bother to) locate the record and conducted the examination without it, with one psychiatrist making it a point of pride that he could easily diagnose most cases "blind."

In his observations of the examinations, the interviewer was instructed to rate how well the patient responded by noting his behavior during the interview, whether he answered the orientation and concept questions correctly, and whether he denied and explained the allegations which resulted in his hospitalization. If the patient's behavior during the interview obviously departed from conventional social standards (e.g., in one case the patient refused to speak), if he answered the orientation questions incorrectly, or if he did not deny and explain the petitioners' allegations, the case was rated as meeting the statutory requirements for hospitalization. Of the 26 examinations observed, eight were rated as Criteria Met.

If, on the other hand, the patient's behavior was appropriate, his answers correct, and he denied and explained the petitioners' allegations, the interviewer rated the case as not meeting the statutory criteria. Of the 26 cases, seven were rated as Criteria Not Met. Finally, if the examination was inconclusive, but the interviewer felt that more extensive investigation might have established that the criteria were met, he rated the cases as Criteria Possibly Met. Of the 26 examined, 11 were rated in this way. The interviewer's instructions were that whenever he was in doubt he should avoid using the rating Criteria Not Met.

Even giving the examiners the benefit of the doubt, the interviewer's ratings were that in a substantial majority of the cases he observed, the examination failed to establish that the statutory criteria were met. The relationship between the examiners' recommendations and the interviewer's ratings are shown in the following table. The interviewer's ratings suggest that the examinations established that the statutory criteria were met in only eight cases, but the examiners recommended that the patient be retained in the hospital

Table 1 / Observer's Ratings and Examiners' Recommendations

Observer's Ratings		CRITERIA MET	CRITERIA POSSIBLY MET	CRITERIA NOT MET	TOTAL
Examiners'	Commitment	7	9	2	18
Recommendations	30-day Observation	1	2	3	6
	Release	0	0	2	2
	Total	8	11	7	26

in 24 cases, leaving 16 cases which the interviewer rated as uncertain, and in which retention was recommended by the examiners. The observer also rated the patient's expressed desires regarding staying in the hospital, and the time taken by the examination. The ratings of the patient's desire concerning staying or leaving the hospital were: Leave, 14 cases; Indifferent, 1 case; Stay, 9 cases; and Not Ascertained, 2 cases. In only one of the 14 cases in which the patient wished to leave was the interviewer's rating Criteria Met.

The interviews ranged in length from five minutes to 17 minutes, with the mean time being 10.2 minutes. Most of the interviews were hurried, with the questions of the examiners coming so rapidly that the examiner often interrupted the patient, or one examiner interrupted the other. All of the examiners seemed quite hurried. One psychiatrist, after stating in an interview (before we observed his examinations) that he usually took about thirty minutes, stated:

> "It's not remunerative. I'm taking a hell of a cut. I can't spend 45 minutes with a patient. I don't have the time, it doesn't pay."

In the examinations that we observed, this physician actually spent 8, 10, 5, 8, 8, 7, 17, and 11 minutes with the patients, or an average of 9.2 minutes.

In these short time periods, it is virtually impossible for the examiner to extend his investigation beyond the standard orientation questions, and a short discussion of the circumstances which brought the patient to the hospital. In those cases where the patient answered the orientation questions correctly, behaved appropriately, and explained his presence at the hospital satisfactorily, the examiners did not attempt to assess the reliability of the petitioner's complaints, or to probe further into the patient's answers. Given the fact that in most of these instances the examiners were faced with borderline cases, that they took little time in the examinations, and that they usually recommended commitment, we can only conclude that their decisions were based largely on a presumption of illness. Supplementary observations reported by the interviewer support this conclusion.

After each examination, the observer asked the examiner to explain the criteria he used in arriving at his decision. The observer also had access to the examiner's official report, so that he could compare what the examiner said about the case with the record of what actually occurred during the interview. This supplementary information supports the conclusion that the examiner's decisions are based on the presumption of illness, and sheds light on the manner in which these decisions are reached:

1. The "evidence" upon which the examiners based their decision to retain often seemed arbitrary.

2. In some cases, the decision to retain was made even when no evidence could be found.

3. Some of the psychiatrists' remarks suggest prejudgment of the cases.

4. Many of the examinations were characterized by carelessness and haste.

The first question, concerning the arbitrariness of the psychiatric evidence, will now be considered.

In the weighing of the patient's responses during the interview, the physician appeared not to give the patient credit for the large number of correct answers he gave. In the typical interview, the examiner might ask the patient fifteen or twenty questions: the date, time, place, who is President, Governor, etc., what is 11x10, 11x11, etc., explain "Don't put all your eggs in one basket," "A rolling stone gathers no moss," etc. The examiners appeared to feel that a wrong answer established lack of orientation, even when it was preceded by a series of correct answers. In other words, the examiners do not establish any standard score on the orientation questions, which would give an objective picture of the degree to which the patient answered the questions correctly, but seem at times to search until they find an incorrect answer.

For those questions which were answered incorrectly, it was not always clear whether the incorrect answers were due to the patient's "mental illness," or to the time pressure in the interview, the patient's lack of education, or other causes. Some of the questions used to establish orientation were sufficiently difficult that persons not mentally ill might have difficulty with them. Thus one of the examiners always asked, in a rapid-fire manner: "What year is it? What year was it seven years ago? Seventeen years before that?" etc. Only two of the five patients who were asked this series of questions were able to answer it correctly. However, it is a moot question whether a higher percentage of persons in a household survey would be able to do any better. To my knowledge, none of the orientation questions that are used have been checked in a normal population.

Finally, the interpretations of some of the evidence as showing mental illness seemed capricious. Thus one of the patients, when asked, "In what way are a banana, an orange, and an apple alike?" answered, "They are all something to eat." This answer was used by the examiner in explaining his recommendation to commit. The observer had noted that the patient's behavior and responses seemed appropriate and asked why the recommendation to commit had been made. The doctor stated that her behavior had been bizarre (possibly referring to her alleged promiscuity), her affect inappropriate ("When she talked about being pregnant, it was without feeling,") and with regard to the question above:

> She wasn't able to say a banana and an orange were fruit. She couldn't take it one step further, she had to say it was something to eat.

In other words, this psychiatrist was suggesting that the patient manifested concreteness in her thinking, which is held to be a symptom of mental illness. Yet in her other answers to classification questions, and to proverb interpretations, concreteness was not apparent, suggesting that the examiner's application of this test was arbitrary. In another case, the physician stated that he thought the patient was suspicious and distrustful, because he had asked about the possibility of being represented by counsel at the judicial hearing. The observer felt that these and other similar interpretations might possibly be correct, but that further investigation of the supposedly incorrect responses would be needed to establish that they were manifestations of disorientation.

In several cases where even this type of evidence was not available, the examiners still recommended retention in the hospital. Thus, one examiner, employed by court A stated that he had recommended 30-day observation for a patient whom he had thought *not* to be mentally ill, on the grounds that the patient, a young man, could not get along with his parents, and "might get into trouble." This examiner went on to say:

> We always take the conservative side. [Commitment or observation] Suppose a patient should commit suicide. We always make the conservative decision. I had rather play it safe. There's no harm in doing it that way.

It appeared to the observer that "playing safe" meant that even in those cases where the examination established nothing, the psychiatrists did not consider recommending release. Thus in one case the examination had established that the patient had a very good memory, was oriented and spoke quietly and seriously. The observer recorded his discussion with the physician after the examination as follows:

> When the doctor told me he was recommending commitment for this patient too (he had also recommended commitment in the two examinations held earlier that day) he laughed because he could see what my next question was going to be. He said, "I already recommended the release of two patients this month." This sounded like it was the maximum amount the way he said it.

Apparently this examiner felt that he had a very limited quota on the number of patients he could recommend for release (less than two percent of those examined).

The language used by these physicians tends to intimate that mental illness was found, even when reporting the opposite. Thus in one case the recommendation stated: "No gross evidence of delusions or hallucinations." This statement is misleading, since not only was there no gross evidence, there was not any evidence, not even the slightest suggestion of delusions or hallucinations, brought out by the interview.

These remarks suggest that the examiners prejudge the cases they examine. Several further comments indicate prejudgment. One physician stated that he thought that most crimes of violence were committed by patients released too early from mental hospitals. (This is an erroneous belief.)[12] He went on to say that he thought that all mental patients should be kept in the hospital at least three months, indicating prejudgment concerning his examinations. Another physician, after a very short interview (8 minutes), told the observer:

> On the schizophrenics, I don't bother asking them more questions when I can see they're schizophrenic because I *know what they are going to say*. You could talk to them another half hour and not learn any more.

Another physician, finally, contrasted cases in which the patient's family or others initiated hospitalization ("petition cases," the great majority of cases) with those cases initiated by the court:

> The petition cases are pretty *automatic*. If the patient's own family wants to get rid of him you know there is something wrong.

The lack of care which characterized the examinations is evident in the forms on which the examiners make their recommendations. On most of these forms, whole sections have been left unanswered. Others are answered in a peremptory and uninformative way. For example, in the section entitled Physical Examination, the question is asked: "Have you made a physical examination of the patient? State fully what is the present physical condition," a typical answer is "Yes. Fair," or, "Is apparently in good health." Since in none of the examinations we observed was the patient actually physically examined, these answers appear to be mere guesses. One of the examiners used regularly in court B, to the question "On what subject or in what way is derangement now manifested?" always wrote in "Is mentally ill." The omissions, and the almost flippant brevity of these forms, together with the arbitrariness, lack of evidence, and prejudicial character of the examinations, discussed above, all support the observer's conclusion that, except in very unusual cases, the psychiatric examiner's recommendation to retain the patient is virtually automatic.

Lest it be thought that these results are unique to a particularly backward Midwestern State, it should be pointed out that this state is noted for its progressive psychiatric practices. It will be recalled that a number of the psychiatrists employed by the court as examiners had finished their psychiatric residencies, which is not always the case in many other states. A still common practice in other states is to employ, as members of the "Lunacy Panel," partially retired physicians with no psychiatric training whatever. This was the case in Stockton, California, in 1959, where the author observed hundreds of hearings at which these physicians were present. It may be indicative of some of the larger issues underlying the question of civil commitment that, in these hearings, the physicians played very little part; the judge controlled the questioning of the relatives and patients, and the hearings were often a model of impartial and thorough investigation.

DISCUSSION

Ratings of the qualifications for involuntary confinement of patients newly admitted to the public mental hospitals in a Midwestern state, together with observations of judicial hearings and psychiatric examinations by the observer connected with the present study, both suggest that the decision as to the mental condition of a majority of the patients is an uncertain one. The fact that the courts seldom release patients, and the perfunctory manner in which the legal and medical procedures are carried out, suggest that the judicial decision to retain patients in the hospital for treatment is routine and largely based on the presumption of illness. Three reasons for this presumption will be discussed: financial, ideological, and political.

Our discussions with the examiners indicated that one reason that they perform biased "examinations" is that their rate of pay is determined by the length of time spent with the patient. In recommending retention, the examiners are refraining from interrupting the hospitalization and commitment procedures already in progress, and thereby allowing someone else, usually the hospital, to make the effective decision to release or commit. In order to recommend release, however, they would have to build a case showing why these procedures should be interrupted. Building such a case would take much more time than is presently expended by the examiners, thereby reducing their rate of pay.

A more fundamental reason for the presumption of illness by the examiners, and perhaps the reason why this practice is allowed by the courts, is the interpretation of current psychiatric doctrine by the examiners and court officials. These officials make a number of assumptions, which are now thought to be of doubtful validity:

1. The condition of mentally ill persons deteriorates rapidly without psychiatric assistance.
2. Effective psychiatric treatments exist for most mental illnesses.
3. Unlike surgery, there are no risks involved in involuntary psychiatric treatment: it either helps or is neutral, it can't hurt.
4. Exposing a prospective mental patient to questioning, cross-examination, and other screening procedures exposes him to the unnecessary stigma of trial-like procedures, and may do further damage to his mental condition.
5. There is an element of danger to self or others in most mental illness. It is better to risk unnecessary hospitalization than the harm the patient might do himself or others.

Many psychiatrists and others now argue that none of these assumptions are necessarily correct.

1. The assumption that psychiatric disorders usually get worse without treatment rests on very little other than evidence of an anecdotal character. There is just as much evidence that most acute psychological and emotional upsets are self-terminating.[13]
2. It is still not clear, according to systematic studies evaluating psychotherapy, drugs, etc., that most psychiatric interventions are any more effective, on the average, than no treatment at all.[14]
3. There is very good evidence that involuntary hospitalization and social isolation may affect the patient's life: his job, his family affairs, etc. There is some evidence that too hasty exposure to psychiatric treatment may convince the patient that he is "sick," prolonging what might have been an otherwise transitory episode.[15]
4. This assumption is correct, as far as it goes. But it is misleading because it fails to consider what occurs when the patient who does not wish to be hospitalized is forcibly treated. Such patients often become extremely indignant and angry, particularly in the case, as often happens, when they are deceived into coming to the hospital on some pretext.

5. The element of danger is usually exaggerated both in amount and degree. In the psychiatric survey of new patients in state mental hospitals, danger to self or others was mentioned in about a fourth of the cases. Furthermore, in those cases where danger is mentioned, it is not always clear that the risks involved are greater than those encountered in ordinary social life. This issue has been discussed by Ross, an attorney:

> A truck driver with a mild neurosis who is "accident prone" is probably a greater danger to society than most psychotics; yet, he will not be committed for treatment, even if he would be benefited. The community expects a certain amount of dangerous activity. I suspect that as a class, drinking drivers are a greater danger than the mentally ill, and yet the drivers are tolerated or punished with small fines rather than indeterminate imprisonment.[16]

From our observations of the medical examinations and other commitment procedures, we formed a very strong impression that the doctrines of danger to self or others, early treatment, and the avoidance of stigma were invoked partly because the officials believed them to be true, and partly because they provided convenient justification for a pre-existing policy of summary action, minimal investigation, avoidance of responsibility and, after the patient is in the hospital, indecisiveness and delay.

The policy of presuming illness is probably both cause and effect of political pressure on the court from the community. The judge, an elected official, runs the risk of being more heavily penalized for erroneously releasing than for erroneously retaining patients. Since the judge personally appoints the panel of psychiatrists to serve as examiners, he can easily transmit the community pressure to them, by failing to reappoint a psychiatrist whose examinations were inconveniently thorough.

Some of the implications of these findings for the sociology of deviant behavior will be briefly summarized. The discussion above, of the reasons that the psychiatrists tend to presume illness, suggests that the motivations of the key decision-makers in the screening process may be significant in determining the extent and direction of the societal reaction. In the case of psychiatric screening of persons alleged to be mentally ill, the social differentiation of the deviant from the non-deviant population appears to be materially affected by the financial, ideological, and political position of the psychiatrists, who are in this instance the key agents of social control.

Under these circumstances, the character of the societal reaction appears to undergo a marked change from the pattern of denial which occurs in the community. The official societal reaction appears to reverse the presumption of normality reported by the Cummings as a characteristic of informal societal reaction, and instead exaggerates both the amount and degree of deviance.[17] Thus, one extremely important contingency influencing the severity of the societal reaction may be whether or not the original deviance comes to official notice. This paper suggests that in the area of mental disorder, perhaps in contrast to other areas of deviant behavior, if the official societal reaction is invoked, for whatever reason, social differentiation of the deviant from the non-deviant population will usually occur.

CONCLUSION

This paper has described the screening of patients who were admitted to public mental hospitals in early June, 1962, in a Midwestern state. The data presented here suggest that the screening is usually perfunctory, and that in the crucial screening examination by the court-appointed psychiatrists, there is a presumption of illness. Since most court decisions appear to hinge on the recommendation of these psychiatrists, there appears to be a large element of status ascription in the official societal reaction to persons alleged to be mentally ill, as exemplified by the court's actions. This finding points to the importance of lay definitions of mental illness in the community, since the "diagnosis" of mental illness by laymen in the community initiates the official societal reaction, and to the necessity of analyzing social processes connected with the recognition and reaction to the deviant behavior that is called mental illness in our society.

Notes

1. John I. Kitsuse, "Societal Reaction to Deviant Behavior: Problems of Theory and Method," *Social Problems*, 9 (Winter, 1962), pp. 247–257.

2. Edwin M. Lemert, *Social Pathology*, New York: McGraw-Hill, 1951; Erving Goffman, *Asylums*, Chicago: Aldine, 1962.

3. For a more general discussion of the presumption of illness in medicine, and some of its possible causes and consequences, see the author's "Decision Rules, Types of Error and Their Consequences in Medical Diagnosis," *Behavioral Science*, 8 (April, 1963), pp. 97–107.

4. Hugh Allen Ross, "Commitment of the Mentally Ill: Problems of Law and Policy," *Michigan Law Review*, 57 (May, 1959), pp. 945–1018.

5. This is the typical phrasing in cases in the *Dicennial Legal Digest*, found under the heading "Mental Illness."

6. Goffman, *op. cit.*, pp. 155, 159.

7. David Mechanic, "Some Factors in Identifying and Defining Mental Illness," *Mental Hygiene*, 46 (January, 1962), pp. 66–75.

8. Esther Lucile Brown, *Newer Dimensions of Patient Care*, Part I, New York: Russell Sage, 1961, p. 60, fn.

9. Luis Kutner, "The Illusion of Due Process in Commitment Proceedings," *Northwestern University Law Review*, 57 (Sept. 1962), pp. 383–399.

10. Other exceptions occurred as follows: the deputy clerks in courts C and D appeared to exercise some discretion in turning away applications they considered improper or incomplete, at step No. 1; the judge in Court D appeared also to perform some screening at step No. 5. For further description of these exceptions see "Rural-Urban Differences in the Judicial Screening of the Mentally Ill in a Midwestern State." (In press)

11. In interviews with the judges, the following criteria were named: Appropriateness of behavior and speech, understanding of the situation, and orientation.

12. The rate of crimes of violence, or any crime, appears to be less among ex-mental patients than in the general population. Henry Brill and Benjamin Maltzberg, "Statistical Report Based on the Arrest Record of 5354 Ex-patients Released from New York State Mental Hospitals During the Period 1946–48." Mimeo available from the authors; Louis H. Cohen and Henry Freeman, "How Dangerous to the Community Are State Hospital Patients?", Connecticut State Medical Journal, 9 (Sept. 1945), pp. 697–700; Donald W. Hastings, "Follow-up Results in Psychiatric Illness," Amer. Journal of Psychiatry, 118 (June 1962), pp. 1078–1086.

13. For a review of epidemiological studies of mental disorder see Richard J. Plunkett and John E. Gordon, Epidemiology and Mental Illness. New York: Basic Books, 1960. Most of these studies suggest that at any given point in time, psychiatrists find a substantial proportion of persons in normal populations to be "mentally ill." One interpretation of this finding is that much of the deviance detected in these studies is self-limiting.

14. For an assessment of the evidence regarding the effectiveness of electroshock, drugs, psychotherapy, and other psychiatric treatments, see H. J. Eysenck, Handbook of Abnormal Psychology, New York: Basic Books, 1961, Part III.

15. For examples from military psychiatry, see Albert J. Glass, "Psychotherapy in the Combat Zone," in Symposium on Stress, Washington, D.C., Army Medical Service Graduate School, 1953, and B. L. Bushard, "The U.S. Army's Mental Hygiene Consultation Service," in Symposium on Preventive and Social Psychiatry, 15–17 (April 1957), Washington, D.C.: Walter Reed Army Institute of Research, pp. 431–43. For a discussion of essentially the same problem in the context of a civilian mental hospital, cf. Kai T. Erikson, "Patient Role and Social Uncertainty—A Dilemma of the Mentally Ill," Psychiatry, 20 (August 1957), pp. 263–275.

16. Ross, op. cit., p. 962.

17. Elaine Cumming and John Cumming, Closed Ranks, Cambridge, Mass: Harvard University Press, 1957, 102; for further discussion of the bipolarization of the societal reaction into denial and labeling, see the author's "The Role of the Mentally Ill and the Dynamics of Mental Disorder: A Research Framework," Sociometry, 26 (December, 1963), pp. 436–453.

23 / A Case of a "Psychotic" Navaho Indian Male

DONALD P. JEWELL

INTRODUCTION

Increased psychological and ethnological rapprochement has resulted in a greater understanding of American subgroups and the processes of acculturation. Examples of this integrated approach are to be seen in Barnouw's study of Chippewa Indian acculturation[1] and, on the individual level, Devereux's psychotherapy of an alcoholic Sioux.[2]

Sometimes identified as the "culture-personality" orientation, this approach has reached a degree of clarification which justifies consistent designation. It is suggested here that it be defined as ethnopsychological. It is an approach which, as Kluckhohn has shown, has about a century of development.[3] Ethnopsychology has generally concerned itself with the definition of general normal personality characteristics of other cultures, only occasionally with the neurotic individual, and rarely with the psychotic.

PURPOSE OF THIS STUDY

The writer had the opportunity recently to make a rather extensive observation of a Navaho Indian institutionalized as a psychotic in a California state mental hospital. By drawing from the literature of Navaho ethnopsychology and the writer's own experience among the Navaho people, it was hoped that the dynamics of the patient's maladjustment would be revealed. It was also anticipated that some sort of psychotherapy would evolve.

This report is a summary of those endeavors to understand and assist the Navaho patient. Cultural and linguistic obstacles prohibited an ideal approach, but enough was accomplished to permit considerable insight into the patient's behavior. There were features about the patient's personality which would not fit harmoniously with concepts of psychiatric symptomatology derived from European culture, those concepts dealing particularly with the dynamics of the patient's diagnosis of catatonic schizophrenia. The unique characteristics of this individual's personality leads, in fact, to the question as to what extent he should be considered psychotic, and whether that consideration should be viewed from Navaho or Anglo perspective.

During his many interviews with the patient, some of them with the aid of a Navaho interpreter, the writer developed an increasing awareness that to call the patient psychotic was an arbitrary matter. When this Navaho is referred to as psychotic, then, it is merely because he carried such a diagnosis during his 18 months of hospitalization as a mental patient.

ORIENTATION

Considerable literary attention has been given to the general psychological characteristics of Navaho Indians.[4] These have related psychological findings to ethnological contexts, and so offer a background against which the atypical Navaho individual may be examined.

On the behavioral level, the Navahos are in many ways unique, not only with respect to white people, but other Indian tribes as well. One of their most characteristic traits may be seen in crisis situations. Kluckhohn and Leighton describe it as a passive resistance, the individual masking his fear by quiet unmovingness, an appearance of stoicism. If forced into action, the response is a mechanical, apparently uncomprehending behavior.[5]

Another form of withdrawal is often expressed in periods of depression, apparently a morbid preoccupation with health.[6]

These being salient aspects of the typical Navaho personality, the question now arises as to how those traits would be characterized on the psychotic level. Under prolonged psychological stress, what would develop from the stoicism and moods of morbid preoccupation?

In an endeavor to answer this question a survey was made of those mental hospitals which would most likely be caring for Navaho patients. The Bureau of Indian Affairs' policy is not to concentrate Indian patients, but to subsidize their care in whatever hospital they may have been committed. It is thus possible that a few Navahos may be hospitalized some distance from their reservation area of New Mexico, Utah, and Arizona, and have not been located in this survey. It is felt, however, that a survey of those mental hospitals in the Southwest only would be adequate to show general trends. The findings are summarized in the following table.

Diagnosis	Number	Sex and Age
Psychosis with syphilis of the C.N.C.	2	1f: 47; 1m: 31
Psychosis with cerebral arteriosclerosis	1	1f: 62
Psychosis due to trauma (organic)	1	1m: 47
Epilepsy	8	6m: 20, 24, 29, 33 37, 39; 2f: 20, 32
Schizophrenia, Simple Type	1	1m: 25
Schizophrenia, Mixed Type	1	1f: 26
Schizophrenia, Hebephrenic Type	1	1f: 30
Schizophrenia, Catatonic Type	7	4m: 26, 28, 28, 36; 3f: 20, 30, 38
Depressed State	1	1f: 37
Manic Depressive Psychosis, Manic Type	1	1m: 42

Legend: f: female; m: male

Summary of survey of Navaho Indian mental patients hospitalized in southwestern United States, excluding mental defectives. (Acknowledgement of the hospitals cooperating in this survey must be regretfully omitted due to the need to protect the identity of the patients.)

Elimination of the organic psychoses leaves one manic, one depressive, and 10 schizophrenics. Of the schizophrenics, seven are catatonic. This is an unusually high incidence of catatonic schizophrenia, and seems to indicate that Navahos are predisposed toward that particular psychosis. This immediately suggests that the above described stoicism has been carried to pathological extremes, and possibly that the stoicism is actually a transient form of catatonia. It was with this problem in mind that the Navaho patient discussed in this report was studied.

THE PATIENT

The patient was a 26-year-old Navaho male. For purposes of anonymity he will be referred to as Bill. He came to the writer's attention through a survey of Indian patients at the hospital. He was the only Navaho of 13 Indian patients scattered throughout the various wards and cottages, and of the 4,000 general patient population.

The outlook for examination and therapy seemed at first quite discouraging. The patient was in a cottage ordinarily reserved for the most regressed patients. Unlike most of the others in this cottage, however, he was not there because of repeated failure of such routine therapies as shock treatment, occupational therapy, etc. It was unusual for a patient in his condition, who had been at the hospital for eight months, not to have received at least electric shock treatment.

A preliminary period was spent at the cottage, observing Bill's behavior. He was very withdrawn. Most of his day was spent in inactive sitting or sleeping. He would rouse himself only for eating or attending to other personal needs. He would assist with floor waxing, dish washing, or other activities the attendants might require of him, but in a perfunctory and apathetic manner. His behavior was not patently catatonic, but certainly suggestive of it.

Most of the attendants reported never having heard Bill speak. A few, however, indicated that Bill would occasionally approach them and, in almost unintelligible English, ask if he could go home.

Shortly thereafter Bill was brought to the writer's office where he was greeted in Navaho. Bill responded in that language, glancing briefly at the writer before returning his gaze to the floor.

This closer inspection of Bill revealed occipital flattening, resulting from the cradle board as a child, and the pierced ear lobes of a conservative Navaho. During this first interview he complained about the close hair cuts he received at the hospital, further evidence that he belonged to the old fashioned, "long hair" conservatives of the reservation.

The interview proceeded very slowly, but gradually a system of communication began to evolve. By utilizing mutually understood Navaho and English words, by means of pantomime, and with the aid of penciled sketches, the system became increasingly refined during the following interviews.

Bill was seen three hours a week for three months. The writer then took an eight months leave of absence from the hospital, during which time he spent several months in Bill's home area near Shiprock, New Mexico.

While in the Shiprock area, the writer endeavored to locate Bill's family to advise them of the patient's circumstances. Bill had previously drawn a map indicating the approximate location of his family's *hogans* (dwellings), but it proved impossible to find them. The *hogans* were located about five miles from the nearest road, and even if a horse and interpreter had been available the chances of locating the specific *hogans* were slight. The situation was complicated by the fact that the family did not have American names and the writer did not know their Navaho names. Missionaries and Bureau of Indian Affairs personnel were consequently given the problem of finding the family but several months elapsed before they were equipped with sufficient information to do so.

Although he could not communicate with Bill's family, the writer succeeded in talking with several Navahos who had known Bill, and in obtaining ecological and further case history material.

Shortly after the writer's return to the hospital a Navaho interpreter was brought in from the Sherman Institute, a large Indian school not far from the hospital. Interviews with the patient through the interpreter corroborated the case history material obtained, and further satisfied the writer in his clinical evaluation of the patient. Both of these areas are separately discussed in the following text.

CASE HISTORY

The gathering of Bill's history extended over a period of 11 months, and was obtained piecemeal from a variety of sources. In summarizing, however, this material will be integrated for greater coherency.

Bill was born in a part of the reservation noted for being both very conservative and poverty-stricken. Only 50 miles away is the markedly contrasting community of Shiprock, considered to be one of the most acculturated Navaho communities. It is also prospering from recently developed uranium operations in the region.

During his early years Bill saw very little of Shiprock, and was reared in the traditional Navaho way. He was born during an eclipse (it is not known whether of the sun or moon), and was thus destined to take part in a periodic ceremony identified to the writer as the "Breath of Life" sing. The first of this series of ceremonies was held while he was still an infant, the second about six years ago. During the ceremony he inhales the breath of a great deity, and is thus assured of continued good health in the respiratory and vocal organs.

Bill lived with his immediate family until he was six years of age. He had only one younger sister at that time, although the family was later to include seven living siblings. He did not become well acquainted with his family, however, as he was given to his grandfather when he was six years old. The grandfather, a widower, lived several miles deeper into the reservation and required Bill's assistance as a sheep herder.

Bill worked for his grandfather as a sheep herder until he was 17, except for one interruption when, at the age of 15, he spent 50 days in the Shiprock hospital with a back ailment. Bill reports that the old man never talked to him.

At his grandfather's death Bill went to work for the railroad in Colorado. This was cut short by an illness which confined him to the Navaho Medical Center in Fort Defiance, Arizona. The illness was diagnosed as tuberculosis, pulmonary, moderately advanced. He was in the hospital for eight months and was discharged in the summer of 1944.

Bill returned to railroad employment, and worked in Utah, Oregon, and Nebraska. He was always part of Navaho crews and thus never exposed to acculturative influences. His father and a younger brother were also part of these crews.

Bill returned home for a brief visit in 1949, accompanied by his brother and father. He had saved $1,022. Subsequently, he went to Phoenix, Arizona to pick cotton, a job that had been found for him by the employment agency at Shiprock. This was his first trip from home without a family member.

The employment at Phoenix did not last long and in December, 1949, on the advice of an Indian friend he went to Barstow, California seeking railroad employment. At the section camp there his attempt to find work was unsuccessful, and after three days he started by bus back to Phoenix.

On this return trip he stopped for dinner at Colton. A white man he met there promised to obtain railroad employment for him. The stranger said that he required funds for this effort and in some way relieved Bill of his savings which had now dwindled to $725.

Bill returned home penniless, pawned some jewelry, borrowed some money, and returned to Colton to try to find the man who had taken his savings. He also looked for Navahos who might have information about employment. The many hours of waiting around the bus station searching for his man apparently caused suspicion, for he was arrested for vagrancy.

In jail he met some Navahos with whom he went to Barstow after his release. But in Barstow he was still unable to find employment and after six days he was completely out of funds. He started walking toward Phoenix, and was picked up by a man driving a truck. This man gave Bill one day's employment which allowed funds for a return to Barstow and another attempt to find work.

He managed to raise a little money doing odd jobs about the section camp near Barstow, and then returned to San Bernardino on the first lap of his return to Phoenix and home. It occurred to him that if he could get to a hospital, the officials there would send him to a reservation hospital, from whence he would be sent home. This was logical thinking: on the reservations, the hospitals, schools, and trading posts are the major source of assistance in all sorts of troubles.

As this idea occurred to Bill, he noticed a woman dressed in white whom he took to be a nurse. He approached her and endeavored to explain that he was sick, but his endeavors were misinterpreted and he was taken to jail.

At the county jail Bill was apparently mistaken for a Mexican since a

Mexican interpreter had tried to interview him. When the interview failed he was transferred to the psychopathic ward. Interviewed by the medical examiner there, he reportedly demonstrated an anguished appearance and repeated, "Me sick." He was diagnosed as Schizophrenia, Catatonic Type, and delivered to the state mental hospital.

Upon admission to the hospital, Bill was first taken to be a Filipino. The psychiatric admission note indicated that he was, ". . . confused, dull, and preoccupied. He has a look of anguish and appears to be hallucinating. . . . He repeats, 'I don't know.' " He was diagnosed as Dementia Praecox, which was later specified as Hebephrenic Type.

Several months later the psychiatrist on Bill's cottage tested him for *cerea flexibilitas* (waxy flexibility) and, finding it to be present, altered the diagnosis to Catatonic Type.

Eight months after his admittance he was discovered by the writer.

PSYCHOLOGICAL ASPECTS

Concomitant with gathering the case history material presented above, endeavors were made to evaluate the patient's intelligence and personality. The lack of culturally-biased examining techniques made this extremely difficult.

Bill's performance on the various tests that were administered led to a conclusion that his probable I.Q. was in the vicinity of 80. This had to take into consideration the patient's slowness. At best, a Navaho refuses to be put under pressure of time, and to what extent Bill's slowness was cultural rather than psychotically pathological was a question of primary concern.

Bill's apathetic and withdrawn behavior has already been described. For diagnostic purposes, however, this syndrome is confused by cultural factors. It is common for Navahos, with their morbid fear of hospitals, to demonstrate just such a withdrawal patterning.[7] It is not known whether or not this would reach a stage of *cerea flexibilitas* or how long this behavior will persist. Accordingly it was concluded that Bill's apparent catatonia should not be accepted as a symptom of schizophrenia until underlying signs of schizophrenic processes could be detected.

During the first interview Bill was given the Draw A Person Test. The figure he drew was indistinct and without facial features and clearly reflected his withdrawal.

On the seventh interview the test was again given. Compared with the earlier attempt, the second drawing clearly reflected an improvement. It probably indicated the therapeutic benefits derived from the extensive individual treatment the patient was receiving.

The second drawing filled the paper, the facial features were portrayed, the arms were extended, and the drawing generally implied those signs which are held to indicate good contact with reality.

Although Bill's second drawing seems to imply considerable personality change, no changes could be observed in his behavior. He continued to appear apathetic and withdrawn. On several occasions he indicated his reluctance to talk because, "me no good this place," pointing to his chest. This suggested the characteristic organ cathexes of schizophrenia. However, the patient's thinking behind this statement was made clear during the later interviews through an interpreter.

Bill was concerned about the fact that he had not completed the second series of the "Breath of Life" ceremony. This matter had gone too long unattended, and he assumed that he must conserve his vocal energies until they could be supplemented by the breath of the deity. He expressed a great need to return home to pursue the ceremony.

In continued endeavor to detect schizophrenic underlay of his apparent catatonia, Bill was given a series of tests, none of which revealed responses normally associated with schizophrenia.

During the early course of the interviews with Bill, although not satisfied that the patient was not psychotic, the writer recommended that the best therapeutic environment for him would be his own home. This recommendation was not acted upon, partly because no one knew where his home was, or how he could be supervised there, but chiefly because he continued to appear catatonic.

Later, as the writer became convinced that the catatonia—if such it could be termed—was not symptomatic of underlying schizophrenia, efforts were renewed to release the patient. The outcome of these endeavors are summarized in the following section.

OUTCOME

As mentioned earlier, the final interviews with Bill were carried on with the aid of a Navaho interpreter. Bill conversed quite freely with the other Navahos and expressed gratitude at being able to talk to someone in his own language. The conversations did not add much to the history and understanding previously gained, but did offer an opportunity to inquire for the presence of hallucinations, delusions, and more subtle clues of schizophrenic thinking. Unless Bill's anxiety regarding the uncompleted "Breath of Life" ceremony could be considered bizarre, nothing of significance was elicited.

The interpreter's reaction to the interviews represented their most significant outcome. He was a professional interpreter, with vast experience in interviewing Navaho youths in strange environments. He expressed a strong conviction that Bill's behavior and attitudes were not unusual under the circumstances.

The interpreter communicated his feelings to the superintendent of the Sherman Institute who took an immediate and active interest in the case. After several interviews with Bill, satisfied that he could observe nothing about Bill's behavior which could be considered atypical under the circumstances, the superintendent offered to accept him into the flexible program of the Sherman Institute.

Bill was accordingly released under custody of the superintendent and careful plans were made to assure his adjustment at the school. At first, he was quartered in the school hospital, but allowed to participate in the school's social and recreational activities. He was employed with the animal husbandry and gardening program.

The writer's last visit to the Sherman Institute disclosed that Bill's adjustment had been quite rapid. He had put on weight and after about two weeks announced that he "felt right at home, now."

It had been difficult at first, because in spite of all precautions the students had learned something of Bill's past hospitalization. To the Navahos the hospital symbolizes death, and death is particularly abhorrent to them as they have no clearly structured concepts of an after-life. The students consequently shied away from Bill a little when he arrived, but he has since found acceptance.

He will go back to the reservation in the spring, at the close of the school year, and attend to the unfinished business of the "Breath of Life" ceremony.

CONCLUDING DISCUSSION

In the course of this Navaho's commitment and 18 months of hospitalization, he was routinely examined by several psychiatrists, all of whom concurred with the diagnosis of schizophrenia. Without verbal communication with the patient, diagnosis was necessarily derived from observation of his overt behavior. Diagnosis was apparently confident as the patient was not referred to staff clinic or for psychological testing, the normal procedure with questionable cases.

Most of the psychiatrists' diagnostic observations were based on information received from the attendants of Bill's cottage, who reported the patient's withdrawn and apathetic behavior. Upon closer examination the patient would demonstrate *cerea flexibilitas*. Because of these factors the patient was assumed to be catatonic and hence schizophrenic.

Actually, many of the classic symptoms of catatonia were not present in this patient. He was not markedly stuporous or mute; he was clean in his personal habits and would eat willingly; he tended to doze as he sat rather than stare fixedly into space as does the typical catatonic. The writer, too, examined Bill for *cerea flexibilitas*, but learned later that the patient held grotesque positions because he thought it was expected of him.

With the assumption, however, that the patient's overt behavior could be interpreted as symptomatic of catatonic schizophrenia, it remains to be explained why testing and closer observation did not reveal the underlying ego disintegration which should be expected.

General personality traits of the Navaho people, as briefly reviewed earlier in this paper, could possibly imply a potential for schizophrenic disintegration. Navahos do not have the imaginative activity and the inner control which is so important to adjustment in the Anglo world. The scales are balanced, however, by a defense of rigidity and constriction. In a threatening situation they strive to maintain ego structure by psychic withdrawal.

The few tests that were applicable in examining Bill did not permit a very intensive examination of the dynamics of his withdrawal, but all indications were that he continued to maintain ego strength. He could account for his acts rationally, he performed very well with conceptualization, he maintained orientation for time and place, and could hold in mind simultaneously various aspects of situations or problems. His visuo-motor performance exhibited no signs of distorted perspective. Many of his expressions could be considered naive, but hardly bizarre.

The apparent incongruity between the patient's overt behavior and underlying personality dynamics, although not fully understood psychologically, should not be considered as psychotic manifestation. Culturally derived, it can probably be explained as a defense mechanism characterized by an extreme and sustained withdrawal.

To what extent Bill's case may be typical of other Navaho patients diagnosed as catatonic schizophrenia cannot, of course, be proposed. It would be necessary to know if those patients were similarly diagnosed on the basis of overt behavior alone.

It is also unknown to what degree Bill may personify on-reservation Navaho youth. Superficially at least, his history appears quite typical. His lack of school, his years as a sheep herder for his grandfather, his attack of tuberculosis, and his railroad employment, are circumstances and events common to many Navahos. His grandfather's apparent lack of affection implies an almost feral existence for the growing boy, but even this situation is not unusual. It is, in fact, difficult to discern some way in which this patient could be atypical as evaluated against his cultural background. Except for his possible low intelligence, he appears to represent a typical Navaho youth, a fact heavy with implication when his 18 months of hospitalization as a mental patient is considered.

The previously cited survey of hospitalized Navaho mental patients shows an amazingly small percentage of the total Navaho population (which is about 65,000). This is probably because few Navahos are currently coming in very close contact with Anglo structure.

Of the catatonic schizophrenics, it would be of value to know more about the details of their admission. If they were referred from the reservation it probably meant that they were considered psychotic within the Navaho milieu; if, on the other hand, they were referred by agencies off the reservation (as was Bill), it would imply an evaluation derived from Anglo perspective. This will become a more poignant problem with increasing off-reservation movement of the Navaho people.

In addition to what this study may imply with respect to the Navaho Indians, it is hoped also that it may illustrate the need to consider the influence of cultural environment in any study of individual personality. The psychiatric approach usually concerns itself with the abnormal personality, and evaluates the individual according to concepts of what constitutes the normal personality. Too often these concepts are preconceived and stereotyped, giving very little consideration to the individual's cultural frame of reference. This factor naturally varies in proportion to the degree of the individual's acculturation.

The cultural factor seems to be particularly important in reconciling overt behavior with covert personality dynamics. This is often a difficult reconciliation even with patients of the general American cultural patterning, and becomes increasingly more difficult the farther removed the individual is from acculturation.

The need to consider emotional maladjustment with respect to cultural factors has long been recognized. It has, however, been somewhat of an academic acknowledgment which demands greater practical application on the clinical level.

Notes

1. Barnouw, V., "Acculturation and Personality Among the Wisconsin Chippewa," *American Anthropologist*, Memoir Number 72, Vol. 52, 1950.
2. Devereux, G., *Reality and Dream*, International Universities Press, Inc., 1950.
3. Kluckhohn, C., "The Influence of Psychiatry on Anthropology in America During the Past One Hundred Years," eds. J. K. Hall, C. Zilboorg, and E. A. Bunker, *One Hundred Years of American Psychiatry*, Columbia University Press, 1947, pp. 589–617.

4. Henry, W., "The Thematic Apperception Technique in the Study of Culture-Personality Relations," *Genetic Psychology Monographs*, Vol. 35, 1947, pp. 3–135; Kluckhohn, C., and Leighton, D., *Children of the People*, Harvard University Press, 1948.

5. Kluckhohn and Leighton, *ibid.*, p. 108.

6. *Ibid.*, p. 110.

7. *Ibid.*, pp. 108–109.

24 / The Role of Teachers' Nominations in the Perpetuation of Deviant Adolescent Careers

DELOS H. KELLY

In their rather recent paper, Cicourel and Kitsuse (1968) initially argue to the effect that any organization generally provides within its organizational structure or makeup several distinct *career lines* that can be pursued by its members. They contend, furthermore, that *entry* into an existing career line is often a function of not only how the "organization" perceives but also *types* its members. Cicourel and Kitsuse also seem to suggest, at least by implication, that the social actor is often afforded relatively little opportunity, if any, to participate in those decisions that may be critical in determining which type of career he may be shunted into. To provide a measure of substance to these initial claims, the authors draw heavily upon the materials they obtained from their two empirical examinations of a specific organization: *the American high school* (Cicourel and Kitsuse, 1963). They begin their analysis of this institution by defining the construct: "adolescent career."

According to their usage, an *adolescent career* can "... be defined as the product of social typing, classifying, and processing of adolescents by the personnel of any social organization or set of organizations (Cicourel and Kitsuse, 1968: 125–126)." Cicourel and Kitsuse (1968: 126) go on to argue that the school system, through its interaction and contacts with other agencies, plays an extremely important role in *selecting-out* students to fill the specific career lines, both deviant and non-deviant, that exist within its organizational structure:

> The school system may be conceived as an organization which *produces*, in the course of its activities, *a variety of adolescent careers* including the delinquent. Because the school occupies a strategic position as a coordinating agency between the activities of the family, the police, and the peer group vis-a-vis adolescents, it also provides a *"clearing house"* which receives and releases information from and to other agencies concerning adolescents . . . *the interpretations and actions of parents, police, and peer group may affect the activation, maintenance and alteration of various careers within the high school.* [Italics mine.]

Once the major career lines are in existence, Cicourel and Kitsuse argue that school personnel begin to identify behavioral or "adolescent problems" among its students; these initial designations then provide the major basis for the typing and subsequent placement of students. In effect, the "working ideology" of the school contains a set of "conceptual packages" or "diagnostic stereotypes" (Scheff, 1968) that serve the important function of identifying students for placement in the existing career lines.

> *The organizational structure of the school and its activities create a variety of "adolescent problems" which are identified in the vocabulary and syntax of its personnel.* The "problems" may be grouped under three rough headings: Those pertaining to (1) the student's academic activities, (2) student infraction of rules of conduct, and (3) the emotional problems of students. School personnel frequently refer to those they consider "academic problems" as "over-achievers," and "opportunity students." Among the *labels* applied to students in the second category are "trouble-makers," "hoods," and "delinquents." In the third category are students who are considered "nervous," "withdrawn and unsocial," and "isolates" (Cicourel and Kitsuse, 1968: 126). [Italics mine.]

It is these *social type designations* that provide ". . . bases for a variety of careers" (Cicourel and Kitsuse, 1968: 126). Cicourel and Kitsuse then go on to delineate the three career lines they uncovered in the school under analysis: (1) the academic, (2) the emotional, and (3) the delinquent (Cicourel and Kitsuse, 1968: 127–135).

Selection of students for entry into these career lines becomes the primary responsibility of the *guidance counselor* and, in the majority of the cases where a discrepancy in placement may arise, his decision generally overrides the expressed desires of the student and his family members.

> . . . For example, parents may insist that their child be placed in an academic program regardless of his prior academic record. *Thus, in principle, a student has the right, on the approval of his parents, to choose between the curricula, a right which he, however, may not know he has.* Even where the right is invoked, the classification of the students as an "academic problem" by the school personnel may have major consequences for the organizational processing of his declared choice of curriculum. If an "underachiever," "over-achiever," or an "opportunity student" declares his decision to follow a college-preparatory curriculum, *the counselor may decide that he is "not college material" or "not adequately motivated" and thus unlikely to successfully complete such a curriculum.* In such circumstances, *the counselor frequently attempts to persuade the student or his parents to change to the vocational curriculum, or he may refuse to allow the student to enroll in certain elective courses because the courses may be considered "too difficult for him"* (Cicourel and Kitsuse, 1968: 127–128). [Italics mine.]

The actual *criteria* employed in the selection of students, it was noted, were often *non-academic* in nature; this was most evident in Cicourel and Kitsuse's analysis of the delinquent career line. They point out that students who may be typed with reference to *infractions of conduct rules* can generally expect to be singled-out for special observation and treatment on the part of teachers, counselors, administrators, and the like.

> . . . Like academic careers, a review of the student's folder or biographical materials received from the junior high school, may lead admissions personnel to *alert* teachers, counselors, and administrators to his history of "difficulties." The labeling of the student as a "trouble-maker," "truant," "fresh," etc., may provide the occasion for *singling him out for special handling and treatment.* For example, he may be more closely supervised, his academic progress more frequently reviewed, his parents requested to come in for conferences, counseling advised, etc. Thus, the student's *cumulative folder and the interpretations and actions which may follow from it* are important sources of data for the investigation of delinquent as well as academic careers (Cicourel and Kitsuse, 1968: 130). [Italics mine.]

Cicourel and Kitsuse thus argue, on the basis of their data, that the guidance counselor plays an extremely strategic and critical role in both typing and classifying students. Through use of available information (e.g., police-school contacts, school records, and other biographical material), along with his own personal assessments of the appropriate student "ability" and "motivational" factors, he not only initially labels but also subsequently places students into specific career lines. Thereafter, through a process of formal and informal communication, these initial career decisions become known to teachers and other school personnel.

In extending the Cicourel-Kitsuse thesis, it can be argued that this type of interaction becomes especially important in the maintenance and *perpetuation* of a deviant adolescent career. Teachers and other third parties are asked, in a sense, to validate the status (e.g., delinquent) being conferred upon a student, and the student, on the other hand, is expected to become committed to this status and its associated roles. Becker (1963) has commented rather extensively on the processes that are often involved in the *imputation* of a deviant identity to a social actor.

He argues that *public labeling* is generally the most important step in the initiation of a deviant career, particularly in view of the effect it has on an actor's *public identity*. This labeling, moreover, often results in his being placed in a new status.

> One of the most crucial steps in the process of building a stable pattern of deviant behavior is likely to be the experience of being caught and publicly labeled as a deviant. Whether a person takes this step or not depends not so

much on what he does as on what other people do, on whether or not they enforce the rule he has violated (Becker, 1963: 31).

... being caught and branded as deviant has important consequences for one's further social participation and self-image. *The most important consequence is a drastic change in the individual's public identity.* Committing the improper act and being publicly caught at it place him in a *new status.* He has been revealed as a *different kind of person* from the kind he was supposed to be. He is labeled a "fairy," "dope fiend," "nut" or "lunatic," and *treated accordingly* (Becker, 1963: 31–32). [Italics mine.]

Becker, in drawing upon Hughes' (1945) distinctions, argues, furthermore, that certain statuses in our society assume a certain priority, particularly in terms of structuring perceptions and reactions. Such statuses can be effectively termed *master statuses.* The label or status "social deviant" is one such example.

... *Some statuses,* in our society as in others, *override all other statuses and have a certain priority.* Race is one of these. Membership in the Negro race, as socially defined, will override most other status considerations in most other situations; the fact that one is a physician or middle-class or female will not protect one from being treated as a Negro first and any of these other things second. *The status of deviant* (depending on the kind of deviance) *is this kind of master status.* One receives the status as a result of breaking a rule, and the identification proves to be more important than most others. *One will be identified as a deviant first, before other identifications are made* ... (Becker, 1963: 33). [Italics mine.]

This identification or labeling process, Becker claims, sets in motion a *self-fulfilling prophecy* which eventually results in the exclusion of the social actor from participation in many conventional groups and activities.

Treating a person as though he were generally rather than specifically deviant produces a *self-fulfilling prophecy. It sets in motion several mechanisms which conspire to shape the person in the image people have of him.* ... In the first place, *one tends to be cut off,* after being identified as deviant, from participation in more conventional groups, even though the specific consequences of the particular deviant activity might never of themselves have caused the *isolation* had there not also been the *public knowledge* and *reaction* to it. ... (Becker, 1963: 34). [Italics mine.]

PROCEDURES AND INITIAL OBSERVATIONS

By not only integrating but also extrapolating from the works of particularly Cicourel and Kitsuse, and Becker, it would seem that several important questions need to be systematically researched: (1) What major adolescent career lines or types appear to exist within a specific educational institution? (2) What criteria are used to select-out students for placement or entry into the existing career lines? (3) Of those school personnel involved in the decision-making process, which individual or group of individuals is given the primary responsibility for applying these criteria in the selection or classifying process? (4) What role does the student and his or her family play in the selection process? (5) Once the initial social type designations and associated career decisions have been made or activated by the appropriate school personnel, how does this information become disseminated to other involved parties? (6) Once the students and their social type designations become known to these other third parties (e.g., teachers and administrators), how is this knowledge used not only in terms of the initial confirmation process but also in terms of how the affected students are subsequently processed and treated? That is, what role, for example, do teachers play in the validation, maintenance, and perpetuation of a deviant adolescent career? (7) Can the existing social type designations and associated labels within a school be legitimately viewed as master statuses?, and (8) Does designation as a social type set into motion a self-fulfilling prophecy and, further, does this generate a conscious shaping or molding process whereby the involved students eventually conform to the image others (e.g., teachers) have of them?

Each of these questions obviously deserves careful consideration. In this research, I will be concerned primarily with examining question number six, particularly that aspect dealing with the critical role that teachers presumably play in the perpetuation of a specific "deviant" adolescent career. However, I will, where necessary (e.g., establishing the existence of career lines, both deviant and non-deviant), also consider briefly other questions and concerns.

Data to be used in the present study were gathered from a combination of sources. Initially, in the Spring of 1974, a trained, student assistant spent approximately twenty hours per week for twelve weeks observing the actual operation of a middle school (grades five thru eight) in western New York State. The school itself is situated in primarily a rural setting.

During this stay, the assistant was asked to record all observations and comments that took place between or among the various school personnel. Thereafter, and similar to Cicourel and Kitsuse's strategy, the vocabulary and syntax of the field observations and notes were examined in an effort to delimit the career lines that seemed to be reflected in the "working ideology" of the school. The results of this initial analysis revealed that, and again somewhat comparable to Cicourel and Kitsuse's findings, three rather distinct career lines appeared to exist as part of the organizational makeup of the school: (1)

the academic, (2) the emotional-troublemaker, and (3) the vocational. Further analyses indicated, however, that, with the exception of the academic career line, types two and three could not really be viewed as distinct types. Rather, there appeared to be a high degree of blending or overlap between the two. This became most evident from the repeated observation that many of the students with emotional or behavioral problems were situated in the vocational career line and vice versa.

Of even greater significance is the observation that not only is a clearly-defined and highly stratified, six level track system operative but that track position overrides most other status considerations. In fact, there is a high degree of correspondence between a specific social type designation and track location. The finding that track levels one and two (the highest) contain the "academic types," whereas levels three thru six (the lowest) include the "non-academic types" provides support for this claim. Thus the "theory of office" (Rubington and Weinberg, 1968) or "working ideology" of the school that is applied during the identifying and processing of students is founded primarily upon the track system. This means, furthermore, that the educational decision-makers really have only two career options avilable to them: (1) the academic (i.e., track levels one and two) and (2) the non-academic (i.e., track levels three thru six). Associated with these major social type designations, however, are several important subtypes, the most prominent being the emotional, troublemaker, and vocational. It can be noted, further, that there is substantial variation within categories of these subtypes; this is particularly noticeable for the vocational career line.

Specifically, and no doubt partly due to the recent emphasis being placed on demonstrating reading competence, a new sub-type has evolved in this school over the last two years. This career option can be effectively termed the "vocatonal-remedial," and is available primarily to those students located in track levels three thru six who are not only destined, so to speak, for a vocational career but who also exhibit various reading problems. That is, students exhibiting these corresponding traits are more likely to be selected-out for placement in the existing remedial reading program. As might also be expected in terms of preceding comments, many of those students exhibiting emotional, behavioral, and discipline problems seem to have been rather systematically relegated to this Program. In fact, it seems most accurate to state that there is a great deal of "stigma" (Goffman, 1963) surrounding the reading program. The negative perceptions and reactions that emerged during several of the assistant's unstructured interviews with various school personnel (including several of those students enrolled in the Program, selected teachers and peers, and

two administrators) provide a clear measure of support for this assertion. These preliminary "interviews" seem to additionally indicate
that a few of the teachers view the Program as a convenient "dumping
ground" that can be used to not only dispose of but also punish the
"academic misfits" encountered.

Given these initial observations, particularly those with respect to
the "stigma" surrounding the remedial reading program plus the
negative perceptions and reactions exhibited on the part of selected
teachers, then a decision was made to examine more systematically
and rigorously the role that teachers might actually play in shunting
students into what available evidence seems to clearly suggest is a
deviant career line. This study was initiated in September of 1974.

I was, at this time, given complete access to the school records of all
sixth and seventh grade pupils attending the school under study.
Thereafter, a data sheet containing all available demographic, social,
school, and family information was compiled for each student. At this
time, too, each fifth and sixth grade teacher was asked to nominate
("We are in the process of selecting students for placement in The
Remedial Reading Program. Would you please list those students you
feel should be placed in this Program?") those students they felt
needed remedial reading. All teachers returned the completed form;
however, and as might be expected on the basis of previous observations, none of the teachers who had taught the track level one and two
students nominated any candidates.

It should be noted that no attempt was made to specify the actual
criteria teachers should use in the nomination process. This strategy
was deliberate and was in line with my attempt to assess, at least after
the fact, both the academic and non-academic criteria that appeared to
have been employed. The teachers were required, therefore, to apply
their own standards in selecting the nominees from all those students
they had taught during the preceding year. Thus, in addition to the
information gathered through formal and informal communication
with other school personnel, the teachers had available to them two
sources of data on which to base their decisions: (1) classroom performance and (2) student records. Quite often, it can be noted, teachers
referred to these records. To determine whether students actually met
the criteria for placement in the Remedial Reading Program, the
school's Reading Specialist was contacted. This Consultant, who was
not, for obvious reasons, informed of all aspects of the present study,
agreed to develop a list of those sixth and seventh grade students
whom she felt could benefit from special treatment. This assessment
was to be based upon the results that had been obtained from the
administration of two tests in September.

Specifically, and as an initial screening device, all students had been administered the Stanford Achievement Test (SAT); this provided the Consultant with a reading comprehension grade level score. Thereafter, all those students reading at their current grade level or below were given the more comprehensive Stanford Diagnostic Reading Test (SDRT). Similar to the SAT, a reading comprehension grade level score can be obtained from the results. This SDRT score served as the major criterion in deciding which students should be placed in the Program. It should be emphasized, however, that the SDRT score is used in conjunction with other information provided by the Test (e.g., vocabulary usage, syllabication, blending, sound discrimination, and rate of reading). The Consultant thus had several pieces of data on which to render a decision.

The completed list, as compiled independently by the Consultant, was composed of three groupings of students in terms of the following standards: (1) Students definitely meeting the criteria for placement in the Program (*Criteria Met*). This comprised those pupils reading two or more years below their current grade level in terms of the reading comprehension grade level score (SDRT) and who also exhibited a similar level of general performance with respect to the SDRT Sub-Tests; (2) Students possibly meeting criteria for placement (*Criteria Possibly Met*). This included those pupils reading one or more years below their current level but less than two and who exhibited a similar level of general performance with respect to the SDRT Sub-Tests; and (3) Students not meeting the preceding criteria for placement (*Criteria Not Met*). These pupils were reading somewhat below, at, or above their grade level and did not exhibit any major problems or deficiencies in terms of the Sub-Tests. Table 1 compares these evaluations with the Teachers' Nominations.

FINDINGS

As is apparent, a substantial amount of disagreement exists between the Teachers' Nominations and the Reading Specialist's Evaluations. This is most evident from the observation that, out of the 17 names submitted by the fifth grade teachers, 9 (or 52.9 percent) do not meet the criteria for placement in remedial reading. A similar but noticeably less pronounced pattern is exhibited by the data on the sixth grade teachers. In this case, 6 out of the 23 nominees (or 26 percent) do not meet the criteria. When those students possibly meeting the criteria for placement are combined with those that do not, the pattern becomes even more striking. These pupils comprise 77.5 percent of the total nominees. The important thing to note, however, is that, overall, 15 out of the 40 nominees (or 37.5 percent) do not meet the

Table 1 / Teachers' Nominations and Reading Specialist's Evaluations (In Frequencies)

Teachers' Nominations	Reading Specialist's Evaluations			
	(1) CRITERIA MET	(2) CRITERIA POSSIBLY MET	(3) CRITERIA NOT MET	TOTAL
Fifth Grade Teachers Student Should Be Placed in Remedial Reading Program	2	6	9	17
Sixth Grade Teachers Student Should Be Placed in Remedial Reading Program	7	10	6	23
Total	9	16	15	40

minimal criteria to warrant placement in the Program. This initial finding could be due to several factors. A very real possibility concerns the type of information available to the teachers.

No SDRT scores existed prior to the nomination process; however, all teachers are not only required to teach a period of reading each day but are also required to record a quarterly reading grade for each student. This grade is determined on the basis of reading tests developed and administered by the individual teachers. Thus the possibility exists that the teachers may have used these grades as the major academic criterion upon which to base the selection of the candidates. If this is accurate, then reading grades should meaningfully distinguish the nominees from the non-nominees. The information contained in Table 2 provides little support for such an expectation.

This is apparent from the observation that there is no statistically significant difference between the nominees and the non-nominees in terms of their average reading scores; this holds for both grade levels. Past enrollment in a remedial reading program, however, does distinguish the nominees from the non-nominees. The findings for the seventh graders, it can be noted, are similar in certain respects. However, and in addition to the remedial reading variable, mean number of years failed also approaches statistical significance.

Further analyses of such background variables as sex, race (there were only two non-whites enrolled in the two classes), father's and mother's occupation, number of siblings, and recorded disciplinary problems fail to produce any statistically significant differences between the nominees and the non-nominees. One additional observation, however, should be noted.

Table 2 / Selected Student Attributes, by Nomination Status and Grade Level

| Student Attribute | Grade Level | | | |
| | SIXTH | | SEVENTH | |
	(1) NOMINEES	(2) NON-NOMINEES	(3) NOMINEES	(4) NON-NOMINEES
Reading Score (Mean)	79	81	77	80
IQ (Mean)	106	103	98	102
Years Failed (Mean)	.33	.36	.81	.61
Past Enrollment in Remedial Reading (Proportion)	1.00	.40*	.65	.31*

* p ≤ .01.

Analyses of the list of nominees submitted by each teacher did produce some glaring discrepancies between the teachers' recommendations and the Reading Specialist's evaluations; this was particularly evident from the names submitted by one teacher. Two of the candidates were reading at grade level 10.5+ (SDRT Score). When this teacher was subsequently interviewed by the Specialist, it became rather apparent that the teacher not only looked unfavorably upon the Program itself but that she also viewed it as a convenient place that could be used to punish those students exhibiting a "bad attitude." It is perhaps also significant to note that these two students had been enrolled in a remedial reading program in the past.

DISCUSSION

These results provide general support for many of the notions developed earlier. This is partially evident from the initial observation that, within this school, two major career lines (i.e., the "academic" and the "non-academic"), as differentiated primarily on the basis of track level, were in existence. Associated with the non-academic line, however, were several deviant subtypes and their corresponding social type designations, the foremost being, at least in terms of our purposes and analyses, the vocational-remedial. Actual analysis of the entry routes and selection criteria employed in the nomination of students to fill this career line produced some interesting findings, particularly with regard to the crucial and important role the teacher plays in initially typing and subsequently shunting a student into this career subtype.

Specifically, the combination of data sources considered seemed to clearly suggest that the actor played virtually no role in the nomination process. Rather, the selection of candidates was made, without consultation, by the student's teacher. Analyses of the actual academic and non-academic criteria that appeared to have been employed in the selection process indicated further that, instead of selecting on the basis of immediate classroom performance (i.e., reading grades), many teachers appeared to have invoked other non-academic criteria, the most notable being whether or not the student had been enrolled in remedial reading in the past. This observation seems to suggest that, at least in this school, the label *remedial reader* can be effectively viewed as a *master status*. This suggests, further, that instead of considering present academic performance, some teachers appear to look, retrospectively, to a student's past history, and if the student has been involved with remedial reading, then such involvement increases his or her chances of being selected again. Such an observation thus underscores the important manner in which one's cumulative record (both the formal and informal aspects) can be used in the initiation and perpetuation of a specific social type or public identity. Such an observation also underscores the extremely critical role that selected teachers may play in the perpetuation of a deviant adolescent career.

References

Becker, H. S. *Outsiders: Studies in the sociology of deviance.* New York: Free Press, 1963.

Cicourel, A. V., and Kitsuse, J. I. *The educational decision-makers.* Indianapolis: Bobbs-Merrill, 1963.

———. The social organization of the high school and deviant adolescent careers. In E. Rubington and M. S. Weinberg (Eds.), *Deviance: The interactionist perspective.* New York: Macmillan, 1968.

Goffman, E. *Stigma: Notes on the management of spoiled identity.* Englewood Cliffs, N.J.: Prentice-Hall, 1963.

Hughes, E. C. Dilemmas and contradictions of status. *American Journal of Sociology*, 1945, *50*, 353–359.

Rubington, E., and Weinberg, M. S. *Deviance: The interactionist perspective*. New York: Macmillan, 1968.

Scheff, T. J. Typification in rehabilitation agencies. In E. Rubington and M. S. Weinberg (Eds.), *Deviance: The interactionist perspective*. New York: Macmillan, 1968.

25 / Court Processing of Delinquents

ROBERT M. EMERSON

A NOTE ON TOTAL DENUNCIATION

Consideration of the structural features of total denunciation provides additional insight into the processes of establishing moral character in the juvenile court. For a successful total denunciation must transcend routine denunciation by *foreclosing* all possible defenses and by *neutralizing* all possible sources of support.

Foreclosure of defenses available to the delinquent . . . has two related elements. First, in order to discredit moral character totally, it must be clearly demonstrated that the denounced delinquent has been given a great many "breaks" or "chances" which he has, how-ever, rejected and spoiled. Such a demonstration is necessary to prove that the case is "hopeless," that the delinquent youth's character is so ruined as to preclude any possibility of reform. The role of the disre-garded "chance" is clearly seen in the following case, where a proba-tion officer convinces both judge and public defender to go along with his punitive recommendation by proving that the youth has received chances not even officially reported:

> Two escapees from reform school were brought into court on a series of new complaints taken out by the police. Public defender argued that these complaints should be dismissed and the boys simply returned to the school. The probation officer, however, argued strongly that the boys should be found delinquent on the new complaints (this would require reconsidera-tion of their cases by the Youth Correction Authority, perhaps leading to an extension of their commitment). The probation officer described how one of his colleagues had worked hard on one of these cases earlier, giving the boy a great many chances, none of which did any good. The judge accepted the probation officer's recommendation.
>
> After the hearing, the public defender admitted that he felt the probation officer had been right, acknowledging the validity of his picture of the character of this boy: "I did not realize he was such a bastard. . . . Appar-ently one of the probation officers had given him a lot of breaks. He had him on so many cases that he should be shot."

Second, it must be made to appear that the delinquent himself "messed up" the chances that he had been given. It should be established not only that the youth misbehaved on numerous occasions, but also that he did so in full knowledge of the possible consequences and with no valid excuse or extenuating circumstances. In this way, responsibility or "fault" for the imminent incarceration must fall completely on the denounced delinquent. Any official contribution to the youth's "messing up" (e.g., an official's intolerance) must be glossed over so that the delinquent bears total blame.

Court probation is in fact constructed so that responsibility for "messing up," should it occur, unavoidably falls on the delinquent . . . . Probationers are constantly warned that they will be committed if there is any further misconduct, and they are given a number of "breaks" on this condition. As one probation officer commented about a youth who had been "given a break" by the judge: "This way, if he gets committed, he knows he has it coming." Furthermore, the constant warnings and lectures against getting into trouble that occur throughout probation tend to undermine in advance the possibility of defending subsequent misbehavior. For example, it is difficult for a youth to excuse a new offense as the product of peer group influence when he has continually been warned to stay away from "bad friends."

A second key element in a successful total denunciation is the neutralization of all possible sources of support. There are several components in this neutralization. First, the assessment of discredited and "hopeless" character must be made to appear as a general consensus among all those concerned in the case. A delinquent without a spokesman—with no one to put in a good word for him—stands in a fundamentally discredited position.

Here the stance taken by the delinquent's lawyer, normally a public defender, becomes crucial. A vigorous defense and pitch by a lawyer often might dispel the appearance of consensus and weaken the denunciation. This occurs very rarely, however, because of court cooptation of the public defender. Working closely with the probation staff, the public defender comes to share their values and indexes of success and failure in delinquency cases. Consequently, he will generally concur with the court's highly negative assessments of delinquent moral character. As a public defender noted in response to a question about how he usually handled his cases in the juvenile court:

> Generally I would find the probation officer handling the case and ask him: "What do you have on this kid? How bad is he?" He'll say: "Oh, he's bad!" Then he opens the probation folder to me, and I'll see he's got quite a record. Then I'll ask him, "What are you going to recommend?" He'll say,

"Give him another chance. Or probation. Or we've got to put him away."

But probation officers don't make this last recommendation lightly. Generally they will try to find a parent in the home, "someone who can keep him under control, someone who can watch him." But if the probation officer has given the kid a number of chances, it is a different story: "He's giving the kid chances and he keeps screwing up. . . . [Commitment will then be recommended.] And I say the kid deserves it. Before a kid goes away he's really got to be obnoxious—he will deserve it."

Adoption of probation standards for assessing delinquent character becomes crucial in total denunciation. The public defender is then in the position of arguing on behalf of a youth whose moral character has been totally discredited in his eyes and who he feels should indeed be committed. His courtroom defense will generally reflect this assessment. He will make only the most perfunctory motions of arguing that the delinquent be let off, and he will do so in a way that communicates an utter lack of conviction that this is a desirable course of action. Or, as in the following case, he will not even go through the motions of making a defense but will explicitly concur with the recommended incarceration and the grounds on which it rests:

A policeman told of finding an 11-year-old Negro boy in a laundry where a coin box had been looted. The officer reported that the boy had admitted committing the offense. Public defender waived cross-examination, and the judge found the youth delinquent.

Probation officer then delivered a rather lengthy report on the case. The boy had been sent to the Boys' Training Program and, while no great trouble, did not attend regularly. He had also recently been transferred to the Harris School and had been in trouble there. Probation officer recommended that the prior suspended sentence be revoked and the boy committed to the Youth Correction Authority.

Judge then asked the public defender if he had anything he wanted to say. Public defender: "The record more or less speaks for itself. He does not seem to have taken advantage of the opportunities the court has given him to straighten out." Then, after briefly reconferring with the probation officer, the judge ordered the commitment. Public defender waived the right of appeal.

Second, the denouncer must establish that in "messing up" and not taking advantage of the chances provided him, the denounced has created a situation in which there is *no other alternative open* but commitment to the Youth Correction Authority. In some cases, this may involve showing that the youth is so dangerous that commitment to the Authority is the only effective way he can be restrained; in others, demonstration that by his misbehavior the youth has completely destroyed all possible placements, including the one he has been in. It is only by dramatically showing in these ways that "there is nothing we can do with him" that the proposed commitment can be made to appear as an inevitable and objective necessity.

The fact that many total denunciations concentrate on proving that nothing else can be done with the case reflects the court's basic resistance to unwarrantable agency attempts to "dump" undesirable cases onto them for incarceration. The court feels that most of these institutions are too ready to give up on cases that from the court's point of view are still salvageable. To overcome this suspiciousness, the denouncer must not only present the youth's character as essentially corrupt and "hopeless," but also show that every effort has been made to work with him and every possible opportunity afforded him. The denouncer, in other words, must take pains to avoid appearing to be merely getting rid of a difficult and troublesome case simply to make his own work easier. This requires showing both that persistent efforts have been made to work with the case and that at the present time even extraordinary efforts cannot come up with anything as an alternative to incarceration.

A final aspect of demonstrating that there is no viable alternative to incarceration involves isolating the denounced delinquent from any kind of reputable sponsorship. In the usual case, where a parent acts as sponsor, successful total denunciation requires either that the parent be induced to denounce the youth and declare him fit only for incarceration or that the parent be discredited. In other cases, where the sponsor is a parental substitute, this sponsor must similarly be led to denounce the youth or be discredited. In this way, for example, sponsors who seek too aggressively to save delinquents considered overripe for commitment by other officials may encounter attacks on their motives, wisdom, or general moral character. This not only undermines the viability of any defense of character made by the sponsor, but also effectively isolates the delinquent by showing the unsuitability of his sponsorship as an alternative to commitment.

COUNTER-DENUNCIATION

As noted earlier, the courtroom proceeding routinely comes to involve a denunciation of the accused delinquent in the course of a confrontation between him and his accusers. This fact creates the conditions for the use of *counter-denunciation* as a defensive strategy. This strategy seeks to undermine the discrediting implications of the accusation by attacking the actions, motives and/or character of one's accusers.

The underlying phenomenon in counter-denunciation has been noted in a number of other contexts. McCorkle and Korn, for example, have analyzed the concept of the "rejection of the rejectors" as a defensive reaction to imprisonment (1964, p. 520). Similarly, Sykes and Matza explain the "condemnation of the condemners" in the process of neutralization in the following terms: "The delinquent shifts the focus of attention from his own deviant acts to the motives and behaviors of those who disapprove of his violations" (1957, p. 668). The concept of counter-denunciation, in contrast, focuses on the communicative work which accomplishes this shift of attention. Furthermore, it gains relevance as a defense against attempted character discrediting. Use of this strategy, however, is extremely risky in the court setting. While counter-denunciation may appear to the delinquent as a "natural" defense as he perceives the circumstances of his case, it tends to challenge fundamental court commitments and hence, even when handled with extreme care, often only confirms the denunciation.

It is striking that counter-denunciation has the greatest likelihood of success in cases where the complainant or denouncer lacks official stature or where the initiative rests predominantly with private parties who have clearly forced official action. Under these circumstances the wrongful quality of the offense can be greatly reduced if not wholly eliminated by showing that the initiator of the complaint was at least partially to blame for the illegal act. For example:

A 16-year-old Negro boy, Johnny Haskin, was charged with assault and battery on two teenaged girls who lived near his family in a public housing project. Although a juvenile officer brought the case into court, he was clearly acting on the initiative of the two girls and their mother, for he had had no direct contact with the incident and did not testify about it. He simply put the two girls on the stand and let them tell about what happened. This was fairly confused, but eventually it appeared that Johnny Haskin had been slapping the younger sister in the hall of the project when the older girl had pulled him off. He had then threatened her with a knife. The girls admitted that there had been fighting in the hall for some time, and that they had been involved, but put the blame on Johnny for starting it. Mrs. Haskin, however, spoke up from the back of the room, and told about a gang of boys coming around to get her son (apparently justifying Johnny's carrying a knife). And Johnny himself denied that he had started the fighting, claiming that the younger girl had hit him with a bat and threatened him first.

Judge then lectured both families for fighting, and placed Johnny on probation for nine months, despite a rather long prior record.

In this case, by establishing that the girls had also been fighting, the boy was at least partially exonerated. The success of this strategy is seen in the fact that the judge lectured both families, and then gave the boy what was a mild sentence in light of his prior court record.

Similarly, the possibility of discrediting the victim, thereby invalidating the complaint, becomes apparent in the following "rape" case:

> Two Negro boys, ages 12 and 13, had admitted forcing "relations" on a 12-year-old girl in a schoolyard, the police reported. After a full report on the incidents surrounding the offense, the judge asked the policemen: "What kind of girl is she?" Officer: "I checked with Reverend Frost [the girl's minister and the person instrumental in reporting this incident] and he said she was a good girl."

As the judge's query implies, the reprehensibility of this act can only be determined in relation to the assessed character of the girl victim. Had the police or the accused brought up evidence of a bad reputation or incidents suggesting "loose" or "promiscuous" behavior, the force of the complaint would have been undermined.

In the above cases, successful counter-denunciation of the complainants would undermine the moral basis of their involvement in the incident, thereby discrediting their grounds for initiating the complaint. But this merely shifts part of the responsibility for an offense onto the complaining party and does not affect the wrongful nature of the act per se. Thus, by denouncing the general character of the complainant and the nature of his involvement in the offense, the accused does not so much clear himself as diminish his guilt. If the offense involved is serious enough and the culpability of the complainant not directly related to the offense, therefore, this strategy may have little impact.

For example, in the homosexuality-tinged case of car theft described earlier . . . both the accused and his father tried to support their contention that the car owner was lying by pointing to his discredited character. But the "victim's" homosexuality had no real connection with the act of stealing the car nor with the threatened physical violence it entailed, and hence did not affect the judge's evaluation of the act and of the delinquent's character. Under these circumstances, the soiled nature of the victim simply was not considered sufficiently extenuating to dissolve the reprehensibility of the act.[1]

In general, then, a successful counter-denunciation must discredit not only the general character of the denouncer but also his immediate purpose or motive in making the complaint. Only in this way can the counter-denunciation cut the ground out from under the wrongfulness of the alleged offense. For example:

> An 11-year-old Negro boy was charged with wantonly damaging the car of an older Negro man, Frankie Williams, with a BB gun. With the boy was his mother, a respectably dressed woman, a white lawyer, and a white couple who served as character witnesses.
>
> A juvenile officer brought the case in and then called Mr. Williams up to testify. The witness told of going outside to shovel his car out of the snow

several weeks previously and finding his windshield damaged in several places. He had noticed the boy at this time leaning out of the window of his house with a BB gun. Laywer then cross-examined, getting Williams to admit that he had been bickering with the family for some time, and that a year before the mother had accused him of swearing at her son and had tried to get a court complaint against him. (Judge ruled this irrelevant after Williams had acknowledged it.) Williams seemed flustered, and grew angry under the questioning, claiming that because of the boy's shooting he would not be able to get an inspection sticker for his car.

Juvenile officer then told judge that although he had not investigated the case, his partner reported that the marks on the windsheield were not consistent with a BB gun. Williams had also admitted that he had not looked for any BB pellets. On the basis of this evidence, the judge found the boy not delinquent. He then severely warned all parties in the case: "I'm going to tell you I do not want any more contests between these two families. Do you understand?"

Here, by showing that the complainant had both a selfish motive for complaining about his damaged windshield (to help get it repaired) and a grudge against the defendant and his family, as well as bringing out the lack of concrete evidence to substantiate the charge, the lawyer was able to get the complaint totally dismissed.

Similarly, the circumstances of the following case were such as to suggest initially that complaints had been taken out to intimidate or at least get even with boys against whom there was some resentment:

Two teenaged Negro boys were brought to court for breaking windows. Case was continued, and policeman gave the following account of what had happened. Several weeks previously there had been a disturbance and some windows broken in a middle class section of the city. There were six boys apparently involved, including these two. One of the occupants of the home had come out and begun shooting at the boys, who were on the other side of the street, "allegedly to protect his property." One of these two boys had been hit in the leg, and another man (apparently a passerby) had also been hit. The shooter, named Barr, "is now up before the grand jury" for this, but meanwhile had taken out complaints against these two boys. A private attorney representing the two accused then took over, explaining how his clients had just been summonsed to testify against Barr. Lawyer next questioned the cop about why complaints had been brought only against these two of the six boys, including the one who had been shot, and the other who had been a witness to the shooting. Cop replied that the other boys had been investigated, but there was nothing against them.

Here the boys' lawyer successfully established that the complaints against his clients had been initiated by the defendant in a related criminal action, suggesting an attempt to discredit in advance their testimony against him. The judge responded by continuing the case, releasing both boys to the custody of their parents, even though one had a long record.

Finally, successful counter-denunciation requires that the denounced provide a convincing account for what he claims is an illegitimate accusation. The court will reject any implication that one person will gratuitously accuse another of something he has not done. The youth in the following case can provide this kind of account:

Five young boys were charged with vandalism and with starting a fire in a public school. Juvenile officer explained that he had investigated the incident with the school principal, getting two of the boys to admit their part in the vandalism. These two boys had implicated the other three, all of whom denied the charge.

The judge then took over the questioning, trying to determine whether the three accused had in fact been in the school. In this he leaned heavily on finding out why the first two boys should lie. One of the accused, Ralph Kent, defended himself by saying he had not been at the school and did not know the boy who had named him. Judge asked how this boy had then been able to identify him. Kent replied that he had been a monitor at school, and one of his accusers might have seen him there. And he used to take the other accuser to the basement [lavatory] because the teacher would not trust him alone for fear he would leave the school.

The two other boys continued to deny any involvement in the incident, but could provide no reason why they should be accused unjustly. The judge told them he felt they were lying, and asked several times: "Can you give me a good reason why these boys would put you in it?" Finally he pointed toward Kent and commented: "He's the only one I'm convinced wasn't there." He then asked Kent several questions about what he did as a monitor. When it came to dispositions, Kent was continued without a finding while the four other boys were found delinquent.

In this situation an accused delinquent was able to establish his own reputable character in school (later confirmed by the probation report on his school record), the discredited character of one of his accusers, and a probable motive for their denunciation of him (resentment toward his privileges and position in school) in a few brief sentences. It should be noted, however, that this successful counter-denunciation was undoubtedly facilitated by the fact that denouncers and denounced were peers. It is incomparably more difficult for a youth to establish any acceptable reason why an adult should want to accuse and discredit him wrongfully.

Counter-denunciation occurs most routinely with offenses arising out of the family situation and involving complaints initiated by parents against their own children. Here again it is possible for the child to cast doubt on the parents' motives in taking court action, and on the parents' general character:

A Negro woman with a strong West Indian accent had brought an incorrigible child complaint against her 16-year-old daughter. The mother reported: "She never says anything to me, only to ask, 'Gimme car fare, gimme lunch money.' . . . As for the respect she gave me I don't think I have to tolerate her!" The daughter countered that her mother never let her do anything, and simply made things unbearable for her around the house. She went out nights, as her mother claimed, but only to go over to a girl friend's house to sleep.

This case was continued for several months, during which time a probation officer worked with the girl and the court clinic saw mother and daughter. The psychiatrist there felt that the mother was "very angry and cold." Eventually an arrangement was made to let the girl move in with an older sister.

In this case the daughter was effectively able to blame her mother and her intolerance for the troubled situation in the home. But in addition, counter-denunciation may also shift the focus of the court inquiry from the misconduct charged to the youth onto incidents involving the parents. This shift of attention facilitated the successful counter-denunciation in the following case:

A 16-year-old white girl from a town some distance from the city was charged with shoplifting. But as the incident was described by the police, it become clear that this offense had occurred because the girl had run away from home and needed clean clothes. Police related what the girl had said about running away: She had been babysitting at home and was visited by her boyfriend, who had been forbidden in the house. Her father had come home, discovered this, and beaten her with a strap. (The girl's face still appeared somewhat battered with a large black-and-blue mark on one cheek, although the court session occurred at least three days after the beating.) She had run away that night.

The rest of the hearing centered not on the theft but on the running away and the incident which precipitated it. After the police evidence, the judge asked the girl: "How did you get that mark on your face?" Girl: "My father hit me." Judge: "With his fist?" Girl (hesitating): "Yes, it must have been his fist." Later in the proceeding, the judge asked the girl specifically why she had run away. She emphasized that she had not tried to hide anything; the kids had been up until eleven and the boy had left his bike out front. "I didn't try to hide it. I told them he'd been there."

With this her father rose to defend himself, arguing with some agitation: ". . . His clothes were loose. Her clothes were loose. Her bra was on the floor. . . . She was not punished for the boy being in the house, but for what she did." Girl (turning toward her father): "What about my eye?" Father: "She got that when she fell out of the bed (angrily, but directed toward the judge)." Girl (just as angrily): "What about the black and blue marks?" Father: "Those must have been from the strap."

The relatively high probability of successful counter-denunciation in cases arising from family situations points up the most critical contingency in the use of this protective strategy, the choice of an appropriate object. Denouncers with close and permanent relations with the denounced are particularly vulnerable to counter-denunciation, as the accusation is apt to rest solely on their word and illegitimate motives for the denunciation may be readily apparent. But again, where relations between the two parties are more distant, counter-denunciation has more chance of success where the denouncer is of more or less equivalent status with the denounced. Thus, the judge can be easily convinced that a schoolmate might unjustly accuse one from jealousy, but will reject any contention that an adult woman would lie about an attempted snatching incident.

While a denounced youth has a fair chance of successfully discrediting a complainant of his own age, and some chance where the complainant is a family member, counter-denunciations directed against officials, particularly against the most frequent complainants in the juvenile court, the police, almost inevitably fail. In fact, to attempt to counterattack the police, and to a lesser extent, other officials, is to risk fundamentally discrediting moral character, for the court recoils against all attacks on the moral authority of any part of the official legal system.

One reflection of this is the court's routine refusal to acknowledge complaints of *unfair* treatment at the hands of the police. On occasion, for example, parents complain that their children were arrested and brought to court while others involved in the incident were not. Judges regularly refuse to inquire into such practices:

> Two young Puerto Rican boys were charged with shooting a BB gun. After police testimony, their mother said something in Spanish, and their priest-translator explained to the judge: "What they've been asking all morning is why they did not bring the other two boys." The judge replied: "I can only deal with those cases that are before me. I can't go beyond that and ask about these other boys that are not here."

Similarly, in this same case the judge refused to inquire into a complaint of police brutality when the mother complained that one boy had been hit on the head, saying: "The question of whether he was injured is not the question for me right now."

But beyond this, the court will often go to great lengths to protect and defend the public character of the police when it is attacked during a formal proceeding. To accuse a policeman of acting for personal motives, or of dishonesty in the course of his duties, not only brings immediate sanctions from the court but also tends to discredit basically the character of the delinquent accuser. . . .

References

McCorkle, Lloyd W., and Richard Korn. 1964. "Resocialization Within Walls." In David Dressler (ed.), *Readings In Criminology and Penology.*

New York: Columbia University Press.
Sykes, Gresham M., and David Matza. 1957. "Techniques of Neutralization:
A Theory of Delinquency." *American Sociological Review*, 22:664–70.

Note

1. Note, however, that even though this denunciation succeeded, the denouncer suffered both discrediting and penalty. Immediately after the delinquency case had been decided the police took out a complaint for "contributing to the delinquency of a minor" against him, based on his admitted homosexual activities with the youth. This "contributing" case was brought before the juvenile court later that same morning, complainant and accused changed places, and the first denouncer was found guilty, primarily from what he had revealed about his behavior earlier in establishing the delinquency complaint.

26 / Court Responses to Skid Row Alcoholics

JACQUELINE P. WISEMAN

Matching sentences with men who plead guilty is thus the judge's true concern. This task must be handled within the pressures created by restricting drunk court to a morning session in one courtroom, regardless of the number of men scheduled to be seen that day.

Up until last year (when drunk arrests were temporarily reduced because of the large number of hippies and civil rights demonstrators in jail), 50 to 250 men were often sentenced within a few hours. Appearance before the judge was handled in platoons of five to 50. This meant the judge decided the fate of each defendant within a few short minutes. Thus judicial compassion attained assembly-line organization and speed.

As a court observer noted:

> The Court generally disposes of between 50 and 100 cases per day, but on any Monday there are 200 to 250 and on Monday mornings after holiday weekends the Court may handle as many as 350 cases. I would estimate that, on the average, cases take between 45 seconds and one minute to dispose of.[1]

Later, with drunk arrests drastically curtailed, the court handled no more than 50 cases in an average morning, and perhaps 125 on the weekends, according to the observer.[2] Right after a civil rights demonstration that resulted in many arrests, only 33 persons were observed in drunk court. This reduction in the quantity of defandants, however, did not appear to increase the length of time spent on each person. Rather, it seemed to reduce it. The observer noted the average length of time per person was 30 seconds, although the size of platoons was reduced from 50 to 15 or 20.

SENTENCING CRITERIA

How is the judge able to classify and sentence a large, unwieldy group of defendants so quickly? The answer is he utilizes social characteristics as indicators to signify drinking status—just as in an arrest situation the policeman looked for social characteristics to identify alcoholic trouble-making potential, combined with the arrestee's legal impotence. The effect is essentially the same: the men are objectified into social types for easy classification. In the case of the judge, the legal decision process must be more refined than for a policeman's arrest, no-arrest decision. Therefore, the judge's sentencing criteria are more complex, as they must include all possible decision combinations.

From court observations, plus interviews with court officers and judges, three primary criteria for typing defendants in drunk court emerge:

The General Physical Appearance of the Man   Is he shaky and obviously in need of drying out? Here, some of the judges ask the men to extend their hands before sentencing and decide the sentence on the degree of trembling.

Physical appearance may actually be the most potent deciding factor. As one court officer put it, when asked how the judges decide on a sentence:

> Primarily by appearance. You can tell what kind of shape they're in. If they're shaking and obviously need drying out, you know some are on the verge of the DT's so these get 10 to 15 days [in jail] to dry out. . . .

One of the seasoned judges said that his criteria were as follows:

> I rely on his record and also his "looks." Their "looks" are very important. I make them put their hands out—see if they are dirty and bloody in appearance.[3]

Past Performance   How many times have they been up before the court on a drunk charge before? A record of past arrests is considered to be indicative of the defendant's general attitude toward drinking. The longer and more recent the record, the greater the need for a sentence to aid the defendant to improve his outlook on excessive liquor consumption. (This is in some contradiction to the presumed greater need the man must have for drying out, since previous recent jailings mean that he could not have been drinking for long.)

The previous comment, plus the answer by a court officer to the question, "Who get's dismissed?" illustrates this criteria for sentencing:

> A person with no previous arrests [gets dismissed]. If they have had no arrests, then the judge hates for them to have a conviction on their record. *The more arrests they've had and the more recently they've had them, the more likely they are to get another sentence.* (Emphasis mine.) . . .

The Man's Social Position   Does he have a job he could go to? Is he married? Does he have a permanent address, or will he literally be on the streets if he receives a dismissal?

For these data, dress is an all-important clue, age a secondary one. A man who looks down-and-out is more likely to receive a sentence than the well-dressed man. According to a court officer:

> If they look pretty beat—clothes dirty and in rags, then you figure that they need some help to stop drinking before they kill themselves. . . .

> If they're under 21 we usually give them a kick-out. If they are a business man or a lawyer we have them sign a civil release so they can't sue and let them go. . . .

An observer reports that a judge freed a young man with the following remarks:

> I am going to give you a suspended sentence and hope that this experience will be a warning to you. I don't want you to get caught up in this cycle. . . .

Transients form a category of their own and get a special package deal—if they will promise to leave town, they draw a suspended sentence or probation. The parallel between this practice and the police policy of telling some Skid Row drunks to "take a walk" need only be mentioned. The following interchanges are illustrative:

> *Judge:* I thought you told me the last time you were in here that you were going to leave Pacific City.
>
> *Defendant:* I was supposed to have left town yesterday. I just got through doing time.
>
> *Judge:* Go back to Woodland. Don't let me see you in here again or we are going to put you away. Thirty days suspended. . . .
>
> *Defendant:* I am supposed to leave with the circus tomorrow. If I don't go, I will be out of work for the whole season.
>
> *Judge:* You promised to leave three times before. Thirty days in the County Jail. . . .

By combining the variables of physical appearance, past performance, and social position, a rough description of social types expected in drunk court, and matching sentences for each type is shown in Table 1.

OTHER SENTENCING ASSISTANCE

Even with the aid of a simplified mental guide, the judge cannot be expected to assemble and assimilate sufficient material on each man, review it, mentally type the man, and then make a sentencing decision

Table 1 / Paradigm of Social Types and Sentences in Drunk Court

Social Type	Probable Sentence
A young man who drank too much: a man under 40, with a job, and perhaps a wife, who has not appeared in court before.	A kick-out or a suspended sentence.
The young repeater: same as above, but has been before judge several times (may be on way to being an alcoholic.)	Suspended sentence or short sentence (five–ten days) to scare him, or possible attendance at Alcoholism School.
The repeater who still looks fairly respectable. (Image vacillating between an alcoholic and a drunk.)	30-day suspended sentence, with possible attendance at Alcoholism School.
Out-of-towner (social characteristics not important as they have nonlocal roots.) Therefore not important as to whether overindulged, a chronic drunk, or an alcoholic.	Suspended sentence on condition he leave town. Purpose is to discourage him from getting on local loop and adding to taxpayer's load.
The middle-aged repeater who has not been up for some time. (May be an alcoholic who has relapsed.)	Suspended sentence with required attendance at Alcoholism School or given to custody of Christian Missionaries.
The derelict-drunk who looks "rough," i.e., suffering withdrawal, a hangover, has cuts and bruises, may have malnutrition or some diseases connected with heavy drinking and little eating; a chronic drunk; seedy clothing, stubble beard, etc.	30–60–90 day sentence depending on number of prior arrests and physical condition at time of arrest. (Has probably attended Alcoholism School already.)
The man who looks gravely ill (probably a chronic alcoholic).	County hospital under suspended sentence.

in less than a minute. Thus, it is not surprising that almost all drunk court judges employ the aid of one assistant and sometimes two court attachés who are familiar with the Row and its inhabitants. These men are known as court liaison officers. Because of personal familiarity with chronic drunkenness offenders, the liaison officers are able to answer questions about each accused person quickly and to recommend a case disposition. Such persons obviously operate as an informal screening board.

The most important court helper in Pacific City is a man who knows most of the Row men by sight and claims also to know their general outlook on alcohol and life. Known to the defendants as "the Rapper," this man often sits behind the judge and suggests informally who would benefit most from probation and assignment to Alcoholism School, who might need the "shaking-up" that jail provides, and who ought to be sent to alcoholic screening at City Hospital and perhaps on to State Mental Hospital. As each man is named, the Rapper whispers to the judge, who then passes sentence.[4]

In Pacific City, the man who was the Rapper for a period of time was an ex-alcoholic who could claim intimate knowledge of the chronic drunkenness offender because he had drunk with them. A relative of the Rapper was highly placed in city politics, and the Rapper made no secret of the fact that his appointment was politically engineered.[5] During the course of the study (several times in fact), the Rapper himself "fell off the wagon" and underwent treatment at Northern State Mental Hospital, one of the stations on the loop. While there, the Rapper told about his recent job with the court and how he helped the judge:

> Each man arrested has a card with the whole record on it. We would go over the cards before the case came up. We see how many times he's been arrested. I could advise the judge to give them probation or a sentence. Many times, the family would call and request a sentence. I would often arrange for them to get probation plus clothes and a place to stay at one of the halfway houses. Oh, I'll help and help, but when they keep falling off—I get disgusted.[6]

The Christian Missionaries also send a liaison man to the drunk court sessions. He acts as Rapper at special times and thereby also serves in an informal screening capacity. Sponsorship by this organization appears to guarantee that the defendant will get a suspended sentence. For instance, this interchange was observed in court several times:

> *Judge*, turning to Missionary representative: "Do you want him [this defendant]?" (Meaning, "Will you take him at one of your facilities?")
>
> *Missionary:* (Nods "Yes.")
>
> *Judge:* "Suspended sentence." . . .

Another observer discussed this arrangement with a veteran judge:

> *Interviewer: Isn't there any attempt made to consider the men for rehabilitation?*
>
> The men are screened by the Christian Missionaries usually. The Christian Missionaries send someone down to the jail who tries to help them. They

talk with the men and screen them. Nobody does the job that the Christian Missionaries do in the jails.

Interviewer: The Court abdicates the screening of defendants to the Christian Missionaries, then?

Not completely. We try to keep a record. Some of these men we can help but most we can't. I know by heart all of their alibis and stories.[7]

Another important informal court post is filled by an employee who is known to some of the men as "the Knocker." The job of the Knocker is to maintain the personal records of the men who appear before drunk court and to supply the judge with this information. A court observer reported the following:

The Knocker spoke to the judge in just about every case. However, I do not know what he said. He may just be reading to the judge the official records, or he may be giving his personal judgement about the possibility of the defendant being picked up again in the near future. One thing seems clear: the judge receives his information from the Knocker just before he hands out the sentence.

Sometimes it is difficult to distinguish the Knocker (who merely gives information to the judge) from the Rapper (who "suggests" the proper sentence.) In 1963, two of these court liaison officers worked together. An interview with one partner is quoted below:

Interviewer: What do you do?

Up here we act as a *combination district attorney and public defender.* We are more familiar with these guys than the judges are. The judges alternate. We have the previous arrest records. A lot of times, guys will give phony names. It may take us a while to catch up with them. We try to remember if we have seen a guy before. (Emphasis mine.)

Interviewer: How does a judge decide whether to sentence the men and if so, for how long?

We help him out on that. If a guy has been in three times in four weeks, they should get a minimum of 30 days. They need to dry out. You know, if a man has been arrested three times in four weeks, you ask yourself the question: "How many times has he been drunk that he wasn't arrested?" Also, you look at the condition of a man—he may even need hospitalization.

Interviewer: You mean you can tell whether a man ought to be sent to jail by looking at him?

Some of them look a lot more rough looking than others. You can tell they have been on a drunk for more than one day. They are heavily bearded. They have probably been sleeping in doorways or on the street. You can tell they have been on a long drunk. . . .

Thus perhaps the most revealing aspect of the sentencing procedure is the virtual absence of interest in the *charge* and the judge's role as spokesman for the court officer's decision. This may account for the fact the judge seldom discusses the case with the defendant, except in a jocular, disparaging way. . . . The following interchanges, which illustrate this attitude, were witnessed by observers:

> *Defendant:* I was sleeping in a basement when a man attacked me with a can opener.
>
> *Judge:* Did you also see elephants? . . .
>
> *Judge:* What is your story this time?
>
> *Defendant:* (As he begins to speak, Judge interrupts.)
>
> *Judge:* You gave me that line yesterday; 30 days in the County Jail. . . .

JUSTIFYING THE SENTENCING PROCESS

How does the municipal court judge, serving in drunk court sessions, allow himself to be a party to such extra-legal activities as platoon sentencing, the heavy reliance on advice from "friends of the court," and the utilization of extraneous social characteristics in setting the sentence? Why is there not a conflict with his self-image of judicial compassion for the individual and scrupulous attention to legal niceties?

For some judges, this conflict is resolved by falling back on the alcoholism-as-an-illness view of drunkenness, and by redefining many of the men who appear before him as *patients* rather than defendants. Thus, when asked to describe their duties, drunk court judges often sound like physicians dealing with troublesome patients for whom they must prescribe unpleasant but necessary medicine, rather than judges punishing men for being a public annoyance. As an example of this:

> I know that jail isn't the best place for these men, but we have to do something for them. We need to put them someplace where they can dry out. You can't just let a man go out and kill himself. . . .
>
> This is a grave and almost hopeless problem. But you have to try some kind of treatment. Often they are better off in jail than out on the street. . . .

The drunk court judges sometimes add the wish that the city provided a more palatable alternative to the County Jail, but then reiterate the view that it is better than no help at all.

Court attachés have essentially the same attitude:

> Some of these guys are so loaded that they will fall and break their skull if you don't lock them up. Half of these guys have no place to stay anyway except a dingy heap. They are better off in jail. . . .

> The whole purpose of the law is to try to help them. It's for the protection of themselves and for others, that's the way the law reads. For example, say you're driving through here [Skid Row] and you hit a drunk. He could get killed and if you don't stop and render aid, you could become a criminal. . . .

> Giving them 30 days in County Jail is sometimes a kindness. *You are doing them a favor, like a diabetic who won't take his insulin.* Sometimes you must hurt him to help him. (Emphasis mine.). . . .

Like the Skid Row police, the officers, the judge and his coterie are reinforced in their definition of the situation as clinical, and of themselves as diagnosticians and social internists, by the fact that relatives often call the court and ask that a man be given time in jail for his own good. The judge usually complies. Furthermore, as has been mentioned, there is at the jail a branch of the Out-Patient Therapy Center that was originally established to work for the rehabilitation of alcoholics. . . . Having this jail clinic allows the drunk court judge to say:

> I sentence you to 30 days and I will get in touch with the social worker at the County Jail and she will help you.[8]

> I sentence you to therapy with the psychologists at the County Jail. (Also reported by court observers.)

Creation of the Pacific City Alcoholism School also allows the judge to feel that he is fulfilling both judicial and therapeutic duties, giving the defendant a suspended sentence on the condition that he will attend the lecture sessions.

Where the name of the social worker or psychologist of Alcoholism School is not invoked as part of the sentence, an awareness of alcoholism as an illness is frequently used as an introductory statement to indicate the reasoning of the courts for giving a jail sentence.

> We realize that you men are sick and need help. Any action I might take, therefore, should not in any sense be construed as punishment. Jail in this case is not a punitive measure, but to help you with your alcoholism problem.

However, the uneasiness of the judge with the jailing of alcoholics has other indicators. The captain of the County Jail, for instance, reports that inmates serving time for public drunkenness have only to write a letter requesting modification and it is almost automatically forthcoming, something not true for modification requests of prisoners convicted of other misdemeanors.[9]

That drunk court's methods and procedures of handling the Row men go against the judicial grain also seems to be indicated by the fact court officers claim a new judge must be "broken in" to drunk court before he operates efficiently. When the judge first arrives, he will sentence differently from an experienced judge and in the direction of greater leniency. This upsets the established pattern.

The result is he is taken in hand and guided to do "the right thing" by the veteran court aids. As one court aid put it:

> Most of the judges are pretty good—they rely on us. Sometimes you get a new judge who wants to do things his way. We have to break them in, train them. This court is very different. We have to break new judges in. It takes some of them some time to get adjusted to the way we do things.[10]

The high rate of recidivism of chronic drunkenness offenders leads some experts to question the value of jail as a cure for alcoholism or chronic drunkenness.[11] Publicly, at least, the judges appear to hold to the view that the current arrest and incarceration process *can* be helpful, but that often the alcoholic simply does not respond to "treatment" permanently and needs periodic "doses" of jail-therapy. As one judge put it:

> Some men have simply gone so far that you can't do anything for them. They are hopeless. All we can do is send them to jail to dry out from time to time.[12]

Notes

1. Frederic S. LeClercq, "Field Observations in Drunk Court of the Pacific City Municipal Court" (unpublished memorandum, 1966), p. 1.
2. These observations were made almost two years after LeClercq made his.
3. LeClercq, "Field Observations in Drunk Court," p. 12.
4. The use of a "Rapper" is apparently not a local phenomenon. Bogue notes it also in his study of the Chicago Skid Row. See Donald J. Bogue, *Skid Row in American Cities* (Chicago: University of Chicago, 1963), p. 414.
5. When the Rapper started drinking again, he was not replaced; rather, court officers and an official of the Christian Missionaries fulfilled his duties.
6. The Rapper was under treatment again for alcoholism at State Mental Hospital when he made this statement. . . . Kurt Lewin discusses this phenomenon of rejection of one's own (if they are a minority group of some type) in "Self-Hatred Among Jews," Chap. 12 of *Resolving Social Conflict* (New York: Harper Publishing Company, 1945).
7. LeClercq, "Field Observations in Drunk Court," p. 11.
8. Reported by inmate in County Jail on public drunkenness charge.
9. Source: Captain, County Jail.
10. LeClercq, "Field Observations in Drunk Court," p. 7.
11. As previously mentioned, the chief deputy of County Jail puts the number of recidivists at 85 percent of the total admissions in any one year. A small "loop," made by a chronic drunkenness offender who goes between municipal jail and Skid Row, has been well chronicled by Pittman and Gordon in *The Revolving Door* (Glencoe, Ill.: The Free Press, 1958).
12. Statement made by Municipal Judge from city near Pacific City.

27 / Characteristics of Total Institutions

ERVING GOFFMAN

INTRODUCTION

Total Institutions

Every institution captures something of the time and interest of its members and provides something of a world for them; in brief, every institution has encompassing tendencies. When we review the different institutions in our Western society we find a class of them which seems to be encompassing to a degree discontinuously greater than the ones next in line. Their encompassing or total character is symbolized by the barrier to social intercourse with the outside that is often built right into the physical plant: locked doors, high walls, barbed wire, cliffs and water, open terrain, and so forth. These I am calling total institutions, and it is their general characteristics I want to explore. This exploration will be phrased as if securely based on findings but will in fact be speculative.

The total institutions of our society can be listed for convenience in five rough groupings. *First*, there are institutions established to care for persons thought to be both incapable and harmless; these are the homes for the blind, the aged, the orphaned, and the indigent. *Second*, there are places established to care for persons thought to be at once incapable of looking after themselves and a threat to the community, albeit an unintended one: TB sanitoriums, mental hospitals, and leprosoriums. *Third*, another type of total institution is organized to protect the community against what are thought to be intentional dangers to it; here the welfare of the persons thus sequestered is not the immediate issue. Examples are: Jails, penitentiaries, POW camps, and concentration camps. *Fourth*, we find institutions purportedly established the better to pursue some technical task and justifying themselves only on these instrumental grounds: Army barracks, ships, boarding schools, work camps, colonial compounds, large mansions from the point of view of those who live in the servants' quarters, and so forth. *Finally*, there are those establishments designed as retreats from the world or as training stations for the religious: Abbeys, monasteries, convents, and other cloisters. This sublisting of total institutions is neither neat nor exhaustive, but the listing itself provides an empirical starting point for a purely denotative definition of the category. By anchoring the initial definition of total institutions in this way, I hope to be able to discuss the general characteristics of the type without becoming tautological.

Before attempting to extract a general profile from this list of establishments, one conceptual peculiarity must be mentioned. None of the elements I will extract seems entirely exclusive to total institutions, and none seems shared by every one of them. What is shared and unique about total institutions is that each exhibits many items in this family of attributes to an intense degree. In speaking of "common characteristics," then, I will be using this phrase in a weakened, but I think logically defensible, way.

Totalistic Features

A basic social arrangement in modern society is that we tend to sleep, play and work in different places, in each case with a different set of coparticipants, under a different authority, and without an overall rational plan. The central feature of total institutions can be described as a breakdown of the kinds of barriers ordinarily separating these three spheres of life. *First*, all aspects of life are conducted in the same place and under the same single authority. *Second*, each phase of the member's daily activity will be carried out in the immediate company of a large batch of others, all of whom are treated alike and required to do the same thing together. *Third*, all phases of the day's activities are tightly scheduled, with one activity leading at a prearranged time into the next, the whole circle of activities being imposed from above through a system of explicit formal rulings and a body of officials. *Finally*, the contents of the various enforced activities are brought together as parts of a single overall rational plan purportedly designed to fulfill the official aims of the institution.

Individually, these totalistic features are found, of course, in places other than total institutions. Increasingly, for example, our large commercial, industrial and educational establishments provide cafeterias, minor services and off-hour recreation for their members. But while this is a tendency in the direction of total institutions, these extended facilities remain voluntary in many particulars of their use, and special care is taken to see that the ordinary line of authority does not extend to these situations. Similarly, housewives or farm families can find all their major spheres of life within the same fenced-in area, but these persons are not collectively regimented and do not march through the day's steps in the immediate company of a batch of similar others.

The handling of many human needs by the bureaucratic organization of whole blocks of people—whether or not this is a necessary or effective means of social organization in the circumstances—can be taken, then, as the key fact of total institutions. From this, certain important implications can be drawn.

Given the fact that blocks of people are caused to move in time, it becomes possible to use a relatively small number of supervisory personnel where the central relationship is not guidance or periodic checking, as in many employer-employee relations, but rather surveillance—a seeing to it that everyone does what he has been clearly told is required of him, and this under conditions where one person's infraction is likely to stand out in relief against the visible, constantly examined, compliance of the others. . . .

In total institutions . . . there is a basic split between a large class of individuals who live in and who have restricted contact with the world outside the walls, conveniently called *inmates*, and the small class that supervises them, conveniently called staff, who often operate on an 8-hour day and are socially integrated into the outside world. Each grouping tends to conceive of members of the other in terms of narrow hostile stereotypes, staff often seeing inmates as bitter, secretive and untrustworthy, while inmates often see staff as condescending, highhanded and mean. Staff tends to feel superior and righteous; inmates tend, in some ways at least, to feel inferior, weak, blameworthy and guilty. Social mobility between the two strata is grossly restricted; social distance is typically great and often formally prescribed; even talk across the boundaries may be conducted in a special tone of voice. These restrictions on contact presumably help to maintain the antagonistic stereotypes. In any case, two different social and cultural worlds develop, tending to jog along beside each other, with points of official contact but little mutual penetration. It is important to add that the institutional plan and name comes to be identified by both staff and inmates as somehow belonging to staff, so that when either grouping refers to the views or interests of "the institution," by implication they are referring to the views and concerns of the staff.

The staff-inmate split is one major implication of the central features of total institutions; a second one pertains to work. In the ordinary arrangements of living in our society, the authority of the workplace stops with the worker's receipt of a money payment; the spending of this in a domestic and recreational setting is at the discretion of the worker and is the mechanism through which the authority of the workplace is kept within strict bounds. However, to say that inmates in total institutions have their full day scheduled for them is to say that some version of all basic needs will have to be planned for, too. In other words, total institutions take over "responsibility" for the inmate and must guarantee to have everything that is defined as essential "layed on." It follows, then, that whatever incentive is given for work, this will not have the structural significance it has on the outside. Different attitudes and incentives regarding this central feature of our life will have to prevail.

Here, then, is one basic adjustment required of those who work in total institutions and of those who must induce these people to work. In some cases, no work or little is required, and inmates, untrained often in leisurely ways of life, suffer extremes of boredom. In other cases, some work is required but is carried on at an extremely slow pace, being geared into a system of minor, often ceremonial payments, as in the case of weekly tobacco ration and annual Christmas presents, which cause some mental patients to stay on their job. In some total institutions, such as logging camps and merchant ships, something of the usual relation to the world that money can buy is obtained through the practice of "forced saving"; all needs are organized by the institution, and payment is given only after a work season is over and the men leave the premises. And in some total institutions, of course, more than a full day's work is required and is induced not by reward, but by threat of dire punishment. In all such cases, the work-oriented individual may tend to become somewhat demoralized by the system.

In addition to the fact that total institutions are incompatible with the basic work-payment structure of our society, it must be seen that these establishments are also incompatible with another crucial element of our society, the family. The family is sometimes contrasted to solitary living, but in fact the more pertinent contrast to family life might be with batch [block] living. For it seems that those who eat and sleep at work, with a group of fellow workers, can hardly sustain a meaningful domestic existence. Correspondingly, the extent to which a staff retains its integration in the outside community and escapes the encompassing tendencies of total institutions is often linked up with the maintenance of a family off the grounds.

Whether a particular total institution acts as a good or bad force in civil society, force it may well have, and this will depend on the suppression of a whole circle of actual or potential households. Conversely, the formation of households provides a structural guarantee that total institutions will not arise. The incompatibility between these two forms of social organization should tell us, then, something about the wider social functions of them both.

Total institutions, then, are social hybrids, part residential community, part formal organization, and therein lies their special sociological interest. There are other reasons, alas, for being interested in them, too. These establishments are the forcing houses for changing persons in our society. Each is a natural experiment, typically harsh, on what can be done to the self.

Having suggested some of the key features of total institutions, we can move on now to consider them from the special perspectives that seem natural to take. I will consider the inmate world, then the staff world, and then something about contacts between the two.

THE INMATE WORLD

Mortification Processes

It is characteristic of inmates that they come to the institution as members, already full-fledged, of a *home world*, that is, a way of life and a round of activities taken for granted up to the point of admission to the institution. It is useful to look at this culture that the recruit brings with him to the institution's door—his *presenting culture*, to modify a psychiatric phrase—in terms especially designed to highlight what it is the total institution will do to him. Whatever the stability of his personal organization, we can assume it was part of a wider supporting framework lodged in his current social environment, a round of experience that somewhat confirms a conception of self that is somewhat acceptable to him and a set of defensive maneuvers exercisable at his own discretion as a means of coping with conflicts, discreditings and failures.

Now it appears that total institutions do not substitute their own unique culture for something already formed. We do not deal with acculturation or assimilation but with something more restricted than these. In a sense, total institutions do not look for cultural victory. They effectively create and sustain a particular kind of tension between the home world and the institutional world and use this persistent tension as strategic leverage in the management of men. The full meaning for the inmate of being "in" or "on the inside" does not exist apart from the special meaning to him of "getting out" or "getting on the outside."

The recruit comes into the institution with a self and with attachments to supports which had allowed this self to survive. Upon entrance, he is immediately stripped of his wonted supports, and his self is systematically, if often unintentionally, mortified. In the accurate language of some of our oldest total institutions, he is led into a series of abasements, degradations, humiliations, and profanations of self. He begins, in other words, some radical shifts in his *moral career*, a career laying out the progressive changes that occur in the beliefs that he has concerning himself and significant others.

The *stripping processes* through which *mortification of the self* occurs are fairly standard in our total institutions. Personal identity equipment is removed, as well as other possessions with which the inmate may have identified himself, there typically being a system of nonaccessible storage from which the inmate can only reobtain his effects should he leave the institution. As a substitute for what has been taken away, institutional issue is provided, but this will be the same for large categories of inmates and will be regularly repossessed by the institution. In brief, standardized defacement will occur. . . . Family, occupational, and educational career lines are chopped off, and a stigmatized status is submitted. Sources of fantasy materials which had meant momentary releases from stress in the home world are denied. Areas of autonomous decision are eliminated through the process of collective scheduling of daily activity. Many channels of communication with the outside are restricted or closed off completely. Verbal discreditings occur in many forms as a matter of course. Expressive signs of respect for the staff are coercively and continuously demanded. And the effect of each of these conditions is multiplied by having to witness the mortification of one's fellow inmates. . . .

In the background of the sociological stripping process, we find a characteristic authority system with three distinctive elements, each basic to total institutions.

First, to a degree, authority is of the *echelon* kind. Any member of the staff class has certain rights to discipline any member of the inmate class. . . . In our society, the adult himself, however, is typically under the authority of a *single* immediate superior in connection with his work or under authority of one spouse in connection with domestic duties. The only echelon authority he must face—the police—typically are neither constantly nor relevantly present, except perhaps in the case of traffic-law enforcement.

Second, the authority of corrective sanctions is directed to a great multitude of items of conduct of the kind that are constantly occurring and constantly coming up for judgment; in brief, authority is directed to matters of dress, deportment, social intercourse, manners and the like. . . .

The third feature of authority in total institutions is that misbehaviors in one sphere of life are held against one's standing in other spheres. Thus, an individual who fails to participate with proper enthusiasm in sports may be brought to the attention of the person who determines where he will sleep and what kind of work task will be accorded to him.

When we combine these three aspects of authority in total institutions, we see that the inmate cannot easily escape from the press of judgmental officials and from the enveloping tissue of constraint. The system of authority undermines the basis for control that adults in our society expect to exert over their interpersonal environment and may produce the terror of feeling that one is being radically demoted in the age-grading system. On the outside, rules are sufficiently lax and the individual sufficiently agreeable to required self-discipline to insure that others will rarely have cause for pouncing on him. He need not constantly look over his shoulder to see if criticism and other sanctions are coming. On the inside, however, rulings are abundant, novel, and closely enforced so that, quite characteristically, inmates live with chronic anxiety about breaking the rules and chronic worry about the consequences of breaking them. The desire to "stay out of trouble" in a total institution is likely to require persistent conscious effort and may lead the inmate to abjure certain levels of sociability with his fellows in order to avoid the incidents that may occur in these circumstances.

It should be noted finally that the mortifications to be suffered by the inmate may be purposely brought home to him in an exaggerated way during the first few days after entrance, in a form of initiation that has been called *the welcome*. Both staff and fellow inmates may go out of their way to give the neophyte a clear notion of where he stands. As part of this *rite de passage*, he may find himself called by a term such as "fish," "swab," etc., through which older inmates tell him that he is not only merely an inmate but that even within this lowly group he has a low status.

Privilege System

While the process of mortification is in progress, the inmate begins to receive formal and informal instruction in what will here be called the *privilege system*. Insofar as the inmate's self has been unsettled a little by the stripping action of the institution, it is largely around this framework that pressures are exerted, making for a reorganization of self. Three basic elements of the system may be mentioned.

First, there are the house rules, a relatively explicit and formal set of prescriptions and proscriptions which lay out the main requirements of inmate conduct. These regulations spell out the austere round of life in which the inmate will operate. Thus, the admission procedures through which the recruit is initially stripped of his self-supporting context can be seen as the institution's way of getting him in the position to start living by the house rules.

Second, against the stark background, a small number of clearly defined *rewards or privileges* are held out in exchange for obedience to staff in action and spirit. It is important to see that these potential gratifications are not unique to the institution but rather are ones carved out of the flow of support that the inmate previously had quite taken for granted. On the outside, for example, the inmate was likely to be able to unthinkingly exercise autonomy by deciding how much sugar and milk he wanted in his coffee, if any, or when to light up a cigarette; on the inside, this right may become quite problematic and a matter of a great deal of conscious concern. Held up to the inmate as possibilities, these few recapturings seem to have a reintegrative effect, re-establishing relationships with the whole lost world and assuaging withdrawal symptoms from it and from one's lost self.

The inmate's run of attention, then, especially at first, comes to be fixated on these supplies and obsessed with them. In the most fanatic way, he can spend the day in devoted thoughts concerning the possibility of acquiring these gratifications or the approach of the hour at which they are scheduled to be granted. The building of a world around these minor privileges is perhaps the most important feature of inmate culture and yet is something that cannot easily be appreciated by an outsider, even one who has lived through the experience himself. This situation sometimes leads to generous sharing and almost always to a willingness to beg for things such as cigarettes, candy and newspapers. It will be understandable, then, that a constant feature of inmate discussion is the *release binge fantasy*, namely, recitals of what one will do during leave or upon release from the institution.

House rules and privileges provide the functional requirements of the third element in the privilege system: *punishments*. These are designated as the consequence of breaking the rules. One set of these punishments consists of the temporary or permanent withdrawal of privileges or abrogation of the right to try to earn them. In general, the punishments meted out in total institutions are of an order more severe than anything encountered by the inmate in his home world. An institutional arrangement which causes a small number of easily controlled privileges to have a massive significance is the same arrangement which lends a terrible significance to their withdrawal.

There are some special features of the privilege system which should be noted.

First, punishments and privileges are themselves modes of organization peculiar to total institutions. . . . And privileges, it should be emphasized, are not the same as prerequisites, indulgences or values, but merely the absence of deprivations one ordinarily expects one would not have to sustain. The very notions, then, of punishments and privileges are not ones that are cut from civilian cloth.

Second, it is important to see that the question of release from the total institution is elaborated into the privilege system. Some acts will become known as ones that mean an increase or no decrease in length of stay, while others become known as means for lessening the sentence.

Third, we should also note that punishments and privileges come to be geared into a residential work system. Places to work and places to sleep become clearly defined as places where certain kinds and levels of privilege obtain, and inmates are shifted very rapidly and visibly from one place to another as the mechanisms for giving them the punishment or privilege their cooperativeness has warranted. The inmates are moved, the system is not. . . .

Immediately associated with the privilege system we find some standard social processes important in the life of total institutions.

We find that an *institutional lingo* develops through which inmates express the events that are crucial in their particular world. Staff too, especially its lower levels, will know this language, using it when talking to inmates, while reverting to more standardized speech when talking to superiors and outsiders. Related to this special argot, inmates will possess knowledge of the various ranks and officials, an accumulation of lore about the establishment, and some comparative information about life in other similar total institutions.

Also found among staff and inmates will be a clear awareness of the phenomenon of *messing up*, so called in mental hospitals, prisons, and barracks. This involves a complex process of engaging in forbidden activity, getting caught doing so, and receiving something like the full punishment accorded this. An alteration in privilege status is usually implied and is categorized by a phrase such as "getting busted." Typical infractions which can eventuate in messing up are: fights, drunkenness, attempted suicide, failure at examinations, gambling, insubordination, homosexuality, improper taking of leave, and participation in collective riots. While these punished infractions are typically ascribed to the offender's cussedness, villainy, or "sickness," they do in fact constitute a vocabulary of institutionalized actions, limited in such a way that the same messing up may occur for quite different reasons. Informally, inmates and staff may understand, for example, that a given messing up is a way for inmates to show resentment against a current situation felt to be unjust in terms of the informal agreements between staff and inmates, or a way of postponing release without having to admit to one's fellow inmates that one really does not want to go.

In total institutions there will also be a system of what might be called *secondary adjustments*, namely, technics which do not directly challenge staff management but which allow inmates to obtain disallowed satisfactions or allowed ones by disallowed means. These practices are variously referred to as: the angles, knowing the ropes, conniving, gimmicks, deals, ins, etc. Such adaptations apparently reach their finest flower in prisons, but of course other total institutions are overrun with them too. It seems apparent that an important aspect of secondary adjustments is that they provide the inmate with some evidence that he is still, as it were, his own man and still has some protective distance, under his own control, between himself and the institution. . . .

The occurrence of secondary adjustments correctly allows us to assume that the inmate group will have some kind of a *code* and some means of informal social control evolved to prevent one inmate from informing staff about the secondary adjustments of another. On the same grounds we can expect that one dimension of social typing among inmates will turn upon this question of security, leading to persons defined as "squealers," "finks," or "stoolies" on one hand, and persons defined as "right guys" on the other. It should be added that where new inmates can play a role in the system of secondary adjustments, as in providing new faction members or new sexual objects, then their "welcome" may indeed be a sequence of initial indulgences and enticements, instead of exaggerated deprivations. Because of secondary adjustments we also find *kitchen strata*, namely, a kind of rudimentary, largely informal, stratification of inmates on the basis of each one's differential access to disposable illicit commodities; so also we find social typing to designate the powerful persons in the informal market system.

While the privilege system provides the chief framework within which reassembly of the self takes place, other factors characteristically lead by different routes in the same general direction. Relief from economic and social responsibilities—much touted as part of the therapy in mental hospitals—is one, although in many cases it would seem that the disorganizing effect of this moratorium is more significant than its organizing effect. More important as a reorganizing influence is the *fraternalization process*, namely, the process through which socially distant persons find themselves developing mutual support and common *counter-mores* in opposition to a system that has forced them into intimacy and into a single, equalitarian community of fate. It seems that the new recruit frequently starts out with something like the staff's popular misconceptions of the character of the inmates and then comes to find that most of his fellows have all the properties of ordinary decent human beings and that the stereotypes associated with their condition or offense are not a reasonable ground for judgment of inmates. . . .

Adaptation Alignments

The mortifying processes that have been discussed and the privilege system represent the conditions that the inmate must adapt to in some way, but however pressing, these conditions allow for different ways of meeting them. We find, in fact, that the same inmate will employ different lines of adaptation or tacks at different phases in his moral career and may even fluctuate between different tacks at the same time.

First, there is the process of *situational withdrawal.* The inmate withdraws apparent attention from everything except events immediately around his body and sees these in a perspective not employed by others present. This drastic curtailment of involvement in interactional events is best known, of course, in mental hospitals, under the title of "regression." . . . I do not think it is known whether this line of adaptation forms a single continuum of varying degrees of withdrawal or whether there are standard discontinuous plateaus of disinvolvement. It does seem to be the case, however, that, given the pressures apparently required to dislodge an inmate from this status, as well as the currently limited facilities for doing so, we frequently find here, effectively speaking, an irreversible line of adaptation.

Second, there is the *rebellious line.* The inmate intentionally challenges the institution by flagrantly refusing to cooperate with staff in almost any way. The result is a constantly communicated intransigency and sometimes high rebel-morale. Most large mental hospitals, for example, seem to have wards where this spirit strongly prevails. Interestingly enough, there are many circumstances in which sustained rejection of a total institution requires sustained orientation to its formal organization and hence, paradoxically, a deep kind of commitment to the establishment.

Third, another standard alignment in the institutional world takes the form of a kind of *colonization.* The sampling of the outside world provided by the establishment is taken by the inmate as the whole, and a stable, relatively contented existence is built up out of the maximum satisfactions procurable within the institution. Experience of the outside world is used as a point of reference to demonstrate the desirability of life on the inside; and the usual tension between the two worlds collapses, thwarting the social arrangements based upon this felt discrepancy. Characteristically, the individual who too obviously takes this line may be accused by his fellow inmates of "having found a home" or of "never having had it so good." Staff itself may become vaguely embarrassed by this use that is being made of the institution, sensing that the benign possibilities in the situation are somehow being misued. Colonizers themselves may feel obliged to deny their satisfaction with the institution, if only in the interest of sustaining the counter-mores supporting inmate solidarity. They may find it necessary to mess up just prior to their slated discharge, thereby allowing themselves to present involuntary reasons for continued incarceration. It should be incidentally noted that any humanistic effort to make life in total institutions more bearable must face the possibility that doing so many increase the attractiveness and likelihood of colonization.

Fourth, one mode of adaptation to the setting of a total institution is that of *conversion*. The inmate appears to take over completely the official or staff view of himself and tries to act out the role of the perfect inmate. While the colonized inmate builds as much of a free community as possible for himself by using the limited facilities available, the convert takes a more disciplined, moralistic, monochromatic line, presenting himself as someone whose institutional enthusiasm is always at the disposal of the staff. . . . Some mental hospitals have the distinction of providing two quite different conversion possibilities—one for the new admission who can see the light after an appropriate struggle and adopt the psychiatric view of himself, and another for the chronic ward patient who adopts the manner and dress of attendants while helping them to manage the other ward patients with a stringency excelling that of the attendants themselves. . . .

While the alignments that have been mentioned represent coherent courses to pursue, few inmates, it seems, carry these pursuits very far. In most total institutions, what we seem to find is that most inmates take the tack of what they call *playing it cool*. This involves a somewhat opportunistic combination of secondary adjustments, conversion, colonization and loyalty to the inmate group, so that in the particular circumstances the inmate will have a maximum chance of eventually getting out physically and psychically undamaged. Typically, the inmate will support the counter-mores when with fellow inmates and be silent to them on how tractably he acts when alone in the presence of the staff. Inmates taking this line tend to subordinate contacts with their fellows to the higher claim of "keeping out of trouble." They tend to volunteer for nothing, and they may even learn to cut their ties to the outside world sufficiently to give cultural reality to the world inside but not enough to lead to colonization. . . .

Culture Themes

A note should be added here concerning some of the more dominant themes of inmate culture.

First, in the inmate group of many total institutions there is a strong feeling that time spent in the establishment is time wasted or destroyed or taken from one's life; it is time that must be written off. It is something that must be "done" or "marked" or "put in" or "built" or "pulled." . . . As such, this time is something that its doers have bracketed off for constant conscious consideration in a way not quite found on the outside. And as a result, the inmate tends to feel that for the duration of his required stay—his sentence—he has been totally exiled from living. It is in this context that we can appreciate something of the demoralizing influence of an indefinite sentence or a very long one. We should also note that however hard the conditions of life may become in total institutions, harshness alone cannot account for this quality of life wasted. Rather we must look to the social disconnections caused by entrance and to the usual failure to acquire within the institution gains that can be transferred to outside life—gains such as money earned, or marital relations formed, or certified training received.

Second, it seems that in many total institutions a peculiar kind and level of self-concern is engendered. The low position of inmates relative to their station on the outside, as established initially through the mortifying processes, seems to make for a milieu of personal failure and a round of life in which one's fall from grace is continuously pressed home. In response, the inmate tends to develop a story, a line, a sad tale—a kind of lamentation and apologia—which he constantly tells to his fellows as a means of creditably accounting for his present low estate. While staff constantly discredit these lines, inmate audiences tend to employ tact, suppressing at least some of the disbelief and boredom engendered by these recitations. In consequence, the inmate's own self may become even more of a focus for his conversation than it does on the outside.

Perhaps the high level of ruminative self-concern found among inmates in total institutions is a way of handling the sense of wasted time that prevails in these places. If so, then perhaps another interesting aspect of inmate culture can be related to the same factor. I refer here to the fact that in total institutions we characteristically find a premium placed on what might be called *removal activities*, namely, voluntary unserious pursuits which are sufficiently engrossing and exciting to lift the participant out of himself, making [him] oblivious for the time to his actual situation. If the ordinary activities in total institutions can be said to torture time, these activities mercifully kill it.

Some removal activities are collective, such as ball games, woodwork, lectures, choral singing and card playing; some are individual but rely on public materials, as in the case of reading, solitary TV watching, etc. No doubt, private fantasy ought to be included too. Some of these activities may be officially sponsored by staff; and some, not officially sponsored, may constitute secondary adjustments. In any case, there seems to be no total intitution which cannot be seen as a kind of Dead Sea in which appear little islands of vivid, enrapturing activity.

Consequences

In this discussion of the inmate world, I have commented on the mortification process, the reorganizing influences, the lines of response taken by inmates under these circumstances, and the cultural milieu that develops. A concluding word must be added about the long-range consequences of membership.

Total institutions frequently claim to be concerned with rehabilitation, that is, with resetting the inmate's self-regulatory mechanisms so that he will maintain the standards of the establishment of his own accord after he leaves the setting. In fact, it seems this claim is seldom realized and even when permanent alteration occurs, these changes are often not of the kind intended by the staff. With the possible exception presented by the great resocialization efficiency of religious institutions, neither the stripping processes nor the reorganizing ones seem to have a lasting effect. No doubt the availability of secondary adjustments helps to account for this, as do the presence of counter-mores and the tendency for inmates to combine all strategies and "play it cool." In any case, it seems that shortly after release, the ex-inmate will have forgotten a great deal of what life was like on the inside and will have once again begun to take for granted the privileges around which life in the institution was organized. The sense of injustice, bitterness and alienation, so typically engendered by the inmate's experience and so definitely marking a stage in his moral career, seems to weaken upon graduation, even in those cases where a permanent stigma has resulted.

But what the ex-inmate does retain of his institutional experience tells us important things about total institutions. Often entrance will mean for the recruit that he has taken on what might be called a *proactive status*. Not only is his relative social position within the walls radically different from what it was on the outside, but, as he comes to learn, if and when he gets out, his social position on the outside will never again be quite what it was prior to entrance. . . . When the proactive status is unfavorable, as it is for those in prisons or mental hospitals, we popularly employ the term "stigmatization" and expect that the ex-inmate may make an effort to conceal his past and try to "pass."

28 / Blacks and Cons: The Working of the Prison Inmate Culture

LEO CARROLL

Given the existing relations between staff members and prisoners, the pressures toward racial integration and cooperation among prisoners that are exerted through the formal organization of the prison are not strong, positive supports for such behavior. Hence . . . while prisoners accept demographic integration in settings subject to administrative control, there is only limited biracial interaction in these settings. However, other pressures contravene prisoner predispositions toward racial avoidance. Unlike the pressures exerted through the formal organization, these pressures have their origin within the informal social organization of the prison, deriving from objects and activities that are of a salient interest to large segments of the prisoner population: drugs, sex, keeping the peace and meeting the public. These objects and activities constitute focal concerns of the inmate subculture. To some extent they function as superordinate goals, "goals which are compelling and highly appealing to members of two or more groups in conflict but which cannot be attained by the resources and energies of the groups separately,"[1] drawing black and white prisoners into relations of exchange and cooperation. Contact does not always lead to harmonious relations, however. The scarcity of drugs, the symbolic meaning of sex, and differing interests with respect to the staff and the public introduce elements of interracial competition and conflict into the relationships that develop around these objects and activities. Whatever the form of interaction involved, however, each of these concerns draws differing segments of the black and white prisoners into contact, and thus they provide links across the color bar. . . .

DRUGS

"Dope fiends are color blind." "When it comes to drugs, color don't make no difference." Statements such as these summarize the unanimous view of the prisoners at ECI. In their eyes, race is not a bar to exchange and cooperation in the network of relationships that surround traffic in drugs. While this view is not entirely accurate, the high demand for drugs amid a limited supply secured at considerable risk does in fact minimize the significance of race. In no other activity is biracial interaction so extensive.

Five distinct activities underlie the web of relations arising from drug usage: "connecting," "stashing," "dealing," "scoring," and "fixing." For drugs to enter the prison economy, a connection with an outside source must be established and the drugs must be carried into the prison. Once inside the walls, the drugs must be "stashed" in a secure place or with a secure prisoner not immediately associated with the owner but to whom he has ready access. If profit is to be realized the drugs must be advertised and numerous transactions executed. These transactions comprise "dealing." "Connecting," "stashing," and "dealing," then refer to the procurement and distribution of drugs; "scoring" and "fixing" are consumer activities. "Scoring" refers to the purchase of a supply from a dealer, and less directly to a number of ancillary activities such as raising the necessary money and securing a set of "works," paraphernalia with which to use the drugs. "Fixing" denotes the actual consumption of drugs.

Connecting and Stashing

Connecting. It is a common belief that a major conduit for drugs into a prison is the custodial force. While this may be true at other institutions, there was no evidence to suggest it at ECI. In fact, prisoners claimed that due to lax security it was so easy to secure drugs through visitors that it was not worth the risk or the price to bribe a guard. Most typically, the connections developed by prisoners at ECI are regular visitors with whom they were associated prior to their confinement. As few inmates have interracial friendships outside the prison, this fact alone makes for segregation in "connecting." There is an additional reason, however. The best connection is one that is inconspicuous. For this reason female connections are preferred. In an institution with no matrons to search female visitors, female connections run less risk of detection than do male. Moreover, the intimacy expected and permitted between prisoners and their female visitors provides ample opportunity for the drugs to be passed successfully. Nothing, however, draws the attention of the officers more quickly than does an interracial visit with a female. Thus, the combination of racial and sexual identities operates to make the most reliable connection one between prisoners and females of the same race, and the most unreliable one between prisoners and females of different races.

The successful acquisition of drugs from a visitor is only the first step in "connecting." The second step is the transportation of the supply from the visiting room into the prison itself. Official policy calls for all prisoners to be searched thoroughly before leaving the visiting room. The sheer number of those receiving visits, however, permits a careful search of only a few. For the majority of those making a connection, then, the transportation of the supply into the prison is not a great problem. They are able to conceal the drugs on their person in such a manner as to transport them successfully without assistance. Those known or suspected of using drugs, however, run a higher risk of search. This problem is circumvented by means of prior arrangements with a prisoner who is not a user or at least not known to the officers as one. Being careful to leave the visiting room at the same time, the prisoner making the connection passes the supply to his "front man."a On occasion, this form of collaboration may involve a black and a white; most commonly, it does not. Again, a requisite of a successful connection is inconspicuousness. . . . Communication between blacks and whites is uncommon. Even a fleeting contact in a public area such as the visiting room is thus liable to draw the suspicious attention of an officer. Thus, the extensive segregation characteristic of routine activities impedes biracial cooperation in at least this one illicit activity.

Stashing. Transporting drugs into the prison shades into the second activity, "stashing." A prisoner in possession of drugs is in a highly vulnerable position. Not only must he conceal them from the staff, he must also conceal them from other prisoners who might hijack his supply. Drugs, then, must be "stashed." Prisoners with only a small supply intended only for their personal use may conceal the drugs in an area near their cell or work assignment. Those with a larger supply intended for sale prefer a more secure "stash." In return for a share of the profit, "dealers" frequently hire non-users to hold their supplies. In the case of known or suspected "dealers," this arrangement is often an extension of the "front man" collaboration. Where such collaboration is not necessary, it is an arrangement independent of the transportation of drugs into the prison. In neither instance, however, does "stashing" entail extensive biracial cooperation. As a "stash" has control of the supply, he must be trusted not to "deal" himself. Trust is no more characteristic of black-white relations in the prison than it is in the surrounding community, and this absence of trust precludes extensive biracial collaboration in this activity.b

a This term possibly has its origins in the subculture of professional or organized crime where a "front" is a legitimate enterprise utilized to cover illegal activities.
b One black dealer, however, commented that he always uses a white prisoner for a "stash." His reason is that he believes all blacks are users and would try to steal some of his supply. Descriptions of dealing by other blacks suggest that he is an exception.

Dealing

The difficulties associated with "connecting" and with raising the necessary money place severe limits on the amount of drugs any one prisoner is able to acquire. Moreover, large-scale "dealing" is likely to be curtailed by inmate leaders if not by the staff. The white "mafia" view drug use as a potential threat to their interest in tranquillity; the black "revolutionaries" see it as genocide. For the most part, "dealing" remains a small-time but pervasive activity engaged in by "dope fiends" and "half-steppers." The consuming interest of "dope fiends"—black and white—compels them to "deal" despite the risks involved. "Dope fiends" must sell a portion of their supply to raise the cash necessary to maintain their connection. Moreover, if they should lose their connection or consume their supply in the period between visits, the cash on hand from "dealing" enables them to score from another "dealer." Thus, while the incumbents of distributive and consumptive roles are largely the same individuals, there is a continual movement from one role to the other.

The high risks entailed by "dealing" make the sale of supplies an urgent matter. To avoid detection by the staff or hijacking by other inmates, the "dealer" must dispose of his supply as quickly as possible. One limit on his ability to sell is the difficulty prisoners face in raising money. Because of this obstacle "dealers" must sell to the largest possible market. To enlarge the potential market and at the same time to protect themselves and their supply, "dealers" hire "runners." The function of the "runner" is to spread the word that drugs are available, to collect the cash and return it to the "dealer," and to distribute the drugs. "Runners," however, are never in control of the drug supply and usually are not informed of its location. The relation between a "runner" and a "dealer" does not involve the degree of trust between a "dealer" and a "stash." As few prisoners have close associations with inmates of the other race, and being under pressure to sell quickly, it is expedient for both black and white "dealers" to use "runners" of the other race. It is at the point of distribution and sales that black and white prisoners are drawn into exchange relations in drug-related activities.

> When the word gets out there's some dope in here you be seein' black dudes and white dudes together all over the place, tryin' to get them enough bread to buy a bundle. All discrimination just leaves, man. They be puttin' their cash together and buyin' a bundle. Then they all be crowdin' 'round for their turn at the needle. It's somethin' else.

Scoring and Fixing

Scoring. As this comment suggests, the quality of biracial interaction in "scoring" and "fixing" differs from that involved in "dealing."

In "dealing," the relations are strictly on an exchange basis, such as those between a buyer and seller or an employer or employee. By contrast, "scoring" and "fixing" draw black and white users into cooperative relations.[2] Two conditions account for this biracial cooperation. First is the price of drugs. The dangers associated with "connecting" and "dealing," and the consequent proliferation of middle-men, greatly inflate the price of drugs in the prison. Heroin selling for five dollars on the outside brings twenty dollars on the inside. Few prisoners have this amount of cash at their disposal. Thus, they are forced into collaborative relations, and their knowledge of the "dealer's" interest in a quick sale combined with their own overwhelming desire to "score" draws them into collaboration with others who have the cash regardless of race. A second pressure toward cooperation is the scarcity of "works." Prisoners in a position to "score" may lack the implements necessary to use the drugs. Quite often, therefore, a user with a good set of "works" is brought into the confederation. Again, greater importance attaches to his having the necessary paraphernalia than to his race. Economic and instrumental concerns induce a measure of biracial cooperation in "scoring."

At the same time, however, the high valuation accorded drugs and their scarcity in the prison produces both intra- and interracial conflict and competition. Both "dealers" and users are in highly vulnerable positions. Despite the precautions taken by the "dealers," other prisoners may be able to trace the path to the supply and "beat" the "dealer" out of drugs and possibly his profits. Conversely, "dealers" and "runners" may conspire to "beat" users by refusing to deliver the drugs after collecting the money, perhaps claiming that they themselves have been beaten. As the term "beat" connotes, the buying and selling of drugs is viewed as a competitive game, one norm of which is "never trust a junkie." An inmate enters the game with the expectation that others will attempt to "beat" him and takes whatever precautions he can to protect himself. If he is "beat," however, he has little recourse other than to suffer the loss. He cannot take his case to the custodians, nor can he usually gain the support of the most influential inmate leaders, as they themselves are opposed to drug use. And, as those who are "beat" are usually low-status or newly-arrived prisoners having few friends or allies, physical retribution is often not an alternative. Still, the frequent thievery associated with the drug traffic does give rise to occasional encounters between small groups of black and white prisoners, and is a continual threat to the harmonious coexistence of the two groups.

Fixing. Norwithstanding the factors of compulsion and suspicion that underlie biracial cooperation in "scoring" and "fixing," such cooperation at times leads to more spontaneous and intimate forms of interracial behavior. There are not enough drugs in the prison for any prisoner to maintain a physical addiction. Unlike addicts on the street, users in the prison are "fixing" to "get high" rather than to ward off the pains of withdrawal. "Fixing" is a festive occasion, and the period of time between "scoring" and "fixing," a time during which the confederates share a mutual excitement at the prospect of "getting off," may be characterized by biracial joking, horseplay, and other gestures of intimacy:

> B.J. (black) looked at his watch and said to "Street Cat" (black), "It's 'bout time to go see that friend of yours ain't it?" "Street Cat" nodded and communicated his desire that I not accompany them by saying "We got some business to take care of." I watched as they walked across the grass and sat on one of the benches. Several minutes later Bob E. (white) came up to them. "Street Cat" and B.J. jumped off the bench and all three exchanged hand slaps with B.J. and "Street Cat" exclaiming, "You're my man! You're my man!" For several minutes they engaged in a highly animated conversation accompanied by backslapping and laughter. When the buzzer rang to clear the yard, the three went into South State together, "Street Cat" with his arm draped around Bob's shoulder. . . . After lockup I walked past "Street Cat" and B.J.'s cells. Both were "spaced out."

As the activities surrounding drugs in the prison come closer to the actual consumption of drugs, the significance of race as a barrier to interaction decreases. Where "connecting" and "stashing" are largely segregated, "dealing" entails biracial exchange relations, "scoring" draws blacks and whites into collaboration, and in "fixing" there is some semblance of interracial cohesion. It is only in the moments preceding "fixing," however, that black and white users interact freely and without any apparent awareness of race. Having "fixed," users retreat to their cells and in their cells they retreat into their own inner worlds. The next day the quest for drugs may find them aligned in an entirely different combination, and perhaps attempting to "beat" the very same individual with whom they were so intimate.

HOMOSEXUAL BEHAVIOR

[Earlier] I noted that to judge by inmate verbalizations the deprivation of heterosexual contact and means of sexual satisfaction are the most severe deprivations experienced by prisoners at ECI. In response to this felt deprivation, there exists among the prisoners a variety of homosexual relationships analogous in form to heterosexual relationships in the free community: marriage, prostitution, rape, and seduction. These relationships have both intra- and interracial aspects. Here, however, I am concerned with their interracial dimension.

Marriage and Prostitution

Marriage. Studies of prisons for women have found homosexual marriages to be the basic unit of the informal inmate social structure.[3] In contrast, discussions of homosexuality in prisons for men have emphasized its largely physical and occasionally violent nature.[4] The structure of sexual relationships at ECI is consistent with the findings of this prior research. Homosexual marriages are rare. During the period of study, I became aware of only six such unions. Three of these were intraracial involving white "fags" and "wise guys,"[5] and three were interracial, being liaisons between older black prisoners in an active role and young white "punks." These few interracial marriages appeared more similar to the dyadic relations found among female prisoners than to the intraracial marriages among the whites. Unlike the marriages among the whites, the interracial marriages seemed to be of long duration. All three lasted throughout the study period, two having been formed prior to the study and one commencing after I had been in the prison about five months. In one case, the black partner refused a raise to minimum custody presumably to maintain the marriage. Also, unlike the marriages among whites, the partners are publicly as well as privately intimate. I observed no instance in which one degraded or demeaned the other and public displays of concern and affection were relatively common.[6]

That three of the six known homosexual marriages were interracial with blacks in the active role may be explicable, at least partially, in terms of the psychological process of projection. Psychologically oriented studies of race relations have made extended comment upon cross-racial sexual attraction.[7] Presumably, the internalization of white standards of beauty, the deprecation of blackness, and the power and prestige of whites relative to blacks combine to make whites attractive sexual objects to blacks of the opposite sex. Conversely the caste patterning of sex makes sexual relations with blacks a forbidden fruit for whites. Presumably, whites project onto blacks many of their repressed sexual desires and fantasies, coming to view blacks as more animal than human and possessed of vigorous, insatiable appetites for sex. Given this line of reasoning, it is at least plausible that the deprivation of heterosexual contact and the inability of older black prisoners to establish close associations with other blacks predisposes them to transfer their attraction to white females onto white males who have been collectively defined as "female." By providing the white partner with affection, material comforts, and some degree of protection from abuse, older black prisoners are able to establish intimate relations with partners whom, by virtue of projection and transference, they value highly.

However, one not need resort to psychodynamic explanations of this sort to explain the attraction of the white partner to the relationship. After having been abused sexually, facing the prospect of either future abuse or extended isolation in segregation, and being deprived of friendship, the rewards offered by a marriage relation must be appealing to many white "punks." Abuse does not end with the establishment of the relationship, however. Other inmates, both black and white, view such marriages negatively. Where the black "revolutionaries" and "half-steppers" are in conflict on the question of liaisons with black "fags," they agree on the question of marriage to a white "fag." Any black who becomes so attached to a white is a "tom," and each of three blacks in homosexual unions with whites were excluded from the Afro-American Society, ostracized from black peer group activities, and subjected to continual assault and verbal taunts from other blacks. In similar fashion, the white partner is the object of verbal taunts from other whites, ostracized, and occasionally assaulted sexually. These common external pressures to which both partners to the marriage are subject may in fact be a force sustaining their cohesion. Interracial marriages, to a large extent, appear to be intimate bonds grounded in adversity, relations of support and consolation between individuals who collectively constitute a disaffiliated and abused segment of the prisoner population.

Prostitution. The most common form of sexual relationship at ECI is prostitution. For the most part, however, this relation is an intraracial one. Nonetheless, the following two excerpts, the first from an interview with a white "fag" and the second from an interview with a white "stand-up guy," suggest that "fags" of both races are attracted to sexual relations with active partners of the other race and at least occasionally sell their sexual favors across the color line.

> I'm a homosexual and I don't care if the guy I'm with is white or colored. The only thing with me is he's gotta be a man. I won't go with no weaklings. . . . I been with colored guys on the outside and I liked it. Most of the time it's better than it is with whites. . . . I can't explain it really. It's just better, more exciting or something. . . . In here I never gone with no colored guys. I'd like to. I think most of us would. . . . It's like I said before, it's just better. And they respect ya more. They treat you better than white guys do. . . . I'm scared. If I left Frankie for a colored guy he and the others might kill me. I get together with one or two now and then but I always keep it behind closed doors.

> I was walking through the wing the other day when one of them black fags, the one that calls herself 'Ellen,' called me into the corner. She asked if I wanted a hand job. Now I ain't one to pass up an opportunity like that! So I let her do it. She's a real pro! It was the best job I ever had. She didn't ask for

nothin' but I gave her a carton and figgered that was it. Yesterday I'm in the yard with Joe H. and she comes and sits on the bench beside me and starts rubbin' her hand up my leg. Then she says, 'Tony, I'd like to marry you.' I damn near fell off the bench. At first I thought she was just screwing around but than I seen she was serious and I told her to bug off. . . . None of them black fags appeal to me. I ain't seen one I'd like to lay. Havin' a fag or a kid in here is like havin' a broad on the street. You like to show her off, ya know? It might be a big thing for a black guy to have a white kid, I don't know. But it sure as hell ain't no big thing for a white guy to have a black kid. Especially when there's so many nice white kids running around.

Presumably, the attraction of "fags" to active partners of the opposite race is explicable in terms of projection as noted above in the case of the attraction of black "toms" to white "punks." Standing in opposition to the attraction of the "fags," however, is a combination of strong social disapproval and a lack of attraction to the relationship, at least on the part of potential white partners. Unlike "punks," white "fags" are highly valued by other white prisoners. Their disaffection from a relationship with a "wise guy" in favor of a relation with a black is thus likely to result in open conflict in which the "fag" would probably be the ultimate victim. In similar fashion, the rationale behind admitting black "fags" to membership in the Afro-American Society, at least in part, is to prevent them from embarassing other blacks by establishing open relations with whites. The involvement of the black "fags" in both the formal and informal activities of the Afro-American Society operates to keep their activities under close surveillance in much the same manner as do the pseudo-marriages between "wise guys" and "fags" among the whites. Finally, there is apparently little attraction to such relationships by potential white partners. As seen by them, a marriage or a relation with a "kid" should enhance one's status. But a marriage to a black "fag" would reduce one's status rather than enhance it.[c] For these reasons, then, prostitution of a biracial nature is relatively uncommon at ECI, occurring only in the form of secretive and fleeting acts.

Rape and Seduction

Certainly not the least of many gains that have accrued to white males by virtue of their dominance over blacks in this country has been in the area of sex. From the beginning of slavery white males have been

[c] This may not be true if the black "fag" were a true "drag queen." Both black and white prisoners frankly admitted their desire for a black "queen" who had been released just prior to the study. Unlike the "fags" present during the study, this "fag" apparently had had silicone injections to simulate female breasts, wore female undergarments and long hair. Both black and white prisoners competed and fought for his (her) attentions.

accorded access to black as well as to white females. At the same time, reciprocal access to white females has been denied to black males by the not infrequent use of crude violence and the atmosphere of fear thus created. This caste patterning of sexual relations has had implications for black males beyond the asymmetrical access to females. More importantly, it has degraded the black male through repeated demonstration of his inability to protect black women.[8] Indeed, the issue of the sexual dominance of white males has been so salient in the history of race relations in this country that some writers have suggested that racial conflict may well have its roots in mutual lust and jealousy.[9]

One need not subscribe to such a view to recognize that culturally patterned sexual tensions are of considerable importance to the understanding of race relations in the prison. In the prison, where the significance of sex is intensified by the deprivation of heterosexual contact and where black and white males live close together, the role of sex in racial conflict is thrown into sharp relief. In the confines of the prison, the rage of black males at their psychological emasculation is vented against white males.

Rape.   An analysis of prison disciplinary records and interviews with informants places the number of sexual assaults at ECI at 40 to 50 per year. More striking than the number of sexual attacks is the extent to which they are interracial. Each of my 21 informants—black and white prisoners and staff members alike—estimated that 75 percent or more of the sexual assaults involve black aggressors and white victims.[10] The following case study, condensed from an interview with one white victim, is illustrative of the process of sexual assault, the motives of the aggressors, and the career of the victim.

> Alan entered ECI in April, 1970 to serve an 18-month sentence for Breaking and Entering. He is 5′6″ tall and weighs about 135 lbs. At the time he entered ECI he was twenty years old, had graduated from high school, and had never been confined previously. By his own admission he was "scared to death" at the prospect of sexual assault.
>
> Soon after he arrived black inmates began to harass him, calling him "white trash," a "white whore," and threatening "to make a little girl out of (him)." When two black inmates cornered him in his cell one evening before lockup and threatened to throw acid over him—it turned out to be orange juice—he submitted to them, allowing them to commit buggery. Terrified, he requested protective custody.
>
> After one month in protective custody, however, the strain of being locked in a cell for 23 hours a day and never being allowed out of the wing proved to be too much, and he requested return to the population. Soon after his return to the population he was approached by Willie, a large and powerful

black inmate. Willie told him that he didn't approve of what the others had done, felt sorry for Alan, and would take care of him. He gave Alan a carton of cigarettes and signed over a five dollar store order to him. Over the next several weeks the relationship developed into what Alan considered a real friendship. He was no longer harassed and his fears abated. One evening Willie told Alan to "get off" with him. Alan accepted, but when he arrived at the back side of the third tier in the lower South State block, he found himself confronted with five or six other blacks. Willie demanded that he "take care of us." "I been taking care of you, now you gotta take care of me and my friends." Alan refused and tried to struggle free but was overpowered. Willie held him down by the head and shoulders while the others took turns committing buggery upon him.

Then he was forced to commit fellatio upon Willie. As Alan remembers it, during all of this time he was repeatedly called a "white punk," a "white bitch," and asked questions such as "How does it feel to have a black p—k in you, white boy?" He was warned that if he told the guards, they would kill him.

"If I was to go back to PCU (protective custody) they'd want to know why and I couldn't tell 'em. Besides I couldn't stand it back there anyway. So I decided to stay out and give it up if I had to." Over the next several months Alan was subjected to repeated assaults of a similar nature by a large number of black inmates. Then in September, a well-known white inmate asked him to be his "kid." Alan entered a relationship with this prisoner and several of his friends. They provide him with cigarettes and store orders, and since entering the relation he has not been assaulted.

Interviews with other informants confirmed the essential details of Alan's story and indicated that with minor variations his experience is typical of those white prisoners who come to be labeled as "punks" or "kids." Invariably, the victims are considerably younger than other inmates and physically underdeveloped for their age, have completed more years of formal education than the average prisoner, are on their first sentence, and often have long hair. In short they possess many characteristics that might be symbolic of femininity in an all male population. Frequently, as in the case of Alan, the prospective victim is subjected to a period of harassment and threat. Such verbal abuse probably increases the excitement of the aggression, but it serves more practical purposes as well. First, it is a means of discovering if the victim has friends who may come to his assistance. If he has ties with any inmates who are able to mobilize any significant number in his defense, then the attack will be stopped. Second, as happened to Alan, verbal aggression is a means of manipulating the victim into a position of trust and dependence upon an inmate who may in fact be the prime mover in the plot against him. Such manipulation facilitates an undetected assault. On occasion, such tactics of intimidation and manipulation are unnecessary, however. Some young white prisoners, by virtue of their political identifications, are predisposed to friendship with blacks. By reason of their overtures of friendship, however, they may find themselves ensnared in a situation that culminates in sexual assault.

At ECI sexual assaults are termed "train jobs," indicating the group nature of the attack. While all interracial assaults involve several blacks attacking a white victim, the composition of the attacking group changes as more and more black prisoners become involved. The one exception is the "ripper." The "ripper" is that prisoner who plans and initiates the attack. After the initial assault, usually undertaken with several of his closest associates, the "ripper" commonly makes his "punk" available to others in subsequent attacks. As the victim becomes less resistant to particular acts, these later attacks may force him into more degrading acts, for example buggery to fellatio. At some point—either when the victim has become completely submissive or a new victim is being manipulated or perhaps when all those interested have been involved—the attacks cease. At this point, white inmates may come forward to offer the victim protection in return for his services.

Sexual assaults of this type are acts of open, direct, and violent aggression, which from a psychological perspective are closely akin to homicide. Given the nature of the act, it is obvious that the largely black-onto-white character of these assaults is not explicable solely in terms of conditions immediately associated with confinement. Factors such as the deprivation of heterosexual contact, the proximity of black and white males, the prison definitions of homosexual behavior, and the greater solidarity of the blacks make such assaults possible. But the motive force behind them has its roots deep within the entire socio-historical context of black-white relations in this country. The prison is merely an arena within which blacks may direct aggression developed through 300 years of oppression against individuals perceived to be representatives of the oppressors.

According to frustration-aggression theory, the instigation to aggression is greatest when a strong drive is repeatedly frustrated in a nearly total manner.[11] Historically, such has been the condition of the black male in relation to one of his strongest drives, the affirmation of his masculinity. In American society masculinity traditionally has been affirmed by qualities such as assertiveness, self-determination, power over others, and the ability to provide for and protect a wife and family. It is precisely such attributes that have been denied black males, first by slavery and more recently by the legacy of racism. One consequence of the structure of race relations in this country has been the development among black males of an image of themselves as emasculated and dependent beings, and a rage at white males as the perpetrators of their condition.[12] In the prison, the subservience of black males to the authority of white-dominated institutions is immediately visible and other means of self-affirmation are denied them. Under such conditions, black rage undoubtedly increases. Such an anger is articulated by black prisoners when speaking of the motives behind their sexual aggression against whites:

> Every can I been in that's the way it is. . . . It's gettin' even I guess. . . . You guys been cuttin' our b—s off ever since we been in this country. Now we're just gettin' even.

> To general way of thinking it's 'cause they're confined and they got hard rocks. But that ain't it at all. It's a way for the black man to get back at the white man. It's one way he can assert his manhood. Anything white, even a defenseless punk, is part of what the black man hates. It's part of what he's had to fight all his life just to survive, just to have a hole to sleep in and some garbage to eat. . . . It's a new ego thing. He can show he's a man by making a white guy into a girl.

> The black man's just waking up to what's been going on. Now that he's awake, he's gonna be mean. He's been raped—politically, economically, morally raped. He sees this now, but his mind's still small so he's getting back this way. But it's just a beginning.

Any internalized inhibitions black prisoners may have regarding such attacks are neutralized by several conditions.[13] First, the very prevalence of anti-white sentiments provides strong group support and approval for the assaults. While two or three black prisoners have a reputation as "rippers," black informants agree that virtually all black prisoners play the role at some time in their prison career. Generally, this occurs soon after their arrival as they seek the support and acceptance of other "brothers." The instigation of a sexual assault, then, is to some extent an initiation rite by which black prisoners demonstrate their manhood and blackness to their peers.

A second condition that may neutralize inhibitions against the act is contained in the rationales offered above. It is an act of revenge. It is a retaliation in kind for the violent attacks of white males against black people. It is thus justifiable and even moral in a sense.

Finally, there is the definition accorded homosexual behavior by the prisoner subculture. Inmate definitions resolve any threats to the participants' masculine self-images by defining only the behavior of the passive participant as homosexual. Not only do such definitions alleviate anxiety concerning masculinity, they also function to make the act an assertion of manhood. In a population in which normal male-female comparisons are lacking, a greater stress is placed upon physical toughness as an indicator of masculinity. The ability to force another male into a degrading sexual act is thus a symbol of manhood. In short, there exist within the black prisoner subculture several rationalizatons for the sexual assault of white males.

From the perspective of the theory of frustration-aggression, the characteristics of the victims of these attacks take on added significance. The strongest aggressive responses evoked by frustration are directed against the source of the frustration, and may be generalized to other objects to the degree that these objects are perceived as similar to the frustrating object and exempt the aggressor from retaliatory responses.[14] Seen in this light, the assault of young and isolated white males may be interpreted as aggression that is displaced from the primary objects of frustration—the white custodians, and the class they represent—out of fear of their retaliatory power. A similar consideration of power potential is probably operative with respect to the more dominant white male prisoners. Here, however, there is an additional consideration. The dominant white male prisoners may not be perceived by the blacks as representatives of the oppressive class. They share with the black prisoners a criminal identity; they also have been rejected and labeled as outcasts by those in power and react to them with bitter hostility. Given this consideration, there appear to be several reasons for the selection of victims. First, their youth and physical underdevelopment are suggestive of femininity in an all-male world. Second, their isolation precludes retaliatory responses. Third, their lack of a criminal identity and their higher than average education may lead black prisoners to perceive them as members of the white middle class, which they regard as their prime oppressor.

Seduction.　　There is one final question to be treated. When the rape of white females by black males traditionally draws such a violent response from the white population, and when even consensual relations between white women and black men are subject to strong social disapproval, why is it that the homosexual rape of white males at ECI does not arouse the racial consciousness of the white prisoner population and precipitate a retaliatory response? The answer to this question lies in the fact that the white inmate leaders are the direct beneficiaries of these assaults. While they may lack the intense anger involved in these attacks, they also need to affirm their masculinity, and these assaults create and maintain a class of inmates upon whom the white leaders depend for the satisfaction of that need. In response to my questioning, one white leader was quite candid about the tacit biracial cooperation in this regard:

> Sometimes if I really need a "kid" and I see one that looks real good, then I might slip the word over to the spooks that he's really gay. Most of the time though I just sit back and watch the action. I wait till it looks like they're done with him then I come on like a knight in shining armor, see. I take him under my wing and start doing things for him and promise to keep the

others away. After what he's been through it ain't nothing for him to take care of me and a coupla others. He's glad to do it.

Rather than oppose these assaults, white inmates use the fear generated in the victims to seduce them into more permanent roles as "punks" and "kids." Thus, what from the perspective of particular individuals is a situation of brutal, physical conflict is—from the broader perspective of group relations—a form of symbiotic cooperation.

Notes

1. Muzafer Sherif, "Superordinate Goals in the Reduction of Intergroup Conflict," *American Journal of Sociology*, 63 (January, 1958), 349–50.

2. Exchange refers to a relation in "which one person or group acts for the express purpose of receiving a reward" from another. Cooperation is "joint or collaborative behavior toward some goal in which there is a common interest." Robert A. Nisbet, *The Social Bond: An Introduction to the Study of Society* (New York: Alfred A. Knopf, 1970), pp. 63, 66.

3. David A. Ward and Gene G. Kassebaus, *Women's Prison: Sex and Social Structure* (Chicago: Aldine, 1965); Rose Giallombardo, *Society of Women: A Study of a Women's Prison* (New York: John Wiley and Sons, 1966); Esther Heffernan, *Making It in Prison: The Square, the Cool, and the Life* (New York: John Wiley and Sons, 1972), ch. 5.

4. Donald Clemmer, *The Prison Community* (2d. ed.; New York: Holt, Rinehart and Winston, 1958), ch. 10; Gresham M. Sykes, *The Society of Captives: A Study of a Maximum Security Prison* (Princeton N.J.: Princeton University Press, 1958), pp. 95–99; Arthur V. Huffman, "Sex Deviation in a Prison Community," *Journal of Social Therapy* 6 (Third Quarter, 1960), 170–81; John H. Gagnon and William Simon, "The Social Meaning of Prison Homosexuality," *Federal Probation*, 32 (March 1968), 23–29.

5. See Chapter 4 for a discussion of the meaning of these terms, and for a discussion of homosexual marriages among white inmates.

6. Several studies in institutions for females have noted that racial differences appear to function as a substitute for sex differences in homosexual marriages and that the disproportionate number of such unions involve black and white partners. See Giallombardo, p. 3 and diagrams on pp. 177, 183.

7. John Dollard, *Caste and Class in a Southern Town* (3d ed.; Garden City N.Y.: Doubleday Anchor Books, 1957), chs. 7, 14, 17; Gordon W. Allport, *The Nature of Prejudice* (Garden City N.Y.: Doubleday Anchor Books, 1958), ch. 23; Calvin C. Hernton, *Sex and Racism in America* (New York: Grove Press, 1965); William H. Grier and Price M. Cobbs, *Black Rage* (New York: Bantam Books, 1968), chs. 3–5.

8. Dollard, chs. 7, 14, 17; Grier and Cobbs, chs. 3–5; Hernton, ch. 3.

9. J. W. Johnson, *Along This Way* (New York: Viking Press, 1933), p. 170 quoted by Dollard, p. 135. For an indication of the impact of black-white sexual conflict on the psychological development of one black militant leader, and the significance he attributes to the role of white sexual dominance as a factor in racial conflict, see Eldridge Cleaver, *Soul on Ice* (New York: Dell, 1968). See especially the essays entitled "The Allegory of the Black Eunuchs" and "The Primeval Mitosis," wherein he analyzes the structure of American race relations from a perspective that blends Marxism with Freudianism.

10. A study of sexual assaults in the Philadelphia prison system revealed that in 56 percent of the incidents the aggressor was black and the victim was white. None of the incidents involved white aggressors and black victims. In 29 percent of the incidents, both the aggressor and the victim were black and in 15 percent both were white. See Alan J. Davis, "Sexual Assaults in the Philadelphia Prison System and Sheriff's Vans," *Trans-Action* 6 (December 1968), p. 15. In general, these findings conform to the

estimates of my informants at ECI. The lower frequency of interracial assaults involving black aggressors and the higher frequency of intraracial assaults involving blacks may be the result of several factors. First, in the Philadelphia system 80 percent of the population were black. There were thus proportionately fewer potential white victims. Moreover, the larger the black population, the more likely it will become polarized into conflicting factions, for example between what I have termed "revolutionaries" and "half-steppers," thus making sexual assaults among blacks more likely. Second, the time of the studies may be important. The ideology of brotherhood did not become a strong force at ECI until 1967. The study in Philadelphia was from June 1966 to July 1968. It is possible then that the brotherhood ideology, a major factor preventing intraracial sexual assaults among blacks, was not fully institutionalized at that time. In any event, the findings of this study confirm my main contention that the majority of sexual assaults involve black aggressors and white victims.

11. Leonard Berkowitz, *Aggression: A Social Psychological Analysis* (New York: McGraw-Hill, 1962), ch. 2.

12. In this regard, see the essays by Cleaver and the analysis by Grier and Cobbs, ch. 4.

13. Berkowitz, ch. 4.

14. Ibid., ch. 5.

29 / The Moral Career of the Mental Patient

ERVING GOFFMAN

Traditionally the term *career* has been reserved for those who expect to enjoy the rises laid out within a respectable profession. The term is coming to be used, however, in a broadened sense to refer to any social strand of any person's course through life. The perspective of natural history is taken: unique outcomes are neglected in favor of such changes over time as are basic and common to the members of a social category, although occurring independently to each of them. Such a career is not a thing that can be brilliant or disappointing; it can no more be a success than a failure. In this light, I want to consider the mental patient, drawing mainly upon data collected during a year's participant observation of patient social life in a public mental hospital,[1] wherein an attempt was made to take the patient's point of view.

One value of the concept of career is its two-sidedness. One side is linked to internal matters held dearly and closely, such as image of self and felt identity; the other side concerns official position, jural relations, and style of life, and is part of a publicly accessible institutional complex. The concept of career, then, allows one to move back and forth between the personal and the public, between the self and its significant society, without having overly to rely for data upon what the person says he thinks he imagines himself to be.

This paper, then, is an exercise in the institutional approach to the study of self. The main concern will be with the *moral* aspects of career—that is, the regular sequence of changes that career entails in the person's self and in his framework of imagery for judging himself and others.[2]

The category "mental patient" itself will be understood in one strictly sociological sense. In this perspective, the psychiatric view of a person becomes significant only in so far as this view itself alters his social fate—an alteration which seems to become fundamental in our society when, and only when, the person is put through the process of hospitalization.[3] I therefore exclude certain neighboring categories: the undiscovered candidates who would be judged "sick" by psychiatric standards but who never come to be viewed as such by themselves or others, although they may cause everyone a great deal of trouble;[4] the office patient whom a psychiatrist feels he can handle with drugs or shock on the outside; the mental client who engages in psychotherapeutic relationships. And I include anyone, however robust in temperament, who somehow gets caught up in the heavy machinery of mental hospital servicing. In this way the effects of being treated as a mental patient can be kept quite distinct from the effects upon a person's life of traits a clinician would view as psychopathological.[5] Persons who become mental hospital patients vary widely in the kind and degree of illness that a psychiatrist would impute to them, and in the attributes by which laymen would describe them. But once started on the way, they are confronted by some importantly similar circumstances and respond to these in some importantly similar ways. Since these similarities do not come from mental illness, they would seem to occur in spite of it. It is thus a tribute to the power of social forces that the uniform status of mental patient can not only assure an aggregate of persons a common fate and eventually, because of this, a common character, but that this social reworking can be done upon what is perhaps the most obstinate diversity of human materials that can be brought together by society. Here there lacks only the frequent forming of a protective group-life by ex-patients to illustrate in full the classic cycle of response by which deviant subgroupings are psychodynamically formed in society.

This general sociological perspective is heavily reinforced by one key finding of sociologically oriented students in mental hospital research. As has been repeatedly shown in the study of nonliterate societies, the awesomeness, distastefulness, and barbarity of a foreign culture can decrease in the degree that the student becomes familiar with the point of view to life that is taken by his subjects. Similarly, the student of mental hospitals can discover that the craziness or "sick behavior" claimed for the mental patient is by and large a product of the claimant's social distance from the situation that the patient is in, and is not primarily a product of mental illness. Whatever the refinements of the various patients' psychiatric diagnoses, and whatever the special ways in which social life on the "inside" is unique, the researcher can find that he is participating in a community not significantly different from any other he has studied.[6] Of course, while restricting himself to the off-ward grounds community of paroled patients, he may feel, as some patients do, that life in the locked wards is bizarre; and while on a locked admissions or convalescent ward, he may feel that chronic "back" wards are socially crazy places. But he need only move his sphere of sympathetic participation to the "worst" ward in the hospital, and this too can come into social focus as a place with a livable and continuously meaningful social world. This in no way denies that he will find a minority in any ward or patient group that continues to seem quite beyond the capacity to follow rules of social organization, or that the orderly fulfilment of normative expectations in patient society is partly made possible by strategic measures that have somehow come to be institutionalized in mental hospitals.

The career of the mental patient falls popularly and naturalistically into three main phases: the period prior to entering the hospital, which I shall call the *prepatient phase*; the period in the hospital, the *inpatient phase;* the period after discharge from the hospital, should this occur, namely, the *ex-patient phase.*[7] This paper will deal only with the first two phases.

THE PREPATIENT PHASE

A relatively small group of prepatients come into the mental hospital willingly, because of their own idea of what will be good for them, or because of wholehearted agreement with the relevant members of their family. Presumably these recruits have found themselves acting in a way which is evidence to them that they are losing their minds or losing control of themselves. This view of oneself would seem to be one of the most pervasively threatening things that can happen to the self in our society, especially since it is likely to occur at a time when the person is in any case sufficiently troubled to exhibit the kind of symptom which he himself can see. As Sullivan described it,

> What we discover in the self-system of a person undergoing schizophrenic changes or schizophrenic processes, is then, in its simplest form, an extremely fear-marked puzzlement, consisting of the use of rather generalized and anything but exquisitely refined referential processes in an attempt to cope with what is essentially a failure at being human—a failure at being anything that one could respect as worth being.[8]

Coupled with the person's disintegrative re-evaluation of himself will be the new, almost equally pervasive circumstance of attempting to conceal from others what he takes to be the new fundamental facts about himself, and attempting to discover whether others too have discovered them.[9] Here I want to stress that perception of losing one's mind is based on culturally derived and socially engrained stereotypes as to the significance of symptoms such as hearing voices, losing temporal and spatial orientation, and sensing that one is being followed, and that many of the most spectacular and convincing of these symptoms in some instances psychiatrically signify merely a temporary emotional upset in a stressful situation, however terrifying to the person at the time. Similarly, the anxiety consequent upon this perception of oneself, and the strategies devised to reduce this anxiety, are not a product of abnormal psychology, but would be exhibited by any person socialized into our culture who came to conceive of himself as someone losing his mind. Interestingly, subcultures in American society apparently differ in the amount of ready imagery and encouragement they supply for such self-views, leading to differential rates of *self*-referral; the capacity to take this disintegrative view of oneself without psychiatric prompting seems to be one of the questionable cultural privileges of the upper classes.[10]

For the person who has come to see himself—with whatever justification—as mentally unbalanced, entrance to the mental hospital can sometimes bring relief, perhaps in part because of the sudden transformation in the structure of his basic social situations; instead of being to himself a questionable person trying to maintain a role as a full one, he can become an officially questioned person known to himself to be not so questionable as that. In other cases, hospitalization can make matters worse for the willing patient, confirming by the objective situation what has theretofore been a matter of the private experience of self.

Once the willing prepatient enters the hospital, he may go through the same routine of experiences as do those who enter unwillingly. In any case, it is the latter that I mainly want to consider, since in America at present these are by far the more numerous kind.[11] Their approach to the institution takes one of three classic forms: they come because they have been implored by their family or threatened with the abrogation of family ties unless they go "willingly"; they come by force under police escort; they come under misapprehension purposely induced by others, this last restricted mainly to youthful prepatients.

The prepatient's career may be seen in terms of an extrusory model; he starts out with relationships and rights, and ends up, at the beginning of his hospital stay, with hardly any of either. The moral aspects of this career, then, typically begin with the experience of abandonment, disloyalty, and embitterment. This is the case even though to others it may be obvious that he was in need of treatment, and even though in the hospital he may soon come to agree.

The case histories of most mental patients document offense against some arrangement for face-to-face living—a domestic establishment, a work place, a semipublic organization such as a church or store, a public region such as a street or park. Often there is also a record of some *complainant*, some figure who takes that action against the offender which eventually leads to his hospitalization. This may not be the person who makes the first move, but it is the person who makes what turns out to be the first effective move. Here is the *social* beginning of the patient's career, regardless of where one might locate the psychological beginning of his mental illness.

The kinds of offenses which lead to hospitalization are felt to differ in nature from those which lead to other extrusory consequences—to imprisonment, divorce, loss of job, disownment, regional exile, noninstitutional psychiatric treatment, and so forth. But little seems known about these differentiating factors; and when one studies actual commitments, alternate outcomes frequently appear to have been possible. It seems true, moreover, that for every offense that leads to an effective complaint, there are many psychiatrically similar ones that never do. No action is taken; or action is taken which leads to other extrusory outcomes; or ineffective action is taken, leading to the mere pacifying or putting off of the person who complains. Thus, as Clausen and Yarrow have nicely shown, even offenders who are eventually hospitalized are likely to have had a long series of ineffective actions taken against them.[12]

Separating those offenses which could have been used as grounds for hospitalizing the offender from those that are so used, one finds a vast number of what students of occupation call career contingencies.[13] Some of these contingencies in the mental patient's career have been suggested, if not explored, such as socio-economic status, visibility of the offense, proximity to a mental hospital, amount of treatment facilities available, community regard for the type of treatment given in available hospitals, and so on.[14] For information about other contingencies one must rely on atrocity tales: a psychotic man is tolerated by his wife until she finds herself a boy friend, or by his adult children until they move from a house to an apartment; an alcoholic is sent to a mental hospital because the jail is full, and a drug addict because he declines to avail himself of psychiatric treatment on the outside; a rebellious adolescent daughter can no longer be managed at home because she now threatens to have an open affair with an unsuitable companion; and so on. Correspondingly there is an equally important set of contingencies causing the person to by-pass this fate. And should the person enter the hospital, still another set of contingencies will help determine when he is to obtain a discharge— such as the desire of his family for his return, the availability of a "manageable" job, and so on. The society's official view is that inmates of mental hospitals are there primarily because they are suffering from mental illness. However, in the degree that the "mentally ill" outside hospitals numerically approach or surpass those inside hospitals, one could say that mental patients *distinctively* suffer not from mental illness, but from contingencies.

Career contingencies occur in conjunction with a second feature of the prepatient's career—the *circuit of agents*—and agencies—that participate fatefully in his passage from civilian to patient status.[15]

Here is an instance of that increasingly important class of social system whose elements are agents and agencies, which are brought into systemic connection through having to take up and send on the same persons. Some of these agent-roles will be cited now, with the understanding that in any concrete circuit a role may be filled more than once, and a single person may fill more than one of them.

First is the *next-of-relation*—the person whom the prepatient sees as the most available of those upon whom he should be able to most depend in times of trouble; in this instance the last to doubt his sanity and the first to have done everything to save him from the fate which, it transpires, he has been approaching. The patient's next-of-relation is usually his next of kin; the special term is introduced because he need not be. Second is the *complainant*, the person who retrospectively appears to have started the person on his way to the hospital. Third are the *mediators*—the sequence of agents and agencies to which the prepatient is referred and through which he is relayed and processed on his way to the hospital. Here are included police, clergy, general medical practitioners, office psychiatrists, personnel in public clinics, lawyers, social service workers, school teachers, and so on. One of these agents will have the legal mandate to sanction commitment and will exercise it, and so those agents who precede him in the process will be involved in something whose outcome is not yet settled. When the mediators retire from the scene, the prepatient has become an inpatient, and the significant agent has become the hospital administrator.

While the complainant usually takes action in a lay capacity as a citizen, an employer, a neighbor, or a kinsman, mediators tend to be specialists and differ from those they serve in significant ways. They have experience in handling trouble, and some professional distance from what they handle. Except in the case of policemen, and perhaps some clergy, they tend to be more psychiatrically oriented than the lay public, and will see the need for treatment at times when the public does not.[16]

An interesting feature of these roles is the functional effects of their interdigitation. For example, the feelings of the patient will be influenced by whether or not the person who fills the role of complainant also has the role of next-of-relation—an embarrassing combination more prevalent, apparently, in the higher classes than in the lower.[17] Some of these emergent effects will be considered now.[18]

In the prepatient's progress from home to the hospital he may participate as a third person in what he may come to experience as a kind of *alienative coalition*. His next-of-relation presses him into coming to "talk things over" with a medical practitioner, an office psychiatrist, or some other counselor. Disinclination on his part may be met by threatening him with desertion, disownment, or other legal action, or by stressing the joint and explorative nature of the interview. But typically the next-of-relation will have set the interview up, in the sense of selecting the professional, arranging for time, telling the professional something about the case, and so on. This move effectively tends to establish the next-of-relation as the responsible person to whom pertinent findings can be divulged, while effectively establishing the other as the patient. The prepatient often goes to the interview with the understanding that he is going as an equal of someone who is so bound together with him that a third person could not come between them in fundamental matters; this, after all, is one way in which close relationships are defined in our society. Upon arrival at the office the prepatient suddenly finds that he and his next-of-relation have not been accorded the same roles, and apparently that a prior understanding between the professional and the next-of-relation has been put in operation against him. In the extreme but common case the professional first sees the prepatient alone, in the role of examiner and diagnostician, and then sees the next-of-relation alone, in the role of advisor, while carefully avoiding talking things over seriously with them both together.[19] And even in those nonconsultative cases where public officials must forcibly extract a person from a family that wants to tolerate him, the next-of-relation is likely to be induced to "go along" with the official action, so that even here the prepatient may feel that an alienative coalition has been formed against him.

The moral experience of being third man in such a coalition is likely to embitter the prepatient, especially since his troubles have already probably led to some estrangement from his next-of-relation. After he enters the hospital, continued visits by his next-of-relation can give the patient the "insight" that his own best interests were being served. But the initial visits may temporarily strengthen his feeling of abandonment; he is likely to beg his visitor to get him out or at least to get him more privileges and to sympathize with the monstrousness of his plight—to which the visitor ordinarily can respond only by trying to maintain a hopeful note, by not "hearing" the requests, or by assuring the patient that the medical authorities know about these things and are doing what is medically best. The visitor then nonchalantly goes back into a world that the patient has learned is incredibly thick with freedom and privileges, causing the patient to feel that his next-of-relation is merely adding a pious gloss to a clear case of traitorous desertion.

The depth to which the patient may feel betrayed by his next-of-relation seems to be increased by the fact that another witnesses his betrayal—a factor which is apparently significant in many three-party situations. An offended person may well act forbearantly and accommodatively toward an offender when the two are alone, choosing peace ahead of justice. The presence of a witness, however, seems to add something to the implications of the offense. For then it is beyond the power of the offended and offender to forget about, erase, or suppress what has happened; the offense has become a public social fact.[20] When the witness is a mental health commission, as is sometimes the case, the witnessed betrayal can verge on a "degradation ceremony."[21] In such circumstances, the offended patient may feel that some kind of extensive reparative action is required before witnesses, if his honor and social weight are to be restored.

Two other aspects of sensed betrayal should be mentioned. First, those who suggest the possibility of another's entering a mental hospital are not likely to provide a realistic picture of how in fact it may strike him when he arrives. Often he is told that he will get required medical treatment and a rest, and may well be out in a few months or so. In some cases they may thus be concealing what they know, but I think, in general, they will be telling what they see as the truth. For here there is a quite relevant difference between patients and mediating professionals; mediators, more so than the public at large, may conceive of mental hospitals as short-term medical establishments where required rest and attention can be voluntarily obtained, and not as places of coerced exile. When the prepatient finally arrives he is likely to learn quite quickly, quite differently. He then finds that the information given him about life in the hospital has had the effect of his having put up less resistance to entering than he now sees he would have put up had he known the facts. Whatever the intentions of those who participated in his transition from person to patient, he may sense they have in effect "conned" him into his present predicament.

I am suggesting that the prepatient starts out with at least a portion of the rights, liberties, and satisfactions of the civilian and ends up on a psychiatric ward stripped of almost everything. The question here is *how* this stripping is managed. This is the second aspect of betrayal I want to consider.

As the prepatient may see it, the circuit of significant figures can function as a kind of *betrayal funnel*. Passage from person to patient may be effected through a series of linked stages, each managed by a different agent. While each stage tends to bring a sharp decrease in adult free status, each agent may try to maintain the fiction that no further decrease will occur. He may even manage to turn the prepatient over to the next agent while sustaining this note. Further, through words, cues, and gestures, the prepatient is implicitly asked by the current agent to join with him in sustaining a running line of polite small talk that tactfully avoids the administrative facts of the situation, becoming, with each stage, progressively more at odds with these facts. The spouse would rather not have to cry to get the prepatient to visit a psychiatrist; psychiatrists would rather not have a scene when the prepatient learns that he and his spouse are being seen separately and in different ways; the police infrequently bring a prepatient to the hospital in a strait jacket, finding it much easier all around to give him a cigarette, some kindly words, and freedom to relax in the back seat of the patrol car; and finally, the admitting psychiatrist finds he can do his work better in the relative quiet and luxury of the "admission suite" where, as an incidental consequence, the notion can survive that a mental hospital is indeed a comforting place. If the prepatient heeds all of these implied requests and is reasonably decent about the whole thing, he can travel the whole circuit from home to hospital without forcing anyone to look directly at what is happening or to deal with the raw emotion that his situation might well cause him to express. His showing consideration for those who are moving him toward the hospital allows them to show consideration for him, with the joint result that these interactions can be sustained with some of the protective harmony characteristic of ordinary face-to-face dealings. But should the new patient cast his mind back over the sequence of steps leading to hospitalization, he may feel that everyone's *current* comfort was being busily sustained while his long-range welfare was being undermined. This realization may constitute a moral experience that further separates him for the time from the people on the outside.[22]

I would now like to look at the circuit of career agents from the point of view of the agents themselves. Mediators in the person's transition from civil to patient status—as well as his keepers, once he is in the hospital—have an interest in establishing a responsible next-of-relation as the patient's deputy or *guardian*; should there be no obvious candidate for the role, someone may be sought out and pressed into it. Thus while a person is gradually being transformed into a patient, a next-of-relation is gradually being transformed into a guardian. With a guardian on the scene, the whole transition process can be kept tidy. He is likely to be familiar with the prepatient's civil involvements and business, and can tie up loose ends that might otherwise be left to entangle the hospital. Some of the prepatient's abrogated civil rights can be transferred to him, thus helping to sustain the legal fiction that while the prepatient does not actually have his rights he somehow actually has not lost them.

Inpatients commonly sense, at least for a time, that hospitalization is a massive unjust deprivation, and sometimes succeed in convincing a few persons on the outside that this is the case. It often turns out to be useful, then, for those identified with inflicting these deprivations, however justifiably, to be able to point to the cooperation and agreement of someone whose relationship to the patient places him above suspicion, firmly defining him as the person most likely to have the patient's personal interest at heart. If the guardian is satisfied with what is happening to the new inpatient, the world ought to be.[23]

Now it would seem that the greater the legitimate personal stake one party has in another, the better he can take the role of guardian to the other. But the structural arrangements in society which lead to the acknowledged merging of two persons' interests lead to additional consequences. For the person to whom the patient turns for help—for protection against such threats as involuntary commitment—is just the person to whom the mediators and hospital administrators logically turn for authorization. It is understandable, then, that some patients will come to sense, at least for a time, that the closeness of a relationship tells nothing of its trustworthiness.

There are still other functional effects emerging from this complement of roles. If and when the next-of-relation appeals to mediators for help in the trouble he is having with the prepatient, hospitalization may not, in fact, be in his mind. He may not even perceive the prepatient as mentally sick, or, if he does, he may not consistently hold to this view.[24] It is the circuit of mediators, with their greater psychiatric sophistication and their belief in the medical character of mental hospitals, that will often define the situation for the next-of-relation, assuring him that hospitalization is a possible solution and a good one, that it involves no betrayal, but is rather a medical action taken in the best interests of the prepatient. Here the next-of-relation may learn that doing his duty to the prepatient may cause the prepatient to distrust and even hate him for the time. But the fact that this course of action may have had to be pointed out and prescribed by professionals, and be defined by them as a moral duty, relieves the next-of-relation of some of the guilt he may feel.[25] It is a poignant fact that an adult son or daughter may be pressed into the role of mediator, so that the hostility that might otherwise be directed against the spouse is passed on to the child.[26]

Once the prepatient is in the hospital, the same guilt-carrying function may become a significant part of the staff's job in regard to the next-of-relation.[27] These reasons for feeling that he himself has not betrayed the patient, even though the patient may then think so, can later provide the next-of-relation with a defensible line to take when visiting the patient in the hospital and a basis for hoping that the relationship can be re-established after its hospital moratorium. And of course this position, when sensed by the patient, can provide him with excuses for the next-of-relation, when and if he comes to look for them.[28]

Thus while the next-of-relation can perform important functions for the mediators and hospital administrators, they in turn can perform important functions for him. One finds, then, an emergent unintended exchange or reciprocation of functions, these functions themselves being often unintended.

The final point I want to consider about the prepatient's moral career is its peculiarly *retroactive* character. Until a person actually arrives at the hospital there usually seems no way of knowing for sure that he is destined to do so, given the determinative role of career contingencies. And until the point of hospitalization is reached, he or others may not conceive of him as a person who is becoming a mental patient. However, since he will be held against his will in the hospital, his next-of-relation and the hospital staff will be in great need of a rationale for the hardships they are sponsoring. The medical elements of the staff will also need evidence that they are still in the trade they were trained for. These problems are eased, no doubt unintentionally, by the case-history construction that is placed on the patient's past life, this having the effect of demonstrating that all along he had been becoming sick, that he finally became very sick, and that if he had not been hospitalized much worse things would have happened to him—all of which, of course, may be true. Incidentally, if the patient wants to make sense out of his stay in the hospital, and, as already suggested, keep alive the possibility of once again conceiving of his next-of-relation as a decent, well-meaning person, then he too will have reason to believe some of this psychiatric work-up of his past.

Here is a very ticklish point for the sociology of careers. An important aspect of every career is the view the person constructs when he looks backward over his progress; in a sense, however, the whole of the prepatient career derives from this reconstruction. The fact of having had a prepatient career, starting with an effective complaint, becomes an important part of the mental patient's orientation, but this part can begin to be played only after hospitalization proves that what he had been having, but no longer has, is a career as a prepatient.

THE INPATIENT PHASE

The last step in the prepatient's career can involve his realization— justified or not—that he has been deserted by society and turned out of relationships by those closest to him. Interestingly enough, the patient, especially a first admission, may manage to keep himself from coming to the end of this trail, even though in fact he is now in a locked mental hospital ward. On entering the hospital, he may very strongly feel the desire not to be known to anyone as a person who could possibly be reduced to these present circumstances, or as a person who conducted himself in the way he did prior to commitment. Consequently, he may avoid talking to anyone, may stay by himself when possible, and may even be "out of contact" or "manic" so as to avoid ratifying any interaction that presses a politely reciprocal role upon him and opens him up to what he has become in the eyes of others. When the next-of-relation makes an effort to visit, he may be rejected by mutism, or by the patient's refusal to enter the visiting room, these strategies sometimes suggesting that the patient still clings to a remnant of relatedness to those who made up his past, and is protecting this remnant from the final destructiveness of dealing with the new people that they have become.[29]

Usually the patient comes to give up this taxing effort at anonymity, at not-hereness, and begins to present himself for conventional social interaction to the hospital community. Thereafter he withdraws only in special ways — by always using his nickname, by signing his contribution to the patient weekly with his initial only, or by using the innocuous "cover" address tactfully provided by some hospitals; or he withdraws only at special times, when, say, a flock of nursing students makes a passing tour of the ward, or when, paroled to the hospital grounds, he suddenly sees he is about to cross the path of a civilian he happens to know from home. Sometimes this making of oneself available is called "settling down" by the attendants. It marks a new stand openly taken and supported by the patient, and resembles the "coming out" process that occurs in other groupings.[30]

Once the prepatient begins to settle down, the main outlines of his fate tend to follow those of a whole class of segregated establishments — jails, concentration camps, monasteries, work camps, and so on — in which the inmate spends the whole round of life on the grounds, and marches through his regimented day in the immediate company of a group of persons of his own institutional status.[31]

Like the neophyte in many of these "total institutions," the new inpatient finds himself cleanly stripped of many of his accustomed affirmations, satisfactions, and defenses, and is subjected to a rather full set of mortifying experiences: restriction of free movement; communal living; diffuse authority of a whole echelon of people; and so on. Here one begins to learn about the limited extent to which a conception of oneself can be sustained when the usual setting of supports for it are suddenly removed.

While undergoing these humbling moral experiences, the inpatient learns to orient himself in terms of the "ward system."[32] In public mental hospitals this usually consists of a series of graded living arrangements built around wards, administrative units called services, and parole statuses. The "worst" level involves often nothing but wooden benches to sit on, some quite indifferent food, and a small piece of room to sleep in. The "best" level may involve a room of one's own, ground and town privileges, contacts with staff that are relatively undamaging, and what is seen as good food and ample recreational facilities. For disobeying the pervasive house rules, the inmate will receive stringent punishments expressed in terms of loss of privileges; for obedience he will eventually be allowed to reacquire some of the minor satisfactions he took for granted on the outside.

The institutionalization of these radically different levels of living throws light on the implications for self of social settings. And this in turn affirms that the self arises not merely out of its possessor's interactions with significant others, but also out of the arrangements that are evolved in an organization for its members.

There are some settings which the person easily discounts as an expression or extension of him. When a tourist goes slumming, he may take pleasure in the situation not because it is a reflection of him but because it so assuredly is not. There are other settings, such as living rooms, which the person manages on his own and employs to influence in a favorable direction other persons' views of him. And there are still other settings, such as a work place, which express the employee's occupational status, but over which he has no final control, this being exerted, however tactfully, by his employer. Mental hospitals provide an extreme instance of this latter possibility. And this is due not merely to their uniquely degraded living levels, but also to the unique way in which significance for self is made explicit to the patient, piercingly, persistently, and thoroughly. Once lodged on a given ward, the patient is firmly instructed that the restrictions and deprivations he encounters are not due to such things as tradition or economy — and hence dissociable from self — but are intentional parts of his treatment, part of his need at the time, and therefore an expression of the state that his self has fallen to. Having every reason to initiate requests for better conditions, he is told that when the staff feels he is "able to manage" or will be "comfortable with" a higher ward level, then appropriate action will be taken. In short, assignment to a given ward is presented not as a reward or punishment, but as an expression of his general level of social functioning, his status as a person. Given the fact that the worst ward levels provide a round of life that inpatients with organic brain damage can easily manage, and that these quite limited human beings are present to prove it, one can appreciate some of the mirroring effects of the hospital.[33]

The ward system, then, is an extreme instance of how the physical facts of an establishment can be explicitly employed to frame the conception a person takes of himself. In addition, the official psychiatric mandate of mental hospitals gives rise to even more direct, even more blatant, attacks upon the inmate's view of himself. The more "medical" and the more progressive a mental hospital is—the more it attempts to be therapeutic and not merely custodial—the more he may be confronted by high-ranking staff arguing that his past has been a failure, that the cause of this has been within himself, that his attitude to life is wrong, and that if he wants to be a person he will have to change his way of dealing with people and his conceptions of himself. Often the moral value of these verbal assaults will be brought home to him by requiring him to practice taking this psychiatric view of himself in arranged confessional periods, whether in private sessions or group psychotherapy.

Now a general point may be made about the moral career of inpatients which has bearing on many moral careers. Given the stage that any person has reached in a career, one typically finds that he constructs an image of his life course—past, present, and future—which selects, abstracts, and distorts in such a way as to provide him with a view of himself that he can usefully expound in current situations. Quite generally, the person's line concerning self defensively brings him into appropriate alignment with the basic values of his society, and so may be called an *apologia*. If the person can manage to present a view of his current situation which shows the operation of favorable personal qualities in the past and a favorable destiny awaiting him, it may be called a *success story*. If the facts of a person's past and present are extremely dismal, then about the best he can do is to show that he is not responsible for what has become of him, and the term *sad tale* is appropriate. Interestingly enough, the more the person's past forces him out of apparent alignment with central moral values, the more often he seems compelled to tell his sad tale in any company in which he finds himself. Perhaps he partly responds to the need he feels in others of not having their sense of proper life courses affronted. In any case, it is among convicts, 'wino's,' and prostitutes that one seems to obtain sad tales the most readily.[34] It is the vicissitudes of the mental patient's sad tale that I want to consider now.

In the mental hospital, the setting and the house rules press home to the patient that he is, after all, a mental case who has suffered some kind of social collapse on the outside, having failed in some over-all way, and that here he is of little social weight, being hardly capable of acting like a full-fledged person at all. These humiliations are likely to be most keenly felt by middle-class patients, since their previous condition of life little immunizes them against such affronts; but all patients feel some downgrading. Just as any normal member of his outside subculture would do, the patient often responds to this situation by attempting to assert a sad tale proving that he is not "sick," that the "little trouble" he did get into was really somebody else's fault, that his past life course had some honor and rectitude, and that the hospital is therefore unjust in forcing the status of mental patient upon him. This self-respecting tendency is heavily institutionalized within the patient society where opening social contacts typically involve the participants' volunteering information about their current ward location and length of stay so far, but not the reasons for their stay—such interaction being conducted in the manner of small talk on the outside.[35] With greater familiarity, each patient usually volunteers relatively acceptable reasons for his hospitalization, at the same time accepting without open immediate question the lines offered by other patients. Such stories as the following are given and overtly accepted.

> I was going to night school to get a M.A. degree, and holding down a job in addition, and the load got too much for me.

> The others here are sick mentally but I'm suffering from a bad nervous system and that is what is giving me these phobias.

> I got here by mistake because of a diabetes diagnosis, and I'll leave in a couple of days. [The patient had been in seven weeks.]

> I failed as a child, and later with my wife I reached out for dependency.

> My trouble is that I can't work. That's what I'm in for. I had two jobs with a good home and all the money I wanted.[36]

The patient sometimes reinforces these stories by an optimistic definition of his occupational status: A man who managed to obtain an audition as a radio announcer styles himself a radio announcer; another who worked for some months as a copy boy and was then given a job as a reporter on a large trade journal, but fired after three weeks, defines himself as a reporter.

A whole social role in the patient community may be constructed on the basis of these reciprocally sustained fictions. For these face-to-face niceties tend to be qualified by behind-the-back gossip that comes only a degree closer to the 'objective' facts. Here, of course, one can see a classic social function of informal networks of equals: they serve as one another's audience for self-supporting tales—tales that are somewhat more solid than pure fantasy and somewhat thinner than the facts.

But the patient's *apologia* is called forth in a unique setting, for few settings could be so destructive of self-stories except, of course, those stories already constructed along psychiatric lines. And this destructiveness rests on more than the official sheet of paper which attests that the patient is of unsound mind, a danger to himself and others— an attestation, incidentally, which seems to cut deeply into the patient's pride, and into the possibility of his having any.

Certainly the degrading conditions of the hospital setting belie many of the self-stories that are presented by patients; and the very fact of being in the mental hospital is evidence against these tales. And of course, there is not always sufficient patient solidarity to prevent patient discrediting patient, just as there is not always a sufficient number of 'professionalized' attendants to prevent attendant discrediting patient. As one patient informant repeatedly suggested to a fellow patient:

If you're so smart, how come you got your ass in here?

The mental hospital setting, however, is more treacherous still. Staff has much to gain through discreditings of the patient's story— whatever the felt reason for such discreditings. If the custodial faction in the hospital is to succeed in managing his daily round without complaint or trouble from him, then it will prove useful to be able to point out to him that the claims about himself upon which he rationalizes his demands are false, that he is not what he is claiming to be, and that in fact he is a failure as a person. If the psychiatric faction is to impress upon him its views about his personal make-up, then they must be able to show in detail how their version of his past and their version of his character hold up much better than his own.[37] If both the custodial and psychiatric factions are to get him to cooperate in the various psychiatric treatments, then it will prove useful to disabuse him of *his* view of their purposes, and cause him to appreciate that they know what they are doing, and are doing what is best for him. In brief, the difficulties caused by a patient are closely tied to his version of what has been happening to him, and if cooperation is to be secured, it helps if this version is discredited. The patient must "insightfully" come to take, or affect to take, the hospital's view of himself.

Notes

1. The study was conducted during 1955–56 under the auspices of the Laboratory of Socio-environmental Studies of the National Institute of Mental Health. I am grateful to the Laboratory Chief, John A. Clausen, and to Dr. Winfred Overholser, Superintendent, and the late Dr. Jay Hoffman, then First Assistant Physician of Saint Elizabeths Hospital, Washington, D.C., for the ideal cooperation they freely provided. A preliminary report is contained in Goffman, "Interpersonal Persuasion," pp. 117–193; in *Group Processes: Transactions of the Third Conference*, edited by Bertram Schaffner: New York, Josiah Macy, Jr. Foundation, 1957. A shorter version of this paper was presented at the Annual Meeting of the American Sociological Society, Washington, D.C., August 1957.

2. Material on moral career can be found in early social anthropological work on ceremonies of status transition, and in classic social psychological descriptions of those spectacular changes in one's view of self that can accompany participation in social movements and sects. Recently new kinds of relevant data have been suggested by

psychiatric interest in the problem of "identity" and sociological studies of work careers and "adult socialization."

3. This point has recently been made by Elaine and John Cumming, *Closed Ranks*; Cambridge, Commonwealth Fund, Harvard Univ. Press, 1957; pp. 101–102. "Clinical experience supports the impression that many people define mental illness as 'That condition for which a person is treated in a mental hospital.' . . . Mental illness, it seems, is a condition which afflicts people who must go to a mental institution, but until they do almost anything they do is normal." Leila Deasy has pointed out to me the correspondence here with the situation in white collar crime. Of those who are detected in this activity, only the ones who do not manage to avoid going to prison find themselves accorded the social role of the criminal.

4. Case records in mental hospitals are just now coming to be exploited to show the incredible amount of trouble a person may cause for himself and others before anyone begins to think about him psychiatrically, let alone take psychiatric action against him. See John A. Clausen and Marian Radke Yarrow, "Paths to the Mental Hospital," *J. Social Issues* (1955) 11:25–32; August B. Hollingshead and Fredrick C. Redlich, *Social Class and Mental Illness*; New York, Wiley, 1958: pp. 173–174.

5. An illustration of how this perspective may be taken to all forms of deviancy may be found in Edwin Lemert, *Social Pathology*; New York, McGraw-Hill, 1951; see especially pp. 74–76. A specific application to mental defectives may be found in Stewart E. Perry, "Some Theoretic Problems of Mental Deficiency and Their Action Implications," *Psychiatry* (1954) 17:45–73; see especially p. 68.

6. Conscientious objectors who voluntarily went to jail sometimes arrived at the same conclusion regarding criminal inmates. See, for example, Alfred Hassler, *Diary of a Self-made Convict*; Chicago, Regnery, 1954; p. 74.

7. This simple picture is complicated by the somewhat special experience of roughly a third of ex-patients—namely, readmission to the hospital, this being the recidivist or "repatient" phase.

8. Harry Stack Sullivan, *Clinical Studies in Psychiatry*; edited by Helen Swick Perry, Mary Ladd Gawel, and Martha Gibbon; New York, Norton, 1956; pp. 184–185.

9. This moral experience can be contrasted with that of a person learning to become a marihuana addict, whose discovery that he can be 'high' and still 'op' effectively without being detected apparently leads to a new level of use. See Howard S. Becker, "Marihuana Use and Social Control." *Social Problems* (1955) 3:35–44; see especially pp. 40–41.

10. See footnote 2: Hollingshead and Redlich, p. 187, Table 6, where relative frequency is given of self-referral by social class grouping.

11. The distinction employed here between willing and unwilling patients cuts across the legal one, of voluntary and committed, since some persons who are glad to come to the mental hospital may be legally committed, and of those who come only because of strong familial pressure, some may sign themselves in as voluntary patients.

12. Clausen and Yarrow; see footnote 4.

13. An explicit application of this notion to the field of mental health may be found in Edwin M. Lemert, "Legal Commitment and Social Control," *Sociology and Social Research* (1946) 30:370–378.

14. For example, Jerome K. Meyers and Leslie Schaffer, "Social Stratification and Psychiatric Practice: A Study of an Outpatient Clinic," *Amer. Sociological Rev.* (1954) 19:307–310. Lemert, see footnote 5; pp. 402–403. *Patients in Mental Institutions*, 1941; Washington, D.C., Department of Commerce, Bureau of Census, 1941; p. 2.

15. For one circuit of agents and its bearing on career contingencies, see Oswald Hall, "The Stages of a Medical Career," *Amer. J. Sociology* (1948) 53:227–336.

16. See Cumming, footnote 3; p. 92.

17. Hollingshead and Redlich, footnote 4; p. 187.

18. For an analysis of some of these circuit implications for the inpatient, see Leila C. Deasy and Olive W. Quinn, "The Wife of the Mental Patient and the Hospital Psychiatrist." *J. Social Issues* (1955) 11:49–60. An interesting illustration of this kind of analysis may also be found in Alan G. Gowman, "Blindness and the Role of Companion," *Social Problems* (1956) 4:68–75. A general statement may be found in Robert Merton, "The Role Set: Problems in Sociological Theory," *British J. Sociology* (1957) 8:106–120.

19. I have one case record of a man who claims he thought *he* was taking his wife to

see the psychiatrist, not realizing until too late that his wife had made the arrangements.

20. A paraphrase from Kurt Riezler, "The Social Psychology of Shame," *Amer. J. Sociology* (1943) 48:458.

21. See Harold Garfinkel, "Conditions of Successful Degradation Ceremonies," *Amer. J. Sociology* (1956) 61:420–424.

22. Concentration camp practices provide a good example of the function of the betrayal funnel in inducing cooperation and reducing struggle and fuss, although here the mediators could not be said to be acting in the best interests of the inmates. Police picking up persons from their homes would sometimes joke good-naturedly and offer to wait while coffee was being served. Gas chambers were fitted out like delousing rooms, and victims taking off their clothes were told to note where they were leaving them. The sick, aged, weak, or insane who were selected for extermination were sometimes driven away in Red Cross ambulances to camps referred to by terms such as "observation hospital." See David Boder, *I Did Not Interview the Dead*; Urbana, Univ. of Illinois Press, 1949; p. 81; and Elie A. Cohen, *Human Behavior in the Concentration Camp*; London, Cape, 1954; pp. 32, 37, 107.

23. Interviews collected by the Clausen group at NIMH suggest that when a wife comes to be a guardian, the responsibility may disrupt previous distance from in-laws, leading either to a new supportive coalition with them or to a marked withdrawal from them.

24. For an analysis of these nonpsychiatric kinds of perception, see Marian Radke Yarrow, Charlotte Green Schwartz, Harriet S. Murphy, and Leila Calhoun Deasy, "The Psychological Meaning of Mental Illness in the Family," *J. Social Issues* (1955) 11:12–24; Charlotte Green Schwartz, "Perspectives on Deviance: Wives' Definitions of their Husbands' Mental Illness," *Psychiatry* (1957) 20:275–291.

25. This guilt-carrying function is found, of course, in other role-complexes. Thus, when a middle-class couple engages in the process of legal separation or divorce, each of their lawyers usually takes the position that his job is to acquaint his client with all of the potential claims and rights, pressing his client into demanding these, in spite of any nicety of feelings about the rights and honorableness of the ex-partner. The client, in all good faith, can then say to self and to the ex-partner that the demands are being made only because the lawyer insists it is best to do so.

26. Recorded in the Clausen data.

27. This point is made by Cumming, see footnote 3; p. 129.

28. There is an interesting contrast here with the moral career of the tuberculosis patient. I am told by Julius Roth that tuberculous patients are likely to come to the hospital willingly, agreeing with their next-of-relation about treatment. Later in their hospital career, when they learn how long they yet have to stay and how depriving and irrational some of the hospital rulings are, they may seek to leave, be advised against this by the staff and by relatives, and only then begin to feel betrayed.

29. The inmate's initial strategy of holding himself aloof from ratifying contact may partly account for the relative lack of group-formation among inmates in public mental hospitals, a connection that has been suggested to me by William R. Smith. The desire to avoid personal bonds that would give license to the asking of biographical questions could also be a factor. In mental hospitals, of course, as in prisoner camps, the staff may consciously break up incipient group-formation in order to avoid collective rebellious action and other ward disturbances.

30. A comparable coming out occurs in the homosexual world, when a person finally comes frankly to present himself to a "gay" gathering not as a tourist but as someone who is "available." See Evelyn Hooker, "A Preliminary Examination of Group Behavior of Homosexuals," *J. Psychology* (1956) 42:217–225; especially p. 221. A good fictionalized treatment may be found in James Baldwin's *Giovanni's Room*; New York, Dial, 1956; pp. 41–63. A familiar instance of the coming out process is no doubt to be found among prepubertal children at the moment one of these actors sidles *back* into a room that had been left in an angered huff and injured *amour-propre*. The phrase itself presumably derives from a *rite-de-passage* ceremony once arranged by upper-class mothers for their daughters. Interestingly enough, in large mental hospitals the patient sometimes symbolizes a complete coming out by his first active participation in the hospital wide patient dance.

31. See Goffman, "Characteristics of Total Institutions," pp. 43–84; in *Proceedings*

of the Symposium of Preventive and Social Psychiatry; Washington, D.C., Walter Reed Army Institute of Research, 1958.

32. A good description of the ward system may be found in Ivan Belknap, *Human Problems of a State Mental Hospital*; New York, McGraw-Hill, 1956; see especially p. 164.

33. Here is one way in which mental hospitals can be worse than concentration camps and prisons as places in which to "do" time; in the latter, self-insulation from the symbolic implications of the settings may be easier. In fact, self-insulation from hospital settings may be so difficult that patients have to employ devices for this which staff interpret as psychotic symptoms.

34. In regard to convicts, see Anthony Heckstall-Smith, *Eighteen Months*; London, Wingate, 1954; pp. 52–53. For 'wino's' see the discussion in Howard G. Bain, "A Sociological Analysis of the Chicago Skid-Row Lifeway;" unpublished M.A. thesis, Dept. of Sociology, Univ. of Chicago, Sept., 1950; especially "The Rationale of the Skid-Row Drinking Group," pp. 141–146. Bain's neglected thesis is a useful source of material on moral careers.

Apparently one of the occupational hazards of prostitution is that clients and other professional contacts sometimes persist in expressing sympathy by asking for a defensible dramatic explanation for the fall from grace. In having to bother to have a sad tale ready, perhaps the prostitute is more to be pitied than damned. Good examples of prostitute sad tales may be found in Sir Henry Mayhew, "Those that Will Not Work," pp. 210–272; in his *London Labour and the London Poor*, Vol. 4; London, Griffin, Bohn, and Cox, 1862. For a contemporary source, see *Women of the Streets*, edited by C. H. Rolph; London, Zecker and Warburg, 1955; especially p. 6. "Almost always, however, after a few comments on the police, the girl would begin to explain how it was that she was in the life, usually in terms of self-justification." Lately, of course, the psychological expert has helped out the profession in the construction of wholly remarkable sad tales. See, for example, Harold Greenwald, *Call Girl*; New York, Ballantine, 1958.

35. A similar self-protecting rule has been observed in prisons. Thus, Hassler, see footnote 6, in describing a conversation with a fellow-prisoner; "He didn't say much about why he was sentenced, and I didn't ask him, that being the accepted behavior in prison" (p. 76). A novelistic version for the mental hospital may be found in J. Kerkhoff, *How Thin the Veil: A Newspaperman's Story of His Own Mental Crack-up and Recovery*; New York, Greenberg, 1952; p. 27.

36. From the writer's field notes of informal interaction with patients, transcribed as near verbatim as he was able.

37. The process of examining a person psychiatrically and then altering or reducing his status in consequence is known in hospital and prison parlance as *bugging*, the assumption being that once you come to the attention of the testers you either will automatically be labeled crazy or the process of testing itself will make you crazy. Thus psychiatric staff are sometimes seen not as *discovering* whether you are sick, but as *making* you sick; and "Don't bug me, man," can mean, "Don't pester me to the point where I'll get upset." Sheldon Messenger has suggested to me that this meaning of bugging is related to the other colloquial meaning, of wiring a room with a secret microphone to collect information usable for discrediting the speaker.

30 / Schizophrenic Patients in the Psychiatric Interview: An Experimental Study of their Effectiveness at Manipulation

BENJAMIN M. BRAGINSKY
DOROTHEA D. BRAGINSKY[1]

The present investigation is concerned with the manipulative behavior of hospitalized schizophrenics in evaluative interview situations. More specifically, the study attempts to answer the question: Can schizophrenic patients effectively control the impressions (impression management, Goffman, 1959) they make on the professional hospital staff?

Typically, the mental patient has been viewed as an extremely ineffectual and helpless individual (e.g., Arieti, 1959; Becker, 1964; Bellak, 1958; Joint Commission on Mental Illness and Health, 1961; Redlich & Freedman, 1966; Schooler & Parkel, 1966; Searles, 1965). For example, Redlich and Freedman (1966) described the mental patient and his pathological status in the following manner: "There is a concomitant loss of focus and coherence and a profound shift in the meaning and value of social relationships and goal directed behavior. This is evident in the inability realistically to implement future goals and present satisfactions; they are achieved magically or through fantasy and delusion . . . [p. 463]." Schooler and Parkel (1966) similarly underline the mental patients' ineffectual status in this description: "the chronic schizophrenic is not Seneca's 'reasoning animal,' or Spinoza's 'social animal,' or even a reasonably efficient version of Cassirer's 'symbol using animal'. . . . Since he violates so many functional definitions of man, there is heuristic value in studying him with an approach like that which would be used to study an alien creature [p. 67]."

Thus, the most commonly held assumptions concerning the nature of the schizophrenic patient stress their ineffectuality and impotency.

In this context one would expect schizophrenics to perform less than adequately in interpersonal situations, to be unable to initiate manipulative tactics, and, certainly, to be incapable of successful manipulation of other people.[2]

In contrast to the above view of the schizophrenic, a less popular orientation has been expressed by Artiss (1959), Braginsky, Grosse, and Ring (1966), Goffman (1961), Levinson and Gallagher (1964), Rakusin and Fierman (1963), Szasz (1961, 1965), and Towbin (1966). Here schizophrenics are portrayed in terms usually reserved for neurotics and normal persons. Simply, the above authors subscribe to the beliefs that: (a) the typical schizophrenic patient, as compared to normals, is not deficient, defective, or dissimiliar in intrapsychic functioning; (b) the typical schizophrenic patient is not a victim of his illness; that is, it is assumed that he is not helpless and unable to control his behavior or significantly determine life outcomes; (c) the differences that some schizophrenic patients manifest (as compared to normals) are assumed to be more accurately understood in terms of differences in belief systems, goals, hierarchy of needs, and interpersonal strategies, rather than in terms of illness, helplessness, and deficient intrapsychic functioning. This orientation leads to the expectation that schizophrenic patients do try to achieve particular goals and, in the process, effectively manipulate other people.

There is some evidence in support of his viewpoint (e.g., Artiss, 1959; Braginsky, Holzberg, Finison, & Ring, 1967; Levinson & Gallagher, 1964). Furthermore, a recent study (Braginsky et al., 1966) demonstrated that schizophrenic patients responded, on a paper-and-pencil "mental status" test, in a manner that would protect their self-interests. Those who wanted to remain in the hospital (chronic patients) presented themselves as "sick," whereas those who desired to be discharged (first admissions) presented themselves as "healthy." That is, they effectively controlled the impressions they wished to make on others. Their manipulative performance, however, was mediated by an impersonal test.

Therefore, the following question is asked: Can schizophrenics engage in similar manipulative behaviors in a "face-to-face" interview with a psychologist? That is, will chronic schizophrenics who desire to remain in the hospital and live on open wards present themselves in an interview situation when they perceive that their open ward status is being questioned as (a) "healthy" and, therefore, eligible for open ward living, and in another interview situation when their residential status is being questioned as (b) "sick" and, therefore, ineligible for discharge? If so, are their performances convincing to a professional audience (i.e., psychiatrists)?

METHOD

A sample of 30 long-term (more than 2 continuous years of hospitalization) male schizophrenics living on open wards was randomly selected from ward rosters. Two days prior to the experiment the patients were told that they were scheduled for an interview with a staff psychologist. Although each patient was to be interviewed individually, all 30 were brought simultaneously to a waiting room. Each patient interviewed was not allowed to return to this room, to insure that patients who had participated would not communicate with those who had not.

Each patient was escorted to the interview room by an assistant, who casually informed the patient in a tone of confidentiality about the purpose of the interview (preinterview induction). Patients were randomly assigned by the assistant to one of three induction conditions (10 to each condition). The interviewer was unaware of the induction to which the patients were assigned, thereby eliminating interviewer bias.

Induction Conditions

Discharge induction. Patients were told: "I think the person you are going to see is interested in examining patients to see whether they might be ready for discharge."

Open ward induction.[3] Patients were told: "I think that the person you are going to see is interested in examining patients to see whether they should be on open or closed wards."

Mental status induction.[4] Patients were told: "I think the person you are going to see is interested in how you are feeling and getting along in the hospital."

After greeting each patient the interviewer asked: "How are you feeling?" Patients who responded only with physical descriptions were also asked: "How do you feel mentally?" whereas those who only gave descriptions of their mental state were asked: "How are you feeling physically?" The patients' responses were tape-recorded. The interview was terminated after 2 minutes,[5] whereupon the purpose of the experiment was disclosed.

Three staff psychiatrists from the same hospital separately rated each of the 30 tape-recorded interviews during two 40-minute sessions. The psychiatrists had no knowledge of the experiment, and they were unfamiliar with the patients; they were told by the experimenter that these were mental patients residing in the hospital and that as a group they represented a wide range of diagnostic categories.

The psychiatrists rated the patients on the following dimensions: (a) the patient's degree of psychopathology, using a five-point scale ranging from "not at all ill" to "extremely ill"; (b) the amount of hospital control a patient needed, ranging on an eight-point scale from complete freedom ("discharge") to maximum control ("closed ward, continual observation"); and (c) the structural or qualitative aspects of the patient's speech, such as pressure of speech, affect, volume, etc. The score for each patient's speech characteristic was based on the sum of the psychiatrist's rating of 14 Lorr scale items (Lorr, 1953). Each item was rated on an eight-point scale ranging from not at all atypical to extremely atypical verbal behavior.

Predictions

If long-term patients are both motivated to live on open wards and to remain in the hospital and if, in addition, they effectively engage in impression management in order to realize these desires, then the following would be expected:

1. Psychiatrists will rate patients in the discharge and the mental status conditions as being similar with respect to psychopathology and need for hospital control. Mental status interviews are generally used by the hospital to evaluate patients for discharge; therefore, the mental status and discharge conditions offer the same potential consequences for patients. Thus, patients in both conditions will give the impression of being "sick" and in need of hospital control in order to decrease the probability of discharge. The purpose of including the discharge induction was to present the consequences of the interview as explicitly as in the open ward induction.

2. Psychiatrists will rate the patients in the open ward condition significantly less mentally ill and less in need of hospital control than patients in the discharge and mental status conditions. That is, patients in the open ward condition will give the impression of being "healthy" in order to maximize their chances of remaining on an open ward.

Subjects

The mean age of the patients was 47.4 years ($SD = 8.36$). The mean educational level of the group was 8.05 years of schooling ($SD = 3.44$). The median length of hospitalization was 10 years. In terms of diagnostic categories, 43% of the sample was diagnosed as chronic undifferentiated schizophrenic, 37% as paranoid schizophrenic, 10% as catatonic, and the remaining 10% as simple schizophrenic. There were no differences between the three experimental groups on any of the above variables.

RESULTS AND DISCUSSION

The reliability coefficients of the three psychiatrists' combined ratings of the patient interviews were as follows: (a) ratings of psychopathology—$r = 89, p < .01$; (b) need for hospital control—$r = .74, p < .01$; (c) normality of speech characteristics—$r = .65, p < .01$. Thus, it was concluded that there was significant agreement between the three psychiatrists.

The means of the psychopathology ratings by experimental condition are presented in Table 1. The ratings ranged 1–5. The analysis of variance of the data yielded a significant condition effect ($F = 9.38, p < .01$). The difference between the open ward and discharge conditions was statistically significant ($p < .01$; Turkey multiple-range test). In addition, the difference between the open ward and the mental status condition was significant ($p < .01$). As predicted, there was no significant difference between the discharge and mental status conditions.

The means of the ratings of need for hospital control are presented in Table 1. These ratings ranged 1–8. The analysis of these data indicated a significant difference between the means ($F = 3.85, p < .05$). Again, significant differences (beyond the .05 level) were obtained between the open ward and the discharge conditions, as well as between the open ward and mental status conditions. No difference was found between the discharge and mental status conditions.

Table 1 / Mean Psychopathology and Need-for-Hospital-Control Ratings by Experimental Condition

Rating	OPEN WARD		MENTAL STATUS		DISCHARGE	
	M	SD	M	SD	M	SD
Psychopathology	2.63	.58	3.66	.65	3.70	.67
Need for hospital control	2.83	1.15	4.10	1.31	4.20	1.42

On the basis of these analyses it is clear that patients in the open ward condition appear significantly less mentally ill and in less need of hospital control than patients in either the discharge or mental status conditions. Obviously the patients in these conditions convey different impressions in the interview situation. In order to ascertain the manner by which the patients conveyed these different impressions, the following three manipulative tactics were examined: (a) number of positive statements patients made about themselves, (b) number of negative statements made about themselves (these include both physical and mental referents), and (c) normality of speech characteristics (i.e., how "sick" they sounded, independent of the content of speech). The first two indexes were obtained by counting the number of positive or negative self-referent statements a patient made during the interview. These counts were done by three judges independently, and the reliability coefficient was .95. The third index was based on the psychiatrists' ratings on 14 Lorr scale items of the speech characteristics of patients. A score was obtained for each patient by summing the ratings for the 14 scales.

Ratings of psychopathology and need for hospital control were, in part, determined by the frequency of positive and negative self-referent statements. The greater the frequency of positive statements made by a patient, the less ill he was perceived ($r = -.58, p < .01$) and the less in need of hospital control ($r = -.41, p < .05$). Conversely, the greater the frequency of negative statements, the more ill a patient was perceived ($r = .53, p < .01$) and the more in need of hospital control ($r = .37, p < .05$). It is noteworthy that patients were consistent in their performances; that is, those who tended to say positive things about themselves tended not to say negative things ($r = -.55, p < .01$).

When self-referent statements were compared by condition, it was found that patients in the open ward condition presented themselves in a significantly more positive fashion than patients in the discharge and mental status conditions. Only 2 patients in the open ward condition reported having physical or mental problems, whereas 13 patients in the mental status and discharge conditions presented such complaints ($X^2 = 5.40, p < .05$).

The frequency of positive and negative self-referent statements, however, cannot account for important qualitative components of the impressions the patients attempted to convey. For example, a patient may give only one complaint, but it may be serious (e.g., he reports hallucinations), whereas another patient may state five complaints, all of which are relatively benign. In order to examine the severity of symptoms or complaints reported by patients, the number of "psychotic" complaints, namely, reports of hallucinations or bizzare delusions, was tallied. None of the patients in the open ward condition made reference to having had hallucinations or delusions, while nine patients in the discharge and mental status conditions spontaneously made such reference ($X^2 = 4.46, p < .05$).

In comparing the structural or qualitative aspects of patient speech no significant differences were obtained between experimental conditions. Patients "sounded" about the same in all three conditions. The majority of patients (80%) were rated as having relatively normal speech characteristics. Although there were no differences by condition, there was a significant inverse relationship ($r = -.35, p < .05$) between quality of speech and the number of positive statements made. That is, patients were consistent to the extent that those who sounded ill tended not to make positive self-referent statements.

In summary then, the hypotheses were confirmed. It is clear that patients responded to the inductions in a manner which maximized the chances of fulfilling their needs and goals. When their self-interests were at stake patients could present themselves in a face-to-face interaction as either "sick" or "healthy," whichever was more appropriate to the situation. In the context of this experiment "sick" impressions were conveyed when the patients were faced with the possibility of discharge. On the other hand, impressions of "health" were conveyed when the patients' open ward status was questioned. Moreover, the impressions they conveyed were convincing to an audience of experienced psychiatrists.

One may argue, however, that the differences between the groups were a function of differential anxiety generated by the inductions rather than a function of the patients' needs, goals, and manipulative strategies. More specifically, the discharge and the mental status conditions would generate more anxiety and, therefore, more pathological behavior than the open ward condition. As a result, the psychiatrists rated the patients in the discharge and mental status conditions as "sicker" than patients in the open ward condition. According to this argument, then, the patients who were rated as sick were, in fact, more disturbed, and those rated healthy were, in fact, less disturbed.

No differences, however, were found between conditions in terms of the amount of disturbed behavior during the interview. As was previously mentioned, the psychiatrists did not perceive any differences by condition in atypicality of verbal behavior. On the contrary, the patients were judged as sounding relatively normal. Thus, the psychiatrists' judgments of psychopathology were based primarily on the symptoms patients reported rather than on symptoms manifested. Patients did not behave in a disturbed manner; rather, they told the interviewer how disturbed they were.

The traditional set of assumptions concerning schizophrenics, which stresses their irrationality and interpersonal ineffectuality, would not only preclude the predictions made in this study, but would fail to explain parsimoniously the present observations. It is quite plausible and simple to view these findings in terms of the assumptions held about people in general; that is, schizophrenics, like normal persons, are goal-oriented and are able to control the outcomes of their social encounters in a manner which satisfies their goals.

References

Arieti, S. *American handbook of psychiatry.* New York: Basic Books, 1959.

Artiss, K. L. *The symptom as communication in schizophrenia.* New York: Grune & Stratton, 1959.

Becker, E. *The revolution in psychiatry.* London: Collier-Macmillan, 1964.

Bellack, C. *Schizophrenia: A review of the syndrome.* New York: Logos Press, 1958.

Braginsky, B., Grosse, M., & Ring, K. Controlling outcomes through impression-management: An experimental study of the manipulative tactics of mental patients. *Journal of Consulting Psychology,* 1966, 30, 295–300.

Braginsky, B., Holzberg, J., Finison, L., & Ring, K. Correlates of the mental patient's acquisition of hospital information. *Journal of Personality,* 1967, 35, 323–342.

Goffman, E. *The presentation of self in everyday life.* New York: Doubleday, 1959.

Goffman, E. *Asylums.* New York: Doubleday, 1961.

Joint Commission on Mental Illness and Health. *Action for mental health.* New York: Basic Books, 1964.

Levinson, D. S., & Gallagher, E. B. *Patienthood in the mental hospital.* Boston: Houghton-Mifflin, 1964.

Lorr, M. Multidimensional scale for rating psychiatric patients. *Veterans Administration Technical Bulletin,* 1953, 51, 119–127.

Rakusin, J. M., & Fierman, L. B. Five assumptions for treating chronic psychotics. *Mental Hospitals,* 1963, 14, 140–148.

Redlich, F. C., & Freedman, D. T. *The theory and practice of psychiatry.* New York: Basic Books, 1966, 29, 67–77.

Schooler, C., & Parkel, D. The overt behavior of chronic schizophrenics and its relationship to their internal state and personal history. *Psychiatry,* 1966, 29, 67–77.

Searles, H. F. *Collected papers on schizophrenia and related subjects.* New York: International Universities Press, 1965.

Szasz, T. S. *The myth of mental illness.* New York: Hoeber-Harper, 1961.

Szasz, T. S. *Psychiatric justice.* New York: Macmillan, 1965.

Towrin, A. P. Understanding the mentally deranged. *Journal of Existentialism,* 1966, 7, 63–83.

Notes

1. The authors would like to express their appreciation to Doris Seiler and Dennis Ridley for assisting with the data collection.

2. This statement is explicitly derived from formal theories of schizophrenia and not from clinical observations. It is obvious to some observers, however, that schizophrenics do attempt to manipulate others. The discrepancy between these observations

and traditional theoretical assumptions about the nature of schizophrenics is rarely, if ever, reconciled.

3. It may be suggested that the open ward induction was meaningless, since no patient enjoying open ward status would believe that he could be put on a closed ward on the basis of an interview. At the time this experiment was being conducted, however, this hospital was in the process of reorganization, and open and closed ward status was a salient and relevant issue.

4. Mental status evaluation interviews are typically conducted yearly. Thus, patients who have been in the hospital for more than a year expect to be interviewed for the purposes of determining their residency status.

5. Although, admittedly, psychiatrists would never base decisions concerning mental status and discharge on a 2-minute interview, it was adequate for the purposes of this study (namely, to determine if mental patients effectively engage in impression management). The 2-minute response to the single question provided sufficient information for psychiatrists to form reliable impressions of the patients. Interestingly, the typical mental status interview conducted by these psychiatrists is rarely longer than 30 minutes.

31 / Two Studies of Legal Stigma

RICHARD D. SCHWARTZ
JEROME H. SKOLNICK

Legal thinking has moved increasingly toward a sociologically meaningful view of the legal system. Sanctions, in particular, have come to be regarded in functional terms.[1] In criminal law, for instance, sanctions are said to be designed to prevent recidivism by rehabilitating, restraining, or executing the offender. They are also said to be intended to deter others from the performance of similar acts and, sometimes, to provide a channel for the expression of retaliatory motives. In such civil actions as tort or contract, monetary awards may be intended as retributive and deterrent, as in the use of punitive damages, or may be regarded as a *quid pro quo* to compensate the plaintiff for his wrongful loss.

While these goals comprise an integral part of the rationale of law, little is known about the extent to which they are fulfilled in practice. Lawmen do not as a rule make such studies, because their traditions and techniques are not designed for a systematic examination of the operation of the legal system in action, especially outside the courtroom. Thus, when extra-legal consequences—e.g., the social stigma of a prison sentence—are taken into account at all, it is through the discretionary actions of police, prosecutor, judge, and jury. Systematic information on a variety of unanticipated outcomes, those which benefit the accused as well as those which hurt him, might help to inform these decision makers and perhaps lead to changes in substantive law as well. The present paper is an attempt to study the consequences of stigma associated with legal accusation.

From a sociological viewpoint, there are several types of indirect consequences of legal sanctions which can be distinguished. These include differential deterrence, effects on the sanctionee's associates, and variations in the degree of deprivation which sanction imposes on the recipient himself.

First, the imposition of sanction, while intended as a matter of overt policy to deter the public at large, probably will vary in its effectiveness as a deterrent, depending upon the extent to which potential offenders perceive themselves as similar to the sanctionee. Such "differential deterrence" would occur if white-collar anti-trust violators were restrained by the conviction of General Electric executives, but not by invocation of the Sherman Act against union leaders.

The imposition of a sanction may even provide an unintended incentive to violate the law. A study of factors affecting compliance with federal income tax laws provides some evidence of this effect.[2] Some respondents reported that they began to cheat on their tax returns only *after* convictions for tax evasion had been obtained against others in their jurisdiction. They explained this surprising behavior by noting that the prosecutions had always been conducted against blatant violators and not against the kind of moderate offenders which they then became. These respondents were, therefore, unintentionally educated to the possibility of supposedly "safe" violations.

Second, deprivations or benefits may accrue to non-sanctioned individuals by virtue of the web of affiliations that join them to the defendant. The wife and family of a convicted man may, for instance, suffer from his arrest as much as the man himself. On the other hand, they may be relieved by his absence if the family relationship has been an unhappy one. Similarly, whole groups of persons may be affected by sanctions to an individual, as when discriminatory practices increase because of a highly publicized crime attributed to a member of a given minority group.

Finally, the social position of the defendant himself will serve to aggravate or alleviate the effects of any given sanction. Although all three indirect consequences may be interrelated, it is the third with which this paper will be primarily concerned.

FINDINGS

The subjects studied to examine the effects of legal accusation on occupational positions represented two extremes: lower-class unskilled workers charged with assault, and medical doctors accused of malpractice. The first project lent itself to a field experiment, while the second required a survey design. Because of differences in method and substance, the studies cannot be used as formal controls for each other. Taken together, however, they do suggest that the indirect effects of sanctions can be powerful, that they can produce unintended harm or unexpected benefit, and that the results are related to officially unemphasized aspects of the social context in which the sanctions are administered. Accordingly, the two studies will be discussed together, as bearing on one another. Strictly speaking, however, each can, and properly should, stand alone as a separate examination of the unanticipated consequences of legal sanctions.

Study I. The Effects of a Criminal Court Record on the Employment Opportunities of Unskilled Workers

In the field experiment, four employment folders were prepared, the same in all respects except for the criminal court record of the applicant. In all of the folders he was described as a thirty-two year old single male of unspecified race, with a high school training in mechanical trades, and a record of successive short term jobs as a kitchen helper, maintenance worker, and handyman. These characteristics are roughly typical of applicants for unskilled hotel jobs in the Catskill resort area of New York State where employment opportunities were tested.[3]

The four folders differed only in the applicant's reported record of criminal court involvement. The first folder indicated that the applicant had been convicted and sentenced for assault; the second, that he had been tried for assault and acquitted; the third, also tried for assault and acquitted, but with a letter from the judge certifying the finding of not guilty and reaffirming the legal presumption of innocence. The fourth folder made no mention of any criminal record.

A sample of one hundred employers was utilized. Each employer was assigned to one of four "treatment" groups.[4] To each employer only one folder was shown; this folder was one of the four kinds mentioned above, the selection of the folder being determined by the treatment group to which the potential employer was assigned. The employer was asked whether he could "use" the man described in the folder. To preserve the reality of the situation and make it a true field experiment, employers were never given any indication that they were participating in an experiment. So far as they knew, a legitimate offer to work was being made in each showing of the folder by the "employment agent."

The experiment was designed to determine what employers would do in fact if confronted with an employment applicant with a criminal record. The questionnaire approach used in earlier studies[5] seemed ill-adapted to the problem, since respondents confronted with hypothetical situations might be particularly prone to answer in what they considered a socially acceptable manner. The second alternative—studying job opportunities of individuals who had been involved with the law—would have made it very difficult to find comparable groups of applicants and potential employers. For these reasons, the field experiment reported here was utilized.

Some deception was involved in the study. The "employment agent"—the same individual in all hundred cases—was in fact a law student who was working in the Catskills during the summer of 1959 as an insurance adjuster. In representing himself as being both an adjuster and an employment agent, he was assuming a combination of roles which is not uncommon there. The adjuster role gave him an opportunity to introduce a single application for employment casually and naturally. To the extent that the experiment worked, however, it was inevitable that some employers should be led to believe that they had immediate prospects of filling a job opening. In those instances where an offer to hire was made, the "agent" called a few hours later to say that the applicant had taken another job. The field experimenter attempted in such instances to locate a satisfactory replacement by contacting an employment agency in the area. Because this procedure was used and since the jobs involved were of relatively minor consequence, we believe that the deception caused little economic harm.

As mentioned, each treatment group of twenty-five employers was approached with one type of folder. Responses were dichotomized: those who expressed a willingness to consider the applicant in any way were termed positive; those who made no response or who explicitly refused to consider the candidate were termed negative. Our results consist of comparisons between positive and negative responses, thus defined, for the treatment groups.

Of the twenty-five employers shown the "no record" folder, nine gave positive responses. Subject to reservations arising from chance variations in sampling, we take this as indicative of the "ceiling" of jobs available for this kind of applicant under the given field conditions. Positive responses by these employers may be compared with those in the other treatment groups to obtain an indication of job opportunities lost because of the various legal records.

Of the twenty-five employers approached with the "convict" folder, only one expressed interest in the applicant. This is a rather graphic indication of the effect which a criminal record may have on job opportunities. Care must be exercised, of course, in generalizing the conclusions to other settings. In this context, however, the criminal record made a major difference.

From a theoretical point of view, the finding leads toward the conclusion that conviction constitutes a powerful form of "status degradation"[6] which continues to operate after the time when, according to the generalized theory of justice underlying punishment in our society, the individual's "debt" has been paid. A record of conviction produces a durable if not permanent loss of status. For purposes of effective social control, this state of affairs may heighten the deterrent effect of conviction—though that remains to be established. Any such contribution to social control, however, must be balanced against the barriers imposed upon rehabilitation of the convict. If the ex-prisoner finds difficulty in securing menial kinds of legitimate work, further crime may become an increasingly attractive alternative.[7]

Another important finding of this study concerns the small number of positive responses elicited by the "accused but acquitted" applicant. Of the twenty-five employers approached with this folder, three offered jobs. Thus, the individual accused but acquitted of assault has almost as much trouble finding even an unskilled job as the one who was not only accused of the same offense, but also convicted.

From a theoretical point of view, this result indicates that permanent lowering of status is not limited to those explicitly singled out by being convicted of a crime. As an ideal outcome of American justice, criminal procedure is supposed to distinguish between the "guilty" and those who have been acquitted. Legally controlled consequences which follow the judgment are consistent with this purpose. Thus, the "guilty" are subject to fine and imprisonment, while those who are acquitted are immune from these sanctions. But deprivations may be imposed on the acquitted, both before and after victory in court. Before trial, legal rules either permit or require arrest and detention. The suspect may be faced with the expense of an attorney and a bail bond if he is to mitigate these limitations on his privacy and freedom. In addition, some pre-trial deprivations are imposed without formal legal permission. These may include coercive questioning, use of violence, and stigmatization. And, as this study indicates, some deprivations not under the direct control of the legal process may develop or persist after an official decision of acquittal has been made.

Thus two legal principles conflict in practice. On the one hand, "a man is innocent until proven guilty." On the other, the accused is systematically treated as guilty under the administration of criminal law until a functionary or official body—police, magistrate, prosecuting attorney, or trial judge or jury—decides that he is entitled to be free. Even then, the results of treating him as guilty persist and may lead to serious consequences.

The conflict could be eased by measures aimed at reducing the deprivations imposed on the accused, before and after acquittal. Some legal attention has been focused on pre-trial deprivations. The provision of bail and counsel, the availability of habeas corpus, limitations on the admissability of coerced confessions, and civil actions for false arrest are examples of measures aimed at protecting the rights of the accused before trial. Although these are often limited in effectiveness, especially for individuals of lower socioeconomic status, they at least represent some concern with implementing the presumption of innocence at the pretrial stage.

By contrast, the courts have done little toward alleviating the post-acquittal consequences of legal accusation. One effort along these lines has been employed in the federal courts, however. Where an individual has been accused and exonerated of a crime, he may petition the federal courts for a "Certificate of Innocence" certifying this fact.[8] Possession of such a document might be expected to alleviate post-acquittal deprivations.

Some indication of the effectiveness of such a measure is found in the responses of the final treatment group. Their folder, it will be recalled, contained information on the accusation and acquittal of the applicant, but also included a letter from a judge addressed "To whom it may concern" certifying the applicant's acquittal and reminding the reader of the presumption of innocence. Such a letter might have had a boomerang effect, by reemphasizing the legal involvement of the applicant. It was important, therefore, to determine empirically whether such a communication would improve or harm the chances of employment. Our findings indicate that it increased employment opportunities, since the letter folder elicited six positive responses. Even though this fell short of the nine responses to the "no record" folder, it doubled the number for the "accused but acquitted" and created a significantly greater number of job offers than those elicited by the convicted record. This suggests that the procedure merits consideration as a means of offsetting the occupational loss resulting from accusation. It should be noted, however, that repeated use of this device might reduce its effectiveness.

The results of the experiment are summarized in Table 1. The differences in outcome found there indicate that various types of legal records are systematically related to job opportunities. It seems fair to infer also that the trend of job losses corresponds with the apparent punitive intent of the authorities. Where the man is convicted, that intent is presumably greatest. It is less where he is accused but acquitted and still less where the court makes an effort to emphasize the absence of a finding of guilt. Nevertheless, where the difference in punitive intent is ideally greatest, between conviction and acquittal, the difference in occupational harm is very slight. A similar blurring of this distinction shows up in a different way in the next study.

Study II: The Effects on Defendants Of Suits for Medical Malpractice

As indicated earlier, the second study differed from the first in a number of ways: method of research, social class of accused, relationship between the accused and his "employer," social support available to accused, type of offense and its possible relevance to occupational adequacy. Because the two studies differ in so many ways, the reader is again cautioned to avoid thinking of them as providing a

Table 1 / Effect of Four Types of Legal Folder on Job Opportunities (in per cent)

	No record	Acquitted with letter	Acquitted without letter	Convicted	Total
	(N = 25)	(N = 25)	(N = 25)	(N = 25)	(N = 100)
Positive response	36	24	12	4	19
Negative response	64	76	88	96	81
Total	100	100	100	100	100

rigorous comparative examination. They are presented together only to demonstrate that legal accusation can produce unanticipated deprivations, as in the case of Study I, or unanticipated benefits, as in the research now to be presented. In the discussion to follow, some of the possible reasons for the different outcomes will be suggested.

The extra-legal effects of a malpractice suit were studied by obtaining the records of Connecticut's leading carrier of malpractice insurance. According to these records, a total of 69 doctors in the State had been sued in 64 suits during the post World War II period covered by the study, September, 1945, to September, 1959.[9] Some suits were instituted against more than one doctor, and four physicians had been sued twice. Of the total of 69 physicians, 58 were questioned. Interviews were conducted with the approval of the Connecticut Medical Association by Robert Wyckoff, whose extraordinary qualifications for the work included possession of both the M.D. and LL.B. degrees. Dr. Wyckoff was able to secure detailed response to his inquiries from all doctors contacted.

Twenty of the respondents were questioned by personal interview, 28 by telephone, and the remainder by mail. Forty-three of those reached practiced principally in cities, eleven in suburbs, and four in rural areas. Seventeen were engaged in general practice and forty-one were specialists. The sample proved comparable to the doctors in the State as a whole in age, experience, and professional qualifications.[10] The range was from the lowest professional stratum to chiefs of staff and services in the State's most highly regarded hospitals.

Of the 57 malpractice cases reported, doctors clearly won 38; nineteen of these were dropped by the plaintiff and an equal number were won in court by the defendant doctor. Of the remaining nineteen suits, eleven were settled out of court for a nominal amount, four for approximately the amount the plaintiff claimed and four resulted in judgment for the plaintiff in court.

The malpractice survey did not reveal widespread occupational harm to the physicians involved. Of the 58 respondents, 52 reported no negative effects of the suit on their practice, and five of the remaining six, all specialists, reported that their practice *improved* after the suit. The heaviest loser in court (a radiologist), reported the largest gain. He commented, "I guess all the doctors in town felt sorry for me because new patients started coming in from doctors who had not sent me patients previously." Only one doctor reported adverse consequences to his practice. A winner in court, this man suffered physical and emotional stress symptoms which hampered his later effectiveness in surgical work. The temporary drop in his practice appears to have been produced by neurotic symptoms and is therefore only indirectly traceable to the malpractice suit. Seventeen other doctors reported varying degrees of personal dissatisfaction and anxiety during and after the suit, but none of them reported impairment of practice. No significant relationship was found between outcome of the suit and expressed dissatisfaction.

A protective institutional environment helps to explain these results. No cases were found in which a doctor's hospital privileges were reduced following the suit. Neither was any physician unable later to obtain malpractice insurance, although a handful found it necessary to pay higher rates. The State Licensing Commission, which is headed by a doctor, did not intervene in any instance. Local medical societies generally investigated charges through their ethics and grievance committees, but where they took any action, it was almost always to recommend or assist in legal defense against the suit.

DISCUSSION

Accusation has different outcomes for unskilled workers and doctors in the two studies. How may these be explained? First, they might be nothing more than artifacts of research method. In the field experiment, it was possible to see behavior directly, i.e., to determine how employers act when confronted with what appears to them to be a realistic opportunity to hire. Responses are therefore not distorted by the memory of the respondent. By contrast, the memory of the doctors might have been consciously or unconsciously shaped by the wish to create the impression that the public had not taken seriously the accusation leveled against them. The motive for such a distortion might be either to protect the respondent's self-esteem or to preserve an image of public acceptance in the eyes of the interviewer, the profession, and the public. Efforts of the interviewer to assure his subjects of anonymity—intended to offset these effects—may have succeeded or may, on the contrary, have accentuated an awareness of the danger. A related type of distortion might have stemmed from a desire by doctors to affect public attitudes toward malpractice. Two conflicting motives might have been expected to enter here. The doctor might have tended to exaggerate the harm caused by an accusation, especially if followed by acquittal, in order to turn public opinion toward legal policies which would limit malpractice liability. On the other hand, he might tend to underplay extra-legal harm caused by a legally insufficient accusation in order to discourage potential plaintiffs from instituting suits aimed at securing remunerative settlements and/or revenge for grievances. Whether these diverse motives operated to distort doctors' reports and, if so, which of them produced the greater degree of distortion is a matter for speculation. It is only suggested here that the interview method is more subject to certain types of distortion than the direct behavioral observations of the field experiment.

Even if such distortion did not occur, the results may be attributable to differences in research design. In the field experiment, a direct comparison is made between the occupational position of an accused and an identical individual not accused at a single point in time. In the medical study, effects were inferred through retrospective judgment, although checks on actual income would have no doubt confirmed these judgments. Granted that income had increased, many other explanations are available to account for it. An improvement in practice after a malpractice suit may have resulted from factors extraneous to the suit. The passage of time in the community and increased experience may have led to a larger practice and may even have masked negative effects of the suit. There may have been a general increase in practice for the kinds of doctors involved in these suits, even greater for doctors not sued than for doctors in the sample. Whether interviews with a control sample could have yielded sufficiently precise data to rule out these possibilities is problematic. Unfortunately, the resources available for the study did not enable such data to be obtained.

A third difference in the two designs may affect the results. In the field experiment, full information concerning the legal record is provided to all of the relevant decision makers, i.e., the employers. In the medical study, by contrast, the results depend on decisions of actual patients to consult a given doctor. It may be assumed that such decisions are often based on imperfect information, some patients knowing little or nothing about the malpractice suit. To ascertain how much information employers usually have concerning the legal record of the employee and then supply that amount would have been a desirable refinement, but a difficult one. The alternative approach would involve turning the medical study into an experiment in which full information concerning malpractice (e.g., liable, accused but acquitted, no record of accusation) was supplied to potential patients. This would have permitted a comparison of the effects of legal accusation in two instances where information concerning the accusation is constant. To carry out such an experiment in a field situation would require an unlikely degree of cooperation, for instance by a medical clinic which might ask patients to choose their doctor on the basis of information given them. It is difficult to conceive of an experiment along these lines which would be both realistic enough to be valid and harmless enough to be ethical.

If we assume, however, that these methodological problems do not invalidate the basic finding, how may it be explained? Why would unskilled workers accused but acquitted of assault have great difficulty getting jobs, while doctors accused of malpractice—whether acquitted or not—are left unharmed or more sought after than before?

First, the charge of criminal assault carries with it the legal allegation and the popular connotation of intent to harm. Malpractice, on the other hand, implies negligence or failure to exercise reasonable care. Even though actual physical harm may be greater in malpractice, the element of intent suggests that the man accused of assault would be more likely to repeat his attempt and to find the mark. However, it is dubious that this fine distinction could be drawn by the lay public.

Perhaps more important, all doctors and particularly specialists may be immune from the effects of a malpractice suit because their services are in short supply.[11] By contrast, the unskilled worker is one of many and therefore likely to be passed over in favor of someone with a "cleaner" record.

Moreover, high occupational status, such as is demonstrably enjoyed by doctors,[12] probably tends to insulate the doctor from imputations of incompetence. In general, professionals are assumed to possess uniformly high ability, to be oriented toward community service, and to enforce adequate standards within their own organization.[13] Doctors in particular receive deference, just because they are doctors, not only from the population as a whole but even from fellow professionals.[14]

Finally, individual doctors appear to be protected from the effects of accusation by the sympathetic and powerful support they receive from fellow members of the occupation, a factor absent in the case of unskilled, unorganized laborers.[15] The medical society provides advice on handling malpractice actions, for instance, and referrals by other doctors sometimes increase as a consequence of the sympathy felt for the malpractice suit victim. Such assistance is further evidence that the professional operates as "a community within a community,"[16] shielding its members from controls exercised by formal authorities in the larger society.

In order to isolate these factors, additional studies are needed. It would be interesting to know, for instance, whether high occupational status would protect a doctor acquitted of a charge of assault. Information on this question is sparse. Actual instances of assaults by doctors are probably very rare. When and if they do occur, it seems unlikely that they would lead to publicity and prosecution, since police and prosecutor discretion might usually be employed to quash charges before they are publicized. In the rare instances in which they come to public attention, such accusations appear to produce a marked effect because of the assumption that the pressing of charges, despite the status of the defendant, indicates probable guilt. Nevertheless, instances may be found in which even the accusation of first degree murder followed by acquittal appears to have left the doctor professionally unscathed.[17] Similarly, as a test of the group protection hypothesis, one might investigate the effect of an acquittal for assault on working men who are union members. The analogy would be particularly instructive where the union plays an important part in employment decisions, for instance in industries which make use of a union hiring hall.

In the absence of studies which isolate the effect of such factors, our findings cannot readily be generalized. It is tempting to suggest after an initial look at the results that social class differences provide the explanation. But subsequent analysis and research might well reveal significant intra-class variations, depending on the distribution of other operative factors. A lower class person with a scarce specialty and a protective occupational group who is acquitted of a lightly regarded offense might benefit from the accusation. Nevertheless, class in general seems to correlate with the relevant factors to such an extent that in reality the law regularly works to the disadvantage of the already more disadvantaged classes.

CONCLUSION

Legal accusation imposes a variety of consequences, depending on the nature of the accusation and the characteristics of the accused. Deprivations occur, even though not officially intended, in the case of unskilled workers who have been acquitted of assault charges. On the other hand, malpractice actions—even when resulting in a judgment against the doctor—are not usually followed by negative consequences and sometimes have a favorable effect on the professional position of the defendant. These differences in outcome suggest two conclusions: one, the need for more explicit clarification of legal goals; two, the importance of examining the attitudes and social structure of the community outside the courtroom if the legal process is to hit intended targets, while avoiding innocent bystanders. Greater precision in communicating goals and in appraising consequences of present practices should help to make the legal process an increasingly equitable and effective instrument of social control.

Notes

1. Legal sanctions are defined as changes in life conditions imposed through court action.
2. Richard D. Schwartz, "The Effectiveness of Legal Controls: Factors in the Reporting of Minor Items of Income on Federal Income Tax Returns." Paper presented at the annual meeting of the American Sociological Association, Chicago, 1959.
3. The generality of these results remains to be determined. The effects of criminal involvement in the Catskill area are probably diminished, however, by the temporary nature of employment, the generally poor qualifications of the work force, and the excess of demand over supply of unskilled labor there. Accordingly, the employment differences among the four treatment groups found in this study are likely, if anything to be *smaller* than would be expected in industries and areas where workers are more carefully selected.
4. Employers were not approached in pre-selected random order, due to a misunderstanding of instructions on the part of the law student who carried out the experiment during a three and one-half week period. Because of this flaw in the experimental procedure, the results should be treated with appropriate caution. Thus, chi-squared analysis may not properly be utilized. (For those used to this measure, $p < .05$ for table 1.)
5. Sol Rubin, *Crime and Juvenile Delinquency*, New York: Oceana, 1958, pp. 151–156.
6. Harold Garfinkel, "Conditions of Successful Degradation Ceremonies," *American Journal of Sociology*, 61 (March, 1956), pp. 420–24.
7. Severe negative effects of conviction on employment opportunities have been noted by Sol Rubin, *Crime and Juvenile Delinquency*, New York: Oceana, 1958. A further source of employment difficulty is inherent in licensing statutes and security regulations which sometimes preclude convicts from being employed in their pre-conviction occupation or even in the trades which they may have acquired during imprisonment. These effects may, however, be counteracted by bonding arrangements, prison associations, and publicity programs aimed at increasing confidence in, and sympathy for, ex-convicts. See also. B. F. McSally, "Finding Jobs for Released Offenders," *Federal Probation*, 24 (June, 1960), pp. 12–17; Harold D. Lasswell and Richard C. Donnelly, "The Continuing Debate over Responsibility: An Introduction to Isolating the Condemnation Sanction," *Yale Law Journal*, 68 (April, 1959), pp. 869–99; Johs Andeneas, "General Prevention—Illusion or Reality?", *J. Criminal Law*, 43 (July–August, 1952), pp. 176–98.
8. 28 United States Code, Secs. 1495, 2513.
9. A spot check of one county revealed that the Company's records covered every malpractice suit tried in the courts of that county during this period.
10. No relationship was found between any of these characteristics and the legal or extra-legal consequences of the lawsuit.
11. See Eliot Freidson, "Client Control and Medical Practice," *American Journal of Sociology*, 65 (January, 1960), pp. 374–82. Freidson's point is that general practitioners are more subject to client-control than specialists are. Our findings emphasize the importance of professional as compared to client control, and professional protection against a particular form of client control, extending through both branches of the medical profession. However, what holds for malpractice situations may not be true of routine medical practice.
12. National Opinion Research Center, "Jobs and Occupations: A Popular Evaluation," *Opinion News*, 9 (Sept., 1947), pp. 3–13. More recent studies in several countries tend to confirm the high status of the physician. See Alex Inkeles, "Industrial Man: The

Relation of Status to Experience, Perception and Value," *American Journal of Sociology*, 66 (July, 1960), pp. 1–31.

13. Talcott Parsons, *The Social System*, Glencoe: The Free Press, 1951, pp. 454–473; and Everett C. Hughes, *Men and their Work*, Glencoe: The Free Press, 1958.

14. Alvin Zander, Arthur R. Cohen, and Ezra Scotland, *Role Relations in the Mental Health Professions*, Ann Arbor: Institute for Social Research, 1957.

15. Unions sometimes act to protect the seniority rights of members who, discharged from their jobs upon arrest, seek re-employment following their acquittal.

16. See William J. Goode, "Community Within A Community: The Professions," *American Sociological Review*, 22 (April, 1957), pp. 194–200.

17. For instance, the acquittal of Dr. John Bodkin Adams after a sensational murder trial, in which he was accused of deliberately killing several elderly women patients to inherit their estates, was followed by his quiet return to medical practice. *New York Times*, Nov. 24, 1961, p. 28, col. 7. Whether the British regard acquittals as more exonerative than Americans is uncertain.

32 / Rejection: A Possible Consequence of Seeking Help for Mental Disorders

DEREK L. PHILLIPS

The nonconformist, whether he be foreigner or 'odd ball,' intellectual or idiot, genius or jester, individualist or hobo, physically or mentally abnormal—pays a price for 'being different' unless his peculiarity is considered acceptable for his particular group, or unless he lives in a place or period of particularly high tolerance or enlightenment.[1]

The penalty that *mentally ill* persons pay for "being different" is often rejection by others in the community. Following the increased interest of social scientists in the public's attitudes toward the mentally ill,[2] this research investigates some of the factors involved in the rejection of mentally ill individuals.

This paper presents the results of a controlled experiment in influencing people's attitudes toward individuals exhibiting symptoms of mental illness. The research attempts to determine the extent to which people's attitudes toward an individual exhibiting disturbed behavior are related to their knowledge of the particular help-source that the individual is using or has used. The term "help-source" here refers to such community resources as clergymen, physicians, psychiatrists, marriage counselors, mental hygiene clinics, alcohol clinics, and mental hospitals, each of which is frequently concerned with persons having emotional problems.

Most studies concerned with attitudes toward the mentally ill have focused on the individual's behavior as the sole factor determining whether or not he is rejected by others. Other research has considered the importance of psychiatric treatment or hospitalization in *identifying* the individual as mentally ill and, subsequently, leading to his rejection.[3] But as far as could be determined, no study has been made of the importance of utilizing other help-sources in determining or influencing public attitudes toward individuals exhibiting disturbed behavior.

In a number of studies respondents have been asked whether they considered various *descriptions* to be those of mentally ill persons, and some respondents were found unable to recognize certain serious symptoms of disturbed behavior. Star, for example, asking 3500 respondents about six case abstracts of mentally ill persons, found that 17 per cent of the sample said that none of these imaginary persons was sufficiently deviant to represent what they meant by mental illness. Another 28 per cent limited their concept of mental illness to the paranoid, the only description where violence was a prominent feature of the behavior.[4] Elaine and John Cumming, asking questions about the same six descriptions of deviant behavior, found that the majority of people dismissed the descriptions, even when they were clinically grave, as normal, with such comments as "It's just a quirk, it's nothing serious."[5]

Sharply in disagreement with these findings, however, are the results of studies by Lemkau and Crocetti, and by Dohrenwend, Bernard and Kolb. Using three of the Star abstracts, Lemkau and Crocetti found that 91 per cent of their sample identified the paranoid as mentally ill, 78 per cent identified the simple schizophrenic, and 62 per cent identified the alcoholic.[6] Dohrenwend and his associates, interviewing "leaders in an urban area," used the six Star abstracts. They report that "all saw mental illness in the description of paranoid schizophrenia; 72 per cent saw it in the example of simple schizophrenia; 63 per cent in the alcoholic; about 50 per cent in the anxiety neurosis and in the juvenile character disorder; and 40 per cent in the compulsive-phobic."[7] These findings, although somewhat inconsistent, do indicate some public ignorance concerning the signs and symptoms of mental illness. More important here, they tell us nothing about how the public *feels* toward the individuals in these case abstracts.

Hospitalization is another cue that has been found to influence recognition of a person as mentally ill. The Cummings state, "Mental illness, it seems, is a condition which afflicts people who must go to a mental institution, but up until they go almost anything they do is fairly normal."[8]

Apparently some people can correctly identify symptoms of mental illness and others cannot, while for some the mentally ill are only those who have been in a mental hospital. But it seems equally important to ask whether people *reject* individuals displaying symptoms of mental illness or those who have been hospitalized. In part, the task of this research was to determine the extent to which people reject various descriptions of disturbed behavior. An additional cue — the *help-source* that the individual described is utilizing — was presented to the respondents in order to ascertain the importance of the help-source in determining rejection of mentally ill individuals. Four help-sources that people with mental disorders often consult[9] — the clergyman, the physician, the psychiatrist, and the mental hospital — were represented.

Several recent studies have been concerned with the help-sources that people suggest using for mental disorders, as well as the ones they actually have used.[10] Considerable evidence from these studies indicates that people have strong negative attitudes toward psychiatrists and mental hospitals and toward individuals using either of these help-sources.[11] But there seems to be no evidence of negative attitudes toward clergymen or physicians, or toward people consulting these two help-sources. Further, the fact that people with emotional problems are more likely to consult clergymen and physicians than psychiatrists and mental hospitals[12] suggests the absence of strong negative attitudes toward the latter and those utilizing them. Gurin points out that they ". . . are the areas most people turn to with their personal problems; they are the major 'gatekeepers' in the treatment process, either doing the treating themselves or referring to a more specialized professional resource."[13] Both the clergyman and the physician are professionally involved in what are usually defined as "the private affairs" of others. They have what Naegele calls ". . . legitimate access to realms beyond public discussion."[14]

Although it is probably true that the public does not hold negative attitudes toward clergymen and physicians, I suggest that an individual consulting either of these help-sources may more often lose face, and more often be regarded as deviant, than an individual exhibiting the same behavior who does not consult one of these professional resources. How does this come to be so?

As Clausen and Yarrow point out, "There is an ethic of being able to handle one's own problems by oneself, which applies not only to psychiatric problems."[15] Similarly, Ewalt says, "One value in American culture compatible with most approaches to a definition of positive mental health appears to be this: An individual should be able to stand on his own two feet without making undue demands or impositions on others."[16] In another statement of this view, Kadushin reports that, in answer to the question "Would you tell people in general that you came here?" (the Peale-Blanton Religio-Psychiatric Clinic), a respondent replied ". . . I wouldn't tell people in general. I know that there's still a stigma attached to people who seek psychiatric aid, and I guess I'm ashamed that I couldn't manage my own problem."[17]

Thus, an outside observer's knowledge that a person is consulting any of the four help-sources discussed may have at least two important consequences for the individual with a behavior problem: (1) He is defined as someone who *has* a problem. Moreover, the further along the continuum from clergyman to mental hospital the individual moves, the more his problem is seen as a serious one, and individuals consulting a psychiatrist or a mental hospital are very often defined as "mentally ill" or "insane." (2) The individual is defined as unable to handle his problem by himself.

I am suggesting that the reported inability of some persons to recognize certain serious symptoms of disturbed behavior is due to difficulty in evaluating an individual's behavior, and that knowledge about what help-source the individual is utilizing helps others decide whether he is "deviant" or has a problem that he cannot cope with himself. And an important social consequence for the person who, because of his behavior or choice of help-source, is defined as deviant may be *rejection*.

These considerations led to formulation of the following hypothesis: Individuals exhibiting identical behavior will be increasingly rejected as they are described as not seeking any help, as utilizing a clergyman, a physician, a psychiatrist, or a mental hospital.

METHOD

To test this hypothesis, interviews were conducted with a systematic sample[18] of 300 married white females selected from the addresss section of the City Directory of Branford, a southern New England town of approximately 17,000 population.[19] The sample was so small that the need to control for a number of variables was obvious. Thus, males,[20] non-whites, and unmarried respondents were excluded from the sample.

The interviews took place in the respondents' homes and were of 20 to 40 minutes duration. Each respondent was given five cards, one at a time, describing different behaviors. The interviewer read each description aloud from the interview schedule as the respondent followed by reading the card.

Case abstract (A) was a description of a paranoid schizophrenic, (B) an individual suffering from simple schizophrenia, (C) an anxious-depressed person, (D) a phobic individual with compulsive features, and (E) a "normal" person. The first four abstracts were, in the main, the same as those developed by Shirley Star, formerly of the National Opinion Research Center in Chicago.[21] The fifth abstract, that of the "normal"[22] individual, was developed expressly for this research.[23]

The five case abstracts were presented in combination with information about what help-source an individual was utilizing, in the following manner:

(1) Nothing was added to the description of the behavior—this was, of course, the absence of any help.

(2) Affixed to the description was the statement: "He has been going to see his clergyman regularly about the way he is getting along."

(3) Affixed to the description was the statement: "He has been going to see his physician regularly about the way he is getting along."

(4) Affixed to the description was the statement: "He has been going to see his psychiatrist regularly about the way he is getting along."

(5) Affixed to the description was the statement: "He has been in a mental hospital because of the way he was getting along."

This research required an experimental design permitting classification of each of the two independent variables (behavior and help-source) in five categories.[24] Observations for all possible combinations of the values of the two variables would have been desirable, but this clearly was not feasible. Hence the observations were arranged in the form of a Graeco-Latin Square[25] so as to obtain a large amount of information from a relatively small number of observations. Specifically, this type of design enables us to discover: (a) the influence of different types of behavior in determining rejection, and (b) the influence of different help-sources in determining rejection.

The 300 respondents were divided at random into five groups of 60 individuals each. Every individual in each group saw five combinations of behavior and help-source, but no group or individual saw any given behavior or any given help-source more than once. In order to assure that the rejection rates were not affected by the *order* in which individuals saw the combinations, the experiment was designed so that each behavior and each help-source was seen first by one group, second by another, third by another, fourth by another, and last by the remaining group.[26]

Thus, in the Graeco-Latin Square design, three variables were considered (behavior, help-source, and order). The data were classified in five categories on each of these variables. See Figure 1, where the letters in each cell indicate a description of behavior, and the numbers in each cell indicate the help-source utilized. In the top left-hand cell, for example, the letter A indicates that the paranoid schizophrenic was the description seen first by Group 1, and that he was described as seeing help-source 1 (that is, he was not described as seeking any help). Similarly, in the bottom right-hand cell, the letter

Figure 1 / The Graeco-Latin Square Design*

	Order				
	1	*2*	*3*	*4*	*5*
Group 1	A1	B2	C3	D4	E5
Group 2	B3	C4	D5	E1	A2
Group 3	C5	D1	E2	A3	B4
Group 4	D2	E3	A4	B5	C1
Group 5	E4	A5	B1	C2	D3

* N for each cell in the table is 60.

D indicates that the phobic-compulsive person was the abstract seen fifth by Group 5, and that he was described as consulting help-source 3 (a physician).

After reading each combination of behavior and help-source, the respondents were asked a uniform series of questions. These questions made up a social distance scale, indicating how close a relation the respondent was willing to tolerate with the individuals in the case abstracts. This scale was used as the measure of *rejection*, the dependent variable in the research.

The social distance scale consisted of the following items: (1) "Would you discourage your children from marrying someone like this?" (2) "If you had a room to rent in your home, would you be willing to rent it to someone like this?" (3) "Would you be willing to work on a job with someone like this?" (4) "Would you be willing to have someone like this join a favorite club or organization of yours?" (5) "Would you object to having a person like this as a neighbor?"[27]

The range of possible scores for each combination of help-source and behavior was from zero (when no items indicated rejection) through five (when all items indicated rejection). A test of reproducibility was applied and the resulting coefficient was .97, indicating that the scale met acceptable standards; i.e., was a unidimensional scale.

It should be emphasized that each combination of behavior and help-source was seen by 60 respondents. It also bears repeating that each respondent was presented with five combinations of behavior and help-source. Thus, each respondent contributed a rejection score (on the social distance scale) to each of five cells out of the 25 cells in Figure 1. An analysis of variance of the form generally applied to planned experiments was carried out.[28]

RESULTS AND DISCUSSION

Table 1 presents the mean rejection rate for each combination of behavior and help-source. An individual exhibiting a given type of behavior is increasingly rejected as he is described as seeking no help, as seeing a clergyman, as seeing a physician, as seeing a psychiatrist, or as having been in a mental hospital. The relation between the independent variable (help-source) and the dependent variable (rejection) is statistically significant at the .001 level. Furthermore, the reversal in the "paranoid schizophrenic" row is the only one among 25 combinations.[20]

The relation between the other independent variable (behavior) and rejection is also significant at the .001 level. In fact, the F obtained

Table 1 / Rejection Scores[a] for Each Help-Source and Behavior Combination[b]

Behavior	Help-Source Utilized					
	NO HELP	CLERGYMAN	PHYSICIAN	PSYCHIATRIST	MENTAL HOSPITAL	TOTAL
Paranoid Schizophrenic	3.65	3.33	3.77	4.12	4.33	3.84
Simple Schizophrenic	1.10	1.57	1.83	2.85	3.68	2.21
Depressed-Neurotic	1.45	1.62	2.07	2.70	3.28	2.22
Phobic-Compulsive	.53	1.12	1.18	1.87	2.27	1.39
Normal Individual	.02	.22	.50	1.25	1.63	.72
Total	1.35	1.57	1.87	2.56	3.04	—

$$F = 23.53, \quad p < .001$$

[a] Rejection scores are represented by the mean number of items rejected on the Social Distance Scale.

[b] N for each cell in the table is 60.

for the relation between behavior and rejection ($F = 64.52$ is much higher than the F obtained for the relation between help-source and rejection ($F = 23.53$). In other words, when a respondent was confronted with a case abstract containing both a description of their individual's behavior and information about what help-source he was utilizing, the description of behavior played a greater part (i.e., accounted for more variance) than the help-source in determining how strongly she rejected the individual described.

As was indicated earlier, the main purpose of this presentation is to show the extent to which attitudes toward an individual exhibiting symptoms of mental illness are related to knowledge of the particular help-source that he is utilizing. The importance of the type of behavior is of secondary interest here; I have investigated the relation between behavior and rejection mainly to ascertain the *relative* importance of each of the two elements presented in the case abstracts. The relation between behavior and rejection will be fully treated in a future paper.

The totals at the bottom of Table 1 show that the largest increase in the rejection rates occurs when an individual sees a psychiatrist. That is, the rejection rate for individuals described as consulting a physician (1.87) differs from the rejection rate for individuals described as consulting a psychiatrist (2.56) to a degree greater than for any other comparison between two adjacent help-sources. The second largest over-all increase in rejection occurs when the individual is described as having been in a mental hospital, and the smallest net increase (.20) occurs when the individual sees a clergyman, compared to seeking no help at all.

Probably the most significant aspect of the effect of help-source on rejection rates is that, for four of the five case abstracts, the biggest increase in rejection occurs when the individual is described as consulting a psychiatrist, and in three of the five abstracts the second largest increase occurs when the individual is depicted as having been in a mental hospital. Not only are individuals increasingly rejected as they are described as seeking no help, as seeing a clergyman, a physician, a psychiatrist, or a mental hospital, but they are *disproportionately* rejected when described as utilizing the latter two help-sources. This supports the suggestion made earlier that individuals utilizing psychiatrists and mental hospitals may be rejected not only because they have a health problem, and because they are unable to handle the problem themselves, but also because contact with a psychiatrist or a mental hospital defines them as "mentally ill" or "insane."

Despite the fact that the "normal" person is more an "ideal type" than a normal person, when he is described as having been in a mental hospital he is rejected more than a psychotic individual described as not seeking help or as seeing a clergyman, and more than a depressed-neurotic seeing a clergyman. Even when the normal person is described as seeing a psychiatrist, he is rejected more than a simple schizophrenic who seeks no help, more than a phobic-compulsive individual seeking no help or seeing a clergyman or physician.

As was noted previously, there is one reversal in Table 1. The paranoid schizophrenic, unlike the other descriptions, was rejected more strongly when he was described as not utilizing any help-source than when he was described as utilizing a clergyman. The paranoid was described in the case abstract as suspicious, as picking fights with people who did not even know him, and as cursing his wife. His behavior may be so threatening and so obviously deviates from normal behavior, that the respondents feel that he is socially less objectionable when he takes a step to help himself. In other words, the individual *obviously* in need of professional help is in a sense "rewarded" for seeking at least one kind of help, that of the clergyman. And though the paranoid schizophrenic is increasingly rejected when he is described as utilizing a physician, a psychiatrist, and a mental hospital, the relative amount of increase is much less than for the other four case abstracts.

Mentally ill persons whose behavior does not deviate markedly from normal role-expectations may be assigned responsibility for their own behavior. If so, seeking any professional help is an admission of inability to meet this responsibility. An individual whose behavior is markedly abnormal (in this instance, the paranoid schizophrenic) may not, however, be considered responsible for his behavior or for his recovery, and is, therefore, rejected less than other individuals when he seeks professional help.

CONTROLS

To determine whether the findings were spurious, the relation between help-source and rejection was observed under several different controls. The association was maintained within age groups, within religious affiliation groups, within educational attainment groups, and within groups occupying different positions in the status hierarchy.[30] The association was also maintained within groups differing in authoritarianism.[31]

But when (1) experience with someone who had sought help for emotional problems[32] and (2) attitude toward the norm of self-reliance,[33] were controlled, the relation between help-source and rejection was specified.

Table 2 presents the rejection rates for respondents reporting a relative who sought help, those reporting a friend who sought help,

Table 2 / Rejection Scores[a] for All Cases by Help-Source and Acquaintance with Help-Seekers

| Help-Source Utilized | Acquaintance | | |
	RELATIVE (N = 37)	FRIEND (N = 73)	NO ONE (N = 190)
No help-source	2.35	1.45	1.12
Clergyman	2.06	1.45	1.51
Physician	1.30	1.58	2.09
Psychiatrist	2.08	2.53	2.66
Mental Hospital	2.38	2.82	3.25

[a] Rejection scores are represented by the mean number of items rejected on the Social Distance Scale.

and those who knew no one who sought help for emotional problems. For ease of presentation and interpretation, the rejection rates for the five case abstracts have been combined.[34]

There are two points of interest in Table 2. One is the difference in rejection rates *among* the three groups of respondents. But because these interesting differences are peripheral to the central concern here, I will focus, instead, on the second point of interest. This is the consistent increase —*within* two of the three groups of respondents — in rejection scores for persons not seeking any help, utilizing a clergyman, a physician, a psychiatrist, or a mental hospital.

Respondents *not* acquainted with a help-seeker as well as those acquainted with a help-seeking *friend* adhere to the pattern of rejection previously demonstrated in Table 1. But respondents with a help-seeking *relative* deviate markedly from this pattern. They reject persons not seeking help more than they do persons consulting a clergyman, physician, or psychiatrist, and almost as much as those utilizing a mental hospital. And they reject persons consulting a clergyman more than those consulting a physician.

Perhaps respondents with help-seeking relatives are more able to recognize the behavior in the abstracts as that of persons who *need* help and therefore they reject them strongly when they do not seek help. A similar explanation may apply to the rejection of persons using a clergyman. That is, these respondents may see the clergyman as not being what Parsons calls "technically competent help"[35] and equate seeing him with not seeking help. The comparatively low rejection of persons consulting a physician may reflect the respondents' belief that a physician is one of the professional resources that one *should* utilize for emotional problems, and that a physician brings the least stigma to the user; whereas the psychiatrist and the mental hospital, though both competent resources, tend to stigmatize the user much more.[36]

The reader will recall that one of the case abstracts presented to the respondents was that of a "normal" individual. Since respondents with a help-seeking relative may reject the non-help-seeking cases because they are recognized as needing help, including the description of the normal person may "distort" the findings. The rejection rates for the four mentally ill abstracts have, therefore, been separated from those for the normal person and presented in Table 3. Inspection of this table reveals the same pattern found in Table 2, except that the rejection rate for persons utilizing each help-source is somewhat higher than in Table 2.[37]

Turning now to the relation between adherence to the norm of self-reliance and rejection of persons described as using the various help-sources, the data in Table 4 indicate that the association between help-source and rejection is maintained even among those who do not strongly adhere to the norm of self-reliance.[38] Among respondents agreeing either strongly or somewhat to the norm of self-reliance there is a consistent increase in rejection of persons as they moved from no help to the mental hospital. Respondents *not* adhering to the norm of self-reliance, however, reject persons not seeking help more

Table 3 / Rejection Scores[a] for All Mentally Ill Cases by Help-Source and Acquaintance with Help-Seekers

Help-Source Utilized	Acquaintance		
	RELATIVE (N = 37)	FRIEND (N = 73)	NO ONE (N = 190)
No help-source	2.81	1.64	1.16
Clergyman	2.20	1.65	1.86
Physician	1.51	1.91	2.46
Psychiatrist	2.45	2.88	2.90
Mental Hospital	3.04	3.14	3.51

[a] Rejection scores are represented by the mean number of items rejected on the Social Distance Scale.

Table 4 / Rejection Scores[a] for All Cases by Help-Source and Adherence to the Norm of Self-Reliance

Help-Source Utilized	Adherence to Norm of Self-Reliance		
	DISAGREE (N = 28)	AGREE SOMEWHAT (N = 128)	AGREE STRONGLY (N = 144)
No help-source	1.79	1.39	1.22
Clergyman	1.68	1.56	1.52
Physician	1.67	1.87	2.00
Psychiatrist	2.43	2.52	2.65
Mental Hospital	2.64	3.09	3.23

[a] Rejection scores are represented by the mean number of items rejected on the Social Distance Scale.

than they do persons seeing a clergyman or a physician.[39]

This pattern is similar to the one followed by respondents who had help-seeking relatives (see Table 2),[40] and the same general interpretation may be appropriate. Respondents who do not agree that people should handle their own problems may view people seeing a clergyman as "handling their own problems." If this is true, then those not adhering to the norm of self-reliance would be expected to reject persons who see a clergyman, as well as those who seek no help.

Thus, for the great majority of respondents, who either (1) have not had experience with a relative who sought help for emotional problems, or (2) adhere to the norm of self-reliance, help-source and rejection are strongly associated.[41]

On the other hand, respondents who have had experience with a help-seeking relative deviate quite sharply from the rejection pattern of the majority, as do those who do not adhere to the norm of self-reliance. Nevertheless, this deviant pattern appears to make sense theoretically. Those acquainted with a help-seeking relative, having had more exposure to sick-role prescriptions, may be highly rejecting of persons not seeking help because they feel that people should seek "technically competent help." Respondents not adhering to the norm of self-reliance may reject non-help-seekers for a similar reason. They too may feel that handling one's own problems is inappropriate, and that people should seek competent help. And, as suggested previously, both groups may equate help from a clergyman with no help at all.[42]

CONCLUSIONS AND IMPLICATIONS

On the basis of these findings from a southern New England town, the source of help sought by mentally disturbed individuals appears to be strongly related to the degree to which others in the community reject them. Individuals are increasingly rejected as they are described as utilizing no help, as utilizing a clergyman, a physician, a psychiatrist, or a mental hospital.

Controls for age, religion, education, social class, and authoritarianism failed to diminish the relationship, but controls for experience with an emotionally disturbed help-seeker and for adherence to the norm of self-reliance tended to specify it. Respondents who had had experience with a help-seeking relative deviated markedly from the pattern followed by the rest of the sample, as did respondents not adhering to the norm of self-reliance. Both of these groups rejected people seeking no help more than they did those consulting a clergyman or a physician, and respondents with help-seeking relatives also reject non-help-seekers more than those consulting a psychiatrist. Both groups rejected persons seeing a clergyman more than those seeing a physician.

The evidence presented here suggests that a mentally ill person who seeks help may be rejected by others in the community. The findings also have implications for what Mechanic and Volkart call "the inclination to adopt the sick role."[43] We can easily imagine an individual who, because he fears the stigma attached to the help-seeker, does not utilize a professional resource for his problems. Avoiding the possibility of rejection, he also denies himself technically competent help.[44]

Thus the utilization of certain help-sources involves not only a *reward* (positive mental health), but also a *cost* (rejection by others and, consequently, a negative self-image);[45] we need to assess the net balance of gains and losses resulting from seeking help for problems of disturbed behavior.

The present analysis has been concerned with the rejection of help-seekers in hypothetical situations. Future research should be designed so that it would be possible to examine the rejection of help-seekers in "real" situations. Hopefully, the present research will provide some understanding and raise significant questions about the consequences of seeking help for problems of disturbed behavior in our society.

Notes

1. Joint Commission on Mental Illness and Health, *Action for Mental Health*, New York: Science Editions, 1961, p. 69.
2. See, for example, John A. Clausen and Marian R. Yarrow, "Paths to the Mental Hospital," *The Journal of Social Issues*, 11 (November, 1955), pp. 25–32; Elaine and John Cumming, *Closed Ranks: An Experiment in Mental Health Education*, Cambridge: Harvard University Press, 1957; Bruce P. Dohrwend, Viola W. Bernard, and Lawrence C. Kolb, "The Orientations of Leaders in an Urban Area Toward Problems of Mental Illness," *The American Journal of Psychiatry*, 118 (February, 1962), pp. 683–691; Howard E. Freeman and Ozzie G. Simmons, "Mental Patients in the Community," *American Sociological Review*, 23 (April, 1958), pp. 147–154; Gerald Gurin, Joseph Veroff, and Sheila Feld, *Americans View Their Mental Health*, New York: Basic Books, 1960; E. Gartly Jaco, *The Social Epidemiology of Mental Disorders*, New York: Russell Sage Foundation, 1960; Paul V. Lemkau and Guido M. Crocetti, "An Urban Population's Opinion and Knowledge about Mental Illness," *The American Journal of Psychiatry*, 118 (February, 1962), pp. 692–700; Jum C. Nunnally, Jr., *Popular Conceptions of Mental Health*, New York: Holt, Rinehart and Winston, 1961; Glen V. Ramsey and Melita Seipp, "Public Opinions and Information Concerning Mental Health," *Journal of Clinical Psychology*, 4 (October, 1948), pp. 397–406; Charlotte Green Schwartz, "Perspectives on Deviance—Wives' Definitions of Their Husbands' Mental Illness," *Psychiatry*, 20 (August, 1957), pp. 275–291; Shirley Star, "The Place of Psychiatry in Popular Thinking," paper presented at the meeting of the American Association for Public Opinion Research, Washington, D.C., May 1957; Julian L. Woodward, "Changing Ideas on Mental Illness and Its Treatment," *American Sociological Review*, 16 (August, 1951), pp. 443–454.
3. See Clausen and Yarrow, *op. cit.*, and Cumming and Cumming, *op. cit.*
4. Star, *op. cit.*
5. Elaine and John Cumming, "Affective Symbolism, Social Norms, and Mental Illness," *Psychiatry*, 19 (February, 1956), pp. 77–85.
6. Lemkau and Crocetti, *op. cit.*, p. 694.
7. Dohrenwend, Bernard and Kolb, *op. cit.*, p. 635.
8. Cumming and Cumming, *Closed Ranks, op. cit.*, p. 102.
9. See, for example, Gurin, *et al, op. cit.*
10. Dohrenwend, *et al., op. cit.*,; Gurin, *et al., op. cit.*; Ramsey and Seipp, *op. cit.*; Woodward, *op. cit.*
11. Clausen and Yarrow, *op. cit.*; Cumming and Cumming, *op. cit.*; Frederick C. Redlich, "What the Citizen Knows About Psychiatry," *Mental Hygiene*, 34 (January, 1950), pp. 64–70; Star, *op. cit.*
12. Gurin, *et al., op. cit.*, p. 307.
13. *Ibid.*, p. 400.
14. Kasper D. Naegele, "Clergymen, Teachers, and Psychiatrists: A Study in Roles

and Socialization," *The Canadian Journal of Economic and Political Science*, 22 (February, 1956), p. 48.

15. Clausen and Yarrow, *op. cit.*, p. 63.

16. Jack K. Ewalt, intro., Marie Jahoda, *Current Concepts of Positive Mental Health*, New York: Basic Books, 1958, p. xi.

17. Charles Kadushin, "Individual Decisions to Undertake Psychotherapy," *Administrative Science Quarterly*, 3 (December, 1958), p. 389.

Gurin, *et al.*, report that 25 per cent of their respondents who had problems but did not utilize help tried to solve the problems by themselves, *op. cit.*, pp. 350–351.

18. The sample was drawn from the address section of the Directory, with every 15th address marked for interview. The first address was drawn randomly from the first 15 entries; thereafter every 15th address was included until the total sample of 300 was obtained.

19. Twenty-eight of the households drawn in the original sample refused to be interviewed. In each of these cases, a substitution was made by selecting an address at random from the same street. Four of these substitutes refused to be interviewed, necessitating further substitution. Also requiring substitution were three addresses that could not be located and six wives of household heads who were divorced, separated, or widowed, rather than married. Selecting substitutes from the same neighborhood was done on the assumption that persons living in the same neighborhood would resemble one another in certain important ways; they were more likely, than people living in different neighborhoods, to be of similar socio-economic status. Although the possibility of bias still exists, so few substitutions were necessary that, hopefully, the effect is minimal.

20. In a pre-test with a sample of 32 women and 28 men, no significant differences were found between the rejection rates of men and women.

21. Star, *op. cit.*

22. The normal person was described as follows: "Here is a description of a man. Imagine that he is a respectable person living in your neighborhood. He is happy and cheerful, has a good enough job and is fairly well satisfied with it. He is always busy and has quite a few friends who think he is easy to get along with most of the time. Within the next few months he plans to marry a nice young woman he is engaged to."

23. My purpose was to determine (a) whether the rejection of the mentally ill descriptions might in part be accounted for by individuals who rejected everyone regardless of behavior; and (b) whether the utilization of a help-source alone could influence rejection, or whether it was the "combination" of deviant behavior and the use of a help-source that led to rejection.

24. The advantages of including tests of different combinations of two or more variables within one experiment have been cited by several writers concerned with experimental design. For example, D. J. Finney, *The Theory of Experimental Design*, Chicago: The University of Chicago Press, 1960, p. 68, notes the following advantages: "(1) To broaden the basis of inferences relating to one factor by testing that factor under various conditions of others; (2) To assess the extent to which the effects of one factor are modified by the level of others; (3) To economize in experimental material by obtaining information on several factors without increasing the size of the experiment beyond what would be required for one or two factors alone."

25. For two excellent explanations of the Graeco-Latin Square design see, Finney, *op. cit.*, and E. F. Lindquist, *Design of Experiments in Psychology and Education*, Boston: Houghton Mifflin, 1953.

26. In addition, to 50 per cent of the respondents, the paranoid, the depressed individual, and the "normal" person were presented as males, with the simple schizophrenic and the phobic-compulsive individual presented as females. The other half of the sample saw a reversed order—the simple schizophrenic and the compulsive individuals as males, and the paranoid, depressed, and "normal" persons as females. Since both the male case abstracts and the female case abstracts were rejected in accordance with the pattern shown in Table 1, they will not be discussed further in this paper. The findings for the *differences* in the *absolute* rejection of males and females exhibiting a given behavior and utilizing the same help-source will be the subject of a forthcoming paper.

27. The above order duplicates the order of "closeness" represented by the scale. The items, however, were administered to each respondent in a random fashion.

28. See, for example, Lindquist, *op. cit.*, chs. 12 and 13.

29. Following Lindquist, neither orders nor interaction was found to be statistically significant at the .20 level. See Lindquist, *op. cit.*, pp. 273–281.

30. For details of the classification procedures, see pp. 82–88 of the author's doctoral dissertation, of which this research is a part: "Help-Sources and Rejection of the Mentally Ill," unpublished Ph.D. Dissertation, Yale University, 1962.

31. For details of the authoritarian scale, see *ibid.*, p. 77.

32. The question was: "We've been talking about people with worries and problems. Have any of your close friends or relatives had any psychiatric treatment or gone to a hospital or professional person, or community agency, regarding emotional problems?" If the respondent answered in the affirmative, she was asked who this person was.

33. Attitude toward self-reliance was measured by the respondent's reaction to the following statement: "People should be expected to handle their own problems," with a choice of four responses—strongly agree, agree somewhat, disagree somewhat, and strongly disagree.

34. Because our primary interest is in the effect of help-source rather than behavior, rejection rates will hereafter be presented in combined form only.

35. Talcott Parsons, *The Social System*, Glencoe, Ill.: The Free Press, 1950, p. 437. Parsons states that ". . . the fourth closely related element [in the sick role] is the obligation—in proportion to the severity of the condition, of course—to seek *technically competent* help, namely in the most usual case, that of a physician and to *cooperate* with him in the process of trying to get well." He makes this point again in "Definitions of Health and Illness in the Light of American Values and Social Structure," in E. Gartly Jaco (ed.), *Patients, Physicians and Illness*, Glencoe, Ill.: The Free Press, 1958, pp. 165–187.

36. We might expect those with help-seeking friends to reject in the same pattern as those with help-seeking relatives. Although both groups of respondents have had experience with someone who sought help, those whose experience was with friends probably were not so involved in the other's welfare and therefore had less intimate a knowledge of the help-sources people consult for emotional problems.

37. This is not surprising in light of the generally low rejection of the "normal" person.

38. Only 9 per cent disagreed (either somewhat or strongly) with the statement about people handling their own problems. This finding lends support to the proposition that people in our society are expected to handle their own problems.

39. Again we ignore differences *among* the various groups of respondents. Our primary interest is in determining whether the relation between help-source and rejection is maintained *within* each group.

40. It should be recalled that the latter respondents also rejected persons not seeking help more than persons seeing a psychiatrist; the findings with respect to experience with a help-seeking relative and non-adherence to the norm of self-reliance are not entirely similar.

41. It would have been desirable to control for experience and attitude toward self-reliance simultaneously, but there were too few (13) respondents who reported experience with a help-seeking relative *and* did not adhere to the norm of self-reliance.

42. The small number of respondents with a help-seeking relative (37), and the small number not adhering to the norm of self-reliance (28), make these findings, as well as their interpretation, highly tentative.

43. David Mechanic and Edmund A. Volkart, "Stress, Illness, and the Sick Role," *American Sociological Review*, 26 (February, 1961), pp. 51–58.

44. Jaco, *op. cit.*, points out that "If mental disease carries a stigma in a particular community, it is likely that many families will use extreme measures to conceal the fact that a member is mentally ill; even to the extent of preventing him from obtaining psychiatric treatment in that area." (p. 18)

45. For an interesting presentation of cost and reward, see George C. Homans, *Social Behavior: Its Elementary Forms*, New York: Harcourt, Brace & World, 1961, ch. 5.

Part 5 / Noninstitutional Deviance

In part four I described how institutional careers may be initiated and perpetuated. The material in that section examined how various types of institutional processing may affect people. An equally important concern is the way in which noninstitutional careers may evolve. It may be recalled that such careers or activities generally arise as a result of the actor's own desires and needs; this means that frequently the actor plays an assertive role in moving into a particular type of activity, as well as consciously structuring and presenting a specific image of self to others. Often, too, as indicated in the general introduction, there may be a degree of overlap between institutional and noninstitutional careers—for instance, prostitutes, skid row alcoholics, homosexuals, and thieves may be arrested and thus pulled into, rather than intentionally entering, the institutional career. The selections in this part describe events such as these.

Structures

"Voluntary Associations Among Social Deviants" by Edward Sagarin analyzes the rise of a relatively new type of formal association: organizations of social deviants. He argues initially that while there have been numerous studies of voluntary associations such as those of alcoholics and gamblers, there has been no real attempt to examine fully the ways in which deviants organize themselves. There is, thus, a lack of information with respect to how structured formal associations arise. Sagarin also rightly points out that it is difficult to specifically delineate the boundaries that characterize "deviant organizations." He then argues that the major difference between "deviants" and "nondeviants" is the fact that deviants share some *negative* trait in common. Thereafter, Sagarin describes various types of "deviant organizations," as well as some of the reasons why organizations evolve. The need to *escape from stigma* seems to be the major catalyst. The actual escape appears to exhibit two major patterns: (1) the deviant may decide to conform by giving up the stigmatizing behavior, or (2) the deviant may try to reform or change society's norms with respect to the behavior in question. Sagarin adds an interesting twist to these possibilities by noting that joining an association may actually "increase stigma, by transferring the individual from an invisible to a visible member of the social disproved category." Joining, however, is not without its advantages. Through membership, a certain degree of anonymity may be guaranteed. A vehicle also exists which can be used to reduce social disapproval. These processes and possibilities are evident in several of the selections that follow, particularly in the material on lesbianism.

Lewis Yablonsky, in "The Delinquent Gang as a Near-Group," offers an interesting analysis of how delinquent gangs may arise—an analysis that has direct applicability to other settings. He suggests initially that contrary to the ideas of many, the structure of such collectivities as juvenile gangs may not be especially rigid or formal. Yablonsky supports this thesis by analyzing the events surrounding the killing of the polio victim Michael Farmer. His analysis, as corroborated by depth interviews with gang boys, indicates that many males have a distorted view of what the organizational structure of their "grouping" looks like. For example, not only are definitions of membership vague, but the leadership itself is frequently self-appointed. Yablonsky suggests additionally that a "group fulfilling prophecy" may actually be operative. Specifically, gang workers and the media may *project structure* onto a grouping where virtually none exists, and the involved actors may then live up to these expectations. Several excerpts from case materials are offered in support of this phenomenon. Yablonsky's analysis is not only useful as far as sensitizing one to structural or quasi-structural elements that may characterize groupings, but it also provides some insight into why actors may violate criminal or deviant categories (part two). His data seem to suggest, for example, that peer pressure and influence motivated the killing of Michael Farmer. It should be noted, too, that some juveniles may be what Lemert would term career deviants—that is, they may view themselves as gang members and act accordingly—while others are not.

Entering and Learning Deviant Cultures

The statements by Sagarin and Yablonsky indicate that some groupings may have a semblance of structure, while others may not. If, however, an activity or profession exhibits a certain degree of structure, a person can gain initial entry or exposure through various channels. Once individuals obtain entry into a profession, career, or occupation, they must learn the existing culture and traditions. A similar requirement exists with respect to the institutional deviant. Failure to meet expectations may result in such penalties as ostracism or exclusion from the group. (The general social psychological processes involved in learning deviant cultures were highlighted in my discussion of the cultural transmission model in part two.)

Charles H. McCaghy and James K. Skipper, Jr., in "Lesbian Behavior as an Adaptation to the Occupation of Stripping," provide an excellent account of how particular settings may actually give rise to homosexual behavior. Central to their thesis is the argument that the nature of the stripping occupation itself can "predispose" or motivate (part two) selected females toward lesbian activity. They support their contention by presenting an organizational analysis of the stripping occupation. Three major conditions appear to give rise to the lesbian behavior: (1) the absence of affective and meaningful relationships with others, (2) bad or unsatisfactory experiences and relationships with males, and (3) an occupational structure which allows for a wide range of sexual behavior and experimentation. The researchers also acknowledge the fact that while most research indicates that homosexual careers begin outside institutional settings, theirs provides an analysis of how situational conditions relative to a selected occupation may contribute to the incidence of homosexual behavior. They suggest that the stripping occupation or profession may be analogous to prison settings, particularly in terms of those structural arrangements that seem to give rise to homosexual activity. McCaghy and Skipper's data also seem to indicate that some females may be career lesbians while others are not. For example, some revert to heterosexual relations upon leaving the profession. This also happens to some individuals upon leaving institutions.

Similarly to McCaghy and Skipper's work, Samuel E. Wallace's investigation, "Ways of Entering the Skid Row Culture," provides an account of how people may move into various careers and occupations. Wallace focuses on the skid rower. He argues that three types of individuals have been "recruited" for the skid row culture: (1) the occupational itinerants, (2) the welfare clients, and (3) the skid row *aficionados*. Wallace then describes those conditions that may "push" or motivate (see part two) these respective categories of individuals into the culture. The welfare client, for example, may be sent to skid row for food, clothing, and lodging. Afterwards, and due to initial exposures such as these, the individual may become progressively committed to the values of the skid row culture—a process that frequently produces the career of the skid rower. Wallace also partially describes the normative structure that guides interaction among the skid rowers.

"Becoming a Taxi-Dancer: The Significance of Neutralization in a Semi-Deviant Occupation" by Lawrence K. Hong and Robert W. Duff offers a week-by-week analysis of how, once exposure is gained, females become taxi-dancers. Of major concern to Hong and Duff is the effect that involvement in what some would consider to be a semideviant occupation has upon the dancer's self-image. One way of dealing with threats or potential threats to one's identity is to develop an effective set of rationalizations. (This, it may be recalled, is a central feature of the cultural transmission model discussed in part two.) The researchers describe how this comes about. During the first week, for example, and through the encouragement of co-workers and the management, the females begin to internalize a set of "neutralization techniques" that can be used to legitimate their involvement in the profession. Thereafter, and especially during weeks two and three, the females begin to learn more and more of the appropriate techniques. By the fourth week, however, the females have learned most of the existing "neutralization techniques," and they have also become committed to the occupation—that is, they come to view themselves as taxi-dancers. Hong and Duff also discuss how females may gain entry, such as through contacts with other dancers, as well as some of the reasons why they may elect to become dancers, such as financial considerations.

Barbara Sherman Heyl, in "The Madam as Teacher: The Training of House Prostitutes," describes the socialization of house prostitutes. Heyl's major focus is placed upon the "female trainer-trainee relationship" that exists at the house level. Once the novice enters the house she becomes trained by the "madam." A major portion of the content of the training involves instruction in the appropriate sexual techniques—fellatio, coitus, and "half and half." The newcomer is also taught the house rules, such as the amount of time to be spent with a customer and the specific sums of money to be charged for various types of sexual services, client management, and how to "hustle." Throughout this training, an attempt is made to effectively isolate the novice from her prior life-style and associations. This specific process is important in structuring an occupational identity as a "professional" (i.e., a view of self as a professional or career prostitute). Heyl argues further that unlike the case of the call girl, for example, training is an important requirement for the house prostitute; this is due primarily to the structure of the profession. Specifically, established houses require close interaction among their participants and thus they hire only the trained prostitute. Like the Hong and Duff study, Heyl's offers a most excellent application of the cultural transmission model discussed in part two. The research also graphically illustrates how the existing theory of the office and associated stereotypes become inculcated within the house prostitute—a process that may produce the career or secondary deviant.

Patterns and Variations

Implicit in the preceding statements is the notion that careers and activities exhibit various patterns. There are obviously several types of prostitutes and criminals. "Female Delinquency: Minor Girls and Major Crimes" by Freda Adler with Herbert M. Adler underscores this fact. Specifically, the researchers describe the changing patterns of female crime and delinquency over the last few years. The authors also offer some hypotheses as to why an increasingly large number of females may violate deviant or criminal categories—one such being the recent more liberated attitudes of females. Several excerpts from interview data are offered in partial support of the investigators' claims.

Bonnie E. Carlson's research, "Battered Women and Their Assailants," provides some recent data on wife abuse. Not only does she initially discuss some of the stereotypes surrounding domestic violence—for instance, that women actually instigate the assaults—but she also presents some revealing patterns. For example, the educational level of the assailants is quite low when compared with the total male population. Of the victims, 43 percent worked outside the home; however, only three subjects were engaged in professional occupations. Thirty-four percent of the victims earned less than $6,000, or were supported by Aid to Families with Dependent Children (AFDC), and close to one-third of the assailants (29 percent) were unemployed. Carlson then offers some observations on how domestic violence may affect children reared in such homes. She also describes the accommodative strategies, such as leaving and returning to the assailants (see part three), that may be involved.

"A Criminogenic Market Structure: The Automobile Industry" by Harvey A. Farberman provides an illustration of how powerful elites may establish policies that cause others to commit crimes. His focus is on the automobile industry, particularly in terms of how large manufacturers actually create a "criminogenic market structure" through their pricing policy—a policy geared to high volume and low per-unit profit. Such a policy, Farberman argues, places a financial squeeze on the new-car dealer. The squeeze also "sets in motion a downward spiral of illegal activities," some of which include illegal "kickbacks" or the use of "short-sales." Not only does the research provide an excellent introduction to the phenomenon of "white collar-organizational crime," but it also provides content to the "conflict model" described in part two, especially those statements relating to how the powerful create criminal or deviant categories that may be violated by the less powerful—in this case the car dealers who, in turn, bilk the public through, for instance, use of "service repair rackets."

The research by Jay Corzine and Richard Kirby in "Cruising the Truckers: Sexual Encounters in a Highway Rest Area" extends the concern for patterns and variations in types of activities and careers by examining how homosexuals cruise truckers. The researchers initially present an analysis of the setting, and then describe the participants, as well as the normative structure that guides interaction. They note additionally that cruisers can be divided into two major types: (1) "the gay" and (2) "the ambisexual." Of particular interest are the ways that intrusions are handled.

Effects of Deviant Careers

Involvement in activities and careers which are commonly viewed as deviant by others is not without its personal and social effects. The lesbian schoolteacher serves as an excellent case in point. Such a person is aware that she is engaging in potentially discrediting behavior. Thus, she must manage her "front" in such a manner as to avoid detection by socially significant straights. She often finds it necessary to turn to other homosexuals in an effort to find a sense of belonging and social support. Such involvement in the gay culture also provides the lesbian with a set of rationalizations that can be used to deal with threats to her personal and social identity. (Many of these processes were noted in the article by Sagarin.) My research, "The Structuring and Maintenance of a Deviant Identity: An Analysis of Lesbian Activity," is meant to provide content to many of these notions.

From an initial study of fifty lesbians, I analyze the cases of two: Pat and Toni. Pat is a high-school teacher and Toni is a researcher. Both are what would be termed "secret" or covert homosexuals. I am concerned initially with describing those events that produced a realization on the part of the females that they preferred other females (i.e., their "coming out"). I then describe how the females maintained their "deviant" identity. Important to this process is their involvement in the gay culture. Such activity, as well as the rather constant need to engage in duplistic or "phony" behavior, is not without its personal costs. The effects are most noticeable in the case of Toni. It appears that involvement in the gay culture, as well as the concomitant need to protect her public identity, has produced an erosion of Toni's self-image. Pat, by contrast, appears to possess a positive image of self.

"The Social Integration of Peers and Queers" by Albert J. Reiss, Jr., provides an account of how peers who engage in homosexual behavior protect their identity. Reiss notes initially that not only are the peers aware of the fact that they are engaging in what some would term "deviant" behavior, but they must also come to grips with any threats such involvement may have upon their personal and public identity. One way this can be accomplished is to view the homosexual exchange as a strict financial transaction. Reiss then describes the manner in which the peers become recruited into the activity, as well as the content of the norms governing the transaction. For example, one of the norms is that "the sexual transaction must be limited to mouth-genital fellation." Furthermore, "both peers and queers, as participants, should remain affectively neutral during the transaction." Reiss observes that breaches of the normative code by the adult fellator are frequently met with violence. Such violence (or the threat of violence) serves as an important instrument of social control as far as keeping the customer in line, and it also reduces the possibility that the peer will view himself as a homosexual, at least in the career sense.

Edwin M. Lemert, in "Role Enactment, Self, and Identity in the Systematic Check Forger," offers an interesting variation on the two previous articles. He is concerned with how the occupation of forgery affects a person's identity. The evidence indicates that the check forger often experiences an identity crisis. The crisis arises primarily as a result of the activity itself. Specifically, not only is the forger constantly on the move, but he is unable to establish any meaningful relationships or contacts with others—contacts which are important in the structuring, presentation, and maintenance of a specific personal and public identity. This frequently means that the "self becomes amorphous." Lemert argues that given this particular condition of self, the forger often exhibits a sense of relief when arrested. Not only is the identity problem partially solved, but an identity is imputed to the forger, even though it is a deviant or criminal one. As Lemert points out, the check forger "is much like the actor who prefers bad publicity to none at all."

33 / Voluntary Associations Among Social Deviants

EDWARD SAGARIN

During the past twenty or thirty years, a new type of formal association has begun to flourish in the United States; it is the organization of the social deviant. The members of such a voluntary association may consist of alcoholics, gamblers, narcotic addicts, or ex-convicts, among others. Although there have been studies of individual organizations of the nature listed above, as yet there has been no effort to study the entire phenomenon of the formation of organizations of this category. No one has attempted to make a list of such groups, such as Fox did for voluntary associations on a national scale,[1] and no one has attempted to count them, as has been done for voluntary associations in many community studies.[2] There has been no effort even to list the types of deviants that are conceptualized in this manner, to cite those that have structured formal associations, and to locate the similarities and differences in aims, goals, structures, or other organizational phenomena or characteristics. A preliminary paper of this type must perforce be broad and general, sketchy rather than exhaustive. The present paper is hence not an effort to fill the many lacunae, but to point the way to a few directions that might prove fruitful for further investigation and study.

THE CONCEPT OF DEVIANCE

Deviance is one of the most elusive concepts in the realm of sociology; and without defining deviance, it becomes extremely difficult to draw the boundary lines around the more specific heading of "deviant organizations" or "voluntary associations among social deviants."

Deviance is sometimes used synonymously and interchangeably with lawbreaking, criminality, delinquency, abnormality, rule- or norm-violence, nonconformity, or aberrance. Without attempting an exhaustive study of the various approaches to the definition of the term, but merely making some delineations in order to be able to define the nature of the organizations under study, one might start by seeing deviant as the antonym of normative. Eliminating the concepts that are related to deviance and may overlap with it, but should not be confused therewith, the term is not meant to describe a statistically small proportion of the populace; not meant to refer to the neurotic, abnormal, psychotic, schizophrenic, maladjusted, pathological, or unhealthy; does not refer to that which is dysfunctional for society; and is not meant to describe a subcultural variation where that subculture is recognized as a legitimate part of the larger society.[3]

Albert Cohen offers a definition which I find most useful as a point of departure; namely, that behavior is deviant "which violates . . . expectations which are shared and recognized as legitimate within a social system."[4]

For Howard S. Becker, in a definition to which I shall return, "deviant behavior is behavior that people so label."[5] This is of course a sociological, as well as a logical, truism; but it is also true that obedient, docile, permissive, aggressive, hostile, antisocial, or any other kind of behavior is behavior that people so label. This does not tell us the characteristics of the behavior that lead people to attach the given label.

Clinard, in one of the standard textbooks on the subject, differentiates between social problems and deviance, and cites soil erosion as an example of the former that is not part of the latter. For Clinard, social disapproval is one criterion for a definition of behavior as deviant: "Only those situations in which behavior is in a disapproved direction, and of sufficient degree to exceed the tolerance limit of the community, constitute deviant behavior."[6]

Merton differentiates between the nonconformist and the deviant, the former typically appealing to a higher morality, the latter seeking to conceal his rule-breaking.[7] It is a differentiation that will prove valuable in viewing the characteristics of groups under consideration at this time.

Finally, for Parsons, "deviance is a motivated tendency for an actor to behave in contravention of one or more institutionalized normative patterns."[8] Deriving from his total view of the social system as one in which there is a strain toward integration, Parsons goes on to state that deviance is "defined by its tendency to result either in change in the state of the interactive system, or in re-equilibration by counteracting forces, the latter being the mechanisms of social control."[9]

The concepts of deviance have been summarized and criticized on several occasions.[10] This paper being devoted to organizations of deviants, rather than deviance itself, the frame of reference used here will be briefly outlined.

While it is undoubtedly true, as Becker states, that a deviant is a person who has been defined as a deviant by significant persons (himself and others), and while this emphasizes the relativistic natures of such a definition, with the possibility that how people see others is subject to pressure, influence, and change, nevertheless Becker's statement is not a definition and should not be confused with one. It merely delineates the self-other process by which the placing of a person, or a group of persons, in the category of deviant is made, but it fails to note the characteristics that deviants have in common, and those which are utilized by oneself and others to give persons that label.

Deviance, as here used, is a category that is socially defined in a negative manner. The deviant group is a collectivity of persons who share some trait, characteristic, or behavior pattern in common, which attribute is defined negatively, and which is of sufficient significance to themselves and to others to differentiate them from all those persons not sharing this attribute. The negative definition, however, is one of disapproval, as with intoxication, rather than of disadvantage, as with blindness.[11]

THE VOLUNTARY ASSOCIATION

To the phenomenon of the deviant group, let us now overlay that of the voluntary association. Several definitions of the phrase "voluntary association" have been made, and one might utilize that of Maccoby:

> The distinguishing characters of the voluntary association are that it be private, nonprofit, voluntary in that entrance rests on mutual consent while exit is at the will of either party, and formal in that there are offices to be filled in accordance with stipulated rules. These traits serve to differentiate the voluntary association from public and governmental bodies; profit-making corporations and partnerships; family, clan, church, nation and other groups into which the individual is born; informal friendship groups, cliques, or gangs.[12]

For over a century, observers coming to the American shores from abroad, and others native to this country, have taken note of what has come to be described as the "proliferation of associations" in a "nation of joiners."[13] The first and classic example of such a commentary was made by Alexis de Tocqueville, who stressed that Americans form organizations for a wide variety of purposes:

> Americans of all ages, all conditions, and all dispositions constantly form associations . . . religious, moral, serious, futile, general or restricted, enormous or diminutive . . . If it is proposed to inculcate some truth or to foster some feelings by the encouragement of a great example, they form a society."[14]

Charles and Mary Beard, writing in the 1920's, stated that "the tendency of Americans to unite with their fellows for varied purposes" had become "a general mania," and declared that "it was a rare American who was not a member of four or five societies."[15] Although there was ample evidence of this being the organizational or the associational society, some writers, and particularly Komarovsky,[16] later questioned whether group-belonging was as ubiquitous as stated by the Beards, and found it to be very much of a middle-class phenomenon, indulged in by those who had the leisure time and the money.

Nevertheless, many forces did make for a strong development of associations in American life. The organizational society had deep historical roots, as traced by Schlesinger.[17] Urbanization, which developed so rapidly in this country, reduced the individual to a depersonalized cipher in a mass society, in which the urbanite, in the words of Wirth, was "bound to exert himself by joining with others of similar interests into organized groups to obtain his ends."[18] Industrialization, in the words of Fox, brings "highly differentiated roles and role clusters such that ... there is a strong tendency of some units to become relatively isolated from one another," and these insulated groups develop formal structure.[19] The decline of the extended family, and the inability of the family to continue to provide a large part of the educational, cultural, social, recreational and other needs of many Americans, leaves the individual, in the view of Rose, with "a need to turn relatively frequently to voluntary associations for self-expression and satisfaction of his interests."[20] This could be seen as an interactive process, cumulative in its dynamic mechanism: that is, if voluntary associations do rise to fill the gaps left by the weakening of the extended family, then to the extent that such vacuums are abolished, to that extent is there a strengthening of the forces tending to drive the extended family into further decline in the society.

In this situation, the American is left with a feeling, to use the expression of the Kluckhohns, that he is "unanchored, adrift upon a meaningless voyage."[21] The predilection of Americans for joining would, in part, the Kluckhohns state, be "a defense mechanism against the excessive fluidity of our social structure."[22]

ORGANIZATIONS OF DEVIANTS

It would be logical to conceptualize organizations of fanatics, unpopular political and religious minorities, and others, as voluntary associations of deviants. Any formal and structured group of crusaders who are either strongly opposed by the overwhelming majority of the people (as the Communist party), or by the major value of the society (as the Klu Klux Klan), or who are generally considered "crackpots" because of their program or policies, might be so labeled. In a sense, modern-day sabbatarians, religious snake cultists, social nudists, apocalyptic groups that have decided that the world will end on a given day—all are organizations of deviants.[23] However, these people are the twentieth-century missonaries in their own land, the true believers of Eric Hoffer,[24] rather than social deviants in the sense in which that phrase can be applied to alcoholics. The exploration of the nature of the difference is the task of sociological analysis.

Another group of organizations have been conceptualized under the heading of "criminal societies." They are collectivities of people who have banded together for self-protection or for mutual assistance, in order the better to continue their criminal activities or to protect themselves from apprehension and arrest. MacNamara has summarized the literature of such types of organizations.[25] While it will be necessary here to differentiate between criminal societies and the groups under study, let it be said that the former are often nothing more than gangs; and while they have strong norms and definitely recognized leadership, it is often difficult to speak of formal organization. This writer would emphasize that Murder, Inc., was not incorporated, and that the name was given to it by persons who never established the existence of a formal organization; that the "Appalachian convention" was not a convention, and that the supposed "delegates" attending the nonconvention were not delegates; and that there is considerable question as to whether there is such an entity in the U.S.A. at this time as the Mafia. However, if there should be established that an adult criminal gang exists as a formal association, having structure, by-laws, and a sharp line of demarcation between member and nonmember, such a collectivity could be conceptualized as an association of deviants, yet not quite in the same sense as A.A. and the other groups here under study.

Wherein do groups, of alcoholics, narcotic addicts, and homosexuals, as examples, differ from right- or left-wing fanatics, religious sectarian true believers, Klansmen, or criminals? I would suggest that this difference resides in one respect that becomes crucial for a sociological investigation; namely, that in the former groups—alcoholics and others—deviance resides in the individual who has certain attributes (traits, characteristics, or behavior patterns), and that belonging to the organization may make them more visible, but does not in and of itself confer the traits upon the actor. On the other hand, in the latter types—political, religious, racist, and others—to the extent that the collectivity is deviant, it is the act of joining that confers this status upon the individual, rather than any trait or behavior pattern that the actor brought to the association.

In other words, believing in right- or left-wing politics, or in a way-out religious faith, does not constitute deviance, but the belief is translated into action by the fact of joining with others in an organizational form. However, being homosexual, alcoholic, or addicted to certain types of drugs, constitutes the deviance—if it is so defined in one's society—and joining with others in an organization merely increases the visibility, the possibility of detection, the degree of vulnerability, but not the deviance itself.

WHY ORGANIZATION?

A voluntary association is looked upon as a response to a felt need of a large number of people who share a common interest. If this is so, then one must determine not so much why organizations of social deviants, of the type here described, have been formed; but rather why, in the long tradition of America as a nation of joiners, they did not appear on the scene until the 1930's, and did not become prominent until the period during and after the second World War.

It would be interesting for the social historian to trace the nature of the American society in the years between the first and second World Wars that became a fertile soil for the development of organizations of social deviants. The wars had a great effect in accelerating the rate of change of moral values. Urbanization was proceeding with great rapidity, and the society was characterized by a great amount of geographic mobility—two factors that permitted people to interact with others in a nameless and faceless manner.

Prohibition made the nation deeply aware of the problem of alcoholism, and it should be emphasized that the alcoholics formed the first organization that caught on, and that became the prototype for so many others. And then there was the depression, with a mass rootlessness on the one hand, and a challenging of the accepted ways on the other.

Among these factors, one should consider the changing attitude toward mental illness and the growing sympathy for all those suffering from mental and emotional difficulties. Psychoanalysis became a byword in the home, it was no longer a disgrace to be under therapy, and eventually a President of the United States would make no secret of the fact that there was a retarded member of his family.

These were among the forces that created a social climate favorable for the first time in American history for the formation of voluntary associations among social deviants.

To this one should add the very simple concept of imitation. A great deal of social interaction tends to be epidemiological, and particularly when one group obtains publicity or apparent success, it becomes a model for others, in the same or somewhat similar situation, to ask themselves, "If they can do it, why can't we?" The success among these organizations was Alcoholics Anonymous, out of which grew, in the most direct manner, Synanon,[26] and in an indirect manner, numerous other associations which embraced either the word or the concept of anonymity.

SOCIOLOGICAL REPORTS ON DEVIANT ORGANIZATIONS

Most comment by sociologists on organizations of social deviants (as a general category) has been favorable, encouraging, and even enthusiastic, although it has frequently been based on the most casual observation and on the most naive and unquestioning acceptance of the image that the deviants wished to project as a vision of reality.

Becker writes that deviants have become "more self-conscious, more organized, more willing to fight with conventional society than ever before. They are more open in their deviance, prouder of what they are and less willing to be treated as others want to treat them without having some voice in the matter."[27] After briefly reviewing some homosexual organizations, Synanon, and the LSD movement headed by Leary and Alpert, he writes that "all three groups exemplify the increasing militancy, organization and self-consciousness of deviant worlds and their growing unwillingness to let respectable society have its own way with them unchallenged." He states, further, that the police "will not prevent homosexual defense groups from winning further allies in the respectable world and pressing their fight for equal rights."

Goffman has referred to the publications sponsored by social deviants as giving voice to "shared feelings, consolidating and stabilizing for the reader his sense of the realness of 'his' group and his attachment to it. Here the ideology of the members is formulated—their complaints, their aspirations, their politics."[28]

Schur, writing of the groups that have come to be known as "homophile organizations," notes:

> Whatever their public influence, these groups appear to function for some homosexuals as a symbol of hope and reassurance of the worthiness of their cause, and to provide some solace to those isolated homosexuals who may have felt left out of homosexual life as well as heterosexual society.[29]

While all of these comments might be considered "correct," they give a partial picture of organizations of social deviants, and usually a favorable one. This writer suggests that underlying all of these statements is a sense of injustice and of moral outrage, of righteous indignation at the cruel social hostility displayed against socially harmless deviance, and hence support for such measures as would constitute retaliation and self-defense. Many sociologists seem to be ideologically predisposed to see the usefulness and good in such organizations. In some instances, it may be because the organizations constitute a challenge to the world of respectability; in others, because they seem to embrace the aspirations of the underdog. For example, if Schur conceptualizes homosexuals as people committing "crimes without victims," as he does, he is tempted to become a special pleader for such people, and from this he is likely to want to see their organizations as helpful to those in distress.

THE SHARED CHARACTERISTIC

The fundamental attribute that seems to tie these organizations together is the motivation behind their formation, namely, *the escape from stigma.* The idea of stigma as a social force, explaining human attitudes and behavior, has been explored with deep insights by Goffman.[30] For Goffman, stigma refers to an attitude that is deeply discrediting.[31] If a characteristic is known about or is easily perceivable, one is dealing, in Goffman's terminology, with the plight of the discredited; if easily concealed or difficult to perceive, then it would be a matter of the discreditable.[32]

Applying this to groups of deviants, it is clear that political, religious, racist and other such organizations are not formed or joined as a mechanism in the search for means to neutralize or reduce social stigma. Groups of noisy and militant motorcyclists, such as Hell's Angels, are likewise not designed to reduce the stigma for the individual or the collectivity.[33]

The escape from stigma takes on two divergent and usually mutually exclusive patterns, although there may be some convergence. These two patterns constitute, as I see it, the most important single factor differentiating some of these groups from others, and enabling the student to make meaningful hypotheses and attempt prediction of group life. They are:

1. The deviant may escape from stigma by conforming to the norms of the society; that is, by "reforming," by relinquishing the stigmatizing behavior; or

2. He may escape from stigma by reforming the norms of society, by reducing the sanctions against his behavior; that is by changing, not himself, but the rule-making others. In this case, he is obtaining from society a relinquishment of the stigmatization of his behavior.

Nevertheless, there may be an apparent contradiction in this view, in that the act of joining may increase the stigma, by transferring the individual from an invisible to a visible member of the socially disapproved category. But this is met in two ways: first, by protection of the individual, through anonymity; and second, by utilizing the greater visibility as a mechanism for the reduction of social disapproval.

Conceptualized in this manner, one might foresee that groups in which individuals would seek to reduce their deviant behavior (i.e., escape from deviance) would gain wide social approval from the greater society, except from those who are geographically and in other ways so close to the deviants that the congregation of individuals in an organization becomes threatening. Furthermore, these groups would function very much like group therapy; would often turn to religious or pseudo-religious concepts for reinforcement; would embrace many middle-class aims in order to return to a life of propriety, while scoffing at the hypocrisy of the middle-class that rejects and opposes them. Such a group would paint the deviant as a worthwhile individual, a soul to be saved, but deviance as immoral, sinful, and self-defeating. It would frown on members who stray, attempt to exert extreme pressure through inner group loyalty, and would develop a pattern of over-conformity in the area of the deviance itself. This last characteristic would in fact result in a harsher condemnation of the disapproved behavior than is found in the general population; a fear of the "enlightened," the liberal, and the permissive view, all butressed by a moralistic stance and reinforced by religion; for to those seeking to relinquish their deviance, any suggestion that the consequences of the behavior would be less severe if only social attitudes were to change becomes a threat to the organization and its program, and a temptation to return to the abandoned pattern. The personality characteristic attracted to such a group consists primarily of those who are in need of authority figures and ego reinforcement; these are the compliant and submissive, who nevertheless have a strong component of aggression and are going to transfer this from self-direction and society-direction to group-direction, during the therapeutic process. As penitents, they will both comply and gripe, willingly accept and let off steam.

The second group, those who are seeking to alleviate the definition of their condition as deviant, shares some of these attributes, but not all, and even when it shares them, it does so for entirely different reasons and hence with different consequences. Seeking to change the public attitude toward the deviance, such a group may turn to religion, not for moral support, but for a respectable front and a respectable ally. There would be a reinforcement of the ego, not through group therapy, but in a process of mutual reinforcement of one's deviant values and deviant ways of structuring reality. The middle-class norms would be scoffed at, but not entirely rejected, because acceptance by society might be viewed merely as more easily attainable if one is moralistic, law-abiding, and conforming in most respects. The group must thumb its nose at society, in order to foster pride in the deviant; and at the same time must become obsequious before society; in order the better to beg for acceptance. Such a group is likely to attract rebels and nonconformists, and yet use a facade of squares as front men and window dressing. It might vacillate between ultraconformity, as an expression of anticipatory socialization, and rebellion and rejection, as an expression of the reaction formation against the society that has thrown them out. Because of the enhanced stigmatization that ensues when one joins a group of this type, the organization is likely to attract some neurotics and personality misfits who require social disapproval and ridicule; together with rebels who relish any battle with the world of respectability. Because of the unceasing aggressive nature of the struggle against society and the small degree of success that can be seen, such groups are likely to have considerable membership turnover, and to have bitter internecine battles for leadership, fission, competition between organizations, skullduggery, and the like.

The two groups will travel in diametrically opposite directions in their attitude toward the deviance with which each is involved. The first category will condemn, moralistically and scientifically, unwavering in pointing the finger to the road of eternal damnation that awaits the one who slips backward; and the second category will likewise invoke science, philosophy, and ideology, but for the eternal condemnation of those who condemn them. The latter type of organization will seek to convince the world without, as well as the members within, that their deviance is normal, natural, moral, socially useful, and that all who deem otherwise are deluded and ignorant hypocrites, if not repressed deviants themselves. Both types of organizations will present a distorted image of themselves; they will fall victim to the temptation, almost inherent in the nature of organization, to project a self-image that glorifies and "prettifies." But the first type will show its members as being almost saintly because they are renouncing deviance, and by contrast the devils are not only the lost souls who have not seen the light, but opponents in the world of respectability. In the second type of group, there is a glorification of the deviant (member and nonmember alike), and the devils are those in the world of respectability who scoff at such an image.

EXAMPLES, PROTOTYPES, AND CASE HISTORIES

Of the first group, the best-known and most successful has been Alcoholics Anonymous, described in great detail by many, and subjected to a thorough sociological analysis by Gellman.[34] The success of A.A. and its generally favorable publicity resulted in a rash of other groups that attempted to emulate the structure and form, though usually not the content, of the prototype. These included organizations of narcotic addicts, gamblers, self-styled neurotics, overweight persons, and others. The proliferation of "anonymous" groups of this sort seemed to indicate in some instances a dissatisfaction with A.A. as an instrument for solving other problems (such as drug addiction); but in other instances it indicated merely that A.A. had attained a positive status of its own, that it was "the thing" and "proper" to belong; and that the stigma of being deviant was not only overcome, but a positive esteem was attached, if one had the "ailment" and then was able to renounce it, particularly through A.A.

The abilities of these organizations to accomplish the manifest goals, particularly for the individual member, have not been examined, except for A.A. and Synanon. In the latter instance, one should note that Synanon has certain structural features that differentiate it from voluntary associations, and that this may be a matter of significant conceptual formation, and not one of semantic quibbling. Synanon is a total institution; in fact, it rejects addicts who will not relinquish their occupation and life on the world outside, and move in, family and all.[35] The voluntary association is a segment of one's life, not one's entire life.

Synanon could perhaps better be analyzed as a correctional hospital, offering group therapy and aid in "kicking the habit," but using unusual methods to accomplish that goal. It is a hospital in which there is voluntary self-induction, and that depends to an enormous extent on inner-group norms and loyalties for its success. To slide back into deviance is a betrayal of the people who have become one's "family" and who have placed trust in the former addict.

Setting aside Synanon and similar groups, and looking only at those organizations where one goes occasionally in order to interact with others like oneself, it is doubtful if either continuity or success will be found in groups other than A.A. The failure of some of these groups— if they do fail—may be due to their own definition of their behavior as deviant, which definition was not made by significant others previous to the group formation. The searching out of companions with a similar problem is suspect; for unlike the alcoholic, or the addict, most of these people did not feel that they had a crippling problem making them into nonfunctioning persons, until A.A. caught on, and they thought it might be "campy" or "cool" to get similarly involved. Their organizations, with "anonymity" written into the title, seem to be the work of the poseur and the romantic rebel. There is an exploitation of the status attained by A.A., rather than a search for strength to change one's own behavior. Among the groups of this type are fat persons, neurotics, gamblers, and even their women's auxiliaries.

The contradiction in this situation would seem to be largely as follows: that whereas A.A. seeks to function by building up self-confidence and ego reinforcement, the act of joining a similar group among gamblers accomplishes the very reverse. A.A. infuses in the individual the belief that alcoholism is an evil which he can overcome to the point of functioning, although he is never free from the danger of falling back (this latter being an excellent device to retain the member and hence strengthen the organization). Hence, for A.A. there is no category of *ex*-alcoholics; there are only "sober" alcoholics, the term applying not to people who are in a temporary and brief state of sobriety between their states of intoxication, but who are in a long and hopefully permanent state of sobriety *after* their state of intoxication. The hold of A.A. is that the sober alcoholic is, in this view, a likely victim for relapse, if he is not strengthened, which is accomplished through inner-group cohesion and mutual reinforcement.

Alcoholics, then, to use the terminology of Becker, are deviants because they are so defined, and the actor then defines himself and accepts the uncomplimentary view of self. Gamblers—whatever financial difficulties there may be in their homes due to their habits—are deviants only if they so define themselves, and the act of joining an organization would seem to be a step in such a definition. Certainly the large number of people who flock to the race track, avidly watch for the announcement of the winning number in the daily newspaper, take or give bets in the shop or office, or who follow each day's stock market gyrations, are hardly social deviants. To compare these people with social drinkers, and then to state that the voluntary association is meant to aid compulsive gamblers who are more akin to compulsive alcoholics, offers a point of clarification. However, it is doubtful if the compulsive gambler sees himself as deviant until he joins with others in an organization in which he is compelled to take this view, and the association is therefore more likely to prove ego damaging than ego reinforcing, even if it is successful in aiding some people to overcome their habit (a point which is very doubtful, indeed).

There are factors in Neurotics Anonymous that make it difficult to take this group seriously. Again, there is no reason to believe that being neurotic carries with it a deviance of its own, with stigma. These people would seem to be stigmatizing themselves by joining with others, not because they expose themselves to public view, but because they redefine themselves as having stigma. Furthermore, whereas it is possible to understand people giving each other strength, through sanctions, rewards, disapprovals, appeals to group norms and loyalties, in order to refrain from drinking, taking narcotics, or even gambling, it is difficult to see how they can obtain strength from one another to refrain from being neurotic. With proper guidance and leadership, the pseudo-organization could be a form of group therapy, with the group a little larger and the price somewhat smaller, but in such an instance the organizational structure is merely a front that might attract people to the therapy.

A number of studies have been made of organizations of ex-mental patients,[36] and there have been some reports of structured groups of ex-convicts.[37] These types of groups have in common that they are joined by people who have a stigma from which they are seeking to escape. However, they bridge the gap between our two conceptual categories, in that they are both seeking to live by the norms of the society in all respects, and at the same time to reduce the stigma that society has toward the group. There is no contradiction because they socially define themselves with the prefix "ex," and they do not see mental patients or convicts in a derogatory manner, but view them rather with sympathy. They function in a manner not unlike A.A. in many respects, but have a greater problem in convincing the world "out there"—in addition to themselves—that they are members of a category that can be trusted to manage their lives.

Of the deviants who have organized so as to escape from deviance by influencing the society to redefine them as nondeviant noncon- formists, the most prominent are the homosexuals.[38] They call their groups "homophile" organizations, a euphemistic term that is meant to project an image of people involved in love relationships, rather than sex relationships, with members of their own sex. Organizations of this character indignantly deny the unhealthy, neurotic, or abnor- mal character of homosexuality, a denial necessary (in their view) to gain acceptance both from others and from themselves; and at the same time they display the very neuroticism that is denied in many ways, of which the appeal to sadomasochistic interest among their members is one of the most apparent.[39] They state that they are not seeking to proselytize for homosexuality, and particularly for its spread; yet their literature urges that homosexuality be considered on a par with heterosexuality,[40] and that children be exposed to both ways of life in an impartial manner so as to be able to make a free choice.[41]

One could cite many other examples of the contradictions in which Mattachine societies, the Daughters of Bilitis, and other groups of this nature are entrapped. The problem seems to be as follows: Since the aim of the groups is to escape from stigma by having the behavior redefined as nondeviant, the organizations seek to sponsor that redef- inition by painting a portrait of homosexuals as psychologically healthy, well-functioning, loving, nonpromiscuous persons, even if this is in contravention to one's knowledge of reality. Whether prob- lems of this sort are inherent in any group of social deviants seeking acceptance of their deviance is a matter for further investigation; utilizing classic sociological theory, particularly that of Michels[42] and of Mannheim,[43] and modern organizational theory, particularly of Selznick,[44] one is tempted to answer such a question in the affirmative. That is, an organization of deviants, seeking acceptance without change in themselves, will attract and hold deviant members if it can reinforce their self-image as normal and healthy persons; and will be able to score some short-range successes with greater ease if it displays such a picture of the deviant to the conforming public.

SOCIAL CONTROL AND DEVIANT GROUPS

The question of in-group control on the behavior of deviants is summarized by Albert Cohen, but it is limited, in Cohen's concept, to the participants in the group.[45] It is possible, however, that deviant associations may be utilized by the society to reach the large mass of unorganized individuals who, precisely because of some single attribute which is socially disapproved, are beyond the confines of ordinary communication and control.

One is reminded in this respect of a passage from Durkheim:

> A society composed of an infinite number of unorganized individuals, that a hypertrophied state is forced to oppress and contain, constitutes a veritable sociological monstrosity . . . A nation can be maintained only if, between the State and the individual, there is intercalated a whole series of secondary groups near enough to the individuals to attract them strongly in their sphere of action and drag them, in this way, into the general torrent of social life.[46]

Organizations of homosexuals have cooperated with authorities to disseminate information on venereal disease, to attempt to place homosexuals on jobs, to aid in locating criminals who prey on the homosexual community, and in numerous other ways. While this is not the first instance of the utilization of socially disapproved persons as intermediaries for communicating with and controlling the unorganized mass, it may be a special form that will prove significant in the future of organizations of social deviants.

Notes

1. Sherwood Dean Fox, "Voluntary Association and Social Structure," Unpublished Doctoral Dissertation, Department of Social Relations, Harvard, 1952.

2. In Boulder, Colo., Bushee counted 268: Frederick A. Bushee, "Social Organizations in a Small City," *American Journal of Sociology*, 51: 217–226 (1945); in Yankee City, Warner and Lunt found 357; W. Lloyd Warner and Paul S. Lunt: *The Social Life of a Modern Community*, Yale University Press, New Haven, 1941, p. 303; in

Middletown, the Lynds discovered 548: Robert S. and Helen Merrill Lynd: *Middletown: A Study in American Culture*, Harcourt, Brace & World, New York, n.d. (original publication, 1929), p. 285. Numerous other community studies included a count of voluntary associations.

3. Some of these differentiations are taken from Marshall B. Clinard: *Sociology of Deviant Behavior*, Holt, Rinehart and Winston, New York, 1963.

4. Albert K. Cohen, "The Study of Social Disorganization and Deviant Behavior," in Robert K. Merton, Leonard Broom, and Leonard S. Cottrell, Jr.; Eds.: *Sociology Today: Problems and Prospects*, Basic Books, New York, 1959, p. 462.

5. Howard S. Becker: *Outsiders: Studies in the Sociology of Deviance*, Free Press of Glencoe, New York, 1963, p. 9.

6. Clinard, *op. cit.* p. 22.

7. Robert K. Merton: *Social Theory and Social Structure*, Rev. Ed., Free Press of Glencoe, Glencoe, Ill., 1957, pp. 360–361.

8. Talcott Parsons: *The Social System*, Free Press of Glencoe, Glencoe, Ill., 1951, p. 250.

9. *Idem.*

10. Among other such summaries, see Jack P. Gibbs, "Conceptions of Deviant Behavior: The Old and the New," *Pacific Sociological Review*, 9: 9–14 (Spring 1966).

11. This differentiation does not seem to be made by any of those writing on the subject. See, for example, the articles collected in Howard S. Becker, Ed.: *The Other Side: Perspectives on Deviance*, Free Press of Glencoe, New York, 1964.

12. Herbert Maccoby, "The Differential Political Activity of Participants in a Voluntary Association," *American Sociological Review*, 23: 524–532 (1958). Maccoby notes that his definition is a modification of one found in the following document: *Our Cities: Their Role in the National Economy*, Report of the Urbanism Committee to the National Resources Committee, Washington, D.C., U.S. Government Printing Office, 1937, p. 24.

13. The history of these observations is given by Herbert Coldhamer, "Some Factors Affecting Participation in Voluntary Associations," Unpublished Doctoral Dissertation, University of Chicago, Chicago.

14. Alexis de Tocqueville: *Democracy in America*, Vintage Press Ed., Random House, n.d., Vol. 2, p. 114.

15. Charles and Mary Beard: *The Rise of American Civilization*, Macmillan Co., New York, 1927, Vol. 2, pp. 730–731.

16. Mirra Komarovsky, "The Voluntary Associations of Urban Dwellers," *American Sociological Review*, 11: 686–698 (1946).

17. Arthur M. Schlesinger, Sr.: *Paths to the Present*, Macmillan Co., New York, 1949, Ch. 2, "Biography of a Nation of Joiners." This essay appeared originally, in essentially the same form but more fully annotated, in *American Historical Review*, 50: 1–25 (1944–45).

18. Louis Wirth, "Urbanism as a Way of Life," in Paul K. Hatt and Albert J. Reiss, Jr.: *Cities and Society: The Revised Reader in Urban Sociology*, Free Press, Glencoe, Ill., 1957, pp. 46–63. This essay appeared originally in *American Journal of Sociology*, 44, 1938.

19. Fox, *op. cit.*

20. Arnold M. Rose: *Theory and Method in the Social Sciences*, University of Minnesota Press, Minneapolis, 1954.

21. Clyde and Florence Kluckhohn, "American Culture: Generalized Orientations and Class Patterns," in L. Bryson, L. Finkelstein, and R. M. MacIver, Eds.: *Conflicts of Power in Modern Culture*, Harper Bros., New York, 1947, pp. 249–250.

22. *Idem.*

23. Some of these groups are investigated in Hadley Cantril: *The Psychology of Social Movements*, John Wiley, New York, 1963.

24. Eric Hoffer, *The True Believer*, Harper and Bros., New York, 1951.

25. Donal E. J. MacNamara, "Criminal Societies," *Encyclopedia Americana*, 1955.

26. Lewis Yablonsky: *The Tunnel Back: Synanon*, Macmillan Co., New York, 1965, pp. 48*ff.*

27. Howard S. Becker, "Deviance and Deviates," *Nation*, 201: 115–119, (Sept. 20, 1965).

28. Erving Goffman: *Stigma: Notes on the Management of Spoiled Identity*, Prentice-Hall, Englewood Cliffs, N.J., 1963, p. 25.

29. Edwin M. Schur: *Crimes Without Victims: Deviant Behavior and Public Policy: Abortion, Homosexuality, Drug Addiction*, Prentice-Hall, Englewood Cliffs, N.J., pp. 96–97.

30. Goffman, *op. cit., passim*.

31. *Ibid.*, p. 4.

32. *Idem.*

33. This group is briefly discussed by Robert Shellow and Derek V. Roemer, "The Riot That Didn't Happen," *Social Problems*, 14: 221–233 (1966).

34. Irving Peter Gellman: *The Sober Alcoholic: An Organizational Analysis of Alcoholics Anonymous*, College and University Press, New Haven, Conn., 1964.

35. Yablonsky, *op. cit.*

36. H. Wechsler, "The Expatient Organization: A Survey," *Journal of Social Issues*, 14, 47–53 (1960). Goffman, *op. cit.*, p. 22, cites other references.

37. Goffman, *op. cit. pp.* 22–23. An organization of this type is said to exist in Canada, and is called "Dead Numbers." See *News Letter of the John Howard Society of Alberta*, 9 (4) (May 1966).

38. Organizations of this type are discussed in the writer's doctoral dissertation: Edward Sagarin, "Structure and Ideology in an Association of Deviants," Unpublished Doctoral Dissertation, New York University, New York, 1966.

39. *Ibid.*

40. *Ibid.*

41. *Ibid.*

42. Robert Michels: *Political Parties: A Sociological Study of the Oligarchial Tendencies of Modern Democracy*, Collier Books, New York, 1962.

43. Karl Mannheim: *Ideology and Utopia: An Introduction to the Sociology of Knowledge*, Harcourt, Brace & World, New York, n.d.

44. Philip Selznick, "Foindations of the Theory of Organization," *American Sociological Review*, 13: 25–35 (1948).

45. Albert K. Cohen: *Deviance and Control*, Prentice-Hall, Englewood Cliffs, New Jersey, 1966.

46. Emile Durkheim: *The Division of Labor in Society*, Free Press of Glencoe, New York, 1964, p. 28.

34 / The Delinquent Gang as a Near-Group

LEWIS YABLONSKY

This paper is based on four years of research and direct work with some thirty delinquent gangs in New York City. During this period I directed a crime prevention program on the upper West Side of Manhattan for Morningside Heights, Inc., a community social agency sponsored by fourteen major institutions including Columbia University, Barnard, Teacher's College, Union Theological Seminary, and Riverside Church.

Approaches used in data gathering included field study methods, participant observation, role-playing, group interaction analysis, and sociometry. The data were obtain through close daily interaction with gang boys over the four-year period during which I was the director of the project.

Although data were obtained on 30 gangs, the study focused on two, the Balkans and the Egyptian Kings. It was the latter which committed the brutal killing of a polio victim, Michael Farmer, in an upper west side park of New York City. The trial lasted over three months and received nation-wide attention. These two groups were intensively interviewed and contributed heavily to the formulation of a theory of near-groups. In addition to the analysis of the gang's structure, a number of delinquent gang war events produced vital case material.

There is a paucity of available theory based on empirical evidence about the structure of delinquent gangs. Two landmarks in the field are Thrasher's *The Gang* and Whyte's *Street Corner Society*. Some recent publications and controversy focus on the emergence of gangs and their function for gang members. Professor Cohen deals with gangs as sub-cultures organized by working-class boys as a reaction to middle-class values.[1] In a recent publication Block and Nederhoffer discuss gangs as organizations designed to satisfy the adolescent's striving for the attainment of adult status.[2]

Although partial group structuring has been extensively discussed in sociological literature on "groups," "crowds," and "mobs," my gang research revealed that these collectivity constructs did not seem to adequately describe and properly abstract the underlying structural characteristics of the delinquent gang. Consequently, I have attempted here to construct a formulation which would draw together various described social dimensions of the gang under one conceptual scheme. I call this formulation Near-Group Theory.

NEAR-GROUP THEORY

One way of viewing human collectivities is on a continuum of organization characteristics. At one extreme, we have a highly organized, cohesive, functioning collection of individuals as members of a sociological group. At the other extreme, we have a mob of individuals characterized by anonymity, disturbed leadership, motivated by emotion, and in some cases representing a destructive collectivity within the inclusive social system. When these structures are observed in extreme, their form is apparent to the observer. However, in viewing these social structures on a continuum, those formations which tend to be neither quite a cohesive integrated group nor a disturbed malfunctioning mob or crowd are often distorted by observers in one or the other direction.

A central thesis of this paper is that mid-way on the group-mob continuum are collectivities which are neither groups nor mobs. These are structures prevalent enough in a social system to command attention in their own right as constructs for sociological analysis. Near-groups are characterized by some of the following factors: (1) diffuse role definition, (2) limited cohesion, (3) impermanence, (4) minimal consensus of norms, (5) shifting membership, (6) disturbed leadership, and (7) limited definition of membership expectations. These factors chracterize the near-group's "normal" structure.

True groups may manifest near-group structure under stress, in transition, or when temporarily disorganized; however, at these times they are moving toward or away from their normative, permanent structure. The near-group manifests its homeostasis in accord with the factors indicated. It never fully becomes a *group* or a *mob*.

THE GANG AS A NEAR-GROUP PATTERN

Some recent sociological theory and discourse on gangs suffers from distortions of gang structure to fit a group rather than a near-group conception. Most gang theorizing begins with an automatic assumption that gangs are defined sociological groups. Many of these misconceived theories about gangs in sociological treatises are derived from the popular and traditional image of gangs held by the general public as reported in the press, rather than as based upon empirical scientific investigation. The following case material reveals the disparities between popular reports of gang war behavior and their organization as revealed by more systematic study.

The official report of a gang fight, which made headlines in New York papers as the biggest in the city's history, detailed a gang war between six gangs over a territorial dispute.* The police, social workers, the press, and the public accepted a defined version of groups meeting in battle over territory. Research into this gang war incident, utilizing a near-group concept of gangs, indicates another picture of the situation.

N. Y. Daily News

NIP 200—PUNK FIGHT NEAR COLUMBIA CAMPUS
by Grover Ryder and Jack Smee

A flying squad of 25 cops, alerted by a civilian's tip, broke up the makings of one of the biggest gang rumbles in the city's turbulent teen history last night at the edge of Columbia University campus on Morningside Heights.

N. Y. Herald Tribune

POLICE SEIZE 38, AVERT GANG BATTLE—
RIVERSIDE PARK RULE WAS GOAL

Police broke up what they said might have been "a very serious" battle between two juvenile factions last night as they intercepted thirty-eight youths.

N. Y. Times

GANG WAR OVER PARK BROKEN BY POLICE

The West Side police broke up an impending gang fight near Columbia University last night as 200 teen-agers were massing for battle over exclusive rights to the use of Riverside Park.

N. Y. Journal-American

6-GANG BATTLE FOR PARK AVERTED NEAR GRANT'S TOMB
COPS PATROL TROUBLE SPOT

Police reinforcements today patrolled Morningside Heights to prevent a teen-aged gang war for "control" of Riverside Park.

World-Telegram and Sun

HOODLUM WAR AVERTED AS COPS ACT FAST
38 to 200 Seized near Columbia
by Richard Graf

Fast police action averted what threatened to be one of the biggest street gang

* New York Newspaper Headlines—June 11, 1955:

fights in the city's history as some 200 hoodlums massed last night on the upper West Side to battle over "exclusive rights" to Riverside Park.

Depth interviews with 40 gang boys, most of whom had been arrested at the scene of the gang fight, revealed a variety of reasons for attendance at the battle. There were also varied perceptions of the event and the gangs involved reported simply in the press as "gangs battling over territory." Some of the following recurring themes were revealed in the gang boys' responses.

Estimates of number of gang boys present varied from 80 to 5,000.

Gang boys interviewed explained their presence at the "battle" as follows:

> I didn't have anything to do that night and wanted to see what was going to happen.
>
> Those guys called me a Spic and I was going to get even. [He made this comment even though the "rival" gangs were mostly Puerto Ricans.]
>
> They always picked on us. [The "they" is usually a vague reference.]
>
> I always like a fight; it keeps up my rep.
>
> My father threw me out of the house; I wanted to get somebody and heard about the fight.

The youth who was responsible for "calling on" the gang war—the reputed Balkan Gang leader—presented this version of the event:

> That night I was out walkin' my dog about 7:30. Then I saw all these guys coming from different directions. I couldn't figure out what was happening. Then I saw some of the guys I know and I remembered we had called it on for that night.
>
> I never really figured the Politicians [a supposed "brother Gang" he had called] would show.

Another boy added another dimension to "gang war organization":

> How did we get our name? Well, when we were in the police station, the cops kept askin' us who we were. Jay was studying history in school—so he said how about The Balkans. Let's call ourselves Balkans. So we told the cops—we're the Balkans—and that was it.

Extensive data revealed this was not a case of two organized groups meeting in battle. The press, public, police, social workers, and others projected group conceptions onto a near-group activity. Most of the youths at the scene of the gang war were, in fact, participating in a kind of mob action. Most had no real concept of belonging to any gang or group; however, they were interested in a situation which might be exciting and possibly a channel for expressing some of their aggressions and hostilities. Although it was not necessarily a defined war, the possibilities of a stabbing or even a killing were high—with a few hundred disturbed and fearful youths milling around in the undefined situation. The gang war was not a social situation of two structured teen-aged armies meeting on a battlefield to act out a defined situation; it was a case of two near-groups in action.

Another boy's participation in this gang war further reveals its structure. The evening of the fight he had nothing to do, heard about this event and decided that he would wander up to see what was going to happen. On his way to the scene of the rumored gang fight he thought it might be a good idea to invite a few friends "just to be on the safe side." This swelled the final number of youths arriving at the scene of the gang fight, since other boys did the same. He denied (and I had no reason to disbelieve him) belonging to either of the gangs and the same applied to his friends. He was arrested at the scene of "battle" for disorderly conduct and weapon-carrying.

I asked him why he had carried a knife and a zip gun on his person when he went to the gang fight if he did not belong to either of the reputed gangs and intended to be merely a "peaceful observer." His response: "Man, I'm not going to a rumble without packin'." The boy took along weapons for self-defense in the event he was attacked. The possibility of his being attacked in an hysterical situation involving hundreds of youths who had no clear idea of what they were doing at the scene of a gang fight was, of course, great. Therefore, he was correct (within his social framework) in taking along a weapon for self-protection.

These characteristic responses to the situation when multiplied by the numbers of others present characterizes the problem. What may be a confused situation involving many aggressive youths (belonging to near-groups) is often defined as a case of two highly mechanized and organized gang groups battling each other with definition to their activities.

In another "gang war case" which made headlines, a psychotic youth acted out his syndrome by stabbing another youth. When arrested and questioned about committing the offense, the youth stated that he was a member of a gang carrying out retaliation against another gang, which was out to get him. He attributed his assault to gang affiliation.

The psychotic youth used the malleable near-group, the gang, *as his psychotic* syndrome. Napoleon, God, Christ, and other psychotic syndromes, so popular over the years, may have been replaced on city streets by gang membership. Not only is it a convenient syndrome, but some disturbed youths find their behavior as rational, accepted, and even aggrandized by many representatives of society. Officials such as police officers and social workers, in their interpretation of the incident, often amplify this individual behavior by a youth into a group gang war condition because it is a seemingly more logical explanation of a senseless act.

In the case of the Balkans, the societal response of viewing them as a group rather than a near-group solidified their structure. After the incident, as one leader stated it, "lots more kids wanted to join."

Another gang war event further reveals the near-group structure of the gang. On the night of July 30, 1957, a polio victim named Michael Farmer was beaten and stabbed to death by a gang varyingly known as the Egyptian Kings and the Dragons. The boys who participated in this homicide came from the upper West Side of Manhattan. I had contact with many of these boys prior to the event and was known to others through the community program I directed. Because of this prior relationship the boys cooperated and responded openly when I interviewed them in the institutions where they were being held in custody.*

Responses to my interviews indicated the near-group nature of the gang. Some of the pertinent responses which reveal this characteristic of the Egyptian King gang structure are somewhat demonstrated by the following comments made by five of the participants in the killing. (These are representative comments selected from over ten hours of recorded interviews.)

> I was walking uptown with a couple of friends and we ran into Magician [one of the Egyptian King gang leaders] and them there. They asked us if we wanted to go to a fight, and we said yes. When he asked me if I wanted to go to a fight, I couldn't say no. I mean, I could say no, but for old time's sake, I said yes.
>
> Everyone was pushin' and I pulled out my knife. I saw this face—I never seen it before, so I stabbed it.
>
> He was laying on the ground and lookin' up at us. Everyone was kicking, punching, stabbing. I kicked him on the jaw or someplace; then I kicked him in the stomach. That was the least I could do was kick 'im.
>
> They have guys watching you and if you don't stab or hit somebody, they get you later. I hit him over the head with a bat. [Gang youths are unable to articulate specific individuals of the vague "they" who watch over them.]
>
> I don't know how many guys are in the gang. They tell me maybe a hundred or a thousand. I don't know them all. [Each boy interviewed had a different image of the gang.]

These comments and others revealed the gang youths' somewhat different perceptions and rationale of gang war activity. There is a

*The research and interviewing at this time was combined with my role as consultant to the Columbia Broadcasting System. I assisted in the production of a gang war documentary narrated by Edward R. Murrow, entitled "Who Killed Michael Farmer?" The documentary tells the story of the killing through the actual voices of the boys who committed the act.

limited consensus of participants as to the nature of gang war situations because the gang structure—the collectivity which defines gang war behavior—is amorphous, diffuse, and malleable.

Despite the fact of gang phenomena taking a diffuse form, theoreticians, social workers, the police, the press, and the public autistically distort gangs and gang behavior toward a gestalt of clarity. The rigid frame of perceiving gangs as groups should shift to the fact of gangs as near-groups. This basic redefinition is necessary if progress is to be made in sociological diagnosis as a foundation for delinquent gang prevention and correction.

THE DETACHED GANG WORKER

The detached-worker approach to dealing with gangs on the action level is increasingly employed in large cities and urban areas throughout the country. Simply stated, a professional, usually a social worker, contacts a gang in their milieu on the street corner and attempts to redirect their delinquent patterns into constructive behavior.

Because of the absence of an adequate perceptual framework, such as the near-group concept, detached gang workers deal with gang collectivities as if they were organized like other groups and social organizations. The following principle stated in a New York City Youth Board manual on the detached gang worker approach reveals this point of view[3]:

> Participation in a street gang or club, like participation in any natural group, is a part of the growing-up process of adolescence. Such primary group associations possess potentialities for positive growth and development. Through such a group, the individual can gain security and develop positive ways of living with other individuals. Within the structure of his group the individual can develop such characteristics as loyalty, leadership, and community responsibility (p. 107).

This basic misconception not only produces inaccurate reports and theories about gang structure but causes ineffectual work with gangs on the action level. This problem of projecting group structure onto gangs may be further illuminated by a cursory examination of detached gang-worker projects.

Approaching the gang as a group, when it is not, tends to project onto it a structure which formerly did not exist. The gang worker's usual set of notions about gangs as groups includes some of the following distortions: (1) the gang has a measurable number of members, (2) membership is defined, (3) the role of members is specified, (4) there is a consensus of understood gang norms among gang members, and (5) gang leadership is clear and entails a flow of authority and direction of action.

These expectations often result in a group-fulfilling prophecy. A group may form as a consequence of the gang worker's view. In one case a gang worker approached two reputed gang leaders and told them he would have a bus to take their gang on a trip to the country. This gang had limited organization; however, by travel-time there were 32 gang members ready to go on the trip. The near-group became more organized as a result of the gang worker's misconception.

This gang from a near-group point of view was in reality comprised of a few disturbed youths with rich delusional systems who had need to view themselves as leaders controlling hordes of other gang boys in their fantasy. Other youths reinforce this ill-defined collectivity for a variety of personal reasons and needs. The gang, in fact, had a shifting membership, no clarity as to what membership entailed, and individualized member images of gang size and function.

The detached worker, as an agent of the formal social system, may thus move in on a gang and give a formerly amorphous collectivity structure and purpose through the projection of group structure onto a near-group.

NEAR-GROUP STRUCTURE

Research into the structure of 30 groups revealed three characteristic levels of membership organization. In the center of the gang, on the first level, are the most psychologically disturbed members—the leaders. It is these youths who require and need the gang most of all. This core of disturbed youths provides the gang's most cohesive force. In a gang of some 30 boys there may be five or six who are central or core members because they desperately need the gang in order to deal with their personal problems of inadequacy. These are youths always working to keep the gang together and in action, always drafting, plotting, and talking gang warfare. They are the center of the near-group activity.

At a second level of near-group organization in the gang, we have youths who claim affiliation to the gang but only participate in it according to their emotional needs at given times. For example, one of the Egyptian Kings reported that if his father had not given him a "bad time" and kicked him out of the house the night of the homicide, he would not have gone to the corner and become involved in the Michael Farmer killing. This second-level gang member's participation in the gang killing was a function of his disturbance on that particular evening. This temporal gang need is a usual occurrence.

At a third level of gang participation, we have peripheral members who will join in with gang activity on occasion, although they seldom identify themselves as members of the gang at times. This type of gang member is illustrated by the youth who went along with the Egyptian Kings on the night of the Farmer killing, as he put it, "for old time's sake." He just happened to be around on that particular evening and went along due to a situational condition. He never really "belonged" to the gang nor was the defined by himself or others as a gang member.

The size of gangs is determined in great measure by the emotional needs of its members at any given point. It is not a measure of actual and live membership. Many of the members exist only on the thought level. In the gang, if the boys feel particularly hemmed in (for paranoid reasons), they will expand the number of their near-group. On the other hand, at other times when they feel secure, the gang's size is reduced to include only those youths known on a face-to-face basis. The research revealed that, unlike an actual group, no member of a near-group can accurately determine the number of its membership at a particular point in time.

For example, most any university department member will tell you the number of other individuals who comprise the faculty of their department. It is apparent that if there are eight members in a department of psychology, each member will know each other member, his role, and the total number of members of the department. In contrast, in examining the size of gangs or near-group participation, the size increases in almost direct relationship to the lack of membership clarity. That is, the second- and third-level members are modified numerically with greater ease than the central members. Third level members are distorted at times to an almost infinite number.

In one interview, a gang leader distorted the size and affiliations of the gang as his emotional state shifted. In an hour interview, the size of his gang varied from 100 members to 4,000, from five brother gangs or alliances to 60, from about ten square blocks of territorial control to include jurisdiction over the five boroughs of New York City, New Jersey, and part of Philadelphia.

Another characteristic of the gang is its lack of role definition. Gang boys exhibit considerable difficulty and contradiction in their roles in the gang. They may say that the gang is organized for protection and that one role of a gang is to fight. How, when, whom, and for what reason he is to fight are seldom clear. The right duties and obligations associated with the gang member's role in the gang varies from gang boy to gang boy.

One gang boy may define himself as a protector of the younger boys in the neighborhood. Another defines his role in the gang as "We are going to get all those guys who call us Spics." Still other gang boys define their participation in the gang as involuntarily forced upon them, through their being "drafted." Moreover, few gang members maintain a consistent function or role within the gang organization.

Definition of membership is vague and indefinite. A youth will say he belongs one day and will quit the next without necessarily telling any other gang member. I would ask one gang boy who came into my office daily whether he was a Balkan. This was comparable to asking him, "How do you feel today?"

Because of limited social ability to assume rights, duties, and obligations in constructive solidified groups, the gang boy attaches himself to a structure which requires limited social ability and can itself be modified to fit his momentary needs. This malleability factor is characteristic of the near-group membership. As roles are building blocks of a group, diffuse role definitions fit in adequately to the near-group which itself has diverse and diffuse objectives and goals. The near-group, unlike a true group, has norms, roles, functions, cohesion, size, and goals which are shaped by the emotional needs of its members.

GANG LEADERSHIP CHARACTERISTICS

Another aspect of near-groups is the factor of self-appointed leadership, usually of a dictatorial, authoritarian type. In interviewing hundreds of gang members one finds that many of them give themselves some role of leadership. For example, in the Egyptian Kings, approximately five boys defined themselves as "war counselors." It is equally apparent that, except on specific occasions, no one will argue with this self-defined role. Consequently, leadership in the gang may be assumed by practically any member of the gang if he so determines and emotionally needs the power of being a leader at the time. It is not necessary to have his leadership role ratified by his constituents.

Another aspect of leadership in the gang is the procedure of "drafting" or enlisting new members. In many instances, this pattern of coercion to get another youth to join or belong to the gang becomes an end in itself, rather than a means to an end. In short, the process of inducing, coercing, and threatening violence upon another youth, under the guise of getting him to join, is an important gang leader activity. The gang boy is not truly concerned with acquiring another gang member, since the meaning of membership is vague at best; however, acting the power role of a leader forcing another youth to do something against his will becomes meaningful to the "drafter."

474 / LEWIS YABLONSKY

GANG FUNCTIONS

In most groups some function is performed or believed to be performed. The function which it performs may be a constructive one, as in an industrial organization, a P.T.A. group, or a political party. On the other hand, it may be a socially destructive group, such as a drug syndicate, a group of bookies, or a subversive political party. There is usually a consensus of objectives and goals shared by the membership, and their behavior tends to be essentially organized group action.

The structure of a near-group is such that its functions not only vary greatly and shift considerably from time to time, but its primary function is unclear. The gang may on one occasion be organized to protect the neighborhood; on another occasion, to take over a particular territory; and on still another, it may be organized in response to or for the purpose of racial discrimination.

The function of near-groups, moreover, is not one which is clearly understood, known, and communicated among all of its members. There is no consensus in this near-group of goals, objectives, or functions of the collectivity — much near-group behavior is individualistic and flows from emotional disturbance.

A prime function of the gang is to provide a channel to act out hostility and aggression to satisfy the continuing and momentary emotional needs of its members. The gang is a convenient and malleable structure quickly adaptable to the needs of emotionally disturbed youths, who are unable to fulfill the responsibility and demands required for participation in constructive groups. He belongs to the gang because he lacks the social ability to relate to others and to assume responsibility for the relationship, not because the gang gives him a "feeling of belonging."

Because of the gang youth's limited "social ability," he constructs a social organization which enables him to relate and to function at his limited level of performance. In this structure norms are adjusted so that the gang youth can function and achieve despite his limited ability to relate to others.

An example of this is the function of violence in the near-group of the gang. Violence in the gang is highly valued as a means for the achievement of reputation or "rep." This inversion of societal norms is a means for quick upward social mobility in the gang. He can acquire and maintain a position in the gang through establishing a violent reputation.

The following comments by members of the Egyptian Kings illustrate this point:

If I would of got the knife, I would have stabbed him. That would have gave me more of a build-up. People would have respected me for what I've done and things like that. They would say, "There goes a cold killer."

It makes you feel like a big shot. You know some guys think they're big shots and all that. They think, you know, they got the power to do everything they feel like doing.

They say, like, "I wanna stab a guy," and the other guy says, "Oh, I wouldn't dare to do that." You know, he thinks I'm acting like a big shot. That's the way he feels. He probably thinks in his mind, "Oh, he probably won't do that." Then, when we go to a fight, you know, he finds out what I do.

Momentarily, I started to thinking about it inside: den I have my mind made up I'm not going to be in no gang. Then I go on inside. Something comes up den here come all my friends coming to me. Like I said before, I'm intelligent and so forth. They be coming to me—then they talk to me about what they gonna do. Like, "Man, we'll go out here and kill this guy." I say, "Yeah." They kept on talkin' an talkin'. I said, "Man, I just gotta go with you." Myself, I don't want to go, but when they start talkin' about what they gonna do, I say, "So, he isn't gonna take over my rep. I ain't gonna let him be known more than me." And I go ahead just for selfishness.

The near-group of the gang, with its diffuse and malleable structure, can function as a convenient vehicle for the acting out of varied individual needs and problems. For the gang leader it can be a super-powered organization through which (in his phantasy) he dominates and controls "divisions" of thousands of members. For gang members, unable to achieve in more demanding social organizations, swift and sudden violence is a means for quick upward social mobility and the achievement of a reputation. For less disturbed youths, the gang may function as a convenient temporary escape from the dull and rigid requirements of a difficult and demanding society. These are only some of the functions the near-group of the gang performs for its membership.

NEAR-GROUP THEORY AND SOCIAL PROBLEMS

The concept of the near-group may be of importance in the analysis of other collectivities which reflect and produce social problems. The analysis of other social structures may reveal similar distortions of their organization. To operate on an assumption that individuals in interaction with each other, around some function, with some shared mutual expectation, in a particular normative system as always being a group formation is to project a degree of distortion onto certain types of collectivities. Groups are social structures at one end of a continuum; mobs are social structures at another end; and at the center are near-groups which have some of the characteristics of both, and yet are characterized by factors not found fully in either.

In summary, these factors may include the following:

1. Individualized role definition to fit momentary needs.
2. Diffuse and differential definitions of membership.
3. Emotion-motivated behavior.
4. A decrease of cohesiveness as one moves from the center of the collectivity to the periphery.
5. Limited responsibility and sociability required for membership and belonging.
6. Self-appointed and disturbed leadership.
7. A limited consensus among participatns of the collectivities' functions or goals.
8. A shifting and personalized stratification system.
9. Shifting membership.
10. The inclusion in size of phantasy membership.
11. Limited consensus of normative expectations.
12. Norms in conflict with the inclusive social system's prescriptions.

Although the gang was the primary type of near-group appraised in this analysis, there are perhaps other collectivities whose structure is distorted by autistic observers. Their organization might become clearer if subjected to this conceptual scheme. Specifically, in the area of criminal behavior, these might very well include adult gangs varyingly called the "Mafia," the "National Crime Syndicate," and so-called International Crime Cartels. There are indications that these social organizations are comparable in organization to the delinquent gang. They might fit the near-group category if closely analyzed in this context, rather than aggrandized and distorted by mass media and even Senate Committees.

Other more institutionalized collectivities might fit the near-group pattern. As a possible example, "the family in transition" may not be in transition at all. The family, as a social institution, may be suffering from near-groupism. Moreover, such standardized escape hatches of alcoholism, psychoses, and addictions may be too prosaic for the sophisticated intellectual to utilize in escape from himself. For him, the creation and perpetuation of near-groups requiring limited responsibility and personal commitment may be a more attractive contemporary form for expressing social and personal pathology. The measure of organization or disorganization of an inclusive social system may possibly be assessed by the prevalence of near-group collectivities in its midst. The delinquent gang may be only one type of near-group in American society.

Notes

1. Cohen, Albert K., *Delinquent Boys* (Glencoe: The Free Press, 1955).
2. Block, Herbert, and Arthur Nederhoffer, *The Gang* (New York: The Philosophical Library, 1958).
3. Furman, Sylvan S., *Reaching the Unreached* (New York: Youth Board, 1952).

35 / Lesbian Behavior as an Adaptation to the Occupation of Stripping

CHARLES H. McCAGHY
JAMES K. SKIPPER, JR.

In recent publications Simon and Gagnon (1967a and b) contend that too frequently students of deviant behavior are prepossessed with the significance of the behavior itself and with the "exotic" trappings which accompany it. One finds exhaustive accounts of the demographic characteristics of deviants, the variety of forms their behavior may take, and the characteristics of any subculture or "community," including its argot, which emerge as a direct consequence of a deviant status. Furthermore, Simon and Gagnon chide researchers for being locked into futile searches for ways in which inappropriate or inadequate socialization serves to explain their subjects' behavior.

Simon and Gagnon argue that these research emphases upon descriptions of deviant behavior patterns and their etiology provide an unbalanced and misleading approach to an understanding of deviants. Deviants do or, at least, attempt to accommodate themselves to the "conventional" world, and they play many roles which conform to society's expectations. Yet, for the most part, deviants' learning and playing of nondeviant or conventional roles are either ignored by researchers or interpreted strictly as being influenced by a dominant deviant role. The focus of most research obscures the fact that with few exceptions a deviant role occupies a minor portion of the individuals' behavior spectrums. What is not recognized is the influence which commitments and roles of a nondeviant nature have upon deviant commitments and roles. To illustrate their contention, Simon and Gagnon discuss how homosexual behavior patterns are linked with the identical concerns and determinants which influence heterosexuals: aging problems, identity problems, making a living, management of sexual activity, etc. The authors argue convincingly for damping concern over ultimate causes of homosexuality and for concentrating on factors and contingencies shaping the homosexual role. In their words: "Patterns of adult homosexuality are consequent upon the social structures and values that surround the homosexual after he becomes, or conceives himself as, homosexual rather than upon original and ultimate causes" (Simon and Gagnon, 1967b:179).

Since past research on homosexuals has been dominated by an emphasis upon the sexual feature of their behavior and its consequences, it is fitting that Simon and Gagnon draw attention to linking deviant with nondeviant behaviors or roles. However, since in their scheme the choice of sexual object is taken as given, a complementary perspective is still needed to gain an understanding of the process by which individuals engage in homosexual behavior. We suggest a structural approach. Because sexual behavior, deviant or not, emerges out of the context of social situations, it would seem that the structure of certain situations might contribute to becoming involved in homosexual behavior and to the formation of a homosexual self-concept. We are not suggesting such structures as "ultimate" causes; rather, we are saying that different social structures may provide conditions, learning patterns, and justifications differently favorable to the occurrence of homosexual contacts and self-concepts. This is not strictly a matter of etiology, then, but an epidemiological concern over differential incidences of deviance, regardless of how episodic or pervasive homosexual behavior may be for an individual case.

A pertinent, albeit extreme, example here is the incidence of homosexual behavior occurring among incarcerated populations. A large proportion of prisoners can be identified as "jail house turnouts": those whose homosexual behavior is limited to within an institutional setting (Sykes, 1965:72, 95–99; Ward and Kassebaum, 1965:76, 96). Evidence indicates that contingencies and opportunities inherent in the prison setting are related to the onset and possible continuation of homosexual behavior. There is no question that for some prisoners homosexual behavior emerges as an adaptation to the prison structure which not only curtails avenues of heterosexual release, but deprives inmates of meaningful affective relationships they would otherwise have (Gagnon and Simon, 1968b; Giallombardo, 1966:133–157).

We have little reliable information concerning the incidence of homosexuality among various populations outside the setting of total institutions.[1] Most researchers agree that homosexuals will be found across the entire socieconomic spectrum (Kinsey *et al.*, 1948:639–655; Kinsey *et al.*, 1953; 459–460, 500; Gerassi, 1966; Leznoff and Westley, 1956). There is, however, continual speculation that relatively high proportions of male homosexuals are contained in certain occupational groups such as dancers, hair dressers, etc. Assuming this speculation to be correct it is still unclear which is prior: occupational choice or commitment to homosexual behavior. The sociological literature is replete with examples of how occupation influences other aspects of social life; there is no apparent reason why choice of sexual objects should necessarily vary independently. This is not to say that occupations are as extreme as total institutions in their control over life situations regarding sexual behavior. We do suggest that *some* occupations, like the prison setting, may play a crucial role in providing pressures, rationales, and opportunities leading to involvement in, if not eventual commitment to, homosexual behavior.

In the course of conducting a study of the occupational culture of stripping, we found that homosexual behavior was an important aspect of the culture which apparently stemmed less from any predisposition of the participants than from contingencies of the occupation.

NATURE OF THE RESEARCH

The principal research site was a midwestern burlesque theater which employed a different group of four touring strippers each week. With the permission and support of the theater manager, two male researchers were allowed access to the back stage dressing room area during and after afternoon performances. The researchers were introduced to each new touring group by the female stage manager, a person whom the girls trusted. After the stage manager presented them as "professors from the university who are doing an anthology on burlesque," the researchers explained that they were interested in how persons became strippers and what these persons thought about stripping as an occupation. After this, the researchers bided their time with small talk, card playing, and general questions to the girls about their occupation.[2] The purposes of this tactic were to make the girls more comfortable and to allow the researchers to survey the field for respondents.

The primary data were gathered through in-depth interviews with 35 strippers.[3] Although there was no systematic method of selecting respondents from each touring group, an attempt was made to obtain a range of ages, years in the occupation, and salary levels. There were only four cases of outright refusals to be interviewed, one coming after the girl had consulted with a boyfriend. In six cases no convenient time for the interview could be arranged because the potential subjects were "busy." It was impossible in these instances to determine whether the excuses really constituted refusals. In general, the researchers found the girls eager to cooperate and far more of them wanted to be interviewed than could be accommodated.

The interviews, lasting an average of an hour and a half, were conducted in bars, restaurants, and, on occasion, backstage. Although difficult at times, the interviewing took place in a manner in which it was not overheard by others. In all but one case, two researchers were present. Interviews were also conducted with others, both male and female, whose work brought them in contact with strippers: the theater manager, stage manager, union agent, and sales persons selling goods to strippers backstage. The interviews were semi-structured and designed to elicit information on background, the process of entering the occupation, and aspects of the occupational culture.

INCIDENCE OF HOMOSEXUALITY

Ideally, in order to posit a relationship between the occupation and homosexual contacts it would be necessary to establish that the incidence of such behavior is relatively higher among strippers than in other female occupations. However, statistics comparing rates of homosexuality among specific female occupational groups are simply not available. Ward and Kassebaum (1965:75, 148–149) did find as part of female prison lore that lesbianism is prominent among models and strippers. In our research the restricted sample and relatively brief contact with the subjects did not allow us to ascertain directly the extent of homosexual behavior among strippers. We were, however, able to gauge the salience of such behavior in the occupation by asking the subjects to estimate what proportion of strippers had homosexual contacts. Estimates ranged from 15 to 100 percent of the girls currently being at least bisexual in their contacts; most responses fell within the 50 to 75 percent range. We also have evidence, mostly self-admissions, that nine of the thirty-five respondents (26 percent) themselves engaged in homosexual behavior while in the occupation, although in no case did we request such information or have prior evidence of the respondents' involvement. We did make some attempt to include subjects in the sample whom we suspected were maintaining relatively stable homosexual relationships. But these deliberate efforts were futile. In two cases strippers known to be traveling with unemployed and unrelated female companions refused to be interviewed, saying they were "too busy."

Despite our inability to fix an exact proportion of strippers who had engaged in homosexuality, it is clear from the subjects' estimates and their ensuing discussions that such behavior is an important facet of the occupation. The estimates of 50 to 75 percent are well above Kinsey's finding that 19 percent of his total female sample had physical sexual contact with other females by age 40 (1953:452–453). This difference is further heightened when we consider that a large majority of our sample (69 percent) were or had been married; Kinsey found that only three percent of married and nine percent of previously married females had homosexual contacts by age 40 (1953:453–454).

CONDITIONS CONTRIBUTING TO HOMOSEXUALITY

More relevant to the hypothesis of this paper, however, are the conditions of the occupation which our subjects claimed were related to the incidence of homosexual behavior, whatever its magnitude. It was evident from their discussions that a great part, if not most, of such behavior could be attributed to occupational conditions. Specifically, conditions supportive of homosexual behavior in the stripping occupation can be classified as follows: 1) isolation from effective social relationships; 2) unsatisfactory relationships with males; and 3) an opportunity structure allowing a wide range of sexual behavior.

Isolation from affective social relationships. Evidence from our research indicates that in general strippers have difficulty maintaining permanent affective social relationships, judging by their catalogues of marital difficulties and lack of persons whom they say they can trust. Aside from such basic inabilities, it is apparent that the demands of the occupation as a touring stripper make it exceedingly difficult for the girls to establish or maintain immediate affective relationships, even on a temporary basis. The best way to demonstrate this is to describe their working hours. Generally, strippers on tour spend only one week in each city and work all seven days from Friday through Thursday evening. They must be in the next city by late Friday morning for rehearsal. Their working day usually begins with a show about 1 P.M. and ends around 11 P.M., except on Saturday when there may be a midnight show. Although the girls' own acts may last only about 20 minutes in each of four daily shows, they also perform as foils in the comedians' skits. As a consequence, the girls usually are restricted to the theater every day from 1 to 11 P.M. except for a two and a half hour dinner break. After the last show most either go to a nearby nightclub or to their hotel rooms to watch television. Many girls spend over 40 weeks a year on tour.

Such working conditions effectively curtail the range of social relationships these girls might otherwise have. It should not be surprising that a nearly universal complaint among strippers is the loneliness they encounter while on tour. One girl claimed: "When you are lonely enough you will try anything." By itself this loneliness is not necessarily conducive to homosexual activities since, aside from other girls in the troupe, there is isolation from females as well as from males. But strippers find that contacts with males are not only limited but often highly unsatisfactory in content, and homosexuality can become an increasingly attractive alternative.

Unsatisfactory relationships with males.   As stated above, women prisoners claim that lesbianism is very frequent among strippers. Data from our research tends to confirm this rumor. There is also some evidence that homosexual behavior is relatively frequent among prostitutes (Ward and Kassebaum, 1965:126–132). It is a curious paradox that two occupations dedicated to the sexual titillation of males would contain large numbers of persons who frequently obtain their own gratification from females. Tempting as it may be to turn to some exotic psychoanalytic explanations concerning latent homosexuality, the reasons may not be so covert. Ward and Kassebaum (1965:126–132) and others (Benjamin and Masters, 1964:245–246n) note that among prostitutes homosexual behavior may result less from inclination or predisposition than from continual experiences which engender hostility toward males in general.

A recurring theme in our interviews was strippers' disillusionment with the male of the species. This disillusionment often begins on stage when the neophyte first witnesses audience reactions which prove shocking even to girls who take off their clothes in public. Due to lighting conditions the stripper is unable to see beyond the second row of seats but from these front rows she is often gratuitously treated to performances rivaling her own act: exhibitionism and masturbation. There is no question that strippers are very conscious of this phenomenon for they characterize a large proportion of their audience as "degenerates." This term, incidentally, occurred so often in the course of our interviews it could be considered part of the stripper argot. Strippers know that "respectable" people attend their performances, but they are usually out in the dark where they cannot be seen. Furthermore, a sizeable proportion of these "respectables" are perceived by strippers to be "couples," hence most of the unattached male audience is suspect.

There is no indication that strippers on tour have more off-stage contact with their audience than does any other type of performer. But the precedent set by the males in rows one and two persists for strippers even in their off-stage contacts with men. They find that their stage identifications as sex objects are all too frequently taken at face value. Initially, strippers may find this identification flattering but many eventually become irritated by it. As one subject put it:

> If a guy took me out to dinner and showed me a good time, I'd sleep with him. But most of them just call up and say "Let's fuck."

When checking into hotels while on tour most girls register under their real rather than their stage name. Several girls pointed out to us that the purpose of this practice was to eliminate being phoned by their admirers. Furthermore, many of the girls avoid identifying themselves in public as strippers, preferring to call themselves dancers, entertainers, and the like. This enables them not only to steer clear of a pariah label but to minimize unwelcome sexual reactions which they feel the name "stripper" engenders.

When strippers do form relatively prolonged liaisons with males during the course of their stripping career, chances are good that they will result in another embittering experience. In some cases the man will insist that the girl abandon the occupation, something she may not be inclined to do; hence a breakup occurs. But more frequently the girls find themselves entangled with males who are interested only in a financial or sexual advantage. One of our male informants closely connected with the stripping profession claimed, "You know the kind of jerks these girls tie up with? They're pimps, leeches, or weirdos." This, of course is an oversimplification; yet the strippers themselves confirm that they seem to be involved with more than their share of rough, unemployed males who are more than happy to enjoy their paycheck.

Strippers probably are not without fault themselves in their difficulties with heterosexual relationships; in our sample of 35 we found that of the 24 who had ever been married, 20 had experienced at least one divorce. It is evident, however, that their problems are compounded by the exploitive males who gravitate toward them. Under these circumstances contacts with lesbians are often seen as respites from importunate males. One subject claimed that although she did not care to engage in homosexual activities she would frequently go to a lesbian bar where she could "have a good time and not be bothered." Another said that lesbians are the only ones who "treat you like a person." As one reasoned:

> Strippers go gay because they have little chance to meet nice guys. They come in contact with a lot of degenerate types. If they do meet a nice guy chances are he will ask them to stop stripping. If he doesn't he's likely to be a pimp. So the girls got to turn to a woman who understands them and their job. It is very easy for them to listen to the arguments of lesbians who will tell them basically that men are no good and women can give them better companionship.

Our argument should in no way be interpreted to mean that most strippers are anti-male or have completely severed all contacts with males. From our research it appears that the "career" homosexual is the exception among strippers. At best, the majority can be described as bisexual. The point is that experiences gained in the course of their occupation promote the homosexual aspect by generating caution and skepticism where relationships with males are concerned. Limited contacts with males plus the wariness which accompanies these contacts can be instrumental in severely curtailing the sexual activity of strippers outside of prostitution. Thus an opportunity for a warm, intimate relationship unaccompanied by masculine hazards becomes increasingly attractive. According to one of our subjects, when faced by the lesbian ploy, "Men are no good; I can do things for you they can't," many strippers [are] persuaded, at least temporarily.

Opportunity structure allowing a wide range of sexual behavior. The final occupational condition contributing to the incidence of homosexual behavior among strippers involves the existence of both opportunities and tacit support for such behavior. As male researchers we found it difficult to fathom the opportunities available for female homosexual activities. Our respondents pointed out, however, that there is no want in this regard. Strippers on tour have easy access to information on the location of gay bars in any city they play; furthermore, the reception strippers receive in these bars is especially hospitable. More immediate opportunities are available, obviously, with the presence of homosexuals in the touring group itself. The group which, of necessity, spends most of the day together provides the novice stripper with at least an opportunity for sexual experimentation without the risks inherent in becoming involved with complete strangers.

There is some indication also that some strippers experienced in homosexual behavior are not particularly quiescent when obtaining partners. One subject informed us that she avoids touring with certain groups simply because homosexual contacts within the group are an expected mode of behavior and noncompliance is punished by ostracism. She claimed that being on tour was boring enough without having the other girls refusing to talk or associate with her. In this same vein, several of our subjects stated that certain older and established women in the occupation actively recruit partners with promises of career rewards. We were at first skeptical of such "casting couch" tactics among strippers, but the same stories and names recurred so often from such diverse sources that the possibility cannot be ignored.

We do not wish to over-dramatize the pressures placed on the girls by others to engage in lesbian practices. No doubt such pressures do occur, but sporadically. More important is the fact that opportunities for homosexual contacts occur in an atmosphere of permissiveness toward sexual behavior which characterizes the workday philosophy of strippers. The strippers' principal salable product is sex; the music, dancing, and costumes are only accessories. The real product becomes, over time, effectively devoid of any exclusiveness and is treated with the same detachment as grocers eventually view their radishes. For some strippers sexual contacts are regarded not only with detachment but with a sense of indifference:

> I usually don't get kicks out of other women, not really, but there are times. Sometimes you come home and you are just too tired to work at it. Then it's nice to have a woman around. You can lay down on the floor, relax, watch T.V. and let her do it.

Add to this a sense of cynicism regarding sexual mores. Sexual behavior is generally not characterized by strippers as right or wrong by any universal standard but in terms of its presumed incidence in the general society; many of our respondents firmly expressed their view that lesbianism and prostitution are easily as common among women outside the occupation as among strippers. One respondent reasoned:

> Strippers are no different in morality than housewives, secretaries, waitresses, or anybody else. There is a certain amount of laxity of behavior which would occur in anybody, but with the occupational hazard of being lonely and moving from town to town, well, that's the reason.

The end effect of such attitudes is that no stigma is attached to either homosexual behavior or prostitution[4] among strippers as long as the participants are discreet, do not bother others, and do not allow their activities to interfere with the stability of the touring group. It appears, then, that strippers work in a situation where opportunities for homosexuality are not only available but where social pressures restricting sexual choice to males are minimal or non-existent.

SUMMARY

Previous research indicates that most homosexual careers, male or female, begun outside the total institutional setting involve enlistment rather than a system of recruitment through peer group or subcultural pressures (Gagnon and Simon, 1968a:116, 118). As sociologists however, we must not lose sight of the importance of situational conditions as explanatory variables for understanding rates of deviant behavior. We have attempted to demonstrate how sexual behavior may be an adaptation to social factors immediately impinging upon the actors; specifically, we have argued that the stripping occupation may be analogous to the prison setting in that its structural characteristics contribute to the incidence of homosexual behavior.

References

Benjamin, Harry, and R. E. L. Masters
 1964 Prostitution and Morality. New York: Julian Press.
Gagnon, John H. and William Simon
 1968a "Sexual deviance in contemporary America." The Annals of the
   Amer. Acad. of Political and Social Science 376 (March): 106–122.
 1968b "The social meaning of prison homosexuality." Federal Probation
   32 (March): 23–29.
Gerassi, John
 1966 The Boys of Boise: Furor, Vice, and Folly in an American City. New
   York: Macmillan.
Giallombardo, Rose
 1966 Society of Women: A Study of a Woman's Prison. New York: Wiley.
Hollingshead, August B.
 1957 Two Factor Index of Social Position. New Haven: Yale University
   (mimeographed).
Kinsey, Alfred C., Wardell B. Pomeroy, and Clyde E. Martin
 1948 Sexual Behavior in the Human Male. Philadelphia: Saunders.
Kinsey, Alfred C., Wardell B. Pomeroy, Clyde E. Martin, and Paul H. Gebhard
 1953 Sexual Behavior in the Human Female. Philadelphia: Saunders.
Leznoff, Maurice, and William A. Westley
 1956 "The homosexual community." Social Problems 3 (April): 257–263.
Simon, William, and John H. Gagnon
 1967a "Femininity in the lesbian community." Social Problems 15 (Fall):
   212–221.
 1967b "Homosexuality: The formulation of a sociological perspective."
   Journal of Health and Social Behavior 8 (September): 177–185.
Skipper, James K., Jr., and Charles H. McCaghy
 1969 "Stripteasers and the anatomy of a deviant occupation." Paper read at
   American Sociological Association meetings in San Francisco (September, 1969).
Sykes, Gresham M.
 1965 The Society of Captives: A Study of a Maximum Security Prison. New
   York; Atheneum.
Ward, David A., and Gene G. Kassebaum
 1965 Women's Prison: Sex and Social Structure. Chicago: Aldine.

Notes

1. Estimates of the proportion of males having homosexual contacts during imprisonment range between 30 and 45 percent, depending on the institution, characteristics
of the population, and length of sentences (Gagnon and Simon, 1968b:25). In one
women's institution researchers estimated that 50 percent of the inmates had at least
one sexual contact during their imprisonment (Ward and Kassebaum, 1965:92).
2. Data concerning stripteasers and the occupation of stripping may be found in a
paper by Skipper and McCaghy (1969).
3. The social characteristics of the interviewed sample of strippers are as follows: All

were white and ranged in age from 19 to 45, with 60 percent between the ages of 20 and 30. On the Hollingshead (1957) two-factor index of social position, ten came from families in classes I and II, nine from class III, and 12 from classes IV and V. (Family background data were not obtained in four cases.) Their range of education was from seven to 16 years: 22 had graduated from high school, eight of whom had at least one year of college.

4. One perceptive respondent even questioned the rationality of the legal definition of prostitution: There is a very hazy line between what people call prostitution and just going to bed with a man. What is the difference between taking $50 for it, or receiving flowers, going out to dinner, and then the theater, and then getting laid? One has preliminaries, otherwise there is no difference. There is a payment both ways.

36 / Ways of Entering the Skid Row Culture

SAMUEL E. WALLACE

The process of becoming a skid rower is not easy, rapid, or uniform. There are many pitfalls along the way, and the novice must be on the alert ere the Forces of Respectable Society swoop down and snatch up another hapless victim. It is a complex process whose description depends upon one's point of view. To the non-skid rower, the process appears to involve ever-increasing isolation from the larger society accompanied by ever-increasing deviance from its norms. From the point of view of the skid rower, on the other hand, the process is one of increasing participation in the life of the skid row community, and is accompanied by increasing conformity to its norms. In its totality, the process of becoming a skid rower combines both the push out of respectable society with the pull toward the society of skid row. To understand the final product of this process — the completely acculturated skid rower—the investigator must recognize these dual forces of rejection and attraction within the life history of the individual.

The routes to homelessness must first be examined with respect to the person's initial exposure to skid row. Since no one is born into the skid row way of life, it is critical to ask who was the skid rower before he came to skid row? Where did he come from? Where and how did he first meet up with skid row? In short, where are skid row's recruiting offices and who are those attracted to step inside?

Since many are exposed to skid row but nevertheless return to respectable society, a second critical phase in the process occurs at the point of regular participation in the skid row way of life. After having been exposed to skid row, why does a novice continue to take the next step of participation in this deviant community? The reaction of the larger community can only have been against skid row in all its manifestations and yet these negative sanctions fail to stop the fledgling skid rower's pattern of increasing deviance. Exposure followed by participation are the first two stages in the process of becoming a skid rower.

The third and final stage in the process involves conformity to skid row values and the corresponding rejection of the values of the larger society. Just as exposure is not necessarily followed by participation, neither do all who take part in the skid row way of life become full-fledged members of its community. And to understand the entire process, the investigator must be able to account for those who drop out at one point or another between exposure and acculturation.[1]

Throughout the history of the vagrant-skid row subculture, three distinct types of persons appear to have been recruited into the skid row way of life. By far the majority have been drawn from the ranks of those occupations which by their very nature separated men from their fixed places in established society — migratory workers, lumberjacks, soldiers, seamen — occupational itinerants who followed the crops, the seasons, the wars, or the sea.

A second source of recruitment into the skid row way of life has been the welfare client — those displaced and often dispossessed by the crises of war, depression, and natural disaster; those rendered homeless, jobless, and hungry, those who joined bread and soup lines, who sought refuge in municipal shelters and in skid row missions.

The third source of recruits are the skid row *aficionados*, those whose lives and habits made them seek skid row as a kind of sanctuary. The *aficionados* are the wanderers, the alcoholics, the petty criminals, the fringe members of society at large.

The point of entry for the mobile worker usually takes place on the job. The newcomer to one of the temporary, seasonal, or traveling occupations is almost certain to meet among his fellow laborers some who are already members in good standing of skid row society, who are neither temporarily or even accidentally unattached and homeless, but chronically and permanently without kin or community. In working, eating, talking, drinking, sleeping, and living with confirmed skid rowers on the job, the newcomer to the occupation is exposed to his first taste of skid row subculture. He learns of skid row attitudes toward the community, the employer, the police, the welfare worker — and he learns of their attitudes toward him. To defend himself against the condemnation he experiences in dealing with the outside community, and to adjust to his companions on the job, he gradually begins to enter the world of the skid rower. He may take up the camaraderie of sharing, of heavy drinking, of casual womanizing, and other behavior patterns characteristic of the subculture. When the season's work is finished, or when his voyage is over, or when he simply quits his job, the newcomer may return home, or move directly onto skid row.

When and if he returns home, he faces all the usual problems created by his absence. He has learned, however, that if he does not like living with father, mother, sister, brother, wife or children, he does not have to stay at home. He is no longer necessarily or totally committed to the values of home and family life any more than his family is totally committed to accepting him back into their midst. He is now aware of alternative attitudes and an alternative way of life. There are two worlds, he now knows, although he may for the moment feel—with some truth—that he belongs to neither.

It is at this point, and only at this point, that an unsatisfactory home situation becomes relevant in explaining a man's move to skid row. If before he left home he was at constant odds with his family, he may be less inclined than ever to "put up with it"—now that he knows another way of life complete with a few friends open to him. Problems at home plus the weakening of family ties brought about by his absence reinforce his sense of isolation, push him further adrift, and help sever the few remaining roots he has in the world of respectable society. The skid row way of life—a life without care, worry, and responsibility, a life with friends, drink, and plenty of time in which to enjoy them—begins to look better and better.

The welfare client's starting point toward skid row is likely to be more direct. He may, for example, when he applies for relief be sent directly to skid row to be fed, housed, and perhaps even clothed by the very same agencies which cater to the needs of the destitute skid rower. When relief agencies are located in the skid row community, the welfare client can hardly avoid coming into contact with the skid rower and his way of life.

During the Depression this was commonplace. A man separated from wife and family because he could no longer support them, or the single person—young or old—with no resources to fall back on when hard times hit, was cared for by welfare agencies who made little or no distinction between him and any other bum, i.e. skid rower. Modern welfare attitudes, policies, and programs have changed the picture considerably. The temporary loss of a man's role as breadwinner no longer necessarily throws him on bread lines, into municipal shelters, or skid row missions. Home relief, housekeeping and institutional care for the aged, the ill, and the infirm or disabled make it possible for more families to stay together even under conditions of extreme financial stress. And welfare agencies no longer are centered in slum or skid row areas. Destitution, therefore, does not automatically bring the welfare client into contact with skid row as it used to.

Destitution, in any case, has never been in and of itself a sufficient explanation for membership in skid row. When destitution came to the mobile worker, he had already met up with the skid row way of life while on one job or another. He was already an initiate if not a full-fledged member of its society. When destitution created a welfare client, it served merely to introduce him to skid row. He made his first contact in the very process of securing relief. Sometimes he stayed on, demoralized or perhaps seduced by a process social workers referred to as "shelterization." Sometimes he fought back, as this letter written at the height of the Depression by several unwilling inhabitants of a Municipal Shelter illustrates:

> Sir:
> Previous to entering the shelters we considered ourselves to be average contented persons of everyday life. . . . After several months . . . we become aware of a change in our mental attitude. . . .
> Realizing that these conditions will exist for years to come, we are going to leave the shelters no matter what befalls us, because we must get back some sort of normal life again, before we have lost all initiative. The mental strain has become much greater. . . .
> We cannot understand what crime we have committed that this should be done to us. Certainly a man in our place can claim no country of his own, no society to which he belongs, no flag to inspire him.
> So now it is sink or swim. . . .[2]

Skid row *aficionados* are those whose life patterns are inherently deviant and lead them to look for a community where they will find toleration, acceptance, and anonymity. The *aficionado's* pattern of deviancy exists before he makes contact with skid row, and he may be said to be the only type of skid row recruit truly motivated to disengage himself from society and to seek out the refuge of skid row. The salesman whose drinking gets out of hand looks for a place where his excesses will not embarrass friends and relatives, and where word of it will not leak back to his employer. The wanderer uses skid row as an emergency relief station—an interim residence when he is not "on the road." The alcoholic uses skid row to conceal his compulsive drinking from friends and neighbors. The prostitute, in the last stages of her professional life, uses skid row to pick up a few impoverished clients. The petty racketeer uses skid row to escape identification.

Over the years changes have taken place in the volume of these three points of entry into the skid row community, and along with these changes, the population of skid row has expanded or diminished. Since 1940 the mechanization of agriculture, lumbering, construction, and the decline of the railroads have vastly reduced the number of men employed in mobile occupations. No longer are thousands of men shipped from urban centers like Minneapolis and Chicago to isolated camps to fell trees or maintain railroad tracks. Heavy construction along waterways is now almost completely unionized, and so none of these jobs are available to the homeless man. Within the cities themselves, jobs like shoveling snow, washing dishes, and even street cleaning have been largely replaced by machines. In every single activity which formerly provided the homeless man with work, employment possibilities have either been drastically reduced—if not eliminated—or the labor force has been unionized.

Even in the field of agricultural labor the homeless man has been displaced not only by machines but by the immigration of Puerto Ricans or the importation of Mexicans. It has also become easier for men to travel with their families and consequently many of these mobile jobs are taken by family units. Finally, average farm wages are so low that many a homeless man prefers to secure whatever relief benefits may be available to him.

The fact that entry into skid row through the world of work has been greatly reduced in both relative and absolute terms when compared with conditions prevailing before World War II has resulted in a decline of the population of most skid rows throughout the United States. An estimate from the Chicago study indicates that the skid row of 1960 is about one-fourth its relative size of 1920.[3]

The Minneapolis data reveal that the relative size of its skid row population has been steadily declining since at least 1940.[4] Data from other major cities in the United States tell a similar story. The skid row population reached its height in absolute numbers and relative proportions in 1935, and since then has declined in relative proportions in nearly every case and in absolute figures in most. Today's population of skid row contains from one-tenth to one-third of persons who entered through the world of work, this proportion varying according to the importance of casual labor in the area surrounding a particular skid row. In general this means a declining proportion from West to East and North to South.

Contact with skid row subculture through welfare agencies and programs has also considerably diminished but in this case because of changes in the policies and practices of welfare agencies rather than because of a decline in the number of relief recipients. Before World War I, skid row and the typically adjacent slums were the centers of welfare activity—when any such organized program existed. The blind, the lame, the ill, and the impoverished were all cared for, if at all, in these locales. When hard times hit the nation, breadlines and soup kitchens were also set up in slums or skid row. Welfare programs such as home relief and institutional care in specialized areas outside the city itself are relatively recent phenomena.

Today the mobile worker has practically vanished from the American scene, and the welfare client no longer need rub shoulders with the skid rower in the process of securing relief. Both these changes have led to a significant decline in the population of all skid rows throughout the country. The *aficionado*-recruit has also been by and large lost to skid row. He seems to find the climate of today's society more temperate toward some, at least, of his proclivities. Nevertheless, those who do find their way to skid row today travel much the same roads as ever though there are a lot fewer travelers and the proportion using one road rather than another may have altered.

Notes

1. Howard Becker's recent publication had a significant influence on my own work, an influence which is most gratefully acknowledged. He terms this type of analysis a sequential model. Howard S. Becker. *Outsiders: Studies in the Sociology of Deviance.* Glencoe: Free Press, 1963. See particularly Chapter 2, "Kinds of Deviance: A Sequential Model."

2. Robert W. Beasley. *Care of Destitute Men in Chiago.* Chicago: unpublished M.A. thesis, University of Chicago, 1933. See Appendix B. p. 121.

3. Chicago Tenants Relocation Bureau. *The Homeless Man on Skid Row.* Chicago: mimeographed report, 1961.

4. Theodore Caplow, Keith A. Lovald and Samuel E. Wallace. *A General Report on the Problem of Relocating the Population of the Lower Loop Redevelopment Area.* Minneapolis: Minneapolis Housing and Redevelopment Authority, 1958, p. 22.

37 / Becoming a Taxi-Dancer: The Significance of Neutralization in a Semi-Deviant Occupation

LAWRENCE K. HONG
ROBERT W. DUFF

Taxi-dancing, which was one of the most common forms of masculine recreation in the 1920s and 1930s (Cressey, 1932; Nye, 1973), has been regaining its popularity in recent years (Hong and Duff, 1976). In Los Angeles, for example, the number of taxi-dance halls has more than doubled in the last few years; increasing from three in 1971 to eight today. Other American cities where taxi-dance halls may be found include New York, Detroit, and Honolulu. Hundreds of taxi-dance halls may also be found in Asian cities such as Hong Kong, Tokyo, and Manila. The revival of taxi-dance halls in the United States can be partially attributed to an expansion of their functions in recent years. Though supplying female partners for dancing purpose is still their chief function, there is a growing emphasis in the taxi-dance halls of the 1970s toward promoting a "social club" atmosphere. Comfortable sitting areas are provided in the dance halls for customers and hostesses to converse and share nonalcoholic refreshments. Customers are also encouraged to play pool and other games with the dance hostesses. Once a week and on special days, such as Valentine's Day and New Year's Eve, buffet dinners are also served in the dance halls to enhance the convivial atmosphere of the clubs.

Customers are delighted with the new approach adopted by the dance halls. With the increased opportunity to socialize with the hostesses, they find it easier to act out their fantasies and satisfy their needs for romantic involvement. Working as a dance hostess is an unconventional venture for most of the women. First of all, the reality of the job requires the simulation of a romantic relationship between the hostess and the customers. It is obvious that this type of pseudo-relationship is in direct contradiction to both the past and the present ideologies pertaining to female-male relations. Furthermore, the job also runs against some traditional normative expectations, because it requires intimate interactions with customers who may be very different from the hostess in terms of age, race, and cultural background (see Hong and Duff, 1976). Also, the public attitude today still views taxi-dancing as a form of activity bordering on prostitution, in spite of the fact that the occupation is approved by local ordinances.

Who are these women who become taxi-dancers? How do they avoid self-esteem damage? How do they overcome the traditional normative barriers with respect to age and race? How do they protect themselves from the possible negative reactions of friends and relatives?

Based on published reports pertaining to other semi-deviant and deviant occupations (Pittman, 1971; Saulutin, 1971; Riege, 1969; Lopata and Noel, 1967; Bryan, 1965, 1966), we initiated the study with the expectation that taxi-dancers, similar to workers in related occupations, may utilize some forms of justification to neutralize the unpleasantness of their job. However, we felt the previously published comments on the use of justifications are too scanty to allow making reliable inferences on their applicability to taxi-dancers. Furthermore, they are also ambiguous on the role of neutralization in occupational socialization. Hence, we studied the taxi-dancers in Los Angeles, hoping that our research would result in more adequate answers to these (aforementioned) questions.

METHODS

The material of this study was obtained by means of participant observation and intensive interviews. We observed and interviewed more than 70 dance hostesses in Los Angeles over a four year period. We approached the hostesses as customers and were able to develop excellent rapport with them. After about six months from the onset of the study, one of the authors became so well acquainted with a number of the hostesses that he was able to maintain informal social contacts with them outside the dance halls.

In gathering the information, two methods of sampling were employed. The first method is similar to a panel survey design: we chose a number of newly hired hostesses, starting from their first day on the job, and informally interviewed each of them over an average period of two months, with 18 months being the longest. During the first two weeks, the hostesses were interviewed every two or three days. In the subsequent weeks, the interviews were conducted at four or five day intervals. During the entire study period, the hostess' interactions with her customers, other hostesses, and the management were also carefully observed. This method of interview and observation was applied to six different groups of taxi-dancers at different times. The size of the groups ranged from three to five.

Since the first method was too costly in terms of money and time for a large sample, a second method of sampling approximating the cohort survey design was also employed. Slightly more than half of the hostesses were interviewed once or twice and divided into different cohorts according to the length of time they had been on the job. Thus, by comparing the different cohorts, we were able to assess their attitudes and other behaviors over time without having to track the same individuals for an extended period.

In analyzing the data, we compared relevant information from our interviews with Sykes and Matza's (1957) neutralization techniques. In the remainder of this paper, we shall present the findings and the typical responses of the interviewees.

FINDINGS

Recruiting the Hostesses

Young women are recruited to work in the dance halls through newspaper advertisements and the personal efforts of women currently employed as hostesses. Due to the high turnover rate for hostesses, "want-ads" to recruit new women appear in the classified sections of the local newspapers almost every day. However, only about half the hostesses are recruited through the newspapers. Almost an equal number are recruited by women already employed in the dance halls. Many hostesses, after having developed a positive attitude toward their occupation, are eager recruiters; they want their friends and relatives to work with them.

Most of the women hired are young (18 to 25), white, divorced or separated, and have finished high school. They generally come from a working class or lower middle class background. Judging from these personal characteristics, it is evident that they have been purposely selected. The dance hall managers prefer young, white, and unattached women because they can attract more customers, for obvious reasons. Furthermore, they want to hire women of at least lower middle or working class background who have at minimum a high school education to insure that their hostesses possess the types of conversational skills and demeanor that are conducive to nurturing the romantic fantasies of the customers.

For women who want to become taxi-dancers, the main attraction is money. The hostesses are guaranteed $2.00 to $2.50 an hour plus an additional amount for the time they spend with customers. The customers are charged at a rate of $.15 per minute from the time they "check out" a hostess to the time they "check in"; the hostess receives about 50% of this charge as her commission. On average, a hostess can make between $3.60 to $5.40 an hour, which is substantially more than what she can receive from a conventional job.

Typically, a woman seeking employment in a taxi-dance hall knows very little about the job; the revival of taxi-dancing is too recent for the various aspects of this work-role to have become popular knowledge, and she is too young to have any knowledge of its controversial past. During the employment interview, the job is briefly described to her by the manager or the owner. The description typically is vague and accentuates the positives:

> This job is like going to a party every night. If you like to dance and talk to people, this job is perfect for you. The girls sit over there and the customers come over to ask them to dance. You will meet people from all over the world. If you don't like a particular customer, you don't have to dance with him. It is just like in a party, if you don't like a guy, you don't have to dance with him. You'll be paid the same for sitting and talking with a customer as for dancing with him. This is really a fun job.

Those who are personally recruited by friends and relatives are not likely to possess much more information about the job than those who respond to the newspaper want-ads, because their friends and relatives would not have recruited them if they disliked the job. Therefore, almost all the women entering the taxi-dancing career have only a very superficial knowledge of its activities and demands.

Confronting the Reality

During the first day on the job, many hostesses immediately find out that the job is psychologically stressful. The majority of these women, due to their social and educational backgrounds, are conventional in their values and attitudes. They share the dominant values of the outside society and their particular age group with respect to female-male relationships. Hence, they find it intensely uncomfortable when their customers are interested not only in social dancing but also in romantic and/or sexual involvement. Almost invariably the new hostess has some early negative experiences with customers who aggressively demand forms of sexual contact on the dance floor. Oftentimes this is part of a ritual "testing out" of the new hostess by one or more of the regular customers.

Compounding the problem is the disparity in age, race, and cultural background between the hostesses and the customers. Almost half the clientele of the dance halls are foreign-born Mexicans, Chinese, and Filipinos. Although many customers are white, these are usually much older than the hostesses. As a consequence of her early negative experiences coupled with what she discovers about the nature of the clientele, it is not uncommon to find a new hostess feeling depressed during her first week on the job.

Some of the new hostesses may turn down customers whom they had found to be unpleasant from previous occasions. When this occurs too often or when she shows signs of depression, the management will try to console her by jokingly pointing out the intrinsic rewards of her work. She is informed that her job is like "a social worker or a counselor" trying to help these "lonely men who are far away from home" or "who are unhappy with their wives." Similar psychological support also comes from her coworkers, especially if they include friends or relatives who were instrumental in recruiting her.

In our view, the encouragements provided by the management and the coworkers are the first step in a very important socialization process leading the woman to accept her work role as a taxi-dancer. Consciously or unconsciously, the management and her coworkers (which may include friends or relatives) are beginning to supply the new hostess with "justifications" to continue working in the dance hall. As we shall see later, these justifications can be best described as "neutralization techniques" (Sykes and Matza, 1957; Ball, 1966; Priest and McGrath, 1970; Dunford and Kunz, 1973; Rogers and Buffalo, 1974; Friedman, 1974) because it is through the learning of the justifications that the new hostess eventually comes to accept her job. The internalization of these justifications, which becomes intensified during the second and third weeks, appears to be a precondition helping to make the taxi-dancer role acceptable to the young woman.

However, it must be pointed out that many new hostesses have become so depressed and disgusted with the job that they simply quit after the first week. Some of them would leave sooner (and a few do), if the pay period was not on a weekly basis. From our four years of observation, we estimate at least one-fourth of the new hostesses do not return to work after the first week. For those who remain, the next two weeks become the most crucial period in learning to accept the taxi-dancer role.

Learning to Neutralize

About 75% of the new hostesses survive the first week. However, as they enter the second week of their work in the taxi-dance hall, they are still uncertain about whether or not they want the job. But, as compared to those who have left, they feel less depressed about the job, and their attitudes toward the customers are mixed rather than totally negative. It must be mentioned that this mixed feeling does not necessarily represent a progressive change on their part; many of the hostesses have this attitude to begin with. In fact, it was this mixed feeling that had prevented them from quitting work after the first week. When asked about her feeling toward her job, a hostess in her second week of work commented:

> I don't know. You meet a lot of different people in this job. Some are very nice, but some are weird. You have to know how to handle yourself. Sometimes you get a good customer and it is great. Last night, this man just sat and talked with me for hours. He was really nice. If all my customers were like him, it'd be all right.

During the second week, the new hostess also begins to know the management and other hostesses better, and feels more at ease in interacting with them. This is an important development in her socialization process which paves the way for her to learn more "neutralization techniques." Though she was introduced to the techniques during her first week at work, it is in the second and third weeks that she begins to learn most of the techniques through repeated interactions with management and co-workers. It should be noted that hostesses who were recruited by friends and relatives usually have a slight head start on learning the neutralization techniques because their friends or relatives are likely to expose them to a large variety of techniques as early as the first week. Thus, with the additional help from the management and other hostesses, these hostesses tend to master the variety of neutralization techniques much faster than those who were recruited by other means.

The management always attempts to promote a casual and relaxed atmosphere in the dance hall. When business is not busy, the hostesses usually sit around in small groups and chat. Generally, the talks revolve around daily activities and news items of interest to them. But, when a new hostess is present in the group, the conversation inevitably turns to her attitude toward the job and the customers. The new hostess may also have questions concerning the job that she wants to ask the other hostesses. It is in such informal gatherings that the new hostess is exposed to a variety of neutralization techniques.

In addition to being exposed to the "claim of benefits" technique (Friedman, 1974) mentioned earlier—i.e., the idea that the taxi-dancer role is philanthropic—the new hostess is also exposed to other neutralization techniques such as "denial of injury," "denial of victim," and "denial of responsibility" (see Sykes and Matza, 1957; Ball, 1966; Priest and McGrath, 1970; Dunford and Kunz, 1973; Rogers and Buffalo, 1974; Friedman, 1974). For example, the "denial of injury" technique was clearly implied in a conversation between a new hostess and her coworkers overheard by one of the authors. One of the more experienced hostesses, in trying to soothe the guilt feeling of a novice who thought she was leading her customers on by playing along with their romantic interests, commented: "Don't feel bad about it. I do it all the time. They know about it. They are not that foolish." In other words, the new hostess was being informed, albeit erroneously, that the customers were not actually emotionally involved, and that they were aware that the hostesses were feigning involvement as part of the game. Therefore, nobody was hurt in the game, and she should not feel guilty about it. In the same conversation, another hostess, who had been working there for at least six months, injected a comment that can be most appropriately classified as "denial of victim":

> They deserve it. I don't care. All they want is to get you to bed with them. This guy dances with me all the time, and asks me to go to breakfast with him after work. I know what he wants, but he is not going to get anything from me.

In the second comment, the hostess was implying that the customer was the transgressor rather than the victim, and therefore deserving of injury. She was not concerned about hurting the feelings of her customer because he was the wrong-doer.

The "denial of responsibility" is also a common neutralization technique used by the hostesses. A new hostess who feels the job is demeaning is likely to be reminded by her coworkers that "every job is the same." "As long as there are men around, they will proposition you. It doesn't matter whether you work in an office, a factory, or a dance hall." In other words, since there are no alternatives, the hostess is not personally accountable for choosing a job that she finds to be degrading.

At first these justifications are casually passed on to a novice by the experienced hostesses ostensibly as a means of helping her to resolve immediate moral dilemmas, but once they are internalized, they become an effective mechanism that can be activated in the future to render inoperative those internal and external restraints that may pull her away from the taxi-dancing career. At any rate, by the end of the third week, many new hostesses are well versed in the neutralization techniques. When they are asked about their job, inevitably they will respond in terms of justifications.

It is important to point out that the use of neutralization techniques alone is not sufficient to make a new hostess committed to her work. During the second seek, she is still evaluating her job—balancing its benefits (mainly income) with its cost (mainly emotional stress). The utilization of neutralization techniques undoubtedly has helped her in reducing the costs and thus enhancing the potential rewards of the job. But, if the amount of income does not meet her expectations (due to paucity of customers), she is not likely to keep the job for too long, in spite of the reduced psychological cost as a result of neutralization. Similarly, some new hostesses may find the stress of the job so intolerable, either because of failure to internalize the neutralization techniques, or in spite of internalizing them, that they quit the job regardless of the amount of income. In short, neutralization appears to be a necessary factor but not a sufficient factor in influencing the occupational commitment of the taxi-dancers.

Acquiring Steady Customers

There is always competition for the "better" steady customers: those who treat the hostess more like a date, are less sexually aggressive, of higher socioeconomic status, and pay for long periods of time. Frictions between hostesses may result from attempts to steal, or "move in on," a good steady customer. The new hostess is at a disadvantage when she enters into this competition. Many of the more desirable customers are already into steady relationships with the established hostesses. As a result, the new hostess' initial experiences are often with some of the least desirable of the dance hall regulars, including some of the most sexually aggressive. On the other hand, she does have one advantage — she is new. A new face and personality always attract attention in the dance hall, and a new hostess can successfully steal a steady customer from an experienced hostess if she has mastered certain tactics.

These tactics entail the development of an *impression* to each customer that their relationship is exclusive. She argues to each that he is the "only one that really interests" her. "The others are all just part of the job." They "mean nothing" to her. In other words, she must cultivate the romantic interest of the customers by "leading them on." These are, at the same time, the tactics that the experienced hostesses employ to keep their steady customers, and the tactics that the new hostesses must master in order to acquire a steady clientele.

However, it should be emphasized that aggressively stealing, or "moving in on" the steady customers of an established hostess is not a common means by which the new hostess secures her steadies. There are many other customers, including regulars, who do not have steady partners. Usually, it is from this group that the new hostess attempts to recruit her clientele. In addition, the tactic of "leading on" customers, so prevalent among the hostesses, actually insures that a certain turnover of customers will take place. Most customers sooner or later become suspicious of their hostess' performance. Her continual verbal reassurance of fidelity is in constant contradiction to the visual evidence which the customer must confront as he observes her with other steadies. Also, most steady customers are finally frustrated when their relationship never develops beyond the confines of the dance hall; though sometimes a hostess will allow the relationship to extend outside the hall in order to hold a restless but highly desirable customer, or because she has actually become personally interested in the man. In general, however, new hostesses are seen as offering "new possibilities" to the customer who is becoming suspicious, frustrated, or simply bored with his steady hostess, or who has lost his steady partner because she has quit her job.

A few new hostesses learn to apply the tactics of "leading on" the customers as early as the first week on the job. From the perspective of the taxi-dancing profession, these women are "naturals": they do not acquire the tactics from the dance halls but seem to possess exceptional interpersonal skills even before they are taxi-dancers. Most of the new hostesses, however, learn the tactics from the more experienced hostesses! Normally, one would expect the established hostesses to guard the secrets of their success, especially from their potential competitors. But, surprisingly, this is not the case. In fact, they are eager to discuss their tactics with other hostesses, especially the new ones.

Without prying into the psyche of the established hostesses, it is difficult to assess their motives for divulging their secrets. But, a number of hypotheses are possible. First, the hostess may have a compulsion to confess in order to purge herself of the guilt feelings which arise from her leading customers on (cf. Friedman, 1968 on the scatological rites of burglars). This hypothesis would also imply partial failure in the use of neutralization techniques. A second hypothesis may be that the established hostess is attempting to assert her social status by boasting of her exploits with the customers in front of the other hostesses, especially the new ones. Finally, a third interpretation is also possible. The established hostesses may be doing it for self-protection. By sharing her trade secrets with the new hostesses, she may make them feel indebted to her and refrain from "moving in on" her steady customers. Some evidence tends to support the third hypothesis: we do not recall finding any new hostess moving in on the steady clientele of an established hostess, if the latter is friendly to the new hostess starting from her first week on the job.

Enjoying the Work

Upon entering the fourth week of her career, a taxi-dancer usually finds the job sufficiently rewarding to keep it for an indefinite period of time; she is not interested in looking for another job at least in the foreseeable future. Apparently, she has internalized enough justifications to neutralize much of the unpleasantness of the job; she is also likely to have acquired a number of steady customers to keep the job financially rewarding.

From the fourth week onward, there is also a noticeable decrease in her verbalization of justifications. When asked about her job, she is likely to say: "I like it," "It's fun," or "It's an easy job." She also begins to show enthusiasm in her work as indicated by acts in her interactions with coworkers and customers such as smiling, giggling, touching, offering cigarettes and chewing gum, greeting by saying "hi," and saying "see you" when leaving.

Perhaps, the most revealing indications of her new attitude are her willingness to recruit friends and relatives to work as taxi-dancers, and her emerging status consciousness within the dance hall. It is reasonable to assume that unless she sees some positive features in it, she will not ask her friends and relatives to work with her. She would be courting potential damage to her self-esteem by exposing her world of work to her friends and relatives, if she believed that taxi-dancing was demeaning or degrading. Some elements of self-fulfilling prophecy are also at work here: while her emerging positive attitude may lead her to recruit friends and relatives, having friends and relatives working with her may, in turn, legitimize her work and make her attitude toward her job more positive.

Her new attitude can also be seen in her development of status consciousness. She begins to speak with pride about the fact that she has steady customers, that her customers spend a long period of time with her, and that they are the better ones—i.e., they are nice, educated, have a good job, and, most important, do not "grab and grind."

The hostess is extremely proud of herself, if her customers begin to come in to see her on a regular schedule—with time and day prearranged—as determined by *her convenience*. Tardiness and absences on the part of customers are at their own risks; her time will have to be paid even though the customers are not physically present. She is now at the pinnacle of her career, and enjoys it immensely. However, it should be added that even for the successful taxi-dancer, her career will seldom extend for more than two or three years. There are a variety of reasons for this. The hostesses belong to a transient age group. Like other workers in the same age category, they are highly mobile. Many marry and retire. Some find a better job. Some move from the Los Angeles area. Only a few see the job as a long-term endeavor.

DISCUSSION AND SUMMARY

Studies of deviant and semi-deviant occupations, such as call girls (Bryan, 1965, 1966), strippers (Saulutin, 1971), dance instructresses (Lopata and Noel, 1967; Riege, 1969), masseuses (Verlarde and Warlick, 1973), and male prostitutes (Pittman, 1971), have consistently reported that workers in these occupations use justifications to explain or to defend their occupational behaviors. The present study also finds the same tendency among the taxi-dancers. Moreover, we find that the learning of justifications plays a significant role in the occupational socialization of the taxi-dancers. Without learning the various justifications to neutralize the unpleasantness of the job, the novice is not likely to commit herself to the taxi-dancing career. Typically, a taxi-dancer goes through the following process in her occupational socialization which is highlighted by her learning of the neutralization techniques.

(1) The First Week. Before starting her work in the taxi-dance hall, a new hostess knows very little about the job she is about to work. During the job interview, she is given the impression that the job is easy and fun. However, on the first day of her work, she is shocked to find out that many customers have amorous interests in her, and may make sexual advances toward her. Compounding the problem is that many of the customers are either foreign born or older whites. Being young, white, high school educated, and working class in background, she finds it difficult to reconcile her conventional values with the unconventional behaviors in the dance hall. She feels depressed. The management and other hostesses console her by jokingly pointing out the intrinsic values of her work—i.e., she is helping out the "lonely men" and "unhappy husbands." If she has friends or relatives working in the same place, they will take a major role in consoling her too. This is the beginning of her exposure to the neutralization techniques.

(2) The Second and Third Weeks. During the next two weeks, the new hostess is still evaluating her job—balancing its financial benefit with its emotional cost. She is still unsure about the job. But, now she becomes exposed to more neutralization techniques as she interacts more frequently with the management and other hostesses. Besides the "claim of benefit" technique, she is also exposed to others which can be best described as "denial of injury," "denial of victim," and "denial of responsibility" techniques. By the end of the third week, she has a tendency to respond in terms of "neutralization techniques" when asked about her job. If she is recruited by friends or relatives, they may introduce her to these techniques as early as the first week.

(3) The Fourth Week and Beyond. As she enters the fourth week, the hostess is likely to have made a positive resolution about her job. It is apparent that she has neutralized much of the unpleasantness of the job, and found the balance of benefit and cost in favor of keeping the job. She is likely to have acquired the tactics of "leading her customer on," thus enabling her to secure a steady clientele. Gradually, she begins to use fewer neutralization responses, when asked

about her job. Instead she begins to use more positive responses such as "I like it," "It is fun," and so on. Her new positive attitude toward her job is also revealed in her interactions with coworkers, her pride in her customers, and her status consciousness. She shows a genuine interest and enjoyment in her work.

In view of the findings of this study, it appears that the use of justifications by workers in the semi-deviant and deviant occupations may have far greater significance than what had been previously recognized. Former studies seldom pay attention to the role justifications played in occupational socialization. This oversight may be attributed to the method of data collection used in these studies. All the former studies cited in this paper obtained their information by interviewing subjects at one point in time after they had been established in their occupations. On the other hand, we used a longitudinal approach. We interviewed and observed panels of subjects over a period of time beginning from their early days in the profession, and also cohorts of subjects representing various lengths of tenure on the job. Thus, we were able to discover that the justifications were learned, and that they were being used as neutralization techniques with the effect of facilitating commitment to the job.

In conclusion, we would like to emphasize that the use of neutralization techniques is not limited to semi-deviant and deviant occupations. For example, Friedman (1974) has observed that these techniques are also employed by workers in legitimate occupations, such as salesmen and contest interviewers. Future research, therefore, may want to look into the process of learning and the significance of neutralization techniques in other occupations, including the legitimate ones.

References

Ball, R. (1966) "An empirical exploration of neutralization theory." Criminologica 4 (August): 22–32.

Bryan, J. (1966) "Occupational ideologies and individual attitudes of call girls." Social Problems 13 (Spring): 441–450.

———. (1965) "Apprenticeships in prostitution." Social Problems 12 (Winter): 287–297.

Cressey, P. (1932) The Taxi-Dance Hall. Chicago: Univ. of Chicago Press.

Dunford, F. and P. Kunz (1973) "The neutralization of religious dissonance." Rev. of Religious Research 15 (Fall): 2–9.

Friedman, A. (1968) "The scatological rites of burglars." Western Folklore 27 (July): 171–179.

Friedman, N. (1974) "Cookies and contests: notes on ordinary occupational deviance and its neutralization." Sociological Symposium 11 (Spring): 1–9.

Hong, L. and R. Duff (1976) "Gentlemen's social club: revival of taxi-dancing in Los Angeles." J. of Popular Culture 9 (Spring): 827–832.

Lopata, H. and J. Noel (1967) "The dance studio—style without sex." Trans-Action (January/February): 10–17.

Nye, R. (1973) "Saturday night at the paradise ballroom: or, dance halls in the twenties." J. of Popular Culture 7 (Summer): 14–22.

Pittman, D. (1971) "The male house of prostitution." Trans-Action 8 (March/April): 21–27.

Priest, M. and J. McGrath III (1970) "Techniques of neutralization: young adult marijuana smokers." Criminology 8 (August): 185–194.

Riege, M. (1969) "The call girl and the dance teacher: a comparative analysis." Cornell J. of Social Relations 4 (Spring): 58–70.

Rogers, J. and M. Buffalo (1974) "Neutralization techniques." Pacific Soc. Rev. 17 (July): 313–331.

Saulutin, M. (1971) "Stripper morality." Trans-Action 9 (June): 12–27.

Sykes, G. and D. Matza (1957) "Techniques of neutralization: a theory of delinquency." Amer. Soc. Rev. 26 (December): 664–670.

Verlarde, A. and M. Warlick (1973) "Massage parlours: the sensuality business." Society 11 (November/December): 63–74.

38 / The Madam as Teacher: The Training of House Prostitutes

BARBARA SHERMAN HEYL

Although the day of the elaborate and conspicuous high-class house of prostitution is gone, houses still operate throughout the United States in a variety of altered forms. The business may be run out of trailers and motels along major highways, luxury apartments in the center of a metropolis or run-down houses in smaller, industrialized cities. (Recent discussions of various aspects of house prostitution include: Gagnon and Simon, 1973:226–7; Hall, 1973: 115–95; Heyl, 1974; Jackson, 1969:185–92; Sheehy, 1974:185–204; Stewart, 1972; and Vogliotti, 1975:25–80.) Madams sometimes find themselves teaching young women how to become professional prostitutes. This paper focuses on one madam who trains novices to work at the house level. I compare the training to Bryan's (1965) account of the apprenticeship of call girls and relate the madam's role to the social organization of house prostitution.

Bryan's study of thirty-three Los Angeles call girls is one of the earliest interactionist treatments of prostitution. His data focus on the process of entry into the occupation of call girl and permit an analysis of the structure and content of a woman's apprenticeship. He concluded that the apprenticeship of call girls is mainly directed toward developing a clientele, rather than sexual skills (1965:288, 296–7). But while Bryan notes that pimps seldom train women directly, approximately half of his field evidence in fact derives from pimp-call girl apprenticeships. Thus, in Bryan's study (as well as in subsequent work on entry into prostitution as an occupation) there is a missing set of data on the more typical female trainer-trainee relationship and on the content and process of training at other levels of the business in nonmetropolitan settings. This paper attempts to fill this gap.

I. ANN'S TURN-OUT ESTABLISHMENT

A professional prostitute, whether she works as a streetwalker, house prostitute, or call girl, can usually pick out one person in her past who "turned her out," that is, who taught her the basic techniques and rules of the prostitute's occupation.[1] For women who begin working at the house level, that person may be a pimp, another "working girl," or a madam. Most madams and managers of prostitution establishments, however, prefer not to take on novice prostitutes, and they may even have a specific policy against hiring turn-outs (see Erwin (1960:204–5) and Lewis (1942:222)). The turn-out's inexperience may cost the madam clients and money; to train the novice, on the other hand, costs her time and energy. Most madams and managers simply do not want the additional burden.

It was precisely the madam's typical disdain for turn-outs that led to the emergence of the house discussed in this paper— a house specifically devoted to training new prostitutes. The madam of this operation, whom we shall call Ann, is forty-one years old and has been in the prostitution world twenty-three years, working primarily at the house level. Ann knew that pimps who manage women at this level have difficulty placing novices in houses. After operating several houses staffed by professional prostitutes, she decided to run a school for turn-outs partly as a strategy for acquiring a continually changing staff of young women for her house. Pimps are the active recruiters of new prostitutes, and Ann found that, upon demonstrating that she could transform the pimps' new, square women into trained prostitutes easily placed in professional houses, pimps would help keep her business staffed.[2] Ann's house is a small operation in a middle-sized, industrial city (population 300,000), with a limited clientele of primarily working-class men retained as customers for ten to fifteen years and offered low rates to maintain their patronage.

Although Ann insists that every turn-out is different, her group of novices is remarkably homogeneous in some ways. Ann has turned out approximately twenty women a year over the six years while she has operated a training school. Except for one Chicano, one black and one American Indian, the women were all white. They ranged in age from eighteen to twenty seven. Until three years ago, all the women she hired had pimps. Since then, more women are independent (so-called "outlaws"), although many come to Ann sponsored by a pimp. That is, in return for being placed with Ann, the turn-out gives the pimp a percentage of her earnings for a specific length of time. At present eighty percent of the turn-outs come to Ann without a long-term commitment to a pimp. The turn-outs stay at Ann's on the average of two to three months. This is the same average length of time Bryan (1965:290) finds for the apprenticeship in his call-girl study. Ann seldom has more than two or three women in training at any one time. Most turn-outs live at the house, often just a large apartment near the older business section of the city.

II. THE CONTENT OF THE TRAINING

The data for the following analysis are of three kinds. First, tape recordings from actual training sessions with fourteen novices helped specify the structure and content of the training provided. Second, lengthy interviews with three of the novices and multiple interviews with Ann were conducted to obtain data on the training during the novice's first few days at the house before the first group training sessions were conducted and recorded by Ann. And third, visits to the house on ten occasions and observations of Ann's interaction with the novices during teaching periods extended the data on training techniques used and the relationship between madam and novice. In addition, weekly contact with Ann over a four-year period allowed repeated review of current problems and strategies in training turnouts.

Ann's training of the novice begins soon after the woman arrives at the house. The woman first chooses an alias. Ann then asks her whether she has ever "Frenched a guy all the way," that is, whether she has brought a man to orgasm during the act of fellatio. Few of the women say they have. By admitting her lack of competence in a specialized area, the novice has permitted Ann to assume the role of teacher. Ann then launches into instruction on performing fellatio. Such instruction is important to her business. Approximately eighty percent of her customers are what Ann calls "French tricks." Many men visit prostitutes to receive sexual services, including fellatio, their wives or lovers seldom perform. This may be particularly true of the lower- and working-class clientele of the houses and hotels of prostitution (Gagnon and Simon, 1973:230). Yet the request for fellatio may come from clients at all social levels; consequently, it is a sexual skill today's prostitute must possess and one she may not have prior to entry into the business (Bryan, 1965:293; Winick and Kinsie, 1971:180, 207; Gray, 1973:413).

Although Ann devotes much more time to teaching the physical and psychological techniques of performing fellatio than she does to any other sexual skill, she also provides strategies for coitus and giving a "half and half"—fellatio followed by coitus. The sexual strategies taught are frequently a mixture of ways for stimulating the client sexually and techniques of self-protection during the sexual acts. For example, during coitus, the woman is to move her hips "like a go-go dancer's" while keeping her feet on the bed and tightening her inner thigh muscles to protect herself from the customer's thrust and full penetration. Ann allows turn-outs to perform coitus on their backs only, and the woman is taught to keep one of her arms across her chest as a measure of self-defense in this vulnerable position.

After Ann has described the rudimentary techniques for the three basic sexual acts — fellatio, coitus, and "half and half" — she begins to explain the rules of the house operation. The first set of rules concerns what acts the client may receive for specific sums of money. Time limits are imposed on the clients, roughly at the rate of $1 per minute; the minimum rate in this house is $15 for any of the three basic positions. Ann describes in detail what will occur when the first client arrives: he will be admitted by either Ann or the maid; the women are to stand and smile at him, but not speak to him (considered "dirty hustling"); he will choose one of the women and go to the bedroom with her. Ann accompanies the turn-out and the client to the bedroom and begins teaching the woman how to check the man for any cuts or open sores on the genitals and for any signs of old or active venereal disease. Ann usually rechecks each client herself during the turn-out's first two weeks of work. For the first few days Ann remains in the room while the turn-out and client negotiate the sexual contract. In ensuing days Ann spends time helping the woman develop verbal skills to "hustle" the customer for more expensive sexual activities.

The following analysis of the instruction Ann provides is based on tape recordings made by Ann during actual training sessions in 1971 and 1975. These sessions took place after the turn-outs had worked several days but usually during their first two weeks of work. The tapes contain ten hours of group discussion with fourteen different novices. The teaching tapes were analyzed according to topics covered in the discussions, using the method outlined in Barker (1963) for making such divisions in the flow of conversation and using Bryan's analysis of the call girl's apprenticeship as a guide in grouping the topics. Bryan divides the content of the training of call girls into two broad dimensions, one philosophical and one interpersonal (1965: 291–4). The first emphasizes a subcultural value system and sets down guidelines for how the novice *should* treat her clients and her colleagues in the business. The second dimension follows from the first but emphasizes actual behavioral techniques and skills.

The content analysis of the taped training sessions produced three major topics of discussion and revealed the relative amount of time Ann devoted to each. The first two most frequently discussed topics can be categorized under Bryan's dimension of interpersonal skills; they were devoted to teaching situational strategies for managing clients. The third topic resembles Bryan's value dimension (1965: 291–2).

The first topic stressed physical skills and strategies. Included in this category were instruction on how to perform certain sexual acts and specification of their prices, discussion of particular clients, and instruction in techniques for dealing with certain categories of clients, such as "older men" or "kinky" tricks. This topic of physical skills also included discussion of, and Ann's demonstration of, positions designed to provide the woman maximum comfort and protection from the man during different sexual acts. Defense tactics, such as ways to get out of a sexual position and out of the bedroom quickly, were practiced by the novices. Much time was devoted to analyzing past encounters with particular clients. Bryan finds similar discussions of individual tricks among novice call girls and their trainers (1965:293). In the case of Ann's turn-outs these discussions were often initiated by a novice's complaint or question about a certain client and his requests or behavior in the bedroom. The novice always received tips and advice from Ann and the other women present on how to manage that type of bedroom encounter. Such sharing of tactics allows the turn-out to learn what Gagnon and Simon call "patterns of client management" (1973:231).

Ann typically used these discussions of bedroom difficulties to further the training in specific sexual skills she had begun during the turn-out's first few days at work. It is possible that the addition of such follow-up sexual training to that provided during the turn-out's first days at the house results in a more extensive teaching of actual sexual skills than that obtained either by call girls or streeetwalkers. Bryan finds that in the call-girl training—except for fellatio—"There seems to be little instruction concerning sexual techniques as such, even though the previous sexual experience of the trainee may have been quite limited" (1965:293). Gray (1973:413) notes that her sample of streetwalker turn-outs were rarely taught specific work strategies:

> They learned these things by trial and error on the job. Nor were they schooled in specific sexual techniques: usually they were taught by customers who made the specific requests.

House prostitution may require more extensive sexual instruction than other forms of the business. The dissatisfied customer of a house may mean loss of business and therefore loss of income to the madam and the prostitutes who work there. The sexually inept streetwalker or call girl does not hurt business for anyone but herself; she may actually increase business for those women in the area should dissatisfied clients choose to avoid her. But the house depends on a stable clientele of satisfied customers.

The second most frequently discussed topic could be labeled: client management—verbal skills. Ann's primary concern was teaching what she calls "hustling." "Hustling" is similar to what Bryan terms a "sales pitch" for call girls (1965:292), but in the house setting it takes place in the bedroom while the client is deciding how much to spend and what sexual acts he wishes performed. "Hustling" is designed to encourage the client to spend more than the minimum rate.³ The prominence on the teaching tapes of instruction in this verbal skill shows its importance in Ann's training of novices.

On one of the tapes Ann uses her own turning-out experience to explain to two novices (both with pimps) why she always teaches hustling skills as an integral part of working in a house.

Ann as a Turn-out⁴

Ann: Of course, I can remember a time when I didn't know that I was supposed to hustle. So that's why I understand that it's difficult to *learn* to hustle. When I turned out it was $2 a throw. They came in. They gave me their $2. They got a hell of a fuck. And that was it. Then one Saturday night I turned *forty four* tricks! And Penny [the madam] used to put the number of tricks at the top of the page and the amount of money at the bottom of the page—she used these big ledger books. Lloyd [Ann's pimp] came in at six o'clock and he looked at that book and he just *knew* I had made all kinds of money. Would you believe I had turned forty-two $2 tricks and two $3 tricks—because two of 'em got generous and gave me an extra buck! [Laughs] I got my ass whipped. And I was so tired—I thought I was going to die—I was 15 years old. And I got my ass whipped for it. [Ann imitates an angry Lloyd:] "Don't you know you're supposed to ask for more money?!" No, I didn't. Nobody told me that. All they told me was it was $2. So that is learning it the *hard* way. I'm trying to help you learn it the *easy* way, if there is an easy way to do it.

In the same session Ann asks one of the turn-outs (Linda, age eighteen) to practice her hustling rap.

Learning the Hustling Rap

Ann: I'm going to be a trick. You've checked me. I want you to carry it from there. [Ann begins role-playing: she plays the client; Linda, the hustler.]

Linda: [mechanically] What kind of party would like to have?

Ann: That had all the enthusiasm of a wet noodle. I really wouldn't *want* any party with that because you evidently don't want to give me one.

Linda: What kind of party would you *like* to have?

Ann: I usually take a half and half.

Linda: Uh, the money?

Ann: What money?

Linda: The money you're supposed to have! [loudly] 'Cause you ain't gettin' it for free!

Ann: [upset] Linda, if you *ever*, ever say that in my joint . . . Because that's fine for street hustling. In street hustling, you're going to *have* to hard-hustle those guys or they're not going to come up with anything. Because they're going to *try* and get it for free. But when they walk in here, they *know* they're not going to get it for free to begin with. So try another tack—just a little more friendly, not quite so hard-nosed. [Returning to role-playing:] I just take a half and half.

Linda: How about fifteen [dollars]?

Ann: You're leading into the money too fast, honey. Try: "What are you going to spend?" or "How much money are you going to spend?" or something like that.

Linda: How much would you like to spend?

Ann: No! Not "like." 'Cause they don't *like* to spend anything.

Linda: How much *would* you like to spend?

Ann: Make it a very definite, positive statement: "How much are you going to spend?"

Ann considers teaching hustling skills her most difficult and important task. In spite of her lengthy discussion on the tapes of the rules and techniques for dealing with the customer sexually, Ann states that it may take only a few minutes to "show a girl how to turn a trick." A substantially longer period is required, however, to teach her to hustle. To be adept at hustling, the woman must be mentally alert and sensitive to the client's response to what she is saying and doing and be able to act on those perceptions of his reactions. The hustler must maintain a steady patter of verbal coaxing, during which her tone of voice may be more important than her actual words.

In Ann's framework, then, hustling is a form of verbal sexual aggression. Referring to the problems in teaching novices to hustle, Ann notes that "taking the aggressive part is something women are not used to doing; particularly young women." No doubt, hustling is difficult to teach partly because the woman must learn to discuss sexual acts, whereas in her previous experience, sexual behavior and preferences had been negotiated nonverbally (see Gagnon and Simon, 1973:228). Ann feels that to be effective, each woman's "hustling rap" must be her own—one that comes naturally and will strike the clients as sincere. All of that takes practice. But Ann is aware that the difficulty in learning to hustle stems more from the fact that it involved inappropriate sex-role behavior. Bryan concludes that it is precisely this aspect of soliciting men on the telephone that causes the greatest distress to the novice call girl (1965:293). Thus, the call girl's income is affected by how much business she can bring in by her calls, that is, by how well she can learn to be socially aggressive on the telephone. The income of the house prostitute, in turn, depends heavily on her hustling skills in the bedroom. Ann's task, then, is to train the novice, who has recently come from a culture where young women are not expected to be sexually aggressive, to assume that role with a persuasive naturalness.

Following the first two major topics—client management through physical and verbal skills—the teaching of "racket" (prostitution world) values was the third-ranking topic of training and discussion on the teaching tapes. Bryan notes that the major value taught to call girls is "that of maximizing gains and minimizing effort, even if this requires transgressions of either a legal or moral nature" (1965:291). In her training, however, Ann avoids communicating the notion that the novices may exploit the customers in any way they can. For example, stealing or cheating clients is grounds for dismissal from the house. Ann cannot afford the reputation among her tricks that they risk being robbed when they visit her. Moreover, being honest with clients is extolled as a virtue. Thus, Ann urges the novices to tell the trick if she is nervous or unsure, to let him know she is new to the business. This is in direct contradiction to the advice pimps usually give their new women to hide their inexperience from the trick. Ann asserts that honesty in this case usually means that the client will be more tolerant of mistakes in sexual technique, be less likely to interpret hesitancy as coldness, and be generally more helpful and sympathetic. Putting her "basic principle" in the form of a simple directive, Ann declares: "Please the trick, but at the same time get as much money for pleasing him as you possibly can." Ann does not consider hustling to be client exploitation. It is simply the attempt to sell the customer the product with the highest profit margin. That is, she would defend hustling in terms familiar to the businessman or sales manager.

That Ann teaches hustling as a value is revealed in the following discussion between Ann and Sandy—a former hustler and long-time friend of Ann. Sandy, who married a former trick and still lives in town, has come over to the house to help instruct several novices in the hustling business.

Whores, Prostitutes and Hustlers

Ann: [To the turn-outs:] Don't get up-tight that you're hesitating or you're fumbling, within the first week or even the first five years. Because it takes that long to become a good hustler. I mean you can be a whore in one night. There's nothing to that. The first time you take money you're a whore.

Sandy: This girl in Midtown [a small, Midwestern city] informed me—I had been working there awhile—that I was a "whore" and she was a "prostitute." And I said: "Now what the hell does that mean?" Well the difference was that a prostitute could pick her customer and a whore had to take anybody. I said: "Well honey, I want to tell

> you something. I'm neither one." She said: "Well, you *work*." I
> said: "I know, but I'm a *hustler*. I make *money* for what I do."

Ann: And this is what I turn out—or try to turn out—hustlers. Not
prostitutes. Not whores. But hustlers.

For Ann and Sandy the hustler deserves high status in the prostitution business because she has mastered a specific set of skills that, even with many repeat clients, earn her premiums above the going rate for sexual acts.

In the ideological training of call girls Bryan finds that "values such as fairness with other working girls, or fidelity to a pimp, may occasionally be taught" (1965:291–2); the teaching tapes revealed Ann's affirmation of both these virtures. When a pimp brings a woman to Ann, she supports his control over that woman. For example, if during her stay at the house, the novice breaks any of the basic rules—by using drugs, holding back money (from either Ann or the pimp), lying or seeing another man—Ann will report the infractions to the woman's pimp. Ann notes: "If I don't do that and the pimp finds out, he knows I'm not training her right, and he won't bring his future ladies to me for training." Ann knows she is dependent on the pimps to help supply her with turn-outs. Bryan, likewise, finds a willingness among call-girls' trainers to defer to the pimps' wishes during the apprenticeship period (1965:290).

Teaching fairness to other prostitutes is particularly relevant to the madam who daily faces the problem of maintaining peace among competing women at work under one roof. If two streetwalkers or two call girls find they cannot get along, they need not work near one another. But if a woman leaves a house because of personal conflicts, the madam loses a source of income. To minimize potential negative feelings among novices, Ann stresses mutual support, prohibits "criticizing another girl," and denigrates the "prima donna"—the prostitute who flaunts her financial success before the other women.

In still another strategy to encourage fair treatment of one's colleagues in the establishment, Ann emphasizes a set of rules prohibiting "dirty hustling"—behavior engaged in by one prostitute that would undercut the business of other women in the house. Tabooed under the label of "dirty hustling" are the following: appearing in the line-up partially unclothed; performing certain disapproved sexual positions, such as anal intercourse; and allowing approved sexual extras without charging additional fees. The norms governing acceptable behavior vary from house to house and region to region, and Ann warns the turn-outs to ask about such rules when they begin work in a new establishment. The woman who breaks the work norms in a house, either knowingly or unknowingly, will draw the anger of the other women and can be fired by a madam eager to restore peace and order in the house.

Other topics considered on the tapes—in addition to physical skills, "hustling" and work values—were instruction on personal hygiene and grooming, role-playing of conversational skills with tricks on topics not related to sex or hustling ("living room talk"), house rules not related to hustling (such as punctuality, no perfume, no drugs), and guidelines for what to do during an arrest. There were specific suggestions on how to handle personal criticism, questions and insults from clients. In addition, the discussions on the tapes provided the novices with many general strategies for becoming "professionals" at their work, for example, the importance of personal style, enthusiasm ("the customer is always right"), and sense of humor. In some ways these guidelines resemble a beginning course in salesmanship. But they also provide clues, particularly in combination with the topics on handling client insults and the emphasis on hustling, on how the house prostitute learns to manage a stable and limited clientele and cope psychologically with the repetition of the clients and the sheer tedium of the physical work (Hughes, 1971:342–5).

III. TRAINING HOUSE PROSTITUTES—A PROCESS OF PROFESSIONAL SOCIALIZATION

Observing how Ann trains turn-outs is a study in techniques to facilitate identity change (see also Davis, 1971 and Heyl, 1975, chapter 2). Ann uses a variety of persuasive strategies to help give the turn-outs a new occupational identity as a "professional." One strategy is to rely heavily on the new values taught the novice to isolate her from her previous life style and acquaintances. Bryan finds that "the value structure [taught to novice call girls] serves, in general, to create in-group solidarity and to alienate the girl from 'square' society" (1965:292). Whereas alienation from conventional society may be an indirect effect of values taught to call girls, in Ann's training of house prostitutes the expectation that the novice will immerse herself in the prostitution world ("racket life") is made dramatically explicit.

In the following transcription from one of the teaching tapes, the participants are Ann (age thirty-six at the time the tape was made), Bonnie (an experienced turn-out, age twenty-five) and Kristy (a new turn-out, age eighteen). Kristy has recently linked up with a pimp for the first time and volunteers to Ann and Bonnie her difficulty in adjusting to the racket rule of minimal contact with the square world—a rule her pimp is enforcing by not allowing Kristy to meet and talk with her old friends. Ann (A) and Bonnie (B) have listened to Kristy's (K) complaints and are making suggestions. (The notation 'B-K' indicates that Bonnie is addressing Kristy.)

Kristy's Isolation from the Square World

B-K: What you gotta do is sit down and talk to him and weed out your friends and find the ones he thinks are suitable companions for you—in your new type of life.

K-B: None of them.

A-K: What about *his* friends?

K-A: I haven't met very many of his friends. I don't like any of 'em so far.

A-K: You are making the same mistake that makes me so goddamned irritated with square broads! You're taking a man and trying to train *him*, instead of letting the man train you.

K-A: What?! I'm not trying to train him, I'm just. . . .

A-K: All right, you're trying to force him to accept your friends.

K-A: I don't care whether he accepts them or not. I just can't go around not talking to anybody.

A-K: "Anybody" is your old man! He is your world. And the people he says you can talk to are the people that are your world. But what you're trying to do is force your square world on a racket guy. It's like oil and water. There's just no way a square and a racket person can get together. That's why when you turn out you've got to change your mind completely from square to racket. And you're still trying to hang with squares. You can't do it.

Strauss' (1969) concept of "coaching" illuminates a more subtle technique Ann employs as she helps the novice along, step by step, from "square" to "racket" values and life style. She observes carefully how the novice progresses, elicits responses from her about what she is experiencing, and then interprets those responses for her. In the following excerpt from one of the teaching tapes, Ann prepares two novices for feelings of depression over their newly-made decisions to become prostitutes.

Turn-out Blues

Ann: And while I'm on the subject—depression. You know they've got a word for it when you have a baby—it's called "postpartum blues." Now, I call it "turn-out blues." Every girl that ever turns out has 'em. And, depending on the girl, it comes about the third or fourth day. You'll go into a depression for no apparent reason. You'll wake up one morning and you'll say: "Why in the hell am I doing this? Why am I here? I wanna go home!" And I can't do a thing to help you. The only thing I can do is leave you alone and hope that you'll fight the battle yourself. But knowing that it will come and knowing that everybody else goes through it too, does help. Just pray it's a busy night! So if you get blue and you get down, remember: "turn-out blues"—everybody gets it. Here's when you'll decide whether you're going to stay or you're gonna quit.

Ann's description of "turn-out blues" is a good example of Strauss' account (1969:111–2) of how coaches will use prophecy to increase their persuasive power over their novices. In the case of "turn-out blues," the novice, if she becomes depressed about her decision to enter prostitution, will recall Ann's prediction that this would happen and that it happens to all turn-outs. This recollection may or may not end the woman's misgivings about her decision, but it will surely enhance the turn-out's impression of Ann's competence. Ann's use of her past experience to make such predictions is a form of positive leverage; it increases the probability that what she says will be respected and followed in the future.

In Bryan's study the call girls reported that their training was more a matter of observation than direct instruction from their trainer (1965:294). Ann, on the other hand, relies on a variety of teaching techniques, including lecturing and discussion involving other turn-outs who are further along in the training process and can reinforce Ann's views. Ann even brings in guest speakers, such as Sandy, the former hustler, who participates in the discussion with the novices in the role of the experienced resource person. "Learning the Hustling Rap," above, offers an example of role-playing—another teaching technique Ann frequently employs to help the turn-outs develop verbal skills. Ann may have to rely on more varied teaching approaches than the call-girl trainer because: (1) Ann herself is not working, thus her novices have fewer opportunities to watch their trainer interact with clients than do the call-girl novices; and (2) Ann's livelihood depends more directly on the success of her teaching efforts than does that of the call-girl trainer. Ann feels that if a woman under her direction does not "turn out well," not only will the woman earn less money while she is at her house (affecting Ann's own income), but Ann could also lose clients and future turn-outs from her teaching "failure."[5]

The dissolution of the training relationship marks the end of the course. Bryan claims that the sharp break between trainer and trainee shows that the training process itself is largely unrelated to the acquisition of a skill. But one would scarcely have expected the trainee to report "that the final disruption of the apprenticeship was the result of the completion of adequate training" (1965:296). Such establishments do not offer diplomas and terminal degrees. The present study, too, indicates that abrupt breaks in the training relationship are quite common. But what is significant is that the break is precipitated by personal conflicts exacerbated by both the narrowing of the skill-gap between trainer and trainee and the consequent increase in the novice's confidence that she can make it on her own. Thus, skill acquisition counts in such an equation, not in a formal sense ("completion of adequate training"), but rather in so far as it works to break down the earlier bonds of dependence between trainer and trainee.

IV. THE FUNCTION OF TRAINING
AT THE HOUSE LEVEL OF PROSTITUTION

Bryan concludes that the training is necessitated by the novice's need for a list of clients in order to work at the call-girl level and not because the actual training is required to prepare her for such work. But turn-outs at the house level of prostitution do not acquire a clientele. The clients are customers of the house. In fact, the madam usually makes sure that only she has the names or phone numbers of her tricks in order to keep control over her business. If Ann's turn-outs (unlike call girls) do not acquire a clientele in the course of their training, why is the training period necessary?

Although Ann feels strongly that training is required to become a successful hustler at the house level, the function served by the training can be seen more as a spin-off of the structure of the occupation at that level: madams of establishments will often hire only trained prostitutes. Novices who pose as experienced hustlers are fairly easily detected by those proficient in the business working in the same house; to be found out all she need do is violate any of the expected norms of behavior: wear perfume, repeatedly fail to hustle any "over-money" or engage in dirty hustling. The exposure to racket values, which the training provides, may be more critical to the house prostitute than to the call girl. She must live and work in close contact with others in the business. Participants in house prostitution are more integrated into the prostitution world than are call girls, who can be and frequently are "independent"—working without close ties to pimps or other prostitutes. Becoming skilled in hustling is also less important for the call girl, as her minimum fee is usually high, making hustling for small increments less necessary. The house prostitute who does not know how to ask for more money, however, lowers the madam's income as well—another reason why madams prefer professional prostitutes.

The training of house prostitutes, then, reflects two problems in the social organization of house prostitution: (1) most madams will not hire untrained prostitutes; and (2) the close interaction of prostitutes operating within the confines of a house requires a common set of work standards and practices. These two factors differentiate house prostitution from call-girl and streetwalking operations and facilitate this madam's task of turning novices into professional prostitutes. The teaching madam employs a variety of coaching techniques to train turn-outs in sexual and hustling skills and to expose them to a set of occupational rules and values. Hers is an effort to prepare women with conventional backgrounds for work in the social environment of a house of prostitution where those skills and values are expected and necessary.

References

Becker, Howard S.
1970 Sociological Work. Chicago: Aldine.
Barker, Roger G. (ed.)
1963 The Stream of Behavior: Explorations of its Structure and Content. New York: Appleton-Century-Crofts.
Bryan, James H.
1965 "Apprenticeships in prostitution." Social Problems 12 (Winter): 287–97.
1966 "Occupational ideologies and individual attitudes of call girls." Social Problems 13 (Spring): 441–50.
Davis, Nanette J.
1971 "The prostitute: Developing a deviant identity." Pp. 297–332 in James M. Henslin (ed.), Studies in the Sociology of Sex. New York: Appleton-Century-Crofts.
Erwin, Carol
1960 The Orderly Disorderly House. Garden City, N.Y.: Doubleday.
Faulkner, Robert R.
1974 "Coming of age in organizations: A comparative study of career contingencies and adult socialization." Sociology of Work and Occupations 1 (May): 131–73.
Gagnon, John H. and William Simon
1973 Sexual Conduct: The Social Sources of Human Sexuality. Chicago: Aldine.
Gray, Diana
1973 "Turning-out: A study of teenage prostitution." Urban Life and Culture 1 (January): 401–25.
Hall, Susan
1973 Ladies of the Night. New York: Trident Press.
Heyl, Barbara S.
1974 "The madam as entrepreneur." Sociological Symposium 11 (Spring): 61–82.
1975 "The house prostitute: a case study." Unpublished Ph.D. dissertation, Department of Sociology, University of Illinois-Urbana.
Hughes, Everett C.
1971 "Work and self." Pp. 338–47 in The Sociological Eye: Selected Papers. Chicago: Aldine-Atherton.
Jackson, Bruce
1969 A Thief's Primer. Toronto, Ontario: Macmillan.

Kinsey, Alfred C., Wardell B. Pomeroy and Clyde E. Martin
   1948 Sexual Behavior in the Human Male. Philadelphia: W.B. Saunders.
Lewis, Gladys Adelina (ed.)
   1942 Call House Madam: The Story of the Career of Beverly Davis. San Francisco: Martin Tudordale.
Polsky, Ned.
   1969 Hustlers, Beats and Others. Garden City, N.Y.: Doubleday.
Ross, H. Laurence
   1959 "The 'Hustler' in Chicago." Journal of Student Research 1: 13–19.
Sheehy, Gail
   1974 Hustling: Prostitution in Our Wide-Open Society. New York: Dell.
Stewart, George I.
   1972 "On first being a john." Urban Life and Culture 1 (October): 255–74.
Strauss, Anselm L.
   1969 Mirrors and Masks: The Search for Identity. San Francisco: Sociology Press.
Vogliotti, Gabriel R.
   1975 The Girls of Nevada. Secaucus, New Jersey: Citadel Press.
Winick, Charles and Paul M. Kinsie
   1971 The Lively Commerce: Prostitution in the United States. Chicago: Quadrangle Books.

Notes

1. This situation-specific induction into prostitution may be contrasted with the "smooth and almost imperceptible" transition to the status of poolroom "hustler" noted by Polsky (1969:80–1).

2. In the wider context of the national prostitution scene, Ann's situation reflects the "minor league" status of her geographical location. In fact, she trains women from other communities who move on to the more lucrative opportunities in the big city. See the stimulating applications of the concept of "minor league" to the study of occupations in Faulkner (1974).

3. The term "hustling" has been used to describe a wide range of small-time criminal activities. Even within the world of prostitution, "hustling" can refer to different occupational styles; see Ross' description of the "hustler" who "is distinguished from ordinary prostitutes in frequently engaging in accessory crimes of exploitation," such as extortion or robbery (1959:16). The use of the term here is thus highly specific, reflecting its meaning in Ann's world.

4. The indented sections (for example, "Ann as a Turn-out" and "Learning the Hustling Rap") are transcriptions from the teaching tapes. Redundant expressions have been omitted, and the author's comments on the speech tone or delivery are bracketed. Words underlined indicate emphasis by the speaker.

5. These data bear only on the skills and values to which Ann *exposes* the turn-outs; confirmation of the effects of such exposure awaits further analysis and is a study in its own right. See Bryan's (1966) study of the impact of the occupational perspective taught by call-girl trainers on the individual attitudes of call girls. See Davis (1971:315) for a description of what constitutes successful "in-service training" for streetwalkers.

39 / Female Delinquency: Minor Girls and Major Crimes

FREDA ADLER
HERBERT M. ADLER

By legal definition, a juvenile delinquent is someone under eighteen who either commits an adult crime or transgresses into areas which society considers beyond his or her physical, mental, or moral capabilities. All state laws agree that a girl is a juvenile delinquent if she commits an act which would be a criminal offense if done by an adult. In addition, eleven state statutes include thirty-four juvenile offenses not covered by the adult criminal code, but no one state includes them all.[1] For serious or persistent antisocial behavior, most states allow the courts to exercise discretion in determining whether to handle it as a crime (adult) or delinquency (juvenile). While boys tend to be arrested for offenses involving stealing and various sorts of mischief, girls are typically charged with sex offenses which are euphemistically described as "delinquent tendencies," "incorrigibility," or "running away."[2] The sources of case referral also show a sex differential. Whereas law-enforcement agencies apprehend the majority of delinquent boys, a much higher percentage of delinquent girls are brought to court by referral from schools, social agencies, and relatives.[3] The stereotype of gender-typical offenses is self-perpetuating because girls tend to be overprosecuted for sexual misbehavior and under-prosecuted, at least in the middle class, for aggressive misbehavior.[4] This is not to say that teen-age girls are sexually less active than the record indicates, but simply that they are probably less active than boys, whose promiscuity is socially tolerated.

Paradoxically, as girls respond to the leveling of the double standard by imitating male promiscuity,[5] we can predict that they will be prosecuted less because their increased sexual activity will be matched by an increased social tolerance. The same pattern is not likely to apply to aggressive behavior, which is doubly troublesome. This behavior challenges a social stereotype, but unlike sexual transgressions it is not a victimless crime and, therefore, poses a practical threat as well. It is just because female offenses did not threaten social functioning that the entire field of female deviancy has been neglected by criminological research.[6] However good the reasons for neglecting female deviancy may have been in the past, at present we are seeing that sex roles among all classes of juveniles are more alike and thus bear equal research. In both hidden delinquency and overt deviancy, girls of all classes have departed from previously prescribed sex role behavior for the same reason that their sisters are choosing careers over domesticity or sexual experience over chastity.

Because girls were different from boys, it was assumed a generation ago that delinquent girls, like nondelinquent girls, were simpler to understand. A girl's traditional role was restricted to the family; her chief concern was her physical appearance[7] because through it she hoped to attract a proper male; and her prime but perishable claim to respectability was her virginity. Determining the rules of normalcy from the exceptions of delinquency, the conventional female teenager of the first third of the twentieth century moved comfortably in a two-dimensional world bounded by familial fealty and sexual abstinence. The former guaranteed her present security . . . the latter ensured her future prospects. From such a socially restricted habitat, there were only two directions in which she could transgress— disobedience and promiscuity. If she was a runaway, she might well be involved in both. Such "unadjusted" girls were considered to be somewhat amoral as well as unwise, because they frittered away the sexual capital of their irreplaceable virginity in self-defeating efforts to satisfy wishes for security, recognition, and new experiences.[8] Such efforts were often pitiful attempts by girls who lacked grace or material means to achieve respectable status.[9] This type of juvenile led some investigators to the conclusion that male delinquents tend to hurt others while female delinquents tend to hurt themselves.[10] This was not mere pious moralizing, because in the climate of the times, no matter how badly a girl fared at home, it was likely that she would fare worse in the outside world. The skillful management of her sexual behavior was the chief faculty she possessed for coping with a male-dominated society,[11] and it was unlikely that the security which chastity failed to gain for her would be achieved by promiscuity. "Nice" girls can be sexy, never sexual. In the limited confines within which women in general, and girls in particular, were allowed to operate there were very few ways in which she could be either good or bad, and most of them encompassed conformity and sex.

Very likely it is just because of the female's tendency to conform and the victimless nature of her transgressions that the study of female delinquents has been so long neglected. Deviations were primarily from the female sex-role expectation rather than from the criminal statutes.[12] The courts treated the bulk of these youngsters with paternalistic chivalry, meting out relatively mild treatment.[13] But there is another side to chivalry. If it dispenses leniency, it may with equal justification invoke control. In recommendations for institutionalization and in actual sentencing to institutions, females were often treated more harshly than their male counterparts.[14] The court's purpose, however, was less punitive than protective. The rationale is that girls gravitate to delinquent behavior as a result of poor home situations. Sexual misbehavior, so the thinking goes, is common to the distressed female because it represents her misguided efforts to compensate for affectional relationships missing from the home.[15] Therefore, institutionalization was deemed necessary to save the girl from herself or from her family.[16] Whether this was an appropriate judicial response or not, the results of self-report studies indicate that the courts have consistently erred in overestimating the sexual character of female delinquency and underestimating the number of incidents of other female delinquency. These studies suggest that if female deviant behavior were being randomly sampled by the juvenile courts, males would still predominate over females in numbers of offenses, but they would be roughly similar in the kinds of offenses.[17]

Another bias of the juvenile court is material to its treatment of females. It considers itself *parens patriae* (a role of legal parent) in relationship to the juvenile and, therefore, mandated with a special responsibility to reinforce the familial demands for morality (usually sexual) and obedience.[18] In acting as a conservative social force, it tends to uphold the double standard, thereby impinging more restrictively on the rights of female adolescents than on males. The court, like the traditional American family, has sex-differentiated expectations—obedience, dependency, and responsibility from girls, and achievement and self-reliance from boys—and concomitant sex-differentiated sanctions. The "family" court, like the family itself, views the female delinquent more from a social than a legal perspective and consequently brings a much narrower tolerance for sexual deviance to its assessment of the gravity of her offense. In its defense of the social *status quo*, the court is especially sensitive to anything the girl does to challenge the authority of the family or to undermine its sexual mores. It is because of its guardianship of these values that the juvenile court often places more emphasis on females' violations of sex-role expectations than on their violations of the law and sanctions female sexual deviancy more severely than male.

But events create the momentum for change, and the courts often follow where custom leads. By the late fifties and early sixties, a generation of female juveniles, politicized by the Indochina war, liberated by the equal-rights movement, protected by oral contraceptives, and bolstered by unprecedented numbers, was bypassing the normative positions petrified by the family court and recasting social stereotypes in its own unisexual image. The changes had a double impact because they involved two generations which synergized each other's efforts toward full equality: adult women were rediscovering sex at the same time as their fourteen-year-old daughters were heterosexually involved at the same level that their mothers had been at sixteen.[19] The crescendo of rising expectations buoyed by higher education and the opening of hitherto inaccessible jobs widened the female horizon to include the entire landscape of male prerogatives. But in spite of the mercurial pace with which these changes seemed to be progressing, the tempo was in part illusory. It owed its aura of headlong acceleration less to the process of female emancipation, which in retrospect was fairly gradual and orderly, than to the precipitous discrediting of stereotypes, suddenly refuted by events they could no longer rationalize. While the daily life of the juveniles underwent continuous changes,[20] these changes were not accurately reflected by the social institutions which were monitoring them. They suffered from the perhaps inevitable inertia of all bureaucratic structures which make them shift from under-reaction to overreaction. Furthermore, the tendency of social movements to be discovered only after they have already gained momentum gives them the impression of possessing more impetus than they may actually have acquired. In fact, a retrospective evaluation suggests that past female abstinence and conformity was overestimated and was probably less real than apparent. Likewise, the present acceleration of female role changes seems also to be overestimated and is probably more apparent than real. It is our social awareness of these events rather than the events themselves which has shown the sharpest increase. Just as official statistics have overlooked the sexual delinquency of boys, so have they underestimated that area of female delinquency considered typically male.[21] Especially in recent years and especially in the middle class, there is evidence to suggest that if law-enforcement agencies employed identical criteria in making arrests of boys and girls, there would be considerably less variation in the delinquency rates between the two.[22]

The increasing antipathy which teen-age girls feel toward traditional female roles could easily lead to their acquisition of even more social and antisocial male behaviors. Superficially, this new trend toward the unisexual is evidenced by the hair styles, clothing, and other items of fashion which have been adopted or rejected by today's younger females. The traditional crinoline and lace of the fifties gave way to the casual denim of the sixties, which has evolved into the overalls of the seventies.

In the words of one seventeen-year-old high-school girl: "Eyeshadow, make-up, and all of that is a real drag when you really think about it. When you stand back and look at it, the whole thing is a trap ... set by multimillion-dollar conglomerates who want us to believe that we can only be 'whole' as human beings when we smear their product on our faces or spray it under our arms or around our vaginal areas. I want to know that I am me; that I don't need just the right smell or smear-on or bra to be me. Once you really get into yourself as a woman, a lot of the female advertising hype you see becomes absurd."

On a level somewhat deeper and far less visible, teen-age girls are receiving changing role cues from within their own family units. Both in the way parents respond to their boys and girls and in what they expect from them, there are fewer and fewer sexual distinctions.[23] Indeed, even as role models, these parents daily demonstrate the convergence of the sexes. While this has freed the middle-class girl from many restraints, it is also forcing her to compete more actively with boys as well as girls scholastically, athletically, vocationally, and criminally. The era when girls sewed dresses and boys sowed wild oats has yielded to a period when both are expected to achieve a degree of self-sufficiency. Passivity is no longer a self-evident feminine virtue, and status is not automatically conferred on the girl who is docile and chaste. Since delinquent activity, like its adult counterpart, is linked to opportunity and expectation, there is every reason to anticipate that, as egalitarian forces expand, so too will the crime rate of the female young set.

Pressures associated with role convergence make girls of today even more vulnerable than boys to delinquency. Traditionally, the biosocial difficulties surrounding pubescence were balanced by the stabilizing influence of a protective family and community. But that stability has yielded to the necessity, once exclusively male, to make one's way and to prove oneself in the world. In addition, this mandate is an ambiguous one for females because, while they are urged toward equality of education and community participation at one level, they also encounter job discrimination and are urged to reject their intellect at another level.[24] The internal and external conflicts generated by the usual disruptions of puberty plus the role change and the ambiguity of the new role create complex identity problems more intense in nature and scope than those faced by boys.[25] While all classes of female juveniles must negotiate these biosocial rites of passage, the middle-class girl, at least, often has the advantage of attractive parental models with whom she can identify in a relatively conflict-free way. The lower-class girl is less fortunate in this, as in other respects. The frequent absence of the father from the home and, in many cases, the brutal treatment of his wife when he is present[26] provide scant opportunities for healthy identification, while at the same time creating an atmosphere of emotional deprivation congenial to a delinquent subculture.

Thus the emancipation of women appears to be having a twofold influence on female juvenile crimes. Girls are involved in more drinking, stealing, gang activity, and fighting—behavior in keeping with their adoption of male roles.[27] We also find increases in the total number of female deviancies. The departure from the safety of traditional female roles and the testing of uncertain alternative roles coincide with the turmoil of adolescence creating criminogenic risk factors which are bound to create this increase. These considerations help explain the fact that between 1960 and 1972 national arrests for major crimes show a jump for boys of 82 per cent—for girls, 306 per cent.[28]

These figures reflect not only quantitative changes in female delinquency but also alterations in the kinds of deviancy which girls were finding attractive. Promiscuity, of course, is not new, but in recent years in decaying countercultural centers such as New York's East Village pubescent prostitutes, so-called teeny-hookers, have replaced the middle-class flower children of the sixties, and the transformation has been striking. Alcohol, amphetamines, and heroin have replaced marijuana and LSD; commercial sex has replaced Aquarian love; and a street-wise group of emotionally distressed, violence-prone youngsters roam the areas where idealistic flower children once trod. These youngsters are runaways, but not only in the physical sense, for they are psychologically adrift from families and social institutions which once supplied security and structure. While drug and alcohol use are on the increase[29] and are sometimes utilized by pimps in efforts to control teen-agers, they are only one segment of the many varieties of deviancies which grow in such adolescent instability.

> "The greater majority of girls we see," explained one director of a California drug-rehabilitation facility, "are not drug users because they were tricked into it. They are drug users because they themselves decided to enter the drug scene—for a number of often quite complicated reasons. The girls we get here—and we are running almost fifty per cent females now—have a basic problem in recognizing who they are. The problem is essentially one of identity. They have reached the point of identity crisis, and for a number of different reasons it was too much for them. They were unable to cope with it. Instead they hoped to stay high and circumvent the problem and the decisions it necessitated.
>
> "Their real problem is not really the chemicals they put into their bodies. It is deeper. The chemical substances are merely a symptom. These girls haven't the faintest idea who they are. What we do is attempt to take them back inside their own heads . . . back to the crisis to see the reasons they couldn't cope . . . make them recognize what drugs are . . . just an escape route."

That escape route would not be nearly so destructive if it led to viable alternatives. Characteristically, the girls who take drugs have fled from, or perhaps more accurately cut, their previous emotional ties (e.g. family, school, church) and lack the vocational or social skills to perform adequately in new nondeviant groups.[30] Historically, they have been affiliated with the male-dominated gang, either as ancillary sex-objects or as semiautonomous female auxiliary groups. They became Egyptian Cobrettes to their Egyptian Cobras and Vice Queens to their Vice Kings, but until recently they were limited to sexual and housekeeping roles and tended to avoid violent confrontations. But in the growing repertoire of female delinquencies, violence is becoming a more frequent option.

> "I know it's happening, but I'll be damned if it still doesn't shock me when I see it," explained one exasperated sergeant who was slumped in the chair of a district precinct house in Washington, D.C. He was talking about the new problems which girls have created for police. "Last week, for instance, we get a call of a disturbance at the high school. A fight . . . after school. So we get down there and pull up and here is a hell of a crowd yelling and screaming at the kids in the center, who are fighting. I push my way through the crowd—they're going crazy like it is really a mean fight—and when I get to the middle . . . I liked to fell over. Here are two husky broads, and they are fighting . . . now I don't mean any hair-pulling face-scratching kind of thing; I mean two broads squared off and ducking it out. Throwing jabs and hooking in at each other and handling themselves like a couple of goddamned pro sparring partners. I mean, I got to ask myself, What the hell is going on? What in the name of God is happening to these girls any more?"

The new aggressiveness of girls is not isolated to the sergeant's Washington precinct—or to any city, for that matter.

> In New York, Gladys Polikoff has spent the last quarter of a century working with adolescent girls who have been apprehended by and are being processed through the Youth Aid Division of the police department.
> "It's difficult to put a finger on exactly what is happening, but something quite drastic has taken place out there," she observed.
> "Through the fifties, we'd get an occasional girl . . . for shoplifting . . . mostly it was because the girl had taken something for kicks or on a dare . . . strictly a spur-of-the-moment sort of thing. Now, of course, girl shoplifters are quite common; and they are taking specific things for resale or for their own use in a very methodical way. Girls we're seeing now are involved in a whole new range of activities . . . like extortion. A group of girls ganging up on another girl and shaking her down for money. I mean, that was simply unheard of just a few years ago. Now, you don't get the name-calling, hair-pulling that used to go between girls . . . you get vicious physical assault.

Perhaps some of the best points from which to monitor the "new" female delinquent are the prisons where the worst of her number are incarcerated.

At Muncy State Prison for Women in northwestern Pennsylvania, for instance, there has been a radical change in the inmate population.

Sue Goodwin, a prison official who has formerly worked as a probation officer in two major urban areas, feels the change in the general attitude of her charges has become glaringly apparent.

"In the first place," she explained, "there is no question that the adolescents are the hardest inmates to handle. They are the most exuberant, and the ones who rebel the most. And now we have begun to get a whole new breed of adolescent inmates . . . very violent ones. They are no longer the frightened, docile prisoners that women have traditionally been. Instead, they come in here and, within the first two weeks, they have to let everyone know that they are the 'baddest ass' in the place."

As Ms. Goodwin points out, there appears to be a certain level of imitative male machismo competitiveness developing among criminal adolescent girls, who, both in their crimes and their overall attitudes and deportment, are becoming almost indistinguishable from male inmates. In the last half of the sixties, for instance, while national attention was focused on male prisons with their riots and threats of riots, similar occurrences at female institutions went almost unnoticed. At the time, the idea of a riot in a female prison was alien to accepted notions of female behavior. But in spite of its implausibility, it became a reality for the officials at the Indiana Girls' School. There, in late 1966, two hundred adolescent girls reduced the institution to a shambles.[31] A study made during the aftermath of that outbreak revealed that the most aggressive and violent participants and, indeed, the instigators of the riots were drawn from the younger girls in the institution. These girls were the ones most frequently serving time for theft, larceny, burglary, assault, and armed robbery, rather than for the usual "soft" female offenses. Since it is this kind of economic and assaultive crime that is on the increase with the upcoming cadre of female delinquents, we can anticipate even more violence in the entire legal process from arrest through imprisonment.

Of all the forms of adolescent urban violence which have plagued our cities in recent years, none has been quite as socially threatening as that of organized gang warfare. In Philadelphia, New York, Chiago, Los Angeles, and other major urban areas, gangs have terrorized entire neighborhoods, virtually crippled school systems, and injured or killed innumerable persons. None of this is new, but a new factor has been introduced into the equation of violence—the female gang member. Her entrance was gradual and at first peripheral to the male-centered gang activity. Sex was, of course, offered and accepted, as were drugs, but her activity—it was not yet quite a role—was incidental to the main operations.

All members of a society tend to share certain perceptions, so that, ironically, even deviancy conforms to the prescribed patterns. Consequently, we have the paradox of a counterculturally dedicated group—such as the antisocial gang—organized, regulated, and ritualized along structural lines that resemble a corporation staff—complete with specific attitudes toward women. As attitudes of the larger society have changed with regard to women, so, in parallel fashion, have the attitudes of these microsocieties. As establishment women reached for and attained positions integrated within the male power structure, so did their delinquent daughters. By the mid-sixties, police were reporting an increase in arrests of girls for being gang lookouts, carrying weapons, and generally aiding in gang warfare. By the seventies, girls had become more highly integrated in male gang activity and were moving closer to parallel but independent, violence-oriented, exclusively female groups.

In Philadelphia, where male gang violence takes a toll of as many as fifty lives a year, there are no girl gangs per se, but there are numerous aggressively disposed female "cliques."[32] They contain anywhere from a few to a few dozen girls who hang together on their own and engage in typical male mischief. At present they differ from gangs in not having the warlords, runners, and other rigid structural components found in male gang organizations.

> Deborath is a fifteen-year-old who has been a member of such a group for a number of years. She comes from the 21st-and-Montgomery section of the city—a rugged area, with dilapidated housing, a high crime rate and widespread unemployment. A student at William Penn High School, she began her involvement with gangs as a hanger-on with the Valley Gang, an all-male gang from the same area. Although currently connected with a church organization seeking to break down the gangs and gang involvement, she feels no shame about her activities in the past. Her words are spoken with a hint of pride as she tells about her effectiveness on the streets and in violence-oriented gang operations.
>
> She, along with the other girls of her group, did much street fighting, usually rivaling the other male gangs of the area. "A lotta times we'd go down to Norris Street, in enemy territory, and fight their girls. But we never shot anybody," she said, pointing out that, instead, the girls liked to confine their efforts to the use of fists and, only occasionally, pipes, clubs, and bricks as weapons. She admitted to having used a knife on special occasions. "The way it was, if any of the other girls got messed up bad, it was because they asked for it. I mean, now we might beat them up or threaten to stab them, but we weren't like the boys . . . they're mean; they use guns and all. We never used guns."

In the Bronx, more and more angry young damsels have slowly made their debuts into organized deviance. Of the 85 male gangs, almost one-third (23) have female branches, with 160 verified members and perhaps as many as 1000 unverified members. In addition, two groups, The Black Persuaders and the Sedgewick Sisters, each

with a membership of 25, are exclusively female with no male affiliation.[33] As an evolutionary extension of the social course female delinquents are following, these all-girl gangs may be a harbinger of urban
problems to come. Nor can this be dismissed as a problem limited to
the streets of New York. In London there are some thirty gangs of
"bovver birds," violence-prone girls who roam the streets in packs
attacking almost any vulnerable object for no apparent reason other
than the sheer thrill of it.

> ... at night they become birds of prey. Sometimes silently, sometimes
> shrieking, they swoop down in groups on unsuspecting victims in dark
> streets, at lonely bus stops, and in deserted toilets, kicking, biting, scratch-
> ing, punching, they reduce the victim—usually another female—to hys-
> teria and then disappear, stealing perhaps only a few pence.... [They are]
> the newest and in some ways the eeriest street gangs since the Teddy boys
> terrorized London in the fifties.[34]

The term "bovver" is cockney for "bother," which is itself a slang
expression for "fighting," and what distresses the English most is that
the majority of their crimes are not perpetrated for money or other gain
but are apparently committed for the intrinsic satisfaction of violence.
During the past few years these female gangs have become a problem
of major proportions for the British police, who blame them for the
substantial increase in the rate of muggings in London. After reviewing the charges against some of the girls, a judge at Old Bailey declared, "The girls are even tougher than the boys. It was once assumed
that if a man and a woman committed a crime, the woman was under
the domination of the man. I think that's now rubbish from what I've
seen."[35]

> A London probation officer explained, "These girls seem very detached,
> very unmoved. Many of their attacks are for pure game, mostly done on the
> spur of the moment." And another police officer went on to explain why he
> and others were so worried about the trend toward widespread adolescent
> female violence. "These girls, more often than not, wear some sort of
> disguises when they go out ... wigs and masks that are done quite well and
> which make it very hard for a victim to identify the actual attacker. The
> danger is, you see, the girls are much better at this sort of disguise ... plus
> they don't hang about, bragging about what they've done—like a lot of boys
> who hang out in gangs. They're much smarter in their approach to this kind
> of thing ... the problem is they may eventually become better than men,
> and even more numerous, as street criminals."

Another area in which young women have begun to express their
aptitude for assertive behavior is political protest. In the storm of
dissent which swept across the country in the late sixties, the adolescent female was an enthusiastic participant in the demonstrations and
a coequal cell-mate in the jailings. Initially, during the early sixties,

the movements were planned, led, and executed by males while females performed their traditional functions as office workers, coffee makers, and overseers of routine chores. But by the end of the decade, a by now familiar transformation had occurred. Neither the women themselves nor their male coworkers any longer expected that their participation would be limited to typewriters and mimeograph machines. Instead they became active, vociferous, and sometimes violent members of some of the most turbulent confrontations this country has ever experienced.

"It was something that I never really noticed, per se, as it was occurring, but there was a great change in a very short time," explained Lucy, a New Jersey woman who began her career with the peace movement as a telephone canvasser in 1966 at the age of fifteen. By the time she was seventeen she had traveled to Chicago on her own and taken part in the tumultuous Democratic Convention riots—indeed, to this day, she carries a scar on her head where a policeman's club opened a wound which required eight stitches to close. Lucy had been arrested during demonstrations in Philadelphia, New York, Chicago, and Washington, D.C., between 1968 and 1971. She has been tear-gassed, gunned down with high-pressure water hoses, and otherwise buffeted about as a front-rank member of violent demonstrations. She has—by her own account—also slugged her share of policemen and National Guardsmen, as well as "trashed" storefronts and cars during protest activities.

Raised as the daughter of an affluent industrial executive in northern New Jersey, she attended private schools—mainly schools which placed a heavy emphasis on the proper deportment for a young lady of society. In the course of her experiences, Lucy has altered her image of herself as well as of the world around her. The change she has undergone, however, is typical of that experienced by numbers of girls her age.

"When I first became involved in political activity against the war," she explained, "women did have their place. Quite naturally I and the other girls were expected to do the telephone work and run the mimeograph machine as well as the errands and other similar things. It was the girls who did all the work, and the men who directed the show and got all the headlines. ... I think that a great many girls began to see something of themselves in the very things they were demonstrating against. Then things began to happen ... girls moved in and began to do more. I can remember some of the guys balking at it, but it couldn't be stopped. After Chicago and the convention, for instance, I was totally radicalized. There was no way that anyone was going to chain me to a typewriter. I wanted to be out there where the action was. I was as good as any boy out there, and I knew it."

It was girls like Lucy—with their new-found confidence—who helped to keep people like Lieutenant Al Hack of the Washington, D.C., Police Department busy through the peak years of the antiwar movement. The capital city became the focal point for much of the antiwar sentiment. From 1967 to 1971, some of the largest gatherings ever assembled in the United States descended upon Washington in the form of peace demonstrations. Although nonviolent in orientation, many of them were peppered with incidents of violence from both sexes. During those convulsive years of the movement, the demonstrations took on a change in complexion which was somewhat perplexing to Lieutenant Hack and his fellow officers charged with keeping the peace.

"Well, what happened," he explained, "is that we found, all of a sudden, that we were arresting just about as many girls as boys at the demonstrations. That was quite a change from the mid-sixties, when you almost never saw girls in the actual demonstrations. By 1969, they had really changed . . . there were even cases where the front lines of demonstrations were made up of *all* females because the demonstrators knew that most of our men would be less likely to deal harshly with girls than boys. But I think even the men changed after a while . . . they had to change . . . I mean, girls were throwing bricks just as hard as boys, and their language was just as rough. They would throw the trashcans, and rock the busses and cars just like the males. No, toward the end there, we had to change our thinking, I guess. We weren't dealing with males or females . . . we had to worry about dealing effectively with just plain 'demonstrators.' "

The lieutenant's point is an important one. For Washington police handling the demonstrations, as well as for the demonstrators themselves, the gender of the lawbreakers was irrelevant. Setting aside issues of civil disobedience and *agents provocateurs*, it is clear that these were neither male nor female offenders—only offenders. Both were reacting to similar forces in similar ways. Not only in Washington but in New York, London, Moscow, and urban centers around the world, girls have shown a capacity comparable to boys for endangering lives and destroying property. With unwonted irreverence toward the traditions of their mothers, adolescent girls, products of a postwar baby boom which became a teen-age tidal wave, challenged social restrictions on many fronts, including those which limit female activity to established roles. The resulting fluidity of male and female functions often makes an anomic contribution to female delinquency by eroding the structures which have historically protected and restrained girls.

But this blurring of sex boundaries is only one of many factors which have increased the extent and altered the nature of female deviancy. Juvenile delinquency, like adult criminality, is a multiply determined phenomenon. It not only varies with social class and changing social tolerance, but it is defined differently from one jurisdiction to another, and prosecuted differently according to local customs. It can best be understood as an outgrowth of legitimate strivings which have found deviant expression.

Notes

1. Frederick B. Sussman, *Law of Juvenile Delinquency* (New York: Oceana Publications, 1959), pp. 21–22.

2. Albert K. Cohen and James F. Short, Jr., "Juvenile Delinquency," in *Contemporary Social Problems*, eds. Robert K. Merton and Robert A. Nisbet, (New York: Harcourt, Brace & World, 1966 [originally published in 1961]).

3. *Ibid.*

4. Barbara Allen Babcock, "Introduction: Women and the Criminal Law," *The American Criminal Law Review*, Winter 1973, 11:291–94; and Nancy Barton Wise, "Juvenile Delinquency Among Middle Class Girls," in *Middle-Class Juvenile Delinquency*, ed. Edmund W. Vaz (New York: Harper & Row, 1967).

5. Ira L. Reiss, "Sexual Codes in Teen-Age Cultures," *The Annals of the American Academy of Political and Social Science*, November 1961, 338:53–62.

6. For a discussion of deviation from sex-role expectation see, Albert K. Cohen, *Delinquent Boys* (New York: The Free Press, 1955); Ruth R. Morris, "Female Delinquency and Relational Problems," *Social Forces*, 1964, 43:82–89; and Richard A. Cloward and Loyd E. Ohlin, *Delinquency and Opportunity* (New York: The Free Press, 1960).

7. James S. Coleman, *The Adolescent Society* (New York: The Free Press of Glencoe, 1963). See also Elaine Walster, Vera Aronson, Darcy Abrahams, Leon Rottman, "The Importance of Physical Attractiveness in Dating Behavior," *Journal of Personality and Social Psychology*, 1966, 4:508–16. In the latter study it was found that the only important determinant of a boy's liking for his date was her physical attractiveness.

8. In an early work (1923) William I. Thomas viewed the sexually delinquent female as an "unadjusted" girl who used sex as capital in an attempt to satisfy her dominant wishes for security, recognition, new experience and response: W. I. Thomas, *The Unadjusted Girl* (New York: Harper & Row, 1967 [originally published in 1923]). Seymour L. Hallbeck, *Psychiatry and the Dilemmas of Crime* (New York: Harper & Row, 1967), p. 138.

9. Albert K. Cohen and James F. Short, Jr., "Research in Delinquent Subcultures," *Journal of Social Issues*, 158, 14:20–37; Albert J. Reiss, "Sex Offenses: The Maryland Status of the Adolescent," *Law and Contemporary Problems*, Spring 1960, 25:309–33.

10. Clyde B. Vedder and Dora B. Somerville, *The Delinquent Girl* (Springfield, Ill.: Charles C Thomas, 1970), p. 89.

11. James F. Short and Fred L. Strodtbeck, *Group Process and Gang Delinquency* (Chicago: University of Chicago Press, 1965), p. 38.

12. W. W. Wattenberg and F. Saunders, "Sex Differences Among Juvenile Offenders," *Sociology and Social Research*, Sept.–Oct. 1954, 39:24–31; John Cowie, Valerie Cowie, and Eliot Slater, *Delinquency in Girls* (London: Heinemann, 1968); J. D. Atcheson and D. C. Williams, "A Study of Juvenile Sex Offenders," *American Journal of Psychiatry*, 1954, 3:366–70; Gordon H. Barker and William T. Adams, "Comparison of the Delinquency of Boys and Girls," *Journal of Criminal Law, Criminology and Police Science* (December, 1962), 53:471–72.

13. Walter Reckless, *The Crime Problem* (New York: Appleton-Century-Crofts, 1961), p. 83.

14. Yona Cohn, "Criteria for the Probation Officer's Recommendation to the Juvenile Court," in *Becoming Delinquent*, eds. Peter G. Garabedian and Don C. Gibbons (Chicago: Aldine Press 1970); see also, Robert Terry, "Discrimination in the Handling of Juvenile Offenders by Social Control Agencies," in Garabedian and Gibbons, *op. cit.*

15. Wattenberg and Saunders, *op. cit.*; Halleck, *op. cit.*, p. 141.

16. Cohn, *op. cit.*

17. John P. Clark and Edward Haurek, "Age and Sex Roles of Adolescents and Their Involvement in Misconduct: A Reappraisal," *Sociology and Social Research*, 1966, 50:496–508; Wise, *op. cit.*; Martin Gold, *Delinquent Behavior in an American City* (Belmont, California: Brooke, Cole Publishers, 1970).

18. Harry Elmer Barnes and Negley K. Teeters, *New Horizons in Criminology* (Englewood Cliffs, N.J.: Prentice-Hall, 1943), p. 923; Anthony Platt, *The Child Savers* (Chicago: University of Chicago Press, 1969).

19. Elizabeth Hurlock, *Adolescent Development* (3rd ed., New York: McGraw-Hill,

536 / FREDA ADLER AND HERBERT M. ADLER

1967); in another study 2000 adolescents in grades 6, 9, and 12 showed significant increases in opposite-sex preference choice in a sociometric test given in 1963 and compared to 1942: Raymond G. Kuhlen and Nancy B. Houlihan, "Adolescent Heterosexual Interest in 1942 and 1963," *Child Development*, 1963, 36:1049–52.

20. See note 17.
21. Wise, *op. cit.*, pp. 179–80.
22. *Ibid.*, p. 180; Gold, *op. cit.*, pp. 63–64.
23. Wise, *op. cit.*, pp. 181, 188.
24. Gisela Konopka, *The Adolescent Girl in Conflict* (Englewood Cliffs, N.J.: Prentice-Hall, 1966).
25. *Ibid.*
26. *Ibid.*
27. Halleck, *op. cit.*, p. 142.
28. Uniform Crime Reports, Crime in the United States, United States Department of Justice (Washington, D.C.: U.S. Government Printing Office, 1972), p. 124.
29. Reginald G. Smart and Dianne Fejer, *Changes in Drug Use in Toronto High School Students Between 1972–1974*, Project J 183, Addiction Research Foundation, Toronto.
30. James F. Short, Jr., "Introduction: On Gang Delinquency and the Nature of Subcultures," in *Gang Delinquency and Delinquent Subcultures*, ed. James F. Short, Jr. (New York: Harper & Row, 1968).
31. Hanus J. Grosz, Herbert Stern, and Edward Feldman, "A Study of Delinquent Girls Who Participated in and Who Abstained from Participating in a Riot," *American Journal of Psychiatry*, April 1969, 125:1370–79.
32. *The Philadelphia Inquirer*, February 4, 1973.
33. *The New York Times*, May 9, 1972.
34. *Time*, October 16, 1972.
35. *Ibid.*

40 / Battered Women and Their Assailants

BONNIE E. CARLSON

For centuries there have been battered women—or battered or abused wives—but only recently has their battering gained public attention as a social problem. In the past few years numerous professional and lay publications have begun to provide information about the problem in an attempt to educate the public about its causes and consequences, as well as to stimulate the provision of services for its victims. However, little systematic research has been conducted in this area, and the limited data collected tend not to be oriented toward service delivery. Before services can be provided both to the victims of domestic violence and their assailants, it is essential to understand the dynamics of the problem and what services the affected population needs.

Currently, many myths and misconceptions regarding domestic or conjugal violence exist among both the general public and the helping professionals who are likely to be confronted with domestic violence in their work.

As Schultz noted, the prevailing stereotypes regarding battered women are these:

1. They are basically sadomasochistic. That is, they enjoy being abused and have a need to be abused. Therefore the problem is difficult to eradicate since its roots lie deep in the victim's psyche.

2. They actually instigate the assaults through antagonistic verbal behavior (for example, nagging, insults, and so on); if they would refrain from such verbal abuse, the battering would cease.

3. They are "very masculine, outspoken, domineering women" (castrating by implication) who "tend to exploit and profit from their husband's passiveness and dependency."[1]

These stereotypes tend to be based on personal observations and have not been investigated empirically in a systematic fashion. Schultz, for instance, based his observations on a sample of four persons. It is also important to note that the foregoing stereotypes clearly place the cause for the violence within the victim, a phenomenon recently called "blaming the victim."[2]

This article (1) provides information about a population of battered women and their assailants, (2) suggests likely causes of domestic violence, (3) tries to dispel misunderstanding about the problem, and (4) indicates connections between characteristics of the affected population, causes of the problem, and the resulting need for services. The situation has gone beyond the point where professionals in mental health and social service can continue to ignore the problem.

SELECTION OF SAMPLE

In April 1975 the Ann Arbor, Michigan, chapter of the National Organization for Women (NOW) developed a Wife Assault Task Force and began to collect information about local domestic violence in the hope of providing free services to abused women, using volunteers from the community. In January 1976 that hope was realized and the NOW Domestic Violence Project began to offer the following services to battered women: emergency housing, short-term peer counseling by volunteers, legal advice and referral, financial assistance, 24-hour crisis phone coverage, and referral to appropriate social service and mental health agencies. Over 260 victims and their children were served in an 18-month period. This figure is surprisingly high in view of the feminist affiliation of the project. It undoubtedly reflects the desperation of these clients and the inability of existing community resources to meet their need for service. The study reported in this article was based on the 101 cases in the NOW project for which information was most complete.

Limitations of the Data The group of women interviewed in the study cannot be considered representative of all women who are physically abused by their husbands or other men with whom they have primary relationships. Rather, generalizations can only be made to a population of abused women who appeal for assistance to a volunteer nonprofessional women's organization. Substantial amounts of data are missing for certain variables, especially those pertaining to the assailants. When this is true, the number of cases on which the relevant statement is based is indicated. In addition, the data regarding assailants were collected from victims — some of whom were in a state of disequilibrium at the time of the interview — and thus cannot be considered completely valid and unbiased.

FINDINGS

It is hoped that the findings of this study will contribute to the slight knowledge about domestic violence. In many cases the data support hypotheses set forth in the literature or corroborate previous research findings, and this suggests that the data of the study are reasonably valid.

Demographic Characteristics   The total sample consisted of 101 women who were victims of assault. These women were referred to the project from a wide range of sources: 32 percent by social service agencies, 20 percent by the criminal justice system (police, judges, legal aid societies, and so on), 10 percent by friends, 10 percent by the media, and the remainder by miscellaneous sources.

The majority (60 percent) were married at the time of the interview; 22 percent were separated or divorced from the assailant (dispelling the myth that merely moving away from the assailant will solve the problem), 13 percent were unmarried and living with assailant, and 5 percent were single and living apart from the assailant. Seventeen percent of the couples had been together less than one year; 28 percent, one to three years; 33 percent, four to ten years; and 22 percent, 11 or more years. Of the 75 couples for whom information regarding their marital history was available, over half had previously been separated at least once.

An overwhelming majority of the women studied (86 percent) had children; the average number per respondent was 2.23, with only 4 women reporting 5 or more. Forty-five percent of these children were 5 years of age or less, 42 percent were 6 to 15 years of age, and 13 percent were 16 years of age or more. The women themselves were relatively young; 65 percent of them were between 21 and 30 years of age. Half the assailants fell into that age group. In general, the assailants were several years older than the respondents. The racial breakdown was as follows: victims, 72 percent white, 27 percent black, 1 percent Oriental; assailants, 63 percent white and 37 percent black. (Racial data unavailable for 11 assailants.) Of the couples for whom racial information was available, 10 percent consisted of a white woman and a black man, but there were none consisting of a black woman and a white man.

In terms of socioeconomic status, the data are revealing. One-third of the victims had not finished high school, while another 25 percent were high school graduates but had no further formal education; 34 percent had some college or vocational training; only 7 percent had graduated from college. A similar pattern existed among the 58 assailants about whom information was available: 33 percent were high school dropouts, 31 percent were high school graduates, 19 percent had some college training, and only 17 percent were college graduates.

It can be seen that the educational attainment of the assailants was quite low compared with that of the total male population in this age group in the United States, and looked at in the aggregate it appears that victims and assailants have approximately equal educational attainment. But the data are deceptive. They were analyzed by case because the literature indicated an inconsistency in status between victims and assailants, and a different pattern emerged.[3] It was discovered that although both victims and assailants tended to have little education, the woman had more education than her partner in 26 of the 58 couples for whom educational data were available (45 percent). In only 17 of these couples (29 percent) did the man's educational achievement surpass that of the woman. This is unusual, considering that the normative pattern is for men to have higher educational attainment on the average and within any one couple.

Employment data are equally revealing. Of the 43 percent of the victims employed outside the home, only three were employed in professional positions; the remainder worked in clerical, technical, or unskilled jobs. This is clearly reflected in the income data for victims: only seven respondents had independent annual incomes of $9,000 or more. The majority employed outside the home earned $6,000–$9,000 per year. Thirty-four percent earned less than $6,000 or were supported by Aid to Families with Dependent Children. Almost one-third of the assailants (29 percent) were unemployed. Of 64 who were employed, only 12 percent were professionals, whereas 36 percent did unskilled work, 38 percent held semiskilled or technical jobs, and 14 percent were in business, sales, or miscellaneous jobs. The occupational distribution is again reflected in the income statistics: 63 percent earned less than $12,000 per year, with 37 percent earning less than $9,000; only 25 percent earned $15,000 or more. In summary, it can be seen that both victims and assailants, when they were employed, usually held low-status, low-skilled, low-paid jobs. This situation can be expected to bring about many problems because of difficulties in maintaining family income. Unfortunately, income data were available for only 46 assailants; it is not known how representative these data are.

Social Characteristics An equal proportion of victims and assailants (39 percent of each) had received some type of counseling prior to the incident that brought the victims to the NOW project; in 20 percent of those cases counseling had occurred in an inpatient setting. About one-third of the victims had observed violence between their own parents, while one-half of the assailants had observed such violence as children.

A marked disparity between victims and assailants is noted with respect to alcohol and drug abuse. Only a small proportion of the victims admitted to being substance abusers (alcohol, 10 percent; drugs, 5 percent), whereas the victims reported substance abuse to be much more prevalent among their assailants (alcohol, 60 percent; drugs, 21 percent). In addition, victims reported that 27 percent of 92 assailants were child abusers and that 44 percent of 73 assailants had criminal records. Admittedly, the validity of data reported by the victims is somewhat questionable, but these data suggest that the assailants constitute a far more deviant population than do the victims.

Table 1 / Actions Taken by Respondents after Being Assaulted (*N* = 154)[a]

Action Taken	Percentage of Responses
Consulted police	36
Consulted women's group	16
Consulted friend	14
Consulted family member	12
No action taken	6
Consulted social service or mental health agency	4
Consulted religious adviser	2
Other	10

[a] Many respondents gave more than one answer, and up to two responses were coded for each respondent.

Incidence of Assault   Seventy-one respondents provided information regarding the frequency of violence experienced during the past year. For 25 percent of the women, incidents of violence had occurred with their partners only once or twice. Half had been assaulted three to eight times, 14 percent had been assaulted monthly, and 11 percent more frequently than once per month. Victims reported that alcohol was involved in two-thirds of the incidents which brought them to the project, whereas drugs were involved in 12 percent of the cases. In one-half the incidents it was reported that a weapon was involved; 60 percent of the weapons were household objects (for example, a shoe, an electric sander, a hockey stick); 25 percent of the weapons were guns; 16 percent, knives. Half the respondents stated that at some point they had tried to defend themselves against the attacks. Of those who attempted self-defense, 77 percent reported that this increased the intensity of the attack; 21 percent, that it had no effect; and only 2 percent (one respondent), that it decreased the intensity. In almost half the cases the victim was hurt severely enough to require medical attention.

What are victims of domestic violence likely to do after an assault? Information about this is especially important for those contemplating intervention for battered women. Accordingly, respondents were asked what they had done after the most recent assaulting incident.

Up to two responses were coded for each respondent. Results are reported in Table 1.

It can be seen from the table that victims appear to be largely concerned with their own protection immediately after the assault and that 36 percent relied mainly on the police to provide this protection. Only 4 percent sought assistance from social service or mental health agencies. Other than the police, battered women appear to rely mainly on informal networks for obtaining sympathy and assistance, or they do not seek help at all.

It is well known among those who work closely with the criminal justice system that the police spend a substantial portion of their time (up to half, according to Saunders), responding to what police officers call "domestics."[4] Given the amount of interaction occurring between battered women and police agencies, how do victims view the quality of police response? It would appear, as shown in Table 2, that the respondents in this sample viewed the response of the police at least

Table 2 / Police Response to Domestic Violence as Perceived by Victims (N = 77)[a]

Type of Police Response	Percentage of Responses
Concerned and helpful	36
Not helpful at all	20
Provided protection	13
Referred elsewhere	13
Concerned, but not helpful	13
Hostile	4
Primarily concerned with own safety	1

[a] Up to two responses were coded for each of 57 respondents who stated they had called the police in the recent past in response to domestic violence.

somewhat favorably. Table 2 reveals that only 25 percent gave outright negative evaluations ("not helpful at all," "hostile," or "concerned primarily with own safety"). On the other hand, there is obviously room for improvement in the response of police.

Discovering the causes of domestic violence presents an intriguing problem. Table 3 provides some leads to those causes. If bad temper is ignored for the moment, the message comes across clearly—from the perceptions of victims themselves—that financial and interpersonal stresses lead to domestic violence. This differs markedly from the view that the causes of family violence are intrapsychic and therefore primarily require strategies of psychotherapeutic intervention.

FURTHER OBSERVATIONS

A number of important observations can be made about the sample that were not reflected in the data already described. These observations were made during the year the author spent working directly with victims and as a consultant to the project. First, the one trait that seemed to characterize all victims was their devastatingly low self-concept. A factor contributing to this was that many had never worked outside the home. The second striking characteristic was the degree of isolation that most of these women experienced. Many had virtually no close friends or relatives with whom to share the pain and fear in their lives; others had depleted such resources and had found that sisters, mothers, friends, and others no longer wanted to hear about their plight.

Another observation concerns the children who are reared in homes characterized by periodic violence between domestic partners. It is often said that both the victims and their assailants (who should also be viewed as victims — victims of their own past and of their socialization) frequently grew up in homes in which they themselves were beaten severely or in which they saw violence between their parents. The modeling effects of aggression and violence have been well documented by social learning theorists and developmental psychologists. It is known, for example, that one does not have to be rewarded directly for aggressive behavior to learn aggression as a problem-solving strategy. Simply observing aggressive behavior occur without punishment is sufficient for learning such behavior.[5] This clearly suggests that children growing up in violent homes, especially boys, are far more likely to learn such patterns of behavior and to use them when frustrated than are children who do not observe domestic violence in their homes.

The following personal anecdote illustrates the link between observing and performing acts of aggression and violence. The author worked with a client who had been badly beaten by her husband. The victim's 14-year-old son had come home in the middle of the most recent, although by no means the first, attack. The son (who, incidentally, was often beaten so badly by his father that he was covered with bruises) immediately began to defend his mother by attacking his father with a hockey stick. The parents subsequently separated and the home situation improved. But about a year later, whenever the mother disciplined the boy verbally, he would respond by attacking her physically — and this was the same son who had defended her against physical attacks by her husband.

Another observation relates to the victims' intense attachment to and concern for their children. Often this contributed to their fear of leaving the assailant and living independently. Many knew they did not have the education or the skills to support their families adequately on their own. Assailants fed into this fear by threatening to

Table 3 / Causes of Domestic Assault as Perceived by Victims (N = 215)ᵃ

Causes	Percentage of Responses
Money	35
Jealousy	21
Bad temper	15
Sex	7
Children	5
Household care	4
Pregnancy	4
Assailant's job frustration	2
Other	6

ᵃ Up to three responses were coded for each respondent; the mean number of responses per respondent was 2.30.

desert the family and not provide financial support and by threatening to prove that the victim was an unfit mother so the children would be removed from her custody. While the latter threat might not seem realistic to persons with education and an understanding of how the justice system works, it fed into such deep-seated fears of many victims that they reacted as if it were a realistic threat. As a result, it often deterred them from taking the necessary steps to escape from the situation.

SOURCES OF VIOLENCE

This author subscribes to what may be called the social structural view of family violence.[6] Persons holding this view believe that the sources of violence do not lie inside the individual (that is, in mental illness) or in certain subcultures (for example, "the subculture of violence"); rather, they maintain that the sources of family violence are complex structural circumstances creating environmental stresses that are distributed unevenly across the social structure. Poverty is one such environmental stress, and the respondents in this study clearly identified it as a source of stress and resulting violence.

How is it that environmental stress—in particular, stress arising from economic pressures—can lead to violence in a setting that should be supportive and harmonious? A number of social scientists have suggested that the linkage is related to the social and economic resources of family members and to intrafamily roles.[7] As Steinmetz and Straus state:

> When the social system does not provide a family member with sufficient resources to maintain his or her position in the family, violence will tend to be used by those who can do so.[8]

It is obvious that learning—especially learning violence as a response to stress, anger, or frustration—also plays a critical role in the etiology of family violence.

The normative pattern in American families has been for the husband to play the dominant role with respect to decision-making, the allocation of resources, and so on. But to maintain this superior position, certain conditions must be met in the domain of status. Thus for the husband to be dominant, he should have superior talent (as illustrated, for example, by his occupation and educational attainment) and superior resources (income) vis-à-vis his spouse. What happens when the wife, the supposed subordinate, has certain resources or talents superior to those of her husband? The paradigm outlined above predicts violence under such circumstances if there is accompanying structural stress and a history of learned violence as a response to frustration.

Are data available to support such a paradigm? O'Brien studied a sample of 150 divorcing couples and found that 25 had admitted to a history of overt violence.[9] He found that the status of a much higher proportion of the 25 couples was inconsistent (for example, the wife's educational achievement was higher than her husband's) than that of the nonviolent divorcing couples in the remainder of the sample.

A similar pattern was found in the data of this study, although overall educational attainment among both victims and assailants was low. When the status inconsistencies in these data are combined with the existing high level of unemployment (almost one-third of those for whom data were available), the possibility of an explosive situation can be predicted. When legitimate resources are not available as a power base, then violence—the "ultimate resource"—may be the result.[10] These data suggest that it was often the result in this sample. The hypothesis "that male power is associated with violence when the husband is low in resources" is supported by these data.[11]

ALCOHOLISM AND VIOLENCE

The use of alcohol among the violent men described in this report has been little mentioned. Professionals and nonprofessionals across the country who have worked with battered women can attest to its prevalence. Many victims incorrectly identify alcohol abuse itself as the major problem. Alcohol abuse is, in fact, a symptom of structural stress and frustration, but it serves to exacerbate rather than alleviate the problem. Many battered women state that when their husbands or partners are not drinking, these men are able to function normally and fulfill their role responsibilities adequately (for example, the victims often say that the men are good fathers and providers). Many women have been beaten by their partners only when the men were inebriated. Thus it would appear that alcohol use is not the cause of domestic violence, but rather that alcohol breaks down inhibitions, allowing many men to injure a woman who would not normally do so because of strong normative inhibitions against such behavior.

Alcohol abuse has been recognized as a serious national concern. Substantial resources have been committed to resolving the problem and its consequences. One potential consequence of alcohol abuse is domestic violence. Given the high proportion of assailants who are said to have problems with alcohol, it might be concluded that men who are alcohol abusers comprise a high-risk population for domestic violence. If this is the case, one means of intervention on behalf of battered women might be through existing programs for treating alcoholism. In trying to help families resolve their conflicts before they become unmanageable, systematic inquiries might perhaps be made regarding family disagreements and how they are resolved.

LEAVING THE ASSAILANTS

It is often assumed that because the victims of domestic assault do not leave the situation, they must enjoy the battering or need to be treated in such a way. When this assumption is examined closely, it can be seen that nothing is further from the truth. In fact, much evidence suggests that physically leaving the situation may not even solve the problem. Many divorced women (22 percent of the women in this sample were divorced or separated) continue to be abused by husbands who actively seek them out. Furthermore, there are realistic reasons why abused women continue to remain in dangerous situations, some of which Gelles has suggested.[12]

Clear patterns were found in the decisions women made after having been assaulted. It was discovered that the more resources a women had (for example, a job), the more likely she was to seek outside intervention. The frequency and severity of the violence were other factors related to the seeking of outside intervention and the type of intervention sought. Severe and frequent attacks of violence were more likely to lead a women to seek outside help. Women who had been exposed to violence as children—either as observers or recipients—were more likely to remain in the abusive situation. It appears that exposure to family violence at a young age may serve to desensitize girls to its effects and may lead them to expect violent behavior in a marital situation. However, Gelles found that the best predictor of a divorce or separation obtained by an abused wife was the level of family violence in the current family situation.[13]

Few women in the sample sought assistance from local social service or mental health agencies. This may reflect the low socioeconomic status of the sample, but it seems more likely to be an accurate reflection of the fact that established agencies in most communities do not provide the services most needed by assaulted women: emergency housing, financial assistance, legal advocacy, and emotional support. And if these services cannot be provided quickly—in some cases immediately—they are of little use to this client population. Furthermore, such services cannot be effectively provided in an agency office on a one-hour-a-week basis. Victims of domestic violence, if they are to make the changes necessary to leave an abusive situation, require a great amount of time and support. However, help need not be provided solely by professional workers. Nonprofessionals can fill the role adequately as long as they receive sufficient training, do not try to make decisions for the client, and do not label the client as deviant. Victims who choose to stay in their situation and hope to improve it also need support. But if the assailant's environment, either external or internal, does not change in a meaningful way, the prognosis for the improvement of the victim's situation is not favorable.

One type of intervention that could be attempted would be to reduce the status inconsistency between victims and assailants by improving the men's potential to support their families.[14] This, however, would reinforce the status already ascribed to men in the family domain. Intervention—in addition to enhancing the opportunities of men to support their families—should also move toward helping women support themselves and their families, especially women who are rearing children as single parents. An effort in this direction can be seen in a bill recently introduced into Congress by Yvonne Braithwaite Burke titled the "Equal Opportunity for Displaced Homemakers Act." The bill would provide for job counseling, training, and placement, as well as the creation of jobs in both the public and private sectors of the economy, for middle-aged homemakers who depended on their husbands for support until confronted with divorce or widowhood.[15] Since such women have no marketable skills, their prospects for becoming self-supporting are slim. The focus of this congressional bill is on utilizing past skills and experiences rather than merely developing new skills. Former victims of domestic violence who lack formal training or skills are being used effectively across the country as peer counselors who assist other battered women. This illustrates how displaced homemakers could be used to help others as well as support themselves and their families.

Although improving both men's and women's ability to provide for their families is important, the roots of domestic violence go beyond financial insecurity. This can be inferred from the fact that some battered women come from homes in which financial resources are not a central problem.

As long as men believe that responding to stress and frustration with aggression or physical violence is acceptable behavior, the problem of the battered woman will continue to exist. Thus in addition to improving the ability of men and women to support themselves and their families, efforts should be made to eradicate the beliefs that (1) men's status must and should be higher than women's, (2) men who are not dominant and are not physically more powerful than women are in some way not masculine and not adequate, and (3) physical power and coercion are valid means of solving disputes in the family or in any other interpersonal relationships. Until these fundamental changes in attitude have become widely accepted, helping professionals must try to reach out to a victimized population too long ignored. They must recognize that battered women are not women who are mentally ill, but rather are troubled women in need of emotional support as well as tangible assistance.

Notes

1. Leroy G. Schultz, "The Wife Assaulter," *Corrective Psychiatry and Journal of Social Therapy*, 6 (February 1960), pp. 103–111.
2. William Ryan, *Blaming the Victim* (New York: Pantheon Books, 1971).
3. Craig M. Allen and Murray A. Straus, "Resources, Power and Husband-Wife Violence," paper presented at The Annual Meeting of the National Council on Family Relations, August 1975; and John E. O'Brien, "Violence in Divorce-Prone Families," *Journal of Marriage and the Family*, 31 (November 1969), pp. 692–698.
4. Daniel G. Saunders, "Marital Violence: Dimensions of the Problem and Modes of Intervention." Paper presented at the Spring Social Work Symposium, Madison, Wisconsin, April 1976.
5. Albert Bandura, *Aggression: A Social Learning Analysis* (Englewood Cliffs, N.J.: Prentice-Hall, 1973).
6. Richard J. Gelles, *The Violent Home* (Beverly Hills, Calif.: Sage Publications, 1972).
7. O'Brien, op. cit.; and Suzanne K. Steinmetz and Murray A. Straus, "General Introduction: Social Myth and Social System in the Study of Intrafamily Violence," in Steinmetz and Straus, eds., *Violence in the Family* (New York: Harper & Row, 1974).
8. Steinmetz and Straus, op. cit., p. 9.
9. O'Brien, op. cit.
10. Allen and Straus, op. cit.
11. Ibid.

12. Richard J. Gelles, "Abused Wives: Why Do They Stay?" *Journal of Marriage and the Family*, 38 (November 1976), pp. 659–668.

13. Ibid.

14. O'Brien, op. cit.

15. Jane McClure, "Equal Opportunity for Displaced Homemakers Act: The Need for Comprehensive Legislative Reform." Unpublished manuscript, Ann Arbor, Michigan, 1976.

41 / A Criminogenic Market Structure: The Automobile Industry

HARVEY A. FARBERMAN

Sociologists have come under attack for ignoring the role powerful elites play in controlling society's central master institutions by establishing political and economic policies which set the structural conditions that cause other (lower level) people to commit crimes[1] (Gouldner, 1968, 1970; Quinney, 1970; Liazos, 1972; Taylor et al., 1974). My aim here is to suggest how one elite, namely, automobile manufacturers, creates a "criminogenic market structure"[2] by imposing upon their new car dealers a pricing policy which requires high volume and low per unit profit. While this strategy gives the *manufacturer* increased total net aggregate profit (by achieving economies of scale and by minimizing direct competition among oligopolist "rivals"), it places the new car dealer in a financial squeeze by forcing him to constantly free-up and continuously re-cycle capital into fixed margin new car inventory. This squeeze sets in motion a downward spiral of illegal activities which (1) inclines the new car dealer to engage in compensatory profit taking through fraudulent service operations, (2) under certain conditions, generates a "kickback" system which enables used car managers of new car dealerships to exact graft from independent used car wholesalers, and (3) forces the independent used car wholesaler into illegal "short-sales" in order to generate unrecorded cash for kickback payments. I shall present the evidence which provides the grounding for this model as I came upon it in the research process. What follows, then, is a natural history which reconstructs the stages of my investigation.[3]

THE BASE SITE

My principal research site was a medium-sized used car wholesale operation located in an eastern metropolitan area.[4] There are approximately forty other wholesale operations in this area,[5] the top three of which sell between 6,000 and 8,000 cars per year.[6] My base operation, which sold 1,501 cars in 1971 and 2,124 in 1972,[7] carried a 125-car wholesale inventory and a repair shop at one location and a 25-car retail inventory at another location. There were 16 employees altogether, including three partners (an older one who runs the office and two younger ones who function as buyers), three additional buyers (who also sell wholesale when not on the road), a retail manager, a retail salesman, two shop workers, a bookkeeper, and two-to-five drivers. The firm also retains the services of a lawyer and an accountant.[8]

Entry into my principal research site and later into other operations was relatively easy, for during my high school and college days I had made pin money selling used cars on a lot owned by the older partner. Later I came across two old acquaintances from high school days who hustled cars when I did; one is now a new car agency general sales manager, and the other a partner in a "family-owned" new car dealership.

Although I was always more an observer than a participant, I increasingly was expected to answer phone calls, take messages, move cars around the wholesale lot, and deliver cars as part of a "caravan" with the regular drivers.[9] Eventually, I gained access to all files. At about the same time the firm offered me a gasoline credit card, reimbursement for my private telephone bill, maintenance work on my own car, and drivers to pick me up at the airport when I returned from out-of-town trips. I did not decline the maintenance work or the airport service[10]; however, I did break off field appearances—but maintained social contact—when the firm adopted one of my opinions as the basis for its expansion policy, and it became clear that my role as an investigator had somehow given way to that of an advisor or consultant.

From December 1971 to August 1973, I spent an average of one day a week including evenings and weekends at my principal site, on the road, and at the homes of or out socializing with various members of my base organization and their families. Sometimes, though, I would hang around the lot for two or three consecutive days in order to get some sense of the continuity and rhythm of the operation. I always carried a notebook and, when necessary, made entries in full view of all present. I also tape-recorded extensive in-depth interviews with the consent of participants, but only when I knew more or less what I wanted information about, thus not abusing the privilege. These "formal" interviews allowed me to nail down—for the record—what I had observed, participated in, or been told during the course of everyday activity or conversation over the course of nearly two years.

The insight and information gleaned from these informal conversations were the basis for the "formal" interviews, the first of which I held during the sixth month of my field appearances.

SERENDIPITY

I should note here that I did not start out to study a criminogenic market structure. Rather, I wanted to follow up on a speculative hypothesis which grew out of some previous research on low income consumers (Farberman, 1968; Farberman and Weinstein, 1970). As a result of the latter study in particular, I had hypothesized that low income consumers strengthened their bargaining position vis-à-vis high status or expert sales or service people by changing the normative ground of the transaction from universalism to particularism, and thereby were able to coerce the expert other to respond as a concerned friend rather than as a mercenary stranger. Consequently, I began the present investigation to see if I could discover if people who bought used cars employed (wittingly or unwittingly) a set of bargaining tactics. I therefore observed over 50 transactions between retail customers and used car salesmen and, indeed, have been able to identify several bargaining tactics, associate them with distinct types of customers, and provide a theoretical interpretation.[11]

My interest in the systemic nature of occupational crime developed without my realizing it for sometimes, while I wrote up notes in the office after watching a sales transaction, I would vaguely overhear or observe the sales manager and customer "write-up" the deal. I began to notice that occasionally the customer would make out a check *as well as* hand over some cash. This was accompanied by the customer's saying how "taxes were killing the little man" and "if you didn't watch out, the Governor would bleed you to death." Out of simple curiosity I began *deliberately to observe* the "write-ups" — something I had originally paid no attention to since I thought the transaction was actually over after the bargain had been made and the salesman had "closed" the deal. It was at the "write-up," however, that a new research problem emerged, because what I had witnessed — and what, in fact, led me off in a new direction — was an instance of "selling short," or "a short-sale," an illegal act which constitutes the first link in a chain of activity that goes back to Detroit.[12] In the section which follows, I will describe (a) what a "short-sale" is; (b) how it benefits and costs both the retail customer and the dealer; and (c) why the dealer feels compelled to engage in it.

THE SHORT-SALE

A "short-sale" begins to develop when a retail customer observes the sales manager compute and add on to the selling price of the car the state sales tax—a hefty eight percent. Often, the customer expresses some resentment at the tax bite and asks if there is any way to eliminate or reduce it. The sales manager responds in a sympathetic fashion and allies himself with the customer in a scheme to "cut down on the Governor's share of the deal" by suggesting that the customer might make out a check for less than the actual selling price of the car. In turn, the manager will make out a bill of sale for the lesser amount. The customer then will pay the difference between the *recorded* selling price and the *actual* selling price in cash. A car which normally costs \$2,000 would carry an additional 8 percent (or \$160) state sales tax, thus actually costing the customer \$2,160. If a bill of sale which records the selling price as \$1,500 is made out, however, then at 8 percent the taxes would be \$120, for an apparent total of \$1,620. Although the customer still pays \$2,000 for the car (\$1,500 by check and \$500 in cash), he "saves" \$40 in taxes.

Almost as important as saving the \$40 is the obvious delight the customer typically takes at finally discovering himself in a situation where he can "even the odds," "give the big guys what for," and "make sure the little guy gets his two cents too." The attitude and mood which washes through the short-sale suggests a welcome, if minor, triumph in the back-stepping of everyday life. As an observer witnessing this "petty" collusion between little Davids against remote Goliath, I had a rather difficult time identifying it pursuant to the criminal code—as a conspiracy to defraud the government through tax evasion. Obviously, the meaning, value, and sentiment attached to the act by at least one of the participants (the customer) is totally incongruous with the meaning, value, and sentiment attached to it by the criminal code. Thus does a minor victory in everyday life co-exist in the same act with a punishable transgression of law. The victory is often more symbolic than material, however, since, if the customer at any future time has an accident or theft, his insurance company, in part, will initiate compensation calculations based on the selling price recorded in the bill of sale—a sum which understates the actual price paid.

But, if the customer derives both a small material savings and a large measure of delight, what does the dealer derive? For one thing, a lot of money; more precisely, a lot of *unrecorded* cash. At the moment the customer "saves" \$40 in taxes the dealer gains \$500 in cash. The "short sale" to the customer allows the dealer to "steal-from-the-top."

In any given year an accumulation of these short sales can total to tens of thousands of dollars. In an effort to determine if "stealing from the top" was anything other than rank venality, I questioned one of the partners in my principal site.

Q: You've just said that it's [stealing-from-the-top] O.K. for the customer but bad for you. I don't understand that. Jeez, look at the money!

A: Yeah, sure, but who the hell wants to live with any of the retail customers. You see what goes on. They don't know shit about a car. They look at the interior, turn on the radio, check the odometer, kick the tire, push the windshield wiper button, turn on the air conditioner, open up the trunk, look at the paint. What the fuck has any of that got to do with the *condition* of the car? I mean, the way the fucker runs. If I put money into all this crap, I can't put it into improving the mechanical condition. Three weeks later the fucking car falls apart and they're on my ass to fix it. Then I got to live with them. They drive me off the wall. Then that broad down the consumer affairs office wants to know why I don't give the customer a fair shake. Shit, why the hell don't she educate the customers? It would make things a lot easier.

Q: Listen, if they're such a pain, why do you put up with them?

A: What do you mean?

Q: I don't know what I mean, but there is usually a bottom line and it's usually money!

A: Well, if you mean that they bail me out every now and then, sure.

Q: What do you mean?

A: Well, you know those creeps [buyers] I got on the road buying for me, you know what their philosophy is? "If you don't buy, you don't earn." They pay big numbers; what do they care; it's my money. If they get in too high on a package [group of cars] or a piece [one car], and I can't blow [wholesale] it out, then I look for a retail shot [sale]. But that means I can't turn over my money quickly, I got to lay with it out on the lot and hope some yo-yo [retail customer] comes along. Believe me, it's a pain in the ass. This whole business is in and out, in and out. Anything that slows the turnover costs money.

Q: O.K., so retail customers generally are a pain, but you put up with them because they bail you out on bad buys, but that still doesn't get to it. What about those retail sales that are "short" sales, that's where the bread is. That's what I'm trying to get at.

A: All right, listen: A wholesaler runs a big grocery store; if it's not on the shelves, you can't buy it. Without cars to sell, I can't sell cars. Look, we make enough legit, but you can't pay graft by check. Those bums get you coming and going.

Q: What bums?

A: You ever wanta meet a crook, go see a used car manager [of a new car dealership]. They clip a quarter [$25], a half [$50], a yard [$100], maybe more [on each car]. Put a package together and take it out [buy it from them] and they'll zing you for a week's pay. They steal their bosses blind.

Q: So, you have to pay them to get cars. You mean something under the table?

A: Yeah, the "vig."

Q: The what?

A: The grease, the commission, the kickback. How I'm gonna stay in business with no cars? You tell me.

Q: Incidentally, how many of your retail sales do you figure are "short"?

A: Maybe 70-75 per cent. I can't be sure.[13]

Q: Tell me, do you ever wind up with more than you need for the kickbacks?

A: Sure, am I gonna lie to you? So I put a little away [in safety deposit boxes]. You think I'm the only one? But if it's buried, you can't use it. Better it should be in the business; I could use it—besides, who needs the aggravation?

Q: Are you ever able to get it [buried money] back into the business?

A: Yeah.

Q: How?

A: Aw, you know.

Apparently, the dealer's reasons for engaging in "short-sales" include, but are not confined to, rank venality. After all, most, but not all, of the unrecorded money is passed along in the form of "kickbacks"; only the residual excess actually finds its way directly into his own hands, and even this excess must be buried or occasionally laundered.[14] The principal reason the dealer engages in short sales is to come up with kickback cash in order to keep his sources of supply open, and this imperative is more than enough to keep him involved with "short-sales," even though it means he has to deal with retail customers—the very bane of his existence.

The antagonism the dealer holds toward the retail customer is incredibly intense and appears to have two sources. First, it stems from the dealer's apparent inability to sell the customer what the dealer considers to be the *essential* element of a car—namely, its *mechanical condition.* Instead, he is compelled to sell what to him is non-essential—*physical appearance.* If he is to improve the car's physical apperance, then he must skimp on improving its mechanical condition. This, in the long run, works to his own disadvantage since he must "live with the customer" and, in some measure, make good on repairs affecting mechanical condition. Put another way, the wholesaler's *conceptualization* of the car and the retail customer's *conceptualization* of the car do not overlap. Where the wholesaler wishes to sell such *unobservables* as a good transmission, a tight front end, a solid chassis, and an engine without knocks in it, the typical retail customer wishes to buy such *observables* as a nice paint job, a clean interior, etc. The wholesaler and the retail customer basically have a hard time "coming-to-terms," that is, abstracting out of the vehicle the same set of concrete elements to invest with meaning and value. The vehicle literally *means* different things to each of them and the establishment of a shared meaning which is *mutually* valued is extremely problematic.[15]

The second source of the dealer's antagonism stems from his overwhelming dependence on these ignorant customers. This dependence heightens dramatically when the dealer's own professional "house" buyers make bad buys; that is, pay too high a "number," or price for the car, which makes it impossible for the car to be quickly re-wholesaled. If the car is in basically sound mechanical condition, it will be "shaped" out in hopes of "bailing out" through a "retail shot." Though a bad buy can be redeemed through a retail sale, this route of redemption bodes ill for the house buyer since it reflects on his competence. It bodes ill for the dealer as well since he must tie up money, men, and space waiting for a fickle retail customer to get everyone off the hook. Thus, the dealer's antagonism toward the retail customer stems from his own dependence, for short-sales and bail-outs, on ignorant yo-yo's who don't know anything about cars. The dealer's redemption, then, lies in the hands of "idiot saviors," an unhappy situation at best.

KICKBACKS AND SUPPLY

In any event, based on what I had seen, heard, and been told, I concluded that the wholesale used car dealer engaged in "short-sales" principally to insure his supply of used cars. Since this conclusion was derived exclusively from observation and interview, I wanted to check it out against the dealer's inventory files. In the following section, I seek evidence of two things: (a) that the predominant source of the wholesaler's inventory, in fact, is the used car department of new car agencies; and (b) that used car managers in new car agencies universally receive kickbacks.

Accordingly, I classified all vehicles in my base site for the years 1971 and 1972 by their source of origin. Table 1 indicates that, of the 1,501 vehicles bought in 1971, 1,134 or 75.5 percent came from used car departments of new car dealers; of the 2,124 bought in 1972, 1,472 or 69.3 percent came from the same source. These figures corroborate the used car wholesaler's overwhelming dependence on the used car department of the new car agency for supply. They also suggest that there may well be a decreasing supply in the number of used cars available on the market altogether. From 1971 to 1972 there was a 6.2 percent decrease (75.5 to 69.3) in the proportion of cars from used car departments of new car dealers even though the number of new car agencies dealt with increased from 72 to 94.[16]

Table 1 / Units* within, and Vehicles Generated by, Various Sources of Supply

	1971		1972	
Source of Supply	UNITS	VEHICLES	UNITS	VEHICLES
1. Used car depts. of new car agencies	72	1134	94	1472
2. Rental, lease or fleet companies	9	145	18	104
3. Off-the-street customers	116	116	172	172
4. Dealers auctions	2	38	1	38
5. Body and fender shops	6	35	6	105
6. Retail used car dealers	11	27	17	193
7. Wholesale used car dealers	3	6	4	40
	219	1501	312	2124

Source: Dealer's Police Books
* The generic term "units" encompasses "establishments" as in categories 1–2 and 4–7, and customers as in category 3.

Given an overall paucity of used cars on the market, it would seem that used car managers of new car agencies are in a perfect position to exact tribute from the independent used car wholesaler whose major source of supply is in their hand. I thus proceeded to check out the universality of kickbacks. I classified all inventory by the *specific* new car agency it came from, and then asked the older partner of my base operation to indicate at which agencies kickbacks were paid. As shown in column 4 of Table 2, kickbacks were paid on 304 (out of 1,134) vehicles in 1971 and on 614 (out of 1,472) vehicles in 1972. Moreover, column 3—much to my surprise—shows that *all* of these cars come from only *seven* (7) agencies in both 1971 and 1972 and each of these agencies carried a Giant Motors franchise. Note, however, that these seven constitute only a small proportion of the total number of G.M. agencies dealt with, which is 35 in 1971 and 51 in 1972. Moreover, only 10 percent of *all* agencies in 1971 and less than 7 percent in 1972 required kickbacks. Nevertheless, in 1971 these agencies did, in fact, provide nearly 27 percent of all supply coming from used car departments of new car agencies and 20 percent of total supply. Similarly, in 1972 they provided 56 percent of supply from used car departments and 31 percent of all supply.

Table 2 / Kickbacks by Vehicle, Agency, and Franchise

Franchise	No. of Agencies		No. of Vehicles		Kickback Agencies		No. of Kickback Vehicles	
	1971	1972	1971	1972	1971	1972	1971	1972
Giant Motors	35	51	571	976	7	7	304	614
Fore	10	16	159	209	—	—	—	—
Crisis	15	16	256	191	—	—	—	—
U.S.	1	2	1	5	—	—	—	—
Foreign	8	6	143	62	—	—	—	—
Unknown	3	3	4	29	—	—	—	—
	72	94	1,134	1,472	7	7	304	614

A closer examination of these seven G.M. agencies, however, discloses some common characteristics. First, an inspection of their zip codes and street addresses reveal that all seven are located in the same high density, urban area. Second, a rank ordering of all new car agencies by the number of cars they supply, as shown in Table 3, reveals that these seven are the top supply sources and, by agreement among house buyers, are large agencies. Third, the remaining eight agencies among the top 15 supply sources all are located in suburban areas and are described by house buyers as medium sized.

Table 3 / Number of Dealerships by Number of Vehicles Supplied: 1972

Number of Dealerships	Number of Vehicles Supplied
2	100+
1	75+
4	50+
8	25+
79	1+

With this information in hand, I again questioned the older partner of my base operation.

Q: Listen, didn't you know that you only paid kickbacks at large, urban, G.M. agencies? Why did you guys give me the impression that you paid kickbacks to *all* used car managers?
A: Really?
Q: Really, what!?
A: Really, you thought we paid off all the managers? Well, I guess these are the big houses for us—it seems like a lot. I'll tell ya, the hicks are O.K. They don't know from conniving. The city is full of crooks.

Q: Really? Don't you think it has anything to do with these particular agencies, maybe the way they're set up or maybe with G.M.? After all, the other manufacturers have agencies there too.

A: No, it's a freak thing! It just means that seven crooks work at these places.

Q: Aw, come on. I don't believe that.

A: Listen, your barking up the wrong tree if you think it has anything to do with G.M.

Q: But why only at G.M.? and why only at G.M. agencies in the city?

A: Look, there's more G.M. agencies than [Fore] and [Crisis]. G.M. sells more cars, they get more trade-ins, they have solid used cars operations. These crooks go where the action is. They're good used car men, they get the best jobs. But they're crooks. I'm telling you, believe me!

Q: But if they're crooks, and you know it, why don't their bosses know it?

A: Look, the bosses aren't stupid. They know what's going on. If the used car man pushes the cars out, and turns over capital, and doesn't beat the boss too bad—they're happy.

Q: I guess I must be thick, I'm still not convinced.

A: All right. The boss is busy running the new car operation. He brings in a sharp used car man and bank rolls him. The used car man pays rent to the boss for the premises and splits profits with him depending on the deal they work out. O.K.? The used car man takes the trade-ins, he keeps the good stuff and wholesales the bad. He wholesales me an off-model, say, for two grand. He tells his boss, the car brought $1,875.00. I send a check for $1,875.00, and grease him a buck and a quarter. At $1,875.00, he still made a legitimate fifty or a hundred on the car—the boss gets half of that. As long as the used car man doesn't get too greedy, there's no problem. The boss takes a short profit but frees up his capital. Believe me, that's crucial, especially if he's paying one percent a month interest on his bank roll to begin with.

Q: So, what you're saying, is that the best agencies are in the city, that they're G.M., that G.M. dealers know their used car men are beating them, but that they don't get uptight as long as they make something and can free-up their capital.

A: Yeah.

Q: Listen, you've got a point, but isn't there another way to look at this? Isn't it possible that the boss does more than just tolerate being ripped off a little by his used car man? Isn't it possible that he's working with the used car man and beating his own business? In other words, he's splitting the kickbacks or something like that?

A: Look, anything's possible, but all I know is that the used car managers are a bunch of crooks. The bosses, I can't say; as for [Giant Motors], forget it, they're a legit concern.

Q: Maybe you're right but it sure would make sense if the bosses [G.M. dealers] did both—you know, turn over money and beat their own business. Hell, you do it and you're the boss, why shouldn't they?

A: Well, I have to. I don't know about them. Just don't go off half-cocked. Be careful before you lean on anybody.

This interview material has two intriguing aspects. Despite the dealer's strenuous insistence that kickbacks are the artifact of corrupt and venal individual used car managers, there is also the suggestion that such venality can take place precisely because large, urban G.M. agencies sell a lot of cars and therefore have an abundance of trade-ins, the best of which are recycled back into the agencies' used car retail line while the surplus is wholesaled out. The power to determine how this surplus is dispersed into the wholesale market places the used car managers of the involved agencies in the position to demand and receive "kickbacks." Moreover, the new car dealer himself, who is under pressure to free up capital in order to avoid paying excess interest on money borrowed to purchase new car inventory, may have an incentive to "look-the-other-way," and perhaps even split "kickbacks" as long as his used car manager keeps moving cars and freeing capital.

THE FINANCIAL SQUEEZE

In the section which follows, I seek to check out (a) the existence of a financial squeeze on dealers, and (b) whether this squeeze inclines dealers to tolerate or even participate in kickbacks. By way of checking these points, I contemplated interviewing some people in the "kickback" agencies. The more I thought about how to guide myself in such interviews, the more I realized I was facing an interesting dilemma. I wanted to do the interviews precisely because I had discovered that the agencies were paid kickbacks by the wholesalers. Yet, in each case the kickback was being paid specifically to the manager of the used car department of the agency and I was not sure if the manager was acting on his own or was acting with the knowledge of his principal. If he was acting on his own, and I disclosed this, I might then put him in jeopardy. If he was acting with the knowledge of his principal, it was certain I would have an unreliable interview since in these cases I did not have personal bonds strong enough to insure truthful responses. Since I did not wish to deceive or jeopardize any of the respondents, and since I did not feel I could be truthful — as no doubt I would have had to disclose just how I had discovered the "kickback" arrangement, and thus transgress the trust that I had established with the wholesalers and run the risk of jeopardizing their ongoing business relationships with the new car dealers — I developed another approach. I decided to interview G.M. dealers in "non-kickback" agencies and try to elicit information which would allow me to pinpoint the key differences between kickback and non-kickback agencies, thereby nailing down an interpretation of the "kickback" phenomenon.

I managed to arrange interviews with three different dealers. The following quoted interview lasted five hours, was granted on the basis of a personal tie, and therefore is most reliable and valid. In addition, the elicited material is highly representative of the other interviews. The general thrust of my questioning was first to ask the dealer to talk about issues which are problematic in the running of his own business, and then to comment on the "kickback" phenomenon at the urban agencies. I was interested mainly in knowing if the pressure to turn over capital and avoid interest payments would encourage a dealer to "look-the-other-way" on "kickbacks" or even split them.

Q: How long have you been a dealer?
A: A dealer? About 20 years. About five or six years after [I finished] college, my dad and I went in as partners. It's mine now.
Q: Have you enjoyed it?
A: Well, it's been good to me for a goodly number of years, but frankly, during these past three to four years the business has changed markedly. It's a tougher, tighter business. I'm more tied down to it now than ever before. I can't be as active in the community as I would like. You know, that's important to me.
Q: Why is that the case? Is the business expanding?
A: Not really, well it depends on how you measure it. I work harder, have a larger sales and service staff than ever, I've expanded the facilities twice and refurbished the fixtures and touched up several times, and yes, I'm selling more new cars than before, but is the business expanding? Well, I suppose, yes, but not the way I'd like it to.
Q: Could you elaborate on that?
A: Well, the point is—and I know this will sound anomalous, well, maybe not to you—but I wish I could ease off on the number of new cars and pick up somewhere else, maybe on used cars.
Q: Why is that?
A: It boils down to investment-return ratios. The factory [manufacturer] has us on a very narrow per unit profit margin [on new car sales]. But if I had the money and the cars, I could use my capital more effectively in used cars.[17]
Q: In other words, G.M. establishes how much profit you can make on each new car you sell?
A: Just about. And more than that, they more or less determine how much [new car] inventory I have to carry, and the composition of that inventory.
Q: So, you have to take what they give you—even if you don't want or need it. How do you pay for the inventory?
A: I borrow money at prevailing interest rates to finance the inventory. And, sometimes it gets tight. Believe me, if I am unable to sell off that inventory relatively quickly, I'm pressed. I have got to keep that money turning or that interest begins to pinch.
Q: Is it fair to say that you compensate for narrow margins on new cars by making wider margins on used cars?

A: Not really, not in practice, at least not out here [in the suburbs]. Used cars, good used cars, are hard to come by. I imagine the city dealers have an easier time getting trade-ins. We get a lot of repeat customers, but I don't believe they trade up. They just buy new cars. Actually, we tend to pick up additional revenue from our service repair operation. I'm not particularly proud about it, but there is a lot of skimping going on. It's quite complicated. The factory has a terrible attitude toward service repair generally, and the [mechanics] union is overly demanding and inflexible. It's rather demoralizing and, frankly, I'm looking out for myself, too.

Q: Could you expand on that?

A: I prefer you not press me on that.

Q: If you had a choice, how would you prefer to set up your operation?

A: Well, if I had a choice—which I don't—I would rather have a low volume, high margin operation. I could get by with smaller facilities, a smaller staff, put less time into the business, and not constantly face the money squeeze.

Q: Do you think the really large city dealers would prefer the same kind of alternative?

A: I guess so, but it's hard to say. Their situation is somewhat different from mine.

Q: In what way?

A: Well, first of all, some of them, especially if they're located in [megalopolis] have even less control over their operation than I do. Some of them really run factory stores. That is, G.M. directly owns or controls the agency. Those outfits are really high-volume houses. I don't see how they can make a go of it. The factory really absorbs the costs.[18]

Q: You did say that they probably had strong used car operations or, at least, had a lot of trade-ins. Do you think that helps?

A: Possibly.

Q: Do you think a really sharp used car man could do well in that kind of operation?

A: Well, he would do well in any operation in which he had used cars to work with.

Q: He could both retail and wholesale?

A: Oh, yes, if he had the cars to work with.

Q: Is it likely, in the wholesale end, he could demand and receive "kickbacks" from wholesalers?

A: Well, it's been known to happen. You know, those wholesalers, they're always willing to accommodate a friend. But it would only pay them to do that in relatively large operations where they could anticipate a fairly steady flow of cars.

Q: So, it would certainly make sense for them to accommodate friends in large, high volume, urban G.M. agencies?

A: Sure.

Q: Do you suppose the used car managers split kickbacks with their bosses?

A: Well, it's possible, but more than likely, the boss is more interested in moving those cars out quickly any way he can, so he can turn over that money and place it back into new car inventory.

Although this material does not permit any educated guess as to whether the dealers might split kickbacks with their used car managers, it does provide some assurance that new car dealers are under pressure to sell off cars relatively quickly in order to turn over capital and thus reduce interest payments. This pressure may be enough of a stimulus to, at least, incline the dealer to "look-the-other-way" if and when his used car man partakes in graft. As long as the used car man doesn't become too greedy and cut into the boss's pocket, his activity will be tolerated. Of course, we may still speculate, but not conclude, that if a "boss" is merely managing or only controlling a minimal share in a new car agency which is principally owned directly by G.M., he may be inclined to collude with his used car manager against "his own" agency. In any event, it is safe to presume that dealers feel under constant pressure to continuously recycle capital back into new car inventory and to get out from under interest payments. Corroboration of this comes from Vanderwicken (1972:128) who did a financial analysis of a medium-sized Fore agency located in a suburb of Cleveland, Ohio, and reported that:

> The average car is in inventory thirty days before it is sold. Quick turnover is important to a dealer, the instant a car leaves the factory, he is billed for it and must begin paying interest on it. This interest is one of [the dealer's] biggest single expenses.

Additional support also comes from Fendell (1975:11) who asked a New Jersey [Fore] dealer how he was coping with decreasing consumer demand and received the following response:

> I'm making deals I lose money on just to get the interest costs off my back. Those cars sit out there, costing me money every second. [Fore] has been paid in full for them a long time ago.

The dealer went on to say that his interest rates run between 10.25 percent to 11 percent per year.

MANUFACTURERS' PRICING POLICY

The constant and unremitting emphasis on new car inventory and the capital squeeze it places dealers in apparently is no accident. To the contrary, it is the calculated outcome of the manufacturers' pricing policy. According to Stewart Macaulay (1966:8), manufacturers and dealers enter into relationships for the mutual goal of making profit; however, their strategies for making that profit may differ.

> For example, a . . . dealer might be able to make a hundred dollars profit on the sale of one car or a ten dollar profit on each sale of ten cars . . . [it makes a great deal of difference to the manufacturer] because in one case it sells only one car while in the other it sells ten . . . It must sell many units of all the various models it makes. . . .

This imperative to sell *many* cars stems from the manufacturers' effort to achieve economies of scale, that is, savings in production and other costs as a result of massive, integrated, and coordinated plant organization. George Romney, when President of American Motors, testified before a Senate Judiciary Subcommittee on Antitrust and Monopoly and reported that:

> A company that can build between 180,000 and 220,000 cars a year on a one-shift basis can make a very good profit and not take a back seat to anyone in the industry in production efficiency. On a two-shift basis, annual production of 360,000 to 440,000 cars will achieve additional small economies . . . (quoted in Lanzillotti, 1968:266.)

An economist, Joe S. Bain (quoted in Edwards, 1966:162) estimates that an even higher minimal production volume is needed for savings.

> In general, 300,000 units per annum is a low estimate of what is needed for productive efficiency in any one line.

Thus, in order to cut costs to a minimum, the manufacturers—as in days gone by—must continue to engage in mass production,[19] which leads to mass distribution and the need for a dealer network into which the manufacturer can pump massive doses of new cars in a *controlled* fashion. According to economist Lawrence J. White (1971:139), this translates into a "forcing model," which may be defined as "the requirement that the retailer sell a specific number of units as a condition of holding his franchise."[20] In effect, this allows the manufacturer to manipulate dealer inventories in a way that serves the oligopolist interests of an economically concentrated industry. Oligopolist "rivals" recognize their interdependence and avoid direct competition. Placing new dealerships in each other's territory would only call forth counter placements which, rather than expanding total auto sales, would perhaps cut into one's own already established dealerships. Thus,

> it would be better to concentrate on lowering the [profit] margins of existing dealers, which could only be met by equal actions . . . by one's rivals and which . . . has the effect of expanding the overall demand for the product (White, 1971:142.)

All the manufacturer need do then to reduce per unit margins, which increases total net aggregate profit for the manufacturer, is to increase dealer inventory volume. This puts pressure on the dealer to free up capital from alternative investment possibilities such as used cars or to borrow capital at prevailing interest rates. Either way the dealer faces a financial squeeze and has a powerful incentive to sell off his inventory as quickly as possible, which industry trend statistics bear out. Despite the fact that new car dealers can achieve more efficient investment-return ratios from used car inventory—that is, if it is available—the ratio of new to used car sales from 1958 to 1972 per franchised new car dealer reflects an increasing preoccupation with new car sales. Examination of Table 4, column 3, indicates that over the last decade and a half new car dealers have been forced away from used cars and into new cars. In 1958, the ratio of used to new car sales was 1.77, but steadily declined until it reached 1.00 in 1970. And after 1970 it actually reversed itself so that in 1972 it was .81.[21]

Table 4 / Cars Sold per Franchised New Car Dealer: 1958–1972

Year	New	Used	Ratio Used to New
1958	125	221	1.77
1959	168	272	1.62
1960	191	285	1.49
1961	175	271	1.55
1962	208	302	1.45
1963	225	317	1.41
1964	239	311	1.30
1965	283	354	1.25
1966	285	336	1.18
1967	269	328	1.22
1968	302	326	1.08
1969	309	389	1.26
1970	281	292	1.00
1971	331	—	—
1972	354	275	.81

Sources: Compiled from *The Franchised New Car and Truck Dealer Story*, Washington, D.C., National Automobile Dealers Association, 1973, p. 32, and *Automobile Facts and Figures*, Detroit: Automobile Manufacturers Association, 1971, p. 33.

This pressure to slant one's operation overwhelmingly in the direction of new car sales places the dealer in a tight margin operation. Vanderwicken (1972:121) observes that ". . . most people have a vastly exaggerated notion of a car dealer's profits . . . the average car dealer earns less than 1 percent on his volume, a minuscule margin far below that of most other retailers." He also provides a breakdown for the Ford agency he studied. Thus, on a car that the customer paid the dealer $3,337.00, the dealer paid the manufacturer $3,025.00. The dealer's gross margin was therefore $312.00 or 9 percent. (Average gross margin for retailers in other industries runs between 20–25 percent). Nevertheless, of this $312.00 the dealer paid $90.00 in salesman's commission, $43.00 in wages and salaries, $30.00 in advertising, $28.00 in interest, $27.00 miscellaneous, $24.00 in taxes, $22.00 in rent and maintenance, $16.00 in preparation and predelivery work, $9.00 in free customer service, and $7.00 in employee benefits — giving him a net profit of $16.00 per unit. As the boss of the Ford agency remarked, "Our low margins reflect the manufacturer's constant clamor for volume . . . the manufacturer sure as hell gets his . . ." (Vanderwicken, 1972:124).[22]

Should the dealer seek to protest this situation because it locks his time, effort, and money exclusively into fixed margin new car sales, he finds himself under subtle coercion. Quick delivery from the factory becomes problematic and so does a substantial supply of "hot" models (Macauley, 1966:173). Moreover, unfavorable sales comparison with "factory" stores, which sell cars below average retail price, raises questions of effective management (Leonard and Weber, 1970:416). And should such subtle coercion fail to reach home, there is always the threat of franchise termination — a threat which cannot be dismissed as idle given the elimination of over 3,300 dealerships between 1961 when there were 33,500 and 1970 when there were 30,200[23] (NADA, 1973:30). If a franchise is cancelled, it is unlikely that another manufacturer will step in and offer a new franchise or that a new dealer will offer to buy one's premises, equipment, stock, and reputation. Consequently, new car dealers apparently accommodate to this "forcing" procedure and avoid direct reaction. Nevertheless, it appears that they do undertake a form of indirect reaction.

DEALER REACTION

An expert witness who testified before the Senate Judiciary Subcommittee on Antitrust and Monopoly in December 1968 reported on a series of "rackets" which dealers perpetrate on the public in order to supplement their short new car profits. These "rackets" include charging for labor time not actually expended, billing for repairs not actually done, replacing parts unnecessarily, and using rebuilt parts but charging for new parts (Leonard and Weber, 1970). In addition to fleecing customers, they also attempt to retaliate against manufacturers whom they accuse of having a hypocritical attitude on service work. Virginia Knauer (Sheppard, 1972:14), special assistant to the

President for consumer affairs, reports that complaints about auto service repair lead the list of all complaints. According to Knauer, local car dealers themselves complain that the manufacturers simply do not care about service repairs because if they did, they would adequately compensate dealers for pre-delivery inspection and for warranty work and they certainly would not set up—as one of the Big Three did—a regional competition in which prizes were awarded to regions that *underspent* their warranty budgets (Leonard and Weber, 1970). Indeed, the resentment held by the dealers toward the factory on the issue of service work, as well as the manner and magnitude of retribution engaged in by the dealers against the factory, has been of such proportion that one manufacturer, General Motors, recently fired its entire Chevrolet Eastern Zone office, which has jurisdiction over no less than 60 Chevrolet dealers, for colluding with those dealers against the factory, in the cause of more just compensation for dealer's service work (Farber, 1975).

It would seem, then, that the forcing of fixed margin new car inventory works to the manufacturers' advantage by increasing total net aggregate profit without risking direct competition. This high volume low per unit profit strategy, however, precipitates a criminogenic market structure. It forces new car dealers to free up money by minimizing their investment in more profitable used car inventory as well as by borrowing capital at prevailing interest rates. The pressure of interest payments provides a powerful incentive for the dealer to move his inventory quickly. The need to turn money over and the comparatively narrow margins available to the dealer on new car sales alone precipitate several lines of illegal activity: First, it forces dealers to compensate for short new car profit margins by submitting fraudulent warrantee statements to the manufacturers, often with the collusion of the manufacturers' own representatives. Second, it forces dealers to engage in service repair rackets which milk the public of untold sums of money. Third, it permits the development of a kickback system, especially in large volume dealerships, whereby independent used car wholesalers are constrained to pay graft for supply. Fourth, the wholesalers, in turn, in order to generate unrecorded cash, collude with retail customers in "short-sales." Fifth, to the extent that short-sales spawn excess cash, the wholesaler is drawn into burying and laundering money. In sum, a limited number of oligopolist manufacturers who sit at the pinnacle of an economically concentrated industry can establish economic policy which creates a market structure that causes lower level dependent industry participants to engage in patterns of illegal activity. Thus, criminal activity, in this instance, is a direct consequence of legally established market structure.

References

Becker, Howard S.
 1970 Sociological Work: Method and Substance. Chicago: Aldine Publishing Company.
Brown, Joy
 1973 The Used Car Game: A Sociology of the Bargain. Lexington, Mass.: Lexington Books.
Edwards, Charles E.
 1965 Dynamics of the United States Automobile Industry. Columbia: University of Southern Carolina Press.
Farber, M. A.
 1975 "Chevrolet, citing 'policy violations,' ousts most zone aids here." The New York Times. Sunday, January 12, Section L.
Farberman, Harvey A.
 1968 A Study of Personalization in Low Income Consumer Interactions and Its Relationship to Identification With Residential Community, unpublished Ph.D. thesis Department of Sociology, University of Minnesota.
Farberman, H. A., and E. A. Weinstein
 1970 "Personalization in lower class consumer interaction." Social Problems 17 (Spring): 449–457.
Fendell, B.
 1975 "Dealers struggle for survival." The New York Times, Sunday, February 2, Section A.
Gouldner, Alvin
 1970 The Coming Crisis of Western Sociology. New York: Basic Books.
 1968 "The sociologist as partisan: sociology and the welfare state." American Sociologist 3 (May): 103–116.
Huber, Joan
 1973 "Symbolic interaction as a pragmatic perspective: the bias of emergent theory." American Sociological Review 38 (April): 274–284.
Lanzillotti, Robert F.
 1971 "The automobile industry." Pp. 256–301 in W. Adams (ed.), The Structure of American Industry, 4th edition. New York: The Macmillan Company.
Leonard, W. N. and N. G. Weber
 1970 "Automakers and dealers: a study of criminogenic market forces." Law and Society 4 (February): 407–424.
Levine, L.
 1968 "Jerome Avenue." Motor Trend 20 (December): 26–29.
Liazos, A.
 1972 "The poverty of the sociology of deviance: nuts, sluts, and perverts." Social Problems 20 (Summer): 103–120.
Macaulay, Stewart
 1966 Law and the Balance of Power: The Automobile Manufacturers and Their Dealers. New York: Russell Sage Foundation.
Motor Vehicle Manufacturing Association
 1972 1972 Automobile Facts and Figures. Detroit: MVMA.

National Automobile Dealers Association
   1973 The Franchised New Car and Truck Dealer Story. Washington, D.C.:
        NADA, Table 6, p. 30.
Pashigan, Bedros P.
   1961 The Distribution of Automobiles, An Economic Analysis of the
        Franchise System. Englewood Cliffs, N.J.: Prentice-Hall.
Quinney, Richard
   1970 The Social Reality of Crime. Boston: Little, Brown and Company.
Robbins, Harold
   1971 The Betsy. New York: Trident Press.
Rothchild, Emma
   1973 Paradise Lost: The Decline of the Auto-Industrial Age. New York:
        Random House.
Schervish, P. G.
   1973 "The labeling perspective: its bias and potential in the study of
        political deviance." The American Sociologist 8 (May): 47–57.
Sheppard, Jeffrey M.
   1972 The New York Times, Sunday, November 5. Section A.
Smith, R. A.
   1961 "The incredible electrical conspiracy." Parts I and II, Fortune
        (April–May).
Stone, G. P., D. Maines, H. A. Farberman, G. I. Stone, and N. K. Denzin
   1974 "On methodology and craftsmanship in the criticism of sociological
        perspectives." American Sociological Review 39 (June): 456–463.
Taylor, I., P. Walton, and J. Young
   1974 "Advances towards a critical criminology." Theory and Society I
        (Winter): 441–476.
Thio, A.
   1973 "Class bias in the sociology of deviance." The American Sociologist 8
        (February): 1–12.
Vanderwicken, Peter
   1972 "How Sam Marshall makes out with his 'deal.' " Fortune 86 (De-
        cember): 121–130.
White, Lawrence J.
   1971 The Automobile Industry Since 1945. Cambridge: Harvard Univer-
        sity Press.

Notes

1. Typical explanations for this neglect include the observation that sociologists of deviance often work out of a symbolic interactionist perspective, and that this perspective has an ideological-theoretical bias which offers tacit support to power elites (Thio, 1973); that it has a philosophical-methodological bias which focuses attention on the passive, powerless individual and thus cannot conceptualize transcendent, unobservable, active groups (Schervish, 1973); and, finally, that it tends toward a grounded-emergent rather than a logico-theroretic style of theory construction and thus is vulnerable to the unequal power distribution embodied in everyday life and, consequently, has a conservative bias (Huber, 1973). For a reply to some of these points, see Stone et al. (1974).

2. I borrow the term "criminogenic market" from Leonard and Weber (1970), who

contend that the most useful conceptual approach to occupational crime is to see it as a *direct consequence of legally established market structure.* In the present study, by "criminogenic market structure" I mean the deliberate and lawful enactment of policies by those who manage economically concentrated and vertically integrated corporations and/or industries which coerce lower level (dependent) participants into unlawful acts. Those who set the conditions which cause others to commit unlawful acts remain non-culpable, while those who perform under these conditions remain eminently culpable. A micro illustration suggestive of this approach was played out in the heavy electric industry where the U.S. government was able to show that a cartel existed among corporations which resulted in a price-fixing conspiracy. Nevertheless, the actual corporate officials who were indicted and convicted came from the second and third echelon of the corporate hierarchy and, upon exposure, were legally and morally disavowed by the first level echelon. Division heads and vice presidents were censured and repudiated by presidents and directors for contravening corporate policy. Those indicted and convicted, however, never for a moment thought of themselves as contravening corporate policy, nor of having done anything but what was expected of them—their jobs (Smith, 1961). Although this case describes activity *within* a corporation, I wish to extrapolate it to an entire industry. Thus, at the pinnacle of the economically concentrated auto industry sit four groups of manufacturers who control 92 percent of the new car market and who, on the distribution side of the industry alone, set economic conditions which control approximately 31,000 franchised new car dealers, approximately 4,000 used car wholesalers, and approximately 65,000 "independent" used car retailers. Despite the fact that those on the top cause the conditions which compel others into untoward patterns of action, they do not reap the public's wrath. At the same time that new car and used car dealers consistently trail far behind every other occupational grouping in terms of public esteem, there never has been a presidential administration—beginning with Franklin Roosevelt—without an automobile *manufacturing executive* in a cabinet or sub-cabinet position!

3. For a discussion of this presentation format see H. Becker (1970:37).

4. For a breezy, journalistic description of the used car wholesaling scene see Levine (1968:26–29). For sociological insight into various levels of the auto industry see: Brown (1973) for independent used car retailing; Vanderwicken (1972) for franchised new car dealing; and Robbins (1971) for manufacturing.

5. This figure derives from enumeration by wholesalers themselves. I was forced to rely on this source for three reasons. First, the appropriate State Departments of Motor Vehicles informed me that their statistical information does not distinguish between new and used and wholesale and retail dealers. Nevertheless, they intend to introduce such breakdowns within the next few years. Second, the U.S. *Bureau of the Census, County Business Patterns, 1970* places fundamentally different *kinds* of wholesale automobile establishments into the same reporting category. Thus, wholesale body and fender shops, junk yards, auction sales, free-lance wholesalers, and regular wholesalers appear in the same category. Moreover, the census also includes businesses that are legally chartered in a state but not actually doing business there. Consequently, for my purposes the census was not helpful. Third, the various county *Yellow Pages* phone books in which used car wholesalers advertise did not allow me to distinguish "cutbook" wholesalers, who free lance and work out of their home addresses, from regular wholesalers, who have substantial business premises, a staff of employees, and sizeable inventories.

6. This figure also comes from wholesalers themselves.

7. I compiled these figures from the dealers' "Police Book." For each car in stock, dealers must enter 23 items of descriptive information. Detectives from the Motor Vehicle squad routinely inspect this book.

8. Subsequent to the completion of my study, three more operations were opened: a retail lot with a thirty-car capacity, a wholesale lot with a forty-car capacity, and a twelve-stall body and fender shop. Each of these operations was situated on land or in buildings purchased by the corporation. The staff also increased with the addition of three more buyers, two retail salesmen, seven body and fender men, one mechanic, and a pool of part-time drivers which fluctuates from three to ten on any given day.

9. For a discussion of the ratio of observation to participation see Gold (1958:217–233).

10. During one of these trips, I parked my car—a small 1965 Buick Special—on the wholesale lot. As a gag, and in addition to whatever prudential motives may have been involved, the firm sold my car and with the proceeds put me into a large 1970 Oldsmobile. The firm, at considerable expense to itself, and, in the words of one of the partners, "felt that a Professor, who you also call Doctor, should drive around in a better car." At one and the same time the "gag" shows deference to my status, takes liberty with my property (albeit improves it) and coerces me into a more conventional status appearance. This gambit smacks of something approaching a hazing ritual. It is fun, yet it prepares the initiate for further entree into the club by manipulating him into club conventions. I imagine field workers often run this sort of gamut before they gain entrance into the secret place. Unhappily, these experiences usually remain unrecorded.

11. See my forthcoming article "Coming-To-Terms: The Reconciliation of Divergent Meanings and Values in the Sale of Used Cars."

12. Although my initial research problem situated me so that I luckily tripped over and recognized a new problem, the new problem actually links to the old problem so that my understanding of the dynamics of customer/salesman interaction is enlarged by my understanding of the systemic dynamics of "short sales." In fact, deliberate—as opposed to accidental—problem transformation may be integral to the methodology of contextual, vertical analysis.

13. Since the operation in question is primarily a *wholesale* not a retail house, the proportion of retail sales typically do not exceed 25 percent of total sales. Of these, however, about 75 percent are "short" sales. Thus, of 2,124 total sales, 398 are short. At a minimum of $100 stolen from the top per short sale, approximately $39,000 is generated in unrecorded cash. Used car *wholesalers* may well engage in retail selling for cash and, therefore, are clearly different from used and new car *retailers* who *avoid* cash sales in favor of "credit" or "installment" sales. This latter point was vividly disclosed at a hearing before California's Corporations Commissioner when Sears, Roebuck and Company requested a license to make low cost automobile loans *directly* to customers, thus by-passing dealers. Direct loans, in effect, would turn consumers into cash customers. This the dealers emphatically did not want as the following testimony reveals:

Q: . . . Do you want to sell cars for cash?
A: I do not want to sell them for cash if I can avoid it.
Q: You would not want to sell the cars you do for a cash price, then?
A: No, sir.
Q: Does this mean that you are not really in the business of selling automobiles?
A: It does not mean that at all.
Q: But you don't want to sell automobiles for cash?
A: It means that I want to sell cars for the most profit that I can per car. Finance reserve (dealer's share of the carrying charges) and insurance commissions are part of the profit derived from selling a car on time.

Moreover, these dealers have no qualms about extending credit to poor risk customers; the car always can be repossessed and resold (Quoted in Macaulay, 1966:186).

14. *"Burying money"* means putting it in a safety deposit box. Ironically, this money becomes a source of long-term anxiety instead of long term security. First, it remains a concrete symbol of criminality and is at odds with the dealer's self-image. Second, it also always is the target of potential investigatory disclosure although known instances of such activity are virtually unheard of. Third, the dealer resents the accumulation of "idle" cash and is frustrated by his inability to "turn it over" easily and make it productive. *Laundering* occurs in tight money situations when capital *must* be made available. It invokes a symbiotic relationship between the dealer and a "bookie." The bookie is hired on as a "commissioned agent" of the dealership. The dealer "pays" him a weekly salary using a legitimate business check; in return, the bookie gives the dealer an equal amount in cash. The dealer provides the bookie with a W2 form and the bookie declares and pays taxes on this "income." The dealer then "declares" the income

brought in by the bookie. Since this income derives from nonexistent buying or selling it is subtly apportioned and spread over actual transactions. The dealer also periodically writes a letter to the bookie's probation officer testifying to the bookie's reliable and gainful contribution to the business.

15. See my already cited forthcoming article for an elaboration of this.

16. These figures are consistent with national trend figures provided to me by Thomas C. Webb, research assistant, National Automobile Dealers Association (personal communication, March 11, 1974). Estimations of the number of used cars sold "on" and "off" the market in 1960 and 1973 indicate that, of the 20.7 million used cars sold in 1960, 14.9 million or 71.6 percent were sold "on" the market, whereas of the 31.4 million used cars sold in 1973, 18.7 million or 59.6 percent were sold "on" the market. Thus, there was a net decrease of 12.0 percent. A possible explanation for the decreasing supply of used cars on the market may be the consequence of an already established social-economic trend toward the multiple car family. Whereas a decade ago only 15 percent of the total population owned more than one car, today 30 percent do. Indeed, one out of every three families whose head of household is between the ages of 35–44 owns two cars and one out of ten whose head of household is between 45–54 owns three cars (MVMA, 1974:38–39). What this probably means is that cars are *handed down* from husband to wife to children and literally "run-into-the-ground." In other words, we may well be seeing the reemergence of "second-hand" cars. Cars change hands but outside the commercial nexus i.e., "off-the-market." An additional factor which may be contributing to this trend is declining public confidence in auto dealers. Not too long ago a poster showed a picture of former President Nixon with a caption which asked, "Would you buy a used car from this man?" The credibility of the new and used car dealer apparently has never been lower. Confirmation of this comes from several different polls which seek to determine the public image of new and used car dealers compared to other occupational groups. Auto dealers uniformly trail way behind others in terms of the trust they inspire in the buying public (Leonard and Weber, 1970). Still another compatible and contemporary factor is the deteriorating condition of our national economy where the combination of rising prices and decreasing purchasing power inhibit overall consumer demand and thus retard new car sales and accompanying trade-ins.

17. Leonard and Weber (1970:4) estimate that a dealer can make a gross profit margin of $400 on a $2,000 used car but only $150–200 on a $3,200 new car. Indeed the new car dealers I interviewed all indicated a desire to be able to sell more used cars.

18. According to White (1971), Detroit manufacturers generally avoid owning their own retail outlets or "factory" stores since a network of financially independent but exclusively franchised dealers helps to spread the risk of doing business, defrays cost, and provides local management with entrepreneurial incentive. Edwards (1965) also suggests that a franchise dealer system establishes local identity for products as well as provides facilities which handle trade-ins and repairs. Nevertheless, as a matter of prestige and because no individual dealer can afford the extremely high cost of land in this particular megalopolis, manufacturers usually own retail outlets directly.

19. In principle, much the same strategy was used in the early 1900s when Henry Ford introduced mass production techniques and reduced the price of the Model "T" from $950.00 in 1909 to under $300.00 in the early 1920s and, as a result, boosted sales from 12,000 to two million and captured 50 percent of the market (Lanzilloti, 1968). Rothchild (1973) undoubtedly is correct when she observes that the auto industry continues to rely on ancient and probably obsolete formulas.

20. For a further mathematical articulation of this model, see Pashigan (1961:33–34; 52–56) and White (1971:137–145).

21. Interestingly enough, the decreasing ratio of used to new car sales more or less parallels the increasing market penetration of foreign auto makers. In 1963 foreign auto makers held 6.0 percent of the American market; that percentage increased to 14.6 percent by 1972. And the very year the ratio of used to new car sales declined to 1:00 or parity in 1970, G.M. lost nearly 7.1 percent of its previous market share (NADA, 1973:5). Put another way, increasing market penetration by foreign firms may have placed greater pressure on American auto makers to push harder on new car sales. One plausible way to accomplish this would be to require the dealer distribution network to

put still more capital into new car inventory thus enabling the manufacturer to increase the volume of sales and thereby hold its market share. There is another compatible interpretation for the dramatic and unprecedented 7.1 percent market loss sustained by G.M. in a one year period. This interpretation is held widely by dealers themselves, namely, that G.M. was attempting to prevent rumored anti-trust action by the justice department and was inclined to show itself under competitive siege. In the following year, 1971, G.M. recouped all but 1.6 percent of its previous loss and has held subsequently at about 45.4 percent of the total market.

22. The per unit net of $16.00 does not reflect per unit revenue from financing or insurance which can boost that figure by 200 percent. Little wonder retail dealers want to avoid cash customers.

23. It is difficult to know what percentage of these 3,300 was the result of attrition, voluntary termination, bankruptcy, or direct and indirect franchise cancellation. It is probably safe to assume, however, that the existing network of franchises reflect manufacturers' preferences relative to location and pricing strategy.

42 / Cruising the Truckers: Sexual Encounters in a Highway Rest Area

JAY CORZINE
RICHARD KIRBY

On the fringe of conventional society are social networks or institutions which have been termed "sexual marketplaces." As defined by Hooker (1967: 175), they are places "where agreements are made for the potential exchange of sexual services, for sex without obligation or commitment—the 'one night stand'." In this paper, we report an ethnographic study of the encounters which occur in one such marketplace. Our primary focus is on how the setting and rules of behavior which shape interaction allow participants to develop short term sexual relationships while avoiding the consequences of participating in activities stigmatized by the larger society.

Although mutual affection, as well as marriage, is now widely accepted as a basis for sexual relationship (Gagnon and Simon, 1973; Petras, 1973), sexual gratification is still not acceptable as an end in itself. Therefore, like others who engage in stigmatized behavior, participants in sexual marketplaces are faced with the problem of controlling information about their activities (Goffman, 1963: 41–104).[1] Depending on the social status of the individual and his relationships with those who discover the activities, the failure to control information may result in damage to evaluations by significant others and/or removal from social roles through avoidance, ostracism, job dismissal, and divorce. The case of Walter Jenkins, a presidential aide to Lyndon Johnson, who was fired after being arrested in a Washington D.C. "tearoom"[2] provides an example of the possible consequences following disclosure of activities in a sexual marketplace. Accordingly, participants in the sexual marketplace we studied structure their actions to avoid public disclosure. In Goffman's terminology, their situation is that of the "discreditable" person who possesses a stigma which must be hidden from others.

In addition to the problem of information management necessitated by their discreditable situation, participants in sexual marketplaces are faced with the issue of controlling their degree of involvement with sex partners.[3] Traditionally, a sexual relationship in our society has implied the existence of a marital bond or other lasting attachment. On the other hand, the defining characteristic of the one night stand is the lack of commitment between partners. Most participants in sexual marketplaces are interested in quick and easy sex instead of lasting attachments. However, an ability to control the level of affection felt for another person is not automatic. A popular movie, *A Touch of Class*, focused on the often fragile nature of agreements to limit involvement to an exchange of sexual services. The individuals we interviewed during this study were also aware of the difficulty. Their presence in the sexual marketplace is partly attributable to the relative ease with which sex without commitment can be obtained. However, almost all participants take further precautions. Their concern to limit involvement with sex partners is also reflected in the rules which shape interaction during sexual encounters. In addition to controlling information available to outsiders, participants in the sexual marketplace we studied also withhold personal information from each other. This action is an attempt to prevent the relationships between sex partners from escalating beyond an exchange of sexual services.

Whether the relationships involved are homosexual or heterosexual, previous studies of sexual marketplaces (Cavan, 1966; Hooker, 1967; Achilles, 1967; Ponte, 1974; Troiden, 1974; Humphreys, 1975) have uncovered three common characteristics. First, the settings (bars, parking lots, streets, restrooms, and beaches) are public areas providing easy access to large numbers of people. As such, they provide a number of legitimate reasons to explain one's presence. Second, interaction is characterized by a disruption of the normal flow of information. This varies from Cavan's (1966: 21) observation that a norm of bar behavior is that exchanged personal information need not be valid to the almost complete silence with which homosexual acts transpire in public restrooms (Humphreys, 1975: 12–14). Third, "pickups," or meetings between prospective sex partners, are ambiguous or indirect. The pickup seems to be loosely structured to allow an individual to make a tactful withdrawal from the situation.

We contend that the above and other characteristics of the sexual marketplace can be understood as emerging from attempts by participants to withhold selected information from potential sex partners and outsiders. On the one hand, the participant must be able to select, from the individual s/he meets in public settings, those with similar interests—potential sex partners. This selection process involves the communication of the participant's true purpose in the setting. By failure to convey sufficient information or other error, to choose an individual who is uninterested in a sexual encounter is to risk creating a personal affront, "making a scene," which may lead to the intervention of outsiders including the police. On the other hand, to convey information concerning one's personal identity, either during the initial contact or the sexual transaction, is to increase the possibility of difficulties if a partner later attempts to escalate the relationship beyond an exchange of sexual services. The choice of setting and partners, as well as the rules which shape interaction in the sexual marketplace, emerge from the conscious attempts of participants to minimize the risks of public disclosure and relationship escalation.

THE STUDY

In 1972, the authors conducted an ethnographic study of George's, a homosexual or gay bar in Newburgh, a Midwestern city of approximately 100,000 population. On Friday nights, the final performance of the "drag show"[4] at George's was closed with the MC's announcement: "The show is over. Let's go to the truckstops for breakfast." From informants, we learned that those who follow the MC's suggestion are not interested in an early morning meal but in a short term homosexual relationship with a truck driver. These sexual encounters are sought at two highway rest areas and two truck stops which lie along an interstate highway at the edge of the city. During the bar study informants would occasionally mention some aspect of the sexual marketplace which exists in these settings.

Methods

Our initial step in the present study was to contact two patrons of George's who had been reliable informants and also "cruised"[5] truck drivers in the highway rest areas. Conversations with these individuals produced detailed information concerning the sexual marketplace including prospective locations for observation of the interaction and the ways in which sexual encounters typically develop. This information was used in developing a research plan.

Between January and June of 1974, 40 separate observations were conducted in the research settings. These varied in length from two to six hours with a mean time of three hours. Depending on weather conditions observations were made from our parked car or one of the picnic tables in the rest areas. Field notes were taken as sexual activity developed. At no time during the observations was our presence in the settings challenged by others. Later observations which served to validate the findings of the earlier, more intensive study were made by one of the authors between January and March of 1975.

We use the terms "cruiser" and "driver" to refer to the two groups of participants in the sexual marketplace.[6] "Cruisers" are those individuals whose primary purpose in the settings is the formation of short term sexual relationships with truck drivers. The term "driver" is a shortened form of "truck driver" and refers to that group. Attempts were made to interview members of both groups. An estimated 40 informal conversations and 10 semi-structured interviews were conducted with approximately 25 cruisers from the Newburgh area. Our efforts to interview drivers were less successful. Two interviews with drivers which were arranged for us by cruisers serve as a limited basis for understanding how this group perceives their participation in the sexual marketplace.

A third segment of our research effort also produced mixed success. On different occasions both of the authors rode with cooperating individuals as they cruised truck drivers. These efforts were abandoned when it became apparent that the presence of the researcher in the cruiser's car created a situation which disrupted the typical flow of interaction.

The Setting

The area where cruising activities occur is diagrammed in Figure 1. Route 142, a four-lane, divided highway, connects two urban centers in the Midwest and serves as a major route of interstate trucking. Route 24, a two-lane highway, connects Newburgh with a number of smaller cities and towns. Elm Street is a city street which extends beyond Newburgh's limits. The intersection of Routes 142 and 24 is approximately one mile from Newburgh's city limits. Hampton is a small town north of Newburgh.

The Trucker's Home on Elm Street and John's Diner on Route 24 are roadside restaurants or truck stops that orient their services toward the needs of truck drivers. Both have large graveled parking lots which with the highway rest areas discussed below are spots where interstate truck drivers stop to sleep for the night. The Trucker's Home is a favorite of local drivers while John's Diner depends on travelers from the interstate highway for the majority of its patrons. Because of the different clienteles and the location of the restaurants relative to the highway rest areas, John's Diner is preferred as a cruising site.

Two and a half miles from the intersection of Routes 142 and 24 is Rest Area #1. It is a typical highway rest area which provides telephone and restroom facilities, drinking water, picnic tables, and parking space for travelers. Rest Area #2, a mile and a half further from the intersection and on the opposite side of the interstate, is identical in construction and layout. They are surrounded by wooded areas which sometimes serve as locales for sexual activities during the warmer

Figure 1 / The Setting

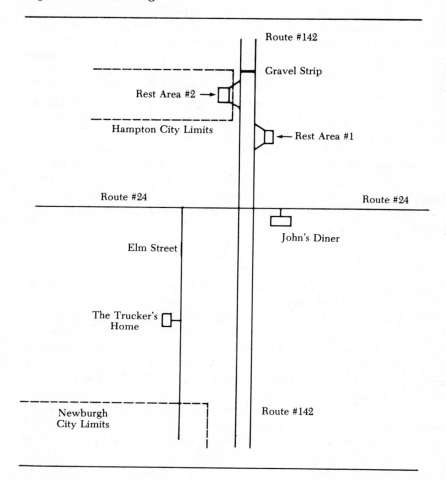

months. At night, the rest areas are unevenly illuminated by mercury lights. While the area surrounding the restrooms and parts of the parking lot are well lighted, most of the rest area is immersed in shadows. A mile from Rest Area #2 is a graveled strip which intersects the median and allows vehicles to change directions on the interstate.

If an individual starts from John's Diner, exits from Route 24 onto the interstate, changes directions on the other side of Rest Area #2, and returns to the diner, the total distance is 12 miles. If he drives through the rest areas and diner parking lot to look for prospective sex partners, the above trip can be completed in about 20 minutes. This is the favorite route of those who cruise truck drivers in the Newburgh area.

Temporal Distribution

The sexual activities at the rest areas, like most human behavior, do not occur randomly in time but are concentrated during both certain hours of the day and certain days of the week. Most sexual encounters occur between the hours of 10:00 PM and 5:00 AM when the largest number of truck drivers have stopped for the night. Besides the relative anonymity offered by darkness, others, especially the police, are usually absent from the diners and rest areas during these hours. As most of the warehouses where interstate truck drivers unload their cargoes are closed on Sunday, there is a reduced number of trucks on the highway or parked for the night on Saturday. Combined with the fact that most cruisers work a standard five-day week, Friday and Sunday are the peak days for cruising activities.

Other factors also influence the incidence of cruising activities in the setting. Bad weather, especially rain or snow, reduces cruising activities for two reasons. Truck drivers who are forced to reduce their speeds during foul weather often drive for longer periods in order to keep on schedule instead of stopping for the night. Also, cruisers — like most individuals — are less likely to leave the shelter of their homes during bad weather. Traffic accidents and speed traps which force reduced speeds also result in fewer trucks stopping in the settings. On nights when few drivers are available many cruisers will curtail their activities unless a successful encounter develops in a short period of time.

Participants

As outlined above, there are two distinct types of participants — cruisers and drivers — involved in the sexual encounters. Besides a mutual interest in the sex without commitment that can be obtained in the marketplace, they have little in common. The characteristic common to cruisers is geography — they live in Newburgh or nearby small towns; that of drivers is occupation — they drive trucks to make a living.

Cruisers can be subdivided into two types. Greg is representative of the first type which corresponds to Humphreys' (1975: 122–125) classification of "The Gay," an unmarried individual who is firmly rooted in the gay subculture. Greg is 28 and has cruised truck drivers for eight years. Married in the past, he considers himself a homosexual and has had no overt heterosexual experience in three years. Highly involved in the local gay community, he also meets sex partners in gay bars and other homosexual cruising areas. Although his family and close friends know Greg is gay, public disclosure would threaten his job as a social worker in an agency which serves mentally retarded adults. Thus, he differs somewhat from Humphreys' description of the gay type in that his job places restrictions on his sexual activities. This is a characteristic shared by a minority of cruisers with high levels of involvement in the gay subculture. Eight of the 10 cruisers we interviewed are of this type.

John represents the second type of cruiser which corresponds to Humphreys' (1975: 117–122) classification of "The Ambisexual," a married individual whose participation in the gay subculture is limited to the search for sex without commitment. John is 38 and has been cruising truck drivers for 18 months. Married and the owner of a business, he feels with justification that the repercussions of public disclosure would be personally disastrous. John began his participation in short term homosexual encounters at a local tearoom frequented by businessmen. After hearing two truck drivers in a restaurant talking about "being bothered by the queers in the rest areas," he decided to find out what they meant. Now his homosexual activities are restricted to cruising truck drivers because in his words: "If you piss them off they don't have the time to give you any trouble about it with the cops." One other cruiser we interviewed is of this type.[7]

During the study we estimated that 50 to 60 individuals cruised trucks in the observed settings. Probably 30% to 40% were of the type represented by John, the ambisexual. As our initial contacts with cruisers were through the local gay subculture, these individuals were more difficult to approach and less willing to talk about their activities. They are underrepresented among the cruisers we interviewed.

The two types of cruisers also differ in the way they first learn about or are recruited into the sexual marketplace. In Newburgh's gay community, knowledge of the settings where truck drivers can be found, specific cruising techniques, and problems to be dealt with are widespread and available on request. Most cruisers with involvement in the subculture learn of the marketplace through others with prior experience. Cruisers with no involvement in the local gay subculture seem to stumble onto the marketplace by chance, by overhearing conversations of others, by being in the settings for other purposes and observing cruising activities, or by other accidental occurrences.

Albert, one of the truck drivers we interviewed, lives and works for a trucking company several hundred miles from Newburgh. For the last five years he has driven the route that takes him past Newburgh and away from his home four days a week. His initiation into the sexual marketplace occurred about four years ago when he was approached by a cruiser in Rest Area #1. Albert explains his acceptance of the proposition by saying: "I was horny that night and decided to give it a go." Since then, he has been involved in sexual encounters with several cruisers and feels these activities provide a safe and dependable outlet for his sexual needs while away from home. He does not consider himself "deviant" and reports no involvement in similar activities when he is home. This type of involvement in homosexual activities, which we believe to be common among drivers, is similar to that discussed by Kinsey et al. (1948: 630–631).

> It has also been pointed out that in certain of the most remote rural areas there is considerable homosexual activity among lumbermen, cattlemen, prospectors, miners, and others engaged in out-of-doors occupations. The homosexual activity rarely conflicts with their heterosexual activity relations, and is quite without the argot, physical manifestations, and other affectations so often found in urban groups. There is a minimum of personal disturbance or social conflict over such activity. It is the type of homosexual experience which the explorer and pioneer may have had in their histories.

Opening Gambits[8]

The majority of cruisers prefer to make the initial approach in the sexual encounter while the driver is sitting in his parked truck. Frequently, a cruiser will first park his car at John's Diner or a rest area where he can observe individuals entering or leaving the buildings in order to look over prospective sex partners. Others prefer to drive slowly by the parked trucks until they see someone who interests them. When this happens the cruiser will stop his car along the driver's side of the truck cab and roll down his window. If the driver rolls down his window or it is open, the cruiser initiates the conversation, usually with the question: "Do you have the time?" An approach style which is used less frequently is described by Roger, a cruiser who has no car and hitchhikes to and from the rest areas.

> I wait in a rest area and look for a truckdriver to leave his truck to go into the restroom. If his appearance appeals to me, I go into the restroom and ask him if he wants to get it on. That's the only method I use. . . . I do not go anyplace with the driver but the tearoom. . . . I'm not going to get myself into a situation that I can't get myself out of.

However, not all truck drivers who are interested in sex sit in their trucks and wait to be approached. Most cruisers with whom we talked during the study reported they had been involved in a sexual encounter where the truck driver had made the initial approach. The first time he engaged in sexual activity with a truck driver, Greg was the one who was approached.

> Actually I became aware of it through a truck driver. I was stopped at a traffic light next to a truck and I was looking at the driver. He motioned me

to pull over past the intersection. When I pulled over, he asked me if I had time for a little action. I've been doing it ever since.

This type of initiation to the possibility of cruising truck drivers was reported by one other respondent. However, the most frequent pattern is for the cruiser to make the initial approach.

A more complex type of approach, called "running a truck" by cruisers, is employed primarily during daytime or early evening hours when few trucks are parked for the night. The cruiser drives toward one of the rest areas in the inside lane of the interstate and allows other traffic to pass him. If he sees a truck driver who interests him, he will change lanes and pull his car to within a few feet of the rear of the truck. Depending on whether it is day or night, he honks the horn or flashes the lights to get the truck driver's attention. The cruiser then passes the truck and when his car is even with the cab waves at the driver. After the truck is passed, the cruiser pulls back into the outside lane and flashes his lights three times. When the cruiser reaches the rest area, he pulls into the entrance and parks his car. If the truck follows, the same approach technique is used as when a truck is initially parked. Although running a truck is a secondary technique and somewhat dangerous on a crowded highway, a few cruisers prefer its almost exclusive use because it virtually eliminates the possibility of approaching a driver who is uninterested in sexual activity.

Midgames

The answer to "Do you have the time?" or other ambiguous opening questions such as "Do you have a match?" determines whether an attempted pickup is made or the encounter is abruptly terminated. A response with a double entendre or indefinite meaning such as "I could find some time," or "that's not all I've got," is perceived by the cruiser as a cue that the driver may be interested in a sexual exchange or as it is usually called, "action." If the response is a direct answer to the question—"it's eight o'clock"; or indicates a hostile attitude—"turn on the radio," the cruiser will terminate the conversation and leave the setting. After the cruiser and driver have a chance to look each other over more closely, sometimes one or both will terminate the encounter because the other is not considered physically attractive. Those cruisers active in the gay subculture share a set of common expectations concerning the characteristics of a "normal" encounter with truck drivers. When actual events differ from what is expected, the result is often confusion, indecisiveness, or the termination of the encounter. These can result when a number of unexpected situations occur including the presence of two men driving for a company which usually employs one man and, ironically, meeting a driver who is not heterosexual.

> I was on my way home from work shortly before midnight. I commuted from a small town and the trip was about thirty minutes. I was cruising a truck with _____ plates and flashed my lights several times. When the driver also flashed the truck lights, I pulled into the rest area. It was not well lighted and when the driver got out I could see tits under the clothing and almost left. When the driver got closer I could see it was a man wearing falsies. When we got into the truck sleeper I found that he was wearing women's underwear. I had never run into anything like that before. He told me that he dressed like that a lot late at night when he was on the road.

Because of our limited number of interviews with truck drivers, we are uncertain if they share a similar set of expectations as to what constitutes a normal encounter. As there is an apparent lack of communication between drivers who frequent the sexual marketplace, they may evaluate emerging encounters more on the basis of past personal experience than by reference to a set of shared subcultural expectations.

If the encounter continues, a difference in styles emerges between individual cruisers. A few favor a rather direct approach and soon follow the opening question with a rather explicit proposition. More often the subsequent conversation is indirect and ambiguous. One or both participants interject statements into the conversation which contain vaguely disguised sexual innuendos—"I'm getting hungry, how about you?" or "I'm sure you know what I'm here for." If the driver has previous experience in the sexual marketplace, he usually understands the cruiser's true purpose. Although frequently no identifying information is exchanged during the encounter, the cruiser and driver may exchange first names which are often fictitious during the midgame stage.

We did not observe the body and eye signals reported by researchers in other gay settings (Hooker, 1967; Humphreys, 1975). Interaction during the approach and midgame stages of the encounter is almost exclusively verbal. Although most encounters occur at night when nonverbal communication is impractical, more important as an explanation for the reliance on verbal communication is that neither group is familiar with the slang or nonverbal gestures which have meaning in the other's subculture. Verbal communication and a rather direct approach also serve to insure that, most of the time, both participants will understand when an agreement for an exchange of sexual services has been reached.

Most cruisers report they will end the conversation with a driver if no agreement can be reached in approximately 10 minutes.

Encounters often end in midgame because one or both participants are suspicious of the other's intentions. Most drivers carry large sums of cash and/or credit cards to pay travel expenses. As a result, they are often on guard against the threat of robbery. Cruisers are aware of the threat of physical violence if they offend a driver. These suspicions are intensified when more than one individual is in either vehicle. The presence of the extra person usually becomes a point of contention in the conversation. Although group sex is reported to occur sometimes when three or more persons are present, a more common outcome is that the lone individual will not leave or trust someone to enter his vehicle. It was this problem which led us to abandon the practice of riding with cruisers. Assurances that we were friends of the cruiser who were "wise"[9] and would remain in the car were not successful in allaying the suspicions of the driver.

Resolutions

There is no role in the sexual marketplace we studied similar to that of "watch queen" (Humphreys, 1975: 26–28) which would have permitted us to observe the exchange of sexual services. Regardless of the location where the exchange occurs, available roles would have required participation in the sexual activity or covert "spying." Therefore, this section is based exclusively on the reports of informants.

Although the sexual exchange occurs in a number of settings—the restrooms at the highway rest areas, the woods at the rest areas, the cruiser's car, or the cruiser's home—the sleeper located in the rear of the truck cab is the favorite location. Like most settings convenient for sleeping, it serves equally well for sexual activities. Another advantage it offers over other settings in the immediate area is its privacy. As homosexual acts between consenting adults conducted in private are legal in the state where Newburgh is located, it is doubtful if any laws are broken when the sexual activity is confined to the sleeper. Another advantage discussed by several informants is that, if the encounter is interrupted by outsiders, both men can claim to be drivers who are sleeping at the same time.

If the initial approach is made at John's Diner or the Trucker's Home, the participants usually move to another setting for the sexual exchange. The stated reason is that the chances of interruption or being recognized, especially by employees, are too great in the parking lots of the truck stops. Although the participants usually move to Rest Area #1, they will sometimes leave the restaurants in the cruiser's car and park on one of the country roads in the area. The cruiser's home is used almost exclusively in those cases where the participants know each other from previous sexual encounters.

The homosexual encounters which occur in tearooms have been the object of the most intensive sociological study of a sexual marketplace (Humphreys, 1975). Accounts of our respondents indicate the payoff stage of rest area encounters differs significantly from that which occurs in tearooms. This finding is also supported by Troiden's (1974) study of sexual activities in a highway rest area. While fellatio is the most common, almost the exclusive, sexual act which occurs in tearooms (Humpreys, 1975: 75), a variety of acts including fellatio, anal intercourse, mutual masturbation, and mutual fellatio were reported as common by our informants. Hugging and kissing, also rare in other settings, were reported as frequent occurrences during the sexual exchanges.

Most of our informants, including both truck drivers, agree that reciprocity is the norm during the sexual exchange. However, the guiding rule is to not force a sex partner into a role in which he is uncomfortable. Some drivers and a few cruisers will reportedly accept only the insertor or, less frequently, the insertee role in fellatio or anal intercourse. Although most cruisers prefer a reciprocal relationship, the option of continuing to cruise is available and seen as preferable to an argument if sexual gratification is not achieved from an encounter.

The resolution stage often lasts two or three hours with periods of conversation alternating with those of sexual activity. The only subject of conversation which is reported to be taboo is enquiries concerning personal information such as name and address. If there have been prior encounters between the participants and mutual trust exists, they will sometimes leave the rest area to go to a local bar or restaurant. When the sexual exchange is completed, the participants dress and use the restroom facilities to wash. Although a few cruisers enter into several completed encounters during the same evening, one encounter is the rule rather than the exception. Both the truck drivers we interviewed reported they never have more than one sexual encounter in an evening.

Although valid personal information is rarely exchanged, five of the 10 cruisers we interviewed reported they have offered phone numbers to drivers or made arrangements to meet them at a future time. As many drivers travel only the route which passes Newburgh, these meetings are not difficult to schedule in advance. The duration of these extended relationships on which we have information varies from one prearranged encounter to regular meetings over a period of four years. Although involvement is usually limited to a series of sexual transactions, some individuals develop friendships which transcend a purely sexual relationship.

Intrusions

As some stages of the sexual encounters occur in public settings, intrusions by others are a constant possibility. During most of the late night encounters we observed, others in the rest areas were apparently sleeping. But at other times, there were numerous individuals using the restrooms, eating at the picnic tables, or simply walking around the grounds. At the truck stops, employees are only a few yards from where approaches are made. Daily shifts of state employees who are responsible for the maintenance of the facilities are always on duty at the rest areas. However, as there is only one employee per shift, there is always one rest area where there are no employees.

Of those who may be present in the settings, only state policemen or the employees at the rest areas are seen as potential threats by cruisers. Even this attitude, like the avoidance of sexual activity at the truck stops, seems to be based more on fear of possible consequences than past behavior of others. The only person who was reported to interfere with the cruising activities is a city policeman from the town of Hampton (Rest Area #2 is within the Hampton city limits) who, while on duty, patrols a road which runs behind Rest Area #2. If cruising activities are visible, he turns on his red light and siren but takes no further action. The usual result is that cruisers will abandon the rest area until the policeman's shift is over.

Besides the sexual encounters, most interaction which occurs in the rest areas is typical of that between strangers in public places. Eye contact is noticeably avoided. Conversations which do occur center on the weather or the rigors of long distance driving. Although the actions of cruisers and drivers violate the common expectations of behavior which should occur in public places, they are almost always ignored. This style of reacting to unusual or unexpected behavior which seems characteristic of public places has been summarized by Lofland (1972:228):

> Once an individual has definitely established himself as an eccentric, he may engage in the most bizarre behavior without exciting the "slightest notice." Almost no matter how peculiar his appearance or his actions, he will be treated as though he looked and acted like a conventional human being.

The interaction of others with the participants in the sexual encounters support Lofland's assertion. At no time did anyone attempt to interfere with or seem to take much notice of the sexual encounters they were witnessing. Only one cruiser remembered anyone being startled or surprised by the cruising activities in the rest area.

I was really brazen when I was younger and I had been cruising this driver in late afternoon. He was interested so we got up in the sleeper for a good round of sex. We were both completely nude and were both fairly uninhibited. It's not easy to dress in the sleeper so we got into the cab to put our clothes back on. About halfway through dressing I looked down and realized that we were being watched by a family in a car that had parked next to the truck. There were this man and his wife and three kids just looking up with bewildered looks on their faces. I was startled for a minute but then finished dressing as nonchalantly as I could and got out of there.

DISCUSSION

The choice of settings and the rules that shape interaction between participants in the sexual marketplace may seem unusual, especially to those whose experience is limited to conventional sexual practices. They are, as stated above, explainable not by reference to some underlying pathology shared by participants but in terms of conscious attempts by participants to control the information available to both their sex partners and outsiders.

The highway rest area, in many ways, provides an ideal setting for individuals who wish to engage in stigmatized behavior. In the contemporary United States, a society where traveling away from one's home is both common and accepted, it is one of a number of institutions including motels, bus stations, and YMCAs that are designed to serve the needs of travelers. Those who frequent these settings are not likely to be from the immediate area; they are, for the most part, strangers both from each other and the local people. As a result, these are locales where people from the local area can engage in stigmatized behaviors with some assurance that they will remain hidden from family and friends. In addition, the highway rest area has two advantages not shared by similar settings. First, they do not currently have the seamy reputation attached to roadside motels, bus stations, and other settings frequented by travelers. Second, although similar institutions are designed to serve travelers, they also employ individuals from the immediate area. In highway rest areas, there are both few employees and a lack of need to interact with them to take advantage, either legitimately or illegitimately, of the provided services. Reputations are likely to remain unblemished regardless of an individual's participation in stigmatized behavior. The cruisers and drivers we interviewed were aware of these advantages. Cruisers who seek out truck drivers as sex partners frequently report that they avoid other local cruising areas. In addition, when the initial approach occurs at a truck stop, the participants usually move to one of the rest areas for the sexual exchange.

The possibility of the relationships formed between cruisers and drivers developing beyond an exchange of sexual services is limited by geographical separation. While cruisers live in Newburgh or the surrounding area, most drivers are from outside the state. The job duties of the long distant truck driver create a situation which is conducive to his acceptance of short term sexual relationships but discourages the development of any lasting attachments. Responsibility for the cargo he hauls and the demands of a strict time schedule limit the opportunity to seek sexual outlets or develop close relationships. This fact is well recognized by cruisers.

> I don't have a steady relationship right now and I really don't want one. Since these men travel so much it's next to impossible to have a permanent relationship with one of them. Likewise, they can make no demands on my time.

> I don't want to settle down. With the kinds of life truck drivers lead they don't make demands on you.

Additional factors minimize the possibility of members of either group becoming interested in more than a transitory exchange of sexual services. Involvement in the sexual marketplace and homosexual activities while serving the needs of both groups has different meanings for them. As discussed above, most drivers maintain a heterosexual self-identity and view their homosexual activity while away from home as simply a convenient sexual outlet. It is doubtful if many drivers would be interested in a long term homosexual relationship if one were easily available. Those cruisers who are ambisexual look upon their homosexual activities as do the drivers: as supplements to the sexual outlet provided by wives or girl friends.

For the cruisers who are active in the gay subculture, involvement with truck drivers has a different meaning. They represent one of several same-sex groups from which prospective sex partners may be drawn. The decision to cruise truck drivers is made for a number of reasons. Two of these, the inability of truck drivers to make demands and the slight chance they will go to the police if offended, have been discussed. Cruisers consider truck drivers to be safe pickups. Another reason is the mystique of masculinity that surrounds the truck driver in our culture and elicits admiration from a significant number of male homosexuals. Several cruisers remarked on this aspect of their attraction for truck drivers.

> I like very masculine men and truck drivers are the epitome of masculinity. They put forth a very masculine image. I like my men to look like men and not the swishy queens you find in bars.

> I like butch, tough numbers which are usually not available in the local bars in this town.

A final attraction of cruising truck drivers is the danger that many cruisers associate with the activity. While the possibility of physical violence is present in some of the encounters, many cruisers embellish stories of past occurrences in a style reminiscent of tales of battle deeds or athletic accomplishments.

> It's more of a challenge. It's a lot like gambling I think. There is an element of danger. Some of these carry a lot of cash for expenses so they are usually armed. I have never met a driver who didn't carry a firearm. If you don't know what you're doing you could get your shit blown away. I've been shot at twice.

Finally, the rule against requesting personal information during the encounters poses a barrier to any participant who would attempt to establish a more involved relationship with a sex partner. The only reliable information a cruiser typically has concerning a driver is the name of his employer painted on the side of the truck. If a driver wishes to end his participation in the sexual marketplace, he may do so effectively by no longer stopping in the settings. Although cruisers sometimes give their phone numbers to truck drivers, they may be easily changed. The driver has neither the time nor the information to pursue a relationship with a cruiser who is not agreeable. The anonymity of the encounter acts as a final safeguard against the possibility of further involvement with a sex partner when it is not desired.

As a final note, there is evidence that the type of sexual marketplace we studied is widespread in the United States. *The 18 Wheeler*, a gay newsletter published on the East Coast, prints stories, cartoons, jokes, pictures, and cruising tips for homosexuals who are interested in truck drivers. The term "fairyland" which refers to roadside parks has in recent years become a standard part of the truck driver's argot. Highway rest areas are also mentioned by Loovis (1974) and Zeh (1975) as locales where sexual activity occurs. In cities combining a well-defined gay subculture and a nearby route of interstate trucking with convenient settings, we would expect the development of a similar sexual marketplace. In an urban society where sex increasingly becomes an activity separated from other social roles, the continued existence of sexual marketplaces in public settings is assured.

References

Achilles, N. (1967) "The Development of the homosexual bar as an institution," pp. 228–244 in J. H. Gagnon and W. Simon (eds.) Sexual Deviance. New York: Harper & Row.

Cavan, S. (1966) Liquor License. Chicago: Aldine.

Gagnon, J. H. and W. Simon (1973) Sexual Conduct: The Social Sources of Human Sexuality, Chicago: Aldine.

Goffman, E. (1963) Stigma: Notes on the Management of Spoiled Identity. Englewood Cliffs, NJ: Prentice-Hall.

Hooker, E. (1967) "The homosexual community," pp. 167–184 in J. H. Gagnon and W. Simon (eds.) Sexual Deviance. New York: Harper & Row.

Humphreys, L. (1975) Tearoom Trade: Impersonal Sex in Public Places. Chicago: Aldine.

Kinsey, A. C. et al. (1948) Sexual Behavior in the Human Male. Philadelphia: W. B. Saunders.

Levitt, E. E. and A. D. Klassen, Jr. (1974) "Public attitudes toward homosexuality: part of the 1970 national survey by the Institute of Sex Research." J. of Homosexuality 1: 29–43.

Lofland, L. H. (1972) "Self-management in public settings: part II." Urban Life and Culture 1: 217–231.

Loovis, D. (1974) Gay Spirit: A Guide to Becoming a Sensuous Homosexual. New York: Grove.

Petras, J. W. (1973) Sexuality in Society. Boston: Allyn & Bacon.

Ponte, M. R. (1974) "Life in a parking lot: an ethnography of a homosexual drive-in," pp. 7–29 in J. Jacobs (ed.) Deviance: Field Studies and Self-Disclosures. Palo Alto, Calif.: National.

Starr, J. R. and D. E. Carns (1972) "Singles in the city." Society/Transaction 9 (February): 43–48.

Troiden, R. R. (1974) "Homosexual encounters in a highway rest stop," pp. 211–228 in E. Goode and R. R. Troiden (eds.) Sexual Deviance and Sexual Deviants. New York: William Morrow.

Warren, C. A. B. (1974) Identity and Community in the Gay World. New York: John Wiley.

Zeh, J. (1975) "Muther truckers!" Advocate 172: 24–26.

Notes

1. As the activities which occur in the sexual marketplace we studied are homosexual, there is an additional stigma attached to them. It should be noted that Levitt and Klassen (1974) found more acceptance of homosexual acts when the partners were involved in a loving relationship than when they had no particular affection for each other.

2. A "tearoom" is a public restroom frequented by males for the purpose of forming transitory homosexual relationships.

3. Of course, the desire to control the degree of involvement in a sexual relationship is not restricted to participants in one night stands and sexual marketplaces. Starr and Carns (1972) who studied singles in Chicago report a widespread rule against intrabuilding dating which serves to forestall difficulties in discontinuing a relationship.

4. The "drag show" is a form of entertainment popular in the gay subculture. It usually consists of a series of male and/or female impersonators who sing or mime to records of popular songs.

5. The term "cruising," as used in the gay subculture, refers to any activity undertaken to find a sex partner.

6. The terms "cruiser" and "driver" are among those used by the participants to designate both members of their own and the opposite group in the encounters.

7. During the study, we discovered no cruisers who would correspond to "Closet Queens" or "Trade," the other types of tearoom participants classified by Humphreys (1975: 104–130).

8. The division of the encounters into the phases of "opening gambits," "mid-games," and "resolutions" is borrowed from Cavan (1966).

9. The term "wise," as used in the gay subculture, refers to heterosexuals who are familiar with at least some aspects of the gay subculture and adopt a nonjudgmental attitude toward homosexuality (Warren, 1974).

43 / The Structuring and Maintenance of a Deviant Identity: An Analysis of Lesbian Activity

DELOS H. KELLY

Recently, many social scientists working in the area of social deviance have aligned themselves with the increasingly popular "labeling" or "interactionist" perspective (e.g., Rubington and Weinberg, 1968, 1973; Schur, 1971). Such an approach highlights the need to consider not only the processes behind the formation of social definitions, rules, and laws (Akers, 1968; Liazos, 1972) but also the conditions under which these standards are applied to social actors (Chiricos et al., 1972; Rushing, 1971). This approach, furthermore, underscores the *problematic* nature of deviance (Becker, 1963; Duster, 1970). What this means in effect is that whether or not a particular social actor will be labeled a deviant depends upon several contingencies, among them the particular behavior in question, the actor involved, and the particular audience (Kelly, 1975). We do know, however, that certain behaviors will generally elicit negative responses (Kitsuse, 1962; Rubington and Weinberg). Female homosexual activity, or lesbianism, is one such behavior (Kitsuse; Simmons, 1969). The many traits and popular stereotypes that have been used to characterize the "lesbian" provide strong support for such a contention.

To many, the lesbian is perceived as embodying the worst in terms of feminine attributes: toughness, aggressiveness, instability, insatiable sexual appetite. Words such as "dyke," "butch," "lesbo," "morphodyke," "queer," and "lady lover" strongly *stigmatize* the lesbian (Goffman, 1963). Words such as these also serve to remind us that the lesbian must attempt to survive in a generally hostile environment. To exist, she must manage her "front"—that is, her behaviors, attitudes, and actions—in such a manner as to avoid detection by selected members of the "straight" society. This means that the lesbian is often forced into leading a dual life-style (Leznoff and

Westley, 1956; Rubington and Weinberg). She becomes, in terms of Becker's argument, a "secret deviant." This particular status requires a constant self-monitoring. Failure to do so may result in detection by socially significant straights such as family members, employers, and friends. This discovery, furthermore, can lead to some very serious consequences. Of major significance is the probability that knowledge of her status will be used to "discredit" her (Goffman). She may, for example, not only lose her job but also become ostracized socially (Winslow, 1974). It is in this sense, then, that the consequences can become most real.

While most would agree that lesbianism is associated with both actual and potential costs, it is evident that relatively little is known about what it is actually like to pursue a deviant life-style in American society, whether focus is given to "deviants" in general or to lesbians in particular. Researchers have, with few exceptions, chosen to *impute* certain drives, conditions, and states to the deviant actors on the basis of inference, not direct observation. Becker (1963:166) argues that a strategy such as this may be partially responsible for the low level of theorizing that characterizes the field of defiance:

> This is not to say that there are no studies of deviant behavior. There are, but they are, on the whole and with a few outstanding exceptions, inadequate for the job of theorizing we have to do, inadequate in two ways. First, there simply are not enough studies that provide us with facts about the lives of deviants as they live them. Although there are a great many studies of delinquency, they are more likely to be based on court records than on direct observation. . . . *Very few tell us in detail what a juvenile delinquent does in his daily round of activity and what he thinks about himself, society, and his activities.* When we theorize about juvenile delinquency, we are therefore in the position of having to *infer* the way of life of the delinquent boy from fragmentary studies and journalistic accounts . . . [italics mine].

This same state of affairs applies to lesbianism (Winslow).

If Becker is correct in his assessment of the state of deviance studies, then it would appear that the only way we can really obtain a better understanding of the lesbian is to immerse ourselves in her world. Attempts should be made to find out how she perceives not only herself but also members of straight society, both socially significant and otherwise. The present study is directed toward these ends.

In particular, questions of the following nature will be explored: (1) How and under what conditions does a female come to view herself as a lesbian? That is, how is a "deviant" or lesbian identity socially *structured*? (2) Once a lesbian identity has been structured, how is it *maintained*? (3) How does a lesbian view herself and her activities—or, more specifically, what is the relationship between a lesbian's own personal identity and her evaluation of self,[1] her feelings of self-esteem? and (4) How does a lesbian *perceive* and *react* to American society, especially its straight members?

The actual data base for our lesbian research was gathered over a period of two and one-half years, and it consists of both structured and unstructured interviews with over fifty self-admitted lesbians. For the purposes of this paper, however, two case studies will be presented. This material is being presented both to *sensitize* researchers and theoreticians to the important analytical concepts and distinctions that have to be made, and to underscore the *problematical* nature of identity formation, maintenance, and transformation.

THE CASE STUDIES

Both females come from white middle-class backgrounds and are in their late twenties.[2] Pat, the first case study, has a master's degree and is currently working on her doctorate at a very reputable university. During the day, she teaches high school. Toni, the second case study, is completing work on her master's degree and has an excellent position as a researcher in a research center.

Pat and Toni share a pleasant apartment on the eastern side of a rather large city. Both currently view themselves as lesbians, but their present relationship is primarily platonic in nature. Each is known as the "butch" or the active female. Although they have been friends since childhood, neither knew that the other was gay until approximately seven years ago.

Throughout high school, their academic training was similar. Both attended the same Catholic grade school, as well as the same all-girl, Catholic high school. Their experiences, however, were quite different.

The Structuring of a "Deviant"[3] or Lesbian Identity

Pat. While growing up, Pat was very close to her mother, a prominent member of the community. By contrast, Pat never held much respect for her father, a retired gambler.[4] Both parents know that Pat is gay. Her father objects but has made no effort to do anything about Pat's life-style. Although Pat's mother does accept this way of life, she does not condone Pat's present choice of dating partners — Pat is currently dating a stripper.

> My mother accepts my love for women but she wants me to date professional women. She thinks my present friends are very low-down people. Toni is my only good friend.

Pat has always felt a certain attraction to her girl friends. Her first actual homosexual experience, as she remembers and defines it now, occurred when she was a senior in high school. At this time, her best friend was leaving to enter the Army. Both girls became very emotional; they hugged and kissed each other profusely. Neither girl gave much thought to these actions, nor did Pat view herself as a lesbian at this time. She continued to date men throughout high school; however, she began to question the quality of her heterosexual contacts:

> I have found my heterosexual relationships to be [satisfying] sexually, emotionally, and mentally. The only difference is that I find my homosexual relations to be far superior.

After graduation from high school, Pat went away to a coed state college. At the beginning of her senior year, Pat and her roommate became involved in homosexual activity. The two girls had lived together the year before and, although their relationship was very close, Pat had no idea that her roommate was gay. During this same period Pat was also engaged to be married. However, she still continued to question the quality of her heterosexual relationships:

> I always felt that there was something animalistic about having sex with a man. No matter how much a man may love and cherish you, he reaches a point where he is all animal and has no control over what he is doing.

The real turning point in Pat's life came when her college roommate took her to a gay bar. Pat liked the experience and began to feel that this was the life for her. Shortly thereafter she not only broke off her engagement but she began a personal crusade to convert all women to her new way of life. It was at this point that she came to view herself as a lesbian.

Pat continued to frequent gay bars and became deeply involved in the gay world. This "coming out" process was associated with extensive learning and training sessions. Experienced lesbians taught her the appropriate language (or argot), techniques, and ways of recognizing the formal agents of social control (e.g., vice squad members). They also provided her with the appropriate justifications that could be used to legitimate her homosexual way of life. Given her strong Catholic education and background, these justifications and associated rationalizations served the additional function of assuaging initial guilt feelings. She came to believe, for example, that among heterosexuals monogamous fidelity to one partner is rare (Hooker, 1967). Gradually, Pat became very committed to her new, satisfying way of life:

> I love the dramatic life. There is such intensity simply because it is not supposed to be happening. It's a very nice feeling . . . I can't explain it.

There is always the threat of it being taken away, but these are also the few things that make it worthwhile.

Involvement with the gay subculture produced further changes in Pat. She began to read a large amount of material on both the lesbian and women's liberation movements. She ultimately became extremely anti-male: "Men are all chauvinists, each of them has been raised by society to be chauvinist."

Toni. Although noticeably less aggressive than Pat, Toni was also a very popular girl. During high school she belonged to a close peer group. In fact, she dated one boy from this group for over three years. Their relationship, however, was terminated when she discovered that the youth was a homosexual. This discovery was especially traumatic for Toni. She refused, thereafter, to become deeply involved with any males.

Following high school, Toni entered and graduated from an all-girl, Catholic college. During her undergraduate days, she did have a few dates. For the most part, however, her social life was limited: "I had no social life at all. I call it my neuter period. I was a nothing, sexless being."

Unlike Pat, Toni discovered her homosexuality somewhat later in life. The process of discovery itself was a gradual one: "When I first came out—had my first sexual experience with a woman—I was not conscious of the gay life. I felt I was only in love with [Pat] and was not attracted to any other woman." Toni did not view herself as a lesbian at that time.

Pat subsequently attempted to convince Toni that she was, in fact, a lesbian, and tried to get her to join the gay culture. Toni initially resisted these efforts. Eventually, however, they began to frequent the gay bars. Over time, and due primarily to influences such as these, Toni began to view herself as a lesbian.

Although Toni has accepted her identity as a lesbian, she exhibits a constant fear that her family will find out: "They would say I was crazy and put me in a mental home." She would like to be near her family, but she feels that she could not really be herself: "I really wish I could get married, just to make them [family] happy. I love them, but I hate to hurt them—so I stay away."

Over time, then, Pat and Toni came to view themselves as lesbians. The acceptance of this particular identity, however, was associated with significant changes in their way of life. For example, to decrease the probability of discovery by socially significant straights, Toni, in particular, found it necessary to move away from the immediate environment of her family into an apartment of her own. To receive a degree of social support for their "deviant" life-style, both women became deeply involved in the culture of the gay world. This involvement not only provided them with an exciting, satisfying way of life but it also supplied them with the appropriate rationalizations that could be used to legitimate it.

> *Pat:* My attitudes toward gay life have changed since I first came out. I have a more realistic perception—the feeling of oppression as a minority group becomes more and more obvious as one becomes further ensconced in the gay life.

Maintaining a "Deviant" Identity (Current Life-Style)

To protect as well as to maintain their identity as lesbians, both females found it necessary to modify their dress habits. Instead of two rather flamboyant butches, one now sees two sophisticated women. However, they still pursue the gay way of life, and they both continue to play the butch role. They have become increasingly aware of what it really means to be a lesbian in our society. Given their ties to certain aspects of the conventional social structure, this awareness is associated with some very real fears. Both realize, for example, that they must continue to play the straight role, particularly if they wish to retain their present positions. This duplicity, however, is not without its costs.

> *Pat:* When I first came out, I saw the ideal, what it could be like for two women. The thing that screws you up is that every social organization negatively reinforces you—church, family, school; this is when the problem hits. Society drives you to neurotic behavior, guilt forces you into leading a double life. In the day I am a femme, the night and weekends a butch. If I want to continue teaching, I must pretend.

> *Toni:* After being in this way of life for seven years, I realize I have my career, family, and friends [straight] to think of. Thus, I'm more conscious of the social and personal pressures that I am certainly under. I have to live for the most part two lives—my straight and gay life—this is difficult at times.

These particular fears and concerns result in a refusal to become intimately involved with not only fellow workers but also other members of the heterosexual world. Such a strategy (or management of front) reduces the possibility that "others" will acquire discrediting information about their style of life.

> *Toni:* I'm always very careful when I have to deal with straight people, and I try for the most part to be pleasant but not too intimate with them. I have been rejected by some very "good"—I thought—straight friends because I happen to love women. I dislike intensely the power, position and chauvinistic attitudes of men in general. Men naturally hate lesbians and try to push them around because they feel [lesbians] are sick. . . .

Pat: I perceive the heterosexual society as a sexist one and therefore because of my new consciousness it is somewhat difficult to function without being grossly hypocritical. In addition society views my life-style as "deviant" and therefore it perpetrates injustices upon me.

As is also perhaps apparent, both girls display a sense of hatred and dislike toward what they consider to be a sexist-oppressive society. Nevertheless, Pat and Toni continue to espouse and lead a way of life that runs counter to the accepted way; they have, however, become more discreet in their methods. Neither, for example, actively participates in any gay liberation movement ("too risky").

Pat: Every woman is a potential lesbian because we are born as sexual beings and it is society that determines whether we become heterosexual or homosexual and unfortunately society places heterosexuality on top priority. I feel very sorry for women who are not allowed to make the choice, if it were really there; there would be a hell of a lot more women who were gay and a hell of a lot more women who were really happy.

In spite of the problems and negative feedback *encountered* and *perceived*, both girls have accepted their identity as lesbians. Wearing the label, however, has produced rather dramatic effects upon their own level of personal esteem.

The Lesbian Identity, Self-Esteem, and Further Perceptions of Society

Pat: For Pat the coming-out process produced a liberating effect. She professes to be happy and satisfied pursuing the gay life and, although she no longer belongs to any gay liberationist movement, she feels that the "feminist ideology is still operating strongly." However, she continues to display an intense hostility toward a world which forces her to play inconsistent and contradictory roles:

It is very natural to feel a hate and a rage toward those who oppress you. It is a healthy response to hate that which oppresses you—one step toward liberation. We must start our own desocialization process.

Through her own desocialization from selected aspects of conventional society, Pat has come to believe that the homosexual way of life is far superior to the heterosexual:

By virtue of our similarity we have a compatibility and an intimacy that is incompatible in heterosexual relations. The heterosexual is overidealistic in assuming that one can find everything in one person. One underestimates her potential by committing herself to a monogamous, heterosexual style of living.

In a very real sense one obtains the impression that Pat has adjusted well to the lesbian way of life. She not only considers it "normal" to be gay but she also accords a high degree of esteem and respect to those women willing to reject the heterosexual way of life: "There is nothing wrong with the nature of the act; the only thing that makes it difficult to function is society's unbelievable oppression against us as a minority group."

Overall, then, one would have to conclude that Pat possesses a favorable image of herself. Most of the "positive reinforcements come from areas that do not directly involve [her] sexual orientation, i.e., family, friends [gay], occupational and academic success." Toni, by contrast, does not possess a similar level of self. This continues to present her with several difficult problems.

Toni: Toni would like to develop a sense of total independence: "I must become self-sufficient." Thus far she has been unable to do so and has come to depend very heavily upon Pat. This particular dependency, however, has produced some serious confrontations between the two women. Several arguments resulted in physical violence.

> I'm sick of living in fear, of being put down, sick of cleaning up after her and her girl, then having her beat me up—am I really that bad?

At one point Toni felt that she could no longer go on. She made no attempt, however, to leave the situation: "Where can I go? I can't move into an apartment alone. Every gay person must have a gay friend. Without a friend you will lead a very miserable and lonely life." Toni, however, has not given up. In an effort to improve her negative self-image, she has become more involved with her work and studies.

> I think it [self-image] is developing positively. I feel more independent now and much more confident. I'm very interested in my work and I hope to get my master's and accomplish something. I want my family to be proud of me, and I want to be respected as a mature intellectual woman. I also feel all of my gay affairs have helped me become more secure in relating to myself.

Although there are some indications that Toni's self-image is developing positively, she has suffered some serious setbacks. Most significantly and most recently, her family discovered [she told them] that she was a lesbian. This discovery placed a definite and predictable strain upon all concerned. Several family members, for example, argued that she was sick and should therefore be committed to a mental institution. No steps, however, have been taken in this direction, nor are any presently anticipated. Toni has also recently moved into an apartment by herself.

DISCUSSION AND IMPLICATIONS

These case materials indicate that accepting a lesbian identity is associated with some significant personal and social consequences. Perhaps of most significance is the observation that lesbians must attempt to exist and operate in a society which generally views lesbianism as a form of sexual perversion. In being aware of and reacting to this general intolerance, Pat and Toni are required, therefore, to lead two rather distinct ways of life. This duplistic type of behavior, however, is not without its costs and has produced rather noticeable strains upon the two females. Of major concern to them are the constant reminders that a very real *discrepancy* exists between their *personal* or actual identity as lesbians and their *public* or social identity as teacher and researcher respectively. For Toni such pressures and conflicts became almost insurmountable. Others have noted a similar pattern of pressures, concerns, and required strategies.

For example, a nurse working in a federal hospital was interrogated intensively by a government investigator flown in from Washington, D.C. Someone suspecting her of being a lesbian had written the local congressman (*Lesbians Speak Out*, 1970). Even though this nurse possessed a "perfect work record," she was subjected to shame and humiliation. Her *suspected* status as a lesbian took priority over her status as an excellent nurse. In effect, the *imputed* status became, in terms of Becker's argument, a "master status." Her other statuses (e.g., nurse, worker, etc.) receded into the background and became of little importance. Accordingly, the investigator reacted to her not as a nurse but as a lesbian.

Incidents and problems such as these, whether *real* or *perceived*, make life difficult for lesbians, psychologically, economically, and socially. And even though many consider their behavior to be normal (as was the case with our two subjects), they do, in a very real sense, feel the "stigma" that is attached to their way of life. To many, this presents additional problems. Some are faced with a struggle within themselves to change, to conform, to be something they do not wish to be. Our own data provide support for this observation, particularly with respect to Toni. Elsewhere, Shelly (1969:310) has commented on these pressures:

> Many of my sisters, confused by the barrage of anti-gay propaganda, have spent years begging to be allowed to live. They have come begging because they believed they were psychic cripples and that other people were healthy and had the moral right to judge them. Many have lived in silence, burying themselves in their careers, like name-changing Jews or blacks who passed for whites . . . many attempt to maintain a love relationship in a society which attempts to destroy love and replace it with consumer goods,

and which attempts to completely destroy any form of love outside the monogamous marriage.

Should lesbians be subjected to such persecution and oppression? Are lesbians really that "different" from "normals"? Should we, as many argue, "tolerate" them? If more people felt this way, would this significantly reduce or eliminate the major living problems confronting lesbians?

Even though manipulating the tolerance aspect would no doubt have some effect, the overall impact would probably be negligible. This contention highlights a more general problem. In effect, any time one is set apart and perceived as being different, this affects the quality of interaction that may take place between the "deviant" and the nondeviant. Toleration does not necessarily imply acceptance. As Liazos (1972:105) emphasizes:

> ... one tolerates only those one considers less than equal, morally inferior, and weak; those equal to oneself, one accepts and respects; one does not merely allow them to exist, one does not "tolerate" them.

Instead of tolerating the lesbian, some have suggested that we need to do away with negative or deviant labels. Given the present structure and prevailing attitudes of American society, this proposition is most unrealistic. On a more practical level, if people could gain more knowledge—and were willing to do so—then many of the stereotypes and misconceptions surrounding the lesbian and her life-style could perhaps be dispelled. That this is no easy task is obvious when one considers the vicious circle that often implicates the lesbian who does, in fact, try to be honest with straights:

> If she divulges her identity, she automatically becomes vulnerable. She faces loss of job, family and friends. Yet, until she opens herself to such possibilities, no one will have the opportunity to come to know and to understand her as the whole person she is. (*Lesbians Speak Out*, 1970:9–10)

Obviously, the task of demythologizing and educating will involve a long and arduous process. Nonetheless, it is a task that many feel needs to be accomplished rapidly and successfully.

References

Akers, R. L. "Problems in the Sociology of Deviance: Social Definitions and Behavior." *Social Forces*, 46 (June 1968): 455–465.

Becker, H. S. *Outsiders: Studies in the Sociology of Deviance*. New York: Free Press, 1963.

Bryan, J. H. "Occupational Ideologies and Individual Attitudes of Call Girls." In Rubington, E. and M. S. Weinberg, eds. *Deviance: The Interactionist Perspective.* 2nd ed. New York: Macmillan, 1973, pp. 315–324.

Chiricos, T. G., P. D. Jackson, and G. P. Waldo. "Inequality in the Imposition of a Criminal Label." *Social Problems,* 19 (Spring 1972): 553–572.

Duster, T. D. *The Legislation of Morality: Laws, Drugs, and Moral Judgment.* New York: Free Press, 1970.

Garfinkel, H. "Conditions of Successful Degradation Ceremonies." *American Journal of Sociology,* 61 (March 1956): 420–424.

Goffman, E. *Stigma: Notes on the Management of Spoiled Identity.* Englewood Cliffs, N.J.: Prentice-Hall, 1963.

Hooker, E. "The Homosexual Community." In Gagnon, J. H. and W. Simon, Eds. *Sexual Deviance.* New York: Harper & Row, 1967, pp. 167–184.

Kelly, D. H. "The Effects of Legal Processing Upon a Delinquent's Public Identity: A Reconsideration." Unpublished manuscript, 1975.

Kitsuse, J. I. "Societal Reaction to Deviant Behavior: Problems of Theory and Method." *Social Problems,* 9 (Winter 1962): 247–256.

Lemert, E. M. *Social Pathology.* New York: McGraw-Hill, 1951.

Lesbians Speak Out. San Francisco: Free Women's Press, 1970.

Leznoff, M., and W. A. Westley. "The Homosexual Community." *Social Problems,* 3 (April 1956): 257–263.

Liazos, A. "The Poverty of the Sociology of Deviance: Nuts, Sluts, and Perverts." *Social Problems,* 20 (Summer 1972): 103–120.

Lofland, J. *Deviance and Identity.* Englewood Cliffs, N.J.: Prentice-Hall, 1969.

McCaghy, C. H., and J. K. Skipper, Jr. "Lesbian Behavior as an Adaptation to the Occupation of Stripping." *Social Problems,* 17 (Fall 1969): 262–270.

Rubington, E., and M. S. Weinberg. *Deviance: The Interactionist Perspective.* 2nd ed. New York: Macmillan, 1973.

Rushing, W. A. "Individual Resources, Societal Reaction, and Hospital Commitment." *American Journal of Sociology,* 77 (November 1971): 511–526.

Schur, E. M. *Labeling Deviant Behavior: Its Sociological Implications.* New York: Harper & Row, 1971.

Shelly, M. "Notes of a Radical Lesbian." In *Sisterhood Is Powerful.* Morgan, Robin, Ed. New York: Random House, 1970, pp. 306–311.

Simmons, J. L. *Deviants.* Berkeley: Glendessary, 1969.

Winslow, R. W., and V. Winslow. *Deviant Reality: Alternative World Views.* Boston: Allyn & Bacon, 1974.

Notes

1. A distinction should be made between a lesbian's personal identity and her evaluation of self. Such a distinction allows us to move away from the tendency, exhibited on the part of many, to assume that a lesbian necessarily possesses a low evaluation of herself. A female may, for example, view herself as a lesbian and yet evaluate herself positively. Bryan's (1966) study of the attitudes of call girls illustrates the often *problematic* nature of this concern. In particular, the call girls, although aware

of the fact that they were engaging in generally frowned-upon behavior, did, with few exceptions, evaluate themselves positively.

2. No claim for representativeness is being made. That is, we have no way of assessing whether these lesbians are representative of lesbians in general. And given the nature of the subject, as well as the potential risks that may be involved, it is doubtful whether such a population can, in fact, be delimited. For a discussion of some of the major problems involved with studies of this type, see particularly the works of Becker, Kitsuse, and Winslow.

3. Similarly to our concerns with personal identity and self-esteem, a distinction should also be made between a lesbian's *public* identity ("How do others view me?") and her *personal* identity ("Who am I?"). Publicly, others may view the lesbian in a positive frame of reference; however, if the female's homosexual activity becomes *known*, then it is highly probable that these significant others will *impute* a negative or "deviant" identity to her (i.e., a lesbian). It is in this sense, then, that a public label or identity is *conferred* upon the lesbian. On a personal level, the female may view herself as a lesbian without evaluating herself in a negative manner. For a discussion of some of these problematic concerns, see Garfinkel (1956), Kelly, Lemert (1951), and Lofland (1969).

4. Many types of "theories" and notions (e.g., biological, psychological, psychiatric) have been advanced to explain why a female becomes a lesbian—that is, displays a sexual preference for females. In this study, however, no systematic framework or effort is being offered to explain such behavior. We are, at least at this stage, more interested in assessing what it means to be a lesbian in American society. For an excellent *structural* account of how "sexual behavior, deviant or not, emerges out of the context of social situations," see particularly the work of McCaghy and Skipper (1969).

44 / The Social Integration of Queers and Peers*

ALBERT J. REISS, JR.

Sex delinquency is a major form of behavior deviating from the normative prescriptions of American society. A large number of behaviors are classified as sex delinquency—premarital heterosexual intercourse, pederasty, and fellation, for example.

Investigation of sex behavior among males largely focuses on the psychological structure and dynamic qualities of adult persons who are described as "sexual types" or on estimating the incidence, prevalence, or experience rates of sex acts for various social groups in a population. There is little systematic research on the social organization of sexual activity in a complex social system unless one includes descriptive studies of the social organization of female prostitution.

An attempt is made in this paper to describe the sexual relation between "delinquent peers" and "adult queers" and to account for its social organization. This transaction is one form of homosexual prostitution between a young male and an adult male fellator. The adult male client pays a delinquent boy prostitute a sum of money in order to be allowed to act as a fellator. The transaction is limited to fellation and is one in which the boy develops no self-conception as a homosexual person or sexual deviator, although he perceives adult male clients as sexual deviators, "queers" or "gay boys."

There has been little research on social aspects of male homosexual prostitution; hence the exploratory nature of the investigation reported here and the tentative character of the findings. Although there are descriptions of "marriage" and of the "rigid caste system of prison homosexuality"[1] which contribute to our understanding of its social organization in the single sex society of deviators, little is known about how homosexual activity is organized in the nuclear communities of America.

A few recent studies discuss some organizational features of male prostitution.[2] Ross distinguishes three types of male homosexual prostitutes on the basis of the locus of their hustling activity:[3] (1) the

---

*The word "queer" is of the "straight" and not the "gay" world. In the "gay" world it has all the qualities of a negative stereotype but these are not intended in this paper. The paper arose out of the perspective of boys in the "straight" world.

bar-hustler who usually visits bars on a steady basis in search of queer clients; (2) the *street-hustler*, usually a teen-aged boy who turns "tricks" with older men; and, (3) the *call-boy* who does not solicit in public. The street-hustler has the lowest prestige among hustlers, partly because his is the more hazardous and less profitable form of activity. One might expect their prestige status in the organized "gay world" to be low since they apparently are marginal to its organization. Street-hustlers, therefore, often become bar-hustlers when they are able to pass in bars as of legal age.

The boys interviewed for this study could usually be classified as street-hustlers, given the principal locus of their activity. Yet, the street-hustlers Ross describes are oriented toward careers as bar-hustlers, whereas none of the boys I studied entered hustling as a career. For the latter, hustling is a transitory activity, both in time and space.

There apparently are crucial differences among hustlers, however, in respect to the definition of the hustler role and the self-concept common to occupants in the role. The hustlers Ross studied are distinguished by the fact that they define themselves as both prostitute and homosexual. The boys I studied *do not define themselves either as hustlers or as homosexual.* Most of these boys see themselves as "getting a queer" only as a substitute activity or as part of a versatile pattern of delinquent activity.[4] The absence of a shared definition of one another as hustlers together with shared definitions of when one "gets a queer" serve to insulate these boys from self-definitions either as street-hustlers or as homosexual.

The boys interviewed in this study regard hustling as an acceptable substitute for other delinquent earnings or activity. Although the sexual transaction itself may occur in a two person *or* a larger group setting, the prescribed norms governing this transaction are usually learned from peers in the delinquent gang. Furthermore, in many cases, induction into the queer-peer transaction occurs through participation in the delinquent group. They learn the prescribed form of behavior with adult fellators and are inducted into it as a business transaction by means of membership in a group which carries this knowledge in a common tradition and controls its practices. In particular, it will be shown that the peer group controls the amount of activity and the conditions under which it is permitted. Finally, it is postulated that this is a shared organizational system between peer hustlers and adult fellators.

There apparently exist the other possible types of males who engage in homosexual sex acts based on the elements of self-definition as homosexual and hustler. John Rechy in several vignettes describes a third type who conceive of themselves as hustlers but do not define themselves as homosexual.[5]

. . . the world of queens and male-hustlers and what they thrive on, the queens being technically men but no one thinks of them that way—always "she"—their "husbands" being the masculine vagrants—"fruit-hustlers"—fleetingly sharing the queens' pads—never considering they're involved with another man (the queen), and as long as the hustler goes only with queens—and with fruits only for scoring (which is making or taking sexmoney, getting a meal, making a pad) *he is himself not considered queer.* (italics mine)[6]

The importance of being defined as nonhomosexual while acknowledging one's role as a hustler is brought forth in this passage:

"Like the rest of us on that street—who played the male role with other men—Pete was touchy about one subject—his masculinity. In Bickford's one afternoon, a good looking masculine young man walked in, looking at us, walks out again hurriedly. 'That cat's queer,' Pete says, glaring at him. 'I used to see him and I thought he was hustling, and one day he tried to put the make on me in the flix. It bugged me, him thinking I'd make it with him for free. I told him to f . . . off, go find another queer like him.' He was moodily silent for a long while and then he said almost belligerently: 'No matter how many queers a guy goes with, if he goes for money, that don't make him queer. You're still straight. It's when you start going for free, with other young guys, that you start growing wings.' "[7]

The literature on male homosexuality, particularly that written by clinicians, is abundant with reference to the fourth possible type— those who define themselves as homosexual but not as hustlers.

THE DATA

Information on the sexual transaction and its social organization was gathered mostly by interviews, partly by social observation of their meeting places. Though there are limitations to inferring social organization from interview data (particularly when the organization arises through behavior that is negatively sanctioned in the larger society), they provide a convenient basis for exploration.

Sex histories were gathered from 18.6 per cent of the 1008 boys between the ages of 12 and 17 who were interviewed in the Nashville, Tennessee, SMA for an investigation of adolescent conforming and deviating behavior. These represent all of the interviews of one of the interviewers during a two-month period, together with interviews with all Nashville boys incarcerated at the Tennessee State Training School for Boys.

As Table 1 discloses, the largest number of interviews was taken with lower-class delinquent boys. There is a reason for this: when it was apparent that delinquents from the lowest social class generally had some contact with adult male fellators, an attempt was made to learn more about how this contact was structured and controlled. Sex histories, therefore, were obtained from all of the white Nashville boys who were resident in the Tennessee State Training School for Boys during the month of June, 1958.

The way sex history information was obtained precludes making reliable estimates about the incidence or prevalence of hustling within the Nashville adolescent boy population. Yet the comparisons among types of conformers and deviators in Table 1 provide an informed guess about their life chances for participation in such an activity.[8]

Only two middle-class boys report experience in the peer-queer transaction. In one case, the boy acquiesced once to solicitation; in the other, the boy had acquired experience and associations in the State Training School for Boys which led to continued participation following his release. Within the lower-class group, it seems clear that the career-oriented delinquent is most likely to report sex experiences with fellators. Roughly three of every five boys report such experiences as contrasted with the peer-oriented delinquent, the type with the next highest relative frequency, where only about one in three report such experiences.

Taking into account the proportional distribution of types of conformers and deviators in a school population of adolescent boys and applying in a very rough way the proportional distribution for type of sex deviation set forth in Table 1, the experience rate with fellators is quite low in a population of all adolescent boys. The peer-queer relationship seems almost exclusively limited to lower-class delinquent boys — particularly career-oriented delinquent boys, where the experience rate is probably very high.

While not of direct concern here, it is of interest that the conformers in Table 1 seem to consist about equally of boys who either report a history of heterosexual and masturbation experience, or masturbation only experience, while hyperconformers either report no sex experience or that they masturbate only.

It might also be inferred from Table 1 that the adolescent conforming boy of lower-class origins in our society is very unlikely to report he never masturbates, though a substantial proportion of middle-class conforming boys maintain they never masturbate and never have masturbated. Although there may be age differences among the class levels in age of onset of masturbation, the class difference may yet be genuine. It is possible, of course, that this difference in masturbation experience reflects only a difference in willingness to report masturbation to a middle-class investigator, i.e., middle-class boys are more likely to hide their sexual experience, even that of masturbation, from

Table 1 / Type of Sex Experience by Conforming-Deviating Type of Boy

Per Cent by Conforming-Deviating Type

Type of Sex Experience	LOWER CLASS				MIDDLE CLASS				ALL CLASSES		
	ORG. CAREER DELINQUENT	PEER ORIENTED DELINQUENT	CONFORMING NON-ACHIEVER	CONFORMING ACHIEVER	PEER ORIENTED DELINQUENT	CONFORMING NON-ACHIEVER	CONFORMING ACHIEVER	HYPER-CONFORMER	NON-CONFORMING ISOLATE	CONFORMING ISOLATE	TOTAL
Total	73	166	250	81	38	86	193	56	24	41	1008
Queers, masturbation, and heterosexual	32.5	27.3	5.1	20.0	—	10.0	—	—	37.5	—	17.6
Queers, masturbation, hetero and animal	30.2	4.5	—	—	5.0	—	—	—	—	—	8.5
Heterosexual only	4.7	11.4	—	—	70.0	30.0	—	—	12.5	—	13.4
Heterosexual and masturbation*	25.6	34.1	33.3	40.0	15.0	10.0	40.0	—	25.0	—	27.3
Masturbation only	2.3	15.9	48.7	40.0	—	10.0	40.0	57.1	25.0	100.0	21.9
Denies sex experience	4.7	6.8	12.8	—	10.0	40.0	20.0	42.9	0.0	—	11.2
Subtotal	43	44	39	5	20	10	10	7	8	1	187
No sex history	41.1	73.5	84.4	93.8	47.4	88.4	94.8	87.5	66.7	97.6	81.4

* Includes 3 cases of heterosexual, masturbation, and animal (2 lower class organized career delinquent and 1 peer oriented delinquent).

others. Nevertheless, there may be class differences in the social organization of sexual experiences, since lower-class boys reported masturbating in groups when they first began to masturbate, while this experience was reported much less frequently by middle-class boys, for whom it is more likely a private matter. The same thing is true for heterosexual experience: lower-class boys, particularly delinquent ones, frequently report they participate in group heterosexual activity in "gang-bangs," while heterosexual experience appears to be a more private experience for the middle-class boy, who does not share his sexual partner with peers. All of this may reflect not only greater versatility in the sex experience of the lower-class male but perhaps a greater willingness to use sex as a means to gratification.

HOW PEERS AND QUEERS MEET

Meetings between adult male fellators and delinquent boys are easily made, because both know how and where to meet within the community space. Those within the common culture know that contact can be established within a relatively short period of time, if it is wished. The fact that meetings between peers and queers can be made easily is mute evidence of the organized understandings which prevail between the two populations.

There are a large number of places where the boys meet their clients, the fellators. Many of these points are known to all boys regardless of where they reside in the metropolitan area. This is particularly true of the central city locations where the largest number of contact points is found within a small territorial area. Each community area of the city, and certain fringe areas, inhabited by substantial numbers of lower-class persons, also have their meeting places, generally known only to the boys residing in the area.

Queers and peers typically establish contact in public or quasi-public places. Major points of contact include street corners, public parks, men's toilets in public or quasi-public places such as those in transportation depots, parks or hotels, and "second" and "third-run" movie houses (open around the clock and permitting sitting through shows). Bars are seldom points of contact, perhaps largely because they are plied by older male hustlers who lie outside the peer culture and groups, and because bar proprietors will not risk the presence of under-age boys.

There are a number of prescribed modes for establishing contact in these situations. They permit the boys and fellators to communicate intent to one another privately despite the public character of the situation. The major form of establishing contact is the "cruise," with the fellator passing "queer-corners" or locations until his effort is recognized by one of the boys. A boy can then signal—usually by nodding his head, a hand gesticulation signifying OK, following, or responding to commonly understood introductions such as "You got the time?"—that he is prepared to undertake the transaction. Entrepreneur and client then move to a place where the sexual activity is consummated, usually a place affording privacy, protection and hasty exit. "Dolly," a three-time loser at the State Training School, describes one of these prescribed forms for making contact:

> "Well, like at the bus station, you go to the bathroom and stand there pretendin' like . . . and they're standin' there pretendin' like . . . and then they motions their head and walks out and you follow them, and you go some place. Either they's got a car, or you go to one of them hotels near the depot or some place like that . . . most any place."

Frequently contact between boys and fellators is established when the boy is hitchhiking. This is particularly true for boys' first contacts of this nature. Since lower-class boys are more likely than middle-class ones to hitch rides within a city, particularly at night when such contacts are most frequently made, they perhaps are most often solicited in this manner.

The experienced boy who knows a "lot of queers" may phone known fellators directly from a public phone, and some fellators try to establish continued contact with boys by giving them their phone numbers. However, the boys seldom use this means of contact for reasons inherent in their orientation toward the transaction, as we shall see below.

We shall now examine how the transaction is facilitated by these types of situations and the prescribed modes of contact and communication. One of the characteristics of all these contact situations is that they provide a *rationale* for the presence of *both* peers and queers in the *same* situation or place. This rationale is necessary for both parties, for were there high visibility to the presence of either and no ready explanation for it, contact and communication would be far more difficult. Public and quasi-public facilities provide situations which account for the presence of most persons since there is relatively little social control over the establishment of contacts. There is, of course, some risk to the boys and the fellators in making contact in these situations since they are generally known to the police. The Morals Squad may have "stake-outs," but this is one of the calculated risks and the communication network carries information about their tactics.

A most important element in furnishing a rationale is that these meeting places must account for the presence of delinquent boys of essentially lower-class dress and appearance who make contact with fellators of almost any class level. This is true despite the fact that the social settings which fellators ordinarily choose to establish contact generally vary according to the class level of the fellators. Fellators of high social class generally make contact by "cruising" past street-corners, in parks, or the men's rooms in "better" hotels, while those from the lower class are likely to select the public bath or transportation depot. There apparently is some general equation of the class position of boys and fellators in the peer-queer transaction. The large majority of fellators in the delinquent peer-queer transaction probably are from the lower class ("apes"). But it is difficult to be certain about the class position of the fellator clients since no study was made of this population.

The absence of data from the fellator population poses difficulties in interpreting the contact relationship. Many fellators involved with delinquent boys do not appear to participate in any overt or covert homosexual groups, such as the organized homosexual community of the "gay world."[9] The "gay world" is the most visible form of organized homosexuality since it is an organized community, but it probably encompasses only a small proportion of all homosexual contact. Even among those in the organized homosexual community, evidence suggests that the homosexual members seek sexual gratification outside their group with persons who are essentially anonymous to them. Excluding homosexual married couples, Leznoff and Westley maintain that there is ". . . a prohibition against sexual relationships within the group . . ."[10] Ross indicates that young male prostitutes are chosen, among other reasons, for the fact that they protect the identity of the client.[11] Both of these factors tend to coerce many male fellators to choose an anonymous contact situation.

It is clear that these contact situations not only provide a rationale for the presence of the parties to the transaction but a guarantee of anonymity. The guarantee does not necessarily restrict social visibility as both the boys and the fellators may recognize cues (including, but not necessarily, those of gesture and dress) which lead to mutual role identification.[12] But anonymity is guaranteed in at least two senses: anonymity of presence is assured in the situation and their personal identity in the community is protected unless disclosed by choice.

There presumably are a variety of reasons for the requirement of anonymity. For many, a homosexual relationship must remain a secret since their other relationships in the community—families, business relationships, etc.—must be protected. Leznoff and Westley refer to these men as the "secret" as contrasted with the "overt" homosexuals,[13] and in the organized "gay world," they are known as "closet fags." For some, there is also a necessity for protecting identity to avoid blackmail.[14] Although none of the peer hustlers reported resorting to blackmail, the adult male fellator may nonetheless hold such an expectation, particularly if he is older or of high social class. Lower-class ones, by contrast, are more likely to face the threat of violence from adolescent boys since they more often frequent situations where they are likely to contact "rough trade."[15] The kind of situation in which the delinquent peer-queer contact is made and the sexual relationship consummated tends to minimize the possibility of violence.

Not all male fellators protect their anonymity; some will let a boy have their phone number and a few "keep a boy." Still, most fellators want to meet boys where they are least likely to be victimized, although boys sometimes roll queers by selecting a meeting place where by prearrangement, their friends can meet them and help roll the queer, steal his car, or commit other acts of violence. Boys generally know that fellators are vulnerable in that they "can't" report their victimization. Parenthetically, it might be mentioned that these boys are not usually aware of their own institutional invulnerability to arrest. An adolescent boy is peculiarly invulnerable to arrest even when found with a fellator since the mores define the boy as exploited.[16]

Situations of personal contact between adolescent boys and adult male fellators also provide important ways to *communicate intent* or to carry out the transaction *without* making the contact particularly visible to others. The wall writings in many of these places are not without their primitive communication value, e.g., "show it hard," and places such as a public restroom provide a modus operandi. The entrepreneur and his customer in fact can meet with little more than an exchange of non-verbal gestures, transact their business with a minimum of verbal communication and part without a knowledge of one another's identity. In most cases, boys report "almost nothing" was said. The sexual transaction may occur with the only formal transaction being payment to the boy.

INDUCTION INTO THE PEER-QUEER TRANSACTION

The peer-queer culture operates through a delinquent peer society. Every boy interviewed in this study who voluntarily established contacts with fellators was also delinquent in many other respects. The evidence shows that contact with fellators is an institutionalized aspect of the organization of lower-class delinquency oriented groups.

This is not to say that boys outside these groups never experience relationships with adult male fellators: some do, but they are not participants in groups which sanction the activity according to the prescribed group standards described below. Nor is it to say that all delinquent groups positively sanction the peer-queer transaction since its distribution is unknown.

How, then, do lower-class delinquent boys get to meet fellators? Most boys from the lowest socioeconomic level in large cities are prepared for this through membership in a delinquent group which has a knowledge of how to make contact with fellators and relate to them. This is part of their common culture. Often, too, the peer group socializes the boy in his first experiences or continuing ones with fellators. The behavior is apparently learned within the framework of differential association.

The peer group actually serves as a school of induction for some of its members. The uninitiated boy goes with one or more members of his peer group for indoctrination and his first experience. Doy L., a lower-class boy at a lower-class school and a two-time loser at the State Training School, explains how he got started:

> I went along with these older boys down to the bus station, and they took me along and showed me how it was done . . . they'd go in, get a queer, get blowed and get paid . . . if it didn't work right, they'd knock him in the head and get their money . . . they showed me how to do it, so I went in too.

In any case, boys are socialized in the subcultural definitions of peer-queer relations by members of their group and many apply this knowledge when an opportunity arises. Within the group, boys hear reports of experiences which supply the cultural definitions: how contacts are made, how you get money if the queer resists, how much one should expect to get, what kind of behavior is acceptable from the queer, which is to be rejected and how. Boys know all this *before* they have any contact with a fellator. In the case of street gangs, the fellators often pass the neighborhood corner; hence, even the preadolescent boy learns about the activity as the older boys get picked up. As the boy enters adolescence and a gang of his own which takes over the corner, he is psychologically and socially prepared for his first experience, which generally occurs when the first opportunity presents itself. Lester H illustrates this; his first experience came when he went to one of the common points of convergence of boys and fellators—The Empress Theatre—to see a movie. Lester relates:

> I was down in the Empress Theatre and this gay came over and felt me up and asked me if I'd go out . . . I said I would if he'd give me the money as I'd heard they did, and I was gettin' low on it . . . so he took me down by the river and blowed me.

In a substantial number of cases, a brother introduces the boy to his first experience, much as he introduces him to other first experiences. Jimmie M. illustrates this pattern. Jimmie describes how he was led into his first heterosexual experience:

> When I was almost 14, my younger brother said he'd screwed this woman and he told me about it, so I went down there and she let me screw her too.

His induction into the peer-queer transaction also occurred through his younger brother:

> Well, my younger brother came home and told me this gay'd blowed him and he told me where he lived . . . And, I was scared to do it, but I figured I'd want to see what it was like since the other guys talked about it and my brother'd done it. So I went down there and he blowed me.

Not all boys belonging to groups which sanction peer hustling accept the practice. Some boys reject the peer-queer transaction while retaining membership in the group. It is not too surprising that such exceptions occur. Although in most delinquent groups some forms of sex activity confer status, it is rarely an absolute requisite for participation in such groups. Some boys in gangs which frequently gang shag, for example, refuse to participate in these activities. "I don't like my meat that raw" appears to be an acceptable "out." Exemption appears possible so long as the boy is acceptable in all, if not most, other respects. A lower-class delinquent boy apparently doesn't "chicken-out" or lose his "rep" if he doesn't want to engage in sex behaviors which most of his peers practice. (The same condition may hold for other practices, such as the use of narcotics.) Jerry P. from a lower-class school is in a group where all the other boys go with fellators; but he refuses to become involved, though he goes so far as to ride in the car with one of the gang's "regular queers." Jerry is in a gang which often gets picked up by a well known "local gay," a David B. Jerry admits: "I ride with B. a lot, but he's never done anything to me; I just can't go for that." When asked how he knew B. was a queer, he replied, "Oh, all the guys say so and talk about doin' it with him. . . . I could, but I just don't want to." Joe C., at a school which crosscuts the class structure, was asked if he had any other kind of sex experiences. His reply shows his rejection of his peer group's pattern of behavior with fellators. "You mean with queers?" "Uh huh." "I don't go with any. Most of my friends queer-bait, but I don't." A friend of his, Roy P., also rejects the activity: "Ain't no sense in queer-baitin'; I don't need the money that bad."

The impression should not be gained that most lower-class boys who are solicited by fellators accept the solicitation. A majority of all solicitations are probably refused when the initial contact is made unless several other conditions prevail. The first is that the boy must be a member of a group which permits this form of transaction, indoctrinates the boy with its codes and sanctions his participation in it. Almost all lower-class boys reported they were solicited by a queer at least once. A majority refused the solicitation. Refusal is apparently easy since boys report that queers are seldom insistent. There apparently is a mutual willingness to forego the transaction in such cases, perhaps because the queer cannot afford the risk of exposure, but perhaps also because the probability of his establishing contact on his next try is sufficiently high so that he can "afford" to accept the refusal. Looked at another way, there must be a set of mutual gains and expectations for the solicitation to be accepted and the transaction to proceed. Boys who refuse to be solicited are not vulnerable for another reason: they usually are members of groups which negatively sanction the activity. Such groups generally "bug" boys who go out with fellators and use other techniques of isolation to discourage the transaction. There also are gangs which look upon queers as "fair game" for their aggressive activity. They beat them, roll, and otherwise put upon them. A third condition that must prevail is that the boy who accepts or seeks solicitation from fellators must view the offer as instrumental gain, particularly monetary gain (discussed below).

There are boys, however, particularly those who are quite young, who report a solicitation from a man which they were unable to refuse but which they subsequently rejected as neither gratifying nor instrumentally acceptable. It is these boys who can be said to be "exploited" by adult fellators in the sense that they are either forced into the act against their will, or are at least without any awareness of how to cope with the situation. One such instance is found in the following report:

> This guy picked me up down at Fourth and Union and said he was going over to East Nashville, so I got in . . . but he drove me out on Dickerson Pike. (What'd he do?) . . . Well, he blowed me and it made me feel real bad inside . . . but I know how to deal with queers now . . . ain't one of 'em gonna do that to me again . . . I hate queers. . . . They're crazy.

There is an important admission in the statement, "But I know how to deal with 'em now." The lower-class boy as he grows older learns how to deal with sexual advances from fellators. Boys exchange experiences on how they deal with them and it becomes quite difficult to "exploit" a lower-class boy who is socialized in a peer group. It is perhaps largely the very young boy, such as the one in the case above, or those isolated from peer groups, who are most vulnerable to solicitation without previous preparation for it.

Lower-class boys, as we have seen, have the highest probability of being in situations where they will be solicited by fellators. But, *the lower-class boy who is a member of a career-oriented gang which positively sanctions instrumental relationships with adult male fellators and which initiates members into these practices, and a boy who at the same time perceives himself as "needing" the income which the transaction provides, is most likely to establish personal contact with adult male fellators on a continuing basis.*

It is suggested that the peer-queer transaction is behavior learned through differential association in delinquent gangs. This cannot be demonstrated without resort to a more specific test of the hypothesis. But, as Sutherland has pointed out, "Criminal behavior is partially a function of opportunities to commit special classes of crimes. . . . It is axiomatic that persons who commit a specific crime have the opportunity to commit that crime. . . . While opportunity may be partially a function of association with criminal patterns and of the specialized techniques thus acquired, it is not entirely determined in this manner, and consequently differential association is not a sufficient cause of criminal behavior."[17] Middle-class boys are perhaps excluded from the peer-queer transaction as much through lack of opportunity to commit this special class of crime in their community of exposure as through any criterion of differential association. The structure of the middle-class area is incompatible with the situational requirements for the peer-queer transaction.

NORMS GOVERNING THE TRANSACTION

Does the peer society have any norms about personal relations with fellators? Or, does it simply induct a boy into a relationship by teaching him how to effect the transaction? The answer is that there appear to be several clear-cut norms about the relations between peers and queers, even though there is some deviation from them.

The first major norm is that *a boy must undertake the relationship with a queer solely as a way of making money; sexual gratification cannot be actively sought as a goal in the relationship.* This norm does not preclude a boy from sexual gratification by the act; he simply must not seek this as a goal. Put another way, a boy cannot admit that he failed to get money from the transaction unless he used violence toward the fellator and he cannot admit that he sought it as a means of sexual gratification.

The importance of making money in motivating a boy to the peer-queer transaction is succinctly stated by Dewey H:

> This guy in the Rex Theatre came over and sat down next to me when I was 11 or 12, and he started to fool with me. I got over and sat down another place and he came over and asked me, didn't I want to and he'd pay me five bucks. I figured it was *easy money* so I went with him . . . I didn't do it before that. That wan't too long after I'd moved to South Nashville. I was a

pretty good boy before that . . . not real good, but I never ran with a crowd that got into trouble before that. But, I met a lot of 'em there. (Why do you run with queers?) It's *easy money* . . . like I could go out and break into a place when I'm broke and get money that way . . . but that's harder and *you take a bigger risk* . . . with a queer it's *easy money*.

Dewey's comments reveal two important motivating factors in getting money from queers, both suggested by the expression, "easy money." First, the money is easy in that it can be made quickly. Some boys reported that when they needed money for a date or a night out, they obtained it within an hour through the sexual transaction with a queer. All a boy has to do is go to a place where he will be contacted, wait around, get picked up, carried to a place where the sexual transaction occurs, and in a relatively short period of time he obtains the money for his service.

It is easy money in another and more important sense for many of these boys. Boys who undertake the peer-queer transaction are generally members of career-oriented delinquent groups. Rejecting the limited opportunities for making money by legitimate means or finding them inaccessible, their opportunities to make money by illegitimate means may also be limited or the risk may be great. Theft is an available means, but it is more difficult and involves greater risk than the peer-queer transaction. Delinquent boys are not unaware of the risks they take. Under most circumstances, delinquents may calculate an act of stealing as "worth the risk." There are occasions, however, when the risk is calculated as too great. These occasions occur when the "heat" is on the boy or when he can least afford to run the risk of being picked up by the police, as is the case following a pickup by the police, being put on probation or parole, or being warned that incarceration will follow the next violation. At such times, boys particularly calculate whether they can afford to take the risk. Gerald L., describing a continuing relationship with a fellator who gave him his phone number, reflects Dewey's attitude toward minimizing risk in the peer-queer transaction: "So twic'd after that when I was gettin' real low and couldn't risk stealin' and gettin' caught, I called him and he took me out and blowed me." Here is profit with no investment of capital and a minimum of risk in social, if not in psychological, terms.

The element of risk coupled with the wish for "easy money" enters into our understanding of the peer-queer relationship in another way. From a sociological point of view, the peer-queer sexual transaction occurs between two major types of deviators—"delinquents" and "queers." Both types of deviators risk negative sanctions for their deviant acts. The more often one has been arrested or incarcerated, the more punitive the sanctions from the larger social system for both types of deviators. At some point, therefore, both calculate risks and seek to minimize them, at least in the very short-run. Each then becomes a means for the other to minimize risk.

When the delinquent boy is confronted with a situation in which he wants money and risks little in getting it, how is he to get it without working? Illegitimate activities frequently provide the "best" opportunity for easy money. These activities often are restricted in kind and number for adolescents and the risk of negative sanctions is high. Under such circumstances, the service offered a queer is a chance to make easy money with a minimum of risk.

Opportunities for sexual gratification are limited for the adult male fellator, particularly if he wishes to minimize the risk of detection in locating patrons, to avoid personal involvement and to get his gratification when he wishes it. The choice of a lower-class male, precisely because of his class position somewhat reduces the risk. If the lower-class male also is a delinquent, the risk is minimized to an even greater degree.

This is not to say that the parties take equal risks in the situation. Of the two, the fellator perhaps is less able to minimize his risk since he still risks violence from his patron, but much less so if a set of expectations arise which control the use of violence as well. The boy is most able to minimize his risk since he is likely to be defined as "exploited" in the situation if caught.

Under special circumstances, boys may substitute other gratifications for the goal of money, provided that these gratifications do not include sexual gratification as a major goal. These special circumstances are the case where an entire gang will "make a night (or time) of it" with one or more adult male fellators. Under these circumstances, everyone is excepted from the subcultural expectations about making money from the fellator because everyone participates and there is no reason for everyone (or anyone) to take money. For the group to substitute being given a "good time" by a "queer" for the prescribed financial transaction is, of course, the exception which proves the rule.

Several examples of group exemption from the prescribed norm of a financial gain were discovered. Danny S., leader of the Black Aces, tells of his gang's group experiences with queers: "There's this one gay who takes us to the Colonial Motel out on Dickerson Pike . . . usually it's a bunch of us boys and we all get drunk and get blowed by this queer . . . we don't get any money then . . . it's more a drinking party." The Black Aces are a fighting gang and place great stress on physical prowess, particularly boxing. All of its members have done time more than once at the State Training School. During one of these periods, the school employed a boxing instructor whom the boys identified as "a queer," but the boys had great respect for him since he taught them how to box and was a game fighter. Danny refers to him in accepting terms: "He's a real good guy. He's fought with us once or twice and we drink with him when we run into him. . . . He's taken us up to Miter Dam a coupla times; he's got a cabin up there on the creek and he blows us. . . . But mostly we just drink and have a real good time." These examples illustrate the instrumental orientation of the gang members. If the expense of the gang members getting drunk and having a good time are borne by a "queer," each member is released from the obligation to receive cash. The relationship in this case represents an exchange of services rather than that of money for a service.

The second major norm operating in the relationship is that *the sexual transaction must be limited to mouth-genital fellation. No other sexual acts are generally tolerated.*[18] The adult male fellator must deport himself in such a way as to re-enforce the instrumental aspects of the role relationsip and to insure affective neutrality.[19] For the adult male fellator to violate the boy's expectation of "getting blowed," as the boys refer to the act, is to risk violence and loss of service. Whether or not the boys actually use violent means as often as they say they do when expectations are violated, there is no way of knowing with precision. Nevertheless, whenever boys reported they used violent means, they always reported some violation of the sub-cultural expectations. Likewise, they never reported a violation of the subcultural expectations which was not followed by the use of violent means, unless it was clearly held up as an exception. Bobby A. expresses the boys' point of view on the use of violent means in the following exchange: "How much did you usually get?" "Around five dollars; if they didn't give that much, I'd beat their head in." "Did they ever want you to do anything besides blow you?" "Yeh, sometimes . . . like they want me to blow them, but I'd tell them to go to hell and maybe beat them up."

Boys are very averse to being thought of in a queer role or engaging in acts of fellation. The act of fellation is defined as a "queer" act. Most boys were asked whether they would engage in such behavior. All but those who had the status of "punks" denied they had engaged in behavior associated with the queer role. Asking a boy whether he is a fellator meets with strong denial and often with open hostility. This could be interpreted as defensive behavior against latent homosexuality. Whether or not this is the case, strong denial could be expected because the question goes counter to the subcultural definitions of the peer role in the transaction.

A few boys on occasion apparently permit the fellator to perform other sexual acts. These boys, it is guessed, are quite infrequent in a delinquent peer population. Were their acts known to the members of the group, they would soon be defined as outside the delinquent peer society. Despite the limitation of the peer-queer sexual transaction to mouth-genital fellation, there are other sexual transactions which the peer group permits members to perform under special circumstances. They are, for example, permitted to perform the *male* roles in "crimes against nature," such as in pederasty ("cornholing" to the boys), bestiality (sometimes referred to as buggery) and carnal copulation with a man involving no orifice (referred to as "slick-legging" among the boys) provided that the partner is roughly of the same age and not a member of the group and provided also that the boys are confined to the single-sex society of incarcerated delinquent boys. Under no circumstances, however, is the female role in carnal copulation acceptable in any form. It is taboo. Boys who accept the female role in sexual transactions occupy the lowest status position among delinquents. They are "punks."

The third major norm operating on the relationship is that *both peers and queers, as participants, should remain affectively neutral during the transaction.* Boys within the peer society define the ideal form of the role with the fellator as one in which the boy is the entrepreneur and the queer is viewed as purchasing a service. The service is a business deal where a sexual transaction is purchased for an agreed upon amount of money. In the typical case, the boy is neither expected to enjoy or be repulsed by the sexual transaction; mouth-genital fellation is accepted as a service offered in exchange for a fee. It should be kept in mind that self-gratification is permitted in the sexual act. Only the motivation to sexual gratification in the transaction is tabooed. But self-gratification must occur without displaying either positive or negative affect toward the queer. In the prescribed form of the role relationship, the boy sells a service for profit and the queer is to accept it without show of emotion.

The case of Thurman L., one of three brothers who are usually in trouble with the law, illustrates some aspects of the expected pattern of affective neutrality. Thurman has had a continuing relationship with a queer, a type of relationship in which it would be anticipated that affective neutrality would be difficult to maintain. This relationship continued, in fact, with a 21 year old "gay" until the man was "sent to the pen." When queried about his relationship with this man and why he went with him, Thurman replied:

> Don't know . . . money and stuff like that I guess. (What do you mean? . . . stuff like that?) Oh, clothes. . . . (He ever bought you any clothes?) Sure, by this one gay. . . . (You mind being blowed?) No. (You like it?) Don't care one way or the other. I don't like it, and I don't not like it. (You like this one gay?) Nope, can't say that I liked anythin' about him. (How come you do it then?) Well, the money for one thing. . . . I need that. (You enjoy it some?) Can't say I do or don't.

More typical than Thurman's expression of affective neutrality is the boy who accepts it as "OK" or, "It's all right; I don't mind it." Most frequent of all is some variant of the statement: "It's OK, but I like the money best of all." The definition of affective neutrality fundamentally requires only that there be no positive emotional commitment to the queer *as a person*. The relationship must be essentially an impersonal one, even though the pure form of the business relationship may seldom be attained. Thus, it is possible for a boy to admit self-gratification without admitting any emotional commitment to the homosexual partner.

Although the peer group prescribes affective neutrality toward the queer in the peer-queer transaction, queers must be regarded as low prestige persons, held in low esteem, and the queer role is taboo. The queer is most commonly regarded as "crazy, I guess." Some boys take a more rationalistic view: "They're just like that, I guess" or, "They're just born that way." While there are circumstances under which one is permitted to like a particular fellator, as in the case of all prejudices attached to devalued status, the person who is liked must be the exception which states the rule. Though in many cases both the boy and the fellator are of very low class origins, and in many cases both are altogether repulsive in appearance, cleanliness and dress by middle-class standards, these are not the standards of comparison used by the boys. The deviation of the queers from the boy's norms of masculine behavior places the fellator in the lowest possible status, even "beneath contempt." If the fellator violates the expected affective relationship in the transaction, he may be treated not only with violence but with contempt as well. The seller of the service ultimately reserves the right to set the conditions for his patrons.

Some boys find it difficult to be emotionally neutral toward the queer role and its occupants; they are either personally offended or affronted by the behavior of queers. JDC is an instance of a boy who is personally offended by their behavior; yet he is unable to use violence even when expectations governing the transaction are violated. He does not rely very much on the peer-queer relationship as a source of income. JDC expresses his view: "I don't really go for that like some guys; I just do it when I go along with the crowd. . . . You know. . . . That, and when I do it for money. . . . And I go along. . . . But . . . I hate queers. They embarrass me." "How?" "Well, like you'll be in the lobby at the theatre, and they'll come up and pat your ass or your prick right in front of everybody. I just can't go for that—not me." Most of the boys wouldn't either, but they would have resorted to violent means in this situation.

Two principal types of boys maintain a continuing relationship with a known queer. A few boys develop such relationships to insure a steady income. While this is permitted within peer society for a short period of time, boys who undertake it for extended periods of time do so with some risk, since in the words of the boys, "queers can be got too easy." The boy who is affectively involved with a queer or his role is downgraded in status to a position, "Ain't no better'n a queer." There are also a few boys affectively committed to a continuing relationship with an adult male homosexual. Such boys usually form a strong dependency relationship with him and are kept much as the cabin boys of old. This type of boy is clearly outside the peer society of delinquents and is isolated from participation in gang activity. The sociometric pattern for such boys is one of choice into more than one gang, none of which is reciprocated.

Street-hustlers are also downgraded within the peer society, generally having reputations as "punk kids." The street-hustler pretty much "goes it alone." Only a few street-hustlers were interviewed for this study. None of them was a member of an organized delinquent group. The sociometric pattern for each, together with his history of delinquent activity, placed them in the classification of nonconforming isolates.

A fourth major norm operating on the peer-queer relationship serves as a primary factor in stabilizing the system. This norm holds that *violence must not be used so long as the relationship conforms to the shared set of expectations between queers and peers.* So long as the fellator conforms to the norms governing the transaction in the peer-queer society, he runs little risk of violence from the boys.

The main reason, perhaps, for this norm is that uncontrolled violence is potentially disruptive of any organized system. All organized social systems must control violence. If the fellator clients were repeatedly the objects of violence, the system as it has been described could not exist. Most boys who share the common expectations of the peer-queer relationship do not use violent means unless the expectations are violated. To use violence, of course, is to become affectively involved and therefore another prescription of the relationship is violated.

It is not known whether adult male fellators who are the clients of delinquent entrepreneurs share the boys' definition of the norm regarding the use of violence. They may, therefore, violate expectations of the peer society through ignorance of the system rather than from any attempt to go beyond the set of shared expectations.

There are several ways the fellator can violate the expectations of boys. The first concerns money: refusal to pay or paying too little may bring violence from most boys. Fellators may also violate peer expectations by attempting to go beyond the mouth-genital sexual act. If such an attempt is made, he is usually made an object of aggression as in the following excerpt from Dolly's sex history:

(You like it?) It's OK. I don't mind it. It feels OK. (They ever try anything else on you?) They usually just blow and that's all. (Any ever try anything else on you?) Oh sure, but we really fix 'em . . . throw 'em out of the car. . . . Once a gay tried that and we rolled him and threw him out of the car. Then we took the car and stripped it (laughs with glee).

Another way the fellator violates a boy's expectations is to introduce considerable affect into the relationship. It appears that affect is least acceptable in two forms, both of which could be seen as "attacks on his masculinity." In one form, the queer violates the affective neutrality requirement by treating the adolescent boy as if he were a girl or in a girl's role during the sexual transaction, as for example, by speaking to him in affectionate terms such as "sweetie." There are many reasons why the feminine sex role is unacceptable to these lower-class boys, including the fact that such boys place considerable emphasis on being "tough" and masculine. Walter Miller, for example, observes that:

> . . . The almost compulsive lower class concern with "masculinity" derives from a type of compulsive reaction-formation. A concern over homosexuality runs like a persistent thread through lower class culture — manifested by the institutionalized practice of "baiting queers," often accompanied by violent physical attacks, an expressed contempt for "softness" or frills, and the use of the local term for "homosexual" as a general pejorative epithet (e.g., higher class individuals or upwardly mobile peers are frequently characterized as "fags" or "queers").[20]

Miller sees violence as part of a reaction-formation against the matriarchal lower-class household where the father often is absent. For this reason, he suggests, many lower-class boys find it difficult to identify with a male role, and the "collective" reaction-formation is a cultural emphasis on masculinity. Violence toward queers is seen as a consequence of this conflict. Data from our interviews suggests that among career-oriented delinquents, violation of the affective-neutrality requirement in the peer-queer relationship is at least as important in precipitating violence toward "queers." There are, of course, gangs which were not studied in this investigation which "queer-bait" for the express purpose of "rolling the queer."

The other form in which the fellator may violate the affective neutrality requirement is to approach the boy and make suggestive advances to him when he is with his age-mates, either with girls or with his peer group when he is not located for "business." In either case, the sexual advances suggest that the boy is not engaged in a business relationship within the normative expectations of the system, but that he has sexual motivation as well. The delinquent boy is expected to control the relationship with his customers. He is the entrepreneur "looking" for easy money or at the very least he must appear as being merely receptive to business; this means that he is receptive only in certain situations and under certain circumstances. He is not in business when he is with girls and he is not a businessman when he is cast in a female role. To be cast in a female role before peers is highly unacceptable, as the following account suggests:

> This gay comes up to me in the lobby of the Empress when we was standin' around and starts feelin' me up and callin' me Sweetie and like that . . . and, I just couldn't take none of that there . . . what was he makin' out like I was a queer or somethin' . . . so I jumps him right then and there and we like to of knocked his teeth out.

The sexual advance is even less acceptable when a girl is involved:

> I was walkin' down the street with my steady girl when this gay drives by that I'd been with once before and he whistles at me and calls, "hi Sweetie." . . . And, was I mad . . . so I went down to where the boys was and we laid for him and beat on him 'til he like to a never come to . . . ain't gonna take nothin' like that off'n a queer.

In both of these instances, not only is the boys' masculinity under attack, but the affective neutrality requirement of the business transaction is violated. The queer's behavior is particularly unacceptable, however, because it occurs in a peer setting where the crucial condition is the maintenance of the boy's status within the group. A lower-class boy cannot afford to be cast in less than a highly masculine role before lower-class girls nor risk definition as a queer before peers. His role within his peer group is under threat even if he suffers *no* anxiety about masculinity. Not only the boy himself but his peers perceive such behavior as violating role expectations and join him in violent acts toward the fellator to protect the group's integrity and status.

If violence generally occurs only when one of the major peer norms has been violated, it would also seem to follow that *violence is a means of enforcing the peer entrepreneurial norms of the system.* Violence or the threat of violence is thus used to keep adult male fellators in line with the boys' expectations in his customer role. It represents social control, a punishment meted out to the fellator who violates the cultural expectation. Only so long as the fellator seeks gratification from lower-class boys in a casual pick-up or continuing relationship where he pays money for a "blow-job," is he reasonably free from acts of violence.

There is another, and perhaps more important reason for the use of violence when the peer defined norms of the peer-queer relationship are violated. The formally prescribed roles for peers and queers are basically the roles involved in all institutionalized forms of prostitution, the prostitute and the client. But in most forms of prostitution, whether male or female, the hustlers perceive of themselves in hustler roles, and furthermore the male hustlers also develop a conception of themselves as homosexual whereas *the peer hustler in the peer-queer relationship develops no conception of himself either as prostitute or as homosexual.*

The fellator risks violence, therefore, if he threatens the boy's self-conception by suggesting that the boy may be homosexual and treats him as if he were.

Violence seems to function, then, in two basic ways for the peers. On the one hand, it integrates their norms and expectations by controlling and combatting behavior which violates them. On the other hand, it protects the boy's self-identity as nonhomosexual and reinforces his self-conception as "masculine."

The other norms of the peer society governing the peer-queer transaction also function to prevent boys in the peer-queer society from defining themselves as homosexual. The prescriptions that the goal is money, that sexual gratification is not to be sought as an end in the relationship, that affective neutrality be maintained toward the fellator and that only mouth-genital fellation is permitted, all tend to insulate the boy from a homosexual self-definition. So long as he conforms to these expectations, *his "significant others" will not define him as homosexual*; and this is perhaps the most crucial factor in his own self-definition. The peers define one as homosexual not on the basis of homosexual *behavior* as such, but on the basis of participation in the homosexual *role*, the "queer" role. The reactions of the larger society, in defining the *behavior* as homosexual is unimportant in their own self-definition. What is important to them is the reactions of their peers to violation of peer group norms which define roles in the peer-queer transaction.

TERMINATING THE ROLE BEHAVIOR

Under what circumstances does a boy give up earning money in the peer-queer transaction? Is it altogether an individual matter, or are there group bases for abandoning the practice? We have little information on these questions since interviews were conducted largely with boys who were still participants in the peer-queer culture. But a few interviews, either with boys who had terminated the relationship or spoke of those who had, provide information on how such role behavior is terminated.

Among lower-class adolescent boys, the new roles one assumes with increasing age are important in terminating participation in the peer-queer relationship. Thus older boys are more likely to have given up the transaction as a source of income. Several boys gave as their reason, "I got a job and don't need that kind of money now." An older boy, who recently married, said that he had quit when he was married. Another responded to the question, "When do you think you'll quit?" with, "When I quit school, I reckon. . . . I don't know a better way to make money afore then." A few boys simply said that they didn't care to make money that way any more, or that since they got a steady girl, they had quit.

The reasons older boys have for giving up the peer-queer transaction as a means of making money is perhaps different for the career-oriented than for the peer-oriented delinquent boy. As career-oriented delinquents get older, the more serious crimes direct their activity and the group is more actively involved in activities which confer status. The boy has a "rep" to maintain. The peer hustler role clearly contributes nothing to developing or maintaining a reputation, and the longer one gets money this way, the more one may risk it. The older career-oriented delinquent boy perhaps gives up peer hustling activity, then, just as he often gives up petty theft and malicious destruction of property. These are activities for younger boys.

As peer-oriented delinquents get older, they enter adult groups where a job becomes one of the acceptable ways of behaving. Many of them may also move out of the "tight little island" of the peer group which inducted them into the activity. If one gets enough money from a job, there is no socially acceptable reason for getting money in the peer-queer transaction. One risks loss of status if one solicits at this age, for this is the age to move from one steady girl to another and perhaps even settle on one and get married, as often one "has to."

Regardless of the reasons for moving out, it seems clear that most boys do move out of their roles as peer hustlers and do not go on to other hustling careers. The main reason perhaps that most boys do not move on in hustling careers is that they never conceived of themselves in a hustling role or as participants in a career where there was a status gradation among hustlers. Hustling, to the peer hustler, is simply another one of the activities which characterizes a rather versatile pattern of deviating acts. It is easier, too, to move out when one has never defined oneself as homosexual. It is in this sense, perhaps, that we have reason to conclude that these boys are not involved in the activity primarily for its homosexual basis. Peer hustlers are primarily oriented toward either delinquent, and later criminal, careers, or toward conventional conformity in lower-class society. They become neither hustlers nor queers.

SUMMARY

This paper explores a special form of male prostitution in American society, a homosexual relationship between adult male fellators and delinquents. It is seen as a financial transaction between boys and fellators which is governed by delinquent peer norms. These norms integrate the two types of deviators into an institutionalized form of prostitution and protect the boys from self-definitions either as prostitutes or as homosexuals.

The conclusions offered in this paper must be regarded as tentative, because of limitations inherent in the data. Study of the fellator population might substantially change the conclusions. Cross-cultural studies also are necessary. Discussion of these findings with criminologists in Denmark and Sweden and exploratory investigations in several larger American cities, however, suggest that the description and explanation offered in this paper will hold for other American cities and for some other social systems.

Notes

1. Arthur V. Huffman, "Sex Deviation in a Prison Community," *The Journal of Social Therapy*, 6 (Third Quarter, 1960), pp. 170–181; Joseph E. Fishman, *Sex in Prison*, New York: The Commonwealth Fund, 1930; Donald Clemmer, *The Prison Community*, Boston: The Christopher Publishing House, 1940, pp. 260–273.

2. William Marlin Butts, "Boy Prostitutes of the Metropolis," *Journal of Clinical Psychopathology*, 8 (1946–1947), pp. 673–681; H. Laurence Ross, "The 'Hustler' in Chicago," *The Journal of Student Research*, 1 (September, 1959), pp. 13–19; Jens Jersild, *Boy Prostitution*, Copenhagen: C. E. Grad, 1956 (Translation of *Den Mandlige Prostitution* by Oscar Bojesen).

3. H. Laurence Ross, *op. cit.*, p. 15.

4. The distinction made here is not intended to suggest that other types of hustlers do not also define themselves in other deviant roles. Hustlers may occupy a variety of deviant roles which are classified as delinquent or criminal; they may be "hooked," blackmailers, thieves, etc.

5. I am indebted to Ned Polsky for bringing Rechy's stories to my attention.

6. John Rechy, "The Fabulous Wedding of Miss Destiny," *Big Table* I, Number 3 (1959), p. 15.

7. John Rechy, "A Quarter Ahead," *Evergreen Review*, Vol. 5, No. 19 (July–August, 1961), p. 18.

8. For a definition of the types of conformers and deviators see Albert J. Reiss, Jr., "Conforming and Deviating Behavior and the Problem of Guilt," *Psychiatric Research Reports*, 13 (December, 1960), pp. 209–210, and Albert J. Reiss, Jr. and Albert Lewis Rhodes, "The Distribution of Juvenile Delinquency in the Social Class Structure," *American Sociological Review*, Vol. 26, No. 5 (October, 1961), pp. 720–732.

9. See, for example, Maurice Leznoff and William A. Westley, "The Homosexual Community," *Social Problems*, 4 (April, 1956), pp. 257–263.

10. *Ibid.*, p. 258.

11. H. Laurence Ross, *op. cit.*, p. 15.

12. The cues which lead to the queer-peer transaction can be subtle ones. The literature on adult male homosexuality makes it clear that adult males who participate in homosexual behavior are not generally socially visible to the public by manner and dress. Cf., Jess Stearn, *op. cit.*, Chapters 1 and 3.

13. *Op. cit.*, pp. 260–261.

14. Ross notes that, failing in the con-man role, some hustlers resort to extortion and blackmail since they provide higher income. See Ross, *op. cit.*, p. 16. Sutherland discusses extortion and blackmail of homosexuals as part of the practice of professional thieves. The "muzzle" or "mouse" is part of the role of the professional thief. See Edwin Sutherland, *The Professional Thief*, Chicago: University of Chicago Press, 1937, pp. 78–81. See also the chapter on "Blackmail" in Jess Stearn, *op. cit.*, Chapter 16.

15. Jess Stearn, *op. cit.*, p. 47.

16. Albert J. Reiss, Jr., "Sex Offenses: The Marginal Status of the Adolescent," *Law and Contemporary Problems*, 25 (Spring, 1960), pp. 322–324 and 326–327.

17. Albert Cohen, Alfred Lindesmith and Karl Schuessler (editors), *The Sutherland Papers*, Bloomington, Indiana: The University of Indiana Press, 1956, p. 31.

18. It is not altogether clear why mouth-genital fellation is the only sexual act which is tolerated in the peer-queer transaction. The act seems to conform to the more "masculine" aspects of the role than do most, but not all possible alternatives. Ross has suggested to me that it also involves less bodily contact and therefore may be less threatening to the peers' self-definitions. One possible explanation therefore for the exclusiveness of the relationship to this act is that it is the most masculine alternative involving the least threat to peers' self-definition as nonhustler and nonhomosexual.

19. Talcott Parsons in *The Social System* (Glencoe: The Free Press, 1951, Chapter III) discusses this kind of role as ". . . the segregation of specific instrumental performances, both from expressive orientations other than the specifically appropriate rewards and from other components of the instrumental complex." (p. 87).

20. Walter Miller, "Lower-Class Culture as a Generating Milieu of Gang Delinquency," *The Journal of Social Issues*, 14 (1958), No. 3, p. 9.

45 / Role Enactment, Self, and Identity in the Systematic Check Forger

EDWIN M. LEMERT

This paper[1] deals with certain consequences which commitment to living by means of passing forged checks have for social roles, self, and identity. Role is a term which summarizes the way or ways in which an individual acts in a structured situation. A situation is structured to the degree that others with whom the individual interacts expect him to respond in certain ways and to the extent that he anticipates their expectations and incorporates them into his behavior. The role reflects these expectations but also reflects claims of other roles and their evaluations by the individual, so that it is always a unique combination of common and diverse elements.

Identity is conceived here as the delimiting, boundary aspects of personality in time and space as perceived and symbolized (named)—the "who I am and who I am not." It has objective as well as subjective aspects, and can exist in degree as well as differ in kind. Self is identity plus evaluation; it is a differentiating and evaluating awareness arising from social interaction, which has cultural content. Both identity and self can be thought of as cognitive structures or as aspects of a common cognitive structure.[2]

The problem addressed is to determine how prolonged enactment of a role or roles fashioned from actions grossly contrary to expectations of authenticity or "genuineness" produces changes in identity and self, and to relate these changes to the forms and limits of face-to-face interaction associated with systematic check forgery.

THE ACT OF FORGERY AND CHARACTERISTICS OF CHECK FORGERS

Check forgery, in contrast to crimes such as assault, robbery, or burglary, is distinguished by its low social visibility. At the time the bogus check is passed there is nothing in the act which reveals that it is deviant or criminal. No special tools or equipment are needed for the crime, as with burglary, nor is any special setting required for the action, as is true with the "store" or the front of a bank, where the confidence man activates his fraudulent enterprises. Furthermore, there are few or no cues in interaction which give feedback to the forger from the victim nor from his own overt responses to indicate that he is behaving contrary to expectations; only later does the act become so defined and then never in direct interaction between the forger and his victim. Here is deviant behavior whose manifest or "existential" qualities do not differentiate or identify the person as a deviant.

Studies of the characteristics of check forgers based upon samples of those in jails, prisons, or on probation show considerable heterogeneity. However, it can be said that in general they more nearly resemble the general middle-class population than they do the populations of jails and prisons. They tend to be native white in origin, male, and much older than other criminals when they commit their first crimes—somewhere in their late 20's or early 30's. Their intelligence averages much higher than that of other criminals and they equal or surpass the general population in years of education completed. Skilled, clerical, professional, and managerial occupations are at least as fully represented among forgers as in the general population, perhaps more so. An impressive small minority have come from prestigeful, wealthy families, or those in which siblings have achieved social eminence, although considerable discounting of forgers' claims on this point is necessary. A high percentage of forgers have been long-time residents in the communities in which they committed their first offenses, but relatively few have lived in so-called "delinquency areas." Forgers are less likely than other criminals to have had a record of delinquency in their youth.

Prior socialization as delinquents or criminals is insufficient to explain the crimes of a large per cent, or even the majority, of persons who pass bad checks. Many have acquired and lived a considerable part of their early adult lives according to conventional middle-class morality. Typically they tend to express aversion to the idea of using violence in interpersonal dealings for whatever purpose. At the same time it must be said that an occasional person comes into forgery via the criminal route—the "short" con man turned forger, or the "old pro" burglar fallen on hard times, who has turned to passing bad checks for a livelihood.

Little effort has been made at systematic personality assessment of check forgers. Yet detectives have for a long time looked upon them as a distinctive criminal type; particularly those designated as professionals.[3]

The professional forger is a man of great ability, and naturally a cunning and suspicious sort of individual. Cautious in extreme, he likes to work in secret, and probably never more than two of his most intimate companions know what he is about until counterfeits he has produced are ready to be put into circulation. He never permits anyone to watch him at work.

Probation officers, prison workers, and parole officers often describe check forgers with such adjectives as "impulsive," "dependent," "lacking ego strength," "unstable," and "immature." In most instances these are reifications of the criminal act itself, more in the nature of invidious labels than separately defined variables demonstrable in case histories of the forgers.

Check forgers with long records who end in prison or those who pass through diagnostic centers are sometimes termed "compulsive"; some observers speak of their having a "disease," underscoring a common belief, "once a check forger always a check forger." Such statements also tend to be circular deductions and serve little useful purpose for analysis or research in the absence of definitions which separate them from the fact of recidivism. Nevertheless, these adjectives indicate that law enforcement people and prison staff members do in some way differentiate check forgers from other convicted criminals, especially in regard to a kind of cyclical pattern and inevitability in their actions.

Check forgers themselves also provide cues and verbalizations which can be inferentially useful for the analysis of their behavior. In jail and prison they often are apathetic toward their predicaments and they seem less inclined than other prisoners to rationalize their behavior. First offenders frequently express continuing deep perplexity about their motivations; some speak of the "other me" as responsible for the check passing; some refer to themselves as "Dr. Jekyll and Mr. Hyde"; and some say that they "must be crazy." Such statements may also come from those with long criminal histories, from those who are "check artists," as well as first offenders. Systematic check forgers seldom have the "businessman" ideology which was attributed to professional thieves by Sutherland.[4]

Check forgery is associated with a wide variety of personal and social contingencies, the nature of which has been dealt with elsewhere in a theory of naïve, i.e., criminally unsophisticated check forgery.[5] Some forgers pass worthless checks only once and quit; others, casual offenders, intersperse periods of stable employment with check writing sorties quickly followed by arrest. Some people imprisoned for bad checks are alcoholics who have unwisely passed worthless checks during a drinking spree, drug addicts "supporting a habit," or gamblers desperately trying to cover losses. The comments which follow are directed not to check forgers in general but to those who have a commitment to check forgery, who develop a system of passing bad checks, and who live according to the dictates of this system as they progressively perceive them. The characteristics of this system have been described in some detail in a previous article.[6] It is only necessary to recapitulate that committed check forgers typically work alone and while they develop a criminal behavior system, it is an individual system. It is neither the same nor the equivalent of professional crime, for it lacks social organization, occupational orientation, careful planning, common rules, a code of behavior, and a special language. In the present context the concern is with the exigencies from which the systems develop and the sociopsychological consequences of the adaptations making up the systems. These revolve around pseudonymity, mobility, and seclusiveness.

PSEUDONYMITY

Once a check forger passes a series of worthless checks, the central fact of his existence becomes the threat of arrest. The business community through the police is strongly organized against the check forger, and when his checks appear, a number of procedures are activated. The more checks he has outstanding the more intensified and widespread are the efforts to apprehend him. Nearly all of these procedures have to do with identification, for once the check forger is identified as working in an area, apprehension and arrest quickly follow. Consequently if he is to survive as a forger he must develop and use techniques which prevent his identification.

Other criminals anticipate and adapt to the threat of arrest through anonymity, e.g., the burglar who works at night, or the bank robbers who work swiftly, sometimes wearing masks, which will confuse witnesses and make subsequent identification difficult or impossible. The confidence man manipulates his victims so that they often remain unaware they have been duped, or so that they fear to go to the police. The check forger cannot use these alternatives as a defense against arrest because he must work during daylight hours and face large numbers of victims who require identification before they will cash his checks. While the forger might "cool out" a few victims in the manner of the con man, he can't psychologically disarm them all, nor can he employ the "fix" with any great degree of success. The district attorney usually has stacks of checks in evidence and numerous complainants ready to testify against him when he is arrested. The check forger by necessity relies upon pseudonyms as the preferred solution to his technical problem.

In a very literal sense the check forger becomes a real life actor, deliberately assuming a variety of roles and identities which both facilitate the cashing of checks and conceal his former or, if preferred, his "real" identity. Thus he may become a spurious customer in a supermarket, a guilty husband purportedly buying his wife a gift, an out-of-town real estate buyer, a corporation executive seeking to set up a branch office, an army officer on leave, or even an investigator for the Department of Internal Revenue.

The systematic forger's problem is the selection or fabrication of roles rather than the learning of new roles. His role models are occupational or leisure time roles of conventional society. Their distinctive quality is their high degree of superficiality.[7] While they require some acting ability, it is of a low order and easily learned. Such roles, as Goffman[8] suggests, are easily put together in response to situational cues from "bits and pieces of performances" which are already in the repertoire of most people.

Some negative learning is done by forgers in jail or prison, in the sense of things not to do, through listening to the stories of other check criminals. This is reflected in an adage followed by some, of "never try another man's stunt." While check forgers are responding to what they expect of others and what others expect of them, they do so in order to maintain deception and avoid arrest. Their behavior is fundamentally more in the nature of strategy or a swiftly moving game than it is a formal or constituted pattern. In this sense it is generically similar to that of the confidence man, representing, however, a lower order of creativity and strategy.

MOBILITY

While the check man employs pseudonyms to avoid exposure when passing his worthless checks, he cannot simply don a different or innocuous identity afterward; he must move on, out of the vicinity of his crime or crimes. This, of course, can be said for other kinds of crimes, but mobility is more or less "built in" the check forger's situation largely because he preys upon resident businessmen, rather than on transients, as do pickpockets or con men.[9] His mobility is shaped by continual awareness of the time required to deposit checks, clear them, and communicate notification of non-payment to law enforcement and business protective agencies. In large part his daily activities are geared to the tempo and rhythms of banking and business, which demarcate the length of time he can pass checks and remain in a given area, ending in a critical interval during which danger of arrest is ubiquitous.[10] Experienced check forgers develop an almost intuitive sense of these points in time which punctuate their periodic movements.

The movements of the systematic check passer take on a circularity of action and motivation in the sense that their mobility begets more mobility. When queried as to why they stay on the move, check forgers usually explain that it is expensive to travel, and also that if they are to impress their businessmen-victims they must appear to have a bank account appropriate to the checks they cash.[11]

> When you're moving around like that you've got to put up a front and look the part. You can't cash checks if you look seedy. How can I impress a clerk that I'm a businessman with a fat bank account if I don't have good quality clothes and stay in better hotels and drive an expensive make of car (rented).

The result of their high levels of expenditure is that forgers usually cash numerous checks in order to defray costs of constant travel and to maintain their prosperous style of life. The local "spreads" of checks stir strong indignation in the business community and quickly mobilize law enforcement people, sensing of which becomes the forger's motivation to move frequently. This suggests one of the main reasons why some check forgers speak of being caught up in something they can't stop.

SECLUSIVENESS

The vulnerability of the forger to recognition and identification impels him away from unnecessary contacts with other persons. Furthermore he must, if he is to remain free from arrest, keep himself from progressive involvement in social relationships, for with intimate interchange of experiences there comes the danger of inadvertent as well as deliberate exposure by others. Free and unguarded interaction, even with persons whom he likes and trusts, becomes an indulgence.

The forger's seclusiveness, in large part a learned response of wariness, is reinforced by his high mobility, which necessarily makes his contacts and interactions of short-lived variety; he simply does not have the time to build up close relationships with the people he meets. His relationships or social activities tend to be those which he can enter and leave quickly, with a minimum of commitment; the roles he enacts apart from the passing of his checks are for the most part casual in nature. In addition to this role selectivity he learns to avoid specific forms of behavior likely to lead beyond casual interaction.

The forger often meets people in settings where drinking is expected behavior, yet he must take care not to drink to the point of intoxication for fear of letting slip revealing or inconsistent facts about himself. If he gets drunk he is likely to do it alone, but this is risky, too, for he might be picked up on a drunk charge and be exposed by a routine fingerprint check. If the forger gambles it is likely to be at a crowded race track or casino, not at a friendly poker game.

The preference for seclusiveness puts its stamp upon the sexual participation of the forger. He is more limited than other criminals in seeking erotic pleasures; for he seldom has a common law wife or a regular traveling companion. Prostitutes are not in keeping with his pseudonyms of respectability, and association with them may lead to unwanted brushes with the police. When he picks up a girl he is apt to be discriminating in his choice, and typically he will treat her lavishly, but seldom will he give her his true name. In this role, as in others, he remains an actor, although at times the temptation to be otherwise is great.

THE EXTRINSIC NATURE
OF CHECK FORGERS' REWARDS

Systematic check forgers are properly described by themselves and by others familiar with their ways as people who like to live fast and well. The money which flows into their hands is spent freely, often with refined taste on clothes, food, drink, travel, and entertainment. Their satisfactions are limited to those which can be had from conspicuous expenditure and display, or those which stem from the honorific qualities of assumed names, titles, or identities which a generous supply of money makes possible in our society. The attendant rewards are the result of automatic or unreflective deference cued by external or immediately recognizable symbols of high economic status. Even the sexual rewards of forgers have much of this quality.

The status pleasures of forgers are further tempered by the fact that they cannot and dare not, for any length of time, assume specific identities of those who are in high positions in a particular local community. They can be rich cattlemen from Texas, but not a particular, known, rich cattleman from Texas. They may use specific identities or impersonations of this sort to pass checks (known as "high powered") but if they are wise they will not register as such persons later at a local hotel.

Some of the rewards which forgers seek arise out of context of private meanings which can be understood only in terms of idiosyncratic life history factors. Thus for some reason they may have disliked bankers or credit managers, and they derive a particular zest or satisfaction from foisting bad checks on these people or on those who work for them. Unfortunately, the rigorous exactions of their criminal technology leave few opportunities for the indulgence in these more subtle gratifications. Furthermore, they have no way of making public these private psychic triumphs, for they have no audience. At best they can only laugh silently later over their beer or pre-dinner cocktail.

THE GROWTH OF ANXIETY

An unavoidable conclusion seems to be that the more successfully the forger plays his roles the greater becomes his anxiety. The more checks he has oustanding the greater is his perception of the danger of arrest, and hence the greater his necessity to move on and devise new identities which conceal his previous behavior. The mounting sense of strain is made real to the forger by occasional "close calls" in which he barely escapes identification and arrest. As the anxiety magnifies it is reflected in jumpiness, stomach upsets, and other physical disturbances. A few check forgers develop acute symptoms, such as stomach ulcers.

> My routine ran like this: I usually picked my city, then after I arrived I opened a savings account with cash. That's on Monday. On Tuesday I deposited some checks to my account, no good, of course. Wednesday I deposited another check and then drew out part of the account in cash. Then I left town. I worked this all over California, depositing maybe $50,000 altogether in I don't know how many banks. I suppose I got about $10,000 in cash. By this time the ulcers kicked up and I laid off in a resort.

Anxiety serves to amplify the suspiciousness of the forger; in some instances it is aggravated into a paranoid-like state, called the "bull horrors" by professional criminals. This is what it implies—abnormal fear of the police. In this state any unusual behavior of a victim, or a chance knock on a hotel room door, may be taken by the forger to mean that he has been discovered or that detectives have arrived to arrest him. At this point it is clear that the symbolic process has been affected; anxiety has begun to distort or interfere with the forger's ability to take over or realistically appraise the responses of others to his actions.

Cooler or highly experienced forgers may be able to objectify the sources of their anxiety and symbolize it in the jargon of the professional criminal as "heat." As one forger put it, "The checks get hot, not me." As a solution to their psychic problems some forgers take a vacation, or "lay off at a resort." In this setting they continue to use a pseudonym but refrain from passing checks during the interim. This has the merit of reducing anxiety attributable to the fear of being recognized by victims or police, but it does not solve what by now has usually become an identity problem. In any event, contingencies or the need for more money are apt to cut short these palliative respites.

PERSONAL CRISIS

Detectives, police, and the check forgers themselves all agree that arrest is inevitable for the person who persists in passing bad checks for any length of time. A few check men manage to evade detection for several years, and one is known to have foiled the FBI for ten years, but these are the rare exceptions which prove the rule. Efficiently organized police work and fortuitous events undeniably have much to do with the forger's ultimate downfall, but from the point of view adopted here, these are constant factors with which he contends. That with which he is unable to cope is a kind of massive personal crisis which inheres in the prolonged enactment of his spurious roles.

That the forger reaches a dead end in his motivation can be inferred from the circumstances and attendant behavior at the time of the arrest. While a number of systematic forgers are apprehended entirely by chance or by police efforts, an impressive number of others engineer their own downfalls. For example, some phone the police or a parole officer and tell them where they can be found. Closely akin are those who foreclose their current criminal careers rather simply by remaining where they are, knowing full well that police or detectives will soon catch up with them, to find them in a resigned mood awaiting their arrival.[12] Still other forgers, like fabled animals wending back to their mythical graveyard to die, return to their home community, there either to court arrest or to arrange for the inevitable in familiar surroundings. In more complex cases an otherwise accomplished check man makes a mistake, knowing at the time that it is a mistake which probably will land him in jail or prison.

> After a weekend of drinking and sleeping with this girl I had known before, I woke up in my room at the Mark Hopkins with a hangover and no money left. I had one check left from those I had been passing in the city. It was over two weeks since I had started passing this series and knew I shouldn't try to cash this one. But I did anyway—and now here I am at Folsom.

When queried as to reasons for their sometimes open, sometimes oblique surrenders to detectives or other law enforcement agents, check forgers frequently refer to a cumulative state of apathy or sense of psychic exhaustion,[13] expressed in such statements as the following:

After that I began to appreciate what a heck of a job it is to pass checks.

In Seattle I got just plain tired of cashing checks.

The thrill I got from passing checks was gone.

I reached a point where I didn't care whether I stayed in Balboa or went to jail.

It's the same thing over and over again; you get tired of running.

It gets to be more and more of an effort.

You have a sense of being caught in something you can't stop.

One meaning that can be readily assigned to such statements is that, assuming satisfactions or rewards of the forger's activities remain unchanged or constant, their costs of acquisition in terms of effort and expenditure of psychic energy (anxiety) increase to a prohibitive point. What started out as "easy" check passing becomes more and more work or sheer labor, until that game is no longer worth the effort.

A second, less apparent implication of the sense of apathy which finally overwhelms the highly mobile check forger was suggested by a thoughtful older inmate of San Quentin prison, who had in his lifetime been both con man and a notorious utterer of very large checks. His interpretation was simply that during the course of a check passing spree, "You come to realize that kind of life has a false structure to it." This in sociological terms speaks of the inherent difficulty of establishing and maintaining identity by reference to purely extrinsic rewards. To admit this is for the forger in effect to admit that the roles he plays, or his way of life, make impossible a stable identity or the validation of a self ideal. An excerpt from an older published autobiography of a forger states the problem clearly.[14]

I could not rid myself of the crying need for the sense of security which social recognition and contact with one's fellows, and their approval furnishes. I was lonely and frightened and wanted to be where there was someone who knew me as I had been before.

At best the forger can seek to use his affluence to buy from others the approval and recognition important to a sense of personal worth. But persons endowed with the intelligence and insight of a systematic check criminal quickly perceive the spurious qualities of such esteem, founded as it is only upon his generosity.

Sure, you get big money. But it's easy come, easy go. You start out on Monday morning with a stack of checks. Maybe it's hard to get started, but after the first check it's easier. You work all week and by Thursday or Friday you have a pocketful of money. Then you pick up a girl and hit the bars and night spots. You have plenty of quick pals to pat you on the back and help you spend that money. Pretty soon it's Monday morning and you wake up with a hangover and empty pockets. You need more money so you start again.

While conspicuous expenditures on goods and services are important means of locating a person with reference to others, close observation of interaction reveals that these are necessary rather than sufficient factors for the purpose. They become most significant when they establish position in a *particular* group within a stratum or social category. The forger, by choice, enacts the form but not the substance of social roles. He lacks, avoids, or rejects contact with reference groups which could validate these roles or fix an underlying identity. He cannot particularize his social interaction, hence has no way of getting appreciation as a separate person. Appreciations must remain superficial imputations to the persons whose real or hypothetical identities he assumes.[15] Apart from the lack of opportunity to do so, the forger dares not put too much of what he regards as his "true self" into these identities; he cannot readily convert them and make them his own either in part or whole. To particularize his interaction to such an end would disclose his essential difference from others, i.e., his commitment to living by passing bogus checks and deceiving others. This disclosure, of course, would destroy the identities or assign him the criminal identity which he does not desire.

When put into a time perspective, the forger's interplay of role and identity has a dialectical quality. The forger sets out on his check writing and passing journey with an initial sense of fulfillment which is exciting or even exhilarating. This is related to the ease of passing checks and the sense of enjoyment of things he has always wanted but could not afford, or to the enactment of roles which on the surface at least are perceived as in keeping with the self-ideal he holds. There is also an awareness of fulfilling or satisfying some of the more highly subjective values previously alluded to. The sense of fulfillment undoubtedly varies from forger to forger in degree and content, depending upon whether he has been in jail, on probation, in prison, or on parole. However, it is present in any case.[16]

The passage of time brings no lasting respite to the fast moving check passer and the tendency is for his anxiety to mount to higher and higher levels. His attempts to cope with this anxiety at most are palliative and may lead to secondary anxieties which are added to his basic anxiety. Reference has already been made to "laying off in a resort" and to the ephemeral nature of the surcease it provides. In addition this may become risky if he is tempted to overstay or to depart from his system.

Some forgers who acutely sense the organized hue and cry against them or who realize that "they are hot" may try to reduce their tensions by "dropping down" to less hazardous methods. Instead of passing payroll checks, checks on accounts of actual persons, or large personal checks, they may cash small checks in supermarkets or drugstores. This is safer, but it is infinitely more labor and less productive. It may mean a jail rather than a prison sentence if the forger is caught, but this merely offers a choice between the lesser of two evils.

> In Minneapolis things began to get real rough. I had trouble getting name cards of businessmen to make my system work and I had this feeling that the FBI was around. Anyway, I had to cash $25 checks in supermarkets and it was damned hard work nearly all day just to get enough to live on, let alone play the horses.

> I'm a thief—a paperhanger. I go for high-powered cashiers checks of $85 to $100. But you won't find any of that high-powered stuff on my record. When I feel the heat is on I drop down to personal checks. Then if I get arrested it is on a less serious charge.

There are, of course, status degradation implications in having to descend to "small time" personal checks. In extreme cases a check man may be driven to engage in forms of petty crime or activities even more compromising to his sense of self-respect. This is apparent in the apologetic tone of the following tersely expressed account of a passage in the life of a long-time check man in jail awaiting the outcome of his trial.

> You have to understand that I'm an old man and I'm so well known that if my checks appear most detectives in the state can tie them to me. I've got to be smart and I have to lay off when things get hot. Once I was living with a pimp and his broad who were both on drugs. It was costing them $40 a day just for the stuff. I went out with the girl at night to help her hustle. Actually I was just doing them a good turn for letting me live with them. Naturally the police didn't come looking for me in places where she hustled, but I kept out of sight as much as possible just the same.

A not uncommon means chosen by check forgers for relief from tension is to increase their alcohol intake, a tendency which has led to some confusion in crime literature between alcoholics who pass checks to get liquor and the bona fide check man. The association between intoxication and felt anxiety and the instrumental quality of liquor for the latter is made vividly clear in the following:

> You asked me if my drinking pattern changed and I can say yes—definitely. I even remember where—in Cincinnati. It was there that my system really began to pay off and I cashed several $400 and $500 checks in the banks. Ordinarily I had one, or at most, two, highballs or a couple of beers before dinner. That night I remember it went up to four drinks, plus a bottle of wine with dinner and liqueur afterwards. I went around in a fog that evening and most nights thereafter.

The urgent need of some forgers to find relief for their troubled inner selves is shown in the willingness to drink liquor despite long established or culturally ingrained attitudes favoring sobriety. Such was the case of a Jewish check forger:

> In reality I am not a drinking man; I dislike any kind of beer or whiskeys, and the only time I actually drink is when I'm in trouble, meaning exactly when I write bad checks. I become very troubled, even though I haven't as yet been apprehended, but I am troubled because I know deep down in my heart that my life of freedom will be short-lived, so to forget my trouble I start drinking. I might add that the first drink tastes like castor oil, and after the first I can tolerate it. When I sober up again I become troubled because of the bogus checks I wrote . . . and, as a fool would figure, I just say to myself I might as well go write checks till I get caught.

While intoxication provides some temporary relief for the troubled forger he knows that it is risky. Furthermore, passing bad checks the next morning with a hangover can be a harrowing experience, which, some forgers say, they have never quite forgotten.

The other significant change which comes with passing time in the criminal cycle of the check forger lies in the meaning or function of the rewards of his labors. The zest and satisfaction originally gained from his large affluence declines. The same is true for such idiosyncratic "thrills," whatever their psychic derivation, he may have originally felt in passing the checks themselves. Whatever reference value they may have had at one time, they are now diminished in their function for delimiting identity and validating self. If the interpretation advanced here is correct, the decline persists until a critical "turning point" is reached, and arrest occurs.

A schematic representation of the three variables involved in the personal crisis is suggested in Fig. 1. The point at which the anxiety gradient and the gradient representing identity and self-validation cross indicates the hypothetical point in time at which personality crisis occurs. While lines with constant and equal gradients are shown in the figure, their application to specific cases might show different slopes, or they might be curvilinear. For maximum clarity objective rewards are shown as constant. In actual cases they might fluctuate or decline somewhat and thus impart a sharper gradient in the decline in self-validation.

THE FORGER'S AVERSION TO CRIMINAL ASSOCIATIONS

It may be protested that the experiences and feelings of the systematic check forger are but similar to those of any person who lives outside the law and plagues society with a long series of crimes. While there is some surface truth in this, it also has to be noted that professional thieves follow hazardous criminal lives yet still manage their occupa-

Figure 1 / Schematic representation of the relationship of anxiety, rewards, and the self-validating function of rewards for the systematic check forger.

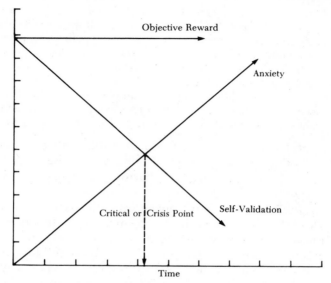

tionally induced anxieties and solve their identity problems. The comparison becomes even more pointed when it is limited to con men, who closely resemble check forgers in their necessary assumption of fictitious identities and in their vulnerability to exposure by victims. Furthermore, con men experience high anxiety levels, fed by the additional probability of exploitation or "shakedowns" by police and detectives if they are recognized.[17]

A significant difference between the check forger and the con man is that the latter retains a locus of the self by means of intimate interaction with other con men.[18] Identity is further maintained by interaction with lesser criminals, and, paradoxically, through accommodative relationships with police.[19] Gambling, drinking, and sexual byplay for the con man tend to take place in the context of primary groups. As such they appear to be more efficient means for relaxing tensions and are less likely than with the forger to generate secondary anxieties. In some cases con men have been able to integrate their criminal forays with a relatively stable family life.

The comparison adumbrated here is intended less to apotheosize the con man than to point up the query as to why check men do not follow his bent and enter into associations with other check criminals or with other types of criminals in their leisure-time pursuits thereby acquiring a criminal identity. In part the answer to this already has been given; such intimacies are contrary to the perceived dictates of the forger's criminal behavior system. The spectre of the stool pigeon who can ruin him with one phone call is never far from the check man's mind, but a loose-tongued male companion in crime, or an angry erstwhile girlfriend can be equally dangerous to him.

It may be that the learned aversions of the check man to close human associations rests upon some kind of pre-criminal personality attributes or selective factors which operate in the recruitment to careers of check passing. This is suggested by the forger's frequent designation of himself as a "lone wolf," which in a number of cases is consistent with a history of family alienation or with a history of marginal participation in social groups. From this perspective, re-cruits to systematic check forgery of necessity would have to be isolate types in order to survive long enough to perfect a system or become anything more than amateurs or casual offenders. Unfortunately, separating learned aversion from predisposition requires kinds of data difficult or impossible to obtain.

Much firmer and less speculative ground for explanation of the check forger's disinclination for criminal colleagues or playfellows is at hand in the middle-class backgrounds of many forgers and their lack of acquaintance with criminal ways until they come to late adulthood. From such facts it can be inferred, as well as demonstrated by verbali-zations of the forgers, that their values or orientation remain conven-tional, "middle class." Put into more specific context, they retain an image of themselves as "nice" persons, of "good" antecedents, or even of refinement, who, as they sometimes phrase it, "wouldn't have the guts to commit any other kind of crime." Associations with other criminals thus become distasteful for them, or even threatening in that they would validate a contradictory, rejected version of the self.

This interpretation is quite consistent with the seclusiveness which carries over into the forger's jail or prison behavior, and his tendency, whenever he can manage it, to occupy intermediary roles on the peripheries of the formal and informal groups in the prison. Examples are the role of a prison runner or that of a bookie in a contraband betting pool.

Such analysis strongly suggests that the problem of the systematic check forger is a special case of self-role conflict, or, more simply, a constantly aggravating moral dilemma. This requires the assumption of something like Sarbin's[20] "constancy principle," i.e., a cognitive structure (the self) tends to maintain its organization despite forces directed toward changing it. From this vantage, the forger's crisis results from the retention of a cognitive picture of himself as essen-tially a "good" person, but playing social roles in a way which violates the expectation of honesty in money matters. The disjunctive relation between the two structures, self and role, gives rise to the perturbations within the organism which are experienced as anxiety.

While this straightforward explanation is attractive, nevertheless it is difficult to reconcile it with the fact that although some forgers experience guilt and remorse, many do not—at least not in any form which can be demonstrated through interview or case history materials. Furthermore, the small minority of systematic forgers with a history of delinquency or of crime beginning in their late teens display the same suspiciousness and avoidance of contacts with other criminals as is found among those who have been categorized as "middle class." Nor is the personal crisis any less exacerbated in the former when it occurs.

For the class of systematic forgers with prior criminal sophistication the roots of dilemma are quite different, revolving about the low or dubious status which check passers hold in the eyes of other criminals. In many ways they are like the nouveau riche, or the "lower-upper" class in a New England town, envied because of their ready possession of money but suspect because of the source of their money.

Check passing is not viewed as a highly skilled criminal vocation[21] and the frequent prison sojourns of forgers implies the lack of any effective solution to the problem of ultimate arrest. The demeanor of forgers can be irritating to less well-educated criminals; in prison they are sometimes disliked because, as one burglar inmate acidly commented, "They like to pretend to be someone they ain't." Back of such attitudes is a vague distrust of the forger, a disapproval of his tendency to try to "con" others inside of the prison as he does on the outside.

It may be that there is a more generalized moral problem for all systematic forgers; the threat of exposure or designation as a "phony" may be the common dilemma which cuts across the psyche of the middle-class forger as well as one who is the product of early criminal socialization. Being a "phony," i.e., defining one's self in terms of a status while lacking the qualifications for the status, may be, as Goffman[22] claims, the "great cardinal sin." Nevertheless, there is good reason to believe that systematic forgers successfully protect themselves from the degradational implications of "phoniness." This they do less through rationalization or other psychodynamic mechanisms than they do by means of selective social participation and managed presentation of the self, which limit organismic involvement in role enactment.

That guilt is seldom more than of marginal importance for the forger so long as he doesn't become "too involved" and so long as he avoids victimizing those with whom he more closely identifies seems clear from the following.

> The only times I felt bad was with the "nice people." Usually when I was
> with people who liked me and I them, I stopped passing checks, or if I did, I

was careful to see that nothing I did could harm them in any way. In Alabama when I went to church with my "friends" I put a check in the collection, but I made sure that it was good, so that they would not be publicly embarrassed later.

Many of the so-called "nice people" who come into the forger's life never learn that he is a "phony" person, or if they do, it is after he has left town. Consequently there is seldom any direct or immediate validation of the stigma. Guilt remains largely retrospective and remote for the forger, without social reinforcement. He "leaves the field" before it can be generated in social interaction.

IDENTITY CRISES AND NEGATIVE IDENTITY

The foregoing argues strongly that the personal crisis of the systematic forger stems less from a moral dilemma than it does from the erosion of identity. So conceived, his problem resides in a neutral component or dimension of the self, namely the sense of separateness and relationship to others, which is assumed to have its own consequences for behavior apart from substantive social value, "good or bad," assigned to it.[23] In a sense the forger fails because he succeeds; he is able to fend off or evade self-degradative consequences of his actions but in so doing he rejects forms of interaction necessary to convert his rewards in positive, status-specific self-evaluations. In time he reaches a point at which he can no longer define himself in relation to others on any basis. The self becomes amorphous, without boundaries; the identity substructure is lost. Apathy replaces motivation, and in phenomenological terms, "life" or "this way of life" is no longer worth living. This is the common prelude to the forger's arrest.

There is, of course, an adaptive aspect to the psychic surrender which precedes or attends the forger's almost casual entry into legal custody, which can be seen quite clearly in the sense of relief which is experienced at the time and also later in jail. From a moral perspective, the forger is "being brought to justice"; he "pays his debt to society." However, from the perspective of this chapter, his apathy or carelessness and subsequent arrest function to end his anxiety which is the subjective aspect of the organized "hue and cry" of modern crime detection. More importantly, they solve his identity problem; arrest immediately assigns the forger an identity, undesirable though it may be, as a jail or prison inmate. In effect, he receives or chooses a *negative identity*,[24] which despite its invidious qualities, is nearest and most real to him. At this juncture he is much like the actor who prefers bad publicity to none at all, or the youth who is willing to be a scapegoat for the group rather than not be part of the group at all.

CONCLUSION

Systematic check forgery comes closest to being a way of life which contains the seeds of its own destruction, or one which generates its own "psychopathology." This pathology, if the term is allowable, is less the product of the structural characteristics of specific roles and their interrelationships than it is of the gamelike manner in which they are chosen, fabricated, and enacted. For this reason, not too much of current "role theory" is germane to the forger's adjustment problems.

Neither role-role conflict nor role-self conflict, nor the availability or nonavailability of institutional ordering of roles (hierarchization, segregation), emphasized by Toby,[25] seem directly relevant to the psychic troubles of the systematic forger. Similarly, the degree of clarity of the roles enacted, stressed by Cottrell,[26] does not seem to have much bearing on his adjustment. Instead, it is the self-perceived or intuited ground rules of the forgery game—pseudonymity, mobility, and seclusiveness—which condition both his success and failure in role playing and adjustment. They do so by placing clear limits on his role involvements.

In this connection Sarbin's[27] concept of the "degree of organismic involvement" obviously becomes centrally important in the behavior of the check man. In fact, his role playing fits rather neatly into the upper two of Sarbin's seven-level classification of roles; the forger, for the most part, is limited to casual roles and dramatic roles (mechanical acting) with the occasional need, perhaps, for "heated acting" (class III).

Skill in "taking-the-role-of-the-other," as conceived by Cottrell, Sarbin, and others, does not seem to be especially important in explaining the forger's ultimate failure in role adjustment, except insofar as it may be temporarily reduced or distorted by isolation and anxiety from extraneous sources. Generally it would have to be conceded that check forgers are "good role takers"; consequently, although their difficulties possibly qualify as "psychopathological," they can scarcely be held to be psychopaths either in Gough's[28] sense of lacking ability to see the self as an object or in Sarbin's sense of being deficient in "tension binding" capacity.

It seems impressively clear that the forger's adjustment difficulties lie primarily in the attenuation of motivation to enact his social roles rather than in their attributes or in the constant aspects of his character. The final bankruptcy of motivation tends to be a dialectical product of prolonged enactment of pseudonymous and casual roles which preclude the establishment of identity. "Establishment" is the term most appropriate to the issue because, as Foote[29] convincingly argues, identity is always problematic. Failing to establish identity, the systematic forger reaches an impasse at which he no longer sees value in everyday existence. Yet valuation, which is at the core of motivation, is problematic, too. Without identity there cannot be valuation.

Notes

1. The original data on which this analysis is based consisted of 75 case studies of check forgers, most of whom were inmates of California penal institutions. Thirty of the 75 were classified as systematic check forgers. For more details on procedure and data see my earlier papers on "naïve" and "systematic" check forgery. Edwin M. Lemert, "An Isolation and Closure Theory of Naïve Check Forgery," *Journal of Criminal Law and Criminology*, 44 (1953), 296–307; Edwin M. Lemert, "The Behavior of the Systematic Check Forger, *Social Problems*, 6 (1958), 141–49.

2. The distinction between identity and self, I will try to show, emerges from the data. For a discussion of several dimensions of the self considered cross-culturally see A. Irving Hallowell, "Self and Its Behavioral Environment," *Explorations Two* (1954), pp. 106–65.

3. Thomas Byrnes, *Professional Criminals of America* (New York: Cassell & Co., 1886), p. 12.

4. Edwin H. Sutherland, *The Professional Thief* (Chicago: University of Chicago Press, 1947), Chap. VI.

5. Lemert, "An Isolation and Closure Theory of Naive Check Forgery," *op. cit.*

6. Lemert, "The Behavior of the Systematic Check Forger," *op. cit.*

7. One forger reported using 285 names during his career. He also argued that the less documentary identification used the less suspicion aroused in the victim. Leonard Hart, "You're a Sucker If You Cash My Check," *Colliers*, February 7, 1953.

8. Erving Goffman, *The Presentation of the Self in Everyday Life* (New York: Doubleday Anchor, 1959), pp. 72ff.

9. Sheldon Messinger thoughtfully suggests that this factor prevents the forger from setting up accommodative relationships with police which are the basis of the fix, by which professional thieves protect themselves—personal communication.

10. In one case, a forger traced his itinerary for the author. It covered a nine-months period, during which he worked in 25 cities between Oakland, California, and Atlanta, Georgia, never remaining longer than two weeks in each.

11. This is only partially revealing of the motivation of the forger; it will become apparent that he also needs large amounts of money to underwrite the kinds of recreation or activities he pursues to relieve his tensions and sense of loneliness.

12. One check man, who spent much of his free time in bars, sensed that bartenders had been alerted to his presence in the area. He brought about his arrest in a bar simply by talking a little louder than was his custom. The owner overheard him and phoned the police.

13. An appropriate descriptive term for this state is not easily found. It resembles the indifference to the threat of death which appeared among some immates of Nazi concentration camps, as a response to "provisional detention without a time limit." See Bruno Bettelheim, "Individual and Mass Behavior in Extreme Situations," *Journal of Abnormal and Social Psychology*, 38 (1948), 434; Elie Cohen, *Human Behavior in the Concentration Camp* (New York: W. W. Norton & Company, Inc., 1953), p. 129. The reaction also suggests the idea of a "breaking point" or limits of effective response under stress. See Eli Ginzberg, *et al., The Ineffective Soldier* (New York: Columbia University Press, 1959). Something of "acute depersonalization" also seems involved. See Paul Schilder, *The Image and Appearance of the Human Body* (London: Kegan Paul, Tench, Trubner and Co., 1935).

14. Roger Benton, *Where Do I Go From Here* (New York: L. Furman, 1936), p. 80.

15. Mills' concept of "status cycles" may be enlightening here. Like the white-collar worker on vacation, the forger seeks to create a "holiday image of self." The difference,

of course, is that there is cultural sanction for the former but not for the forger's holiday image, financed as it is by fraudulent means. C. Wright Mills, *White Collar* (New York: Oxford University Press, 1951), p. 258.

16. One female forger described feelings analogous to sexual orgasm which followed cashing checks in stores.

17. See David Maurer, *The Big Con* (New York: Bobbs-Merrill Company, Inc., 1940). The comparison is best regarded as an historical one, for it is doubtful whether big con games, and con men of the sort described by Maurer, have existed for several decades.

18. While late nineteenth-century check forgers worked in groups, they usually split up after passing a large check on a bank. See Lemert, "Behavior of the Systematic Check Forger," *op. cit.*

19. The best evidence of this is the distinctive names, used by con men in the past, e.g., The Yellow Kid Weil, The Boone Kid Whitney, and The High Ass Kid. Maurer, *op. cit.*

20. Theodore Sarbin, "Role Theory," in *Handbook of Social Psychology*, ed. G. Lindzey (Cambridge: Cambridge University Press, 1954), Chap. 6.

21. ". . . they all (thieves and professional criminals) assume an air of superiority in the presence of the lowly 'short story writer,' as the bum check artist is known in the underworld." Sutherland, *op. cit.*, pp. 76–78.

22. Erving Goffman, "On Cooling Out the Mark," *Psychiatry*, 15 (1952), 451–63.

23. A conception approximating this distinction can be found in D. L. Burham, "Identity Definition and Role Demand in Hospital Careers of Schizophrenic Patients," *Psychiatry*, 24 (1961), 96–122.

24. Erik H. Erikson, "The Problem of Ego Identity," in *Identity and Anxiety*, ed. M. R. Stein, *et al.* (New York: Free Press of Glencoe, Inc., 1960), pp. 60–62.

25. Jackson Toby, "Some Variables in Role-Conflicting Analysis," *Social Forces*, 30 (1950), 324–27.

26. Leonard Cottrell, "The Adjustment of the Individual to his Age and Sex Roles," *American Sociological Review*, 12 (1942), 618–25.

27. Sarbin, *op. cit.*

28. H. G. Gough, "A Sociological Theory of Psychopathology," *American Journal of Sociology*, 53 (1948), 359–66.

29. Nelson N. Foote, "Identification as a Basis for a Theory of Motivation," *American Sociological Review*, 16 (1951), 14–21.

Part 6 / Changing Deviance

Particularly in part four I offered materials demonstrating how a person's public identity becomes transformed into a "deviant" identity. Central to this process is the "status denunciation ceremony," in which a collective effort is made to place an institutional tag upon a person. This status-conferring process was especially evident in those articles dealing with the involuntary processing and incarceration of clients as mental patients. The articles also helped to underscore the fact that the institutional deviant has relatively little to say about his or her processing. It has been emphasized, too, that the identity transformation or change process is generally rather routine.

How the labeled deviant actually perceives and responds to institutional processing is often difficult to judge. As we have seen, some will accept the label, while others will either reject or ignore it. The individual's response, however, is critical in the changing or altering of a "deviant" identity—that is, in moving from a deviant to a nondeviant status, or more generally, having the deviant label removed. For example, if the individual rejects the institutional label, he or she can expect to encounter various types of difficulty. The plight of McMurphy (general introduction) offers an illustration of this. Not only did he reject the "sick role," but his resistance, when viewed from the institution's perspective, was taken as a sign that he needed help. In this instance, the prognosis for change—again from the institution's viewpoint (i.e., their theory of the office and associated diagnostic stereotypes)—was extremely poor. A patient may, however, accept the label and act in accordance with institutional expectations. Such patients thus become willing parties in the transformation process.

Even if individuals decide to conform to social norms, they will most certainly encounter numerous structural and individual barriers—barriers which often reduce the probability that they will elect to change their behavior. Ex-deviants, as I have noted in the general introduction, frequently experience difficulty finding housing and employment; this is due primarily to the fact that others, in general, continue to react to the person as a deviant. What this suggests, moreover, is that institutional processing is most systematic and efficient in tagging individuals as deviants. The reverse process, however, is anything but systematic and efficient. Specifically, there are few, if any, institutional mechanisms and procedures that can be used to systematically remove deviant-institutional labels (and the associated stigma) from individuals. Thus, deviants are often left to fend for themselves. Obviously, giving ex-cons a bit of money and a suit of clothes, without helping them deal with potential structural barriers—such as having to indicate they are ex-cons on job applications—and individual problems—such as feelings of low self-esteem or lack of confidence in self and abilities—is not going to do much by way of "rehabilitating" them. A viable model of change (if desired) or "rehabilitation" must incorporate a concern for both individual and structural factors. The selections following deal with contingencies such as these, particularly in terms of some of the conditions that various types of noninstitutional (e.g., addicts and skid row alcoholics) and institutional (e.g., mental patients and delinquents) deviants can expect to encounter if they choose to change their "deviant" behavior. Throughout the discussion of most of the pieces it is possible to apply the organizational paradigm introduced in the general introduction.

Problems and Issues

Even though the "societal reactions" perspective has been given a major focus in various sections of this volume, it should be emphasized that additional research is needed, especially if we are to learn more about the effects of labeling. "The Labeling Process: Reinforcement and Deterrent?" by Bernard A. Thorsell and Lloyd W. Klemke underscores this need.

Thorsell and Klemke offer several propositions which relate rather directly to the probability of whether people will change their behavior or not. For instance, they note that "if a label can be easily removed, the probability that the stigmatized person is likely to move toward conforming behavior is greater." Not only do their statements provide a useful critique of the labeling perspective, but their comments also help to underscore the difficulty involved in trying to determine the impact of labels; this should have been apparent in many of the selections presented previously. As Thorsell and Klemke note, labeling may terminate behavior, push one into further behavior, or have no effect at all.

"The Cycle of Abstinence and Relapse Among Heroin Addicts" by Marsh B. Ray continues the theme being developed in this section.

Ray is concerned initially with outlining those structural and individual factors that may produce relapse on the part of the heroin addict. A major problem concerns society's reaction to the label. The addict may, for example, experience some initial difficulty deciding where he stands relative to nonaddict groups; this process of evaluation is not without its consequences, and it can play a major role in determining whether a particular person will change his behavior or not. In fact, Ray contends that the process of relapse begins when the addict "develops an image of himself as socially different from nonaddicts, and [it actually] occurs when he redefines himself as an addict." Ray goes on to describe those factors that may promote relapse, the most important of which seem to be contact with other addicts and negative responses received from members of the nonaddict society. Throughout this process of identity assessment, addict and nonaddict identities and values are being compared, particularly in terms of the cost and advantages associated with the addict as opposed to the nonaddict identity.

Jacqueline P. Wiseman's research, "Alcoholics and the Transformation of Deviant Identity," documents some of the barriers that skid row alcoholics can expect to encounter when they leave the institutional role and try to assume a conventional role in society. Of particular relevance are Wiseman's initial comments that not only is the institutional experience of a contrived or artificial nature, but, unlike the middle-class alcoholic, the skid row alcoholic is "not returning to any niche being held for him in society." The alcoholic thus has difficulty finding employment, as well as acceptable living quarters. He also experiences trouble staying sober, and doing so often means avoiding old acquaintances and surroundings; this in turn frequently means spending a great deal of time alone. Wiseman contends that there are only three ways an alcoholic can move off skid row: (1) by becoming a member of an institution, (2) by becoming involved in "alcoholic rehabilitation as a profession," or (3) by dying.

Programs and Strategies

The preceding articles described some of the general problems that may confront individuals who try to change their behavior—that is, transform their "deviant" identity. The remaining selections deal with the notion of identity transformation in greater depth, particularly in terms of *specific* programs and strategies that may be used in the process. Embedded within each program or strategy is a particular theory of the office and its associated diagnostic stereotypes.

Harrison M. Trice and Paul Michael Roman's piece, "Delabeling, Relabeling, and Alcoholics Anonymous," describes the process whereby an alcoholic becomes delabeled "as a stigmatized deviant and relabeled as a former and repentant deviant." Trice and Roman argue initially that there are probably at least three ways in which deviants can be successfully delabeled: (1) by having organizations of deviants change existing norms so that their behavior becomes acceptable, (2) by having organizations develop effective "delabeling" or "status-return" ceremonies, and (3) by developing mutual aid organizations which not only emphasize and require strict conformity to societal or community norms but which also create socially acceptable stereotypes of the deviant. Alcoholics Anonymous provides an example of this latter strategy. Trice and Roman then describe how this organization works. They also stress the fact that AA is not successful with all of its clients. The successful cases seem to exhibit a specific set of personality or self factors—for instance, the successes appeared more "sensitive to responsibility, more serious, and introspective."

Nathan B. Eddy's piece, "Methadone Maintenance for the Management of Persons with Drug Dependence of the Morphine Type," describes a model whereby heroin users are maintained with daily doses of methadone. The program also helps clients become functioning and productive members of society; this type of treatment strategy appears to be a success. Final assessment, however, must await the appropriate evaluation data. Eddy concludes his analysis by offering several precautions which any maintenance program must observe, such as control of the drug and monitoring by urinalysis.

"Treating Schizophrenics in the Community" by Benjamin Pasamanick, Frank R. Scarpitti, and Simon Dinitz summarizes a three-year feasibility study of treating schizophrenics in the community. The research is concerned with examining the relative effectiveness of selected types of treatment strategies; this is accomplished by studying three groups of schizophrenics: (1) hospital controls, (2) drug home-care patients, and (3) placebo home-care cases. The results provide support for the community-based treatment model; this is evident from the finding that over 77 percent of the drug-care patients, as opposed to 34 percent of the placebo patients, remained in the community for the duration of the experiment. The researchers also offer some interesting observations concerning the failures. They conclude their analysis by discussing several important ramifications of their study—implications of which have a direct bearing upon whether or not "deviant" actors can successfully transform their public (and personal) identities.

Ted Palmer's article, "The Youth Authority's Community Treatment Project," presents an evaluation of the effectiveness of California's community-based treatment program for juveniles. His major focus is on the period from 1961–1969, and he is concerned specifically with examining whether juvenile offenders should be left in the community *before* locking them up. The results indicate that diversion may work for some individuals but not for others. This seems most apparent for "power-oriented" youths. Not only did these males show little improvement in their parole performance, but the traditional (institutional) method appears most effective in dealing with these individuals. Overall, Palmer provides an excellent model that can be used to evaluate treatment programs and strategies. His results are important in predicting whether or not institutional and noninstitutional deviants will change their behavior. The results also provide substance to many of those articles (e.g., Goffman's) and statements (e.g., Thorsell and Klemke's) indicating that actors may respond differently to labeling and processing in different settings.

The final selection, Dennis Berg and David Shichor's "Methodological and Theoretical Issues in Juvenile Diversion," offers a recent evaluation of a diversion program, a strategy in corrections and rehabilitation that has received a great deal of funding and attention in the last decade. Underlying this concept, and suggested partially by the works of Pasamanick and Palmer, is the idea that official or institutional processing may not only have a negative impact upon people, but it also appears to be relatively ineffective. Berg and Shichor address some methodological and theoretical issues, and then proceed to analyze the ATSC Project, particularly in terms of whether it is more effective than other methods of treatment. Their findings provide little support for the diversion movement. They do, however, offer several recommendations that may make the ATSC Project a more viable alternative to probation, such as developing better referral guidelines. The results of this study demonstrate very clearly that identity and behavior changes entail a complex set of individual and structural concerns. Processing or treatment may terminate existing behavior, push an individual into further behavior, or have virtually no effect at all.

46 / The Labeling Process: Reinforcement and Deterrent?

BERNARD A. THORSELL
LLOYD W. KLEMKE

The labeling theory approach to the analysis of deviance depicts stable patterns of deviant behavior as products or outcomes of the process of being apprehended in a deviant act and publicly branded as a deviant person. The involvement of an individual in this process is viewed as depending much less upon what he does or what he is than upon what others do to him as a consequence of his actions. Deviant persons are regarded as having undergone a degradation ceremony with the result that they have been relegated to membership in a deviant group. In the process, they are thought to have come to acquire an inferior social status and to have developed a deviant view of the world and all the knowledges, skills, and attitudes associated with that status.

Labeling analysts make a basic distinction between primary and secondary deviance. This distinction has been clearly formulated by Lemert (1967: 17; 1951: 75). In his view, primary deviance is simply any behavior which might cause an individual to be labeled as a deviant person, whereas secondary deviance is behavior which is generated when an individual is placed in a deviant social role as a result of having been labeled and processed as a deviant person. Labeling analysts attach much greater significance to secondary deviance than to primary deviance, except insofar as other persons react to an act which might be labeled as deviant. They view deviance as a product or outcome of the interaction between the individual who performs the deviant act and those who respond to it by labeling the individual as a deviant person.

Thus, the labeling theory approach to the analysis of deviant behavior typically stresses the importance of the impact of societal reaction on the deviant person rather than focusing upon his psychological or sociological characteristics. Apropos of this, the central issue to which labeling analysts have consistently addressed their inquiries is the consequences of having become the target of a label as a deviant person. The labeling process is depicted as resulting characteristically in the reinforcement and crystallization of deviant behavior as a life style. This *negative* result is attributed to what are considered to be typical sequelae of the labeling process, namely, the isolation of the deviant from nondeviant social relationships and a resultant acceptance of a definition of self as a deviant person.[1]

While readily acknowledging the highly significant contributions that this approach has made to our understanding of deviant behavior, this paper takes special note of the fact that a possibly highly important alternative consequence of the labeling process, namely its *positive* effect on future behavior,[2] has been virtually ignored in the work of labeling analysts. Indeed, the treatment of this issue has been limited almost entirely to a concern for the *negative* effect of the labeling process on future behavior. While labeling analysts have demonstrated that the labeling process appears to reinforce and solidify deviant behavior in many cases, they apparently have not seriously considered the possibility that in other cases it might serve to terminate on-going deviance and to deter future deviant behavior. It is somewhat difficult, at first glance, to understand why labeling analysts have failed to examine, to any appreciable extent, the possibility that the labeling process may have positive or deterrent effects on behavior. It does not appear to be for lack of evidence in the literature or in personal experience. For example, depictions by social scientists of social control techniques often point to labeling as a negative sanction and behavioral deterrent. A good case in point is the Bank Wiring Room experiment in the Western Electric Hawthorne Works studies (Roethlisberger and Dickson, 1939). In that experiment, deviants were sanctioned by their work group by being labeled "rate busters," "speed kings," and so forth, when their work output exceeded the group norm defining "a fair day's work." This treatment by their fellow group members was, on the whole, quite successful in pressuring the deviants to conform to the group norm. Moreover, one's own everyday experiences and observations and common sense all lend support to the general contention that labeling by friends, peers, colleagues, and other associates often does result in a cessation of deviant behavior and can serve to deter future deviance.

The ultimate reasons for the failure of labeling analysts to attend to this dimension of the problem are probably many and varied. Although the determination of these reasons is not the central concern of this paper, it seems appropriate to note in passing that at least one of the roots of the labeling theory approach to the analysis of deviance would seem to lie in a larger perspective on the phenomenon which was established by earlier analysts of deviant behavior, most of whom were criminologists.[3] These analysts sought to identify the social and cultural, as contrasted to the individual and psychological, sources of deviance, particularly, crime. Very importantly, they found that the established societal channels for dealing with criminal deviance yielded, on the whole, essentially negative results. The societal agencies and processes involved in apprehension, adjudication, and rehabilitation of the criminal deviant were shown to be largely ineffective in stopping on-going criminal behavior and deterring future crime. Moreover, these agencies and processes were shown to have characteristics which not only failed to rehabilitate the criminal and to deter new criminal behavior, but which actually helped establish and support criminal careers.

This criminological tradition seems to have focused attention almost exclusively on deviance and the labeling process as they take place in an urban, secondary-group-dominated setting where opportunities for personalized observations about behavior are vastly outnumbered by (and thus take second place to) those which are based upon typifications. As a result, it would seem that contemporary labeling analysts, as heirs of this tradition in the study of deviance, have come to center their attention almost exclusively upon the negative outcomes of the labeling process as they typically occur in a mass society setting. Thus, the perspective of contemporary labeling analysts appears to be a carry-over from work within this larger criminological tradition which has been directed at the negative outcomes of the inept and ineffective social control measures characteristic of an urban society.

This approach to deviance and the analytical and empirical results it has produced are highly significant as far as they go. However, it is important to call attention to the fact that it has failed to take into consideration the possibility that the impact of the labeling process may not be uniform in all social settings and across all forms of deviant behavior. For example, there is reason to believe that the effect of the labeling process in a primary group situation may be quite different from that found in a mass society setting. Primary group settings characteristically provide the labeled person much greater exposure to personalized observations by others which may help neutralize the negative stereotypic aspects of the label. Further, as illustrated in the Western Electric Bank Wiring Room research, the effect of labeling in a primary group setting seems to be just the opposite of that observed by labeling analysts in secondary group settings. That is, the labeling process seems to work, for the most part, as a deterrent in the former in sharp contrast to its apparent reinforcing effect upon deviant behavior in the latter. In sum, there is evidence to suggest that the labeling process apparently can function either as a negative, socially disintegrative force or as a positive, socially integrative force, depending upon the social setting and the interpersonal circumstances.

The validity of the currently accepted hypothesis concerning the outcome of the labeling process, therefore, has not to date been completely established. The empirical evidence which lends support to the contention that the labeling process typically results in negative outcomes for future behavior, while significant, is actually very selective in nature and, therefore, satisfies only part of the requirement for the establishment of the validity of this hypothesis. While the data for crime, for example, tend, on the whole, to support the current formulation, it has not been demonstrated that comparably significant data could not be marshalled in support of the converse of the hypothesis with regard to other types of deviant behavior and alternative social settings. Thus, while few, if any, social scientists would contest the idea that the labeling process does in many cases result in negative consequences, it is important to realize that positive outcomes may also be part of the social reality of this phenomenon. The issue is not simply whether the labeling process reinforces or deters future deviance. Rather it is that an examination of the current state of the art in labeling theory forces an increased recognition that both reinforcement *and* deterrence may be outcomes of the labeling process.

At this time, there is no indication that there has been a systematic effort on the part of labeling analysts to evaluate these issues. Moreover, there have been few efforts to undertake the empirical exploration of the implications of labeling theory. In view of this, it seems fair to say that, at this time, the validity of the currently accepted hypothesis that the labeling process typically reinforces deviant behavior seems to rest more upon its repeated assertion by labeling analysts than upon a substantial body of empirical evidence and carefully reasoned conclusions. If this is the case, it seems incumbent upon labeling analysts to entertain the possibility of a systematic empirical exploration of all the possible outcomes of the labeling process.

It is the contention of this paper that the determination of whether the labeling process will result in positive or negative outcomes for future behavior turns upon several conditions of the labeling process which, to date, have received little or no attention from labeling analysts. Several observations regarding these conditions will be examined with the intention of suggesting directions which future research in this area might take.

OBSERVATION NO. 1: THE LABELING PROCESS SEEMS TO HAVE DIFFERENT EFFECTS AT VARIOUS STAGES IN A DEVIANT CAREER.

Given Lemert's distinction between primary and secondary deviance (1951; 1967), it seems likely that labeling will have fewer effects, positive or negative, after the person has moved into the stage of secondary deviance. The primary deviant seems to be more vulnerable to the direct influence of the labeling process inasmuch as he is still "corruptible." At this stage, the label will either tend to end his deviance or it will serve to push him closer to secondary deviance. Tannenbaum (1938) has emphasized how the youthful troublemaker may be propelled into a delinquent career by being so labeled. On the other hand, Cameron (1964: 165) found that the labeling of the novice pilferer as "shoplifter" usually terminated this activity in her subjects. She points out that the novice pilferer does not think of himself before his arrest as a thief and has no peer group support for such a role. Therefore, being apprehended and labeled as such results in his rejection of that role. In this case, the labeling process serves to terminate the on-going deviant behavior and apparently deters further deviance of this type.

In a recent study (Klemke, 1971) of students who had been officially labeled academic failures by having been dropped for poor scholarship from a large state university, it was found that those attending a local community college did not seem to be caught in a self-fulfilling prophecy of failure. Instead, those who had been stigmatized as failures were found to be earning better grades and to have more favorable attitudes toward their academic work than did the non-failure students. This finding runs counter to the labeling analyst's expectation of a negative outcome in this case and indicates again that there is a need to examine all possible outcomes of the labeling process. Thus, while the primary deviant is still "corruptible," he is also still susceptible to the sanctions of the larger society.

OBSERVATION NO. 2: WHEN A LABEL IS ASSIGNED CONFIDENTIALLY, AND THE PERSON SO LABELED IS A NONPROFESSIONAL DEVIANT, THERE APPEARS TO BE A GREATER CHANCE THAT FUTURE DEVIANCE WILL BE AVOIDED.

There is a vast difference between the impact of labeling which is carried out in a limited, confidential manner, as for example, behind the closed doors of a department store manager's office, and that which takes place before a public audience, such as in a court of law. If labeling is done publicly, the processes of alienation and differential treatment, as discussed by Tannenbaum (1938), tend to be set in motion. This outcome would seem to be even more likely if opportunities for acceptance by a deviant subculture were also available.

Such acceptance would certainly enhance the probability that the labeled person might move into secondary deviance. However, it must be noted that even when labeling is carried out publicly, it is not inevitable that the labeled person continues or intensifies his deviant behavior. Indeed, most persons so labeled probably do not. Thus, the majority of young males repeatedly labeled in the manner discussed by Tannenbaum do not turn out to be professional criminals. Moreover, in contemporary mass society such public labeling "ceremonies" are increasingly easier to keep secret, and thereby additional negative reactions from others are avoided.

OBSERVATION NO. 3: WHEN THE DEVIANT PERSON HAS SOME COMMITMENT TO AND IS, THEREFORE, SENSITIVE TO THE EVALUATION OF THE LABELER, THE EFFECT OF THE LABELING PROCESS APPEARS MORE LIKELY TO BE POSITIVE THAN NEGATIVE.

Cameron's research, noted earlier, points out that the labeling techniques utilized in handling shoplifting cases worked well to discourage the amateur pilferer but had little success with experienced shoplifters. This points up the importance of subcultural supports which encourage renunciation of the legitimacy of conventional morality. The "techniques of neutralization" provided by the subculture to nullify conventional morality seem to abrogate any effect, positive or negative, that the labeling process might have on the labeled person. This, in turn, suggests that when the labeler is not a member of the "target's" in-group, his evaluation may not carry the same effect as if he were a member. This observation is borne out empirically in the Western Electric Bank Wiring Room experiment noted earlier (Roethlisberger and Dickson, 1939). In that study, labels applied by members of one's own work group were more effective in controlling deviation from group norms than was labeling carried out by management representatives with respect to formal orders contradicting the group norms concerning daily output. Similarly, it has become an increasingly common observation in treatment and correctional settings, such as Synanon and Alcoholics Anonymous, that labeling by one's peers or significant others seems to be more successful in stopping deviant behavior and rehabilitating the deviant than that carried out by non-peers, such as counselors, psychiatrists, or prison guards applying the same labels.

OBSERVATION NO. 4: IF A LABEL CAN BE EASILY REMOVED, THEN THE PROBABILITY THAT THE STIGMATIZED PERSON IS LIKELY TO MOVE TOWARD CONFORMING BEHAVIOR IS GREATER.

In their research on occupational opportunities, Schwartz and Skolnick (1962) found that the revelation of an arrest record, irrespective of conviction or acquittal, markedly reduces the number of job opportunities for the individual, particularly for the lower-class person. In an effort to cope with this problem, some legal authorities for some time have pressed for the expungement of the records of persons placed on probation or parole. In the U.S., this has been limited, for the most part, to juvenile records in cases where the community views the young person as deserving of a "second chance." In Sweden, however, the present policy in this regard is so advanced that it is a cardinal principle of Swedish penal policy to protect and maintain the anonymity of released offenders, especially released murderers (Playfair and Sington, 1957). The released offender is advised to change his name and to take up residence in a community or part of the country different from the one in which his crime was committed. A job and, if necessary, living accommodations are found for him there. The only member of his new community aware of his true identity is his employer who is sworn to secrecy. In short, the released offender has the opportunity to embark on a new life completely free of any evidence from the past that might stigmatize him. Swedish penal officials report that for decades there have been no cases of homicide offenders who have been released under this program repeating their crimes. These results suggest that by making the realistic removal of such labels feasible, it is possible, in many cases, to initiate and to sustain movement away from deviant behavior.

OBSERVATION NO. 5: THE NATURE OF THE SOCIETAL REACTION WHICH FOLLOWS OR ACCOMPANIES THE APPLICATION OF A LABEL IS OF CENTRAL IMPORTANCE IN DETERMINING WHETHER THE OUTCOME OF THE PROCESS WILL BE POSITIVE OR NEGATIVE.

In the area of mental illness, the difficulties of the person who has been labeled as "sick" once again becoming perceived as "normal" or "well," has been of interest to labeling analysis.[4] An examination of the ways in which the Hutterites deal with persons exhibiting abnormal behavior was carried out by Eaton and Weil (1953). They found that persons so identified became the objects of extensive efforts on the part of friends and the community in general to aid and support the labeled person in becoming reintegrated into the community. This contrasts sharply with the larger societal reaction to the mentally "sick" person in the United States. In American society, the person so labeled characteristically is regarded as someone to be avoided, rejected, and isolated. Viewed from this perspective, the labeling process is essentially a stimulus which can set off a wide range of societal reactions varying from negative, isolative, and socially disintegrative responses to highly positive, supportive, and socially integrative actions. Where societal reactions are positive, supportive, and socially integrative, the labeling process seems to generate a positive atmosphere in which the effect on future behavior is to move it in the direction of greater conformity.

It is important to distinguish between official, institutionalized reactions to deviant acts and the informal reactions of one's significant others. In the study of academic failures mentioned earlier (Klemke, 1971: 16), it was found that official expulsion from the university was countered by positive, supportive reactions from the student's significant others. These positive reactions were instrumental in encouraging the students to reenter college and try again to succeed academically. They also were significant in maximizing the chances for academic success once the student decided to enter the community college for another try. This finding adds still another dimension to the labeling process and its outcomes which has not been adequately examined by labeling analysts.

OBSERVATION NO. 6: A LIBERAL ASSIGNMENT OF POSITIVE LABELS, WITHIN REALISTIC LIMITS, SEEMS TO STIMULATE AND INCREASE THE PREVALENCE OF DESIRABLE BEHAVIOR.

In their apparent preoccupation with the negative effects of the labeling process, labeling analysts have paid little attention to the possibility that an increase in desirable behavior might result from the application of positive labels. That positive labeling can function as a stimulus to desirable behavior is shown in the work of Rosenthal and Jacobson (1968). In their study, teachers in an elementary school were led to believe at the beginning of the school year that certain pupils could be expected to show considerable academic improvement during the coming year. The teachers were told that these predictions were based upon intelligence tests which had been administered at the end of the preceding academic year. The children so designated were labeled "spurters" by the investigators in their conversations with the teachers. In reality, the children designated as "spurters" were chosen at random from the roster of students enrolled at the school by using a table of random numbers. After the school year was in progress, standard intelligence tests were given to all pupils during the year at predetermined itervals. The results indicated clearly that the randomly chosen children labeled as "spurters" improved scholastically considerably more than the rest of the children who were not so designated. Moreover, in addition to depicting the "spurters" as intellectually more alive and autonomous than the other children, their teachers described them as being happier, more interesting, more appealing, and more affectionate, as well as being better adjusted and less in need of social approval. In this case, the application of a positive label clearly generated socially desirable behavior both as perceived by others and as measured by standardized psychological tests.

On the basis of these six observations, it is possible to construct six hypotheses that seem to be amenable to systematic empirical evaluation by the labeling analyst. While there seems to be little doubt that continued observation and reflection could yield additional hypotheses, those suggested here seem sufficient to point the way to a systematic investigation of the converse of the currently accepted hypothesis concerning the outcome of the labeling process. This is the primary purpose of this paper. In order to express the hypotheses as formal statements, it seems to be most convenient to summarize them as follows.

THE LABELING PROCESS IS MORE LIKELY TO TERMINATE EXISTING DEVIANT BEHAVIOR AND TO DETER FUTURE DEVIANCE:

1. If the labeled person is a primary rather than a secondary deviant.
2. If the labeling is carried out in a confidential setting with the understanding that future deviance will result in public exposure.
3. If the labeling has been carried out by an in-group member or significant other.
4. The more easily the label is removable when the deviant behavior has ceased.
5. The more the labeling results in efforts to reintegrate the deviant into the community.

6. If the label is favorable rather than derogatory.

Empirical evaluation of these hypotheses will do much to expand our knowledge concerning the possible positive effects of the labeling process on both on-going deviance and future conduct. Hopefully, in time it will be possible to amass sufficient empirical evidence so that an objective evaluation of the converse of the currently accepted labeling hypothesis will be possible. All of this will do a great deal to enhance our understanding of the labeling process itself as well as its consequences for future behavior. Moreover, research such as this can begin to provide an objective basis for a systematic evaluation of labeling theory as a general theory of deviant behavior.

References

Becker, Howard S. (1963) *Outsiders: Studies in the Sociology of Deviance* (London: Free Press).

Cameron, Mary O. (1964) *The Booster and the Snitch* (London: Free Press).

Eaton, Joseph, and Weil, Robert J. (1953) *Culture and Mental Disorders* (Glencoe: Free Press).

Erickson, Kai (1962) "The Sociology of Deviance," *Social Problems* 9, p. 307.

Kitsuse, John (1962) "Societal Reaction to Deviant Behavior: Problems of Method and Theory," *Social Problems* 9, p. 247.

Klemke, Lloyd W. (1971) "Higher Education Failures Coming to a Community College and Labeling Theory," paper presented at the 1971 Annual Meeting of the Pacific Sociological Association in Honolulu, Hawaii.

Lemert, Edwin (1967) *Human Deviance, Social Problems and Social Control* (Englewood Cliffs, N.J.: Prentice-Hall).

Lemert, Edwin (1951) *Social Pathology* (New York: McGraw Hill Company).

Playfair, Giles, and Sington, Derrick (1957) *The Offenders: Society and the Atrocious Crime* (London: Secker and Warburg).

Roethlisberger, Fritz J., and Dickson, William J. (1939) *Management and the Worker* (Cambridge: Harvard University Press).

Rosenthal, Robert, and Jacobson, Lenore F. (1968) "Teacher Expectations for the Disadvantaged," *Scientific American* 218, p. 19.

Scheff, Thomas J. (1966) *Being Mentally Ill: A Sociological Theory* (Chicago: Aldine).

Schwartz, Richard D., and Skolnick, Jerome H. (1962) "Two Studies of Legal Stigma," *Social Problems* 10, p. 133.

Tannenbaum, Frank (1938) *Crime and the Community* (Boston: Ginn).

Notes

1. See, for example, Becker (1963), Erickson (1962), Kitsuse (1962), Lemert (1951); also Lemert (1967), Scheff (1966).

2. The terms "positive" and "negative," as used in this context, are utilized only to indicate that deviant behavior is usually regarded negatively by the larger society, whereas a reduction in its frequency or its termination is normally regarded positively.

There is no intention of implying that conformity to the norms of the larger society is necessarily better or more desirable than deviance from them. The question as to whether deviance should be discouraged or promoted, while a legitimate and interesting issue, is not at stake here.

3. The work of pioneering analysts, such as Clemmer, Lemert, Reckless, Sutherland, Taft, Tannembaum, and others whose work falls within the framework of this general tradition comes to mind here.

4. See, for example, Scheff (1966).

47 / The Cycle of Abstinence and Relapse Among Heroin Addicts

MARSH B. RAY

Those who study persons addicted to opium and its derivatives are confronted by the following paradox: A cure from physiological dependence on opiates may be secured within a relatively short period, and carefully controlled studies indicate that use of these drugs does not cause psychosis, organic intellectual deterioration, or any permanent impairment of intellectual function.[1] But, despite these facts, addicts display a high rate of recidivism. On the other hand, while the rate of recidivism is high, addicts continually and repeatedly seek cure. It is difficult to obtain definitive data concerning the number of cures the addict takes, but various studies of institutional admissions indicate that it is relatively high,[2] and there are many attempts at home cure that go unrecorded.

This paper reports on a study[3] of abstinence and relapse in which attention is focused on the way the addict or abstainer orders and makes meaningful the objects of his experience, including himself as an object,[4] during the critical periods of cure and of relapse and the related sense of identity or of social isolation the addict feels as he interacts with significant others. It is especially concerned with describing and analyzing the characteristic ways the addict or abstainer defines the social situations he encounters during these periods and responds to the status dilemmas he experiences in them.

SECONDARY STATUS CHARACTERISTICS OF ADDICTS

The social world of addiction contains a loose system of organizational and cultural elements, including a special language or argot, certain artifacts, a commodity market and pricing system, a system of stratification, and ethical codes. The addict's commitment to these values gives him a status and an identity.[5] In addition to these direct links to the world of addiction, becoming an addict means that one assumes a number of secondary status characteristics in accordance with the definitions the society has of this activity.[6] Some of these are set forth in federal and local laws and statutes, others are defined by the stereotypic thinking of members of the larger society about the causes and consequences of drug use.

The addict's incarceration in correctional institutions has specific meanings which he finds reflected in the attitudes adopted toward him by members of non-addict society and by his fellow addicts. Additionally, as his habit grows and the demands for drugs get beyond any legitimate means of supply, his own activities in satisfying his increased craving give him direct experiential evidence of the criminal aspects of self. These meanings of self as a criminal become internalized as he begins to apply criminal argot to his activities and institutional experiences. Thus shop-lifting becomes "boosting," the correctional settings become "joints," and the guards in such institutions become "screws."

The popular notion that the addict is somehow psychologically inadequate is supported by many authorities in the field. In addition, support and definition is supplied by the very nature of the institution in which drug addicts are usually treated and have a large part of their experience since even the names of these institutions fix this definition of addiction. For example, one of the out-patient clinics for the treatment of addicts in Chicago was located at Illinois Neuropsychiatric Institute, and the connotations of Bellevue Hospital in New York City, another treatment center for addicts, are socially well established. Then, too, the composition of the staff in treatment centers contributes substantially to the image of the addict as mentally ill, for the personnel are primarily psychiatrists, psychologists, and psychiatric social workers. How such a definition of self was brought forcefully home to one addict is illustrated in the following quotation:

> When I got down to the hospital, I was interviewed by different doctors and one of them told me, "you now have one mark against you as crazy for having been down here." I hadn't known it was a crazy house. You know regular people [non-addicts] think this too.

Finally, as the addict's habit grows and almost all of his thoughts and efforts are directed toward supplying himself with drugs, he becomes careless about his personal appearance and cleanliness. Consequently non-addicts think of him as a "bum" and, because he persists in his use of drugs, conclude that he lacks "will power," is perhaps "degenerate," and is likely to contaminate others.

The addict is aware that he is judged in terms of these various secondary social definitions, and while he may attempt to reject them, it is difficult if not impossible to do so when much of his interpersonal and institutional experience serves to ratify these definitions. They assume importance because they are the medium of exchange in social transactions with the addict and non-addict world in which the addict identifies himself as an object and judges himself in relation to addict and non-addict values. Such experiences are socially disjunctive and become the basis for motivated acts.

THE INCEPTION OF CURE

An episode of cure begins in the private thoughts of the addict rather than in his overt behavior. These deliberations develop as a result of experience in specific situations of interaction with important others that cause the addict to experience social stress, to develop some feeling of alienation from or dissatisfaction with his present identity, and to call it into question and examine it in all of its implications and ramifications. In these situations the addict engages in private self-debate in which he juxtaposes the values and social relationships which have become immediate and concrete through his addiction with those that are sometimes only half remembered or only imperfectly perceived.

I think that my mother knew that I was addicted because she had heard rumors around the neighborhood. Around that time [when he first began to think about cure] she had been telling me that I looked like a "bum," and that my hair was down the back of my neck and that I was dirty. I had known this too but had shoved it down in the back of my mind somewhere. She used to tell me that to look like this wasn't at all like me. I always wanted to look presentable and her saying this really hurt. At that time I was going to [college] and I wanted to look my best. I always looked at myself as the clever one—the "mystery man"—outwitting the "dolts." I always thought that no one knew, that when I was in my room they thought I was studying my books when actually I wasn't studying at all.

After mother said those things I did a lot of thinking. I often used to sit around my room and think about it and even look at myself in the mirror and I could see that it was true. What is it called . . .? When you take yourself out of a situation and look at yourself . . .? "Self appraisal" . . . I guess that's it. Well I did this about my appearance and about the deterioration of my character. I didn't like it because I didn't want anything to be master over me because this was contrary to my character. I used to sit and look at that infinitesimal bit of powder. I felt it changed my personality somehow.

I used to try staying in but I would get sick. But because I had money I couldn't maintain it [withstand the demands of the withdrawal sickness] and when the pain got unbearable, at least to me it was unbearable, I would go out again. I wanted to be independent of it. I knew then that if I continued I would have to resort to stealing to maintain my habit and this I couldn't tolerate because it was contrary to my character. The others were robbing and stealing but I couldn't be a part of that. I first talked with my uncle about it because my mother was alive then and I thought she would crack up and maybe not understand the problem. I didn't want to be reprimanded, I knew I'd done wrong. I had been through a lot and felt I wanted to be rid of the thing. He was very understanding about it and didn't criticize me. He just talked with me about going to the hospital and said he thought this would be the best way to do it.

In the above example, the meanings of the complex of secondary status characteristics of the addict identity when used as self referents in bringing this identity into question is shown in dramatic fashion.

But the social psychological prerequisites to the inception of an episode of abstinence need not precede physical withdrawal of the drug. It is frequently the case that following the enforced withdrawal that begins a period of confinement in a correctional institution or hospital, the addict engages in self debate in which the self in all of its ramifications emerges as an object and is brought under scrutiny. Such institutional situations constrain the addict's perspectives about himself and have a dual character. On the one hand, they serve to ratify a secondary status characteristic, while on the other, as addicts interact with older inmates of jails and hospitals, they provide daily concrete models of what life may be like in later years as a consequence of continued use of drugs.

On occasion, however, the addict group itself, rather than non-addict society, provides the socially disjunctive experience that motivates the addict to abstain, although the non-addict world and its values are still the reference point. An addict who had been addicted for several years and had had several involuntary cures in correctional institutions describes such an experience as follows:

When I first started using we were all buddies, but later we started "burning" each other. One guy would say, "Well, I'll go 'cop' " [buy drugs]. Then he'd take the "bread" [money] and he'd never come back. I kicked one time because of that. I didn't have no more money and I got disgusted. First I started to swear him up and down but then my inner conscience got started and I said maybe he got "busted" [arrested]. Then I said, "Aw, to hell with him and to hell with all junkies—they're all the same." So I went home and I tried to read a couple of comic books to keep my mind off it. I was very sick but after a couple of days I kicked.

While the above situation may not be typical, it illustrates the same process to be observed in the other examples—a disruption of the social ordering of experience that has become familiar, a calling into question of the addict identity, and the rejection of this identity and the values associated with it. The more typical situations that evoke such conduct would appear to involve a non-addict or some concrete aspect of the non-addict world as the catalytic agent.

THE ADDICT SELF IN TRANSITION

The addict who has successfully completed withdrawal is no longer faced with the need to take drugs in order to avert the disaster of withdrawal sickness, and now enters a period which might best be characterized as a "running struggle" with his problems of social identity. He could not have taken such a drastic step had he not developed some series of expectations concerning the nature of his future relationships with social others. His anticipations concerning these situations may or may not be realistic; what matters is that he has them and that the imagery he holds regarding himself and his potentialities is a strong motivating force in his continued abstinence. Above all, he appears to desire ratification by significant others of his newly developing identity, and in his interactions during an episode of abstinence he expects to secure it.

In the early phases of an episode of cure, the abstainer manifests considerable ambivalence about where he stands in addict and non-addict groups, and in discussions of addiction and addicts, he may indicate his ambivalence through his alternate use of the pronouns "we" and "they" and thus his alternate membership in addict and non-addict society. He may also indicate his ambivalence through other nuances of language and choice of words. Later, during a successful episode of abstinence, the ex-addict indicates his non-membership in the addict group through categorizations that place addicts clearly in the third person, and he places his own addiction and matters pertaining to it in the past tense. For example, he is likely to preface a remark with the phrase "When I was an addict. . . ." But of equal or greater importance is the fact that the ex-addict who is successful in remaining abstinent relates to new groups of people, participates in their experience, and to some extent begins to evaluate the conduct of his former associates (and perhaps his own when he was an addict) in terms of the values of the new group.

> I see the guys around now quite often and sometimes we talk for a while but I don't feel that I am anything like them anymore and I always leave before they "make up" [take drugs]. I tell them, "You know what you are doing but if you keep on you'll just go to jail like I did." I don't feel that they are wrong to be using but just that I'm luckier than they are because I have goals. It's funny, I used to call them "squares" for not using and now they call me "square" for not using. They think that they are "hip" and they are always talking about the old days. That makes me realize how far I've come. But it makes me want to keep away from them, too, because they always use the same old vocabulary—talking about "squares" and being "hip."

Thus, while some abstainers do not deny the right of others to use drugs if they choose, they clearly indicate that addiction is no longer a personally meaningful area of social experience for them. In the above illustration the abstainer is using this experience as something of a "sounding board" for his newly developed identity. Of particular note is the considerable loss of meaning in the old symbols through which he previously ordered his experience and his concern with one of the inevitable consequences of drug use. This is a common experience for those who have maintained abstinence for any length of time.

During the later stages of the formation of an abstainer identity, the ex-addict begins to perceive a difference in his relations with significant others, particularly with members of his family. Undoubtedly their attitudes, in turn, undergo modification and change as a result of his apparent continued abstinence, and they arrive at this judgment by observing his cleanliness and attention to personal neatness, his steady employment, and his re-subscription to other values of non-addict society. The ex-addict is very much aware of these attitudinal differences and uses them further to bolster his conception of himself as an abstainer.

> Lots of times I don't even feel like I ever took dope. I feel released not to be dependent on it. I think how nice it is to be natural without having to rely on dope to make me feel good. See, when I was a "junkie" I lost a lot of respect. My father wouldn't talk to me and I was filthy. I have to build up that respect again. I do a lot of things with my family now and my father talks to me again. It's like at parties that my relatives give, now they are always running up to me and giving me a drink and showing me a lot of attention. Before they wouldn't even talk to me. See, I used to feel lonely because my life was dependent on stuff and I felt different from regular people. See, "junkies" and regular people are two different things. I used to feel that I was out of place with my relatives when I was on junk. I didn't want to walk with them on the street and do things with them. Now I do things with them all the time like go to the show and joke with them and I go to church with my uncle. I just kept saying to myself that "junkies" are not my people. My relatives don't say things behind my back now and I am gaining their respect slow but sure.

In this illustration there may be observed a budding sense of social insight characteristic of abstainers in this period of their development. Another characteristic feature is the recognition that subscription to non-addict values must be grounded in action—in playing the role of non-addict in participation with non-addicts and thus sharing in their values and perspectives.

THE PROCESS OF RELAPSE

The tendency toward relapse develops out of the meanings of the abstainer's experience in social situations when he develops an image of himself as socially different from non-addicts, and relapse occurs when he redefines himself as an addict. When his social expectations and the expectations of others with whom he interacts are not met, social stress develops and he is required to re-examine the meaningfulness of his experience in non-addict society and in so doing question his identity as an abstainer. This type of experience promotes a mental realignment with addict values and standards and may be observed in the abstainer's thoughts about himself in covert social situations, in his direct interpersonal relations with active addicts, and in his experience with representatives of non-addict society. It is in these various settings that his developing sense of self as an abstainer is put to the test.

Experiences with other addicts that promote relapse. Re-addiction most frequently occurs during the period immediately following the physical withdrawal of the drug—the period described earlier as a time of "running struggle" with identity problems for the ex-addict. It is at this point, when the old values and old meanings he experienced as an addict are still immediate and the new ordering of his experience without narcotics is not well established, that the ex-addict seems most vulnerable to relapse. Sometimes the experiences that provoke the questioning of identity that precedes relapse occur within the confines of the very institution where the addict has gone to seek cure. The social expectations of other addicts in the hospital are of vital importance in creating an atmosphere in which identification with the values of non-addict society is difficult to maintain.

> [The last time we talked you said that you would like to tell me about your experiences in the hospital. What were they like?]
>
> Well, during the first time I was at the hospital most of the fellows seemed to hate [to give] the "square" impression, not hate it exactly but refuse to admit [to] it. My own feelings were that everyone should have been a little different in expressing themselves that I would like to accept the extreme opposite. But I felt that I would have disagreements about this with the fellow inmates. They thought I was a very queer or peculiar person that constantly showed disagreement about the problem as they saw it. I never did reach an understanding with them about the problem.

But addicts do not always relapse on first contact with members of the old group. In fact, there is nothing to indicate that addicts relapse only as a result of association. Instead, contacts may go on for some time during which the ex-addict carries on much private self debate, feeling at one point that he is socially closer to addicts and at another that his real interest lies in future new identities on which he has decided. Typically he may also call to mind the reason he undertook cure in the first place and question the rationality of relapsing. An interesting example of the dilemma and ambivalence experienced under these circumstances and the partial acceding to social pressures from the addict group by applying the definitions of that group to one's own conduct are the experiences of another addict.

> [He had entered the hospital "with the key" and after completing withdrawal he stayed at the hospital for three weeks before voluntarily signing out, although the required period of treatment for a medical discharge at the time was four and one-half months.]
>
> This one kid who was a friend of mine came to me one night and said, "Let's get out of here." So I went and checked out too. Then I got to thinking, "I don't want to go home yet—I'm still sick—and what did I come down here for anyway." So I went up and got my papers back from the officer and tore them up. Then I found this kid and told him that I was staying and he said, "Oh we knew you weren't going to do it—we knew you'd chicken out." Then I went back and put my papers through again. I felt they were trying to "put me down."
>
> When we got out I could have had a shot right away because one of these guys when we got to town said he knew a croaker who would fix us up, but I didn't go with them. I didn't care what they thought because I got to figuring that I had went this far and I might as well stay off.
>
> When I got home I stayed off for two months but my mother was hollering at me all the time and there was this one family in the neighborhood that was always "chopping me up." I wanted to tell this woman off because she talked all right to my face but behind my back she said things like she was afraid I would turn her son on because I was hanging around with him. She would tell these things to my mother. I never turned anybody on! She didn't know that but I wanted to tell her. Finally I just got disgusted because nobody wanted to believe me and I went back on.

The experiences of this addict provide an interesting denial of the notion that addicts relapse because of association *per se* and support the thesis that relapse is a function of the kind of object ex-addicts make of themselves in the situations they face.

Relations with non-addicts as a prelude to relapse. While the ex-addict's interaction with addict groups is often a source of experiences which cause him to question the value to him of an abstainer identity, experiences with non-addict groups also play a vital role. In most instances the addict has established a status for himself in the eyes of non-addicts who may be acquainted with his case—members of his family, social workers, law enforcement officers, physicians and so forth. Through gestures, vocal and otherwise, these non-addicts make indications to the ex-addict concerning his membership and right to participation in their group; for example, the right to be believed when he attempts to indicate to the non-addict world that he believes in and subscribes to its values. In his contacts with non-addicts, the former addict is particularly sensitive to their cues.

During the early phases of an episode of abstinence the abstainer enters various situations with quite definite expectations concerning how he should be defined and treated. He indicates his desire for ratification of his new status in many ways, and finds it socially difficult when he sees in the conduct of others toward him a reference to his old identity as an addict. He is not unaware of these doubts about his identity.

> My relatives were always saying things to me like "Have you really quit using that drug now?" and things like that. And I knew that they were doing a lot of talking behind my back because when I came around they would stop talking but I overheard them. It used to burn my ass.

On the other hand, the non-addicts with whom he has experience during this period have their own expectations concerning the abstainer's probable conduct. Based in part on the stereotypic thinking of non-addict society concerning addiction, in part on unfortunate previous experiences, they may exhibit some skepticism concerning the "cure" and express doubt about the abstainer's prognosis.[7]

THE SOCIAL PSYCHOLOGICAL MEANING OF RELAPSE

On an immediate concrete level, relapse requires that the individual reorient himself to the market conditions surrounding the sale of illicit drugs. He must re-establish his sources of supply and, if he has been abstinent for very long, he may have to learn about new fads and fashions in drug use. He may learn, for example, that dolophin is more readily available than heroin at the moment of his return to drug use, that it requires less in the way of preparation, that it calls for such and such amount to safely secure a certain effect, what the effects will be, and so on.

But the ex-addict's re-entrance into the social world of addiction has much deeper meanings. It places demands and restraints upon his interactions and the meaningfulness of his experience. It requires a recommitment to the norms of addiction and limits the degree to which he may relate to non-addict groups in terms of the latter's values and standards. It demands participation in the old ways of organizing conduct and experience and, as a consequence, the readoption of the secondary status characteristics of addiction. He again shows a lack of concern about his personal appearance and grooming. Illicit activities are again engaged in to get money for drugs, and as a result the possibility of more firmly establishing the criminal aspect of his identity becomes a reality.

The social consequence of these experiences and activities is the re-establishment of the sense of social isolation from the non-addict group and a recaptured sense of the meaningfulness of experience in the social world of addiction. It is through these familiar meanings and the reapplication of the symbolic meanings of the addict world to his own conduct that identity and status as an addict are reaffirmed. The ex-addict who relapses is thus likely to comment, "I feel like one of the guys again," or as Street has put it, "It was like coming home."[8]

While repeated relapse on the addict's part may more firmly convince him that "once a junkie, always a junkie" is no myth but instead a valid comment on his way of life, every relapse has within it the genesis of another attempt at cure. From his however brief or lengthy excursions into the world of non-addiction, the relapsed addict carries back with him an image of himself as one who has done the impossible—one who has actually experienced a period when it was unnecessary to take drugs to avoid the dreaded withdrawal sickness. But these are not his only recollections. He recalls, too, his identification of himself as an abstainer, no matter how tentatively or imperfectly this may have been accomplished. He thinks over his experiences in situations while he occupied the status of abstainer and speculates about the possible other outcomes of these situations had he acted differently.

[Originally from Chicago, he experienced the only voluntary period of abstinence in a long career of addiction while living with his wife in Kansas City, Missouri. After an argument with his wife, during which she reminded him of his previous addiction and its consequences for her, he left her and returned to Chicago, where he immediately relapsed. After three weeks he was using about $12 worth of morphine daily.] He reports on his thoughts at the time as follows:

Now and then I'm given to rational thinking or reasoning and somehow I had a premonition that should I remain in Chicago much longer, shoplifting and doing the various criminal acts I did to get money for drugs, plus the criminal act of just using the drug, I would soon be in jail or perhaps something worse, for in truth one's life is at stake each day when he uses drugs. I reflected on the life I had known in Kansas City with Rose in contrast to the one I had returned to. I didn't know what Rose thought had become of me. I thought that more than likely she was angry and thoroughly disgusted and glad that I was gone. However, I wanted to return but first thought it best to call and see what her feelings were.

[At his wife's urging he returned to Kansas City and undertook a "cold turkey" cure in their home. He remained abstinent for a considerable period but subsequently relapsed again when he returned to Chicago.]

Reflections of the above kind provide the relapsed addict with a rich body of material for self-recrimination and he again evaluates his own conduct in terms of what he believes are the larger society's attitudes toward addicts and addiction. It is then that he may again speculate about his own potential for meaningful experiences and relationships in a non-addict world and thus set into motion a new attempt at cure.

SUMMARY

Addiction to narcotic drugs in our society commits the participant in this activity to a status and identity that has complex secondary characteristics. These develop through shared roles and common interpersonal and institutional experience, and as a consequence addicts develop perspectives about themselves and about non-addict values. They evaluate social situations, and in turn are evaluated by the other participants in these situations, in these terms, often with the result that the value of the addict's identity relative to the social world of addiction is brought into question. When this happens the identification of oneself as an addict, committed to the values and statuses of the addict group, is contrasted with new or remembered identities and relationships, resulting in a commitment to cure with its implications of intense physical suffering. In the period following physical withdrawal from heroin, the addict attempts to enact a new social reality which coincides with his desired self-image as an abstainer, and he seeks ratification of his new identity from others in the situations he faces.

But the abstainer's social expectations during a period when he is off drugs are frequently not gratified. Here again, socially disjunctive experiences bring about a questioning of the value of an abstainer identity and promote reflections in which addict and non-addict identities and relationships are compared. The abstainer's realignment of his values with those of the world of addiction results in the redefinition of self as an addict and has as a consequence the actions necessary to relapse. But it should be noted that the seeds of a new attempt at abstinence are sown, once addiction has been re-established, in the self-recriminations engaged in upon remembrance of a successful period of abstinence.

Notes

1. See as examples: C. Knight Aldrich, "The Relationship of the Concept Formation Test to Drug Addiction and Intelligence," *Journal of Nervous and Mental Diseases*, 100 (July, 1944), pp. 30–34; Margaret E. Hall, "Mental and Physical Efficiency of Women Drug Addicts," *Journal of Abnormal and Social Psychology*, 33 (July, 1938), pp. 332–345; A. Z. Pfeffer and Dorothy Cleck, "Chronic Psychoses and Addiction to Morphine," *Archives of Neurology and Psychiatry*, 56 (December, 1946), pp. 665–672.

2. Michael J. Pescor, *A Statistical Analysis of the Clinical Records of Hospitalized Drug Addicts*, Supplement No. 143 to the Public Health Reports, United States Public Health Service (Washington: Government Printing Office, 1943), p. 24; Victor H. Vogel, "Treatment of the Narcotic Addict by the U.S. Public Health Service," *Federal Probation*, 12 (June, 1948), pp. 45–50.

3. The basic data consisted of case histories collected in repeated depth interviews with 17 addicts and abstainers over a two year period. During this time several of the active addicts became abstainers and vice-versa. Additional material was gathered while the author worked for a year as a social worker in a rehabilitation program for addicts.

4. "Object" is employed here in the sense intended by George Herbert Mead in his development of the concept in *Mind, Self and Society* (Chicago: University of Chicago Press, 1934), Part III, pp. 135–226. Two earlier studies have applied this kind of thinking in studying the behavior of addicts, see: L. Guy Brown, "The Sociological Implications of Drug Addiction," *Journal of Educational Sociology*, 4 (February, 1931), pp. 358–69, and Alfred R. Lindesmith, *Opiate Addiction* (Bloomington, Indiana: Principia Press, 1947).

5. Marsh B. Ray, "Cure and Relapse Among Heroin Addicts" (unpublished M.A. thesis, Department of Sociology, University of Chicago, 1958).

6. For a general discussion of the important role that auxiliary status characteristics play in social situations, see Everett C. Hughes, "Dilemmas and Contradictions in Status," *American Journal of Sociology*, 50 (March, 1945), pp. 253–59.

7. Family members may have been subjected to thefts by the addict, or other kinds of trickery, and they tend to be on their guard lest the experience be repeated. Interestingly, the matter of thefts of either money or small household objects (a radio or a clock) is often used by family members as an index as to whether "he's back on that stuff again" or not. His physical appearance is another gauge.

8. Leroy Street (pseudonym) and D. Loth, *I Was A Drug Addict*, Pyramid Books (New York: Random House, 1953), p. 71.

48 / Alcoholics and the Transformation of Deviant Identity

JACQUELINE P. WISEMAN

RETURN VERSUS BREAKING-IN

In the atmosphere of the institution, with the clear, friendly, logical counsel of the average middle-class professional worker, exhortations to reenter society seem to make a great deal of sense. True, much hard work is demanded, but the plans suggested also appear to offer progress and the goal seems worthwhile. Middle-class nondrinkers seem like the world's happiest people from this vantage point.

When asked what he is going to do upon release from an institution, the Skid Row alcoholic typically says:

> I'm hoping to "make it" in the outside world this time. I'm really going to try and not drink and to get back on the track. . . .

> I'm going to try to get back into society. I know that I've been leading an aimless, useless life. It's really no kind of life for anyone, there on Skid Row. . . .

> I'm going to work on my problem. I'm going to try to get back on my feet and live with the respectable world again. . . .

The Skid Row drunk is encouraged in this stance while in the institution by the professional posture of friendship offered by his therapist and other patients. Psychologists and social workers attempt to "gain rapport" with the patient. The alcoholic is also a part of the pseudo-mutual interaction that is a sought characteristic of group therapy sessions. These institutionally-created social success experiences often make the Skid Row man feel quite capable of inserting himself into any desirable primary group in the "outside world."

It is easy to forget that the environment of friendship at the institution is *contrived*[1] for the express purpose of offering the alcoholic a warm, supportive (therapeutic) community, and that the professionals who do this are actually trained to utilize empathetic techniques as part of their jobs.[2] Mainstream society does not concern itself with being therapeutic, however, and the reaction of the man-on-the-street

677

or the boss-on-the-job to the ex-alcoholic is often a cold wind that clears away the haze of such pretensions to easy acceptance. Thus there is minimum transfer of personal adjustment training from the institution to the outside world.[3] Often this is a reality shock of no mean proportions, one sufficient to send the recipient back to the warm unreality of alcohol.

Furthermore, the fact is that the Skid Row alcoholic is really not *returning* to any niche being held for him in society in the same sense that it often is for the middle class alcoholic.[4] Rather, the Skid Row man is trying to break into mainstream society *for the first time* and he usually must do this without the support of friends or relatives as "starters."[5]

Using current occupation as an indicator, Table 1 is quite suggestive of just how much social distance there is between middle-class society, in general, and the average Skid Row alcoholic's position upon release. (Note the absence of professional, semi-professional, managerial, and technical occupations, as well as skilled workers — the backbone of the middle class. Additionally, almost half of the Row men [43 percent] had *no* employment in the preceding month.)

Table 1 / Social Characteristics of Skid Row Men
(As Indicated by Current Occupation)

Occupation (in month preceding interview)	Percent of Skid Row Men in Pacific City (N = 2,582)
General laborers and construction workers	12
Culinary workers	6
Sales and clerical	5
Hotel managers and clerks	2
Teamsters	4
Longshoremen and warehousemen	3
Seamen and stewards	3
Domestics	1
Other	15
Not reported	6
No employment in preceding month	43

Source: *Pacific City Urban Redevelopment Association Report* (1963).

Furthermore, as was mentioned . . . , the Skid Row man is much more often a man of inadequate skills and education than a man who has "skidded," in the social mobility sense of the term, from a relatively high position down to the bottom of the barrel. A number of studies previously cited indicate many Skid Row alcoholics were never in any stratum of society but were "wanderers" or working or living in institution-like settings from early youth.[6] Others relinquished their social niche so long ago and so completely that they have no one waiting for them to "return." (The possible exception is among those men who still have parents living. But here the choice is not too attractive—living with [and possibly caring for] an aged parent.)[7]

DETAILS OF EXECUTING "THE PLAN"

The plan the Skid Row alcoholic is presented for his "return" to middle-class society is not only demanding, in the face of his social class and occupational limitations, but somewhat skimpy as to details. The plan emphasizes only a few of the needs that he must meet and problems he must overcome to lead any sort of satisfactory existence.

Getting a job, a room, and maintaining sobriety (partially through avoidance of drinking friends) is the gist of the plan, but these maxims do not offer a guide to fulfilling other needs and solving other problems without resorting to Skid Row tactics. What is he to do for social contact, contact with the opposite sex? How is he to get the job, the room, and avoid old friends? How can he change from a today-oriented, no-social-stake person to a future-oriented, middle-class person with margin? How is he to feel a *part* of this middle-class society?

Once the Skid Row alcoholic is "on the streets," the plan is not at all so logical or easy to follow as it seemed to be when presented to him in the institution. His framework for constructing meaning must shift from the professional formulas of the return to a society, which is substantially middle-class in concept, to that of the homeless man coping with day-to-day needs in a world that is alien and unfriendly.

This disjunction in viewpoint inside and outside the institution could easily account for the paucity of reasons offered by the Skid Row alcoholic for drinking excessively again, as well as his apparent insincerity about trying to stay dry. The Row men stop drinking while imbued with the rehabilitator's framework; they start drinking when they *see things differently* on the outside; they are at a loss to explain their lapse when they *return to the rehabilitation framework again,* for the decision to drink was not made within this framework.[8]

If these men were to give a detailed account of the framework that makes taking a drink seem like the most feasible thing to do at the time it is done, they would have to recount their life as experienced while trying to follow the reentry plan. In such a description, the following items are pertinent:

SOCIAL STRUCTURE AND EMPLOYMENT OPPORTUNITIES

Even in times of high employment, it is difficult for a Skid Row alcoholic who has made the loop to get a job. In part, this is because (as has been mentioned) his union membership has lapsed during drinking bouts, or he cannot get a job in his trade as an electrician, metal worker, or one of the other crafts because so much of this work is tied in with contracts demanding security clearance for all workers.

To be unbondable means that the Skid Row man cannot work on many jobs connected with the handling of money or expensive equipment. His status as an alcoholic (or ex-alcoholic) means he cannot work around heavy machinery because of high-risk insurance provisions. Add to this his age, his loss of current experience in his field, and the suspiciously long gaps in his job record (which are hard to explain in any case), and the picture of a virtually unemployable man emerges.

Here is what these men say about the agony of job hunting:

> I know what is going to happen. Everything will be going along all right until they find I didn't work for nine months. When they ask why, and I tell them I was in a mental institution for a drinking problem—that's all, brother. They say, "Don't call us, we'll call you." . . .

> I wish that someone would go in ahead of me and say, "Look, this guy is an ex-alcoholic, but he's okay now. He hasn't had a drink for some time and he's really trying to make it." That would clear the air, and then I could go in and talk about my abilities. . . .

> If I get the job by lying about the past, sure as shootin' they find out.[9] I've been told nine months later that my security clearance didn't work out and I would have to leave even though my work was okay. Now, I'm afraid to accept something for fear I'll just lose it. . . .

> My references are so old that there is no use using them. I don't have any recent ones because all the work I've been doing is in institutions. I was an orderly in the mental hospital and I'd like to work as an orderly now, but I don't dare tell where I got my experience. . . .

A final blow to his job-getting ability is his address and lack of telephone:

> Skid Row is a bad address to have to put down on job applications. Right away they suspect you. And you don't have a telephone either so they can

get in touch with you. I sometimes offer to check back from time to time, but you can see they aren't impressed. . . .

What kind of employment can these men get?

The range is limited to menial jobs with low pay. Such jobs often do not involve the man's former skill, or if they do, they are combined with other, low-status tasks. Gardening and "landscaping" the grounds of the numerous colleges and universities that dot the Pacific City area is a major resource for placement of ex-alcoholics by rehabilitation agents. Custodial work or cafeteria jobs are also available at such institutions. Other non-profit institutions such as hospitals and rest homes hire these men as attendants or orderlies.

In Pacific City itself, the Row men must be willing to work as dishwashers, busboys and on other general clean-up jobs. If they are lucky, they may find employment as an elevator operator or night clerk in a cheap hotel. The Row men who were merchant seamen can try to get their papers reinstated and go back to sea.

If he gets a job, the Skid Row alcoholic finds himself torn between fear of failure and anger at what he conceives to be exploitation.

First of all, as his work experience recedes into dim memory, the Row man loses confidence in his abilities to hold a job. Mistakes and problems that cause a secure jobholder some uneasiness cause the ex-alcoholic trying to "make it" to endure true agony. As one man put it:

You aren't "current" on your job anymore. You forget how to do it. You are certain that people are watching you and saying, "He can't handle it." . . .

Another Row man related the following as what he conceived to be *his failure*, and as the reason he ultimately resumed drinking:

I had a good job in the filing department, it was arranged for me by the Welfare Home, and I was doing well when they put me in charge of six young high school drop-outs on a government project to train them for jobs. I couldn't get them to do anything! I worked and worked with them, but they weren't interested in learning. I felt like I was a failure as a supervisor. It made me so nervous I started taking tranquilizers, but they didn't really help, so one day I just walked out and went back to drinking. I couldn't handle that job. It was too much for me. . . .

Furthermore, the Skid Row man trying to stay dry usually feels he is treated differently than the rest of the employees. He is constantly reminded that he is lucky to have a job. He is often paid less than usually offered for the work.[10] He is asked to do things he does not think should be part of the job (such as mopping floors, when he was hired to do gardening). And he is expected to perform these extra tasks in good spirit. His experience is that if society wants him back at all . . .

it is to exploit him. Often he does as he is told for a while, but the moment comes when anger at what he feels to be an injustice gets the better of him. Years of unemployment have not taught him the discipline of patience on the job, nor does he yet have enough social margin to make the cultivation of such forbearance seem worthwhile, being still "now" oriented. He quits, usually telling the boss off in the bargain (which means no recommendation for future job hunting), and the unemployment part of the cycle starts again.

PROBLEMS OF LIVING QUARTERS

The problems of living quarters, once the Row man is "outside" again, come up almost immediately. Based on the type of job he can get, the Row man can usually afford only a single room, perhaps with cooking privileges, and probably near or in Skid Row. As previously mentioned, a single man who is not well dressed has difficulty renting a room, even in parts of the city that cater to laboring-class families or to single professional men. This is why the reformed alcoholic usually is resigned to living in Skid Row or the Tenderloin, where he blends in better. However, he is living in a drinking culture again.

Skid Row men who are given welfare vouchers through arrangements with jail welfare workers, the Christian Missionaries, the Welfare Home, or on direct appeal to the Welfare office, are sent to Skid Row hotels, inasmuch as the budget for such aid is limited and cannot support numerous men in any but the cheapest of rooms.[11] Skid Row cafes are the only eating establishments that take Welfare food tickets. Thus with the aid of Welfare, the Skid Row man finds himself sent to Skid Row, a drinking culture, and told not to start drinking again.

An alternative housing arrangement is the halfway house. There are quite a few such establishments in Pacific City, but they are not popular with the Skid Row man. Halfway houses are, from his point of view, too much like an institution in their scheduling of meals, lights out, and required attendance at AA meetings. Furthermore, these facilities are used by the state parole board to place prison parolees because this solves some surveillance problems. These ex-convicts are avoided by the Skid Row alcoholic unless he has also done some "hard time." Finally, those Skid Row men who have jobs complain they are constantly "hit up" for money by those without jobs.[12] This combination of association with ex-cons and penniless peers makes the halfway house an atmosphere charged with suspicion, uneasiness, and coolness. As one Skid Row man explained it:

> There isn't much friendliness in a halfway house. You have to be careful who you speak to. Either they are broke and want to put the touch on you, or

they are ex-cons and will take advantage of you. As a result, every man sort of keeps to himself. It's a cold and suspicious place. . . .[13]

SOBRIETY AND SOCIABILITY

The resolution not to drink and to avoid old drinking companions means spending most free time alone. As many of these men said:

I ate all my meals alone. Most of the time, I had to cook them in my room on my hot plate. About once a month, I could afford dinner out, but it's really no fun to eat out alone. . . .

Sometimes, I'd go to an early movie, then home, read in bed a while and go to sleep. Those four walls really close in on you after a while. . . .

I was trying to live on Valoda Street in Gadsen District of Pacific City [working class]. It was very lonesome. I finally went to Skid Row where you know everyone. I hadn't even had anything to drink, but was picked up for drunk. . . .

As previously mentioned, most Skid Row alcoholics do not seek support for their abstinence from liquor by attending local Alcoholics Anonymous meetings or by socializing at AA clubs. AA has never had much appeal for the lower-class alcoholic. It is primarily a middle-class organization, focused on helping ex-alcoholics regain their lost status. Skid Row alcoholics dislike what they refer to as "drunkalogs," in which members tell with relish just how low they had sunk while drinking. They dislike what they call the "snottiness" and "holier-than-thou" attitude of the reformed alcoholic (or "AA virgins" as they call them). The only reason Skid Row men go to AA is to convince another person (someone who would be impressed by such atten-dance) that they are really trying to lick the alcohol problem. As one put it:

I plan to join AA. Then people will believe I'm not drinking. As it is now, if I get drunk for three days, they don't count it if I'm sober for three weeks. . . .

Other Skid Row men tell of going to AA meetings out of desperation for *any* companionship and for the refreshments served. After the meeting, they feel a very strong urge to drink so that life becomes a round of early evening AA sessions followed by late evening drinking, and morning hangovers:

It got so that I just went to AA meetings and from there would get a bottle and go to my room and drink—usually Vodka, and then sober up in time for the next AA meeting. . . .

One might ask why the Skid Row alcoholic does not make friends with co-workers on his new job—if he has found one. The answer given by many of the men is that they have nothing in common with the average worker. Experiences on the loop seem to socialize the Row man so that he is unable to enjoy the company of those who do not share such experiences as living in institutions on the circle, fooling the authorities, panhandling, and general Skid Row adventures.[14] This is especially true if the Skid Row alcoholic has been placed in a gardening or groundskeeper job. His co-workers are seldom urban men, and the Skid Row man keenly misses the presence of the "city" and the men who have knowledge of its many-faceted underlife.[15]

Of new on-the-job acquaintances, the Skid Row drinker says:

They don't speak my language. They are square-Johns. . . .

I got so lonesome for someone who talked my language. You can't talk to some jerks. . . .

I want to talk with someone who knows what I'm talking about. Some guys have never done nothing. . . .[16]

THE PROBLEM WITH WOMEN

A Skid Row man trying to "make it" back into society has a particularly complicated problem so far as women are concerned.

. . . The average Skid Row man is usually quite charming and has no trouble attracting female companions on the Row or partners at the State Mental Hospital. However, neither of these types of women is seen by the alcoholic as a good influence for a man who is attempting to stop drinking. What he wants, in his own words, is "a decent woman."

The problem is, though, that he is shy and awkward about pursuing a woman of this type. As one Skid Row man put it:

It's been so long since I been around a decent woman, I don't know how to act. . . .

Furthermore, if the Skid Row man has recently been in jail, at the Christian Missionaries, in a non-coeducational halfway house, or spending his time in all-male company on the Row, he has lost practice in communicating with women. Wallace quotes one such man's insecurity about women:

Now, how shall I ask one of these girls for a dance? No need of introductions, that much I knew. Which would be best, "C'mon kid, let's prance this out?" Or, "May I have this dance?" How I wished these girls were men. I could talk to men.[17]

Another worry is the lack of acceptable credentials.[18]

What can I offer a decent woman? I have no job and no prospects. If I go with a drinking woman, sure as shootin' I'll wind up drinking again. . . .

As noted, the Skid Row alcoholic does have some access to professional women who would like to mother him, but here he must relinquish any hope of being head of the house, and must settle instead for being sort of a house pet.

THE DAILY ROUTINE

What is the daily round like for this man who is trying to gain some social margin so as to get in and stay in the society depicted by the middle-class professional? The mundane experiences of this project form the framework within which the Skid Row man gives up and takes a drink.

A composite description might go something like this: rise early in a lonely room; breakfast fixed on a hot plate, eaten alone in the room, or eaten alone in a cheap restaurant; ride the bus to work (often quite a distance), because an alcoholic usually has lost his driver's license or cannot afford a car and cannot afford to live near work; work all day at a boring, menial, poorly paid job with dull, unsympathetic (to the alcoholic) co-workers and an unsympathetic (to the alcoholic) boss; return at night to eat dinner alone and watch television in the hotel lobby, or read, attempt to freshen his limited wardrobe, or go to bed, knowing a similar day awaits him tomorrow.

Although he may be seeing a welfare worker or a therapist on a regular basis, the dried-out chronic drunk trying to "make it" discovers his relationship with these professionals is not the same as it was in institutions, and he has no claim on their outside social time for informal friendship.

The solitary status of the Skid Row man also affects his opportunities for *experiencing* success. Success, like margin, is an attribute ascribed by others. The Skid Row man has no friends or relatives to reinforce his determination to "make it" or congratulate him on progress. No one (except for an occasional professional therapist) seems even aware of his efforts to prove worthiness. Respectable society is not an entity, and it neither hands out keys to the city nor certificates of social integration. It seems almost impossible for a Skid Row man to know when he has, indeed, "made it." Certainly, merely going through the motions of being respectable will not necessarily elicit immediate recognizable rewards.[19]

The agents of social control counsel "patience" and that "better things will eventually come." But patience means future-orientation, a psychological state of mind that is foreign to a man who has been operating for many years on here-and-now satisfactions.

The story that follows is typical. The man was first interviewed at the Welfare Home for Homeless Men and then seen about a month later, quite by chance, at County Jail. He explained his lapse this way:

> I got a job at the Green Pine Hotel in the suburbs as janitor. I was terribly lonesome. I had no friends. I was on the job there two weeks and then came down to the city. There's quite a few fellows I know around. I want to be with somebody I know once in a while. I liked the job, but I got lonesome. There's nothing to do and no one to talk to. If I had had companionship, it wouldn't have happened. You get lonesome in one room. . . .

Also revealing is the answer to the question, "How were things out there?", asked of a Skid Row alcoholic who had just returned to jail after two weeks of freedom. He replied:

> Pretty rough! Everything moves so fast. No one knows or cares if you are alive. You just don't fit in anywhere. . . .

GOING FULL CIRCLE: "AND THEN I DECIDED TO HELL WITH IT"

In contrast to a return to the society and reality suggested as a goal by professional rehabilitators, there exists also the Skid Row society with its instant warmth, friendliness, and general conviviality. Here, many of the friends of the job-holding Skid Row alcoholic are living on welfare and spending their time drinking, partying, and making out. The dole in Pacific City provides a standard of living probably only slightly lower than the pay of the first menial job available to the alcoholic just discharged from an institution. The room of the "unreformed drunk" may compare favorably with the room in which the struggling "ex-alcoholic" is living. The amount and quality of food each is able to obtain varies but little, even though the unreformed man may be getting part of his daily bread from missions and other charitable organizations.

Furthermore, having once made the loop and learned its machinations, the Skid Row alcoholic trying to "make it" knows that these institutions are always available to him. Compared to the way he is living while trying to make a comeback, some of the stations that he despised and feared at first seem pleasant in retrospect.[20] Old friends are certain to be in any institutions he should choose (or be sent to). Although "admission to society" is so nebulous as to defy definition or provide any feeling of belonging, admission to an institution is just the opposite. While progress toward the goal of reintegration into society is difficult to apprehend, progress in an institution is well marked. On the inside the alcoholic is often told if he has done well on a task, and may be given a higher status job; in therapy, he is praised for "being honest and not holding back"; at the Christian Missionaries he may be promoted to a better room or a larger gratuity; he may even have "institutional margin" on the basis of past performance.[21] Outside the loop station, in Skid Row society, there are the small triumphs of making out and sharing one's cleverness with friends over a bottle.

Thus where the road into respectable society is cold and lonely, Skid Row and the stations of the loop offer conviviality, feeling of accomplishment, as well as an opportunity to forget the struggle.[22] The Row man can stop seeking an idealized society at the end of the rainbow, stop leading a treadmill existence, and return to being seen by his most significant others as a real person again.[23]

An important character in the "Return of the Prodigal Son" story is the respectable brother who stayed at home and out of trouble. In a very true sense, he epitomizes the general attitude of the average citizen toward anyone who strays from the fold too long or too completely and then expects to be granted amnesty merely by some suffering and an apology.

When asked to come to the party given in honor of the returning prodigal son, the self-righteous brother was angry and said to his father:

> Lo, these many years do I serve thee, neither transgress I at any time thy commandment; and yet thou never gavest me a kid, that I might make merry with my friends; but as soon as this thy son was come, which hath devoured thy living with harlots, thou hast killed for him the fatted calf.
>
> Luke 15:29–30

To which the Skid Row alcoholic might reply, as he gives up the fight for acceptance in the rehabilitator's society and returns to Skid Row living and inevitably a loop institution:

> And then I decided to hell with it, and I started drinking again.

CYCLING OUT

Is there any way off the loop? Besides the few who stick it out long enough to get back sufficient social margin to reclaim a lost existence, what other ways are there for Skid Row men to escape?

There appear to be three major ways off Skid Row:

1. Become a live-in servant for an institution (or, once in a while, for a professional woman).

2. Go into alcoholic rehabilitation as a profession.
3. Die.

The first has been amply discussed. Ex-alcoholics may be found at many nonprofit institutions, especially hospitals and rest homes, for some small wages plus board and room. This becomes, then, their new way of life.

The second escape route has possibly been traveled successfully by more alcoholics than is generally known. During the course of this study, the number of ex-alcoholics in positions of agents of social control on the loop was astounding. Ex-alcoholics can be found in administrative positions in the Courts, County Jail, the City Hospital, the State Mental Hospital, Welfare Home for Homeless Men, and the Christian Missionaries.

Other ex-alcoholics are to be found making a career of operating Alcoholics Anonymous clubs, halfway houses, and therapy groups. The newest halfway house for men to be started under the sponsorship of the Pacific City Department of Public Health will be manned by ex-alcoholics.

The factors underlying the success of this maneuver to get off the loop may well center about the fact that "going into rehab work" converts what is a vice in the outside world (i.e., excessive drinking, institutionalization, familiarity with other alcoholics, and absence of recent job experience) into an employable virtue. Indeed, this idea has been formally accepted by many agencies concerned with reform and rehabilitation of deviants.[24] "It takes one to know and understand one" philosophy prevails. Paradoxically, however, the assumption an ex-alcoholic will be more understanding in working with alcoholics has not generally held true if we are to accept the testimony of the men they work with. Alcoholics complain that, "There's nothing colder than an ex-alcoholic," which suggests that once a man makes it to "the right side" he no longer empathizes with former buddies but rather identifies with the associates of his newly-established status—other agents of social control.[25]

Death is the third way off the loop. Six Row men died in Pacific City during the course of this study of such causes as acute alcoholism, cirrhosis of the liver, brutal beatings in an alley, a seizure, and an internal hemorrhage. Men who get off the loop permanently in this way have long ago given up the right for reentrance into society. After a few such attempts they unhesitatingly take a drink the moment they leave an institution. Such men can be roughly divided into two types—both of whom accept the consequences of the bridges they have burned and the lonely life that will be their future.

They are:

1. *The so-called institutionalized man*, the perennial and resigned

loop maker. This includes the chronic drunkenness offender who uses the jail as an emergency hotel in bad weather, the self-admitted State Hospital man who uses that institution for drying out and building up both physically and financially, and the mission rounder who, cursing the hand who feeds him, still goes back when forced by hunger and illness.

2. *The Welfare Skid Row man* who "graduates" to vouchers and settles down to living on what his check provides, plus what he can earn on pick-up jobs. He drinks heavily except on the days he has an appointment with his social worker. Intermittent institutionalizations keep him alive.

Both these types of Row men are trapped on the loop. Death is their only avenue of escape.

Notes

1. This is not to say that professional rehabilitation workers are not sincere in their feelings of friendship toward their patients or clients. It is rather that these friendships are not of the type to carry past quitting time, when the off-duty professional usually prefers the company of persons of his own educational and social background.

Alcoholics are not the only persons to mistake professional friendliness for the genuine thing. The following was overheard at County Jail between ex-state prison inmates who were discussing parole officers:

At least those guys who go by the book, you know what they are going to do. You don't overestimate their show of friendliness and get out of line and get slapped down. (Overheard while observing in the Jail.)

2. See, for instance, William Schofield, *Psychotherapy, the Purchase of Friendship* (Englewood Cliffs, N.J.: Prentice-Hall, 1964).

3. See Robert Rapaport, *Community as Doctor: New Perspectives on a Therapeutic Community* (London: Tavistock Publications, 1959; and Springfield, Illinois: Charles C. Thomas, 1960), for a discussion of the deliberate creation of a permissive, security-oriented atmosphere that is no doubt helpful in reducing anxieties in patients but bears little resemblance to the less well-planned outside world.

4. For the middle-class returnee, the problem is one of breaking down the counter-role relationships that were built up during the heavy drinking period when they were "irresponsible," according to middle-class standards. The middle-class ex-alcoholic's problems in overcoming the dependency relationships he helped to create have been well-chronicled. See Joan K. Jackson, "Family Structure and Alcoholism," *Mental Hygiene* (July 1959), 403–7. Jackson points out that "if the husband does stop drinking, he is usually permitted to exercise his family roles *only on probation*." (Emphasis mine.)

5. At least, there usually are no relatives to whom he is willing or able to return. Sometimes this is by choice. As one man put it:

I got to straighten myself out *before* I go to see my family. I can't let them see me this way. . . .

Another said:

Most of us would starve rather than call our relatives. That relationship is *over*. . . .

6. This is not intended to suggest that the Skid Row alcoholic was not of some higher status before coming to Skid Row. By the very term "bottom of the barrel" Skid Row residents suggest they were higher at *some* time, at least in their own eyes. However, both Donald J. Bogue, in *Skid Row in American Cities* (Chicago: University

of Chicago Press, 1963), pp. 320–22, and Howard M. Bahr, *Homelessness and Disaffiliation* (New York: Columbia University Bureau of Applied Social Research, 1968), pp. 220–30, indicate that these men started out in the lower portion of the status continuum and rose only slightly before losing status. As previously mentioned, skidding from high status to Skid Row happens in only a few well-publicized cases.

Pittman and Gordon's study of the chronic police case inebriate produced the following socio-economic characteristics, scarecely indicative of middle-class status:

Approximately . . .
90 percent are skilled and unskilled workers (as compared with 59 percent of the general population)
75 percent had only a grade school education (as compared with 41 percent of the general population)
85 percent had no permanent residence, lived at a mission or shelter, a hotel or shelter, a hotel or rooming house (as compared with 21 percent of the general population).

See David J. Pittman and C. Wayne Gordon, *Revolving Door* (Glencoe, Ill.: The Free Press, 1958), Chap. 2, "The Sociocultural Profile," pp. 16–58.

Bogue, *Skid Row in American Cities*, pp. 13–14, reports that, "in comparison with the adult population of the city of Chicago as a whole, the . . . Skid Row men are:

a. Foreign born white or "other nonwhite" race (American Indian).
b. Single, widowed, or divorced: half have never married.
c. Middle-aged or older men, concentrated in the ages of 45–74.
d. Very poorly educated, with more than one-fifth being "functionally illiterate" (having completed fewer than five years of elementary school).
e. Unemployed. The unemployment rate among the Skid Row men was more than eight times that of the general population.
f. Not in the labor force, with "unable to work" as the primary reason.
g. Employed as wage or salary workers.
h. Of extremely low income, with almost one-half living on less than $90 per month. Almost one-fourth of the men had received less than $500 in cash during the preceding year.

7. Agents of social control report a large proportion of Skid Row alcoholics keep in contact (usually through correspondence) with their mothers. (Maintenance of this mother-son tie is often cited by those Freudianly inclined group therapy leaders as evidence many alcoholics have not passed the oedipus crisis successfully, are latently homosexual as a result, and thus drink to forget the guilt attached to this perversion. Of course, there are no comparative figures on the proportion of nonalcoholic males who maintain contact with their mothers.)

8. The fact there are an infinite number of mental frameworks, and a given individual may use more than one on the same phenomena, was discussed in chapter 1 to explain how Skid Row may be seen as both a disgusting and exciting place in which to live.

The point is that motivation to act is not, as seen by conventional psychological theory, the result of either inner personality characteristics or external cues alone but is rather the result of the way in which the situation is defined by the actor. The "wisdom" of a given plan of action is dependent upon the ground rules for such wisdom—that is, the theoretical framework by which the ingredients of the situation are "understood." When presumably intelligent individuals do things and later admit they "should have known better," they are referring to the fact they are now viewing the action from another, less sympathetic framework.

9. Joan Emerson has suggested the Skid Row alcoholic (often accused of being a con-artist) apparently does not know how to lie sensibly in an employment interview situation. He either lacks the middle-class job-seeker's training in fictionalizing his job experience and covering up embarrassing spots with plausible excuses, or he has become out of practice in such activity.

10. . . . Skid Row men are often exploited by employers who pay them below-standard or state-minimum wages, taking advantage of their desperate need for work

and money. Bogue, in *Skid Row in American Cities*, p. 492, also noted this in his study of the Chicago Skid Row and incorporated the following into his recommendations for eliminating the area:

The minimum-wage laws are openly broken, both in spirit and in deed, along Skid Row. Some industries . . . manage to get their work done at rates as low as fifty cents an hour, by declaring the men . . . are independent operators. Skid Row hotels and restaurants also pay very low wages to night watchmen, janitors, and dishwashers. By making a tie-in arrangement between salary and room or board, the man gets paid less than the minimum wage, even when his pay check and benefits are given their combined cash value. . . . A careful review of minimum-wage compliance should be made of every hotel, restaurant, mission, employment agency, and firm known to employ numbers of Skid Row men.

11. It seems strange that Pacific City Welfare officials do not see any contradiction in returning an alcoholic to live in a Skid Row hotel after he has been dried out and his health rebuilt at their Welfare Home for Homeless Men. When I was first granted permission to interview men at the Welfare Home for Homeless Men, the director said, as he bemoaned the high rate of recidivism among alcoholics:

If you can tell us why, after all we try to do for these men, that they go right back to Skid Row and drinking, you will be doing a great service with your research project.
. . .

12. Earl Rubington has done some of the few analyses of the problem of operating or living in a halfway house. (The tone of most literature on halfway houses reads like annual reports—glowingly successful.) Rubington outlines the problems faced by ex-alcoholic administrators in "Organizational Strains and Key Roles," *Administrative Science Quarterly*, 9, No. 4 (March 1965), 350–69, and the panhandling problems Skid Row alcoholics face within the halfway house itself. See "Panhandling and the Skid Row Subculture," paper read at 53rd Annual Meeting of the American Sociological Society (Seattle, Washington, August 28, 1958).

13. My limited visits to halfway houses seem to confirm this. They are *very* quiet and the atmosphere is "cold." At one co-educational house, men and women could not eat meals at the same table. There was little talking in either the lounge or the coffee room. The alcoholism units at State Mental Hospital were swinging places by comparison.

14. . . . these subjects constitute a substantial proportion of small talk among Skid Row men.

15. Howard M. Bahr has been engaged in some well-constructed tests of generally-accepted hypotheses concerning life on Skid Row with special emphasis on the area of socialization. His findings seem to indicate Skid Row men develop a rather strong attachment to Skid Row drinking companions, which aid in their identification with the Row and their feelings of alienation off the Row. See Howard M. Bahr and Stephen J. Langfur, "Social Attachment and Drinking in Skid Row Life Histories," *Social Problems*, 14, No. 4 (Spring 1967), 464–72. Also, see Howard M. Bahr, "Drinking, Interaction, and Identification: Notes on Socialization into Skid Row," *Journal of Health and Social Behavior*, 8, No. 4 (December 1967), 272–85.

16. The experience of being "on the other side" apparently does not leave a man unmarked psychologically and, paradoxically, although it is degrading, it is simultaneously a source of pride to have survived it. As a survivor, a man actually feels superior to those who have not had this experience, and this creates a chasm between deviants and non-deviants that may never be closed again. John Irwin, in his study, *The Felon* (Englewood Cliffs, N.J.: Prentice-Hall, 1970), speaks of "the enduring affinity" ex-convicts have for each other—others with the same experience. It is also said that drug addicts at Synanon still consider themselves "hipper" than the nonuser.

17. Samuel E. Wallace, *Skid Row as a Way of Life* (Totowa, N.J.: The Bedminister Press, 1965), p. 174.

18. George Orwell, in *Down and Out in Paris and London* (New York: Harcourt, Brace & World Company, 1933), p. 148, speaks of "the degradation worked in a man who knows that he is not even considered fit for marriage. . . . Cut off from the whole race of women, a tramp feels himself degraded to the rank of a cripple or a lunatic. No humiliation could do more damage to a man's self-respect."

19. Additionally, trying and failing to gain acceptance is much more ego-debilitating

than not trying at all. Like going through college rush week and not getting a bid from a sorority or fraternity, there is no longer any doubt about your social acceptance with a group deemed desirable. The Skid Row alcoholic, in his efforts to get back into society may also encounter a "reality shock" not intended by his rehabilitators — that of finding that he is socially undesirable to the society he seeks, regardless of his efforts to the contrary.

20. Before it happens, the thought of being sent to jail for drunkenness, or going to a mental hospital for "the cure," seems like one of the worst experiences that a man can have. However, when he finds he *can* survive it, going through the same thing again holds fewer terrors. At times he even feels strengthened by the experience. Jack Black, a confessed thief of all trades, explains this phenomenon in terms of his reactions to the whipping post (*You Can't Win* [New York: The Macmillan Co., 1927], p. 278):

> As a punishment, it's a success; as a deterrent it's a failure; if it's half and half, one offsets the other and there's nothing gained. The truth is I wouldn't have quit no matter how I was treated. The flogging just hardened me more, that's all. I found myself somewhat more determined. . . . I had taken everything they had in the way of violence and could take it again. Instead of going away in fear, I found my fears removed. *The whipping post is a strange place to gather fresh confidence and courage, yet that's what it gave me. . . .*

. . . Furthermore, while the quest for society is fraught with uncertainty, life in an institution offers security of rules and regulations plus provisions for all the exigencies of living which are a problematic struggle on "the outside."

21. Howard Bahr's analysis of the relationship of drinking and social disaffiliation to presumed "institutionalization" indicates that it is not the simple one-to-one relationship some persons have thought. Rather, it is a complicated, interactive process. Howard M. Bahr, "Institutional Life, Drinking, and Disaffiliation," a paper read at the 1968 annual meeting of the Society for the Study of Social Problems in Boston.

22. It could be the grinding monotony of regular but boring and often physically demanding work, the lack of desirable or interesting companions, and the bleakness of his living quarters contribute to a certain "flatness" of experience quite unlike the little adventures the Skid Row alcoholic has enjoyed both in institutions and on the Row. Just as soldiers returning from the war find civilian life flat at first so may the Skid Row man find the square life dull.

23. It is indeed a paradox that the Skid Row man must return to an *ad hoc* existence (where neither his past nor his future is seriously affected by present adventures) to feel he is accepted as a real person. Only on Skid Row, where times of pleasure are momentarily "sealed off" from their consequences, can he enjoy himself. When he is working at his low-status job and living his ascetic "attempting-to-make-it" life, he has all the burdens of responsibility to the past and cognizance of the future without any of the rewards.

24. See, for instance, National Institute of Mental Health, *Experiments in Culture Expansion*, Report of proceedings of a conference on "The Use of Products of a Social Problem in Coping with the Problem" (Norco, California, July 1963), and *Offenders as a Correctional Manpower Resource*, Report of a seminar convened by the Joint Commission on Correctional Manpower and Training (Washington, D.C., March 1968). Erving Goffman has called the phenomenon of the deviant using his stigma to advantage as "going into business for himself." "Twelfth-step work" in Alcoholics Anonymous and Synanon (for drug users) are other examples of this phenomenon.

25. An excellent description of the way in which the ex-alcoholic seeks to identify with agents of social control to the extent that he is actually rude to ex-drinking partners is to be found in Earl Rubington's "Grady 'Breaks Out': A Case Study of an Alcoholic's Relapse," *Social Problems*, 11, No. 4 (Spring 1964), 372–80. This phenomenon of upwardly mobile low-caste persons turning with vehemence upon those who were formerly "their own kind" has been noted by many sociologists and psychologists, and has been given many labels including "identification with the aggressor," and "self-hatred of one's membership in a despised group." . . .

49 / Delabeling, Relabeling, and Alcoholics Anonymous

HARRISON M. TRICE
PAUL MICHAEL ROMAN

An increasing amount of research emphasis in social psychiatry in recent years has been placed upon the rehabilitation and return of former mental patients to "normal" community roles (Sussman, 1966). The concomitant rapid growth of community psychiatry as a psychiatric paradigm parallels this interest, with community psychiatry having as a primary concern the maintenance of the patient's statuses within the family and community throughout the treatment process so as to minimize problems of rehabilitation and "return" (Pasamanick *et al.*, 1967; Susser, 1968). Despite these emphases, successful "delabeling" or destigmatization of mental patients subsequent to treatment appears rare (Miller, 1965; Freeman and Simmons, 1963). It is the purpose of this paper to explore an apparent negative instance of this phenomenon, namely a type of social processing which results in *successful* delabeling, wherein the stigmatized label is replaced with one that is socially acceptable.

The so-called labeling paradigm which has assumed prominence within the sociology of deviant behavior offers a valuable conceptualization of the development of deviant careers, many of which are apparently permanent (Scheff, 1966). In essence, labeling theory focuses upon the processes whereby a "primary deviant" becomes a "secondary deviant" (Lemert, 1951: 75–76). Primary deviance may arise from myriad sources. The extent and nature of the social reaction to this behavior is a function of the deviant's reaction to his own behavior (Roman and Trice, 1969), the behavior's visibility, the power vested in the statuses of the deviant actor, and the normative parameters of tolerance for deviance that exist within the community. Primary deviance that is visible and exceeds the tolerance level of the community may bring the actor to the attention of mandated labelers such as psychiatrists, clinical psychologists, and social workers.

If these labelers see fit "officially" to classify the actor as a type of deviant, a labeling process occurs which eventuates in (1) self concept changes on the part of the actor and (2) changes in the definitions of

693

him held by his immediate significant others, as well as the larger community. Behavior which occurs as a consequence of these new definitions is called secondary deviance. This behavior is substantively similar to the original primary deviance but has as its source the actor's revised self concept, as well as the revised social definition of him held in the community.

Previous research and theoretical literature appear to indicate that this process is irreversible, particularly in the cases of mental illness or so-called residual deviance (Miller, 1965; Myers and Bean, 1968). No systematic effort has been made to specify the social mechanisms which might operate to "return" the stigmatized secondary deviant to a "normal" and acceptable role in the community. In other words, delabeling and relabeling have received little attention as a consequence of the assumption that deviant careers are typically permanent.

Conceptually, there appear to be at least three ways whereby delabeling could successfully occur. First, organizations of deviants may develop which have the primary goal of changing the norms of the community or society, such that their originally offending behavior becomes acceptable (Sagarin, 1967). For example, organized groups of homosexuals have strongly urged that children be educated in the dual existence of homosexuality and heterosexuality as equally acceptable forms of behavior.

Secondly, it is possible that the mandated professionals and organizations who initially label deviant behavior and process the deviant through "treatment" may create highly visible and explicit "delabeling" or "status-return" ceremonies which constitute legitimized public pronouncements that the offending deviance has ceased and the actor is eligible for re-entry into the community. Such ceremonies could presumably be the reverse of "status degradation" rituals (Garfinkel, 1957).

A third possible means is through the development of mutual aid organizations which encourage a return to strict conformity to the norms of the community as well as creating a stereotype which is socially acceptable. Exemplary of this strategy is Alcoholics Anonymous. Comprised of 14,150 local groups in the United States in 1967, this organization provides opportunities for alcoholics to join together in an effort to cease disruptive and deviant drinking behavior in order to set the stage for the resumption of normal occupational, marital, and community roles (Gellman, 1964).

The focus of this paper is the apparent success in delabeling that has occurred through the social processing of alcoholics through Alcoholics Anonymous and through alcoholics' participation in the A.A. subculture. The formulation is based chiefly on participant observation over the past 15 years in Alcoholics Anonymous and data from various of our studies of the social aspects of alcoholism and deviant drinking. These observations are supplemented by considerable contact with other "self-help" organizations. These experiences are recognized as inadequate substitutes for "hard" data; and the following points are best considered as exploratory hypotheses for further research.

THE "ALLERGY" CONCEPT

The chronic problem affecting the re-acceptance into the community of former mental patients and other types of deviants is the attribution of such persons with taints of permanent "strangeness," immorality, or "evil." A logical method for neutralizing such stigma is the promulgation of ideas or evidence that the undesirable behavior of these deviants stems from factors beyond their span of control and responsibility. In accord with Parsons' (1951) cogent analysis of the socially neutralizing effects of the "sick role," it appears that permanent stigmatization may be avoided if stereotypes of behavior disorders as forms of "illness" can be successfully diffused in the community.

Alcoholics Anonymous has since its inception attempted to serve as such a catalyst for the "delabeling" of its members through promulgating the "allergy concept" of alcohol addiction. Although not part of official A.A. literature, the allergy concept plays a prominent part in A.A. presentations to non-alcoholics as well as in the A.A. "line" that is used in "carrying the message" to non-member deviant drinkers. The substance of the allergy concept is that those who become alcoholics possess a physiological allergy to alcohol such that their addiction is predetermined even before they take their first drink. Stemming from the allergy concept is the label of "arrested alcoholic" which A.A. members place on themselves.

The significance of this concept is that it serves to diminish, both in the perceptions of the A.A. members and their immediate significant others, the alcoholic's responsibility for developing the behavior disorder. Furthermore, it serves to diminish the impression that a form of mental illness underlies alcohol abuse. In this vein, A.A. members are noted for their explicit denial of any association between alcoholism and psychopathology. As a basis for a "sick role" for alcoholics, the allergy concept effectively reduces blame upon one's *self* for the development of alcoholism.

Associated with this is a very visible attempt on the part of A.A. to associate itself with the medical profession. Numerous publications of the organization have dealt with physicians and A.A. and with physicians who are members of A.A. (*Grapevine*, 1968). Part of this may be related to the fact that one of the co-founders was a physician; and a current long time leader is also a physician. In any event, the strong attempts to associate A.A. with the medical profession stand in contrast to the lack of such efforts to become associated with such professions as law, education, or the clergy.

Despite A.A.'s emphasis upon the allergy concept, it appears clear that a significant portion of the American public does not fully accept the notion that alcoholism and disruptive deviant drinking are the result of an "allergy" or other organic aberration. Many agencies associated with the treatment of alcohol-related problems have attempted to make "alcoholism is an illness" a major theme of mass educational efforts (Plaut, 1967). Yet in a study of 1,213 respondents, Mulford and Miller (1964) found that only 24 percent of the sample "accepted the illness concept without qualification." Sixty-five percent of the respondents regarded the alcoholic as "sick," but most qualified this judgment by adding that he was also "morally weak" or "weak-willed."

The motivation behind public agencies' efforts at promulgating the "illness" concept of behavior disorders to reduce the probability of temporary or permanent stigmatization was essentially upstaged by A.A. Nonetheless, the data indicate that acceptance of the "illness" notion by the general public is relatively low in the case of alcoholism and probably lower in the cases of other behavior disorders (cf. Nunnally, 1961). But the effort has not been totally without success. Thus it appears that A.A.'s allergy concept does set the stage for reacceptance of the alcoholic by part of the population. A more basic function may involve the operation of the A.A. program itself; acceptance of the allergy concept by A.A. members reduces the felt need for "personality change" and may serve to raise diminished self-esteem.

Other than outright acceptance of the allergy or illness notion, there appear to be several characteristics of deviant drinking behavior which reduce the ambiguity of the decision to re-accept the deviant into the community after his deviance has ceased.

Unlike the ambiguous public definitions of the causes of other behavior disorders (Nunnally, 1961), the behaviors associated with alcohol addiction are viewed by the community as a direct consequence of the inappropriate use of alcohol. With the cessation of drinking behavior, the accompanying deviance is assumed to disappear. Thus, what is basically wrong with an alcoholic is that he drinks. In the case of other psychiatric disorders the issue of "what is wrong" is much less clear. This lack of clarity underlies Scheff's (1966) notion of psychiatric disorders as comprising "residual" or relatively unclassifiable forms of deviance. Thus the mentally ill, once labeled, acquire such vague but threatening stereotypes as "strange," "different," and "dangerous" (Nunally, 1961). Since the signs of the disorder are vague in terms of cultural stereotypes, it is most difficult for the "recovered" mental patient to convince others that he is "cured."

It appears that one of the popular stereotypes of former psychiatric patients is that their apparent normality is a "coverup" for their continuing underlying symptoms. Thus, where the alcoholic is able to remove the cause of his deviance by ceasing drinking, such a convincing removal may be impossible in the case of the other addictions and "mental" disorders. Narcotic addiction represents an interesting middle ground between these two extremes, for the cultural stereotype of a person under the influence of drugs is relatively unclear, such that it may be relatively difficult for the former addict to convince others that he has truly removed the cause of his deviance. This points up the fact that deviant drinking and alcoholism are continuous with behavior engaged in by the majority of the adult population, namely "normal" drinking (Mulford, 1964). The fact that the deviant drinker and alcohol addict are simply carrying out a common and normative behavior to excess reduces the "mystery" of the alcoholic experience and creates relative confidence in the average citizen regarding his abilities to identify a truly "dry" alcoholic. Thus the relative clarity of the cultural stereotype regarding the causes of deviance accompanying alcohol abuse provides much better means for the alcoholic to claim he is no longer a deviant.

To summarize, A.A. promulgates the allergy concept both publicly and privately, but data clearly indicate that this factor alone does not account for the observed success at "re-entry" achieved by A.A. members. Despite ambiguity in public definitions of the etiology of alcoholism, its continuity with "normal" drinking behavior results in greater public confidence in the ability to judge the results of a therapeutic program. An understanding of A.A.'s success becomes clearer when this phenomenon is coupled with the availability of the "repentant" role.

THE REPENTANT ROLE

A relatively well-structured status of the "repentant" is clearly extant in American cultural tradition. Upward mobility from poverty and the "log cabin" comprises a social type where the individual "makes good" for his background and the apparent lack of conformity to economic norms of his ancestors. Redemptive religion, emergent largely in American society, emphasizes that one can correct a moral lapse even of long duration by public admission of guilt and repentance (cf. Lang and Lang, 1960).

The A.A. member can assume this repentant role; and it may become a social vehicle whereby, through contrite and remorseful public expressions, substantiated by visibly reformed behavior in conformity to the norms of the community, a former deviant can enter a new role which is quite acceptable to society. The re-acceptance may not be entirely complete, however, since the label of alcoholic is replaced with that of "arrested alcoholic"; as Gusfield (1967) has stated, the role comprises a social type of a "repentant deviant." The acceptance of the allergy concept by his significant others may well hasten his re-acceptance, but the more important factor seems to be the relative clarity by which significant others can judge the deviant's claim to "normality." Ideally the repentant role is also available to the former mental patient; but as mentioned above, his inability to indicate clearly the removal of the symptoms of his former deviance typically blocks such an entry.

If alcohol is viewed in its historical context in American society, the repentant role has not been uniquely available to A.A. members. As an object of deep moral concern, no single category of behavior (with the possible exception of sexual behavior) has been laden with such emotional intensity in American society. Organized social movements previous to A.A. institutionalized means by which repentants could control their use of alcohol. These were the Washingtonians, Catch-My-Pal, and Father Matthews movements in the late 1800's and early 1900's, which failed to gain widespread social acceptance. Thus not only is the repentant role uniquely available to the alcoholic at the present time, but Alcoholics Anonymous has been built on a previous tradition.

SKID ROW IMAGE AND SOCIAL MOBILITY

The major facet of Alcoholics Anonymous' construction of a repentant role is found in the "Skid Row image" and its basis for upward social mobility. A central theme in the "stories" of many A.A. members is that of downward mobility into Skid Row or near Skid Row situations. Research evidence suggests that members tend to come from the middle and lower middle classes (Trice, 1962; Straus and Bacon, 1951). Consequently a "story" of downward mobility illustrates the extent to which present members had drastically fallen from esteem on account of their drinking. A.A. stories about "hitting bottom" and the many degradation ceremonies that they experienced in entering this fallen state act to legitimize their claims to downward mobility. Observation and limited evidence suggests that many of these stories are exaggerated to some degree and that a large proportion of A.A. members maintained at least partially stable status-sets throughout the addiction process. However, by the emphasis on downward mobility due to drinking, the social mobility "distance" traveled by the A.A. member is maximized in the stories. This clearly sets the stage for impressive "comeback accomplishments."

Moral values also play a role in this process. The stories latently emphasize the "hedonistic underworld" to which the A.A. member "traveled." His current status illustrates to others that he has rejected this hedonism and has clearly resubmitted himself to the normative controls and values of the dominant society, exemplified by his A.A. membership. The attempt to promulgate the "length of the mobility trip" is particularly marked in the numerous anonymous appearances that A.A. members make to tell their stories before school groups, college classes, church groups, and service clubs. The importance of these emphases may be indirectly supported by the finding that lower-class persons typically fail in their attempts to successfully affiliate with A.A., i.e., their social circumstances minimize the distance of the downward mobility trip (Trice and Roman, 1970; Trice, 1959).

A.A. AND AMERICAN VALUES

The "return" of the A.A. member to normal role performance through the culturally provided role of the repentant and through the implied social mobility which develops out of an emphasis upon the length of the mobility trip is given its meaning through tapping directly into certain major American value orientations.

Most importantly, members of Alcoholics Anonymous have regained self control and have employed that self control in bringing about their rehabilitation. Self control, particularly that which involves the avoidance of pleasure, is a valued mode of behavior deeply embedded in the American ethos (Williams, 1960). A.A. members have, in a sense, achieved success in their battle with alcohol and may be thought of in that way as being "self-made" in a society permeated by "a systematic moral orientation by which conduct is judged" (Williams, 1960:424). This illustration of self control lends itself to positive sanction by the community.

A.A. also exemplifies three other value orientations as they have been delineated by Williams: humanitarianism, emphases upon practicality, and suspicion of established authority (Williams, 1960:397–470). A definite tendency exists in this society to identify with the helpless, particularly those who are not responsible for their own afflictions.

A.A. taps into the value of efficiency and practicality through its pragmatism and forthright determination to "take action" about a problem. The organization pays little heed to theories about alcoholism and casts all of its literature in extremely practical language. Much emphasis is placed upon the simplicity of its tenets and the straightforward manner in which its processes proceed.

Its organizational pattern is highly congruous with the value, suspicion of vested authority. There is no national or international hierarchy of officers, and local groups maintain maximum autonomy. Within the local group, there are no established patterns of leadership, such that the organization proceeds on a basis which sometimes approaches anarchy. In any event, the informality and equalitarianism are marked features of the organization, which also tend to underline the self control possessed by individual members.

A.A.'s mode of delabeling and relabeling thus appears in a small degree to depend upon promulgation of an allergy concept of alcoholism which is accepted by some members of the general population. Of greater importance in this process is the effective contrivance of a repentant role. Emphasis upon the degradation and downward mobility experienced during the development of alcoholism provides for the ascription of considerable self control to middle-class members, which in turn may enhance their prestige and "shore up" their return to "normality." The repentance process is grounded in and reinforced by the manner in which the A.A. program taps into several basic American value orientations.

A.A.'S LIMITATIONS

As mentioned above, A.A. affiliation by members of the lower social classes is frequently unsuccessful. This seems to stem from the middle-class orientation of most of the A.A. programs, from the fact that it requires certain forms of public confessions and intense interpersonal interaction which may run contrary to the images of masculinity held in the lower classes, as well as interpersonal competence.

Perhaps an equally significant limitation is a psychological selectivity in the affiliation process. A recent followup study of 378 hospitalized alcoholics, all of whom had been intensely exposed to A.A. during their treatment, revealed that those who successfully affiliated with A.A. upon their re-entry into the community had personality features significantly different from those who did not affiliate (Trice and Roman, 1970). The successful affiliates were more guilt prone, sensitive to responsibility, more serious, and introspective. This appears to indicate a definite "readiness" for the adoption of the repentant role among successful affiliates. To a somewhat lesser extent, the affiliates possessed a greater degree of measured ego strength, affiliative needs, and group dependency, indicating a "fit" between the peculiar demands for intense interaction required for successful affiliation and the personalities of the successful affiliates. Earlier research also revealed a relatively high need for affiliation among A.A. affiliates as compared to those who were unsuccessful in the affiliation process (Trice, 1959).

These social class and personality factors definitely indicate the A.A. program is not effective for all alcoholics. Convincing entry into the repentant role, as well as successful interactional participation in the program, appear to require middle-class background and certain personality predispositions.

SUMMARY

In summary, we shall contrast the success of A.A. in its delabeling with that experienced by other self help groups designed for former drug addicts and mental patients (Wechsler, 1960; Landy and Singer, 1961). As pointed out above, the statuses of mental patients and narcotic addicts lack the causal clarity accompanying the role of alcoholic. It is most difficult for narcotic addicts and former mental patients to remove the stigma since there is little social clarity about the cessation of the primary deviant behavior. Just as there is no parallel in this respect, there is no parallel in other self-help organizations with the Skid Row image and the status-enhancing "mobility trip" that is afforded by this image. The primary deviant behaviors which lead to the label of drug addict or which eventuate in mental hospitalization are too far removed from ordinary social experience for easy acceptance of the former deviant to occur. These behaviors are a part of an underworld from which return is most difficult. On the other hand, Alcoholics Anonymous possesses, as a consequence of the nature of the disorder of alcoholism, its uniqueness as an organization, and the existence of certain value orientations within American society, a pattern of social processing whereby a labeled deviant can become "delabeled" as a stigmatized deviant and relabeled as a former and repentant deviant.

References

Anonymous
  1968 "Doctors, alcohol and A.A." Alcoholics Anonymous Grapevine, October, 1968, entire number.
Freeman, H., and O. Simmons
  1963 The Mental Patient Comes Home. New York: Wiley.

Garfinkel, H.
   1957 "Conditions of successful degradation ceremonies." American Journal of Sociology 61 (November): 420–425.
Gellman, I.
   1964 The Sober Alcoholic. New Haven: College and University Press.
Gusfield, J.
   1967 "Moral passage: The symbolic process in public designations of deviance." Social Problems 15 (Winter): 175–188.
Landy, D., and S. Singer
   1961 "The social organization and culture of a club for former mental patients." Human Relations 14 (January): 31–40.
Lang, K., and G. Lang
   1960 "Decisions for Christ: Billy Graham in New York City." Pp. 415–427 in M. Stein et al. (eds.), Identity and Anxiety. New York: The Free Press.
Lemert, E.
   1951 Social Pathology. New York: McGraw-Hill.
Miller, D.
   1965 Worlds That Fail. Sacramento, California: California Department of Mental Hygiene.
Mulford, H.
   1964 "Drinking and deviant drinking, U.S.A., 1963." Quarterly Journal of Studies on Alcohol, 25 (December): 634–650.
Mulford, H., and D. Miller
   1964 "Measuring public acceptance of the alcoholic as a sick person." Quarterly Journal of Studies on Alcohol, 25 (June): 314–323.
Myers, J., and L. Bean
   1968 A Decade Later. New York: Wiley.
Nunnally, J.
   1961 Popular Conceptions of Mental Health. New York: Holt, Rinehart and Winston.
Parsons, T.
   1951 The Social System. Glencoe, Ill.: The Free Press.
Pasamanick, B. et al.
   1967 Schizophrenics in the Community. New York: Appleton, Century, Crofts.
Plaut, T.
   1967 Alcohol Problems: A Report to the Nation. New York: Oxford University Press.
Roman, P., and H. Trice
   1969 "The self reaction: A neglected dimension of labeling theory." Presented at American Sociological Association Meetings, San Francisco.
Sagarin, E.
   1967 "Voluntary associations among social deviants." Criminologica 5 (January): 8–22.
Scheff, T.
   1966 Being Mentally Ill. Chicago: Aldine.

Susser, M.
1968 Community Psychiatry. New York: Random House.
Sussman, M. (ed.)
1966 Sociology and Rehabilitation. Washington: American Sociological Association.
Straus, R., and S. Bacon
1951 "Alcoholism and social stability." Quarterly Journal of Studies on Alcohol 12 (June): 231–260.
Trice, H.
1959 "The affiliation motive and readiness to join Alcoholics Anonymous." Quarterly Journal of Studies on Alcohol 20 (September): 313–320.
1962 "The job behavior of problem drinkers." Pp. 493–510 in D. Pittman and C. Snyder (eds.), Society, Culture and Drinking Patterns. New York: Wiley.
Trice, H., and P. Roman
1970 "Sociopsychological predictors of successful affiliation with Alcoholics Anonymous." Social Psychiatry 5 (Winter): 51–59.
Wechsler, H.
1960 "The self-help organization in the mental health field: Recovery, Inc." Journal of Nervous and Mental Disease 130 (April): 297–314.
Williams, R.
1960 American Society. New York: A. A. Knopf.

50 / Methadone Maintenance for the Management of Persons with Drug Dependence of the Morphine Type

NATHAN B. EDDY

I. BACKGROUND

Through the years the claim has been made repeatedly, sometimes by persons with a wide experience with drug addicts[1,2], that some individuals can lead a reasonably normal life if they are given regularly small to moderate doses of an opiate and are unable to do so if they are not. The Rolliston Committee[3] seemed to accept this view when, in its report to the Home Office of the British Government in 1926, it recommended that whether or not a patient should receive an opiate continuously, essentially the above criterion having been established, be left to the discretion of the physician. The Committee on Drug Addiction of the New York Academy of Medicine[4] subscribed to the same view at least in part, since it said that immediate withdrawal of narcotics was not the best policy and recommended establishment of clinics for narcotic administration. The Scientific Study Group on Treatment of Addiction of the World Health Organization[5] recommended a preparatory phase of treatment before withdrawal but certainly intended eventual abstinence.

Many have disputed the claim for a better life with drugs than without. It is a defeatist attitude; through continued effort the subject ought to be encouraged to meet his conflicts without the shelter of drug action. Also, stabilization on small doses without compulsory supervision is extremely difficult. Persons dependent on opiates prize the thrill of drug action, the acquired euphoric effect, and, whatever the intake load, seek enough drug to give them that thrill. Consequently, on account of developing drug tolerance and shortening of drug action they want more drug and more frequent administration. Their life is not a steady state but a waxing and waning of drug effect and constant drive for repetition of this cycle.

Methadone came to our attention in 1946.[6] It was demonstrated promptly that it was qualitatively morphine-like in its action essentially in all respects, with time-action differences. It substituted for morphine smoothly at a better than one-for-one ratio in persons dependent on large daily doses. Substitution could be effected and the dose reduced subsequently at a rapid rate with days elapsing before the patient was aware that either had taken place. Impending abstinence phenomena could be avoided completely by substitution of remarkably small doses of methadone taken by mouth. Given a choice, former addicts preferred methadone to morphine for its prolonged effect, but many reversed this choice later because of the greater peak thrill which morphine afforded. Chronic administration of methadone caused the rapid development of tolerance and cross-tolerance to other opiates and of a physical dependence of the morphine type. On abrupt withdrawal there was a delay of about 48 hours before any abstinence signs appeared. These signs never reached more than moderate intensity and were slower in their disappearance than after morphine. These differences have led to the employment of oral methadone substitution as an almost routine means of minimizing the withdrawal sickness whatever the opiate upon which the patient is dependent.

Dole[7] and Dole and Nyswander[8] have discussed at length the ineffectiveness for all but a very few narcotic addicts of detoxification with various rehabilitative efforts. Withdrawal of drugs can be accomplished in a hospital without much difficulty, but patients almost always return to drugs after discharge. If treatment is to improve substantially, physicians, according to Dole and Nyswander, must review their attitudes toward addiction. Drug abuse must be approached as a medical rather than a moral issue, and treatment goals must be clearly defined. At present physicians strive for two distinct goals which, if not inconsistent, are at least difficult to reach simultaneously. Elimination of drugs and rehabilitation are both desirable, but one must decide which has priority. The Dole-Nyswander belief and experience assign priority to rehabilitation.

It could be argued that confinement of addicts in a controlled environment is preferable to having them free as criminals in the community. Confinement is needed to protect society when individuals are both destructive and incurable, but it is not therapy. Segregation of addicts, by law or as volunteers, with or without psychotherapy, in jails, hospitals, and sheltered communities has been tried for many years and has not succeeded in transforming more than a small minority into people capable of living a normal life in free society. If a way could be found to change such addicts into productive citizens, society would not only be spared the cost and indignity of massive jails but would also gain support for families now being cared for by public funds and, with improvement of neighborhoods, would diminish the rate of new addictions.

The drug-dependent person experiences psychic and physical drives to drug-seeking behavior as the result of acquired euphorigenic action and impending abstinence phenomena. When tolerance and cross-tolerance to narcotics develop, euphorigenic action is largely suppressed, and if concentration of drug in the body is maintained at a sufficient level, abstinence phenomena are in abeyance. The basic problems may be stated as selection of an agent which would maintain a steady state without euphoria or abstinence, whether street addicts would accept this steady state and stay with such a program, and whether they would under these conditions be motivated to become productive citizens. A review of pharmacological properties and actual clinical trial of agents in a small group of patients during a two-year period led to the selection of methadone and elaboration of the maintenance technique.

II. THE TECHNIQUE (AS DESCRIBED ORIGINALLY)

The original description[9] published in 1965 (see also Nyswander[10]), stressed a distinction between unsupervised distribution of narcotic drugs to addicts for self-administration at times of their choosing and medical prescription of drugs as a treatment or management of the drug-dependent person. The former was the condition in the clinics for addicts which existed briefly around 1920 and has been the objectionable feature in all later efforts to set up centers for the distribution of drugs to addicts. Dole and Nyswander insist that their procedure is not simple administration of drug for maintenance of addiction or substitution of one addiction for another. Their goal is rehabilitation, and drug administration is one tool to that end.

Patients for maintenance have been carefully selected throughout. After the first few were admitted from among those known to the originators of the program, others have been chiefly persons known and recommended by someone already in the program. The criteria have been: males aged 20–50 (during the past two years a smaller number of females have been admitted), mainline diacetylmorphine (heroin) users for several years with a history of failures of withdrawal treatment, not psychotic, and without substantial dependence on other drugs. The program was developed in three phases.

Phase I. Stabilization with methadone hydrochloride in an unlocked hospital ward during a period of about six weeks. The patient was given a complete medical workup, psychiatric evaluation, review of family and housing problems, and job-placement study. After the first week he was free to leave the ward for school, library, shopping, and various amusements, usually but not always with one of the staff.

Patients differed markedly in tolerance to narcotics at the beginning of treatment and in the rate at which they adapted to increasing doses of methadone so individualization of dosage build-up was necessary. If signs of abstinence were apparent on admission, they were relieved with one or two intramuscular doses of morphine (10 mg.) or dihydromorphinone (4 mg.). Methadone hydrochloride was started with 10 to 20 mg. orally twice a day. The dose was increased gradually during the next four weeks to the stabilization level, fifty to 150, occasionally 180, mg. per day. With careful attention to dosage, the patients did not become euphoric, sedated, or sick from abstinence at any stage of treatment. They have felt normal and have not asked for more medication. After reaching maintenance level the daily dosage was adjusted until all was given at one time in the morning. It was made clear to the patients and accepted by them that the amount of medication and the dosage schedule were the responsibility of the medical staff; dosage has not been discussed. The dose was always taken in four ounces of liquid (a fruit-juice equivalent). Urine was analyzed daily for methadone, morphine, and quinine, later also for amphetamine and barbiturate. Sensitivity of analysis was such that a definite positive would be obtained if the patient had taken an average "bag" of heroin during the preceding 24 hours.

Phase 2 began when the patient left the hospital to live in the community. He returned every day for his maintenance medication, taken in the presence of a staff member, and to give a urine specimen. After a time means were provided for a few patients living at a distance to receive from and take, in the presence of a local pharmacist, the daily maintenance dose, returning to the hospital less often than daily; or a few patients on the program for several months were given at one time enough medication for a week-end or for a short trip. The chief help needed in this phase was in obtaining jobs and housing and in resumption of education. Legal help was available if the person got into trouble.

Phase 3 was the goal of treatment. The "ex-addict" became a socially normal, self-supporting person. Those who arrived at this phase were still receiving maintenance medication and were returning one or more times a week to the hospital for counselling and urinalysis. The physicians in charge, while subscribing to the possibility of eventual withdrawal, have taken no steps in that direction and feel that such would still be premature. The difference between phases 2 and 3 is only in the degree of social advancement.

The principal medical problem has been constipation. No signs of drug toxicity have been detected, and neuromuscular functions appeared to be unaffected. The degree of tolerance (cross-tolerance) to other narcotics has been tested in some patients and was present at least to the extent that 40 to 80 mg. of heroin was without effect. It was said,[9] "with methadone maintenance patients found that they could meet addict friends, and even watch them inject diacetylmorphine, without great difficulty. They have tolerated frustrating episodes without feeling a need for diacetylmorphine. They have stopped dreaming about drugs and seldom talk about drugs when together. . . . Unscheduled, but perhaps necessary, experiments in drug usage were made by four patients. These subjects found that they did not "get high" when "shooting" diacetylmorphine with addict friends on the street. Both the patients and their friends were astounded at their lack of reaction to the drug. They discontinued these unrewarding experiments without need for disciplinary measures and have discouraged other patients from repeating the experiment."

If phase 3 is reached "the patient will have established a new routine of life, socially acceptable and consistent with his abilities. He will have developed a long-range outlook for the future; he will have a bank account and friends. At this stage he no longer needs support from older patients or counselors. He looks to the physician as a medical advisor, not as a guardian. The chief danger in this stage is his complacency, since a successfully treated patient ceases to consider himself as an addict. He is likely to feel that continued taking of medication is a needless inconvenience. . . . It is clear, however, that the decision as to continuation should be made by the physician and not by the patient."[11]

Dole and Nyswander admit[11] that phase 3 may not ever be reached. "The problem patients, the disturbed individuals with psychopathology independent of addiction respond less well. These patients may not be recognizable in the initial interview or in phase 1, since addiction and the resultant social pressures cause anxiety and distortion in attitude that cannot be well separated from more fundamental disturbances. [See Dole & Nyswander[12] for their discussion on theories of narcotic addiction.] In the course of treatment however, some patients fail to progress as expected. Psychopathic individuals cause disturbances in the ward and in the out-patient clinic, sometimes episodes of violence. Schizoid individuals remain isolated and may or may not be able to hold a job. Patients with anxiety neurosis may not find a sufficiently protected environment. They may report symptoms of abstinence and be convinced that the medication has been reduced when, in fact, the dose has remained constant and the recurrent symptoms are emotional. Other patients may continue to use alcohol to excess or to have continuing problems of barbiturate, tranquilizer or amphetamine abuse. The problem patients, fortunately, have been a minority in the group that we have treated."

The authors concluded this first report on methadone maintenance:[9] "Methadone has contributed in an essential way to the favorable results, although it is quite clear that giving of medicine has been only part of the program. This drug appears to relieve narcotic hunger and thus free the patient for other interests, as well as protect him from readdiction to diacetylmorphine by establishing a pharmacological block." In the patient maintained on methadone there is still a drug dependence of morphine type and heroin is ineffective because of the phenomenon of cross-tolerance. Unfortunately, Dr. Dole and his associates persist in reference to the "antinarcotic action" of methadone and "blockade" of heroin effect,[13] though their discussion of the principles and objectives in their treatment of addiction indicate that they are aware of the phenomena of tolerance. We suggest that suppression, rather than blockade, more clearly describes the waning of the reaction to heroin.

III. RESULTS

In 1966 Dole and Nyswander[8] reported on 79 patients who had been in their program for three months or more. Of these, 58 had a job, nine were in school and four were involved with both job and school. Sixty-one were fully and eleven partly self-supporting. At the time of the report 120 patients had been admitted and 13 had been discharged because of psychopathic behavior or intractable continuing involvement with barbiturates or alcohol. Each of the dischargers had tried for re-admission. The authors point to the economic saving to the individuals and to society as the result of the cessation of heroin use by the 107 patients still in the program and of the absence or diminished need for hospitalization and incarceration in connection with criminal activity. They estimate conservatively that this saving already amounts to millions of dollars.

In June of this year, 1968, Dole, Nyswander and Warner[14] reported on 863 admissions to the program. There have been 109 discharges, 13 percent— 10 voluntary, 9 for nonheroin drug abuse, 27 for medical disability and 54 for behavior reasons. Nine have died. Criminal behavior has been reduced by 90 percent and about 70 percent are engaged in productive work or are at school.

Others have tried methadone in the management of drug dependence of the morphine type (narcotic addiction) according to the Dole-Nyswander procedure or some modification. See unpublished reports to the Committee on Problems of Drug Dependence, Division of Medical Sciences, National Academy of Sciences, National Research Council[15, 16, 17, 18, 19].

Holmes[15] said that 62 patients, mostly males, had been offered methadone maintenance, employing small doses, 10 to 14 mg. per day. Twenty-six were active out-patients; ten had been steadily occupied and attending the clinic for more than 12 months. Only half of the females had continued on treatment and none at time of report for more than 12 months. He admitted some difficulty with the small doses.

Halliday[16] reported 71 admissions to a program which he called prolonged withdrawal and said that of those who had remained in treatment for a year or more, ten percent showed much improvement and fifteen percent some improvement. Again the methadone doses were small. He regarded his patients as a "hard core" group of narcotic addicts.

Freedman[17, 18] started a small-scale experiment with 15 male, long-time heroin addicts, with many previous treatment failures. His procedure was patterned after that of Dole; the daily methadone dosage ranged from 70 to 180 mg. Of the nine patients who continued on the program three were working regularly and five were looking for work, showing considerable improvement.

Brill, et al.[19] reported nine patients with satisfactory improvement in behavior and discontinuance of heroin abuse. They had some difficulty in arriving at a stabilization dose. The work was carried out in New York and was discontinued because facilities were not available for expansion, and it was considered inefficient to carry so small a group. Jaffe has begun a methadone maintenance program in Chicago. He is endeavoring to institute some of the controls suggested (see below). For example, he is carrying on a schedule of methadone administration as pre-treatment to detoxication and after care. Jaffe believes that his usage of high methadone dosage with long-time commitment to treatment will be as effective as the results reported by Dole and Nyswander.

In 1966 Wieland[20] initiated an experimental program designed to answer two questions: Can Dole-Nyswander findings be replicated in another city by another group of clinicians; can the cost-effectiveness be further improved by starting the treatment on an out-patient basis? Forty-four patients had been admitted and 41 were still under treatment in 1968. Criteria similar to those of Dole and Nyswander were used for admission. Twenty-seven began as out-patients, the others in an institutional setting remaining there for two weeks to two months. The starting dose of methadone was 40 or 60 mg. per day, raised in 10 mg. amounts per day according to individual response. Patients reported one to five times a week, and urinalysis was done at least once a week. Counseling and vocational training were provided as indicated. No difference in the outcome of the initial in- and out-patient groups has been detected. Eighteen patients were working at the beginning of the experiment; they have continued or improved their positions. Fifteen initially unemployed are working or going to school. Eight are still unemployed. None have returned to heroin or become dependent on other drugs. The individual stabilization dosage covered a wide range, 40 to 180 mg. per day. Some patients get their drug from pharmacists through prescriptions. Wieland comments on the need to build up trust in patient and physician. He believes that it may be possible for individual practitioners to treat selected addicts with methadone maintenance as part of their regular office practice. It is still uncertain, in his opinion, if withdrawal of methadone in these patients will be possible eventually.

IV. COMMENTS, CRITICISM, RECOMMENDATION

Eddy has written two accounts of the methadone maintenance program[21, 22] and has participated in discussions of its potentialities and limitations in the Committee on Problems of Drug Dependence, National Academy of Sciences, National Research Council, and in the Expert Committee on Dependence-Producing Drugs, World Health Organization. The former Committee has had first-hand reports from and discussions with Dr. Dole and Dr. Henry Brill, the latter representing the New York State Narcotic Addiction Control Commission. The discussions were at its 28th and 29th Meetings, 1966 and 1967.[23, 24] The WHO Expert Committee discussed the program at its 15th and 16th Meetings, 1967, 1968.[25, 26]

The Committee on Problems of Drug Dependence in 1967 passed unanimously this resolution: "The Committee agreed that there continued to be a need for controlled studies to establish the conditions, potentialities and essential restrictions of a program of management of drug dependent persons by continuing administration of methadone, that this procedure remained a research undertaking, and that it could not be considered an established treatment."

According to the NRC Committee, the following control procedures should be considered:

1. Screening by the Dole-Nyswander criteria of a large number of known addicts (six to eight thousand are expected to come to the attention of the New York State Commission in a year) to determine those who would be and would not be admissible to the

Dole-Nyswander program. Then selection from the acceptable and non-acceptable populations of groups of patients to be put on methadone maintenance under the supervision of the Dole-Nyswander staff and under the supervision of an entirely different outside staff.

2. Selection also from the acceptable and non-acceptable populations of groups to be handled by other treatment modalities; for example, a self-help program, usual detoxification and follow-up, ambulatory withdrawal and follow-up.

3. Adoption of uniform documentation to describe the patient and his history at the time of admission and at intervals during treatment.

4. Adequate identification of the patient for cross-referencing, if he is contacted in more than one situation. For example, if he is involved in anti-social behavior, subject to arrest, etc.

5. Attempted maintenance at different methadone dose levels to determine the amount which will suffice or which is optimal.

6. Withdrawal of methadone after a considerable period of maintenance and apparent rehabilitation.

In 1966 the WHO Expert Committee[25] said, "It must be emphasized that this methadone maintenance program should be looked upon as a research procedure on a limited scale which it is hoped will yield valuable information on the phenomena of drug dependence. However, at present many questions remain unanswered and many investigations to elucidate the precise role of methadone as against that of surrounding conditions need to be initiated. The Committee is of the opinion that in so far as maintenance on methadone is not carried out simply for gratification of the individual but is used as an adjunct to vigorous efforts towards social rehabilitation the employment of this procedure under very carefully controlled conditions will continue to be of considerable scientific interest." This carefully worded, conservative statement was misinterpreted by some as a full endorsement. The Committee did mean to encourage investigative rehabilitation efforts for drug-dependent persons.

The Sixteenth Report of the WHO Expert Committee[26] contains a further statement on methadone maintenance. "On the basis of data now available, the Committee was of the opinion that methadone maintenance for drug dependence of morphine type remains experimental. It is not suitable for utilization by individual physicians but requires for its operation the full support of a multi-disciplinary medical service to effect the therapeutic, social, economic and rehabilitation measures which may be necessary to check for possible relapse to multiple drug use, and also to provide data for scientific evaluation and other research. The Committee believes that despite verified reports of dramatic improvement in patients with a history of repeated treatment failures, methadone maintenance has not yet been adequately evaluated. The techniques of well-designed clinical drug trials including scientifically controlled series and/or comparison groups are required. In these trials it is important that the influence of factors other than methadone itself be evaluated. The various methadone maintenance programs all involve therapeutic elements in addition to any drug effects. To date, patients involved have, in the main, been highly motivated, carefully selected and provided with organized after-care arranged so as to develop a supportive group process. Furthermore, these patients have not been shown to be a representative sample of the drug dependent population in other respects: e.g., age, ethnic grouping and educational level. Finally it must not be forgotten that methadone itself is a drug of dependence and that persons taking it regularly in the methadone program continue to have a drug dependence of morphine type. It will therefore, be necessary to keep in view the question of final withdrawal of methadone from these patients."

The Methadone Maintenance Evaluation Committee of Columbia University School of Public Health, under the chairmanship of Dr. Henry Brill, submitted a progress report[27] as of March 31, 1968, to the New York State Narcotic Addiction Control Commission, covering approximately four years of operation of the methadone maintenance program. According to this report 871 patients had been admitted to various treatment centers; 119 or 14 percent had left the program, of whom 87 had been discharged, 24 had dropped out and 8 had died. The report, however, deals in detail with the two largest groups which include 544 males who have been in the program for three months or longer. At the time of admission, it was known that 28 percent were gainfully employed and 40 percent were receiving welfare support. After five months, 45 percent were employed, after eleven months, 61 percent were employed or in school, and for those in the program for 21 months or longer 85 percent were employed or in school. The proportion receiving welfare support showed a progressive reduction to 15 percent after two years. The pattern is similar for 79 women in the program for three months or longer.

The report indicates further that none of the patients who have continued under care have resumed regular use of heroin ("become re-addicted") but 11 percent have demonstrated repeated use of amphetamines or barbiturates and about five percent have chronic problems with alcohol. The arrest record for the 544 males compared with a contrast group admitted to a detoxification unit and followed for the same length of time, matched only by age, ethnic group and time of admission, is shown in Fig. 1.

The arrest experience of those leaving the program resembles that of the contrast group. A relatively small percentage of those gainfully employed are employed in the program and such employment for the most part is transient. All patients are continuing on maintenance doses of methadone. Periodic medical examinations have revealed no evidence of drug toxicity in liver or kidney function tests or of decreased motor functioning.

The Evaluation Committee concluded, "For those patients selected and treated as described, this program can be considered a success. It does appear that those who remain in the program have on the whole become productive members of society, in contrast to their previous experience, and have, to a large extent, become self-supporting and demonstrate less and less anti-social behavior. It should be emphasized that these are volunteers, who are older than the average street addict and may be more highly motivated. (Their high morale and devotion to the program are phenomenal.) Consequently, generalizations of the results of this program in this population to the general addict population probably are not justified."

Figure 1 / Percentage Distribution of Arrests for 544 Men in Methadone Maintenance Program Three Months or Longer as of March 31, 1968 and Contrast Group According to Months of Observation

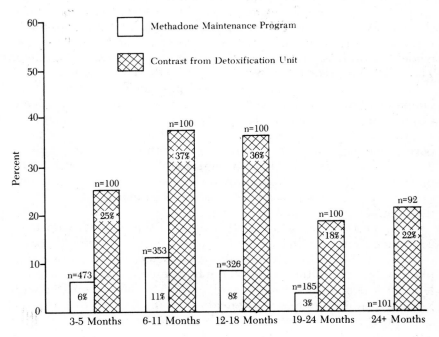

Period of Observation

The Committee made a number of recommendations:

1. Continued intake of new patients as rapidly as current facilities will allow.
2. Expansion of the program to other units which can provide all elements of the current program.
3. Extension of this program (a) to other groups, using different criteria for admission, such as younger patients or a prison population, in order to determine the applicability of this treatment program to a broader segment of the addict population, and (b) to variations in technique, including induction on an ambulatory basis.
4. Further research on the impact of each major component of the program.
5. Continued follow-up and evaluation of all patients currently in the program and any new programs to be developed in order to assess the long-term effects and results.

The points made in these recommendations are essentially those of the suggestions for controls made by the NRC Committee on Problems of Drug Dependence. Dole has subscribed to the desirability of control procedures, though he has not, so far as we know, implemented any of them. He has also discussed at length comparative evaluation.[28]

It is clear, I think, that for a particularly selected group of persistent heroin abusers methadone maintenance has brought about significant social and economic gain at relatively low cost, compared to the loss to the individual and to society in these patients' previous experience. It must be emphasized, however, that until the recommended control studies have been instituted and evaluated, conclusions cannot be drawn in respect to general applicability, nor plans formulated for broad extension of the program as an established treatment modality. Until such controls are carried out and their evaluation is at hand, the program is one of research only. It may be that full evaluation will eventually suggest the desirability as well as advantage of establishment of centers for the application of this treatment modality under a coordinating and supervising authority, wherever there are persons with drug dependence of morphine type in sufficient number to justify the effort. Even so certain precautions and attendant conditions will, I believe, be required:

1. Strict control of the amount and form of drug administration; designed to prevent accumulation or diversion, or recovery of methadone in injectable form.
2. Constant monitoring by urinalysis to determine not only narcotic consumption but also resort to other drugs of abuse.

3. Adequate and uniform record-keeping for meaningful analysis of the patient's history, condition at the beginning and progress in treatment.
4. Such help as is indicated for vocational training, job placement, living adjustment, and interpersonal relationships.
5. Eventual withdrawal of methadone must be kept in mind but insistence upon it should be left in abeyance at present.

The major points presently at issue are:

1. Is this a treatment modality to be recommended and sponsored as an established procedure? No. It is an experimental effort (research) in spite of any claimed or admitted success at least until the recommendations which have been made in respect to it are implemented and evaluated.
2. Is this a treatment modality which can be employed by the individual private physician in the course of his office practice? No. For a physician to establish such rapport with a particular patient as to maintain control over his methadone intake, establish a maintenance dose, and assist him towards rehabilitation, avoiding the risks of accumulations or diversion of methadone or resort to other drugs, is so nearly an ideal situation as not to be taken into account by anyone who is honest and sincere in his approach to this problem. Both the physician and the patient would need more help than would be available to them on an individual basis. The alternative of centers for multi-disciplinary management has been suggested. The prescribing of methadone by the physician for a maintenance regimen is fraught with too many dangers and physicians should be warned against it even to the issuance of a restrictive regulation. Physicians interested in amelioration of the drug-dependence problem and rehabilitation of its victims can and should associate themselves with colleagues similarly interested to provide the necessary controls and safeguards. If there is promise of social and economic gain to the individual and to society, at relatively low cost, in the methadone maintenance, even though it is not a cure for drug dependence, let us proceed to verify this promise, and not jeopardize its potential by attempts to exploit it which involve material risks of drug diversion and actual worsening of the drug-abuse situation.

Notes

1. **Dixon, W. E.,** *Practitioner* 78:642 (1907).
2. Kolb, L. Personal Communications.
3. "Department Committee's Report." *Brit. Med. J.* 1:391 (1926).

4. "New York Academy of Medicine Committee on Public Health." *Bull. New York Acad. Med.* 39:417 (1963).

5. "Scientific Study Group on Treatment and Care of Drug Addicts." *Wld. Health Org. Techn. Rep. Series* No. 181 (1957).

6. Isbell, H., et al., *J. Am. Med. Assn.* 135:888 (1947).

7. Dole, V. P., *New York State J. Med.* 65:927 (1965).

8. Dole, V. P. and Nyswander, M. E., *New York State J. Med.* 66:2011 (1966).

9. Dole, V. P. and Nyswander, M. E., *J. Am. Med. Assn.* 193:646 (1965).

10. Nyswander, M. E., *Hospital Practice* 2: No. 4 (1967).

11. Dole, V. P. and Nyswander, M. E., *Arch. Environ. Hlth.* 14:477 (1967).

12. Dole, V. P. and Nyswander, M. E. *The Addictive States, Association for Research in Nervous and Mental Disease.* Baltimore: Williams & Wilkins, Vol. XLVI, Chapter XXVIII, p. 359. 1968.

13. Dole, V. P. and Nyswander, M. E., *Brit. J. Addict.* 63:55 (1968).

14. Dole, V. P., Nyswander, M. E., and Warner, A. *Proc. First National Conference on Methadone Treatment* (28th meeting). New York: The Rockefeller University, p. 11. 1968.

15. Holmes, S. J. Committee on Problems of Drug Dependence (28th meeting.) App. 10, p. 4522 (1966).

16. Halliday, R. Committee on Problems of Drug Dependence (28th meeting.) App. 14, p. 4599 (1966).

17. Freedman, A. M., Committee on Problems of Drug Dependence (28th meeting.) App. 17, p. 4633 (1966).

18. Freedman, A. M., Fink, M., Sharoff, R., and Zaks, A. Committee on Problems of Drug Dependence (29th meeting.) App. 38, p. 5129 (1967).

19. Brill, L., Jaffe, J. H., and Lasbowitz, D., Committee on Problems of Drug Dependence (29th meeting). App. 40, p. 5145 (1967).

20. Wieland, W. F., *First National Conference on Methadone Treatment.* New York: The Rockefeller University, 31. 1968.

21. Eddy, N. B., *J. Tenn. Med. Assn.* 60:269 (1967).

22. Eddy, N. B., *South. Med. Bull.* 35:39 (1967).

23. Committee on Problems of Drug Dependence, NAS-NRC (28th meeting.), p. 4387. 1966.

24. Committee on Problems of Drug Dependence, NAS-NRC (29th meeting), 1967. p. 4790.

25. "WHO Expert Committee on Dependence-Producing Drugs" (Fifteenth report). *Wld. Hlth. Org. Techn. Rep. Ser.* No. 343, p. 9 (1966).

26. "WHO Expert Committee on Drug Dependence" (Sixteenth report). *Wld. Hlth. Org. Techn. Rep. Ser.* In press (1968).

27. Methadone Maintenance Evaluation Committee, *First National Conference on Methadone Treatment.* New York: The Rockefeller University, p. 3, 1968.

28. Dole, V. P. and Warner, A., *Am. J. Publ. Hlth.* 57:2000 (1967).

51 / Treating Schizophrenics in the Community

BENJAMIN PASAMANICK
FRANK R. SCARPITTI
SIMON DINITZ

This experimental home care program for the treatment of schizophrenics has yielded solid scientific results. The project demonstrated in a most conclusive way that home care under drug medication with systematic public health nursing care is quite feasible both for newly hospitalized and ambulatory schizophrenic patients. Even the minimal type of home care provided proved in every respect at least as effective, and in most respects, clearly superior, to treatment in a hospital. An enriched, expanded, and more comprehensive program such as now envisioned and planned in many community mental health centers can be expected to be even more successful not only in keeping many patients out of the hospital but in restoring them to at least as adequate a level of functioning as they would have achieved from conventional treatment in a state hospital. Whatever additional practical consequences of this investigation may emerge, this study has provided convincing evidence for the validity of the principles of community psychiatric treatment programs at least as these apply to typical state hospital schizophrenic patients. It is also a reasonable inference that other categories of the mentally ill may be successfully treated in this way.

RECAPITULATION

The rigor of the experimental design and the unequivocal nature of the findings have implications for programs rarely found in this field. Several aspects of the enterprise seem to us to warrant recapitulation at this point.

After 3 years of frustration in getting the investigation started, the Institute Treatment Center was finally established in downtown Louisville, Kentucky, in the latter half of 1961. The staff included a director, a part-time psychiatrist, a psychologist, a social worker and five nurses with public health nursing experience. Only one of the nurses had any prior training or experience in psychiatric nursing. A psychiatrist was employed at the hospital to do the initial screening of patients to determine their eligibility for inclusion in the program. Newly admitted state hospital patients had to meet the following criteria to be admitted to the project: a diagnosis of schizophrenia, nonsuicidal or homicidal, be between 18 and 60 years of age, have residence in Louisville or surrounding counties, and have a family or relative willing to provide supervision of the patient at home. State hospital admissions who met these criteria were sent to the Institute Treatment Center for further evaluation. If the ITC staff psychiatrist confirmed the diagnosis and deemed the patient suitable for the program and the family agreed to cooperate, the patient was accepted. Using a deck of random cards, the study director then assigned the patient to one of three groups as follows: home on drugs (40 percent), home on placebo or on inert medication (30 percent), or hospital care (the control group, 30 percent).

State hospital schizophrenic patients do not, of course, include all schizophrenics. Many schizophrenic patients, because their symptoms are not especially florid and can therefore be tolerated more readily, typically remain in the community and are not hospitalized. To have this population represented as well, particularly for the purpose of determining the effectiveness of drug medication, referrals from community sources other than the state hospital and from private physicians were welcomed. In order to qualify for inclusion in the study, these referrals had to meet the same diagnosis, age, residence, family, and other requirements. The only difference from the aforementioned study group resulted from their "ambulatory" status. Their random assignment permitted just two categories: home on drugs or home on placebo.

Shortly after each patient returned home, the public health nurse assigned to the case visited the patient and family. The same nurse made weekly calls the first 3 months, bi-monthly visits during the second 3 months, and monthly visits thereafter. On every visit she left the medication prescribed by the staff psychiatrist. She also completed a written report on the status of the patient which was reviewed by the ITC psychiatrist. Patients and families experiencing difficulties were free to call the treatment center and speak to or make appointments to see the social worker and psychiatrist. Usually, however, it was the nurse who arranged for such consultation.

In order to reach a judgment as to the feasibility of home care and the efficacy of drug therapy, the following instruments, tests, and measures were used:

Psychiatric evaluation. Two instruments (a psychiatric inventory and the Lorr IMPS) were used by the staff psychiatrist to evaluate the mental status of all patients on a regular basis. Home care patients were examined at intake and at 6-month intervals thereafter. Hospital control patients were evaluated at intake and again after 6 and 18 months whether or not they still were hospitalized.

Psychological tests. All groups were studied by the staff psychologist who administered the Wechsler Adult Intelligence Scale, a sequential reaction time test series, and the Bender Gestalt and Porteus Mazes tests. Testing periods were the same as for the psychiatric evaluations.

Social history. A complete social history was taken by the social worker at the time of admission of the patient to the project.

Nurses reports and ratings. The public health nurse completed a mental status rating form (the Lorr IMPS) on each visit to the home care patient. She also completed a behavior chart checklist, a physical status rating sheet, a nursing report, and a monthly report from the responsible relative concerning the patient's functioning.

Hospital control patients were visited by the nurse 1 month after hospital release, and these same instruments were administered at that time.

In all, 152 state hospital patients were involved in the project, 57 drug home care patients, 41 placebo home care cases, and 54 hospital controls. All were followed up for a period ranging from well over 6 months at the least to 30 months. In addition, 29 community drug home care cases and 23 community referred placebo home care patients were in the project for from 6 to 27 months.

The principal substantive findings were these:

1. Over 77 percent of the drug home care patients but only some 34 percent of the placebo cases remained in the community throughout their participation in the project. All controls, of course, were hospitalized. Not only did the program, by averting hospitalization, save a considerable amount of bed-patient time, but this saving permitted in theory at least the possibility of more intensive care for the fewer hospitalized patients.

2. Drug and placebo home care patients in the project for a longer time period were no less successful than those in the program for shorter periods. Thus, it is fair to speak of *prevention* of hospitalization as such rather than merely of *delay* in institutionalization.

3. Patients who failed (13 drug and 27 placebo) and had to be hospitalized usually failed soon after acceptance into the program. Nearly all failures occurred within 6 months.

4. Even after initial hospitalization averaging 83 days and the presumable remission of the grosser symptoms, the *hospital controls*

failed more often at the termination of treatment than did the home care patients.

5. When home care patients failed it was frequently of the "last straw" variety. Either patient behavior was bizarre or dangerous, or the responsible relatives could no longer cope with the patient and his needs. Changes in the family situation sometimes resulted in a lack of supervision of the patient and so precipitated failure.

6. On the more subjective evaluation level—that is, according to the nurses, psychiatrist, and relatives—patients improved in mental status, psychological test performance, domestic functioning, and social participation. These gains were considerable and frequently statistically significant. *In all of the many specific measures, home care patients were functioning as well or better than the hospital control cases.*

7. *Most of the improvement in performance occurred during the first 6 months of the study.* Thereafter functioning improved very little, if at all. In other words, once the acute signs and symptoms abated and functioning returned to a pre-episode level, there was little more gain made.

8. At their best, some of these patients still showed considerable difficulty in performing at what might be termed an adequate level. Both on the instrumental role performance level and on the psychological symptom level, some of the home care patients as well as some of the controls were still exhibiting low quality performance. Perhaps this is really all one might realistically expect, however, from a chronically impaired population.

9. Regarding the community referred drug and placebo patients, nearly 76 percent of the drug and 61 percent of the placebo cases succeeded on home care. Length of time on the project was not a major correlate of failure. In instances of hospitalization, failure occurred early and the precipitants were generally of the same nature. In the case of the state hospital patients, functioning improved, and most of the gains in the psychiatric, psychological, and social functioning measures were registered between intake and the 6 months' testing.

IMPLICATIONS

There were other more specific findings which have been dealt with earlier and need no additional consideration here. From a practical standpoint this research has important implications for several areas of concern: schizophrenia, the community mental health center, patient care cost, and manpower problems.

Schizophrenia

It would have been far less complicated to select either a cross-section of the mentally ill or a nonpsychotic population to test the feasibility of a home care program. Instead, schizophrenics were deliberately chosen for a variety of compelling reasons. First, there is clear professional agreement that the schizophrenias are chronic and disabling disorders, not merely the consequences of difficulties experienced in the everyday process of living and adjusting. If ever a case can be made for mental illness as a disease, schizophrenia would be one of the prime illustrations. Unlike the characterological disorders, the neuroses, the psychosomatic problems, and other clinical entities, there is almost no dispute that schizophrenia fits, by almost any conventional definition, the disease model. This point is important. If so severe an illness as schizophrenia, accounting for about half of all mental hospital resident patients, and nearly a fourth of the new admissions, can be controlled and treated effectively in a community setting, other difficult behavioral problems presumably can also be managed without recourse to institutionalization, except in extreme cases.

Second, it is well to note, too, that all of the "loading" or biasing in this study was in the direction of selecting sicker rather than less impaired schizophrenic patients for study. Two psychiatrists evaluated each patient—one in the state hospital at admission of the patient and the other in the treatment center. Only when both agreed on the diagnosis as schizophrenia was the patient accepted into the program. For this reason, it is likely that very few, if any, nonschizophrenics were included in this investigation.[1]

Third, regardless of the high reliability in the diagnosis of schizophrenia, and the great amount of conflict over the etiology of this disorder, there is no argument at all that schizophrenic patients require protracted care and treatment. The layman's concept of "cure" in the sense of complete remission of symptoms and the absence of later pathology is wholly inadequate. Instead, a more accurate assumption is that schizophrenics are sick continually and that this illness is, at times, exacerbated. On such occasions, hospitalization usually results. When the acute phase passes, the patient continues to be ill but at a level which often permits him to return to the community and remain there until the next major episode.

Our home care data on the state hospital patients offers reasonably good evidence of this. Once the florid symptoms had passed, the patients settled into a routine which showed almost no superior functioning on any level and mostly minimal functioning on all levels. The community referred schizophrenics, while better than the state hospital patients, and despite their lack of episodic flareups, were not functioning at a very high level either. These are not the great innovators, or activists ahead of their time; they are, along with the state hospital patients, the leftovers in society who are and will undoubtedly continue to be burdens to their families and to society until specific preventive or therapeutic measures are developed. In short, they are sick persons who require continuous attention, not only when their symptoms are at a peak but also when the peaks have flattened. Up to now, attention in or out of the hospital has been largely reserved for those patients whose symptoms were exaggerated and who were acutely ill. With limited resources and personnel, the more floridly ill were the most likely to receive what attention was available. Home care offers to all patients continuous management not otherwise possible.

Present evidence from drug and other studies indicates that care given to schizophrenic patients only in times of acute episodes is far from adequate treatment.[2] Indeed, continued drug and other treatment is exceedingly important not only in the control of acute flareups but also in reducing the frequency or eliminating entirely the periodic episodes normally resulting in hospitalization. *This type of continuous care, then, in the absence of knowledge of the etiology or specific treatment of schizophrenia may be, and probably is, the only type of prevention available to us now.* Such secondary prevention is clearly preferable to releasing patients back home without follow-up care and treatment and with the certain knowledge that many will return again for another round of hospitalization. *Thus, in hard terms, nearly half of the hospital control patients, 25 of 54, after an average initial period of 83 days in the state hospital had to be rehospitalized.* This is not only uneconomic but unnecessary since, as this study indicates so definitively, much of both the initial institutionalization and the rehospitalization could have been prevented by even a modest home care program.[3]

It is instructive to compare the community home care approach with the historic hospital treatment accorded the schizophrenic. In the hospital, between acute episodes, patients are mostly left alone to stare vacantly into space, to walk down the corridors and back again, to sit, rock, and hallucinate, or to partake of inmate culture. In time, this lack of normal stimulation—intellectual, interpersonal, even physical—has usually resulted in deterioration and impairment of functioning which was wholly unnecessary.[4] Between episodes, many of these patients could have been released had there been any provision for supervision and aftercare. As a result, because such patients were lost in the institutional process and were not frequently returned to the world outside the hospital walls, schizophrenia became identified in the public (and often in the professional) mind with hopelessness and despair. In the past, instead of questioning the necessity for continued and prolonged hospitalization, the focal point of concern was the humanizing of the institution itself. Hardly anyone, before the advent of the psychoactive drugs plus the other changes described at the outset of this volume, was foolhardy enough to propose seriously that hospitalized schizophrenics could survive the pressures of living in a normal family setting without harm to themselves or to others. Whatever else may eventuate from this investigation and related studies, one conclusion seems warranted: in the absence of considerable deterioration, an acute episode, or grossly exaggerated symptoms, no special reason exists for keeping schizophrenic patients hospitalized.[5] Community facilities now being established and those already in existence are reasonable, preferable, and necessary alternatives.

It is hoped that this study and its findings will serve as a model for demonstration projects and programs for care and treatment of the aged, the retarded, and even the alcoholic and addicted, all of whom have been woefully neglected and shunted aside. The aged and the retarded, in particular, share many of the characteristics of the schizophrenic—chronicity, disabling character of the problem, poor functioning, limited productive or economic potential, and of course, the absence of specific treatment. Like the schizophrenic, too, the senile and retarded numerically constitute an inordinately large number of all those newly admitted and resident in state institutions. Home care and drug and other therapy would seem to be most applicable as a substitute for institutionalization and in reducing the hopelessness and stigma presently associated with these problems.

Notes

1. It is true, of course, that schizophrenia is sometimes confused with the psychoneuroses in middle- and upper-class patients. It is also a fact that there are variations across cultures and countries in the clinical manifestations and signs in which a diagnosis of schizophrenia seems warranted. Thus in England, the presence of hallucinations is not considered nearly as critical as in the United States. Again, while the overall interrater reliability in the diagnosis of schizophrenia is high, the reliability falls precipitously when the specific categories of schizophrenia such as paranoid and hebephrenic and simple are considered. Finally, the longer and more frequently a patient is hospitalized, the more likely that he will ultimately be classified as a schizophrenic. All of these qualifications, while significant, do not alter the fact that of all major functional psychiatric disorders, schizophrenia commands the greatest reliability in diagnosis.

2. Martin Katz and Jonathan Cole, "Research on Drugs and Community Care," A.M.A. Arch. gen. Psychiat., 7 (November, 1962), 345–359.

3. On this point, recent data from Maryland indicate that of 1,984 state hospital psychotic patient admissions, 55 percent were released in 3 months, 74 percent in 6 months, and 85 percent within a year. Of those released within the year, 17 percent required rehospitalization within 3 months, 37 percent in 12 months, and 45 percent in

18 months. (It is these rehospitalizations which were prevented in the home care study.) See "Patterns of Retention, Release and Rehospitalization," Statistics Newsletters, Department of Mental Hygiene, State of Maryland, December 10, 1965.

4. See again, *Mental Disorders: A Guide to Control Methods*, American Public Health Association, 1962, Chapter 1.

5. Even, and perhaps especially, family-less schizophrenics deliberately excluded from this study who might be placed in hostels.

52 / The Youth Authority's Community Treatment Project

TED PALMER

From 1961 to the present, the California Youth Authority (CYA) has been conducting a large-scale, two-part experiment known as the Community Treatment Project (CTP). Part 1 was completed in 1969. Its basic goal was to find out if certain kinds of juvenile offenders could be allowed to remain right in their home communities, if given rather intensive supervision and treatment within a small-sized parole caseload. Here, the main question was: Could CYA parole agents work effectively with some of these individuals *without first locking them up for several months* in a large-sized, State instituion? The 1961–1969 phase of the Youth Authority's experiment was carried out mainly in Sacramento and Stockton, with San Francisco being added in 1965. Within each of these cities all areas or regions were included. We will now describe part 1 of the experiment. After that, we shall turn to part 2 (1969–1974).

WHO PARTICIPATED?

Eight hundred and two boys and 212 girls participated in the 1961–1969 effort. All economic levels and racial backgrounds were included; and in this respect the CTP "sample" proved to be typical of the Youth Authority's population within the State as a whole. Most of the participants were between 13 and 19 years of age when first sent to the CYA and placed into the experiment. Typically, these individuals had been in trouble with the law on 5.8 occasions at the time they were sent to the Youth Authority by the local juvenile court. Their "troubles" had usually begun several years prior to the burglary, auto theft, etc., which typically preceded their CYA commitment.

Certain youths were not allowed to participate in the experiment. For example, it was necessary to exclude everyone who had been sent to the CYA for offenses such as armed robbery, assault with a deadly weapon, or forcible rape. (These nonparticipants were called "ineligibles"; participants were known as "eligibles.") Despite such restrictions, it was still possible to *include* a total of 65 percent of all boys and 83 percent of all girls who had been sent to the CYA for the first time, from the Sacramento, Stockton, and San Francisco Juvenile Courts. Along this line, it should be kept in mind that the presence of such things as the following did not, in themselves, prevent any youths from participating in the 1961–1969 experiment: Marked drug involvement, homosexuality, chronic or severe neurosis, occasional psychotic episodes, apparent suicidal tendencies.

THE PROGRAM

Part 1 of the CYA experiment was conducted in a careful, scientific manner: A "control" group was set up from the start. This made it possible to compare the performance of (1) youths who were placed directly into the intensive CTP program, without any prior institutionalization, against that of (2) "controls"—i.e., youths who were sent to an institution for several months prior to being returned to their home communities and then being given routine supervision within standard-sized parole caseloads which were operated by a different (non-CTP) group of parole agents.[1] Thus, all eligible youths were randomly assigned to either the *experimental (CTP)* or the *control (traditional)* program—both of which were operated entirely by the Youth Authority. Six hundred and eighty-six experimentals and 328 controls eventually became part of the 1961–1969 experiment, and all research costs were picked up by the National Institute of Mental Health (NIMH).

All CYA youths, or "wards," who were assigned to the *experimental* (CTP) part of the program were placed on a caseload which contained no more than 12 youths for each parole agent. Based upon (1) detailed initial interviews, (2) a careful review of written background material, and (3) a joint conference by responsible CTP staff, a "treatment plan" was developed for each experimental youth shortly after his assignment to the program. This plan tried to take into account each youth's major strengths, weaknesses, and interests, together with his overall "level of maturity," and various circumstances of his personal, family life, and social situation. Since the resulting plan could vary a great deal from one youth (or type of youth) to the next, the particular approach used in CTP was referred to as "differential treatment." This feature was separate and apart from that of *community-based treatment* per se.

The caseload of each CTP parole officer was limited to only certain "types" of youth or particular "levels of maturity." That is to say, it included only those youths who exhibited a particular *range* of personality characteristics, or who usually displayed certain distinguishing patterns of behavior. In order to make best use of the CTP parole agent's particular skills and interests, each such agent was selected to work primarily with only *certain types* of youth, or "personality patterns." In this sense, they were paired, or "matched," with all youths who were placed on their caseload; and as a result, they were not expected to be all things to *all kinds* of Youth Authority wards.

Certain principles, strategies, and techniques were followed in connection with all youths who were assigned to Community Treatment Project caseloads. Included were: (1) A determination on the parole agent's part to work with individual youths for a number of years if necessary; (2) careful placement planning (e.g., Exactly *where* is this youth going to live, and with *whom?*), especially during early phases of each ward's parole program; (3) parole agent contact on behalf of youths, with any of several community or volunteer agencies (e.g., probation, employment, school); (4) ready access to the parole agent, by the youths, if and when a need or emergency would arise on the youths' part; (5) flexible agent-youth contacts (office or streets, formal or informal), and on a daily basis if necessary; (6) extensive surveillance by the parole agent (e.g., during evenings or weekends) with respect to the youths' community activities, if and as needed.

The following were among the major program elements which could be made available, depending upon the youth's needs and life-situation of the time: (1) Individual and/or group-centered treatment; (2) group homes, individual foster homes, and other out-of-home placements; (3) an accredited school program which was located within the CTP "community center" building and which included tutoring as well as arts and crafts; (4) recreational opportunities and socializing experiences (e.g., outings and cultural activities) both within and outside the community center.

The next section will contain the main results of the 1961–1969 effort. To help state these findings in a succinct yet meaningful way it will be necessary to: (1) Focus upon the Sacramento-Stockton area alone;[2] (2) talk about boys only—although, later on, the main results for girls will be mentioned as well; and (3) refer to three separate groups, or "types," of youth.

A few words must be said about the three groups of youth: *"Passive Conformist," "Power Oriented,"* and *"Neurotic."* These groups have long been recognized by perhaps the majority of practitioners and theorists. They are usually referred to by names which are similar to the ones which are used in this report. Each group is briefly reviewed in Section A of the Appendix. As to quantities, these groups accounted for *14 percent, 21 percent,* and *53 percent* of the 1961–1969 sample of boys, respectively. (Incidentally, the Passive Conformist group seems to account for a considerably larger proportion of the typical California *probation*—i.e., local city and county—population, when compared with that observed within the CYA.[3]) Thus, taken together, the three groups accounted for 7 of every 8—i.e., 88 percent—of the eligible boys.[4] The remaining 12 percent were made up of four rather rare groups of youth, and will be referred to later on.

For readers who are familiar with "I-level" theory,[5] it should be mentioned that many practitioners and theorists would refer to the Passive Conformists as "immature conformists" (Cfm's). Similarly, one may think of the Power Oriented group as being made up of "cultural conformists" (Cfc's) and "manipulators" (Mp's), whereas the Neurotic group would be comprised of individuals who are often referred to as "neurotic acting-out" (Na's) and "neurotic anxious" (Nx's).

MAIN RESULTS OF THE 1961–1969 EXPERIMENT

A.—First we will talk about the group which was by far the largest—*Neurotics*. These individuals appeared to perform much better within the intensive CTP program than within the traditional program (i.e., institution plus standard parole). For example, Criminal Identification and Investigation (CI&I) "rap sheets,"[6] which covered each ward's entire Youth Authority "career,"[7] showed that the controls were arrested 2.7 times more often than experimentals. (Offenses of minor severity were excluded.[8]) More specifically, the rates of arrest in connection with each month "at risk"—i.e., for *each month on parole, in the community*—were .080 for controls and .030 for experimentals. This amounted to a difference of about 1.4 arrests per youth, per CYA *career*. In practical terms, this would mean 1,400 fewer arrests per career, for every 1,000 "Neurotic" youths in the CTP program as compared with an equal number of these youths within the traditional program.

When offenses of minor severity were included, the arrest rates per month-at-risk were .101 for controls (C's) and .044 for experimentals (E's)—a difference of 130 percent in favor of the latter. Statistically speaking, neither of the C vs. E differences which have been mentioned could be explained on the basis of chance alone.

Additional information and findings are given in Section C of the Appendix. The present set of results, which of course apply to the Neurotic group alone, are probably of greater relevance today than they were during much of the 1961–1969 period. This is because the Neurotic group currently appears to make up an even larger proportion (perhaps 70–75 percent) of the Youth Authority's entire population of males, and of females as well. This increase seems to have been an indirect and rather complicated byproduct of the continually increasing average age of CYA first commitments and, of course, recommitments.

B.—*Power Oriented* youths who participated in the intensive CTP program performed substantially *worse* than those within the traditional program, particularly in connection with followup periods of relatively long duration. This was in spite of their better showing on a 24-month "recidivism index." See the Appendix, for details.

C.—On balance, *Passive Conformists* who participated in CTP performed somewhat better than those in the traditional program, at least while under Youth Authority jurisdiction. However, the subsample of experimentals who received a *favorable discharge* from the CYA performed somewhat worse than their controls in terms of convictions (but somewhat better in terms of arrests), when one looked at the 4-year period immediately following the termination of that jurisdiction. (See the Appendix.)

D.—*The Relatively Rare Types of Youth:* What about the four groups of youth who, when taken together, accounted for the remaining 12 percent of the sample? Basically, too few cases were present within each of these groups to allow for really firm or definite conclusions. Yet, it makes some sense to briefly state the findings which we do have, on at least a tentative or provisional basis, in contrast to reporting nothing at all about these individuals.

In the case of one particular group, however, there happened to be a complete absence of cases within the Sacramento-Stockton, experimental sample; as a result, nothing can be said about them. In I-level terms, these youths are referred to as *"asocialized aggressives"* (Aa's). (I-level terminology will also be used in referring to the three remaining personality types: "Ap's, Se's, and Ci's" (see below)). Aa's, Ap's, Se's and Ci's accounted for *1 percent, 4 percent, 2 percent,* and *5 percent* of the present sample of E + C boys, respectively.

(1) All things considered, the *"asocialized passive"* group (Ap's) seemed to perform somewhat better within the intensive CTP program than in the traditional Youth Authority program. (2) No substantial E vs. C differences were observed in relation to the *"situational emotional reaction"* group (Se's). Youths of this type appeared to perform consistently well, regardless of which particular program they were in. (3) The *"cultural identifier"* group (Ci's)[9] appeared to perform somewhat better in the traditional program than in CTP.

E.—*The Total Group of Boys (Viewed Collectively).* In this section, the results for *all* Sacramento-Stockton boys are reviewed. This includes the 12 percent which had earlier been set aside.

Based on CI&I rap sheets, the arrest rate was found to be .065 among controls and .040 among experimentals, for each month on parole. This 63 percent difference in favor of the intensive, CTP program cannot be explained in terms of "chance." (A similar non-chance difference was found when offenses of minor severity were included.) In practical terms, this would amount to at least 750 fewer arrests per CYA career, for every 1,000 experimentals as vs. 1,000 controls.

On 24-months-parole followup, experimental boys performed significantly better than control boys in terms of recidivism rate: 44 percent vs. 63 percent. (Recidivism is defined in Section C of the Appendix.) Other results are: Fifty percent of the controls, as vs. 69 percent of the experimentals, received a *favorable* discharge from the CYA within 60 months of their first release to the community. Twenty-three percent of the controls, as vs. 16 percent of the experimentals, received an *unfavorable* discharge within 60 months.

It seems clear from the above that boys who participated in the CTP program performed substantially better than those in the traditional program at least during the 2-to-4-year, typical duration of their Youth Authority jurisdiction.

What happened *after* some of these youths left the Youth Authority? If one looks at the subsample of individuals who received a *favorable* discharge from the CYA, control boys were found to have chalked up an average of 1.42 convictions within 48 months after they had left the CYA. The figure for experimentals was 1.67. (Focusing on arrests alone, the figures were 1.72 and 1.94—a difference of 13 percent. As before, nonsevere offenses were excluded.)[10]

It should be mentioned that this 18 percent difference, one which favored the traditional program, seemed to largely reflect the comparatively good performance which was chalked up by what amounted to a relatively large number of *Power Oriented* individuals among the "favorable-dischargee control-subsample," when compared with the performance of the relatively smaller number of control *Neurotics* who had also received a favorable discharge. (As seen in Section C of the Appendix, Neurotic *experimental* boys, taken by themselves, performed better than their controls, after having left the CYA on the basis of a favorable discharge. Very much the opposite was found in the case of Power Oriented experimentals.) In short, the Power Oriented individuals contributed enough "points" to have tipped the postdischarge balance in favor of the control group—i.e., when all youths were counted at the same time and when the performance of the Power Oriented youths was weighted according to the number of such individuals who were present in this subsample of favorable dischargees.

F.—*Girls*. The following relates to the total sample of girls: On balance, these individuals seemed to perform equally well in the traditional program and in CTP. We say "on balance" because control girls appeared to perform better when one focused on certain measures of effectiveness only, whereas results of an opposite nature were noted when still *other* measures were used. Even when these individuals were analyzed separately with regard to each of the three major personality groupings—Passive Conformist, Power Oriented and Neurotic—no really substantial, overall E vs. C differences were observed.

WHAT ABOUT COSTS?

What was the average cost of sending a youth through the traditional program, as compared with that of CTP? In addressing this question, the first thing we found was that costs for *both* programs rose a great deal from 1961 through 1969. This was mainly due to "normal" increases in salaries and wages, price-of-living, etc. Secondly, costs increased more within the *traditional* program than within CTP; moreover, this trend continued into the 1970's. (See below.)

> This "differential rise in costs" was largely related to the greater relative, and total, amount of time which the control youths were spending within the CYA's increasingly expensive-to-operate institutions, beginning in the middle and later 1960's. In other words, it was mainly a reflection of the amount of institutional time which was being accumulated by controls (particularly those whose parole had been revoked on one or more occasions[11]) as compared with that of experimentals. (Experimentals had been revoked and institutionalized less often than controls, on the average.)

The costs which appear below relate to all Sacramento-Stockton boys who had entered either CTP or the traditional program during 1961–1969, and who received either a favorable or an unfavorable discharge as of March 1, 1973. All reception center (NRCC), institution, camp, and parole costs were included. Separate analyses were made on these 162 C's and 192 E's, depending upon the year in which each individual had first entered the program (i.e., the experiment):

> For youths who entered during the experiment's early years, or *"early period,"* 1963 prices were used. For those entering during the *"middle period,"* 1966–67 prices were used. For youths who entered during the later years—the *"recent period"*—1971–72 prices were used.[12]

The average CYA career costs per ward were as follows:

Early period:	C —	$ 5,734;	E —	$ 7,180
Middle period:	C —	8,679;	E —	9,911
Recent period:	C —	14,327;	E —	14,580

Thus, in earlier years the traditional program was noticeably less expensive than CTP. However, the C vs. E "cost-ratio" underwent a definite change as time went by. This was seen in relation to the early, middle, and more recent cost-ratios, respectively: 0.80 to 1;[13] 0.88 to 1; and 0.98 to 1. As a result, the earlier advantage which was observed for the traditional program had largely faded away by the early 1970's. Stated directly, the actual C vs. E cost difference per youth amounted to *$1,446* during the early period, *$1,232* during the middle period, and $253 during the more recent period. When one looks at the 1971–72 data in relation to the duration of the average youth's CYA career, the figure of $253 is found to involve a control/experimental difference of $66 per year, or 18 cents a day.

In light of price increases which have been experienced since the early 1970's, it is possible that the cost-balance has by now tipped in "favor" of the CTP program. Aside from this possibility, one which centers around the above figures alone, it should be pointed out that the 1971–72 "per ward costs" would be at least a few hundred dollars higher for the traditional program than for CTP if *capital outlay costs* were added to the picture. These costs, which were not included in the figures shown above, would relate to the construction of new institutions. They are estimated as being close to $10,000,000 for each "up-to-date," physically secure, 400-bed facility. Finally, the above figures do not take into account the fairly substantial, *non-CYA correctional costs* which were accounted for by unfavorable dischargees who had been sent directly to a State or Federal prison. In this connection, it will be recalled that a greater percentage of controls than experimentals had received a discharge of this type. (Also see footnote 31.)

It appears, then, that current costs for the community program would in no event be substantially greater than those for the traditional program. To all indications they would, in fact, be a little less. This would be highlighted if one focused upon the "Neurotic" youths alone, regardless of whether any post-CYA "career costs" were brought into the picture.

THE PRESENT EXPERIMENT (1969–1974)

Despite the early promise shown by CTP with various groups of youth, it was quite clear by 1965 that there was much room for improvement with regard to still other groups. By 1967–1968, it was the consensus of CTP operations staff, and on-site researchers, that the difficulties and delinquent orientation of 25-to-35 percent of the eligible boys were hardly being influenced by the intensive CTP program. In fact, it had been found that at least one-third of these individuals were again involved in delinquency within a few weeks or months after having entered the program. Much the same was observed with similar types of individuals who had been assigned to the traditional program—i.e., with youths (control subjects) who had spent some 8 or 10 months in a regular CYA institution (or camp) prior to being parolled. These, then, were the type of experiences, findings and impressions which led to the present experiment—part 2 of the Youth Authority's Community Treatment Project.

"Part 2" has several objectives; however, its main thrust relates to the following question: Would many of the above-mentioned youths become less delinquently oriented if they began their CYA career within a certain kind of residential setting (described below), and *not within the community itself?* Thus the title of this 1969–1974 effort: "Settings for the Differential Treatment of Delinquents."[14]

To be sure, the idea of using a residential facility, on a fairly long-term basis if necessary, involved a definite departure from the philosophy which was behind the 1961–1969 effort. Under that philosophy, or set of hypotheses, the treatment-and-control of *all* eligible youths could just as well have begun within the community itself.[15] (Basically, only the research requirement that there be a control group prevented this from actually occurring.) Furthermore, during 1961–1969 the residential setting—in this case NRCC—was to be used (a) only *after* the youths' intensive community program had gotten underway, and (b) on a short-term "temporary detention" basis alone, if at all.

The "Settings" experiment obtains its sample of youths from the greater Sacramento area. This consists entirely of males who (a) may be 13 to 21 years old at intake, and (b) are no longer restricted to being juvenile court commitments. The *key* "ineligibility criteria"—i.e., bases for exclusion—relate to the youths' commitment offense and offense history, as before. However, the present set of offense-criteria allow for the inclusion, within the experiment, of a *broader range* of individuals than was possible in 1961–1969. (See below for details.)

PROCEDURES AND OPERATIONS (1969–1974)

The following question is asked by project staff in connection with each newly committed youth who—in accordance with the above criteria—seems likely to later be judged eligible by the Youth Authority Board:[16] "Within which type of setting would it probably be best to initiate the treatment-and-control of this individual"? The choice is between: (1) Initial assignment to an intensive, CTP-staffed-and-operated residential program—later to be followed by release to the intensive CTP community program (staffed-and-operated as in 1961–1969); (2) direct release to the intensive CTP community program (again as per the 1961–1969 pattern).

The project staffing team approaches the above question by first making a careful study of the individual's interests, limitations, immediate pressures and underlying motivations. The main object is to figure out what the most appropriate, yet practical, short-range and long-range goals might be. The resulting "close look" allows staff to next "check the youth out" in terms of written guidelines which are designed to further focus their attention on the question of *where* the given treatment-and-control plan might best be started. The guidelines relate to certain categories of youth who, as mentioned earlier, were found to be unusually difficult to "reach" during 1961–1969:

> In these guidelines, a number of distinguishing characteristics are spelled out with regard to five groups of individuals. (According to the hypotheses of this experiment, youths who appear to "fit" any one or more of these descriptions "should" begin their CYA career within the above-mentioned residential setting.) More specifically, the guidelines contain short descriptions of (a) certain patterns of interacting with others, (b) outstanding personality characteristics, (c) underlying motivations, and/or (d) immediate pressures and life circumstances.[17] The guidelines are outlined in Section D of the Appendix.

Individuals who are seen as needing an initial period of institutionalization are referred to as "Status 1"; those seen as *not* needing this type of initial setting are termed "Status 2." When the staffing team completes its evaluation of an individual and finalizes his "status," a random drawing is then made to determine whether his initial *placement* is to be within the CTP residential component (i.e., program) or else within its community-based component.[18] All CTP parole agents serve both parts of CTP. (Prior to the youth's actual placement into either one or the other of these CTP settings/components, the Youth Authority Board must declare him eligible for CTP per se. It makes this decision without having learned the outcome of the random drawing.)

> This random assignment procedure results in the establishment of four separate youth-groups—two "residential" and two "community-based," with each of the two containing a subgroup of Status 1 and, in addition, Status 2 individuals. The research team later compares each one of these four youth-groups with each of the remaining three, in terms of community adjustment.[19] With certain planned exceptions, parole agents who participate in the experiment can have caseloads which contain individuals from all four youth-groups.

The parole agent who is assigned to work with a given youth, and who has therefore been part of the staffing team, remains assigned to that youth regardless of whether the latter's placement happens to be within the residential or the community section of CTP at any particular point in time. This helps promote continuity within and across settings, with respect to long-term treatment-and-control efforts.[20]

Before presenting the results to date, a few words should be added about the CTP residential unit. This unit ("Dorm 3") is located at NRCC and is a 5- or 10-minute drive from CTP's community center in Sacramento. Dorm 3 normally houses 23 to 25 youths at any one time—CTP youths (males) exclusively—although the number has ranged from 15 to 32. It is staffed by carefully selected "youth counselors" and "group supervisors," and is readily as well as continuously accessible to all remaining CTP personnel. Some parole agents have their office in the dorm. All dorm staff are individually, and officially, paired-up with one or two agents. This makes for better dorm-agent as well as dorm-dorm coordination of efforts with respect to implementing stated goals and strategies for residence-located youths who are on the caseload of the given agents.

Two additional points. (1) *Expanding CTP's Applicability.* Part of the 1969–1974 effort centers around the following question: Can the CTP approach[21] be applied to a *broader range and variety* of offenders than that which was available in connection with the 1961–1969 experiment? This question is dealt with at two levels: First, the "ineligibility criteria" which were used during 1961–1969 have been trimmed back in order to allow for the inclusion of many individuals who would otherwise be *excluded* on the basis of (a) commitment offenses relating to armed robbery, forcible rape, etc., or (b) offense histories of a particularly disturbed or aggressive-appearing nature.[22] However, the Board will declare these particular youths eligible for CTP only with the understanding that their program is to be initiated within Dorm 3. (For research purposes, all such individuals are therefore analyzed as a separate group. They are called "Category B" youths.[23]) Secondly, and aside from the matter of offenses, all first commitments to the CYA from the Sacramento County Superior Court have been made available for inclusion within CTP. This is the first time that adult court commitments have become part of the CTP studies. No restrictions are applied as to *where* these particular individuals may begin their program; etc. (2) *Terminology.* The following should facilitate the presentation of findings:

RR = Status 1 youths who were *appropriately placed:* These individuals were diagnosed as needing to begin their program within a residential setting. Their program *did* begin within a residential setting (i.e., Dorm 3).

RC = Status 1 youths who were *inappropriately placed:* Diagnosed as needing to begin in a residential setting; however, their program was initiated within a community setting, as in 1961–1969.

CR = Status 2 youths who were *inappropriately placed:* Diagnosed as being able to begin their program within a community setting; however, their program was initiated within a residential setting (i.e., Dorm 3).

CC = Status 2 youths who were *appropriately placed:* Diagnosed as being able to begin their program within a community setting. Their program *did* begin within a community setting, as in 1961–1969.

MAIN FINDINGS TO DATE (1969–1974 EXPERIMENT)[24]

Status 1 youths who were inappropriately placed are performing considerably worse than those who were appropriately placed: 94 percent of the RC's (inappropriately placed) as vs. 58 percent of the RR's (appropriately placed) have chalked up one or more offenses during their first year-and-a-half on parole.[25] The number of offenses per youth is 1.56 among RC's and 0.96 among RR's. For each month at risk the mean rate of offending is .140 among RC's as vs. .066 among RR's—in other words, one offense for every 7.1 months in the case of RC's, and one per 15.2 months among RR's.[26] This 112 percent difference in rate of offending cannot be explained in terms of "chance."[27]

These findings suggest that the delinquent behavior of the Youth Authority's more troubled, troublesome and/or resistive wards may be substantially reduced—provided that they are first worked with in a setting such as is represented by Dorm 3, as distinct from one which is community-based in the usual sense of the term. The scope, and the potential importance, of any such "reductions" should not be thought of as slight: Status 1 youths represent 46 percent of the total CTP sample.[28] It is likely that they comprise a sizable portion of the Youth Authority's total population, as well.[29]

What about the remaining 54 percent—i.e., the *Status 2* youths? (These youths, it will be recalled, are the less troubled, troublesome and/or resistive individuals.) On balance the present findings suggest that there is little if anything to be gained, with regard to parole performance, by initially placing Status 2 youths into a residential facility,[30] even of the type represented by Dorm 3: The average monthly rates of offending are .086 for CR's (inappropriately placed) and .068 for CC's (appropriately placed)—a difference of 26 percent. On the surface, these rates might suggest that an "inappropriate" (in this case, residential) placement would be slightly *detrimental* to the Status 2 youths, at least when compared with the more appropriate, alternate placement. However, this particular difference in rates of offending may be accounted for by "chance" alone. Together with results from three other measures of performance, the overall picture is one of few substantial and consistent CR vs. CC differences.

Inappropriately placed youths (RC's + CR's) are performing worse than appropriately placed youths (RR's + CC's): For each month spent within the community, the mean rate of offending is .107 among "inappropriates" (INP's) and .067 among "appropriates" (APR's). This amounts to one offense for every 9.3 months on parole in the case of INP's, and one per 14.9 months among APR's. This 60 percent difference cannot be accounted for by "chance." Results from the remaining performance-indicators are consistent with this basic finding, although not as clear-cut.

The various findings which have been presented might seem to suggest the obvious: Delinquent behavior can probably be reduced in connection with community and residential programs *alike*, by means of careful diagnosis and subsequent placement of individuals into appropriate rather than inappropriate or less-than-optimal settings and programs. In short, it might be said that it matters *which* youths (or types of youth) are placed into *which* type of setting, and that careful selection may lead to higher rates of success for residential and community-based programs alike. Yet it is recognized that such a viewpoint or conclusion would by no means be universally accepted as being "obvious," within corrections. For one thing, many people feel that nothing really has much effect on delinquent behavior; others believe that one single approach, and perhaps one particular setting, may well contain "the answer" for all but a tiny portion of the population. At any rate, the present findings will hopefully add new information to a long-standing placement issue which many practitioners do regard as being less than entirely obvious in the majority, if not large majority, of cases: Which youths would best be placed into which types of setting, or program?

Two final points in this connection. (1) The difference in rate of offending which is found *between* the Status 1 groups (RC's *vs.* RR's) is considerably larger than that found between the Status 2 groups (CR's *vs.* CC's). More specifically, Status 1 youths who were inappropriately placed are performing *considerably* worse than those who were appropriately placed; however, in the case of Status 2 youths *no substantial differences* are observed between individuals who were inappropriately placed and those who were appropriately placed. This raises the possibility that an initial placement within an inappropriate or less-than-optimal setting might make more of a difference to Status 1 youths than to those diagnosed as Status 2. It may be that the latter, presumably "stronger" individuals are in a better position to compensate for, or otherwise cope with and make the best of, an environment of this nature. (2) The significance, or possible differential significance, of the initial treatment-and-control setting is also suggested by the following: Appropriately placed youths (RR's *and* CC's) are performing about equally well on parole—i.e., regardless of status. However, *inappropriately* placed *Status 1* youths (RC's) are performing substantially worse than inappropriately placed *Status 2* youths (CR's). In other words, appropriate placement may perhaps help to offset or moderate certain pre-existing differences in level of coping ability, on the part of Status 1 vs. Status 2 youths. On the other hand, *inappropriate* or less-than-optimal placement may be more likely to accentuate or activate various differences which relate to their personal or interpersonal liabilities.

Thus far, the CTP approach does seem applicable to categories of offenders other than those which were studied in 1961–1969: Briefly, *Adult Court* commitments have presented few if any special operational problems, or, for that matter, diagnostic problems. Their treatment-and-control requirements differ only slightly from those of Juvenile Court commitments who fall within the 16-and-older age range. In addition, *Category B* youths have presented few unusual or serious operational and diagnostic problems. However, partly because of Board restrictions which are frequently placed upon these individuals with regard to day passes, furloughs or minimum length of residential stay, it has sometimes been difficult to develop treatment-and-control plans which closely resemble those observed in the case of many other residence-located youths. Operations staff nevertheless feel able to engage in productive interactions with most such youths. The parole performance of these individuals has yet to be evaluated in detail.

OVERVIEW AND CONCLUDING REMARKS

Within and outside of corrections, many concerned individuals are currently engaged in an ideological battle over whether to "keep almost all offenders on the streets," or else "lock up nearly all offenders, except for first-timers." This, of course, may be exaggerating the situation to a certain degree; yet at the same time, it may be accurate in its reflection of certain feelings which are often involved. Feelings aside, the facts which have emerged from California's 12-year experiment thus far suggest that both of the above positions may be too extreme, and that a more differentiated or flexible approach may be appropriate. (These considerations would at least apply to the type of individuals who have been studied thus far—youths who have had numerous contacts with the law.) A brief review may illustrate this point:

When an NIMH-funded research team combined several hundred

Youth Authority males into a single study group (one which included the full range of CYA "personality types"), it found that (a) "experimentals" who participated in the intensive, 1961–1969 *community-based program (CTP)* had produced substantially less delinquent behavior than (b) "controls" who had participated in the traditional CYA program. (The experimentals and controls had been well-matched on such characteristics as age, IQ, socioeconomic status, race, etc.) However, the researchers also found that much of this difference in favor of the CTP—i.e., noninstitutional—program was accounted for by youths who were referred to as "Neurotics." During the 1960's, these individuals accounted for half of the CYA's population; they currently account for considerably more. By way of contrast, the *traditional CYA program* was found to have a greater influence than CTP in the case of individuals described as "Power Oriented." This particular group now comprises about one-tenth of the CYA population; it previously accounted for twice that amount.

Quite aside from these particular findings and developments, it was observed, prior to 1969, that roughly one-third of the *total* sample were responding somewhat indifferently, and often quite unfavorably, to the community-based and traditional programs alike. Included within this broad, "difficult-to-reach" category were some individuals from nearly all personality groupings. However, it was the difficult-to-reach Neurotics who accounted for the largest total number. (This was possible despite the relatively positive performance by the Neurotic group as a whole.) Since 1969, the distinguishing characteristics of difficult-to-reach "Neurotics" have been largely singled-out. In many cases (perhaps half) operations staff have helped them to engage in less by way of delinquent behavior while in the community. But before this could occur, it was necessary for these individuals to *begin* their Youth Authority program, (a) not within the community per se, (b) not inside a standard CYA institution, but rather (c) within a *medium-sized, CTP-staffed residential facility*—one which was operated in accordance with the 1961–1969 "differential treatment" philosophy. As to the difficult-to-reach "Power Oriented" youths, this same "residence-first" (CTP facility) approach seems to be resulting in relatively little overall improvement in terms of parole performance. Thus, the *traditional* program may still represent the Youth Authority's best alternative for the majority of these particular individuals—especially the subgroup known as "Cfc's." Finally, during 1961–1969 the "Passive Conformists" (now one-tenth of the population) performed somewhat, though not a great deal better in CTP than within the traditional CYA program. Nevertheless, their response to CTP's residential facility (1969–present) has been unfavorable. Thus, in this particular instance the 1961–1969 type of community-based approach would seem to be the treatment of choice.

CTP's originally stated ideal—that of changing delinquents into lifelong nondelinquents—is not being achieved in the large majority of cases. Obviously, the CTP program does not contain a "special potion" which, after having been taken, is capable of eliminating all traces of delinquency, and of fortifying the youths against every form of stress. Nevertheless, the "differential treatments" and "differential settings" which have been utilized in this program do seem capable of *reducing* the total volume of delinquent behavior on the part of many, but by no means all, eligible males. This holds true during the period of their CYA jurisdiction and, to a lesser extent, subsequent to the termination of that jurisdiction. In order to bring about this "reduction," it has very often seemed unnecessary to initially place these individuals within a residential setting (traditional or otherwise); in many other cases, it has seemed quite necessary. As suggested above, it is what goes on *within* the given setting that seems to count, and not just the setting itself. This, of course, may also vary from one type of youth to another.

Nothing in our experience suggests that it is an easy matter to operate a program such as CTP. Implementation and maintenance of a community-based, intensive differential treatment-and-control program involves critical issues, and requires steadfast commitments, with respect to personnel selection, quality of supervision, administrative support, etc. In one form or another, issues of this nature will also be encountered outside the context of large-sized, State agencies such as the CYA. Although challenges of this type have been adequately met in certain instances, it might be well to recognize the fact that any thoroughgoing implementation of CTP—even of the 1961–1969 approach alone—is, at the present time, probably beyond the reach of most probation and parole departments within the USA on anything other than a limited scale. Even so, worthwhile modifications and adaptations of the California program do seem to be well within the realm of possibility; in several instances, they are already in existence.

Whatever the immediate future may hold for programs such as CTP, the research information which has been gathered since 1961 may continue to be of interest to practitioners, administrators and social scientists who still place value upon the concept of actively and directly intervening in the life of personally troubled, developmentally lacking and/or disturbing-aggressive youths and young adults. This should apply in relation to community-based and residential-centered programs alike.

APPENDIX

Section A

The three groups of youth which were first mentioned on page 4 may be briefly described as follows:

(1) *Passive Conformist:* This type of youth usually fears, and responds with strong compliance to, peers and adults who he thinks have the "upper hand" at the moment, or who seem more adequate and assertive than himself. He considers himself to be lacking in social "know-how," and usually expects to be rejected by others in spite of his efforts to please them.

(2) *Power Oriented:* This group is actually made up of two somewhat different kinds of individuals, who, nevertheless, share several important features with one another. The first likes to think of himself as delinquent and tough. He is often more than willing to "go along" with others, or with a gang, in order to earn a certain degree of status and acceptance, and to later maintain his "reputation." The second type, or "subtype," often attempts to undermine or circumvent the efforts and directions of authority figures. Typically, he does not wish to conform to peers or adults; and not infrequently, he will attempt to assume a leading "power role" for himself.

Passive Conformist and Power Oriented youths are usually thought of as having reached a "middle maturity" level of interpersonal development. The group which is described next is said to have reached a "higher maturity" level. The "level of interpersonal maturity" concept is briefly explained in Section B of this Appendix.

(3) *Neurotic:* Here again, we find two separate personality types which share certain important characteristics with one another. The first type often attempts to deny—to himself and others—his conscious feelings of inadequacy, rejection, or self-condemnation. Not infrequently, he does this by verbally attacking *others* and/or by the use of boisterous distractions plus a variety of "games." The second type often shows various symptoms of emotional disturbance—e.g., chronic or intense depression, or psychosomatic complaints. His tensions and conscious fears usually result from conflicts produced by feelings of failure, inadequacy, or underlying guilt.

Section B

The following are brief definitions of the three main levels of interpersonal maturity which are observed within the CYA:

Maturity Level Two (I^2): An individual whose overall development has reached this level, but has not gone beyond it, views events and objects mainly as sources of short-term pleasure, or else frustration. He distinguishes among individuals largely in terms of their being either "givers" or "withholders," and seems to have few ideas of interpersonal refinement beyond this. He has a very low level of frustration-tolerance; moreover, he has a poor capacity for understanding many of the basic reasons for the behavior or attitudes of others, toward him.

Maturity Level Three (1^3): More than the 1^2, an individual at this level recognizes that certain aspects of his own behavior have a good deal to do with whether or not he will get what he wants from others. Such an individual interacts mainly in terms of oversimplified rules and formulas rather than from a set of relatively firm, and generally more complex, internalized standards or ideals. He understands few of the feelings and motives of individuals whose personalities are rather different than his own. More often than the 1^4 (see below), he assumes that peers and adults operate mostly on a rule-oriented or intimidation/manipulation basis.

Maturity Level Four (1^4): More than the 1^3, an individual at this level has internalized one or more "sets" of standards which he frequently uses as a basis for either accepting or rejecting the behavior and attitudes of himself as well as others. (These standards are not always mutually consistent, or consistently applied.) He recognizes interpersonal interactions in which individuals attempt to influence one another by means other than compliance, manipulation, promises of hedonistic or monetary reward, etc. He has a fair ability to understand underlying reasons for behavior, and displays some ability to respond, on a fairly long-term basis, to certain moderately complex expectations on the part of various peers and adults.

Section C

For the *Neurotic* group, the additional information and findings are as follows:

(1) Despite its known shortcomings, "rate of recidivism" has long been one of corrections' most widely used measures of parole *failure*. As used in this report, recidivism reflects the occurrence of any one or more of the following events: (a) Revocation of the youth's parole by the Youth Authority Board; (b) recommitment of the youth to the CYA, by either a Juvenile or an Adult Court; (c) unfavorable discharge of the youth by the Youth Authority Board, from the CYA itself. Any one of these events is usually the result of some type of police arrest and subsequent conviction. Events (a) and (b), above, are usually followed by a period of incarceration for several months, within one or another of the Youth Authority's large-sized institutions. (See below, regard-

ing (c).) Thus, the higher the recidivism rate, the greater is the amount of "failure" in one sense of the term. Now then, on 24-months parole followup the recidivism rate was 66 percent for controls and 45 percent for experimentals.

(2) Within 60 months from the time of their first release to the community (literally, their date of initial parole), 40 percent of the C's as vs. 77 percent of the E's had been officially released by the Youth Authority Board from the CYA's jursidiction—on the basis of a *favorable discharge*. Also within a period of 60 months, 40 percent of the C's as vs. 17 percent of the E's were released on the basis of an unfavorable discharge. (It should be noted that depending upon an individual's behavior subsequent to one or more prior parole revocations which he may have received, the individual will still be able to eventually obtain *either* a favorable *or* an unfavorable discharge from the CYA.)[31]

(3) What happened *after* the CYA's jurisdiction had ended, in the case of Neurotic youths and young adults who had been given a *favorable discharge* (see (2), above)? At least this much is known: Many of these individuals did not entirely relinquish their delinquent tendencies—despite their experiences within the CYA. Be this as it may, those who had gone through the traditional CYA program seemed, on the average, to have remained somewhat *more* delinquent than those who had completed CTP: Within 48 months after having left the Youth Authority, controls chalked up an average of 1.88 convictions; the figure for experimentals was 1.58. (A somewhat larger C vs. E difference was obtained when one looked at *arrests*, and not simply convictions. As before, arrests of minor severity were not counted.) In practical terms, this would amount to a difference of about 300 convictions for every 1,000 experimental as well as control "favorable-dischargees," over a 4-year span of time. (The reader may note that this analysis of *post-CYA*, CI&I data has been completed on "arrests" and, also, on the "convictions" which related to those arrests. However, because the earlier-mentioned *parole (CYA-time)* CI&I data were first analyzed during 1973, only the "arrest" information has been looked at thus far, with regard to *parole* time. Judging from the "post-CYA" findings on arrests vs. convictions, the "parole time" results for these same two levels of analysis should be very similar to one another.) Using a 10-point scale, the penalties received for each conviction were somewhat more severe among controls than among experimentals—5.75 as vs. 4.25, on the average.

The following results relate to *Power Oriented* youths:

(1) CI&I rap sheets showed an arrest rate of .060 for controls and .071 for experimentals, with regard to each month spent within the community. This difference favored the traditional program by 18

percent. (Again, offenses of minor severity were excluded, although the picture hardly changed when they were included.) (2) On 24-months' parole followup, the recidivism rate was 66 percent for controls and 40 percent for experimentals. (3) Despite the better showing by experimentals on the 24-month recidivism index, it was found that 53 percent of the controls as vs. 43 percent of the experimentals received a favorable discharge from the Youth Authority within 60 months of their first release to parole. Similarly, 15 percent of the C's as vs. 23 percent of the E's received an unfavorable discharge. (4) Within 48 months after being released from the CYA's jurisdiction, the Power Oriented, control *"favorable-dischargees"* had chalked up an average of 1.47 convictions; the figure for experimentals was 2.55. (The C vs. E difference was even larger when one focused upon arrests alone, rather than convictions alone.) This was a 73 percent difference in favor of Power Oriented youths who had successfully completed the Youth Authority's traditional program.

The following relates to *Passive Conformist* youths:

(1) CI&I rap sheets showed an arrest rate of .066 for controls and .037 for experimentals, for each month within the community. This difference favored the CTP program by 78 percent. (2) On 24-months' parole followup, the recidivism rate was 59 percent for controls and 51 percent for experimentals. (3) 54 percent of the C's as vs. 78 percent of the E's received a favorable discharge from the Youth Authority within 60 months of their first release to the community. Similarly, 14 percent of the C's as vs. 6 percent of the E's received an unfavorable discharge. (4) Within 48 months after termination of their CYA jurisdiction, the Passive Conformist, control "favorable-dischargees" had chalked up an average of 1.44 convictions; the figure for experimentals was 1.80. This was a 25 percent difference in favor of the traditional program.

Section D

Basic to the 1969–1974 experiment is the hypothesis that certain youths (five groups in all) would probably derive greater benefit from a course of treatment-and-control which would begin within a residential setting, in contrast to a community setting. Briefly, the groups are:

(1) Youths who are quite disturbed and openly disorganized relative to overall, everyday functioning, and who at times become highly agitated or even delusional when under the pressure of everyday life. (Mostly found among Nx's, Ap's and Aa's.)

(2) Youths who have an intensive drive to prevent other persons from exerting controls upon them, or from substantially influencing

the direction of their lives. They are prepared to use virtually "everything" in their power—including runaway, physical resistance, etc.—to avoid the ongoing confrontation of concerned authority figures, and to avoid involvement in nonexploitive relationships with adults in general. (Mostly found among Mp's and Cfc's—the "Power Oriented" group.)

(3) Youths who are unable to recognize, or who vigorously attempt to deny, the existence and influence of the unusually destructive relationships and loyalty-binds in which they are involved, at home and within the community. Were these youths released directly to the community setting, conditions such as these would undermine the youth/parole agent relationship at a time when this relationship would still be in its formative stage, and would operate so as to lead the youth into delinquent acting-out of a frequency or magnitude sufficient to result in an early parole revocation and removal from the community setting. (Mostly found among Na's and Nx's—the "Neurotic" group.)

(4) Youths who are nonneurotic and of a relatively high level of maturity, but who need to actually be shown that their freedom will definitely be withdrawn if they persist in their delinquent patterns. (Mostly found among Ci's.)

(5) Youths who—operating on the basis of underlying motivations of a self-defeating nature—have become increasingly committed to the use of drugs and/or a drug-using subculture, to the point of feeling little interest in coping with long-range social expectations or pressures, or in interacting with others in a nonexploitive manner. (Mostly found among Na's and Nx's.)

Notes

1. It should be mentioned that experimental and control youths both spent an average of 4 to 6 weeks at the Youth Authority's Northern Reception Center and Clinic (NRCC), immediately after having been committed to the Youth Authority. This period of "routine processing" consisted of necessary medical and dental work, standard diagnostic workups and related achievement testing, appearance before the Youth Authority Board, etc. Upon release from NRCC, youths were either sent to a CYA institution for a period which averaged several months or else they were returned directly to their home community, on parole status.

2. In part, this is because the necessary, detailed analyses have not been completed relative to San Francisco youths. Nevertheless, relevant analyses which have been completed suggest that the overall results may be fairly comparable to those which appear in the present report, for the Sacramento-Stockton location alone.

Of the 1,014 eligibles, 72 percent of the boys and 58 percent of the girls were from the Sacramento-Stockton area.

3. For example, an estimated 25 percent of the overall probation population—in contrast to the 14 percent which was observed during the CYA's 1961–1969 effort.

4. They accounted for 94 percent of the eligible girls.

5. See: Warren, M. Q. et al., "Interpersonal Maturity Level Classification: Juvenile. Diagnosis and Treatment of Low, Middle, and High Maturity Delinquents." (Sac-

ramento: California Youth Authority, 1966), pp. 1–52, (mimeo.).

6. These documents are compiled by the State of California, Department of Justice (D.J.). They are based on reports which are routinely, and directly, received by D.J. from police, probation, and sheriffs' departments throughout California. Among other things, the documents may include listings of antisocial activities which had not been mentioned in the (a) formal suspension reports, and (b) "special incident reports," of Youth Authority parole agents who participated in the 1961–1969 effort. (For a variety of reasons, omissions of this nature occurred significantly more often relative to the traditional program, as compared with the CTP program.)

7. The figures which will next be given refer to all youths who received either a favorable or an unfavorable discharge from the CYA by the close of the 1961–1969 experiment, or shortly thereafter.

8. Arrests of "minor severity" are those which relate to traffic (noninjuries/nonfelonies), runaway, incorrigibility, etc.

9. More recently referred to as higher maturity "delinquent identifiers" (Di's).

10. As indicated in footnote 31, we have not completed the analysis of post-CYA offense behavior on the part of individuals who had received an *unfavorable* discharge.

11. The periods of incarceration which resulted from these revocations are over and beyond the *initial* period of incarceration which was experienced by the controls, but not by the experimentals, shortly after their original commitment to the Youth Authority.

12. In connection with the "recent period" the primary question was: What would the program costs look like on the basis of early 1970 prices—yet in relation to the performance of an actual sample of experimentals and controls who had entered the CYA during the later part of the 1961–1969 effort?

13. Thus, 5,734 divided by 7,180 yields a ratio of 0.80 to 1.

14. As before, the research costs are picked up by NIMH.

15. At any rate, there seemed to be little if any scientific evidence to suggest that it would be *inappropriate or impractical* to begin the treatment-and-control of eligible wards outside of a traditional institutional setting.

16. As in 1961–1969, the Youth Authority Board gives the final, legal approval in regard to eligibility. (In the event that the youth is declared eligible, a "random drawing" will alone determine exactly *where* he is to begin his treatment-and-control. See the text.) Prior to the time that a ward is officially declared eligible, he would be referred to as a "pre-eligible."

17. Since 1969, these descriptions have been found to be largely, though not entirely, mutually exclusive.

18. As a result of the random drawing, it not infrequently happens that a Status 1 youth will have to begin his program within the community setting. By the same token, a Status 2 youth may have to begin within the residential facility. (These "less-than-optimal," initial placements serve an essential function in terms of the research design.) When this type of initial placement is called for, the Operations section of the staffing team prepares what is called a "modified treatment-and-control" plan. This differs in several respects from the "optimal . . . plan" which they had prepared just prior to the drawing. The main object of the modified plan is to (a) develop goals which are appropriate to the less-than-optimal setting in which the youth's program is to be initiated, yet which will remain relevant to the individual's needs, and (b) develop strategies which will allow for and at the same time encourage a maximum use of the resources which are available within the particular setting.

19. The groups which are being compared thus serve as "controls" for one another.

20. In many cases, individuals whose parole is revoked while they are in the community can be placed into, or returned to, the CTP residential facility. This allows them to remain part of the overall program.

21. In the present case this includes the "differential treatment" feature in addition to the community-based aspect per se.

22. That is, regardless of the possible lack of severity of the *commitment* offense itself.

23. All other youths are referred to as "Category A."

24. (a) These results relate to the first 106 eligible "Category A" males who were

paroled as of December 15, 1972. (See footnote 23.) When "Category B" cases are included, the results hardly change. (b) Neurotic, Power Oriented, Passive Conformist, and "rare types" are combined into a single group—74 percent of which is comprised of the Neurotic category alone. (The findings which are reported—more specifically, the differences between comparison groups—are very largely accounted for by the latter individuals. They receive little if any support in relation to the remaining 26 percent of the sample, when the latter are viewed as a single, separate entity.) This population-distribution probably reflects a broader trend within the CYA as a whole. (c) The present results take into account offenses of all severity levels; however, they are virtually unchanged when those of minor severity are excluded. The latter account for 7 percent of the present, 120 offenses. (d) "Offense" is defined as any delinquent act which results in any one or more of the following, official actions: Revocation of parole; court recommitment; adjudicated court referral to CTP; unfavorable transfer from CTP; suspension parole. (During the coming year an analysis of CI&I rap sheets will be undertaken for the first time, relative to the 1969–1974 sample.)

25. As before, "months on parole" is used synonymously with "months in the community" and "months at risk."

26. By using a closely related yet possibly more refined statistical approach, an even larger difference was obtained between RC's and RR's with respect to the average (mean) monthly rate of offending. When the *median* rather than the *mean* was used in relation to this alternate approach, the monthly rate of offending was .180 for RC's and .060 for RR's.

27. Nor can various background factors account for this difference. These factors include age, IQ, socioeconomic status, race, I-level, "subtype," and level of parole risk ("base expectancy").

28. With "Category B" youths included, the figure is 49 percent.

29. In 1968, research staff estimated that 39 percent of all eligible youths would receive a Status 1 diagnosis during the present experiment. Wards who were received by the CYA during the past few years appear to be more involved with delinquency than those received during the 1960's. For example, the present sample of eligible Category A subjects had accumulated an average of 7.1 delinquent contacts by the time of their commitment to the CYA. The figure for 1961–1969 eligibles was 5.8.

30. This is generally consistent with the main results of the 1961–1969 experiment.

31. Taking into account all "groups" of boys—i.e., all nine "subtypes"—50 percent of the experimentals and 50 percent of the controls who received an unfavorable discharge from the Youth Authority were sent to a State or Federal prison immediately upon receipt of their discharge. Their Court sentence commonly specified a maximum of several years' incarceration. Partly because of this, followup (i.e., post-CYA, postprison) analyses have not been completed for the unfavorable dischargee sample.

53 / Methodological and Theoretical Issues in Juvenile Diversion: Implications for Evaluations

DENNIS BERG
DAVID SHICHOR

Diversion is a term used widely in the field of corrections. As is the case with many other terms, there is some ambiguity and confusion regarding the exact meaning of the concept. Diversion means many different things to many different people. (Cressey and McDermott, 1973:7).

The National Advisory Commission on Criminal Justice Standards and Goals uses the term "diversion" in reference to

formally acknowledged and organized efforts to utilize alternatives to initial or continued processing into the justice system. To qualify as diversion, such efforts must be undertaken prior to adjudication and after a legally proscribed action has occurred.

According to this definition, all those modalities in which offenders are dealt with in a way that will halt further official processing after the first encounter with formal agencies (police, or community organizations) would qualify as diversion. These efforts are predicated on the assumption that the existing system often has negative effects upon the offenders, and is not even very efficient in reducing existing crime rates.

Although the general objectives of diversion seem to be widely accepted by people in the field of juvenile corrections, there are nevertheless some criticisms leveled against them. In a recent work, Morris (1974) expresses his concern that attempts at diversion may result in an increase in the number of people brought under social control, since policies which keep our offenders from correctional institutions may at the very same time extend control by formal agencies. Morris predicts that the guilty will be convicted while the innocent will be diverted and supervised. Concerning juvenile justice he points out that:

... the juvenile court itself was a diversionary program, aiming to reduce the impact of the criminal law on the young offender and to divert him to less primitive, rehabilitative controls. However, it had swept more children within the ambit of the criminal law than if the State had not gone coercively into the business of child saving by means of statutes ill defining delinquency. (Morris, 1974:11)

Probation seems to have the same results—namely, the reduction of the extent of incarceration, especially among juveniles, with a concomitant increase in the total number of youngsters under the control of the criminal justice system (Platt, 1969). That is likewise the case with coercive diversion programs devised for drug addicts and alcoholics. Many of the juveniles participating in the diversion programs are status offenders and thus, many believe, should not have been handled by the juvenile justice system in the first place.

In addition, diversion programs are usually based on the therapeutic ideal, with supervision and treatment seen as complementary aspects of one role. An individual in such a position is exposed to opposing demands in which the supervisory role often supersedes the treatment role, and the coercive aspects threaten to detract from the therapeutic ones. Diversion programs can also be easily slanted toward the "medical model" of corrections by keeping juveniles under "treatment" until they progress well enough to be released, instead of retaining them in a program for a determined period of time. This practice can provide a wide discretionary power to the administrative and treatment staff. With the increase in the discretionary power of each individual staff member there tends to be a decrease in the uniformity of treatment method. At the same time the "sick role" is attributed to the participants.

While diversion seems to be an effort to mitigate the adverse effects of processing through the formal social control system, it may nevertheless result in a public definition of the individual as a deviant or delinquent. The introjection of this social labeling often culminates in "secondary deviance," the development of a delinquent self-concept which determines the person's future career and life-style. (Lemert, 1951; Becker, 1963).

The current proliferation of diversion programs in the field of juvenile justice warrants intensive, continuing evaluation of their effectiveness. In fact, if these programs are to be assessed correctly and the maximum benefits derived from them, some means for self-evaluation should be built into them from the outset.

The Present Study

This present study is based on a more detailed evaluation of the Behavioral Assessment and Treatment Services Center (Berg, 1975), which was established and implemented during 1972 in Orange County, California. The major objectives of the (ATSC) project were:

1. to provide a multidisciplinary resource to which the police could refer emotionally disturbed and/or behaviorally disordered juveniles for assessment and/or treatment and as a diversion from the juvenile justice system;

2. to develop a model intake process within the regular juvenile probation system which would maximize diversion from the juvenile justice system at the point of intake;

3. to identify needed service resources and develop appropriate community-based and funded service facilities which would provide service outside of the juvenile justice system.

Virtually all of the referrals received by the ATSC were from the over twenty law enforcement agencies operating within the county. Assessment appointments were arranged for all referrals as the initial intake mechanism. Assessment resulted in release, referral to other agencies or the development of a treatment plan. Parents were encouraged to participate in assessment as well as treatment if necessary. Table 1 provides a summary of the dispositions resulting from referral to the ATSC for those cases selected into the evaluation sample.

Table 1 / Assessment and Treatment Services Center Caseload Dispositions for Referrals Received Between Sept. 1, 1972 and Feb. 28, 1974

Referral Dispositions	N	TOTAL PERCENT	SUBGROUP PERCENT
Referrals	639	100.0	—
Failed to show for assessment	65	10.2	10.2
Assessed	574	89.8	89.8
Found not in need of treatment...........	71	11.1	12.4
Dismissed with ATSC followup	39	6.1	54.9
Treatment not needed	32	5.0	45.1
Found in need of treatment	503	78.7	87.6
Referred to other agency	66	10.3	13.1
Treatment not obtained/other	41	6.4	8.2
Treated at ATSC	396	62.0	78.7
Early Terminations....................	91	14.2	23.0
Violations	28	4.4	7.1
Mutual/normal treatment	277	43.4	69.9

The evaluation of the ATSC attempted to establish the extent to which the program was able to accomplish its stated objectives. This of course required the translation of those objectives into measurable criteria (Glaser, 1973:16; Weiss and Rein, 1971:293). The goals set forward in the ATSC project proposal serve as a good example of the kind of problem which results when the objectives of a project fail to be clearly articulated.

Objective 1, for example, as stated in the project proposal, failed to make reference to any explicit anticipated accomplishment. The fact that a resource was provided and that its existence became known to law enforcement agencies, which in turn referred juveniles to the program, is obvious. Consequently, the operationalization of this objective was based on two major assumptions: (1) that the primary aim of any diversion program is ultimately the reduction of delinquent behavior and the rehabilitation of those who were involved in law-breaking activity; and (2) that this goal is to be accomplished by avoiding the involvement of the juveniles with the formal sanctioning system.

Methodology

The ATSC program did not lend itself to easy evaluation. As is the case with most criminal justice programs, random sampling and randomization were impossible. Thus, the design choice for this study was the pseudo-experimental or quasi-experimental design wherein:

> . . . a treatment process is evaluated by means of information on a treatment group and a 'comparison' group. The latter is chosen in a way that makes it 'similar' to the treatment group. (Adams, 1975:60).

In the present study an effort was made to overcome the problems resulting from the failure to randomize through sample selection procedures and statistical controls by conforming to the "all else being equal" dictum of science. The following measures were taken: (1) In choosing the control population, a select subset of all probation referrals was defined in a way that the resulting set of individuals would approximate the referral characteristics of those who would have been eligible for diversion to the ATSC; thus, it included only initial referrals. (Custody referrals and probation violators were not eligible to participate in ATSC). (2) In a further effort to isolate the effects of differential treatments (ATSC vs. Probation), several variables (e.g., sex, age and previous referral record) were statistically controlled.

The total experimental population included all referrals to the ATSC between September 1, 1972 and February 28, 1974—an eighteen-month period containing 1,305 cases. The starting date was selected as a result of the limited data available on the 277 cases processed prior to this time—that is, during the first three months of the program's operation. The latter date was selected to ensure the availability of at least one year of follow-up information on all cases in the sample.

A systematic random sampling procedure was used whereby every even-numbered referral to ATSC was selected into the sample, excluding re-referrals. This procedure resulted in the selection of a 50 percent random sample of 651 juveniles.

The control group was selected from all initial noncustody referrals received by the Orange County Probation Department during the same period. Restricting the control group to only initial noncustody referrals was an attempt to ensure that the type of cases selected were those which would have been eligible for diversion to the ATSC. Every tenth relevant entry in the probation logbooks was selected into the control group. This procedure resulted in a 10 percent systematic random sample of 1,008 initial noncustody intake cases referred to probation during the eighteen-month period of study.

A wide range of data was collected on the cases referred to the ATSC. These data included detailed personal information, psychological test results, behavioral assessment at the beginning, during and the end of the participation in the program, and a termination form completed at the end of treatment detailing the nature and conditions under which termination took place.

The data on the control group were taken from the probation files and included personal and family data, and information pertaining to the actions taken on the referrals, such as disposition at intake, disposition at court and the dates of intake and termination.

Evaluation Measures: Major Criteria

A variety of procedures were selected for summarizing the subsequent behavior (juvenile justice contact) data. By using several outcome measures, varying aspects of the extent and severity of subsequent behavior could be articulated. Outcome measures included:

(a) the percent of cases having at least one subsequent application for petition;

(b) the percent of cases having at least one subsequent wardship, which is the most serious disposition recorded for each case;

(c) the average number of subsequent referrals;

(d) the average level of severity, measured by the assignment of a weighted severity value to each terminal disposition, (Berg, 1975:17) summed up and divided by N.

ANALYSIS

Selection Bias

The first step of the evaluation was to ascertain the extent of similarity, on the basis of demographic attributes, between the experimental and the control group. This step was instrumental in establishing the comparability of the two groups on basic personal characteristics, thus making it possible to isolate the possible effects of differential correctional treatment.

The comparisons on the two basic demographic variables—sex (Table 2) and age (Table 3)—indicate some significant differences

Table 2 / Sex by Treatment

Sex	ATSC		Probation	
	NUMBER	PERCENT	NUMBER	PERCENT
Male	379	59.4	749	75.6
Female	259	40.6	242	24.4
Total	638	100.0	991	100.0

$X^2 = 47.69$, df=1, p<.001

Table 3 / Age by Treatment

Age	ATSC		Probation	
	NUMBER	PERCENT	NUMBER	PERCENT
Under 13	121	19.2	56	5.7
13–15	340	53.9	405	41.5
Over 15	170	26.9	516	52.8
Total	631	100.0	977	100.0

$X^2 = 135.90$, df=2, p<.001

between the two groups. A significantly greater percent (.001 level) of females were assigned to the ATSC (40.6 percent) than to Probation (24.4 percent). The ATSC cases were found also to be significantly younger than the probation group (on the .001 level). While more than half of the probation sample cases were over 15 years old, only 26.9 percent of the ATSC cases were in that age group.

There was also a significant difference between the two groups in ethnic composition (Table 4). The figures indicate that while the proportion of minority group youngsters was relatively low in both

Table 4 / Ethnicity by Treatment

Ethnicity	ATSC		Probation	
	NUMBER	PERCENT	NUMBER	PERCENT
White	536	94.7	815	86.4
Spanish	20	3.5	92	9.7
Black	6	1.1	21	2.2
Other	4	.7	16	1.7
Total	566	100.0	944	100.0

$X^2=26.5$, df=3, p<.001

programs (ATSC—5.3 percent, probation—13.6 percent), this difference was statistically significant, at the .001 level of significance.

The selection process was also investigated with regard to the
history of delinquent involvement—namely, prior probation referrals. Table 5 contains information concerning the number of prior

Table 5 / Prior Applications for Petitions by Treatment: Number of Applications and Most Serious Prior Referral

Number of Prior Applications for a Petition	ATSC		Probation	
	NUMBER	PERCENT	NUMBER	PERCENT
None	561	91.5	675	77.3
One	42	6.9	128	14.7
Two	8	1.3	45	5.1
Three or More	2	.3	25	2.9
Total	613	100.0	873	100.0

$X^2=55.66$, df=3, p<.001

Most Serious Prior Referral				
None	561	91.5	675	77.3
Dismissed at Intake	30	4.9	89	10.2
Dismissed at Court	15	2.4	44	5.0
Field Supervision	3	.5	52	6.0
Institutional Placement	4	.7	13	1.5
Total	613	100.0	873	100.0

$X^2=58.75$, df=4, p<.001

probation referrals of the participants in both samples within a two-year period prior to the referral, as well as the extent of the most serious prior referral. In both the number and the nature of referrals the findings point out that the two populations were significantly different in their prior juvenile justice contact history.

In the ATSC sample 91.5 percent of the juveniles did not have previous referrals, while in the probation sample this figure was 77.3 percent. In terms of the seriousness of prior referrals, 7.5 percent of the probation sample sustained a prior wardship, while only 1.2 percent of the ATSC cases had similar experience.

These findings indicate that there was a systematic bias in the selection of participants to the ATSC program. There was a clear tendency to select younger juveniles, more girls, more whites and youngsters with fewer and less serious prior delinquent involvement into this program. These findings bring into serious question the degree to which the ATSC program fulfilled a truly diversionary function. How many, for instance, of the juveniles who were referred to the ATSC would have otherwise been placed on probation? There is a good chance that many of them would have been released back to the community without any further processing, or would not have been contacted in the first place. Thus, it can be assumed that ATSC is often used as an "insertion" device (Klein, 1976:74)—i.e., as a way to introduce juveniles into the system.

ANALYSIS OF OUTCOMES

Subsequent Referrals

When the date of referral is taken as the starting point of comparison, it is seen (Table 6) that within twelve months from this date *31.0* percent of the ATSC cases and *34.8* percent of the probation sample had at least one subsequent application for petition filed with the probation department. This difference is not significant on the .05 level.

Within eighteen months of the date of referral the difference between the percent of ATSC cases and probation cases had grown to 9.6 percent (32.8 percent versus 42.4 percent). This difference is significant on the .02 level.

The major reason for the significant difference between the percent of re-referrals after eighteen months was the large difference among males with no prior history of probation referral. Among the ATSC cases this group had 28.9 percent subsequent re-referrals while in probation 44.3 percent from this group had at least one subsequent petition. This difference is statistically significant on the .01 level.

Table 6 / Percent of Cases Upon Which an Application For Petition Was Filed With Probation, Twelve and Eighteen Months From Date of Referral by Sex, Prior Referral History, Age and Treatment

Time From Date of Referral[1]

| | TWELVE MONTHS | | | | | EIGHTEEN MONTHS | | | | |
| | ATSC | | Probation | | | ATSC | | Probation | | |
	N	PERCENT	N	PERCENT	Δ%	N	PERCENT	N	PERCENT	Δ%
All Cases	562	31.0	663	34.8	-3.8	329	32.8	337	42.4	-9.6*
Males Only	342	30.7	497	37.0	-6.3	205	32.2	246	47.2	-15.0*
No Priors	310	28.4	394	33.0	-4.6	187	28.9	210	44.3	-15.4*
Under 13	93	12.9	37	16.2	-3.3	68	16.2	22	18.2	-2.0
13–15	165	35.2	228	36.0	-0.8	101	37.6	142	45.8	-8.2
Over 15	52	34.6	129	32.6	2.0	18	27.8	46	52.2	-24.4
Priors	32	53.1	103	52.4	0.7	18	66.7	36	63.9	2.8
Under 13	4	75.0	12	41.7	—	2	50.0	7	42.9	—
13–15	13	53.8	45	60.0	-6.2	12	83.3	20	70.0	13.3
Over 15	15	46.7	46	47.8	-1.1	4	25.0	9	66.7	—
Females Only	220	31.4	166	28.3	3.1	124	33.9	91	29.7	4.2
No Priors	210	30.5	143	25.2	5.3	120	33.3	76	25.0	8.3
Under 13	24	16.7	2	0.0	—	14	7.1	1	0.0	—
13–15	142	33.1	95	22.1	11.0	88	33.0	58	22.4	10.6
Over 15	44	29.5	46	32.6	-3.1	18	55.6	17	35.3	20.3
Priors	10	50.0	23	47.8	2.2	4	50.0	15	53.3	—

[1]Difference between proportions: *p=.05, **p=.01, ***p=.001

However, when age was controlled for, no significant differences were encountered. Generally, within each age category the ATSC males with no priors had a lower rate of re-referrals than those on probation.[1] The differences tended to increase with age (below 13—2.0 percent; 13–15—8.2 percent; over 15—24.4 percent). Due to the small sample size, even the 24.4 percent difference was not large enough to be statistically significant on the conventional .05 level.

In the other major categories where the sample size was sufficient to make comparisons—males with prior probation experience and females with no prior referrals—the ATSC cases tended to have somewhat higher but not significant rates of re-referral.

Re-referral rates were the lowest in the youngest age group with no prior history of referrals, regardless of sex, treatment, age and follow-up time. The rates were highest for those with prior records, regardless of all the other variables. Male ATSC cases on the whole tended to have lower rates than their probation counterparts, while for females the opposite was true.

Level of Recontact

In comparing the two samples on the percent of cases upon which a petition was filed, significant differences are apparent at the end of both the twelve- and the eighteen-month follow-up periods (Table 7). By the end of twelve months, the date of referral, 22.2 percent of the ATSC and 28.1 percent of the probation cases were petitioned to juvenile court at least once. This difference is significant on the .02 level. By the end of eighteen months these figures were 23.1 percent and 35.9 percent respectively—a difference which is significant on the .001 level.

If personal attributes—age, sex and previous contacts with law enforcement agencies—are controlled, only the difference between males 13–15 years old without prior referral to probation is found to be significant—16.7 percent fewer ATSC boys in this category were returning than boys who finished probation. This difference is statistically significant at the .01 level. The overall female comparisons were slightly favorable for the ATSC program but no real substantive differences emerged.

Generally, the patterns of re-referrals tend to be better for the younger age groups, and worse for those with priors, especially among males.

Wardship

Within eighteen months of the date of referral 19.5 percent of the ATSC and 30.6 percent of the probation cases were declared wards of

Table 7 / Percent Of Cases With At Least One Subsequent Petition Filed Within Twelve And Eighteen Months From Date Of Referral By Sex, Prior Referral History, Age And Treatment

Time From Date of Referral[1]

| | TWELVE MONTHS | | | | | EIGHTEEN MONTHS | | | | |
| | ATSC | | Probation | | | ATSC | | Probation | | |
	N	PERCENT	N	PERCENT	Δ%	N	PERCENT	N	PERCENT	Δ%
All Cases	562	22.2	663	28.1	−5.9*	329	23.1	337	35.9	−12.8***
Males Only	342	21.9	497	29.6	−7.7*	205	23.9	246	40.7	−16.8***
No Priors	310	20.0	394	26.1	−6.1	187	20.3	210	38.6	−18.3***
Under 13	93	8.6	37	10.8	−2.2	68	11.8	22	13.6	−1.8
13–15	165	24.8	228	29.8	−5.0	101	24.8	142	41.5	−16.7**
Over 15	52	25.0	129	24.0	1.0	18	27.8	46	41.3	−13.5
Priors	32	40.6	103	42.7	−2.1	18	61.1	36	52.8	8.3
Under 13	4	50.0	12	33.3	16.7	2	50.0	7	28.6	21.4
13–15	13	46.2	45	53.3	−7.1	12	75.0	20	60.0	15.0
Over 15	15	33.3	46	34.8	−1.5	4	25.0	9	55.6	−30.6
Females Only	220	22.7	166	23.5	−0.8	124	21.8	91	23.1	−1.3
No Priors	210	22.4	143	21.7	0.7	120	21.7	76	19.7	2.0
Under 13	24	16.7	2	0.0	16.7	14	7.1	1	0.0	7.1
13–15	142	23.9	95	17.9	6.0	88	20.5	58	17.2	3.3
Over 15	44	205	46	30.4	−9.0	18	38.0	17	29.4	9.5
Priors	10	30.0	23	34.8	−4.8	4	25.0	15	40.0	−15.0

[1]Difference between proportions: *p=.05, **p=.01, ***p=.001

the court (either under supervision, or in juvenile institutions). As Table 8 indicates, these figures show a statistically significant difference between the two samples at the .001 level. Also, the general pattern described in the analysis of petitioning rate exists in the case of wardship comparisons. In all cases a lower percent of the ATSC graduates were sent to juvenile institutions. Generally, the percent of cases with at least one wardship within eighteen months of the date of referral was lower for the ATSC among all males regardless of prior history. Females, with and without prior referral, showed some favorable differences for the ATSC, while when age groups were compared, the graduates of the Probation Department seem to have a slightly more favorable record.

Re-referrals and Severity of Crime

Concerning the number of re-referrals, it was found that twelve months after the date of the referral an average of .63 applications per case were filed in the ATSC group, compared with .68 in the probation group (Table 9). This difference is not significant. Males with prior referrals have the highest average (1.3 ATSC, 1.2 probation), while the second-highest is for females with prior referrals (.90 ATSC, .91 probation). These figures are in accordance with the patterns found in other studies—namely, that there seems to be an emergence of a core group of delinquent who are getting involved with the social control agencies at a relatively early stage in life, and that many of them tend to continue this involvement, developing a delinquent and later a criminal career.

The only category in which there is a significant difference between the two groups is among females without a prior record in the age group of 13–15 where, unexpectedly, the ATSC "graduates" indicate a significantly higher re-ferral rate on the .01 level than their counterparts in the probation group. Within twelve months of the date of referral, the average severity of the new charges is the lowest among boys under the age of 13 who do not have prior referral record in both groups—somewhat lower in the probation group. The scores are highest among boys 15 years old and older with prior referrals; also in this category, the ATSC group has a higher average severity score than the probation group. The only significant difference, however, between the two groups on the severity scores is found among females 13–15 years old without prior referrals. The girls from ATSC tend to be charged with more serious infractions than girls who were on probation.

Table 8 / Percent Of Cases With At Least One Subsequent Petition Resulting In Wardship, Twelve And Eighteen Months From Date Of Referral By Sex, Prior Referral History, Age and Treatment

Time From Date of Referral[1]

| | TWELVE MONTHS | | | | | EIGHTEEN MONTHS | | | | | |
| | ATSC | | Probation | | | ATSC | | Probation | | |
	N	PERCENT	N	PERCENT	Δ%	N	PERCENT	N	PERCENT	Δ%
All Cases	562	18.1	663	24.4	-6.3**	329	19.5	337	30.6	-11.1***
Males Only	342	17.8	497	25.2	-7.4*	205	19.5	246	33.7	-14.2***
No Priors	310	17.1	394	21.6	-4.5	187	17.1	210	31.4	-14.3***
Under 13	93	6.5	37	5.4	1.1	68	8.8	22	13.6	-4.8
13–15	165	21.8	228	25.9	-4.1	101	23.8	142	35.3	-11.4
Over 15	52	21.2	129	18.6	-2.6	18	11.1	46	28.3	-17.2
Priors	32	25.0	103	38.8	-13.8	18	44.4	36	47.2	-2.8
Under 13	4	25.0	12	24.0	—	2	50.0	7	28.6	—
13–15	13	30.8	45	51.1	-20.3	12	50.0	20	60.0	-10.0
Over 15	15	20.0	46	30.4	-10.4	4	25.0	9	33.3	—
Females Only	220	18.6	166	22.3	-3.7	124	19.4	91	22.0	-2.6
No Priors	210	18.1	143	20.3	-2.2	120	19.2	76	19.7	-0.5
Under 13	24	16.7	2	0.0	—	14	7.1	1	0.0	—
13–15	142	18.3	95	16.8	1.5	88	18.2	58	17.2	1.0
Over 15	44	18.2	46	28.3	-10.1	18	33.3	17	29.4	3.9
Priors	10	30.0	23	34.8	-4.8	4	25.0	15	33.3	- 8.3

[1]Difference between proportions: *p=.05, **p=.01, ***p=.001

Table 9 / Average Number Of Applications For Petition Filed And Average Severity Per Case Of Re-referrals Within Twelve Months Of The Date Of Referral And The Date Of Termination By Age, Sex And Prior Referrals[1]

| | Number of Applications | | | | | Level of Severity | | | | |
| | ATSC | | Probation | | | ATSC | | Probation | | |
	N	X̄	N	X̄	Δ	N	X̄	N	X̄	Δ
All Cases	562	.63	663	.68	-.05	562	1.48	663	1.70	-.22
Males Only	342	.65	497	.76	-.11	342	1.50	497	1.85	-.35
No Priors	310	.58	394	.63	-.05	310	1.31	394	1.56	-.25
Under 13	93	.22	37	.19	.03	93	.49	37	.35	.14
13–15	165	.76	228	.75	.01	165	1.77	228	1.90	-.13
Over 15	52	.64	129	.54	.10	52	1.31	129	1.31	.00
Priors	32	1.3	103	1.2	.10	32	3.31	103	2.94	.37
Under 13	4	2.0	12	.92	—	4	4.50	12	2.00	—
13–15	13	.92	45	1.5	-.57	13	2.46	45	3.69	-1.2
Over 15	15	1.5	46	1.1	.46	15	3.73	46	2.46	1.3
Females Only	220	.60	166	.45	.15	220	1.46	166	1.24	.21
No Priors	210	.59	143	.37	.22*	210	1.45	143	1.04	.41
Under 13	24	.42	2	.00	—	24	1.13	2	.00	—
13–15	142	.68	95	.28	.39**	142	1.67	95	.80	.87*
Over 15	44	.39	46	.57	-.18	44	.93	46	1.59	-.66
Priors	10	.90	23	.91	-.01	10	1.50	23	2.48	-.98

[1]Test for differences between means: *p=.05, **p=.01

Discussion

The primary concerns of the current evaluation can be summarized in two questions:

(1) Were the cases referred to ATSC ones which would have otherwise been referred to probation?

(2) Is the effect of the ATSC treatment on the individuals any different than that which would have resulted if those cases had indeed been referred to probation?

It is hard to arrive at a conclusive answer to these questions on the basis of this study primarily because of the problems of initial design—namely, as mentioned, the unequal selection process into ATSC vs. probation. However, an attempt can be made to derive some logical conclusions which might have implications for the formulation of further treatment policies.

As has been pointed out earlier, what constitutes diversion is both ambiguous and relative. It has been stated that "diversion occurs only when use of the customary process is warranted, but not actualized." Determining when the customary process is warranted is itself a major and controversial problem. Compounding this problem is the great latitude of discretion allowed the various law enforcement agencies (Klein, 1976) regarding the decision to refer juveniles to different programs. Granted, if it is important to establish that each referral to the ATSC did in fact constitute a diversion, some criteria of verification should have been established from the outset. Unfortunately, as was pointed out, no such criteria were set up.

There is a good possibility that not all the referrals to the ATSC were diversions in the strict sense of the word. For example, during 1973–74, 260 (14.4 percent) from the total referrals of 1,801 to the ATSC were referred on an informal basis—that is, no specific code violations were indicated. It is feasible that at least a part of these cases would have been handled informally if the ATSC had not been available. This is quite a widespread phenomenon (Morris, 1974; Lincoln, 1976), as was mentioned before.

At the outset of the program, police were asked to refer emotionally disturbed youngsters and/or those who had some behavior disorder problems to the ATSC. Obviously, these guidelines are very general and almost all juveniles contacted by the police might fit into this broad category. The result is to give the police wide-scale discretion in this matter. At the time of the evaluation process there was no way of assessing whether or not those who were referred to the ATSC were any different on the emotional disturbance/behavioral disorder dimension from those who were referred to probation. (In fact it is not clear whether this dimension was ever uniformly defined for the various agencies.) Without reliable data on this matter, there is no way to establish a meaningful comparison group (referred to probation) against which the subsequent behavior of ATSC referees can be compared.

Taking all these limitations into consideration, this study has compared the subsequent behavior of a sample of ATSC cases with that of a sample of initial noncustody probation referrals. The results of these comparisons generally did not indicate any systematic differences between the two groups.

In the evaluation of the ATSC program, when all the referrals are considered, the group of referrals who failed to keep their assessment appointments showed the poorest pattern of subsequent behavior— that is, within eighteen months of the referral 27.0 percent of this group became the wards of the juvenile court at least once, while among the assessed the comparable figure was 17.2 percent.

The matriculation of cases through the ATSC tends to follow a pattern of positive selection, with those ingressing further into the program generally showing a "better" outcome. Probation, on the other hand, indicates an opposite trend: the deeper the ingression into the formal juvenile justice system, the higher the probability of recidivism. This finding should be pursued by additional studies to determine its significance, since as it stands it might indicate real differences in the treatment impact; it might be mainly an outcome of the selection process for the different programs; or it may indicate that there are different meanings of early termination in the two programs—that is, in ATSC it might indicate that the extreme flexibility of the program allows those youngsters who need it most to drop out earliest, while in probation, where the regulations are stricter, those youngsters are getting out earliest who constitute the best risks in any case.

CONCLUSION

On the basis of the evaluation presented in this study, it is hard to arrive at clear-cut conclusions. To a large degree ATSC appears to be no better and no worse than its counterparts in the juvenile justice system. This is obviously not a very positive, optimistic statement about the program, and it offers no final estimation of its value. However, it would seem that some of the results would be more positive if the selection process were improved. The two immediate steps that should be taken to make ATSC a more viable alternative to probation and certainly a better object for evaluation purposes should be: (a) determining more specifically what persons should participate in the program, and (b) developing better referral guidelines and creating more effective cooperative links between the law enforcement agencies to keep up with them.

This study, besides focusing on a comparison of the outcome of various treatment programs, also highlighted some of the actual research problems which might emerge in their evaluation. While it is known that decision makers frequently fail to use the conclusions of evaluation research (Weiss, 1972), it is still hoped that at least some of the problems of design which emerged in the ATSC Project will be addressed by administrators of juvenile diversion programs.

References

Adams, Stuart. *Evaluative Research in Corrections: A Prochial Guide.* Washington, D.C.; U.S. Department of Justice, L.E.A.A. National Institute of Law Enforcement and Criminal Justice, 1975.

Becker, Howard S. *Outsiders: Studies in the Sociology of Deviance.* New York: Free Press, 1963.

Berg, Dennis. "Behavior Assessment and Treatment Services Center: Evaluation Report." Santa Ana, California: Office of Criminal Justice Planning, 1975.

Carter, Robert and Malcolm W. Klein (eds.). *Back On the Street: The Diversion of Juvenile Offenders.* Englewood Cliffs, N.J.: Prentice-Hall, 1976.

Cressey, Donald R. and Robert A. McDermott. *Diversion from the Juvenile Justice System.* Ann Arbor: National Assessment of Juvenile Corrections, 1973.

Glaser, Daniel. *Routinizing Evaluation: Getting Feedback on Effectiveness of Crime and Delinquency Programs.* Washington, D.C.: N.I.M.H. Center for Studies of Crime and Delinquency, 1973.

Klein, Malcolm W. "Issues in Police Diversion of Juvenile Offenders." In Carter and Klein, *Back On the Street*, pp. 73–104.

Lemert, Edwin M. *Social Pathology.* New York: McGraw-Hill, 1957.

Lincoln, Susanne Bugas. "Juvenile Referral and Recidivism." In Carter and Klein, *Back On the Street*, pp. 321–328.

Morris, Norvel. *The Future of Imprisonment.* Chicago: University of Chicago Press, 1974.

National Advisory Commission on Criminal Justice Standards and Goals. *Corrections.* Washington, D.C.: U.S. Government Printing Office, 1973.

Platt, Anthony. *The Child-Savers: The Invention of Delinquency.* Chicago: The University of Chicago Press, 1969.

Weiss, Carol H. "Utilization of Evaluation: Toward Comparative Study." In Weiss, Carol H. (ed.). *Evaluating Action Programs: Readings in Social*

Action and Education. Boston: Allyn and Bacon, 1972, pp. 318–326.

Weiss, Robert S. and Martin Rein. "The Evaluation of Broad-Aim Programs: A Cautionary Case and a Moral." In Caro, Francis G. (ed.). *Readings in Evaluation Research.* New York: Russell-Sage, 1971, pp. 287–296.

Note

1. This might be due also to the ability of law enforcement agencies to differentiate among the youngsters whom they referred to the two programs.

Acknowledgments (continued from p. iv)

Selections from *Delinquency and Opportunity* by Richard A. Cloward and Lloyd E. Ohlin reprinted with permission of Macmillan Publishing Co., Inc. © The Free Press, a Corporation, 1960.

Selection from *Theoretical Criminology* by George B. Vold © 1958 by Oxford University Press, Inc. Reprinted by permission. Second Edition available Fall, 1979.

Selection from *The Social Reality of Crime* by Richard Quinney, pp. 8-24 reprinted by permission. Copyright © 1970 by Little, Brown and Company (Inc.).

Selection from *Crime and the Community* by Frank Tannenbaum reprinted by permission of the publisher, Columbia University Press.

Selection from *Social Pathology* by Edwin M. Lemert used with permission of McGraw-Hill Book Company. Copyright 1959 by McGraw-Hill Inc.

"On Managing a Courtesy Stigma" by Arnold Birenbaum is reprinted with the permission of the author and the American Sociological Association from *Journal of Health and Social Behavior*, Vol. 11, 1970.

"The Adjustment of the Family to the Crisis of Alcoholism" by Joan K. Jackson is reprinted by permission from *Quarterly Journal of Studies on Alcohol*, Vol. 15, 1954. Copyright by Journal of Studies on Alcohol, Inc., New Brunswick, N.J. 08903.

"The Psychological Meaning of Mental Illness in the Family" by Marian Radke-Yarrow, Charlotte Green Schwartz, Harriet S. Murphy, and Leila Calhoun Deasy is reprinted by permission of The Society for the Psychological Study of Social Issues from *Journal of Social Issues*, Vol. 11, No. 4 (1955).

"Paranoia and the Dynamics of Exclusion" by Edwin M. Lemert is reprinted by permission of the author and The American Sociological Association from *Sociometry*, Vol. 25, 1962.

"Deviance and Respectability: An Observational Study of Reactions to Shoplifting" by Darrell J. Steffensmeier and Robert M. Terry is reprinted with the permission of the authors and the publisher from *Social Forces* 51 (June 1973). Copyright © 1973 by The University of North Carolina Press.

"The Police and the Delinquent in Two Cities" by James Q. Wilson is reprinted with the permission of the author.

"Ascriptive Elements in the Psychiatric Screening of Mental Patients in a Mid-western State" by Thomas J. Scheff with the assistance of Daniel M. Culver is reprinted with the permission of the author and The Society for the Study of Social Problems from *Social Problems*, Vol. 11:4 (Spring 1964).

"A Case of a 'Psychotic' Navaho Indian Male" by Donald P. Jewell reproduced by permission of the author and the Society for Applied Anthropology from *Human Organization*, Vol. 11:32-36, 1952.

"The Role of Teachers' Nominations in the Preparation of Deviant Adolescent Careers" by Delos H. Kelly reprinted by permission of Project Innovation from *Education*, Vol. 96 (1976).

Selections from *Judging Delinquents* by Robert M. Emerson reprinted with permission of the author and Aldine Publishing Company. Copyright © 1969 by Robert M. Emerson.

Selections from *Stations of the Lost: Treatment of Skid Row Alcoholics* by Jacqueline P. Wiseman reprinted by permission of the author. Copyright 1970, by Jacqueline P. Wiseman, University of California-San Diego.

"Characteristics of Total Institutions" by Erving Goffman is reprinted fom *Symposium on Preventative and Social Psychiatry*, Walter Reed Medical Center, Washington D.C., April 15-17, 1957.

Selection from *Hacks, Blacks and Cons: Race Relations in a Maximum Security Prison* by Leo Carroll is reprinted by permission of D. C. Heath and Company. Copyright 1974, D. C. Heath and Company.

"The Moral Career of the Mental Patient" by Erving Goffman is reprinted by special permission of The William Alanson White Psychiatric Foundation, Inc. from *Psychiatry* (1959) 22:123-142. Copyright © 1959 by The William Alanson White Psychiatric Foundation, Inc.

"Schizophrenic Patients in the Psychiatric Interview: An Experimental Study of their Effectiveness at Manipulation" by Benjamin M. Braginsky and Dorothea D. Braginsky is reprinted with the permission of the authors and the American Psychological Association from *Journal of Consulting Psychology* Vol. 31 (1967). Copyright 1967 by the American Psychological Association.

"Two Studies of Legal Stigma" by Richard D. Schwartz and Jerome H. Skolnick is reprinted by permission of the authors and The Society for the Study of Social Problems from *Social Problems,* Vol. 10:2 (Fall 1962).

"Rejection: A Possible Consequence of Seeking Help for Mental Disorders" by Derek L. Phillips is reprinted by permission of the author and the American Sociological Association from *American Sociological Review,* Vol. 28, 1963.

"Voluntary Associations Among Social Deviants" by Edward Sagarin is reprinted from *Criminologica,* Vol. 5 (1967), pp. 8-22 by permission of the Publisher, Sage Publications, Inc. and the author.

"The Delinquent Gang as a Near-Group" by Lewis Yablonsky is reprinted by permission of the author and The Society for the Study of Social Problems from *Social Problems,* Vol. 7:2 (Fall 1959).

"Lesbian Behavior as an Adaptation to the Occupation of Stripping" by Charles H. McCaghy and James K. Skipper, Jr. is reprinted with the permission of the authors and The Society for the Study of Social Problems from *Social Problems,* Vol. 17:2 (Fall 1969).

Selection from *Skid Row as a Way of Life* by Samuel E. Wallace is reprinted by permission of The Bedminster Press, Totowa, New Jersey. Copyright 1965 by The Bedminster Press.

"Becoming a Taxi-Dancer: The Significance of Neutralization in a Semi-Deviant Occupation" by Lawrence K. Hong and Robert W. Duff is reprinted from *Sociology of Work and Occupations,* Vol. 4, No. 3 (August 1977) by permission of the authors and of the Publisher, Sage Publications, Inc.

"The Madam as Teacher: The Training of House Prostitutes" by Barbara Sherman Heyl is reprinted by permission of the author and The Society for the Study of Social Problems from *Social Problems,* Vol. 24:5 (June 1977).

Selection from *Sisters in Crime* by Freda Adler used with permission of McGraw-Hill Book Company. Copyright © 1975 by Freda Adler.

"Battered Women and Their Assailants" by Bonnie E. Carlson is reprinted with permission from *Social Work,* Vol. 22, No. 6 (November 1977), pp. 455-460. Copyright 1977, National Association of Social Workers, Inc.

"A Criminogenic Market Structure: The Automobile Industry" by Harvey A. Farberman is reprinted by permission from *The Sociological Quarterly,* Vol. 16, No. 4, 1975.

"Cruising the Truckers: Sexual Encounters in a Highway Rest Area" by Jay Corzine and Richard Kirby is reprinted from *Urban Life,* Vol. 6, No. 2 (July 1977) by permission of the authors and the Publisher, Sage Publications, Inc.

"The Social Integration of Queers and Peers" by Albert J. Reiss, Jr. is reprinted by permission of the author and The Society for the Study of Social Problems from *Social Problems,* Vol. 9:2 (Fall 1961).

Selection from *Human Deviance, Social Problems, and Social Control* by Edwin M. Lemert is reprinted by permission of Prentice-Hall, Inc., Englewood Cliffs, New Jersey. Copyright © 1967 by Prentice-Hall, Inc.

"Labeling Process: Reinforcement and Deterrent?" by Bernard A. Thorsell and Lloyd W. Klemke is reprinted by permission of the Law and Society Association from *Law and Society Review,* Vol. 6, 1972.

"The Cycle of Abstinence and Relapse Among Heroin Addicts" by Marsh B. Ray is reprinted by permission of the author and The Society for the Study of Social Problems from *Social Problems,* Vol. 9:2 (Fall 1961).

"Delabeling, Relabeling, and Alcoholics Anonymous" by Harrison M. Trice and Paul Michael Roman is reprinted by permission of the authors and The Society for the Study of Social Problems from *Social Problems,* Vol. 17:4 (Spring 1970).

Selection from *Schizophrenics in the Community* by Benjamin Pasamanick, Frank R. Scarpitti, and Simon Dinitz is reprinted by permission of Irvington Publishers, Inc. © Copyright 1967 by the Meredith Corporation.

"The Youth Authority's Community Treatment Project" by Ted Palmer is reprinted by permission of the author from *Federal Probation,* Vol. 38, No. 1 (March 1974).

"Methodological and Theoretical Issues in Juvenile Diversion: Implications for Evaluation" by Dennis F. Berg and David Shichor is reprinted by permission of the authors.